biology
of Insects

DAVID J. HORN
The Ohio State University

1976   W. B. SAUNDERS COMPANY • PHILADELPHIA • LONDON • TORONTO

W. B. Saunders Company: West Washington Square
                          Philadelphia, Pa.   19105

                          1 St. Anne's Road
                          Eastbourne, East Sussex BN21 3UN, England

                          833 Oxford Street
                          Toronto, Ontario M8Z 5T9, Canada

Library of Congress Cataloging in Publication Data

Horn, David J

Biology of insects.

Bibliography: p.

Includes index.

1. Insects.   I. Title.

QL463.H78   595.7   76–1217

ISBN 0–7216–4780–4

Front cover illustration: Monarch butterfly. (Courtesy of Lawrence J. Connor, Ph.D.,
                            The Ohio State University.)

Biology of Insects   ISBN   0-7216-4780-4

Last digit is the print number: 9   8   7   6   5   4   3   2   1

Preface

In a way, this book had its genesis 23 years ago when my brothers and I, armed with cheesecloth-and-broomstick nets, first set forth to see what the insect world had to offer. More recently, I have come to believe that there is a need for a basic text that regards insects as adaptive solutions to problems of survival in a hetero-geneous and largely hostile environment. In this book, I seek to show how insects function and how selective pressures have shaped the exceedingly diverse array that we see around us in both natural and artificial habitats. Although I survey important areas of entomology, I have not attempted to include everything; the field is too diverse to be covered in a single textbook. Moreover, this book should not be considered as an identification guide, of which there are several excellent ones already. Rather, I have been selective in trying to present entomology as a dynamic study of living organisms. Discovery of how insects function and interact with their environment is rewarding and fun, and fun is good.

Writing this book has been mostly fun. I have alternately blessed and cursed the project; it has taught me things I never knew, about insects and about myself. I have a good deal more respect for anyone who writes books.

I am indebted to many people for assistance with tasks great and small. In particular, five people merit my special thanks: Richard Lampert, Biology Editor for W. B. Saunders Co., expertly guided the project from start to finish; he knew when to prod me and when to leave me be. Rosalind S. Horn read and edited several drafts and has given me unqualified love and support when I needed them most. Alice Kolbe produced nearly all the original drawings from my very scratchy, cryptic sketches. Robert Dowell was a darkroom genius; he printed most of the original photographs, some from very fuzzy negatives. Dalene Hoppe typed the entire manuscript quickly and accurately and retyped several sections that some-one, often myself, suggested that I revise.

The following people read and commented on selected sections, whole chap-ters, or several chapters: C. Albrecht, F. M. Carpenter, D. S. Chandler, V. G. Dethier, R. C. Dobson, R. V. Dowell, T. Eisner, W. A. Foster, L. I. Gilbert, R. F. Har-wood, R. P. Holdsworth, H. S. Horn, M. E. Horn, C. D. Johnson, J. Kovarik, G. L. Leibee, W. L. Luckmann, R. F. Morris, R. L. Patton, P. W. Price, E. L. Raffensperger, C. L. Selman, C. G. Summers, S. R. Swier, and T. K. Wood. I am grateful for their assistance and suggestions. The errors and inconsistencies that remain are mine, and I would appreciate hearing of them.

I borrowed illustrative material from many sources and many people. I am sincerely grateful to all those I have acknowledged in the text as sources for photographs, drawings, and tables. My colleagues at The Ohio State University and Ohio Agricultural Research and Development Center have been most helpful in offering advice, support, and encouragement in all my entomological endeavors.

This book is dedicated to Catherine A. and Rosalind B. Horn, two of the best field assistants that Daddy ever had.

D. J. H.

Contents

Part Three

INSECTS AND HUMAN AFFAIRS

Chapter Ten

PEST MANAGEMENT 351

Chapter Eleven

INSECTS AND DISEASE.. 376

Chapter Twelve

BENEFICIAL ASPECTS.. 395

Part One

Insect Diversity

Chapter One

Introduction

One of the most striking things we see in the natural world is the remarkable diversity among insects and their relatives. Insects are found in great abundance and variety nearly everywhere on land and fresh water. Four of every five animal species are insects.

This phenomenal diversity is unique to the insects among animals and has important consequences intimately related to the survival of many other inhabitants of Planet Earth. In terrestrial and freshwater ecological communities, insects are vital links, passing chemical energy from green plants up food chains to predatory insects, birds, and fish. Without insect pollination of flowers or their scavenging on organic detritus, the natural world would not be as we know it.

The diversity of insects has direct economic and social consequences to humanity. Annually, insects cause several billion dollars' worth of damage to crops, forests, and structures. Insect-borne diseases claim millions of lives each year and have had major impact on human history and economic development. On the other hand are beneficial insects, from parasitic and predatory insects that eat pests to bees that produce honey and pollinate flowers, thus ensuring the continued existence of many fruits and vegetables.

The incomparable diversity of form among insects is intrinsically interesting. Insects provide inspiration for poets, artists, and musicians and objects of study for scientists. The latter have found insects to be useful experimental animals because of their small size, high reproductive rate, and ease of laboratory rearing. The great diversity of the insect world is a fertile lure for scientific investigation. That is what this book is about: entomology, the scientific study of insects.

Science is a body of knowledge obtained by rigorous use of the scientific method, which assumes that events in the observable world follow sets of rules or generalizations that, once discovered, can be used to predict subsequent events. The scientific method is sometimes misunderstood by nonscientists (and misused by some scientists), and I therefore will begin by discussing the scientific method, though science is not the only way to view the natural world, as any theologian, and many scientists, will quickly tell you.

An investigation by the scientific method begins with an observation or a series of observations. For example, I have termites in my woodpile but not (I hope) in my garage or house. From observations, a scientist formulates a **hypothesis**, a general rule that could apply to similar situations one has not yet observed and that can be tested by experiment. In my example, I hypothesize that (1) "termites infest only that wood in direct contact with the ground." I could choose other hypotheses, e.g., (2) "excessive human activity keeps termites away" or (3) "termites infest woodpiles but not buildings." A hypothesis is an *educated* guess, and hypothesis 1 seems *most* likely, given what I already know about local termites (i.e., that most of the nest is underground). Hypothesis 3 is obviously unlikely because termites do infest buildings.

Having formulated a hypothesis, a scientist's next step, and the most critical one, is designing and conducting an appropriate experiment. A valid experiment involves: (1) **comparison:** observation of similarities and differences between treatments; (2) **replication:** repetition of experimental treatments; and (3) **probability:** a chance, however small, that the hypothesis is incorrect. Ideally, the investigator attempts to hold all conditions constant except that which he is testing. To test hypothesis 1, I procured 12 wooden blocks (No. 1 pine) nearly identical in all respects. I placed six directly on the ground and elevated six on cinder blocks, and I observed which blocks became termite-infested. The results (Table 1-1) seem straightforward even though termites failed to infest one block on the ground. From my experiment, I therefore accept my hypothesis*: "Termites infest only that wood in direct contact with the ground."

No science is absolute, and hypotheses need to be modified in the light of fresh facts. Though I did not so observe in my few samples, I and others have observed that termites construct earthen tubes from ground to wood (especially along cinder blocks) and so it is not always true that "termites infest only that wood in direct contact with the ground." Perhaps my experiment did not last long enough. For greater validity, my hypothesis must be altered: "Termites are more **likely** to infest wood in direct contact with the ground than wood that is not." Even this hypothesis does not apply to all termites; it holds well in Columbus, Ohio, where all termites nest underground but not in subtropical and tropical areas where drywood termites directly infest above-ground wood.

Hypotheses that stand the tests of repeated, varied experimentation eventually are dignified by being called "theories" or "laws." Such a law might be: "Most termites eat wood or other cellulose-containing plant matter." No theories or laws are immutable (though some are likely to apply in nearly all cases), and the truly objective scientist must constantly ask: What is the experimental evidence for a particular theory? Theories change but facts do not, and there is no substitute for careful observation and well-conceived experimentation. Alterna-

---

*Statistical analysis of these data, using a "chi-square" test (see Bishop, 1966, or another elementary statistics text), shows the probability of error to be $p = 0.002$; by accepting my hypothesis, I am likely to be correct 998 times out of 1000.

Table 1-1. RESULTS OF EXPOSING 5 × 10 × 10 cm. PINE BLOCKS TO TERMITES FOR THREE MONTHS IN MY BACKYARD, COLUMBUS, OHIO, JUNE TO SEPTEMBER, 1974

Location of Blocks	Total Number of Blocks	Termite Infested	Not Infested
On ground	6	5	1
On cinder blocks	6	0	6

tively, a poorly designed experiment can be greatly misleading. Dethier (1962) tells an apocryphal story of an experimenter who wished to know where the organs of hearing are located on the flea. He trained a flea to jump on command, and then he cut off the antennae and commanded "jump." The flea jumped. He successively removed the first two pairs of legs, and the flea continued to jump. After the investigator removed both hind legs, however, the flea no longer jumped on command. "Aha," exclaimed the scientist, "he hears with his hind legs."

Scientific method has limitations. It cannot deal with what cannot be observed and therefore is at the mercy of the technology of instrumentation. As new tools for observation are developed, previously unobservable phenomena can be observed, and new facts, hypotheses, theories, and laws are thereby added to the body of scientific knowledge, even as many older theories and laws must be modified or, occasionally, rejected. For instance, the invention of the microscope was a major early advance that permitted detailed examination of insects and other small organisms and microorganisms. A more recent example is the development of gas chromatography, enabling us to detect minute proportions of such chemicals as DDT and mercury in samples of crops, soil, water, and wildlife, thereby forcing reconsideration of hypotheses explaining the fate of chemicals in the environment. Science and technology often advance together; the hypothesis that termites are more likely to infest wood in contact with the ground is used by builders who avoid building structures with wood parts directly contacting the ground in termite country.

Science also cannot deal with values, as scientific laws are descriptive laws dealing with how things **are** and not how they ought to be. Science can determine where and how termites will (or won't) eat wood but cannot say that termites are thereby good, evil, beautiful, or ugly, nor can science tell us the reason for the termites'—or our—existence.

HISTORY OF ENTOMOLOGY

Because entomology is a body of scientific knowledge accumulated through time, and culturally is a rather new phenomenon, it is worthwhile to look at the history and development of entomology as it is today. Much of what follows is from the review of Smith et al. (1973).

Insects and people have been associated for humanity's entire existence. Prehistoric men and women had lice and fleas and were doubtless subject to insect-borne diseases. Insects and their products probably were often eaten; a cave drawing in Spain depicts a man taking honey from a tree (Pfadt, 1971). As civilization developed, people came into contact and conflict with an increasing variety of insects. Silk culture was practiced in China by 4700 B.C., and the Chinese knew of the insecticidal properties of mercury and arsenic 2000 years ago. Locust swarms plagued ancient China and Egypt, as did maggots and flies in the latter country (Exodus 8:16–24). Scarab beetles were considered sacred in Egypt 4000 years ago. Insects were a staple food for many American Indians, and the Mayans of Central America hurled occupied wasps' nests at enemies.

Scientific study of insects is, however, a relatively recent development. In prehistoric times and in the ancient world, the supernatural was often invoked to explain observed phenomena, and the idea of experimental proof apparently was not entertained. Until the Renaissance, Western entomology was dominated by the works of Aristotle (384–322 B.C.), who stressed **deductive** reasoning: starting with a general premise and reasoning to particular circumstances. Aristotle and, later, Pliny the Elder (23–79 A.D.), though they occasionally made gross errors of fact, were usually careful observers of natural processes and knew, for instance, of insect metamorphosis. Not having microscopes, they did not recognize insect eggs as such; to Aristotle, the pupa was the "egg" stage, the larva an "imperfect" adult. Subsequent generations leaned more heavily on the writings of Aristotle, Pliny, and Scripture than on their own observations for nearly 2000 years in the West. In the Orient, a rather sophisticated technology of insect control was developed over 1000 years ago, though much of this knowledge was suppressed or ignored with the westernization of China.

Like many of aspects of modern Western culture, the scientific method became popular shortly after the Renaissance as scientific intellectuals began questioning established authority. Francis Bacon (1561–1626) is credited with starting the trend away from Aristotle by stressing **inductive** (scientific) reasoning: beginning with observation and formulating a generality from it. Typical of the period was the pioneering work of Redi (1626–1697), who disproved the then-current notion that maggots were spontaneously generated from spoiled meat. Redi placed meat in containers that were uncovered or covered with screen or with parchment and observed that maggots appeared on the uncovered meat and on the screen but not on the parchment-covered meat, and from this he concluded that flies were the source of the maggots (though Redi persisted in the belief that insects occurred spontaneously in plant galls).

Progress in scientific investigation is totally dependent on the observational powers of scientists, and the advancement of the science of entomology has coincided with technological improvements in observational aids. Perhaps *the* major advance in entomology (and in all biology) was the invention of the microscope in 1599, which primitive though it might at first have been, opened up possibilities for detailed observations of insect anatomy. Pioneering in this field were Marcello Malpighi (1624–1697) and Jan Swammerdam (1637–1711), whose painstaking anatomical studies of insects were surprisingly accurate (Fig. 1–1).

From Aristotle and Pliny through Swammerdam and others, many early investigators felt a need to classify living things, and here the insects, with at least 750,000 species, presented a clear challenge. Early classification schemes were cumbersome, depending on lengthy Latin phrases for description of each form, and needed revision often. It remained for Carolus Linnaeus (alias Karl von Linné, 1707–1778) of Sweden to devise a system that worked well. Linnaeus devised what is essentially our modern system of a hierarchy of categories (Table 2–1). Modern taxonomy, the naming and describing of organisms, dates directly from 1758, the year of publication of Linnaeus' *Systema Naturae,* 10th edition. Here was (and is) a system that could be added to and was easy to use, specific names consisting of only two (or three) words, Latin or latinized and hence understandable by all educated men of the day, regardless of their native language. Additional categories have been added since 1758, but the basic hierarchical system remains unchanged. The Linnaean system and the growing colonialism of western Europe ushered in what might be called the "Age of Insect Taxonomy." Explorers such as the British Captains Cook and Bligh sent back countless specimens of new and exciting insect species that kept museum curators and other taxonomists busy and happy year after year describing, naming, and cataloguing insects.

Entomologists of the 18th and 19th centuries were usually amateurs, to

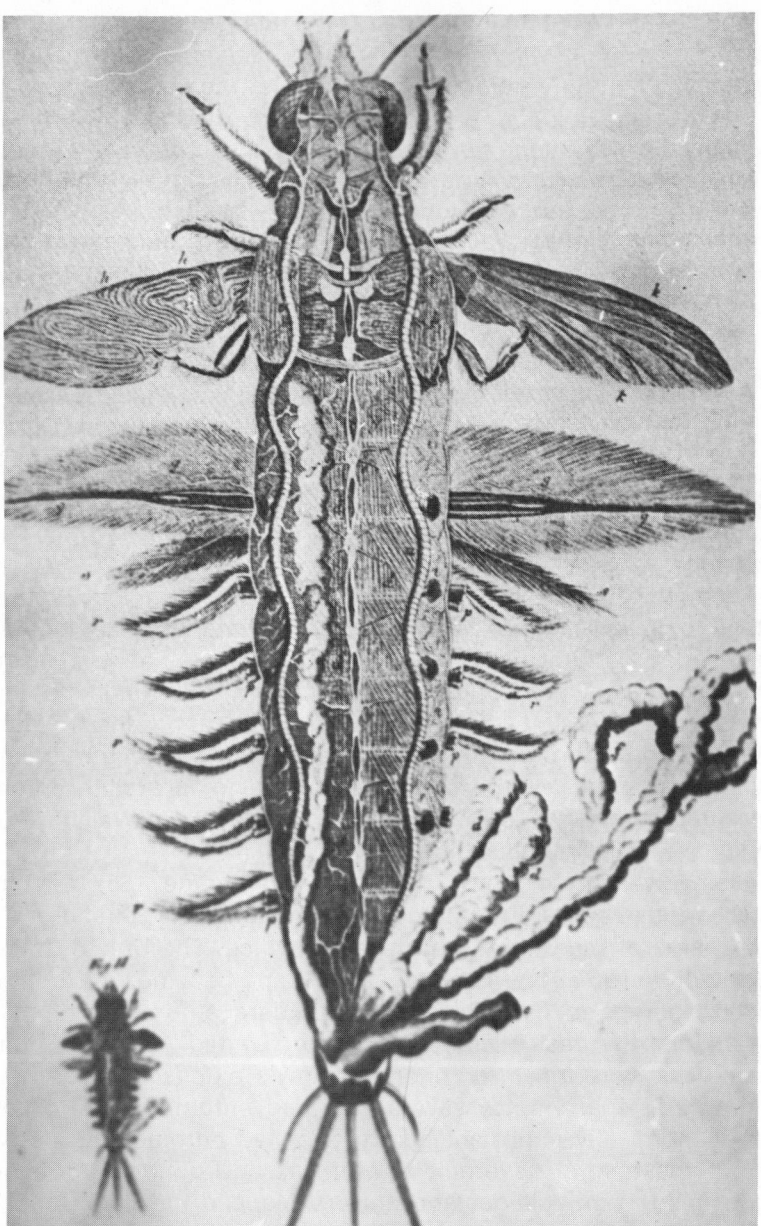

Figure 1–1. Dissection of mayfly nymph by Swammerdam, about 1675. From Essig, E. O. 1942. College Entomology. Macmillan Publishing Co., Inc., New York.

whom entomology was somewhat of a hobby as they pursued other careers. For example, in France, Boisduval (1799–1879) was a medical doctor and country gentleman who dabbled in butterflies and caterpillars and Dejean (1780–1845) was one of Napoleon's generals who collected battlefield beetles. The German Hübner (1761–1826) designed print cloth for a living and provided outstanding illustrations of many beetles and butterflies in his spare time. Osten-Sacken (1826–1903) was a Russian diplomat interested in flies. Overshadowing other early systematists and perhaps most deserving of the title "First Entomologist" was the Dane Johan Christian Fabricius (1745–1808), a student of Linnaeus, who produced the monumental *Systema Entomologiae*, in several volumes (1775–1804). He was the last entomologist to try to cover the insect fauna of the entire world.

The discovery of the many diverse forms of insect (and other) life in areas distant from Europe led directly to evolutionary ideas in the early 19th century. Evolutionary theory took on its essentially modern view with the works of Charles Darwin (1809–1882) and A. R. Wallace (1823–1913). Both had travelled extensively, viewing the diversity of animal species and independently formulating the idea of natural selection, which they published jointly in 1858. This work, *On the Tendency of Species to Form Varieties,* followed by Darwin's *Origin of Species* (1859), reoriented entomological (and biological) observations by postulating evolution of adaptations by natural selection. After Darwin, most entomologists viewed insect biology from an adaptive standpoint; genetic and environmental factors interact to produce the very diverse morphological, behavioral, and physiological characteristics. Comparative studies revealed and still reveal much about evolutionary relationships among insects (see Chapter 2).

Entomology as a profession perhaps began with J. O. Westwood (1805–1893), the first major university (Oxford) professor of entomology. In most institutions, entomology was taught, if at all, as part of natural history courses. In the United States, Harvard University had by the 1850's an extensive insect collection for which a curator was hired, and the first academic departments of entomology were formed in the 1870's at Cornell, Michigan State, and Kansas State Universities. As has been true throughout history, applied entomology was emphasized. As agricultural problems increased, states began to hire state entomologists; among the first were New York (Asa Fitch), Illinois (B. D. Walsh) and Missouri (C. V. Riley).

Federal involvement in entomology began with the 1853 appointment of Townend Glover as Federal Entomologist. At the time, the Bureau of Agriculture was a subdivision of the United States Patent Office. The United States Department of Agriculture (USDA) was created in 1878 and became an executive department in 1888. About then, C. V. Riley initiated federal entomological research activity by aiding the establishment of the United States Entomological Commission. This was the forerunner of today's extensive USDA entomology research programs that employ several hundred entomologists to conduct research on economically important insects. Applied entomology received major support from the federal government with passage of the Morrill Act (1862), providing for land-grant colleges and universities, and the Hatch Act (1887), establishing state agricultural experiment stations. From their beginnings, state universities and experiment stations have been heavily involved in entomological research, teaching, and extension activities.

Progress in medical entomology was directly linked to the mid-19th century recognition of microorganisms and their role in causing diseases. Mosquitoes were first recognized as vectors (carriers) of filariasis in India in 1877, and the late 19th and early 20th centuries saw increasing discoveries of relationships between insects and microorganisms. Of special note is the discovery of transmission of yellow fever by mosquitoes, made by Dr. Walter Reed in 1900. This knowledge enabled the United States to control yellow fever in the Panama Canal Zone by controlling mosquitoes and paved the way for the building of the Panama Canal.

The present century has seen great diversification in entomological studies. In 1900, most entomologists could have been categorized as either taxonomists or applied (and mostly agricultural) entomologists. Medical entomology early became somewhat of a specialty, and refinements in chemical insect control and in microtechniques have led to successive diversification of insect physiologists, toxicologists, and biochemists, while advances in biological ideas have generated insect ecologists, behaviorists, and systematists. Entomology today is therefore a very broad field of endeavor tied together loosely because all "entomologists" study some aspect of those forms of life having an external skeleton and six jointed legs.

SCOPE AND PLAN OF THIS BOOK

This book seeks to introduce you to entomology, the scientific study of insects, by first introducing the theory of adaptation through natural selection. After discussion of the probable evolutionary history of insects, Part One concludes with a survey of the major insect groups to which you are likely to be exposed as a beginning student.

In Part Two, I at first break down the insect to discuss how it functions: how it eats, hears, sees, moves, excretes, and so forth, and than I reassemble the insect to find out how it behaves, develops, reproduces, and interacts with other members of its own species and with other organisms. Finally, in Part Three, I consider insects as they relate to people (other than through the study of insects, which, of course, is what the whole book is about). Economic and medical entomology are considered from the point of view of what constitutes a pest and how pests are controlled. The book ends on a positive note by considering the beneficial aspects of the insect world.

SUMMARY

Entomology is the scientific study of insects. Through the use of the scientific method (observations, hypotheses, and experiments) scientists, including entomologists, have accumulated a vast body of knowledge, science, over the past several hundred years. The latter portion of this introductory chapter summarizes particularly important advances in the history of entomology.

Chapter Two

Evolution of Insects

INTRODUCTION

Insects are a phenomenally numerous and diverse group of organisms. They range in size from tiny beetles and wasps less than a millimeter long to tropical walkingsticks over a foot long and are found in bewildering variety nearly everywhere on land or in fresh water. Estimates of the total number of insect species run from 750,000 to over 2 million; four of every five living animal species are insects. There may be over a million individuals representing 1000 different species in a 1-acre hayfield. The insects are among man's most serious competitors for food, fiber, and forests, and annual cases of insect-carried disease run into the millions. "Success" in evolution can mean many things: long-term survival, sheer abundance, diversity of form, or occupation of diverse environments. By any of these standards the insects are a most successful class of organisms.

Variety, to me, is the insects' outstanding characteristic, making it difficult to discuss general characteristics of insects as a whole. Nevertheless, insects share with us, and with all living things, equipment to meet the basic challenges of survival. We may consider insects as tiny living machines for converting chemical (food) resources into more tiny living machines like themselves. Like us, insects must obtain and utilize food, water, and oxygen, rid themselves of carbon dioxide, urea, and other wastes, and maintain an optimal internal environment for these physiological activities. They also need coordinative, locomotive, protective, and reproductive systems efficient enough for at least a few to escape being eaten, stepped on, poisoned, or frozen long enough to reproduce successfully. These activities are constrained by the limitations of an external skeleton, jointed limbs, and small size, yet insects have become the most diverse of all animal groups. This chapter discusses probable evolutionary pathways that have led to the remarkable diversity of insects.

FEATURES OF INSECTS

Insects are members of the class Insecta in the phylum Arthropoda (see Table 2–1). Other classes of Arthropoda are the Crustacea (lobsters, crabs, crayfish, shrimp, etc.); Arachnida (spiders, scorpions, ticks, and mites); Chilopoda (centipedes); Diplopoda (millipedes); and several minor groups. All Arthropoda are characterized by having jointed legs and a hardened, segmented exter-

10

nal skeleton (exoskeleton). Insects are unique among arthropods in having the following features (Fig. 2–1):

1. Six legs. Traditionally, all six-legged arthropods have been considered insects. As explained in Chapter Three, a few groups of six-legged arthropods are here considered separate classes.

2. Tagmatization: division of the body into three regions: head, thorax, and abdomen. Each of these is thought to have evolved from fusion of several segments: the head from three to five, the thorax from three, and the abdomen from six to eleven. These divisions may not be obvious on some immature insects.

3. Cerci: paired sensory appendages at the end of the abdomen.

4. Malpighian tubules: internal excretory organs associated with the digestive tract (see Fig. 4–23).

5. Wings. A pair is located on each of the second and third segments of the thorax in most adult insects. Some insects, such as lice and fleas, have lost their wings during their evolution, and one order, Thysanura, has never had wings.

The Insecta also share the following characteristics with some (not all) other arthropod classes:

1. Mandibles, or chewing mouthparts, that in some insect groups have become so modified as to no longer be obviously mandibles.

2. A pair of antennae ("feelers") and a pair of compound eyes, composed of many facets (lenses), present in most adult insects.

3. Tracheae, breathing tubes, branching throughout the body and opening through 10 (or fewer) pairs of spiracles (pores).

DIVERSITY AND CLASSIFICATION

Characteristic of insects is great diversity in form; very few insects conform precisely to any generalized structure. The search for unity and recurring pat-

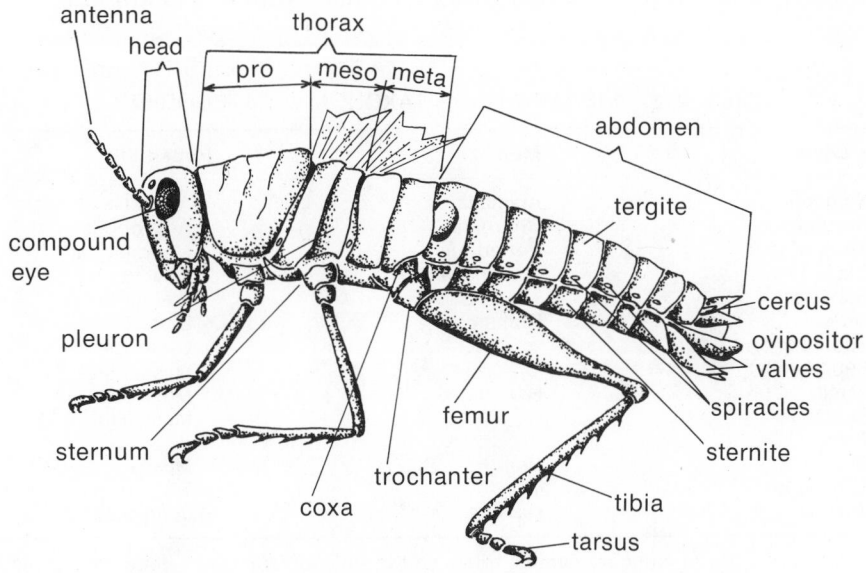

Figure 2–1. External structure of female grasshopper.

terns in insect diversity is the role of systematists—literally, those who systematize, or organize, the diverse array of living things. This ordering and classification is essential to all who study insects, for without a standardized, international system of naming animals and plants, communication among scientists would be extremely difficult. Beginning before Linnaeus (see Chapter One) and continuing today, systematists have used a hierarchy of categories, each of which is subordinate to that preceding. Table 2–1 shows the more commonly used systematic categories and how two common and familiar animals are classified.

The focal point of the classification scheme is the **species.** In the days of Linnaeus, and for a long time thereafter, many systematists believed in special creation—that insect (and other) species had been created "each after its own kind" (Genesis 1:24). This view led to a **typological species concept**; i.e., each form of life was unique and conformed to a "type" or model example. Each published species description described a **type specimen** which was placed in a collection for future reference. Undeniably, many animal and plant species conform enough to model examples, or verbal and pictorial descriptions, to be recognized by scientist and layman alike. However, beginning in the 19th century, the evolutionary views of Darwin and others changed the outlook of most systematists by introducing the notion that species do, in fact, change over time in response to changing environments. Thus, the typological concept has been replaced by a more modern **biological species concept,** wherein a species is viewed as (ideally) a population of organisms that interbreed but are reproductively isolated from all other populations. In actual practice, it is often extremely difficult to determine breeding limits of populations in nature, and specialists must rely on comparative studies (discussed subsequently). Ideally, individuals from interbreeding populations should show more similarity among themselves than with populations with which they do not breed, because of members of an interbreeding population share many identical genes.

It is still necessary to have reference materials for comparative purposes, especially since so many systematists are actively describing insect species around the world. Therefore, when a specialist, after study, decides that he (or she) has a "new" species, he publishes a description, perhaps with an illustration, in which

Table 2–1.   HIERARCHY OF TAXONOMIC CATEGORIES*

Level	Man	House Fly
Kingdom	Animalia	Animalia
Phylum	Chordata	Arthropoda
Subphylum	Vertebrata	Mandibulata
Class	Mammalia	Insecta
Subclass		Pterygota
Order	Primates	Diptera
Suborder		Cyclorrhapha
Superfamily		Muscoidea
Family	Hominidae	Muscidae
Subfamily		Muscinae
Tribe		
Genus	*Homo*	*Musca*
Subgenus		
Species	*sapiens*	*domestica*

*Endings are clues to category names: tribes end in **-ini**, subfamilies in **-inae**, families in **-idae**, superfamilies in **-oidea**, and most insect orders end in **-ptera**.

he designates a **type** or **holotype** specimen. This specimen is usually placed in a large museum collection to serve as a reference thereafter. He may also designate a series of **paratypes,** specimens that illustrate variation within the species, and these may go to several museums as insurance in case the holotype is lost or destroyed. Finally, of course, he gives the insect a name and tells where, in his estimation, it fits into the hierarchy of classification (i.e., to what tribe, subfamily, or family it belongs).

Because there are so many insects, and entomologists, naming of insects (and other animals) must follow certain standardized rules. A species is referred to by two names, the generic (genus) and specific (species) names. These are either Latin or latinized, and in this form are used throughout the world in scientific literature. Customarily, the name of the describer follows the specific name. Higher categories are not usually included with a species name, though in large animal classes such as Insecta, the order and family may be included in parentheses to aid those unfamiliar with insect groups and to provide information for automated literature retrieval systems. Thus, a complete scientific name for the house fly is *Musca domestica* Linnaeus (Diptera:Muscidae). The rules further state that if two people describe the same insect with different names, the first published description shall hold priority. Neither may two different species within a genus hold the same name (though a genus may contain one, several, or many species). An International Commission on Zoological Nomenclature polices these (and other) rules and meets periodically to settle disputes.

Scientific names are standardized for the scientific community, but many insects, particularly economically important species, have common names as well. These may vary according to interest; *Diabrotica undecimpunctata* is called the southern corn rootworm or spotted cucumber beetle, depending on your crop. Especially in the United States, there have been several efforts to standardize common names for more effective communication among economic entomologists. In this book, I use standardized common names from the Entomological Society of America (1970) and scientific names when no common names are available.

STUDYING INSECT EVOLUTION

Insect species are products of evolution, and systematists, in designating species and higher categories (genus, family, etc.), strive for a "natural" or **phyletic** classification: one that reflects the actual evolutionary sequence. Obviously, nobody lives long enough to observe evolution of new species, genera, or families, though evolutionary changes within existing species are well-documented (see subsequent examples). The probable course of evolutionary changes must therefore be inferred from comparative studies. Presumably, populations possessing common characteristics share a common ancestry, and the closer the similarity, the closer the inferred relationship. Conversely, very different insects may be only distantly related. Traditionally, speculation on insect evolution has been based on comparative morphology. For example, the placement of longitudinal wing veins is basically similar in all winged insects. Comstock and Needham (1899), along with others, inferred from this that all winged insects are related, though distantly; insect wings apparently evolved but once. Thus, winged insects are considered a subclass (Pterygota) of the class Insecta.

There are major differences among the wings of insects, however, and these are used to justify classifying winged insects into 23 rather distinct orders (see Chapter Three).

Though comparative morphology has been (and will remain) the major source of systematic data, systematists have compared many other biological characteristics. Evans and Matthews (1973) delineated sand wasp species by comparing their behaviors. Alexander and Moore (1962) found that morphologically nearly indistinguishable species of cicadas could be differentiated by songs. Barber (1951) came to a similar conclusion after studying light-flash patterns among fireflies. Cardé's (1971) studies of tiger moths revealed specific differences in sex pheromones among otherwise similar populations. Other entomologists have compared genetics, activity periods, and biochemistry. Any biological attribute of insects may be subject to evolutionary change and therefore can serve as a basis for comparative studies.

Researchers in insect evolution stress that the choice of characteristics to be compared is critical. Blackwelder (1967) suggested that useful characteristics are those that do not vary greatly but are consistently expressed and can be measured reasonably. In general, the more characteristics measured, the better. By counting legs only, one would group all six-legged arthropods together as insects, deriving from a single ancestral population. If number of abdominal segments, number and location of spiracles, and presence or absence of malpighian tubules are also considered, there is evidence for regarding six legs as having evolved independently in at least three additional arthropod classes (Table 3–1). This complication is **convergent evolution,** in which two forms from separate ancestors evolve similarly in response to similar evolutionary pressures. A classic case is that of mantids and mantispids (Fig. 2–2, *A* and *B*), members of two different orders yet remarkably similar in appearance and habits as adults. In cases of convergent evolution, some differences are usually evident in other characteristics: mantids and mantispids differ in metamorphosis, wing venation, life history, and in more subtle morphological ways (such as number of tarsal segments). Increasingly, systematists use computers to handle the voluminous data generated by measurement of a great many characteristics. There has been much heated debate among systematists as to the relative importance of characteristics in delineating higher taxonomic categories, and the issue is far from settled. Sneath and Sokal (1973) have championed **numerical taxonomy,** in which as many characteristics as possible are measured and analyzed to produce objective taxonomic categories. Numerical methods give equal emphasis to all measured characteristics; Blackwelder's criteria do not apply. Numerical data are especially suited to computer analysis and have become a valuable addition to the systematic toolbox.

Inevitably, it is not possible to measure all morphological, behavioral, biochemical, genetic, physiological, ecological, and geographical data for each of several thousand insects that may be compared in a systematic study. For one thing, it is too time-consuming, and more importantly, most such information may not yet be known. Therefore, classifications, particularly the higher categories, are somewhat subjective and arbitrary. As new information comes to light, classifications may be revised and updated, and this can confuse the non-systematist who may suddenly discover that what he thought was a single genus having many species has just been "split" into several genera comprising a few species each. For instance, the codling moth, which for years had been *Car-*

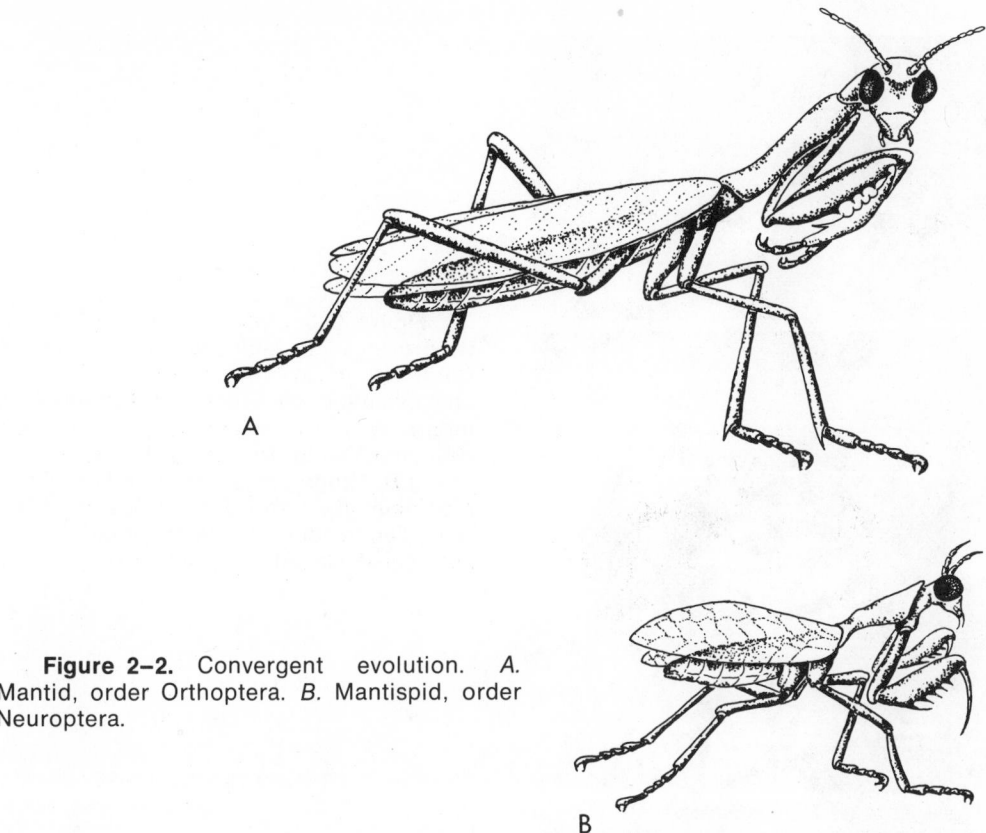

Figure 2–2. Convergent evolution. *A.* Mantid, order Orthoptera. *B.* Mantispid, order Neuroptera.

pocapsa pomonella, family Tortricidae, is now considered to be *Laspeyresia pomonella,* family Olethreutidae. Such temporary annoyances are, however, positive steps toward a classification system that reflects as accurately as possible the actual relationships among living organisms.

The concrete evidence on which to best base the evolutionary history of insects is the record of fossils, preserved remains of insects or their fragments in rock or amber. Being fragile and small, insects of the past have not been preserved nearly so abundantly as have been bones and teeth of vertebrates or mollusk shells. Insect fossils are therefore comparatively rare. Most of them were formed under one of two unusual conditions: (1) an insect falling into a pond was rapidly covered with silt, preventing total decay, and the rock eventually resulting from the silt did not undergo severe stresses; or (2) insects were trapped in sticky pitch exuding from coniferous trees and the resulting resin hardened into amber, preserving insects whole and in relatively good condition inside (Fig. 2–3). When such fossils are discovered and brought to entomologists' attention, it is possible to assign to them an age, based on either the age of the associated rock or measurement of the radioactive decay rate. Geologists have thus assigned names and ages to the various periods in the earth's history (Table 2–2). Some insect fossils, mostly fragments or wings, are known for all geologic periods since the Upper Carboniferous, though most are found in Tertiary sediments.

A

B

Figure 2–3. Insect fossils. *A,* Dragonfly preserved in sedimentary rock. (From Carpenter, F. M. 1973. Geological history and evolution of insects. *In* Tipton, V. J. (ed.). Syllabus/Introductory Entomology. Brigham Young University Press, Provo, Utah.) *B,* Midge preserved in amber. (From McAlpine, J. F., and J. E. H. Martin. 1969. Canadian amber—a paleontological treasure-chest. Canad. Entomol. *101*:819–838.)

Because of the comparative scarcity of insect fossils, the record is incomplete and may over-represent insects associated with water or conifers—the fossil record of dragonflies, for instance, is rather complete. Relatively few insect fossils clearly demonstrate evolutionary relationships among existing insect orders. As new evidence is discovered, views of insect evolution will change. The evidence now available (the best we can do) strongly supports evolution of insect diversity through a series of adaptive radiations.

ADAPTIVE RADIATION AND INSECT EVOLUTION

Insects in their diversity are excellent examples of the phenomenon of **adaptive radiation,** the evolution of a number of rather different organisms from a single ancestral group. In the case of insects, major adaptations that evolved very early are the exoskeleton, small size, wings, and metamorphosis. Each of these apparently was followed by extensive diversification in structure, physiology, and behavior, leading to invasion of numerous habitats in space and time. Before speculating on how adaptive radiation occurred in the insects, we need to consider evolution of adaptations.

An adaptation is any genetically based characteristic—structural, behavioral, or physiological—that aids an organism to survive and reproduce successfully.

Most biologists agree that adaptations arise through evolution, the process in outline being:

1. An organism is composed of structures and behaviors that are mostly under genetic control, and these structures and functions enable it to respond to environmental factors long enough to reproduce.

2. Insect species exist in interbreeding groups, populations, whose members exhibit variation in outward appearance and behavior, a reflection of genetic variation within the population.

3. The environment (e.g., weather, competitors, food supply, predators) to which insects are exposed is likewise variable. This variation may favor certain genetic combinations within populations, so that some individuals will leave more offspring than others, thereby increasing the proportion of their genes in

Table 2–2. OUTLINE OF GEOLOGIC TIME AND ANTIQUITY OF INSECT ORDERS*

Period	Years Since Start	Important Events	Insect Orders
Recent	10,000 years	Rise of civilization	Mallophaga, Anoplura (lice)
Tertiary	60 million	"Age of Mammals"	Embioptera (webspinners), Siphonaptera (fleas) Strepsiptera (twisted-winged insects)
Cretaceous	135 million	Rise of mammals and seed plants	Isoptera (termites), Lepidoptera (butterflies and moths)
Jurassic	185 million	Dinosaurs and origin of birds	Dermaptera (earwigs), Diptera (flies)
Triassic	230 million	Diverse reptiles, origin of early mammals	Hemiptera (bugs), Hymenoptera (ants, bees, wasps)
Permian	280 million	Glaciers and wide-spread extinction	Odonata (dragonflies), Plecoptera (stoneflies), Thysanoptera (thrips), Homoptera (cicadas, etc.), Neuroptera (lacewings), Mecoptera (scorpionflies), Trichoptera (caddisflies), Coleoptera (beetles), Protelytroptera,† Glosselytrodea†
Carboniferous Upper	310 million	Insects and amphibians, major coal formation	Thysanura (bristletails), Ephemeroptera (mayflies), Orthoptera (roaches, etc.), Palaeodictyoptera† Megasecoptera†, Diaphanopterodea†, Protodonata†, Miomoptera†, Protorthoptera†, Caloneurodea†
Lower	345 million	Some coal formation	No known insects
Devonian	405 million	Early amphibians	No known insects
Silurian	425 million	First land plants, diverse fish	No known insects
Ordovician	500 million	Origin of fish	No known insects
Cambrian	600 million	Diverse marine invertebrates	No known insects

*Ranges of orders from Carpenter, F. M. 1973. Geological history and evolution of insects. In Tipton, V. J. (ed.). Syllabus/Introductory Entomology. Brigham Young University Press, Provo, Utah, pp. 77–88.

†Became extinct after Permian period.

the population. This process is natural selection, and the individuals leaving the most offspring are said to have a selective advantage.

4. Over time, a changing environment will therefore bring about genetic changes which will be reflected in the structural, behavioral, and physiological characteristics of insects — their adaptations.*

A well-documented contemporary case illustrating this process is that of the British "salt-and-pepper" moth, *Biston betularia.* When first described in the 18th century, these moths in England were predominantly white with black speckling (Fig. 2–4), with an occasional rare black individual. During the latter half of the 19th century. particularly around industrial cities, the black form became progressively more abundant, so that by 1900 a large proportion of *Biston betularia* was dark. By releasing equal numbers of white and dark moths in both suburban and rural woods, Kettlewell (1973) found that survival of dark moths was greater near cities and survival of white moths was greater away from cities (Table 2–3). He showed further that this was due to the sooty tree trunks exposed to coal smoke near cities; black moths blended better with the dark surface and were not as easy for birds to find. This phenomenon is termed industrial melanism. The opposite result occurred in rural woods, where light-colored lichens provided a background on which lighter moths were protected and dark

---

*A more extensive treatment of natural selection theory may be found in a modern biology text, e.g., Wilson et al., 1973; Keeton, 1972.

Figure 2–4. *Biston betularia* (Lepidoptera:Geometridae), light and dark forms. *A.* On a soot-covered oak trunk near Birmingham, England. *B.* On a lichen-covered tree trunk in unpolluted countryside. (From Kettlewell, H. B. D. 1973. The Evolution of Melanism. The Study of a Recurring Necessity; with Special Reference to Industrial Melanism in the Lepidoptera. Clarendon Press, Oxford.)

Table 2-3. RESULTS OF RELEASE AND RECAPTURE OF DARK AND LIGHT
PEPPERED MOTH, *BISTON BETULARIA,* IN POLLUTED AND
UNPOLLUTED ENGLISH WOODLANDS*

	Light Moths	Dark Moths
Birmingham: polluted woods		
Released	137	447
Recovered	18	123
Per Cent Recovered	13.1	27.5
Dorset: unpolluted woods		
Released	496	473
Recovered	62	30
Per Cent Recovered	12.5	6.3

*From Kettlewell, H. B. D. 1973. The Evolution of Melanism. The Study of a Recurring Necessity;
with Special Reference to Industrial Melanism in the Lepidoptera. Clarendon Press, Oxford.

moths stood out. In this example, an environmental change (air pollution and soot on trees) favored some genes (those causing dark pigment) over others in survival, leading to the adaptation of dark coloration. Newer evidence supporting Kettlewell's theory is that since the 1950's, stringent air pollution controls in Britain have significantly reduced sootiness on tree trunks, and the white moths are becoming increasingly prevalent near cities. Industrial melanism has been demonstrated or suspected in more than 150 species of moths in Europe and North America (Kettlewell, 1973).

The development of resistance to insecticides is further evidence of the evolution of insect adaptations by natural selection. Widespread use of DDT and other synthetic organic insecticides began in 1943. In 1946, 10 insect and mite species were resistant to chemicals that formerly killed them; by 1967 this number had increased to 224, including 97 arthropod species of public health importance (Brown, 1968).

The mechanism for developing resistance has been demonstrated experimentally in laboratory studies on houseflies, cockroaches, and other insects. In any population, there is variability; while most individuals are susceptible to insecticide, some are resistant. Like mosquitoes that remain stationary rather than walking about on DDT-treated walls, these resistant insects may have a genetically based behavior that allows them to avoid contact with a lethal dose. Alternatively, they may possess enzymes that speed detoxification of the poison; resistant houseflies can chemically change to DDT to a less toxic chemical. When insecticides are applied to such a genetically variable population, most of the susceptible insects are killed, whereas the resistant remnant reproduces, passing on to their offspring genes responsible for resistance (Fig. 2–5). The proportion of resistant individuals in the succeeding generation is then greater. If the insecticide is reapplied, the proportion of resistance increases again. It has usually taken several generations for the amount of resistance to increase beyond negligible levels, though once resistance is established in an insect population, it often remains even after the insecticide is no longer applied.

Evolution of such adaptations as industrial melanism and insecticide resistance is relatively minor when compared to evolution of whole orders of insects from wingless ancestors, yet the process of natural selection, operating over vastly longer time periods, is thought to have brought about the great diversity in

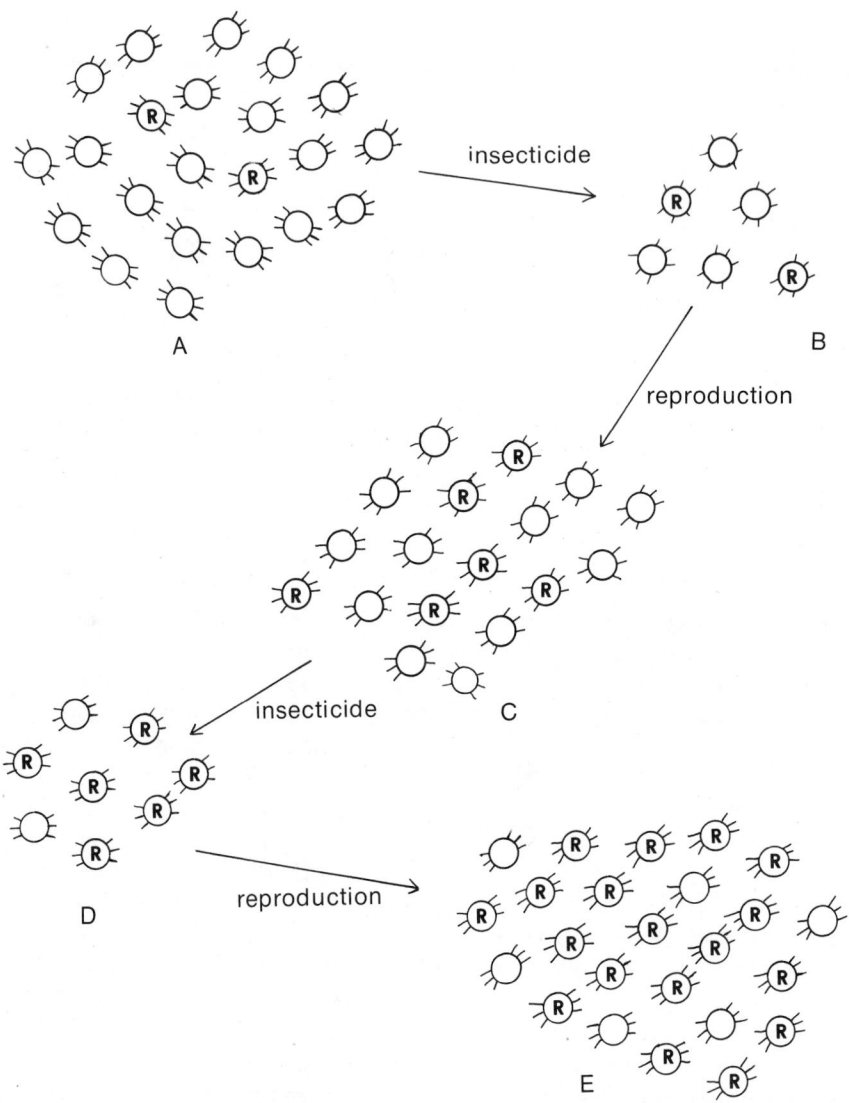

Figure 2–5. Evolution of insecticide resistance. R = resistant insects. *A,* Starting population only 9 per cent resistant. *B,* Insecticide kills 80 per cent of susceptible insects. *C,* Each insect leaves 3 offspring; population is now 33 per cent resistant. *D,* Insecticide again kills 80 per cent of susceptible individuals. *E,* Each insect again leaves 3 offspring. Population is now 75 per cent resistant.

insects that we see today. There is no a priori reason why the same processes that have brought about insecticide resistance in two years or industrial melanism in 50 years could not have changed "primitive"* marine worms into butterflies in 600 million years.

ORIGIN OF INSECTS

Most biologists agree that plant and animal life originally evolved in the seas, because the oldest known fossils are of marine organisms and the chemical reactions of living cells require liquid surroundings similar in some respects to sea water. Among the earliest fossils are those of Annelida (segmented worms) and Arthropoda whose extant (living) members share a number of common characteristics: segmentation, a dorsal blood vessel, a ventral nerve cord, and similarities in early development (see Chapter Seven). These similarities suggest a common ancestry for the two phyla; Arthropoda may have evolved from as yet undiscovered segmented worms, perhaps worms with limblike structures on some or all segments. A frustrating and unavoidable fact is that possession of hard body parts is a prerequisite to being fossilized except under extraordinary circumstances.

Sometime before the Cambrian period (Table 2–2), probably over a span of several million years, an external skeleton and jointed limbs evolved in at least one group of segmented worms. Scientists disagree on how many times exoskeletons evolved. Traditionalists suggest a single arthropodization followed by adaptive radiation, whereas Manton (1964), Cisne (1974), and others point out sufficient anatomical differences among arthropods to suggest at least two, and maybe more, origins of Arthropoda.

A remarkable rainforest animal, *Peripatus,* phylum Onychophora, (Fig. 2–6)

---

*Much of evolutionary literature uses the terms "primitive" and "advanced" or "lower" and "higher" in referring to various life forms. (Thus, insects are "lower and more primitive" than we, who are "higher and more advanced" animals.) These terms are misleading, partly because we (at least I) may attach values to the terms: higher and advanced are "better." Also, one may draw the erroneous conclusion that "advanced" existing animals may have evolved from "primitive" existing animals—that the monkeys are our ancestors. In fact, *all existing* animal and plant species are equally "advanced" in that all presently exist. Throughout this book, therefore, the terms "primitive" and "advanced" will appear in quotation marks.

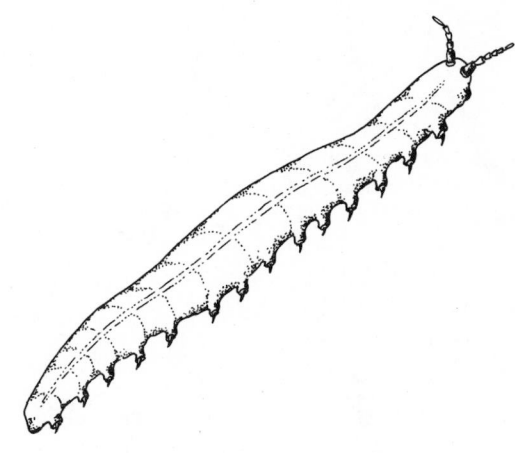

Figure 2–6. *Peripatus,* phylum Onychophora.

that lives under logs and has anatomical and developmental characteristics similar to those of Annelida and Arthropoda, gives us an idea of what such worms may have looked like, though of course Arthropoda did not evolve from present-day Onychophora. Modern Onychophora are unsegmented as adults, though their embryos are segmented. Manton (1949) and others suggest that Onychophora are arthropods whose exoskeleton has become greatly reduced, leaving only the cuticle.

The earliest (Cambrian) extensive animal fossils include arthropods from three subphyla: Trilobita, Chelicerata, and Mandibulata. Of these, the diverse marine Trilobita (Fig. 2–7) became extinct, and Chelicerata gave rise to several living classes, including the diverse Arachnida—spiders, ticks, and scorpions. Mandibulata are probably polyphyletic. Crustacea share with Chelicerata and Trilobita biramous (two-pronged) limbs, extensive cephalic digestive glands, and similarities in head appendages (Manton, 1964). Other mandibulate arthropods (Chilopoda, Diplopoda, Insecta, etc.) have uniramous limbs and head appendages different from those of Crustacea.

Evolution of the exoskeleton has puzzled biologists, who have proposed several hypotheses. The most popular suggests evolution of a hardened exoskeleton in response to predation, and indeed, the few known Precambrian fossils include wormlike creatures with hardened, presumably predatory, jaws. Alternatively, Nicol (1966) hypothesized that a rigid supporting structure evolved in response to increased body size. Blood pressure, maintained by muscle contraction was, and is, the principal means of support for segmented worms. Cisne (1974) suggested that a hardened, supportive exoskeleton is more economical, in terms of energy, than the hydrostatic skeleton of annelids. Muscles are reduced in bulk and number and concentrated across hinged joints for maximum effectiveness with minimal effort (see Chapter Five).

Whatever hypothesis one accepts, certainly evolution of an exoskeleton was prerequisite to a major adaptive radiation among early arthropods. The exoskeleton, composed of a nonliving cuticular layer secreted by underlying epidermal cells (Fig. 5–22), provides form, protection, and locations for muscular attachment. Hardened areas characteristically form plates, or **sclerites,** separated by thinner, membranous cuticle (Fig. 2–8). This arrangement allows for movement

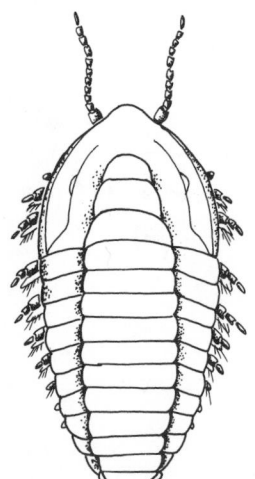

Figure 2–7. Trilobite, member of an extinct arthropod class, Trilobita.

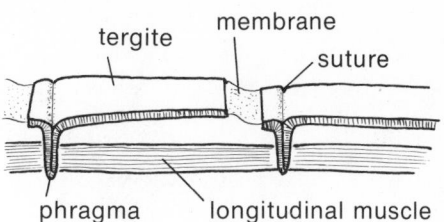

Figure 2–8. Abdominal tergites, showing arrangement of muscle and exoskeleton.

of sclerites relative to one another. Ingrowths of exoskeleton for muscle attachment are often visible externally as pits or sutures.

The jointed limbs that resulted from this sclerite-membrane arrangement allowed increased speed of movement, and in addition, limbs became modified into specialized structures for feeding. Figure 2–9 shows a front view of a grasshopper head (A) and its disassembled mouthparts (B), an example of generalized mandibulate mouthparts. The **labrum** covers the other mouthparts anteriorly, and it looks (and functions) like an upper lip. **Mandibles** are directly behind the labrum. They are heavily sclerotized jaws that bite and grind food particles, be they pieces of grass (in grasshoppers) or pieces of grasshoppers (in mantids). Behind the mandibles are the **maxillae,** bearing **palpi,** fingerlike projections that handle and "taste" food. Behind the maxillae is the **labium,** or lower lip, likewise bearing palpi.

Noting patterns of nerve and muscle attachment to mouthparts (see Chapter Five) and of embryonic development (see Chapter Seven), entomologists are in general agreement that at least the mandibles, maxillae, and labium each represent a pair of limbs greatly specialized for obtaining and handling food. The labium represents a fusion of two limbs. Thus, the insect head is thought to have evolved from fusion of the "primitive head," or **acrostome,** and at least three body segments. (Some have suggested that the labrum and perhaps even compound eyes or antennae may have evolved from limbs, but comparative evidence is not so convincing.) Fossil mandibulate arthropods are found in Cambrian marine deposits, showing the antiquity of modification of limbs for mouthparts. Arthropod morphologists disagree on how many times the evolution of mouthparts from limbs occurred. Certainly Chelicerata, whose mouthparts are exceedingly unlike those of Mandibulata (Chapter Three) represent independent evolution, and differences among Mandibulata are great enough to suggest that Mandibulata are polyphyletic: that limbs evolved into mandibulate mouthparts more than once (Cisne, 1974).

The main advantage of specialized structures for feeding (discussed in detail in Chapter Four) is their efficiency, permitting discontinuous feeding. An animal that feeds discontinuously has time to do other things, like find another meal. Furthermore, specialized feeding structures permit specialized diets, expanding the opportunities for adaptive radiation. Discontinuous feeding was therefore an important **preadaptation*** to survival in the terrestrial environment, where food distribution is not as uniform as in the seas and individual meals often must be searched out.

An exoskeleton was another preadaptation for the earliest arthropods colon-

---

*Any genetically based attribute evolved in one context that has fortuitous survival value in another context.

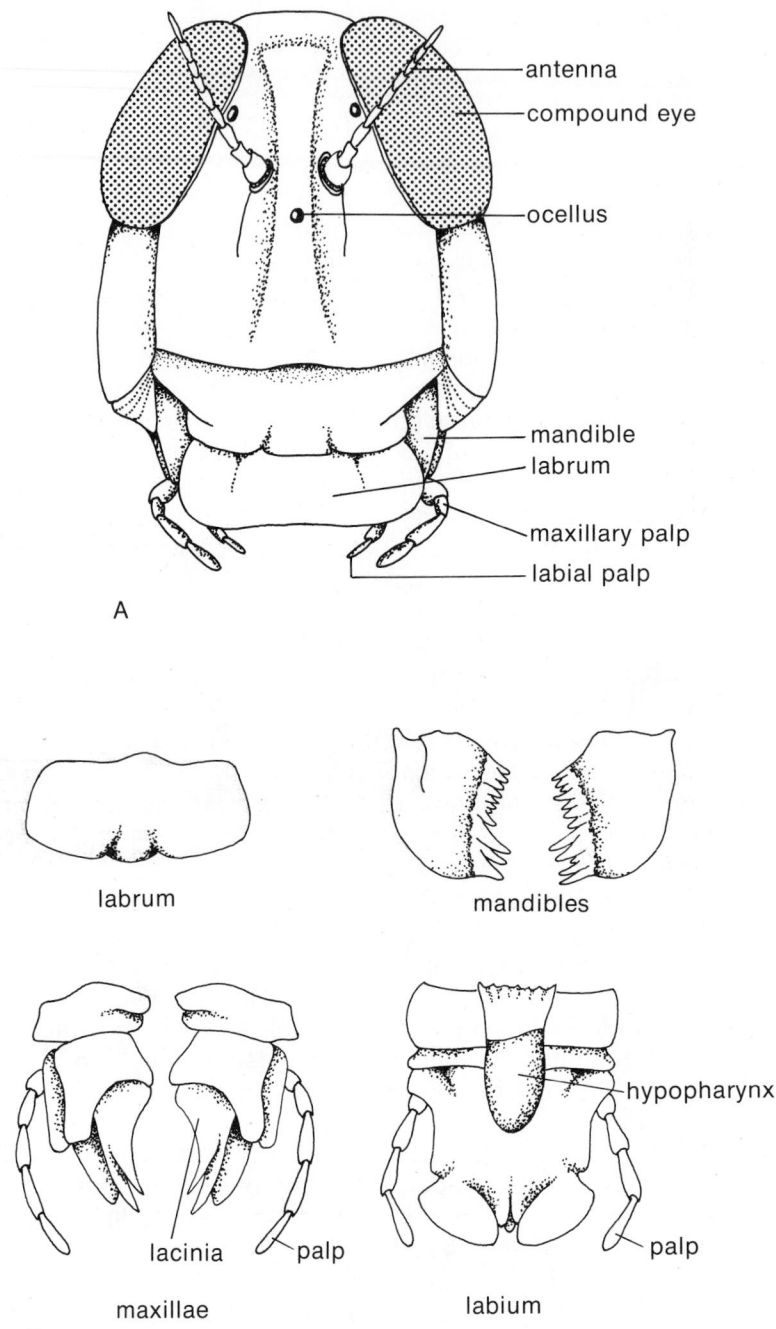

Figure 2–9. Mandibulate mouthparts of grasshopper. *A.* Anterior view of head. *B.* Mouthparts, shown separately.

izing the terrestrial environment. Retention of water is a major survival problem facing terrestrial animals, particularly small ones with a high surface-to-volume ratio (see Chapter Four). The arthropod exoskeleton is rather impermeable to water, thus holding it in. Moreover, the exoskeleton is rigid, providing necessary support since air is not very supportive (which is one reason why there are no terrestrial jellyfish). Support is improved by limbs which raise the bulk of the body off the ground, and this permits faster movement.

The terrestrial environment is, in general, more discrete or "patchy" than the relatively uniform marine environment (with the exception of intertidal and estuarine areas). Favorable areas for survival and reproduction are interspersed with extensive areas of hostile environment. Consider an apple orchard from the standpoint of codling moth larvae within the fruit: inside they are protected from drying, insecticides, and predation, and they live surrounded by food, but outside it's another story and a long way to the next apple. The earliest terrestrial arthropods faced similar obstacles, and small size was then, and is now, a distinct advantage in occupying limited microhabitats. Also, small-sized animals do not eat much, an important advantage in utilizing food in small, specialized parcels. The codling moth spends its entire larvahood in a single apple core.

Terrestrial animals and plants are relative newcomers in the history of life. Plants evidently existed on land somewhat before the earliest terrestrial animals, which arrived (probably) in the Devonian period (Table 2–2). Arthropod ancestors of insects may have been among these first land animals. Though we have no fossil evidence, it is likely that the earliest terrestrial arthropods were small, multilegged, ground-dwelling forms, superficially like present-day centipedes.

According to this view of insect evolution (Martynov, 1925; Carpenter, 1953), several groups of multilegged arthropods colonized the terrestrial environment. Some of their descendants, the centipedes, millipedes, and some minor classes (Chapter Three), have remained multilegged and are not as diverse, abundant, or widespread as are the largest terrestrial arthropod classes, Insecta and Arachnida. The great success of these two classes evidently stems from their small size, loss of abdominal limbs, and **tagmatization,** division of the body into discrete regions.

Abdominal limbs were probably lost from the rear forward (Fig. 2–10) until six remained, perhaps as insects' ancestors moved to more open environments. The paucity of marine insects suggests that leg loss occurred after the insects' ancestors moved onto land. Though no intermediate fossils exist between multileggers and six-leggers, it is suspected that leg loss to six occurred at least three times (Chapter Three). Six legs moved three at a time form a tripod (Fig. 5–26) that is most stable if the center of gravity is located directly over it. Most insects reveal this arrangement, with six legs and wings (if present) attached to a **thorax,** three fused segments in the center of the body. Along with this, the abdomen became shorter (Fig. 2–10), moving the center of gravity forward. This increased the speed at which insects could move about, and this was (and is) a great advantage in surviving in the patchy terrestrial environment. Insects could consequently occupy an increased variety of habitats, and this could have led to adaptive radiation. Tagmatization was therefore a logical consequence of limb loss: The head, meeting the environment first, became a center for sensory and food input; the thorax became a locomotor center, providing strength and muscle attachment for legs (and later, wings); and the abdomen became principally a container for digestive, excretory, and reproductive organs.

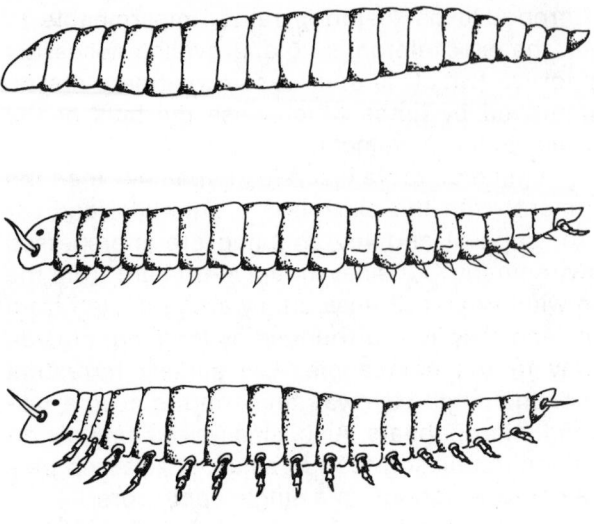

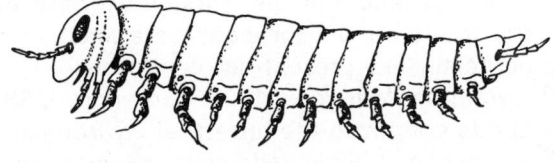

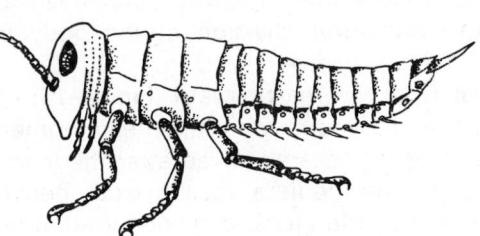

Figure 2–10. Hypothetical steps in evolution of insect from annelid worm. (Redrawn from Snodgrass, R. E. 1935. Principles of Insect Morphology. © 1935 by McGraw-Hill, Inc. Used by permission of McGraw-Hill Book Company.)

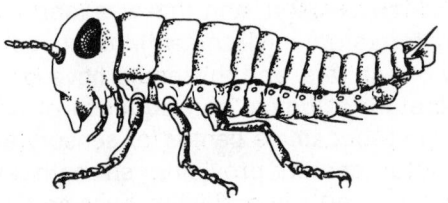

EVOLUTION OF MODERN ORDERS

Bristletails, order Thysanura (Fig. 3–9), are the only existing insect order whose members have never had wings. We presume that the earliest insects were rather like them. However, by the time of the first insect fossils (Carboniferous), not only do insects have six legs and tagmatization, but most of them also have wings. The origin of insect wings has long puzzled entomologists. Because of similarities in wing venation, it is generally, though not universally, believed that insect wings evolved once, probably as outgrowths of the thorax. Certainly they were not modified limbs, because the thorax already had legs and still does. An early hypothesis suggested that these outgrowths were first used to glide short distances, and the most efficient gliders occupied the widest variety of habitats and left the most offspring. Others have suggested that the thoracic gills of aquatic nymphs of mayflylike insects might have been retained by terrestrial adults for gliding. Existing mayflies are quite "primitive" and have aquatic nymphs, and mayflies are among the oldest insect fossils. Wigglesworth (1963) speculated that wings evolved from airfoil lobes in very small insects. Alexander and Brown (1963) suggested that thoracic outgrowths may have originally been used in display for species recognition and sex attraction, with the larger-lobed insects leaving more offspring. As larger display lobes thus evolved, gliding, then flight, followed. Many existing insects do use their wings for display, and this "sexual" hypothesis does account for wings' being limited to adult insects.

However wings evolved, their presence was, and is, a tremendous advantage to very small animals in the terrestrial environment. Wings permit very fast movement, and insects having them can move very quickly through hostile territory from one host plant to another or from one pool to another. In terms of energy, flight is more efficient than walking, too (Schmidt-Nielsen, 1972). As winged insects began flight, an evolutionary opening was created for aerial predators, which was quickly filled by creatures closely resembling contemporary dragonflies, including the celebrated *Meganeura* (Fig. 2–11A). With a 30-inch wingspan, this was the widest insect ever to exist, giving rise to the erroneous popular impression that Paleozoic insects were much larger than those of today. They weren't; the Protodonata are the only known extinct insects larger than those of today.

Wings thus permitted (and still permit) rapid occupation of a tremendous variety of habitats, and insects apparently underwent a spectacular adaptive radiation concurrently with the evolution of wings. This view is consistent with the fossil record; eleven orders appear in the Carboniferous period (Table 2–2; Fig. 2–12). These were diverse insects, ranging in size from minute Miomoptera to the aforementioned giant dragonflies, and from the odd-looking extinct order Paleodictyoptera, rather like mayflies but with sucking mouthparts, to essentially modern Orthoptera, represented by cockroaches very similar to those of today (Fig. 2–11). Forty per cent of Carboniferous and Permian fossils are of cockroaches.

Several Carboniferous insect orders contained insects capable of wing flexing. Ability to flex wings back over the abdomen permitted insects the simultaneous advantages of flight and small size; they could move about rapidly and efficiently, yet hide in and under things when necessary. This permitted occupation of additional terrestrial habitats, with consequent adaptive radiation.

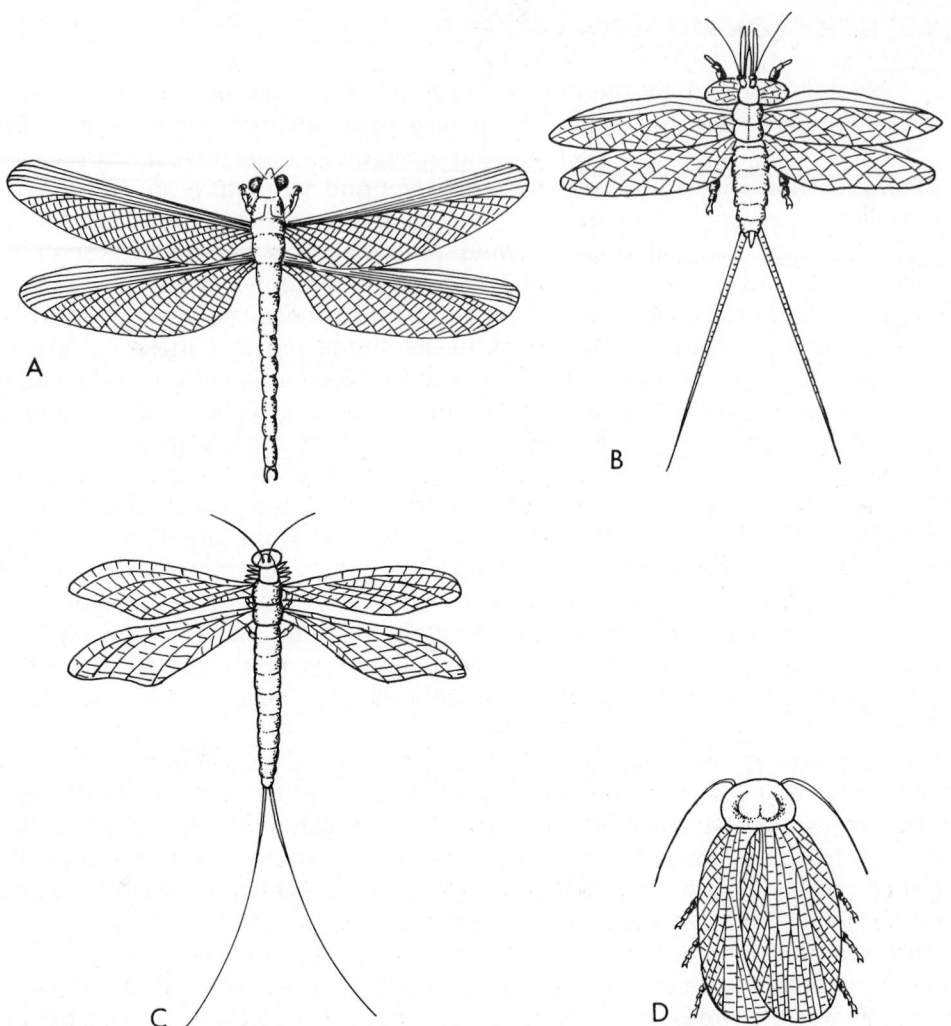

Figure 2–11. Extinct insects from Upper Carboniferous period. *A, Meganeura,* order Protodonata. *B,* Stenodictya, order Palaeodictyoptera. *C,* Mischoptera, order Megasecoptera. *D, Aphthoroblattina,* order Orthoptera. (*B* and *C* redrawn from Carpenter, F. M. 1973. Geological history and evolution of insects. *In* Tipton, V. J. (ed.). Syllabus/Introductory Entomology. Brigham Young University Press, Provo, Utah. *D* redrawn from A Textbook of Geology, Part II, Historical Geology, by C. Schuchert and C. O. Dunbar. © 1933 by John Wiley & Sons, Inc. Reprinted by permission of John Wiley & Sons, Inc.)

All the Carboniferous insects apparently had **gradual metamorphosis** or **hemimetabolous** development (Chapter Seven), in which, normally, eggs hatch into nymphs that look more or less like miniature, wingless adults (Fig. 2–13A) The nymph develops through a series of stages (instars) as it grows, periodically shedding its exoskeleton, or molting. (The insect exoskeleton is incapable of stretching or growing and must be replaced at intervals; see Chapter Seven for details.) Once the winged adult stage is reached, no additional molts occur (with a very few exceptions). We assume that Carboniferous insects had gradual metamorphosis because it occurs today in Ephemeroptera, Odonata, and Orthoptera, and there are fossils of miniature, wingless Paleodictyoptera, Megasecoptera, and Prothorthoptera.

Probably before the beginning of the Permian period, there developed complex (or **holometabolous**) metamorphosis (Fig. 2–13*B*), in which the egg hatches into a larva, specialized for feeding and usually appearing very unlike the adult. The larva molts several times as it grows, until it becomes a pupa, a "resting" (or rearranging) stage from which emerges the winged (usually) adult, specializing in reproduction and dispersal. Eighty-eight per cent of all existing insect species are holometabolous, and this type of metamorphosis permits occupation of more than one habitat by the same insect at different stages of its life. This development again allowed relatively rapid occupation of new habitats and consequent adaptive radiation, particularly among Coleoptera (beetles), which represent about 40 per cent of Permian insect fossils. Coleoptera have retained their dominance; nearly 40 per cent of existing insect species are beetles.

It is difficult to trace the ancestry of modern orders because of a lack of intermediate fossils; a notable exception is *Permotipula* (order Mecoptera), which has wing venation very much like that of earliest craneflies but possesses four wings. Mecoptera are very likely ancestral to at least Diptera, and wing venation similarities suggest mecopteran ancestors for Lepidoptera, Trichoptera, and perhaps Hymenoptera. The origin of Coleoptera is more of a mystery owing to loss and modification of wing veins as the forewings and hindwings became modified (Chapter Three), though "primitive" Neuroptera might have been beetle ancestors. Complex metamorphosis could have evolved more than once before the Permian period, because certain existing Hemimetabola (thrips, order Thysanoptera, and whiteflies, family Aleyrodidae, order Homoptera) have a resting stage very like a pupa. We presume Permian Mecoptera, Neuroptera, and other orders to have been holometabolous because of their morphological similarity to these existing orders, though there are few fossils of their immatures, and it is difficult to tell which larvae became which adults because of the extreme dissimilarities in form.

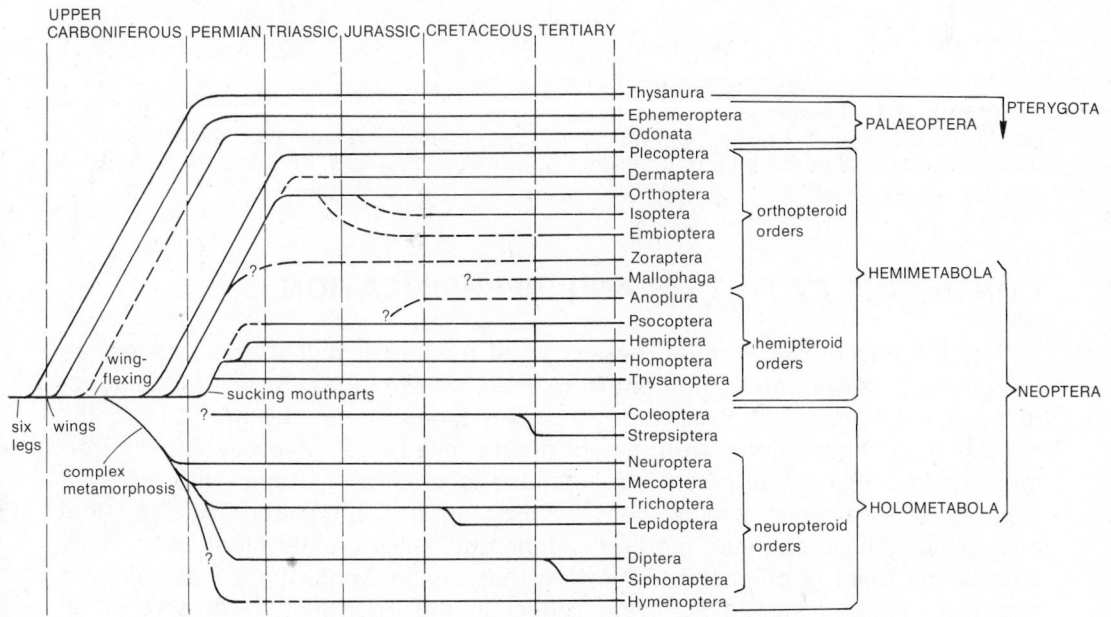

Figure 2–12. Dendrogram of insect evolution.

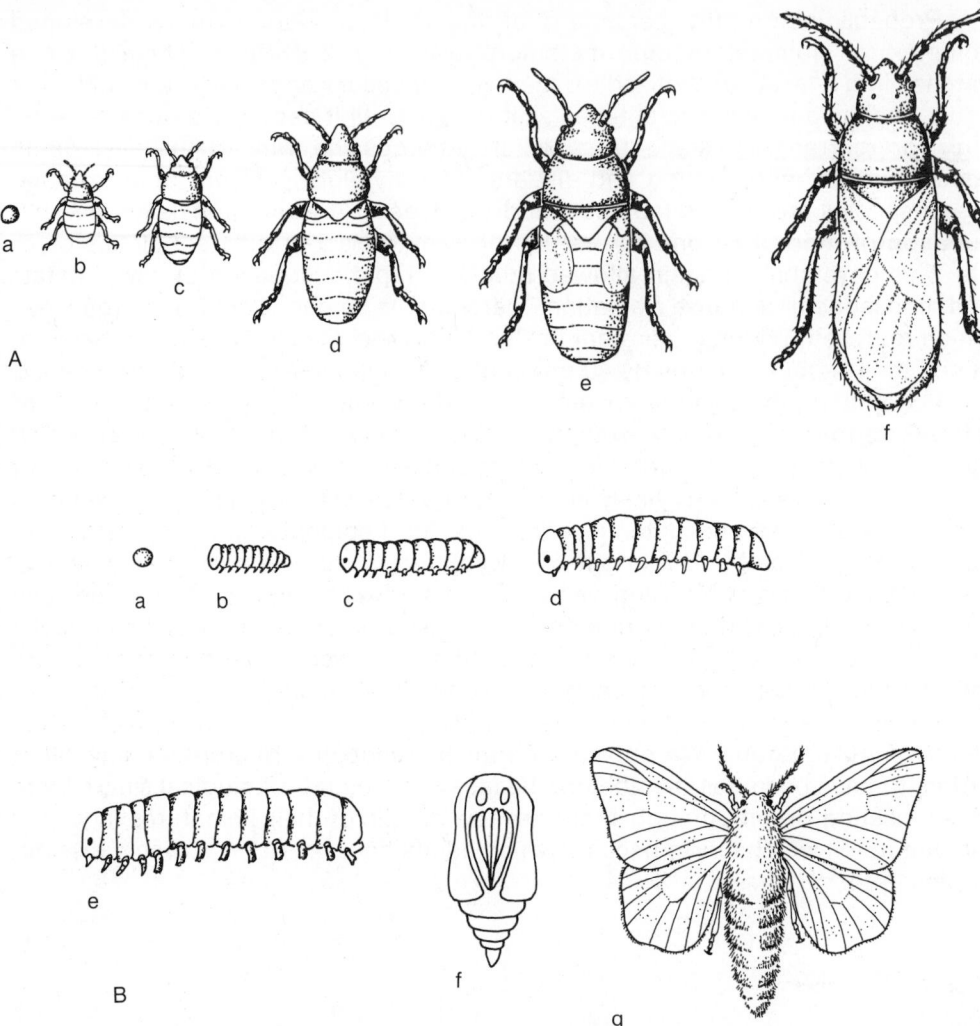

Figure 2–13. Metamorphosis. *A,* Gradual metamorphosis, or hemimetabolous development, in a true bug. Egg *(a)*; nymphs *(b, c, d, e)*; adult *(f)*. *B,* Complex metamorphosis, or holometabolous development, in moth. Egg *(a)*; larvae *(b, c, d, e)*; pupa *(f)*; adult *(g)*.

CONTINUING EVOLUTION AND DIVERSIFICATION

By the end of the Permian period, most modern insect orders existed, although species were quite different from those we see today. Widespread extinction occurred among all animal phyla at this time; among the arthropods, the marine class Trilobita and eight insect orders failed to survive beyond the Permian period. The cause of such extinctions is unknown, though the fact that glaciers and volcanic activity were widespread has suggested to many that climates may have changed markedly, indirectly causing extermination of many animal and plant populations. Following these extinctions, there was renewed adaptive radiation among surviving orders in the Triassic period, and within existing orders additional adaptive radiations have occurred, especially among

Coleoptera (270,000 species), Lepidoptera (150,000 species), and Hymenoptera and Diptera (100,000 species each). Eighty per cent of all existing described insect species occur in these orders.

As new ecological opportunities have become available through evolutionary time, insects have diversified to use them. For example, the evolution of woody and flowering plants, beginning in the Triassic period and continuing at present, produced numerous evolutionary opportunities for adaptive radiation. Wood-boring beetles occurred early on; Triassic tree trunks preserved in Arizona's Petrified Forest contain tunnels very like those made by modern Buprestidae and Scolytidae (Chapter Three). The origin and diversification of Lepidoptera closely parallel that of flowering plants; fossils of complex flowers appear simultaneously with bee fossils (Smart and Hughes, 1973). Close chemical interrelationships between butterflies and food plants (Ehrlich and Raven, 1964), floral adaptations for bee pollination (Chapter Nine), and morphological specialization on bees for handling pollen (Chapter Five) all indicate continued **coevolution** in which plant evolution has caused adaptive changes in insects, and vice versa. Some insect-plant associations are quite old; for instance, *Nepticula* moth leaf mines are found in Miocene oak leaf fossils (Opler, 1973). Evolution of warm-blooded birds and mammals in the late Mesozoic and Cenozoic eras presented opportunity for adaptive radiation among external parasites: lice, fleas, biting flies, and bloodsucking Hemiptera. Insects themselves produced evolutionary opportunities. In complex metamorphosis, insect larvae became a food resource for internally parasitic wasps and flies. Social insects, first found in Cretaceous fossils, adaptively radiated in the Cenozoic era and created a new environment within which evolved cohabitants, **inquilines,** of several insect orders (Chapter Six).

Oligocene amber fossils from the Baltic region of Europe include many genera still existing, showing a greater antiquity among insects than some other animals (including most mammals). As climates have changed, however, insect distributions have moved, and living examples of some Oligocene Baltic beetles are now found far away—some restricted to Australia, another in the southeastern United States. Conversely, Oligocene fossil tsetse flies (Diptera:Glossinidae) have been found in Colorado, while today this family occurs only in Africa. Continental glaciers and associated climatic changes in the past million years forced many distributional changes. For example, as these glaciers retreated, small areas of Arctic vegetation and insects remained behind on high mountains, and today, above the treeline on summits of New Hampshire's White Mountains and in the Colorado Rockies, one can find butterflies (and other insects) nearly indistinguishable from related populations of the high Arctic tundra a thousand miles northward. Such changes in distribution may open possibilities for adaptive radiation. Among the first insect populations established on the Hawaiian Islands (5 million years old) were *Drosophila* flies. There having been a diverse forest but few flies, *Drosophila* species evolved many forms that today number several hundred; three fourths of the world's *Drosophila* are Hawaiian (Carson et al., 1970).

On a global basis, there is every reason to suspect that adaptive radiation in insects continues everywhere today. The diversity of insects we find today, far from being an end result, is merely what we see at a particular moment—our moment—in time. The next chapter discusses these dynamic results of 350 million years of insect adaptive radiation.

SUMMARY

Insects are members of the phylum Arthropoda (animals having an exoskeleton and jointed legs), class Insecta. They are unique in having six legs and three body sections (tagmata): head, thorax, and abdomen. Most adult insects also have four wings.

Insects are by far the most diverse animal class, and their diversity is thought to have arisen by adaptive radiation, the evolution of a number of different forms from a single ancestral population. After a brief review of the hierarchy of biological classification, this chapter discusses how adaptations evolve and gives a probable course of insect evolution based on presently available evidence from fossils and comparative studies of living forms. According to this view, insects probably evolved from "primitive" wormlike arthropods by a series of major adaptive radiations following loss and modification of legs, tagmatization, and evolution of wings and metamorphosis.

Chapter Three

Major Insect Groups

INTRODUCTION

In a book of this size and scope, it is impossible to discuss more than a small minority of the exceedingly diverse results of adaptive radiation among insects. In this chapter, I have compromised by including all insect orders but discussing only those insect families whose members are (1) large (>5 mm.), (2) common (in the United States), or (3) of special biological or economic significance. Borror et al. (1976) present a useful, complete identification manual to North American insect families, and Brues et al. (1954) cover insect families of the world.

I also briefly discuss noninsect terrestrial arthropods here because they are important to understanding insect evolution and the relationship of insects to other arthropods. As explained in the previous chapter, the insects probably are an offshoot of multilegged, mandibulate, terrestrial arthropods that underwent spectacular adaptive radiation following the origin of wings. Among other major evolutionary trends within the Insecta are:

1. Increased compactness, with loss of cerci and ovipositor and shortening of antennae and nerve cord.

2. "Higher" orders having complex metamorphosis and either two functional wings only or a wing-coupling mechanism that allows the four wings to function as two.

3. Specializations for parasitism in many orders. Usually, loss of wings and reduction of eyes, antennae, and legs occur in parasitic insects.

4. More rapid evolution in some groups than in others. Adaptive radiations are probably now occurring in some flies, parasitic wasps, and leaf-mining moths. Identification is perhaps most difficult in such actively evolving insects.

These and other tendencies are evident in the diversity of insects described in the rest of this chapter.

NONINSECT ARTHROPODA

The phylum Arthropoda is traditionally separated into three subphyla: Chelicerata, Mandibulata, and the extinct Trilobita (Barnes, 1974; Borror et al., 1976).

The two existing subphyla differ in several respects, the most important being their mouthparts. In Chelicerata, the first postoral segment of the head bears a pair of clawlike or fanglike **chelicerae** that move vertically (up and down). Mandibulata have paired **mandibles** that operate laterally. Furthermore, Chelicerata lack antennae, whereas Mandibulata normally bear at least one pair. Chelicerata apparently represent a single (monophyletic) evolutionary line. Most evidence suggests that Mandibulata are **polyphyletic**; that is, several arthropod classes with mandibles probably evolved independently and more or less simultaneously (Chapter Two; Cisne, 1974).

Table 3–1 lists major characteristics of the several arthropod classes discussed in the next sections.

SUBPHYLUM CHELICERATA

Classes Xiphosura and Pycnogonida

These are two minor classes of marine chelicerates. Xiphosura are horseshoe crabs (Fig. 3–1), sometimes called king crabs, which are found along the Atlantic and Gulf coasts of the United States where the substrate is sandy or muddy. They feed mostly on worms and have done so, essentially unchanged, since the Paleozoic era. Some are used in experiments on transmission of nerve impulses. Pycnogonida, sea spiders (Fig. 3–2), are uncommon marine predators about which we know very little. King (1975) discusses the biology of Pycnogonida.

Class Arachnida

In contrast to other Chelicerata, the class Arachnida is extremely diverse, having undergone extensive adaptive radiation in the terrestrial environment. It is second only to Insecta in diversity among terrestrial arthropod classes, though there are rather few aquatic or marine arachnids. Because this book is about insects, however, I do not discuss arachnids at a length proportional to their im-

Table 3–1. SUMMARY OF CHARACTERISTICS OF ARTHROPOD CLASSES

Subphylum	Class	Legs	Antennae	Tagmata	Comments
Chelicerata	Xiphosura	10	0	2	marine, intertidal
	Pycnogonida	10	0	2	marine
	Arachnida	8	0	2	terrestrial, diverse
Mandibulata	Crustacea	10 or more	4 (some 0)	2	mostly aquatic, marine
	Diplopoda	60 or more 4 per segment	2 short	2	terrestrial
	Chilopoda	30 or more 2 per segment	2 long	2	terrestrial, predatory
	Pauropoda	18	2 branched	2	rare
	Symphyla	20–24	2	2	
	Collembola*	6	2	3	6 abdominal segments
	Protura*	6	0	3	anamorphosis, no tracheae
	Diplura*	6	2	3	no malpighian tubules
	Insecta	6	2	3	

*Sometimes considered orders within Insecta. All are soil animals, with mouthparts withdrawn into the head and no compound eyes.

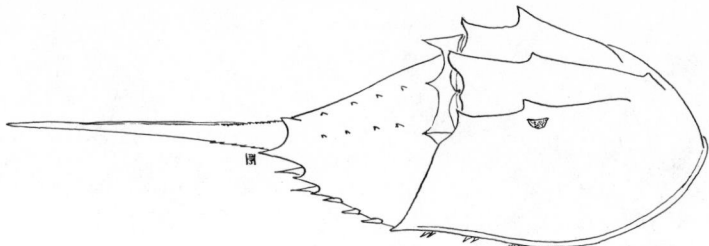

Figure 3–1. Horseshoe crab, class Xiphosura.

portance. Savory (1964) and Snow (1970) are useful references for Arachnida. Cloudsley-Thompson (1958) lists 11 arachnid orders found in the United States. Of these, one is most likely to encounter members of the following six:

Order Araneida.   Araneida (also called Araneae) are the spiders, characterized by fanglike chelicerae, eight legs, and a narrow constriction between the

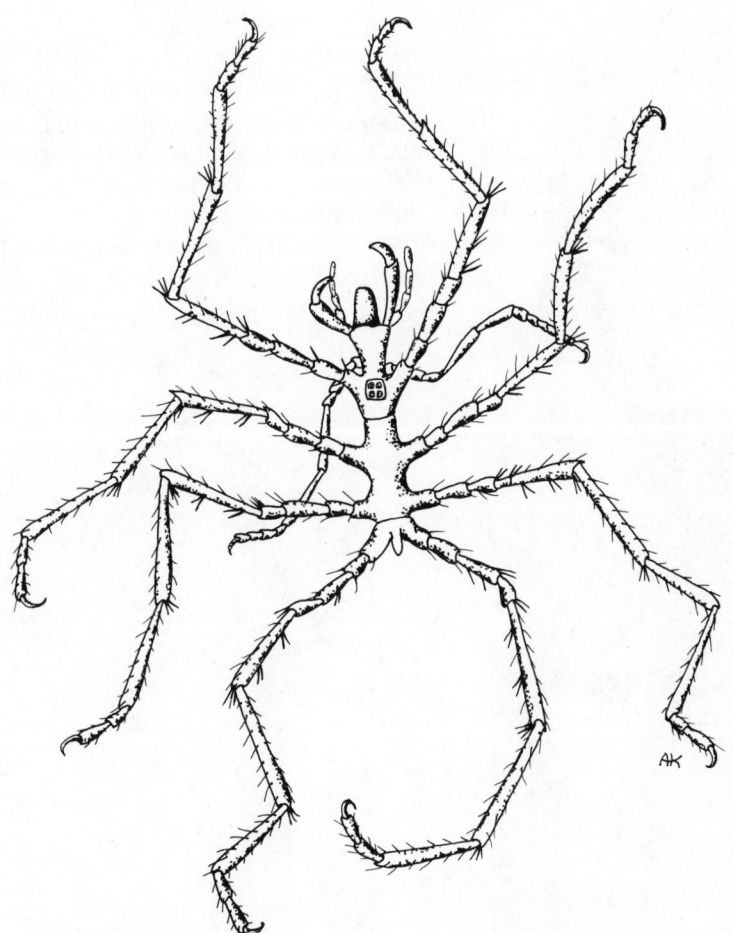

Figure 3–2. Sea spider, class Pycnogonida.

Figure 3–3. Class Arachnida, order Araneida, spiders. *A,* Wolf spider, family Lycosidae. *B,* Wolf spider with young on back.

cephalothorax and abdomen. They are very diverse as a group; over 50 families and many thousand species occur in the United States alone (Kaston and Kaston, 1953). Figure 3–3 illustrates diversity among spiders. All species are predaceous and inject poison into prey through grooves in the chelicerae. They then suck body fluids from their victim. Most spiders feed on insects (and other spiders), though some of the largest tropical species can (and do) eat small fish and birds. The bite of such large spiders is painful, but the danger is exaggerated. There are very few spiders whose bites are seriously harmful to humans; the black widow and brown recluse spiders (Fig. 11–2) are the only two such spiders in the United States (see Chapter Eleven).

Spiders produce silk in abdominal glands and spin it out through **spinnerets** located near the anus. Webs woven with spider silk are familiar to everyone; woe to the insect that becomes ensnared therein. Spiderweb patterns are generally typical and constant for each species. Some spiders do not spin webs but instead either hunt actively or lie in wait among flowers or leaves to pounce on unsuspecting insect prey.

Many spiders oviposit within silken cases (Fig. 3–3C) which females spin and may carry about for a while. When the eggs hatch, emerging young often spin out a few strands of silk from which they float, or "balloon," long distances after the manner of dandelion or thistle seeds. Spiders thus gain some advantages of flight without having wings. They are among the first terrestrial animals to arrive on newly formed islands (Simberloff and Wilson, 1969). If it is true that flight was

Figure 3–3. *Continued.*   *C,* House spider, family Theridiidae, with egg case. *D,* Garden spider, family Araneidae.

a major factor in insects' adaptive radiation (Chapter Two), then spiders' ability to balloon may be partially responsible for their diversity in spite of their rather restricted food habits. Spiders have no metamorphosis; most young look and act like miniature adults. Male spiders are usually smaller than females, and mating may culminate in the male's becoming a meal, from whence the black widow gets her name.

Order Acari.   The order Acari (or Acarina) includes mites and ticks and in terms of form, habitat, and sheer abundance of species, is a group far more diverse than Araneida. Acari are both free-living and parasitic on plants and animals; most are terrestrial, but many are aquatic and some are marine. Huge numbers occur in soil, and many of these species are as yet undescribed. The diversity within the order Acari is probably exceeded by only three or four insect orders. Acari are characterized by having eight legs* and a broad joining between cephalothorax and abdomen. They are small; the largest are about 10 mm. and many are microscopic.

Figure 3–4 shows some examples of this group. Some plant-feeding mites form galls (Fig. 9–23), and others feed freely on leaves, usually crushing or rasping open cells and drinking the contents. Of these, **spider mites** are among the most serious of plant pests, especially on vegetables and fruits and in greenhouses. They combine a short life span with high reproductive potential to very rapidly reach damaging numbers and have developed resistance to many chemical pesticides. Fortunately, spider mites are often eaten by predaceous mites, some of which have proven useful in biological control (Chapter Ten). Mites are parasitic on insects, freshwater and marine invertebrates, fish, reptiles, birds, and mammals, including people. Mange of livestock is caused by mites feeding on skin and hair follicles. **Chiggers** are tiny mites that climb from vegetation to people and burrow to feed on blood on legs, wrists, and waist. The resultant maddening itch must be experienced to be fully appreciated.

Ticks (suborder Ixodides) are parasitic Acari and often attack mammals. Hungry ticks wait among vegetation, usually on tips of leaves or grass blades, and grab onto animals that go by. The tick then locates a suitable point of attachment and feeds on host blood for several days, then, engorged, drops off. Females may lay several thousand eggs after a single blood meal, and ticks can go for months without feeding. Tick bites can generate severe and sometimes fatal reactions in a host, and ticks also transmit serious diseases (Chapter Eleven).

Order Phalangida.   Phalangida, or Opiliones, includes the daddylonglegs or harvestmen (Fig. 3–5A), oval arachnids with extremely long, slender legs (that little children take great delight in removing). Phalangids are common in leaf litter, under bark and logs, and in outbuildings and drafty cellars. They vary in food habits; most are scavengers or feed on plant juices, while a few eat dead or living insects. They have little economic impact.

Order Scorpionida.   Scorpionida, scorpions, look superficially like little lobsters or crayfish (Fig. 3–5B), with clawlike pedipalps used for catching and holding their small insect prey. The posterior portion of the abdomen is narrow and terminates in a sting. The sting is held over the back and is thrust forward to

---

*The first instar of many Acari has but six legs and is called a "larva." The final pair of legs appears when the larva molts.

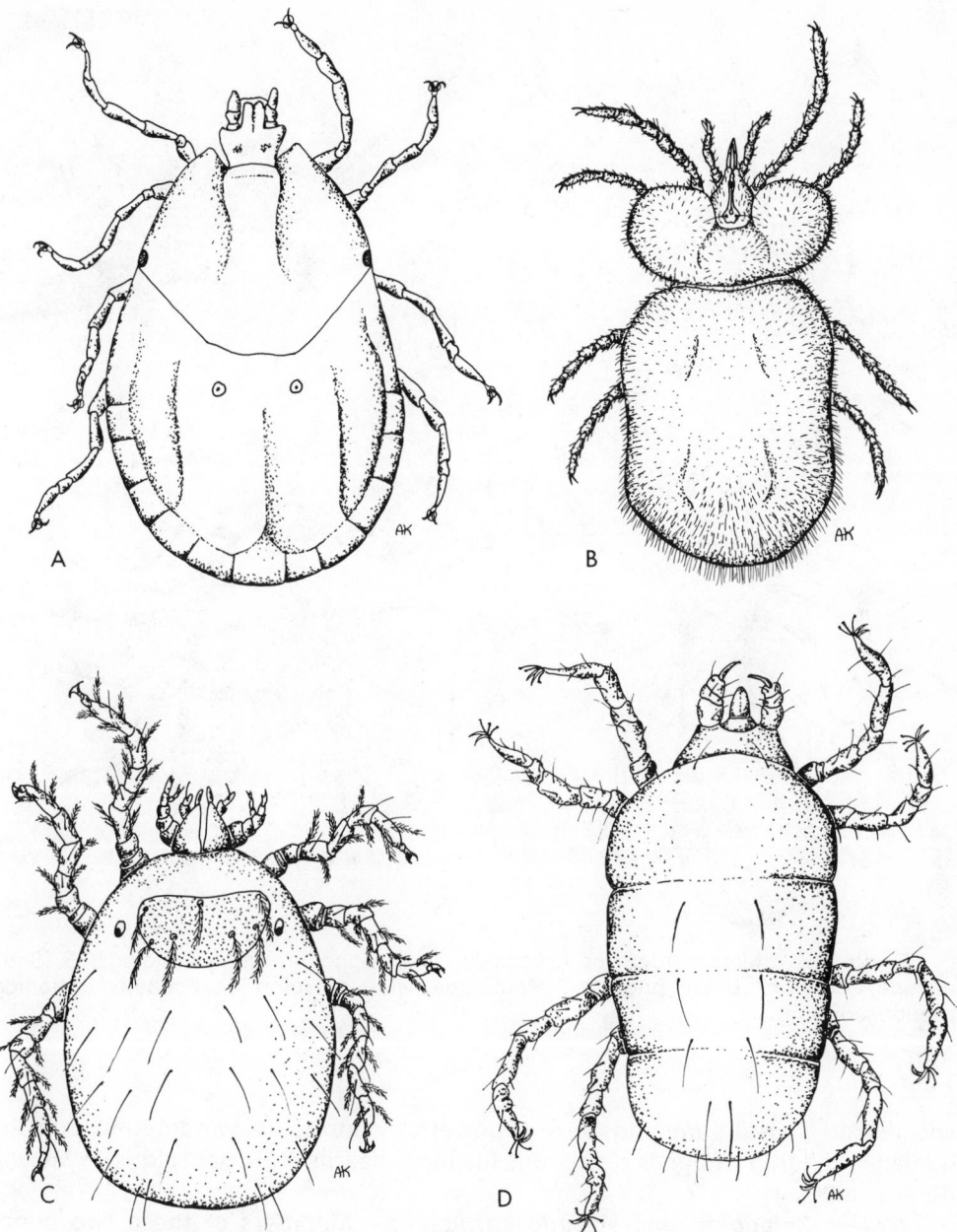

Figure 3–4. Class Arachnida, order Acari. *A,* Tick. *B,* Harvest mite. *C,* Chigger. (Redrawn from U.S. Public Health Service photo.) *D,* Spider mite.

kill prey or to defend against larger predators. Scorpions are nocturnal and secretive, yet abundant enough in warmer climates (including the southeastern and southwestern United States) that one should be careful about putting bare fingers under boards, stones, and other potential hideouts. (These are favored hiding places for poisonous snakes, too.) Scorpions grow to 12 to 13 cm. or more, though the most poisonous species are among the smallest. Two Arizona

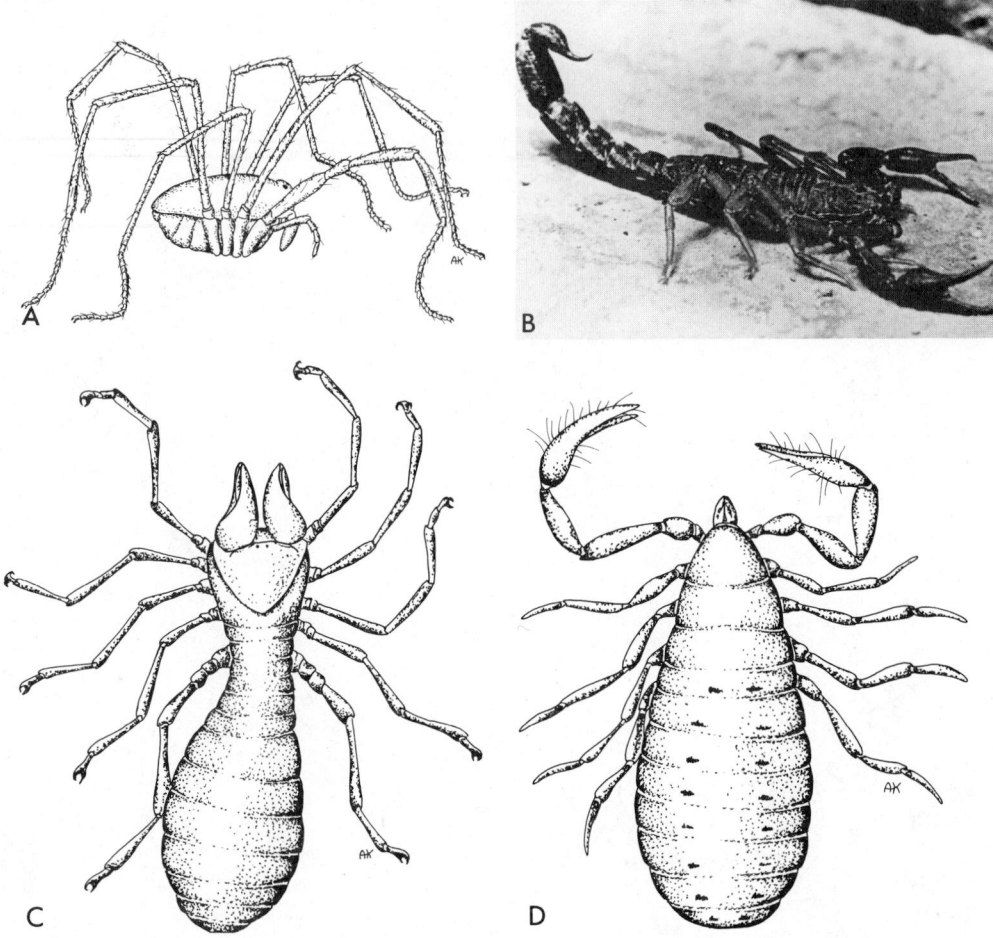

Figure 3–5. Minor orders of Arachnida. *A,* Phalangida, daddy longlegs. *B,* Scorpionida, scorpion. (USDA photo.) *C,* Solpugida, wind scorpion. *D,* Pseudoscorpionida, pseudoscorpion.

species of *Centruroides* possess a powerful neurotoxic venom that can kill humans; children under five account for most deaths from scorpions in Mexico (Baerg, 1929).

Orders Solpugida and Pseudoscorpionida. Members of these two minor orders superficially resemble scorpions, thereby causing public alarm; however, they are quite harmless. Solpugida, or Solfugae (Fig. 3–5*C*), known as wind scorpions or sun spiders, are nocturnal inhabitants of Florida, the southwestern states, and tropical countries, and favor sandy habitats. Some are large (up to 5 cm.), and their enlarged chelicerae, pale appearance, and rapid movements lead people to cringe in terror at their approach. Wind scorpions are harmless except to small insects which they eat. Pseudoscorpionida or Chelonethida (Fig. 3–5*D*), called pseudoscorpions, are tiny (5 mm.), flat arachnids found in leaf litter, under bark and sometimes in buildings. They have clawlike pedipalps, but there the resemblance to scorpions ends; they are harmless scavengers of dead organic matter.

SUBPHYLUM MANDIBULATA

Class Crustacea

Next to Insecta, Crustacea is the most diverse arthropod class, though the major portion of crustacean diversity is found among marine and freshwater forms. These include such familiar and economically important animals as lobsters, crabs, shrimp, crayfish, and barnacles. Crustacea characteristically have two pairs of antennae, 10 or more legs, and the head and thorax closely joined, often fused into a **cephalothorax.** Extreme deviations from this basic appearance are found in some parasitic and sessile Crustacea (Fig. 3–6). Barnacles, for instance, were once considered Mollusca because of their shells.

Most Crustacea are marine and therefore less likely to be encountered by terrestrial entomologists. Small freshwater crustaceans are very common, and many are important food sources for aquatic insects. The only widespread terrestrial crustaceans are sowbugs, or pillbugs (Fig. 3–6E) (order Isopoda). Sowbugs have seven pairs of legs, and some roll into a ball when disturbed. Most are nocturnal and hide by day in or near soil, under bark or leaf litter, or in other such protected, moist places. They scavenge decaying plant and animal matter; some eat portions of living plants and are occasional pests in greenhouses.

"Myriapoda"

Members of four small arthropod classes have many legs, and once were grouped together as a single class "Myriapoda." These groups are now considered to be polyphyletic (of multiple origin); centipedes and millipedes are apparently no more closely related than either group is to insects. Despite this, the multilegged arthropods have certain characteristics in common besides mandibles and nine or more pairs of legs. All are terrestrial but are limited to protected, humid places in or near soil, under bark, logs, and stones, and among dead leaves and brush. They are rather exacting in moisture requirements. They are not nearly as diverse as classes with fewer limbs, and apparently their having many limbs restricts them to protected places.

Class **Diplopoda,** or millipedes (Fig. 3–7A), are the most diverse myriapods, with 10 orders in the United States (Borror et al., 1976). They are mostly cylindrical, with a hardened exoskeleton and short antennae. Typically, each body segment is the result of fusion of two ancestral segments; hence there are two pairs of legs per segment. Most have 28 or more pairs of legs; millipede literally means "a thousand legs," though none has quite that many. Millipedes are primarily scavengers, although a few species feed on young plants and may become pests in greenhouses or outdoor seedbeds. Some release pungent odors containing cyanide and roll into a ball when disturbed.

Class **Chilopoda,** centipedes (four United States orders), have very long antennae and bear on each body segment one pair of legs, totalling 30 or more per animal. The first pair are modified as poison jaws (toxicognaths) for injecting venom into prey. All centipedes are predaceous, and the bite of large southwestern and tropical species (up to 30 cm. long!) can be very painful. The house centipede (Fig. 3–7B) infests buildings, where it preys upon insects and spiders. This beneficence is rarely appreciated by the homeowner who discovers these ghostly, fast-moving creatures scuttling about the kitchen and bathroom. As befits

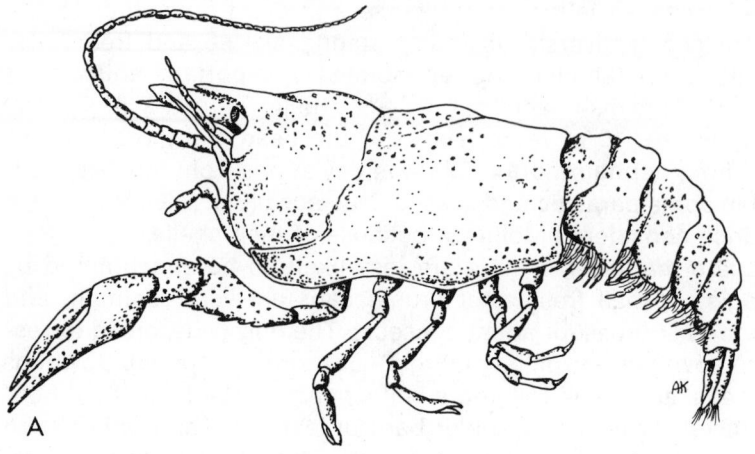

A

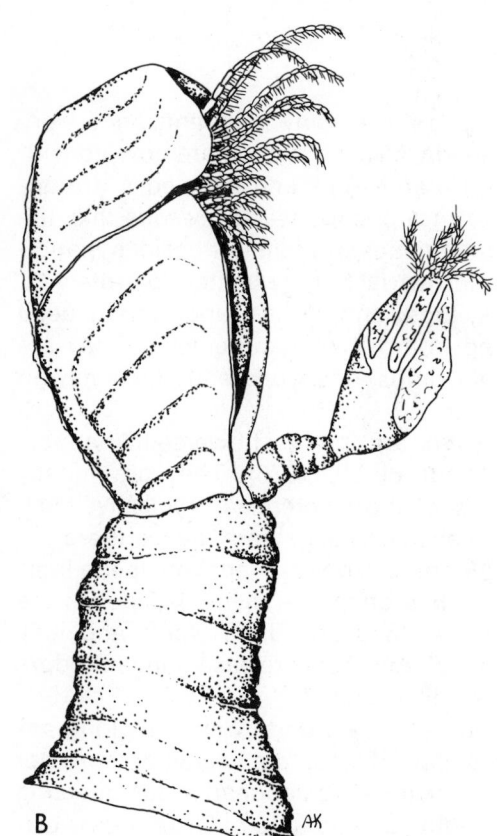

B

Figure 3–6. Class Crustacea. *A,* Crayfish, order Decapoda. *B,* Barnacle, order Cirripedia.

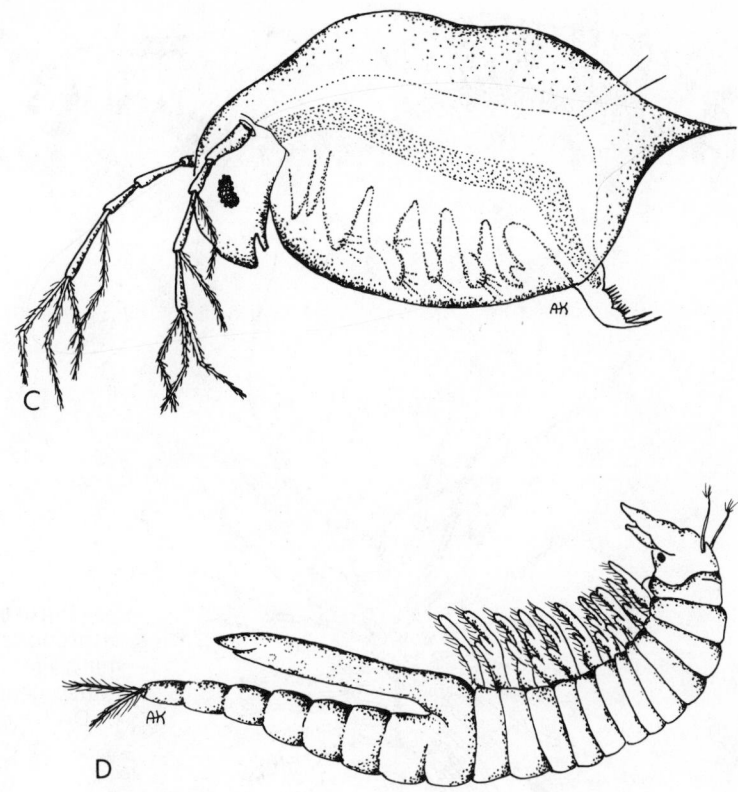

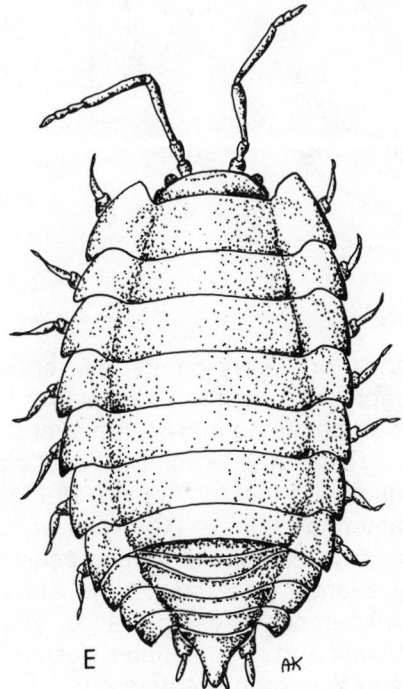

Figure 3–6. *Continued. C,* Water flea *(Daphnia),* order Copepoda. *D,* Fairy shrimp, order Branchiopoda. *E,* Sowbug or pillbug, order Isopoda.

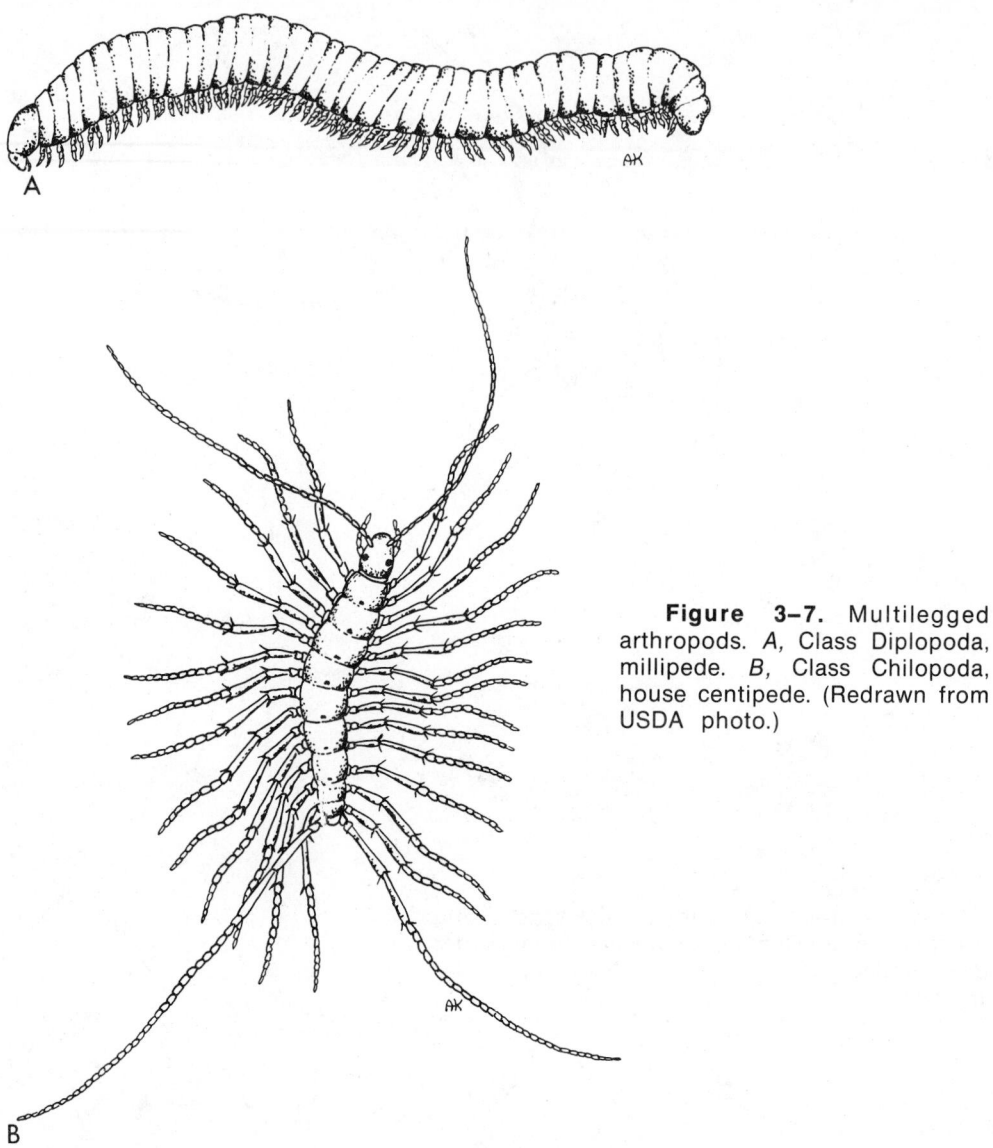

Figure 3–7. Multilegged arthropods. *A,* Class Diplopoda, millipede. *B,* Class Chilopoda, house centipede. (Redrawn from USDA photo.)

their predatory habits, all centipedes are fast-moving. High-speed cinematography has confirmed what our intuition might lead us to expect: at top speed, centipedes do indeed trip over their own legs.

The other two myriapod classes are small and obscure. **Pauropoda** are minute (1 to 2 mm.), pale, 18-legged arthropods with characteristically branched antennae (Fig. 3–7C). They occur in or near soil and are probably scavengers; such obscure, uncommon beasts have rarely been intensively studied. **Symphyla** are larger (to 8 mm.), blind, and have 10 to 12 pairs of legs (Fig. 3–7D). They likewise occur in damp places, and one species, the garden symphylan, feeds on plants and is sometimes pestiferous in greenhouses and outdoors on vegetable and field crop seedlings.

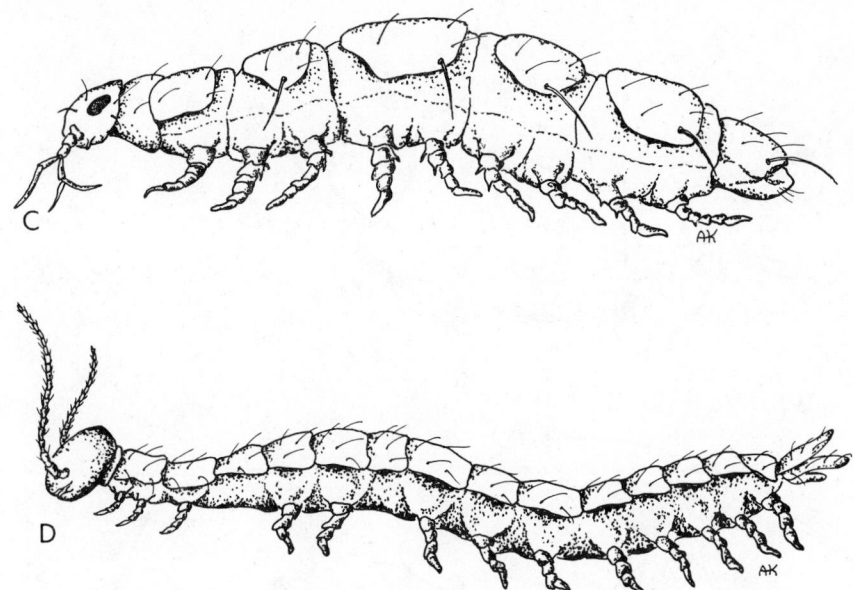

Figure 3-7. *Continued.* *C,* Class Pauropoda. *D,* Class Symphyla.

SIX-LEGGED NONINSECT ARTHROPODS

Traditionally, all six-legged mandibulate arthropods have been considered insects (Ross, 1965; Borror et al., 1976). However, Sharov (1966), Manton (1964, 1972), and others have argued that there are sufficient biological differences to consider that six-legged arthropods are polyphyletic, representing four independent evolutionary lines. Unlike the vast majority of six-leggers, the three groups discussed next all have mouthparts withdrawn into the head, lack compound eyes and wings, and have coxae that do not articulate with the thoracic pleura. These characteristics are probably convergent adaptations to life in the soil. Each group also has enough unique features so that I consider them as classes separate from Insecta and one another. Scudder (1973) has reviewed this taxonomic debate in detail.

Class Collembola

Collembola, **springtails,** are tiny (<6 mm.), incredibly abundant arthropods found in soil and other damp places; 96 per cent of soil arthropods are either Collembola or mites (Evans, 1966). They have no compound eyes but may have lateral ocelli. Most characteristic is an appendage, the **furcula** or "tail", on the fourth or fifth segment of the six-segmented abdomen (Figs. 3-8, *A* and *B,* and 5-28). The furcula is usually folded forward under the abdomen but can be vigorously snapped or sprung against the substrate, thus propelling the springtail several centimeters through the air.

There are two collembolan subclasses, best differentiated by shape; Arthropleona are elongate, whereas Symphypleona are more globular (Fig. 3-8, *A* and *B*). Both are most abundant in soil, leaf litter, and decaying wood and under bark. One species, the snowflea, is sometimes abundant on snow, particularly

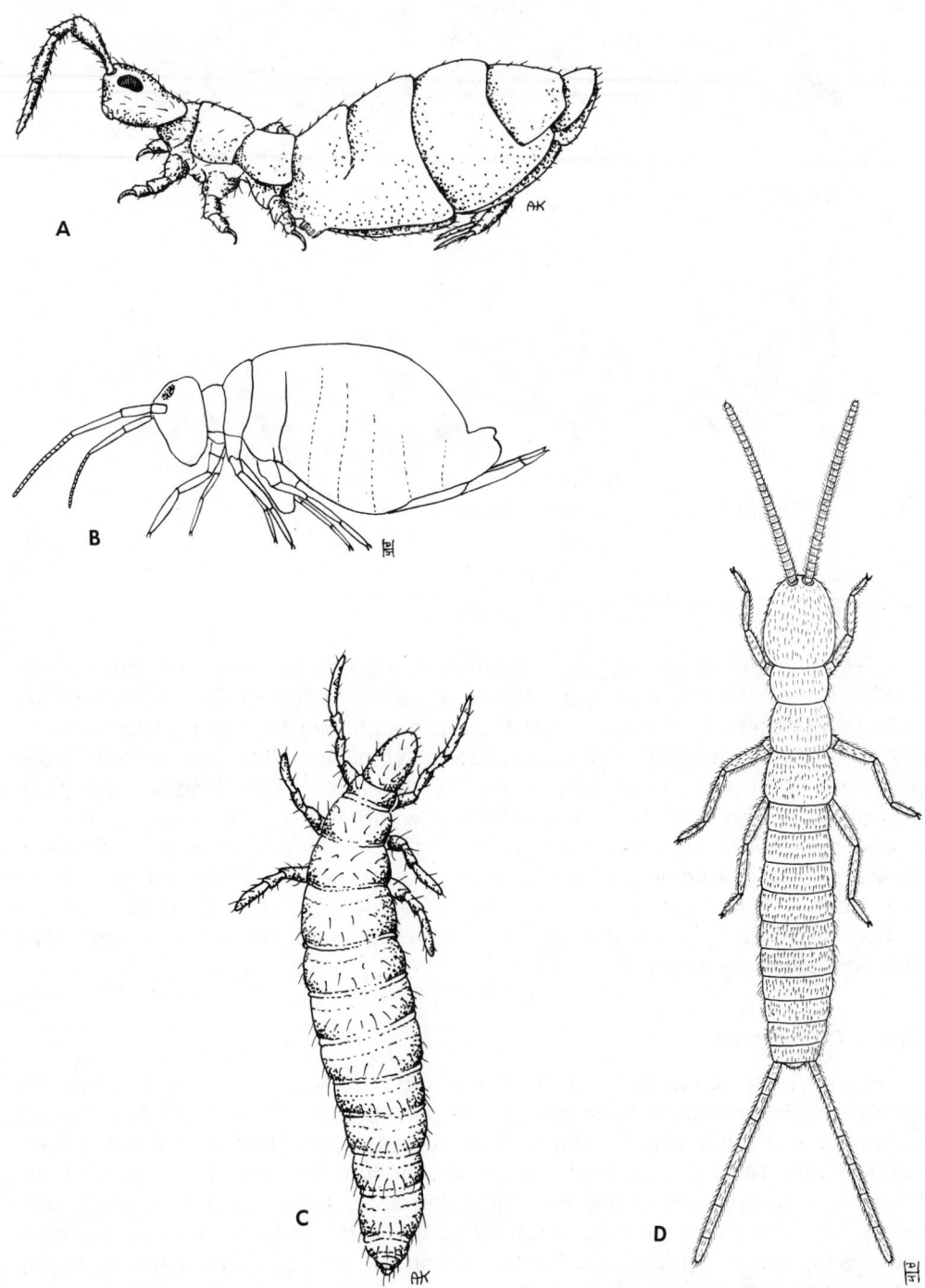

Figure 3–8.   Six-legged noninsect arthropods. *A*, Class Collembola, subclass Arthropleona. *B*, Class Collembola, subclass Symphypleona. *C*, Class Protura. *D*, Class Diplura.

near bases of trees on bright, late winter days. Most springtails are apparently scavengers, though a few are phytophagous and may damage greenhouse plants or flowers. Some prey on soil nematodes. An Australian springtail is a serious pest of alfalfa there. A few tropical springtails are inquilines, or cohabitants, in ant and termite colonies (Chapter Nine). Springtails are **ametabolous**; i.e., there is no metamorphosis, and young look and behave very much like adults. Scott (1961) and Christiansen (1964) have more to say about Collembola. They are apparently a very old group, having been found in Devonian fossils.

Class Protura

The Protura (proturans, Fig. 3–8C) are minute (0.5 to 1.5 mm.), blind, whitish, soil-inhabiting arthropods that are common but seldom seen except by biologists who look for them. They (and other soil "microfauna") can be extracted from soil or litter with a "Berlese funnel" (Fig. 8–1A), which literally cooks them out into the open. Protura have no antennae but instead move about with raised forelegs; these function as sensory structures in place of antennae. Protura undergo three molts, at each of which they add an abdominal segment; they start with nine and end with twelve. Such addition of segments is **anamorphosis**, which occurs only in Protura. They have no economic importance. Tuxen's (1964) monograph covers the world's Protura.

Class Diplura

Diplura (formerly called Entotrophi) are small, blind, soil arthropods, which in the United States are 6 mm. or less, although some tropical species reach 40 mm. Characteristically, they have well-developed cerci which are long and slender in the **Campodeidae,** the most common family (Fig. 3–8D). Other families have forceps or pincerlike cerci. Diplura are of no economic importance; indeed, we know very little of their life history. Smith (1960) summarizes what is known of this class in the United States.

CLASS INSECTA

The insects are by far the largest class of animals. Chapter Two discusses the major features that differentiate insects from other arthropods. Among the insects we find two suborders, **Apterygota** ("without wings") and **Pterygota** ("with wings"). Apterygota consists of the single order Thysanura, whose members bear projections, **styli**, on the ventral abdominal sclerites. Styli are thought to be vestiges of limbs from the insects' multilegged ancestors (Snodgrass, 1935). Apterygota also lack the thoracic sutures and other thoracic modifications (Fig. 5–29) that we find on all Pterygota, including wingless lice and fleas. We thus surmise that Apterygota have never had wings, though they, or insects like them, very likely were ancestors of all winged insects.

SUBCLASS APTERYGOTA

Order Thysanura

Thysanura, **bristletails**, are probably the most "primitive" insects still existing. Table 3–2 lists their major characteristics. Most are recognizable by their

Table 3–2. GENERAL CHARACTERISTICS OF ORDERS OF APTERYGOTA
AND HEMIMETABOLA

Order	Wings*	Mouthparts	Cerci	Comments
Thysanura	none	chewing	long, filamentous	external fertilization
Ephemeroptera	FW > HW	chewing (none in adults)	long, filamentous	aquatic nymphs
Odonata	FW = HW	chewing	short	aquatic nymphs, all predatory
Orthoptera	FW < HW, HW pleated	chewing	short	diverse, all terrestrial
Isoptera	FW = HW (in reproductives)	chewing	1 segment	eat wood, social
Dermaptera	FW < HW, FW hardened	chewing	pincers	
Embioptera	FW = HW (males only)	chewing	short, asymmetrical	subsocial, southern and western U.S. only
Plecoptera	FW < HW	chewing (vestigial in adults)	short	aquatic nymphs
Zoraptera	FW > HW	chewing	1 segment	subsocial, uncommon
Psocoptera	FW > HW	chewing — chisel-like	short	
Mallophaga	none	chewing	none	parasitic on birds and mammals
Anoplura	none	sucking	none	parasitic, mammals only
Homoptera	FW < HW	sucking	none	eat plant sap only
Hemiptera	FW < HW	sucking	none	diverse; aquatic, terrestrial, phytophagous, predatory
Thysanoptera	FW = HW, fringed	rasping, asymmetrical	none	tiny

*FW > HW means forewing larger than hindwing; similarly FW < HW means forewing smaller than hindwing,
and FW = HW, forewing and hindwing equal.

three long terminal filaments, two of which are the cerci (Fig. 3–9). Thysanura are
usually covered with fine scales, and each abdominal segment bears paired styli.
There are four United States families, two of which are common. **Lepismatidae**
includes the silverfish and firebrat (Fig. 3–9), both of which inhabit buildings and

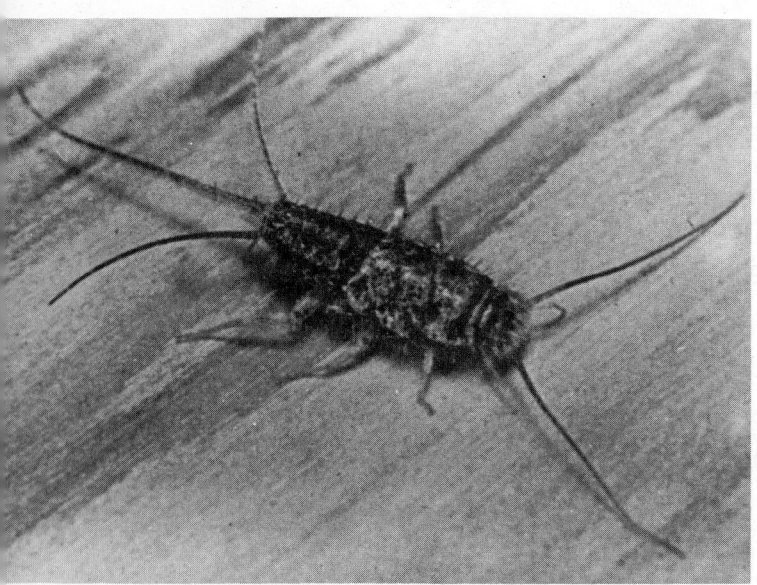

Figure 3–9. Firebrat, order
Thysanura. (USDA photo.)

eat starch, sometimes from paper goods and old books. Silverfish favor cool, damp storage areas, while firebrats are partial to hot, dry areas near furnaces, steam pipes, and such. **Machilidae**, jumping bristletails, are found outdoors among organic debris, especially under dried cow dung. They are scavengers. Among insects, Thysanura are further unique in that they continue molting after reaching adulthood; firebrats have lived as long as 6 to 7 years, through 60 instars. When molting, the female sheds her spermatheca (Fig. 7–2) along with any sperm stored therein; she must mate after each molt if eggs are to be fertile. Males deposit spermatophores externally and females then pick them up; this is another "primitive" characteristic.

SUBCLASS PTERYGOTA: PALEOPTERA

As explained in the previous chapter, there are but two surviving orders of Paleoptera ("old-wings") whose members lack a wing-flexing mechanism. These are Ephemeroptera and Odonata.

Order Ephemeroptera

Ephemeroptera (or Ephemerida) are mayflies, familiar to anyone who spends much time about fresh water. Adults are winged, with forewings much larger than hindwings (Fig. 3–10); a few have no hindwings. Wings are held vertically at rest. Mayflies have short antennae and two or three very long abdominal filaments. Adults lack functional mouthparts and the digestive tract is vestigial. Their life span is usually very short, lasting from several hours to a few days during which they may gather in huge mating swarms. These swarms concentrate individuals for mating and provide some protection from predators, for the combination of short life and huge numbers makes it difficult for predators to overwhelm the swarm. Many are eaten, but enough survive to reproduce. Swarming mayflies are sometimes considered a nuisance around lakeside resorts.

While mayfly adults are rather consistent in appearance, the aquatic nymphs, or naiads, are very diverse (Fig. 3–10), reflecting ecological differences. Some that inhabit swift streams are streamlined and bear holdfasts; others live on lake bottoms, under stones, or in burrows. Some are phytophagous, others predaceous, and many are important as fish food. All have chewing mouthparts and at least four pairs of gills on the ventral surface of the abdomen; most have three abdominal filaments like adults. In contrast to adults, mayfly naiads live a long time—up to three years—during which some may molt 30 to 50 times. When a mayfly naiad emerges from water, it usually molts to a winged but nonreproductive **subimago**. This molts again, usually within a few hours, to a slightly larger, winged, reproductive adult; mayflies are the only insects to molt after having wings.

Mayfly classification might be said to be in taxonomic turmoil; from 3 to 15 United States families are recognized. Identification is complex and is based mainly on wing venation patterns. Edmunds (1962) contains identification keys to mayflies, as do Day (1956) and Needham et al. (1957), which also give authoritative accounts of mayfly biology. Mayflies were once (Carboniferous period) one of the largest insect orders. Many of these early mayflies had all four wings of equal size.

Figure 3–10. Order Ephemeroptera, mayflies. *A*, adult.

Order Odonata

Odonata (dragonflies and damselflies) are medium- to large-sized familiar insects found nearly everywhere, especially near water. Adults typically have huge compound eyes, short bristlelike antennae, a long slender abdomen, and long, narrow, profusely veined wings (Fig. 3–11). They are all aerial predators, catching smaller flying insects in a "basket" formed by their legs and devouring prey while still flying. The male and female often fly about coupled together (Fig. 7–7). Eggs are laid singly, either in open water or within submerged plant stems. Eggs hatch into predaceous aquatic naiads that eat aquatic insects, especially mayfly nymphs. Unwary tadpoles and small fish are also occasionally devoured by Odonata naiads. Odonata are long-lived (as insects go), both as naiads and adults. Most overwinter as naiads, which may live up to 5 years and go through 15 instars.

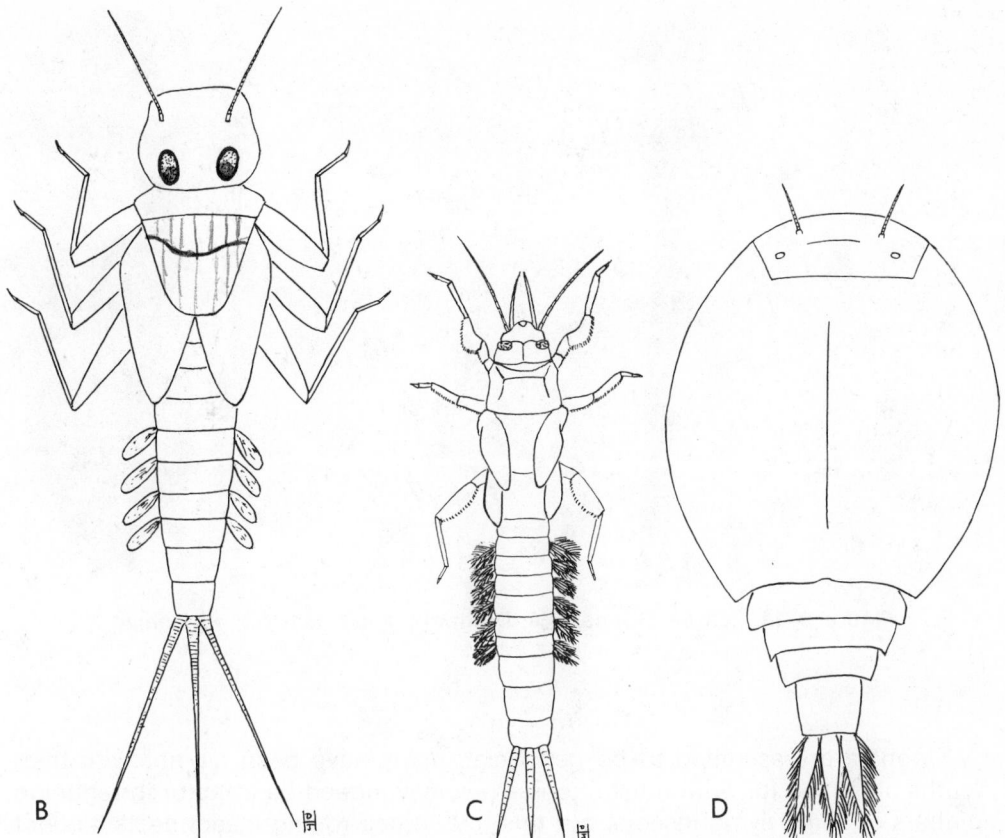

Figure 3-10. *Continued.   B, C,* and *D,* nymphs, or naiads.

American Odonata are divided into two large suborders, **Anisoptera** (dragonflies) and **Zygoptera** (damselflies). (Anisozygoptera, a third suborder, is now restricted to Japan, but its fossils have been found elsewhere.) Anisoptera are larger and stouter, with broader wings which are held outstretched at rest. Their naiads have internal rectal gills (Fig. 4-21*D*). **Zygoptera** have narrower wings and are generally weaker fliers than Anisoptera; moreover, their thorax is tilted backwards (Fig. 3-11*C*), enabling them to fold their wings along their back and hide in vegetation without a wing-flexing mechanism (Chapter Two). Damselfly naiads are narrow, with external caudal gills (usually three) (Fig. 3-11*D*; Fig. 4-21*C*).

Needham and Westfall (1955), Walker (1953, 1958), and Walker and Corbet (1975) are useful guides to identification of Odonata, and Corbet (1963) covers dragonfly biology. There are seven families of dragonflies and three of damselflies in the United States; of these, three are commonest. The large, green or blue, clear-winged dragonflies one often sees patrolling a "beat" several meters up in the air are usually **Aeschnidae**. Members of another common family, **Libellulidae**, often have colorful wing patterns that apparently are used in species recognition, defending territories, and attracting mates (Fig. 3-12). The most common damselflies, clear-winged with light blue or green bodies, are **Coenagrionidae**.

Figure 3–11. Order Odonata. *A*, Dragonfly adult. *B*, Dragonfly naiad.

Odonata are assumed to be beneficial; many have been caught with their mouths crammed full with mosquitoes. They may indeed be a factor in reducing numbers of some flying insects, but this role in controlling insect pests has not been fully investigated.

SUBCLASS PTERYGOTA: NEOPTERA

All the insect orders discussed in the remainder of this chapter have the ability to flex the wings over the back, and this, as explained in Chapter Two, is a great advantage and has resulted in tremendous adaptive radiation. Wing-flexing enables insects to hide in small places, and a subsequent tendency has been modification of forewings into protective structures, especially in Orthoptera, Hemiptera, and Coleoptera.

Neoptera is divided into two categories based on metamorphosis: **Hemimetabola** (or Exopterygota), having gradual metamorphosis; and **Holometabola** (or Endopterygota), with complex metamorphosis. Hemimetabola are subdivided into two complexes, orthopteroid and hemipteroid. The orthopteroid orders (see Table 3–2) are more generalized, having chewing mouthparts, visible cerci, and forewings narrower than hindwings. Their wings often have many crossveins. Hemipteroid orders have specialized, piercing-sucking mouthparts (Fig. 4–4), lack cerci, and have equal-sized wings with relatively few crossveins.

There are a few small orders that, as is obvious from Table 3–2, do not fit neatly into the classifications of orthopteroid and hemipteroid as defined here. In particular, Mallophaga have chewing mouthparts but no cerci, and Psocoptera have no cerci and curious rasping mouthparts that seem midway between chewing and piercing-sucking. These two orders, along with Anoplura and Zoraptera,

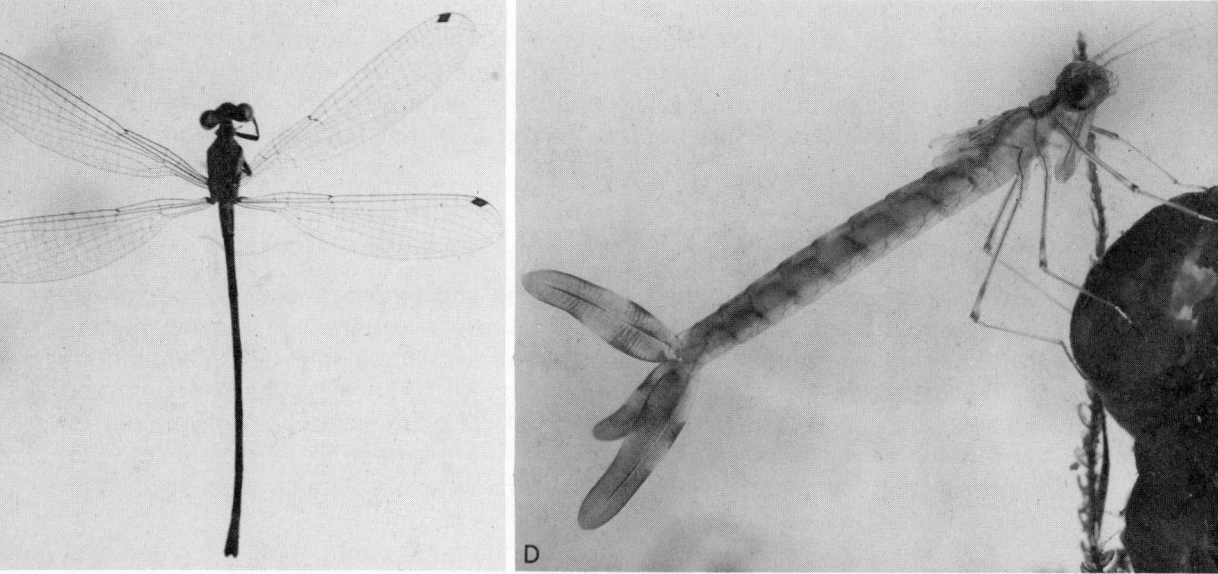

Figure 3–11. *Continued.   C,* Damselfly adult. *D,* Damselfly naiad. (From Tipton, V. J. (ed.). 1973. Syllabus/Introductory Entomology. Brigham Young University Press, Provo, Utah. Photo courtesy of E. S. Ross.)

have each been considered orthopteroid or hemipteroid by one authority or another (e.g., compare Ross [1965] with Borror and DeLong [1971]).

Zoraptera are orthopteroid by my definition and share many characteristics with Psocoptera. Ross (1965) and others suggest that hemipteroid insects developed from orthopteroid ancestors via a psocopteran-like stage. From this perspective, Psocoptera might be viewed as intermediate between the two groups. Both orders of lice are so specialized to parasitic existence as to have lost ances-

Figure 3–12.   Family Libellulidae, showing typical wing patterns.

tral characteristics (including wings) that might aid in determining their relationships. They are different enough from one another, however, that they warrant inclusion in separate orders (though some authors have combined them). They may be *very* distantly related, and their similarity in form may result from convergent evolution. Some authorities consider that biting lice alone may be polyphyletic.

Order Orthoptera

This order includes a variety of common and familiar insects characterized by chewing mouthparts, gradual metamorphosis, and hardened, narrow, protective forewings (tegmina) that fold over more delicate, pleated, membranous hindwings. Some are wingless. The hindlegs of some (e.g., grasshoppers and crickets) are specialized for jumping; others (e.g., cockroaches) have hindlegs for running or walking. Almost all Orthoptera are terrestrial. Fertilization occurs internally; the male deposits sperm within the female's oviduct. Most species (at least outdoors in North America) overwinter as eggs.

Orthoptera are otherwise a diverse lot, and great controversy has raged over whether or not the order is monophyletic. I here regard Orthoptera in its broadest sense, though many other textbook writers (e.g., Fox and Fox, 1964; Ross, 1965) and orthopterists separate the jumping Orthoptera (grasshoppers, etc.) from cockroaches, mantids, and stick-insects. The former are then considered Orthoptera (in the narrow sense), and the latter Dictyoptera (or Cursoria). Some entomologists have gone even further and consider separate orders for cockroaches (Blattaria), mantids (Mantodea), stick-insects (Phasmida), and grylloblattids (Grylloblattodea). The issue is far from resolved, and there is no "right"* classification for the insects here called Orthoptera.

Discussion of major families begins with jumping Orthoptera. Blatchley (1920) and Helfer (1963) are useful guides to identification and biology of Orthoptera.

Most common grasshoppers are **Acrididae** (or **Locustidae**), short-horned grasshoppers, or locusts.† These have short antennae (Fig. 3–13A), and many have brightly colored hindwings which are displayed in flight as part of mating behavior. Males stridulate by rubbing the hind femur against thickened veins on the forewing (Fig. 5–33A). Eggs are laid undergound, usually in groups. All Acrididae are herbivorous, and most prefer grasses but will eat many leafy plants. Some are among the most destructive range and crop pests in existence, particularly in semiarid tropical countries where swarms of many billions periodically destroy much-needed crops. Chapters Six and Nine have more to say about locust swarms.

Tetrigidae, pygmy locusts, are similar to Acrididae but smaller, with a very long pronotum (Fig. 3–13B). They overwinter as adults and are consequently the first grasshoppers of spring.

---

* "Right" in either the sense of a natural phylogenetic classification or of universal acceptance.

†In North America, "locust" in popular parlance refers to cicadas (Homoptera; see page 67). This is because the early English colonists were impressed by mass emergences of 17-year cicadas. Being biblically oriented, they assumed that these cicadas were the same insects that Moses called down upon Egypt (Exodus 10:4–20) and, later, that John the Baptist ate (Matthew 3:4). Properly, "locust" should be reserved for Acrididae, and cicadas should simply be called what they are.

Figure 3–13. Order Orthoptera. *A,* Family Acrididae, short-horned grasshopper. *B,* Family Tetrigidae, pygmy grasshopper.

Tettigoniidae (long-horned grasshoppers, Fig. 3–14*A*) are perhaps the most generalized of jumping Orthoptera. They characteristically are large (more than 20 mm.), usually winged, green or brown insects with long slender antennae and (females) a flattened swordlike ovipositor. They oviposit in or on plants that they eat. They are far more often heard than seen; males (and a few females) possess a file and scraper on the forewings (Fig. 5–33) with which they produce sounds. Most species, including the legendary katydid, "sing" only at night, while a few, particularly those in wet meadows, are active day and night. Most do no commercial harm; an exception is the Mormon cricket *(Anabrus simplex),* a large wingless tettigoniid that occasionally migrates in huge numbers to feed on crops in parts of the western United States. A few Tettigoniidae are predaceous.

Gryllidae (crickets, Fig. 3–14*B*) are similar to tettigoniids in having long antennae and stridulatory tegmina, but they are more cylindrical, with a cylindrical ovipositor and longer cerci. Again, males "sing" by emitting trills or chirps familiar to nearly everyone. Most crickets are scavengers. The most obvious are those found in grass, under boards, or in buildings, where they may infest stored food. Other crickets (subfamily Oecanthinae) live in trees or shrubs, and several have

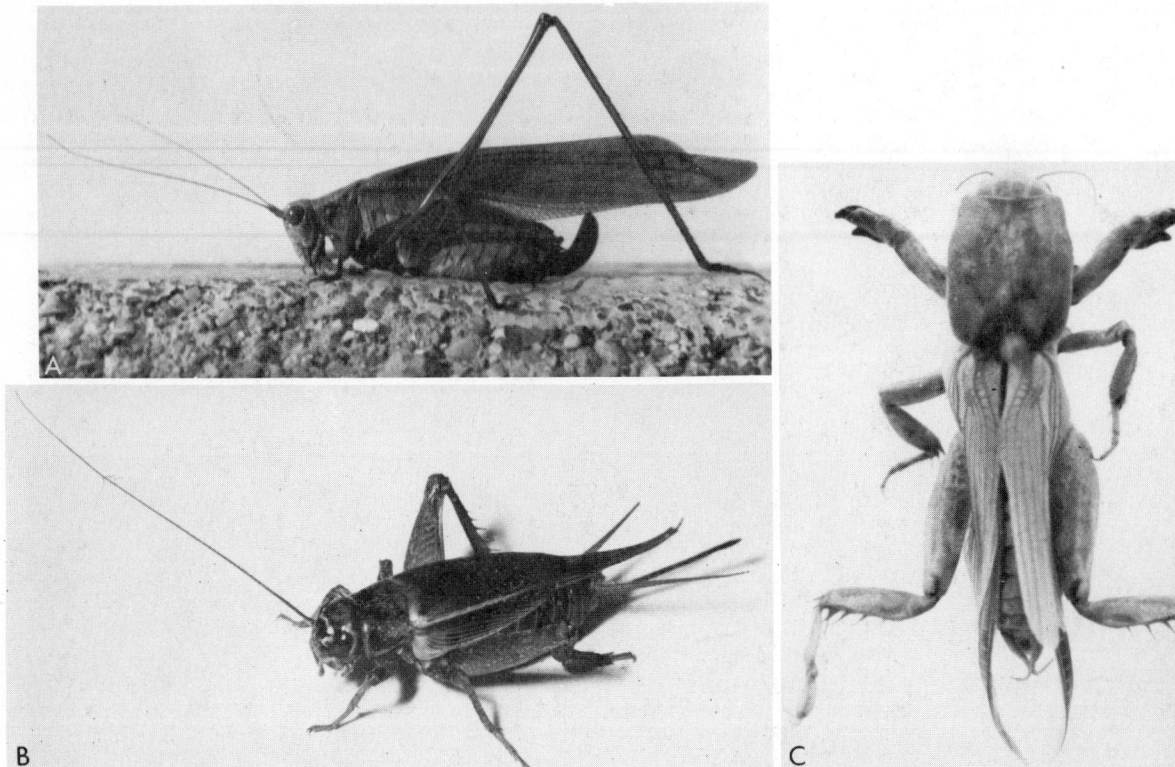

Figure 3–14. Order Orthoptera. *A*, Family Tettigoniidae, long-horned grasshopper. *B*, Family Gryllidae, cricket. *C*, Mole cricket.

earned a reputation for telling temperature (see Chapter Four). Tree crickets may sometimes injure twigs by cutting the bark when ovipositing. Mole crickets (Gryllotalpinae, Fig. 3–14*C*) are uniquely adapted to underground existence. In sandy soils, they sometimes damage vegetable crops.

A small related family, **Gryllacrididae**, contains two common wingless groups. Cave or camel crickets occur in damp cellars and outhouses, and Jerusalem crickets, or "potato bugs" (Fig. 3–14*D*), are common under stones in arid and semiarid regions of the western United States.

Cockroaches were once considered to be a single family, though McKittrick (1964), and most authors since, recognize five United States families. By far the commonest families are **Blattidae**, which are larger (20 to 30 mm.) cockroaches most often found in buildings (Fig. 3–15*A*) and **Blattellidae**, smaller (10 to 15 mm.) slimmer species including the ubiquitous German cockroach (Fig. 3–15*B*) and many woodland cockroaches found under logs, bark, and stones. Cockroaches as a group are rather uniform, being flattened and having a wide pronotum that completely hides the head from above. Their diversity is greatest in the tropics, where many species are very brightly colored, in contrast to most dull brown cockroaches of temperate North America. Cockroaches were even

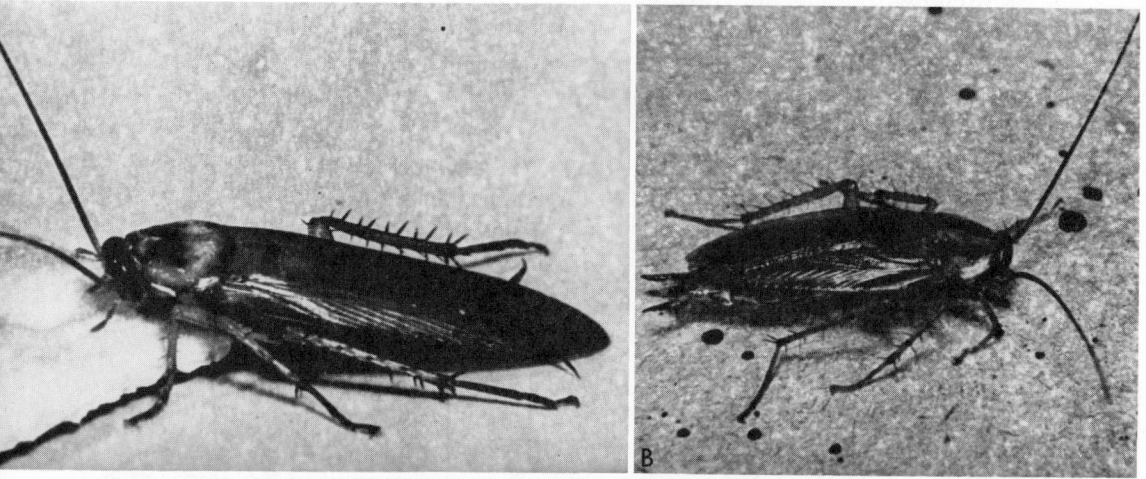

Figure 3–14. *Continued. D,* Jerusalem cricket. (From Tipton, V. J. (ed.). 1973. Syllabus/Introductory Entomology. Brigham Young University Press, Provo, Utah. Photo courtesy of E. S. Ross.)

more diverse in the Paleozoic era; 40 per cent of Permian insect fossils are those of cockroaches.

Cockroaches are typically woodland scavengers, adapted for living under bark, among palm leaves, and in similar places. A few species have taken up a domestic existence and infest buildings, especially those in which food or gar-

Figure 3–15. Order Orthoptera, cockroaches. *A,* American cockroach, family Blattidae. *B,* German cockroach, family Blatellidae. (*A* and *B,* USDA photos.)

bage is abundant. Most prevalent of these are the German, American, Oriental ("waterbug"), and brown-banded cockroaches. People find them unpleasant because they defecate in food, and, though they have not been absolutely proved to carry disease, there is a good chance that they may transmit diseases to people (Chapter Eleven).

Cockroaches lay eggs in an ootheca, or egg case (Fig. 7–9C). Nymphs feed voraciously but grow slowly; the American cockroach takes a year to mature. Cockroaches possess hindgut protozoa that aid in digestion of cellulose. Members of the obscure family **Cryptocercidae**, found in the Appalachian region and the Pacific Northwest, live in loose colonies within logs where they eat wood. Such a cockroach may have been ancestral to termites.

Cockroaches are certainly related to **Mantidae**, the mantids, which are, in effect, highly specialized, predatory cockroaches. Again, the eggs are contained in an ootheca, in which temperate mantids overwinter. Masses of tiny nymphs hatch in spring; they are similar to adults but smaller, with the distinctive and familiar grasping forelegs and lengthened pronotum (Fig. 2–2A). North American mantids are rather uniform in appearance (Northeastern species are introduced), but the group is exceedingly diverse in the tropics (Fig. 9–21), where some species exceed 10 cm. in length. All mantids are predaceous on other insects (including other mantids), which they capture with their forelegs. Females often eat males when mating (Chapters Five and Seven). Because of their predatory habits, mantids are widely touted as beneficial insects to control pests biologically. Alas, mantids are indiscriminate predators, as likely to eat honey bees as houseflies. While their value is thus dubious, they are very interesting insects to watch and do very well in captivity.

The last major group of Orthoptera are the stick-insects, or walkingsticks, **Phasmidae**. Included here are a variety of quite common but cryptic insects that resemble sticks (Fig. 3–16A) or, in the tropics, leaves. All eat leaves, and they may become abundant enough to defoliate portions of a forest. Many are parthenogenetic (without males), the females simply laying viable eggs that drop to the forest floor and may take a year or two to hatch. North American walkingsticks lack wings, but many tropical species have them. Phasmids are most diverse in the Oriental tropics and East Indies, where we find walkingleaves and brightly colored walkingsticks, including the world's longest extant insect (+30 cm.).

In the mountains of western North America and eastern Asia occur unusual and uncommon Orthoptera—the grylloblattids, **Grylloblattidae** (Fig. 3–16B). These insects frequent soil at the edges of subalpine glaciers and snowfields and apparently are scavengers. They are wingless and otherwise display characteristics of both crickets and cockroaches. They may, in fact, be a "missing link" between the two or perhaps are a last remnant of the diverse and widespread Paleozoic order Protorthoptera. Some authorities (e.g., Ross, 1965) place them in a separate order, Grylloblattaria (or Grylloblatodea).

Order Isoptera

Closely allied to Orthoptera are the Isoptera, termites, which might be considered highly specialized social cockroaches. Society is indeed the termites' distinguishing characteristic; they live in highly organized colonies of a few thousand to several million individuals each. Within a colony are several special-

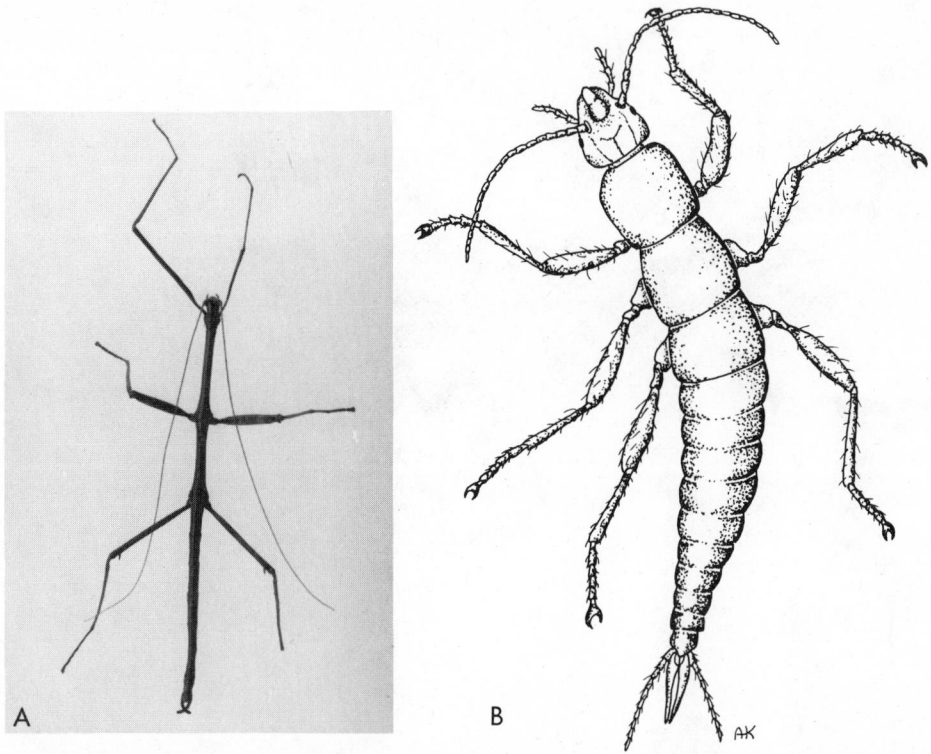

Figure 3–16. Order Orthoptera. *A*, Walkingstick, family Phasmidae. *B*, *Grylloblatta*, family Grylloblattidae.

ized functional forms, or **castes** (Fig. 6–18): workers, blind and pale (in the United States); soldiers, with enlarged mandibles for colony defense; and winged reproductives. The social life of termites is discussed further in Chapter Six and detailed in Skaife (1961). All termites eat wood or other foods heavy in cellulose, which is digested by unique intestinal protozoa. Termites are warm-weather animals; the majority of the 2000 or so species are tropical, and none occur in the extreme northern United States (northern Minnesota and Vermont) or in much of Canada. Because of their inability to distinguish between fallen logs and wooden structures, termites are of major economic importance throughout their range.

Order Dermaptera

Dermaptera, earwigs, are a small group (1000 species) of small to medium (20 mm.) orthopteroid insects whose distinguishing characteristic is pincerlike cerci (Fig. 3–17A). These give earwigs a fearsome appearance, though actually they are quite harmless. Their name derives from an alleged tendency to crawl in the ears of sleeping persons and worm their way into the brain, generating mental aberrations. (They don't do that.) Some earwigs are wingless, while others have short elytra that cover elaborately folded hindwings. Many earwigs can and do fly, and the cerci then aid in stuffing the hindwings back under the elytra when the animal lands. Cerci also function as tongs for holding food (personal observation) and probably are involved in copulation, though nobody seems to have ever watched earwig sexual behavior. Females do guard eggs until hatching and for a short time thereafter.

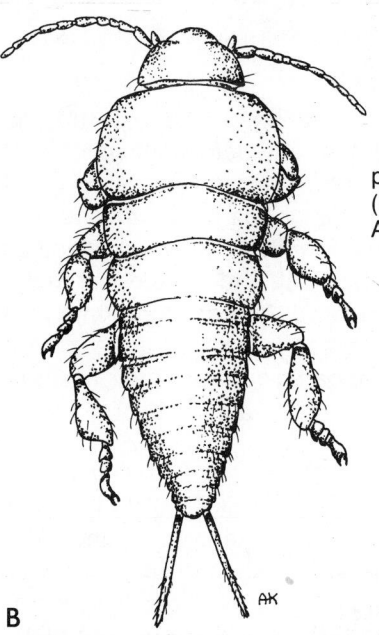

Figure 3–17. Order Dermaptera, earwigs. *A,* European earwig, family Forficulidae. *B,* Parasitic earwig. (Redrawn from Askew, R. R. 1971. Parasitic Insects. American Elsevier Publishing Co., Inc., New York.)

Earwigs are mostly nocturnal scavengers, hiding in litter and debris by day. The European earwig (*Forficula auricularia*) (Fig. 3–17*A*), introduced to both coasts of North America, sometimes chews petals off ornamental flowers and artichokes and may enter houses and pantries.

Members of two families have forsaken the scavenging habit and are ectoparasites of bats (in Southeast Asia) or rats (in South Africa). They may originally have scavenged around the lairs and nests of these animals and gradually moved onto their hosts to disperse and, later, eat. As is often the case with parasitic insects, these earwigs are so highly specialized as to be practically unrecognizable as earwigs (Fig. 3–17*B*).

Order Embioptera

A small (150 species) obscure orthopteroid order contains the webspinners, Embioptera (or Embiidina). They are small (up to 7 mm.), narrow, cylindrical insects with an enlarged first segment of the front tarsi (Fig. 3–18). This contains glands that produce silk from which nymphs and adults construct tunnels. Embioptera are subsocial, forming small colonies in silken tunnels under bark, logs, and rocks. Females guard eggs until hatching, and webspinners of all ages may be found in a single colony. They are apparently scavengers on dead and living plant material. Males sometimes have wings; all known females are wingless. There are three United States families limited to the South and Southwest; the group is primarily tropical. They are of negligible economic importance. Their evolutionary position is unclear, as they bear resemblance to both Isoptera and Plecoptera. E. Ross (1944) gives further information on Embioptera.

Order Plecoptera

Plecoptera, stoneflies, are medium-to-large (5 to 40 mm.) insects found in large numbers near fast-moving rocky streams. Adults have straight, narrow

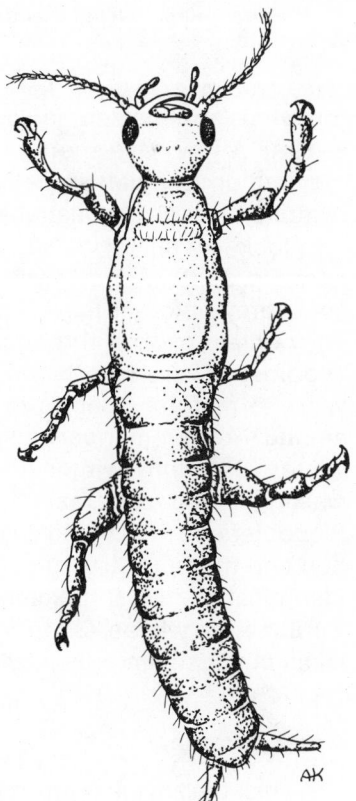

Figure 3–18. Webspinner, order Embioptera.

Figure 3–19. Order Plecoptera, stoneflies. *A,* Adult. *B,* Naiad. (*A* and *B,* Paintings by W. Costello.)

forewings and pleated, fanlike hindwings and prominent cerci and antennae (Fig. 3–19*A*). A few have short wings or are wingless. Mouthparts of many adults are reduced or vestigial; stoneflies generally eat lichens, pollen, or nothing. Stonefly nymphs are aquatic, flattened insects that resemble their respective adults and also look like mayfly naiads except for lacking a median terminal filament. (Compare Fig. 3–10, *B* and *C* with Fig. 3–19*B*). They are mostly phytophagous, though some prey on other insects and in turn are important as food for freshwater fish. They obtain oxygen through filamentous gills under the thorax and (sometimes) abdomen. There may be 20 to 30 instars, as stonefly nymphs take one to four years to mature. Species in several families, especially **Capniidae**, are unusual among North American insects in that they reach adulthood in late fall and winter. On sunny winter days, large numbers of such stoneflies may be found walking about and mating on snow near streams. There are 10 families of Plecoptera in the United States; identification depends on details of wing venation and thoracic structure. Needham and Claasen (1925) is a very good guide to identification. Most common stoneflies collected in spring and summer are **Perlidae**; very large (30 to 40 mm.) stoneflies found about lights near rivers and lakes in midsummer usually belong to the **Pteronarcidae**.

Order Zoraptera

This, the smallest insect order (22 species, 1 family) includes obscure little (1 to 2 mm.) insects (Fig. 3–20) that few entomologists have seen alive. They languished undiscovered until 1913 in sawdust piles, rotten wood, and under bark in the southeastern United States and throughout warmer parts of the world. Superficially, they resemble tiny termites, even to existing in subsocial groups and (in winged forms) shedding wings after mating. They are of note mostly as a bridge between orthopteroid and hemipteroid groups; they have chewing (orthopteroid) mouthparts, and tiny one-segmented cerci, yet they seem hemipteroid in having the forewings larger than hindwings, with few veins. They are very similar to Psocoptera (see next section), of which some entomologists consider them a suborder. Gurney (1938) summarizes what little is known of Zoraptera.

Order Psocoptera

Psocoptera, booklice and barklice, are small (1 to 5 mm.) but common insects that have both orthopteroid and hemipteroid characteristics, as noted earlier. Their mouthparts are mandibulate, but the maxillae bear chisel-like structures that represent a primitive stylus, or beak, foreshadowing the sucking mouthparts of hemipteroids. They have no cerci, and (in winged forms) the forewings are larger than the hindwings (Fig. 3–21). They are best recognized by their rather large head, long antennae, and, if winged, peculiar and unique venation pattern.

The 1000 or so species (11 United States families) are mostly scavengers or lichen feeders, abounding on tree trunks and under bark in gregarious, apparently subsocial, aggregations. Broadhead (1958) discusses the ecology of some Psocoptera; Mockford (1951) and Mockford and Gurney (1956) present useful guides to identification of more common Psocoptera. While most live outdoors, some wingless species inhabit buildings and feed on grain, flour, starch, mold, and such. The booklouse, *Liposcelis divinatorius* (**Liposcelidae**) (Fig. 3–21*B*) is one such species; it sometimes scurries across the pages of old books

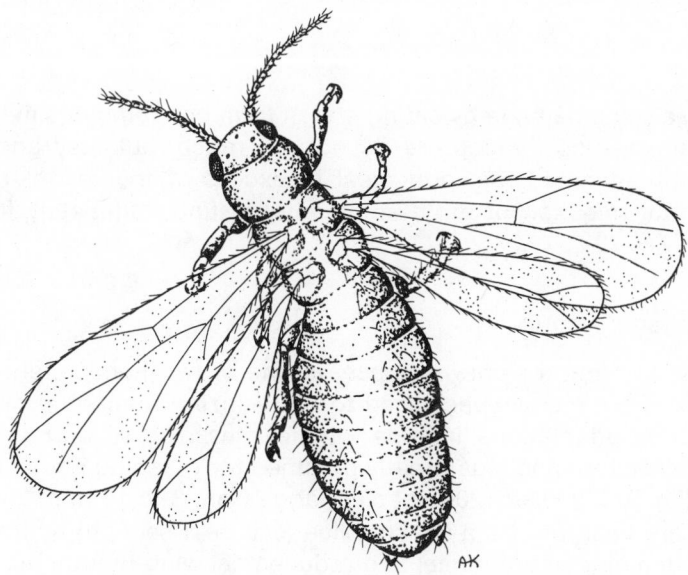

Figure 3–20. Zorapteran, order Zoraptera.

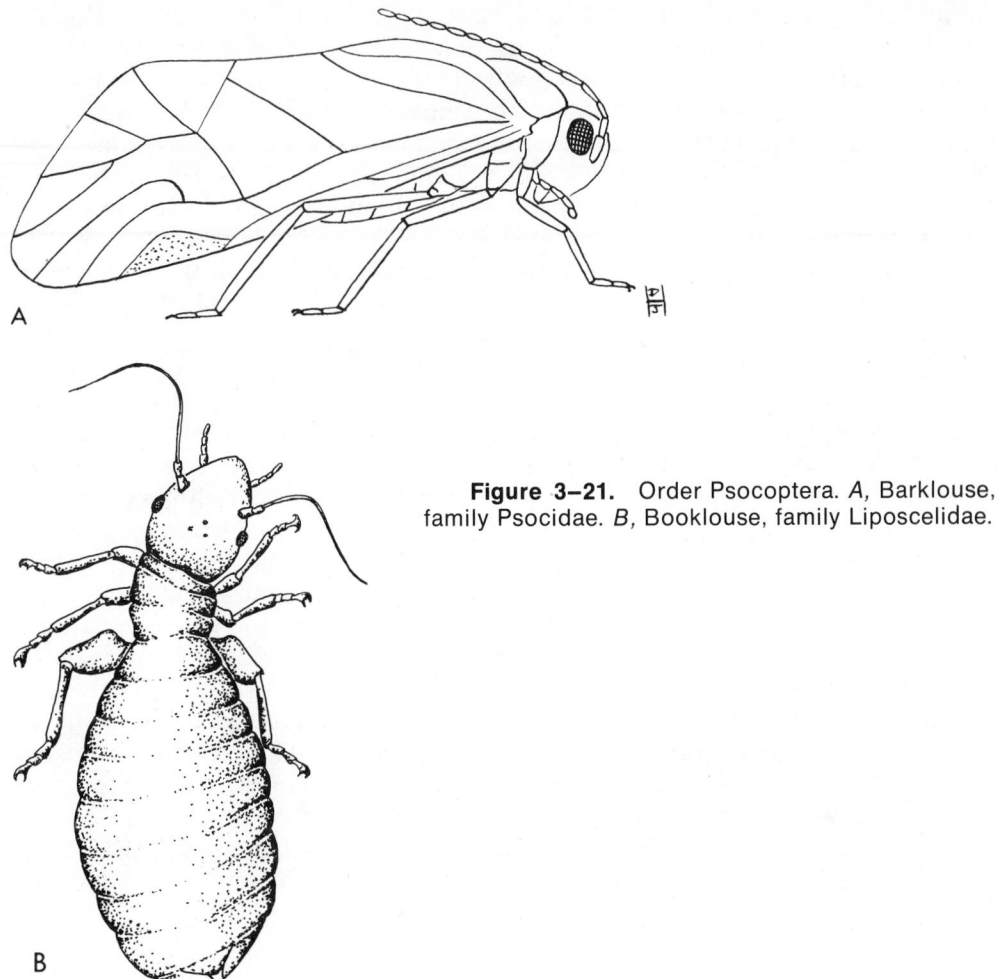

Figure 3–21. Order Psocoptera. *A,* Barklouse, family Psocidae. *B,* Booklouse, family Liposcelidae.

and may cause some damage by eating starch from bookbindings in libraries and archives. Grain-feeding Psocoptera do not eat much, but they and their fragments may contaminate grain and meal in excess of federal tolerance limits, causing outright rejection of grain shipments destined ultimately for breakfast cereal.

Order Mallophaga

Mallophaga, biting (or chewing) lice, is one of two hemimetabolous orders whose members are highly specialized for parasitizing homeotherms (birds and mammals). Such adaptations include winglessness, dorsoventral flattening, a very hard exoskeleton, and legs greatly modified for grasping hairs or feathers of their hosts (Fig. 3–22). The 1200 species range from 3 to 10 mm. long when full grown. They are best told from sucking lice (see next section) by their relatively large head, often hidden antennae, and reduced chewing mouthparts with which they chew the skin of hosts. Most biting lice parasitize birds (Mallophaga are sometimes called bird lice), and the family **Menoponidae** contains some that can cause serious weakening of poultry. **Trichodectidae** includes the relatively few mallophagan parasites of mammals. Horses, sheep, goats, cattle, dogs, and cats are among their hosts and may be severely weakened by large louse populations. They are especially pestiferous on dairy cows in winter. No biting lice parasitize humans.

Lice are very closely associated with their hosts and die within a few hours if removed or if the host dies. Dispersal occurs mostly by contact between infested hosts, and reproduction of lice is controlled by the host's hormones, assuring that louse reproduction is timed to availability of new hosts. Lice are species-specific, and their evolution has closely paralleled that of their hosts. From whence they came remains a mystery, though their mouthparts are similar to those of Psocoptera, some of whom regularly infest nests and lairs of birds and mammals. Presumably, a group of primitive psocids took to chewing skin while it was still on the animal and, over many millions of years, lost their wings and cerci.

Order Anoplura

Anoplura, sucking lice, are superficially very similar to Mallophaga, and the two have at times been combined into a single order ("Phthiraptera"). Some entomologists (e.g., Ross, 1965) suggest that Anoplura may have evolved from Mallophaga; others consider the similarity to be a case of convergent evolution. Like Mallophaga, Anoplura are small (2 to 5 mm.), heavily sclerotized, flattened dorsoventrally, without cerci, and with clawlike tarsi (Fig. 3–23). They have very specialized sucking mouthparts that they withdraw into the narrow head when not in use. The 250 species suck blood, only from mammals. **Haematopinidae**

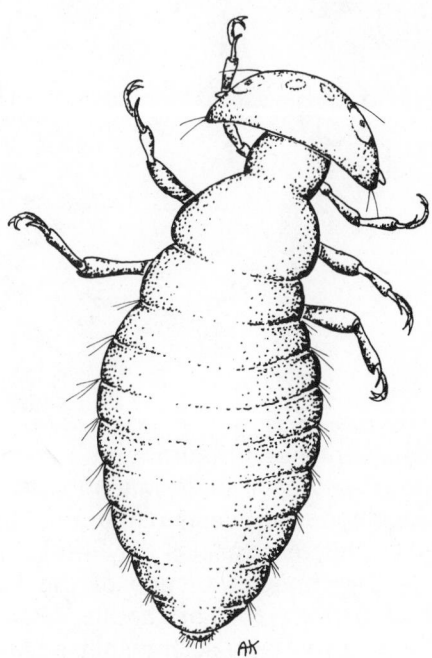

Figure 3–22. Biting louse, order Mallophaga.

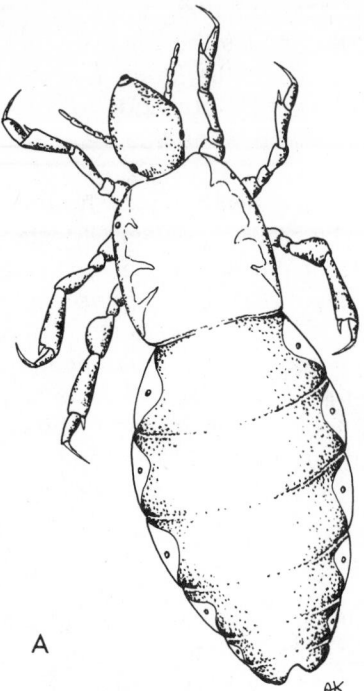

Figure 3–23. Order Anoplura, sucking lice. *A,* Human body louse. *B,* Crab louse.

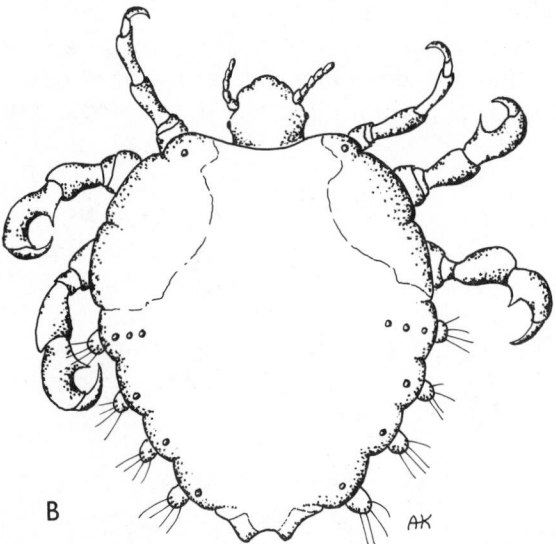

cause intense irritation and some loss of blood to cattle, hogs, horses, sheep, dogs, and cats. As in Mallophaga, associations are species-specific; the cattle-sucking louse infests cattle only, the hog louse only swine, and so forth; moreover, different species may infest different parts of the same animal.

Two species of lice of the family **Pediculidae** infest human beings. The human body louse or "cootie," *Pediculus humanus* (Fig. 3–23A), feeds on human blood and may also transmit epidemic typhus, murine typhus, and trench fever

(Chapter Eleven). Louse-borne diseases are a particular problem when numbers of people are crowded in unsanitary, bathless conditions, as occurs in war zones. The human louse glues its eggs (nits) to hairs or in clothing. (For years, head and body lice were considered separate species.) The other longtime louse associate of people is the pubic or crab louse, *Pthirus pubis* (sometimes placed in a separate family, **Pthiriidae**) (Fig. 3–23*B*). These lice inhabit hairy areas around genitals and, sometimes, underarms. Their feeding produces a maddening itch, but crab lice have not been conclusively proved to transmit disease. Lice are easily eliminated by DDT-impregnated soap and may be held at bay by judicious use of baths and haircuts. They are currently enjoying somewhat of a renaissance as long hair and beards return to fashion.

Order Homoptera

This is the largest order we have encountered thus far, with 32 North American families according to Borror et al. (1976). Their mouthparts are specialized as a "beak," or proboscis, the labium forming a sheath for piercing stylets and for salivary and food canals. In Homoptera, the beak appears to arise from the posterior of the head or from between the forelegs. Another useful identifying characteristic is that wings, when present, usually fold rooflike over the abdomen. One group, scale insects, is so specialized that they bear little resemblance to the rest of the order, and superficially, many do not even resemble insects.

Homoptera are all terrestrial and feed on plant sap exclusively; many are associated with but one or a few plant species. Some authorities (e.g., Ross, 1965, Romoser, 1973) consider Homoptera and Hemiptera (our next order) to be suborders of a single large order. There is certainly great similarity between the two, and some Australian and South American species (family **Peloridiidae**) have characteristics of both Homoptera and Hemiptera. North American families are easily classified into one category or the other, however, and I here follow tradition by calling Homoptera an order. In any event, all insect orders are somewhat subjective (Chapter Two), and Homoptera and Hemiptera, even though separate orders, are very closely related.

Homoptera are divided into two suborders, in each of which considerable adaptive radiation has occurred within the limitation of feeding on plant sap. The suborder Auchenorrhyncha (**Cicadidae** through **Fulgoroidea**) (see next section) is considered more generalized; its members are larger, have short antennae, beak arising from the head, and many wing veins (as Homoptera go). Sternorrhyncha (**Psylloidea** through **Coccidoidea**) are smaller, with longer antennae and beak arising between the forelegs. There are fewer wing veins, and many are wingless and highly specialized for parasitizing plants. Homoptera all suck plant sap and must suck large quantities to obtain needed vitamins and other micronutrients. Because of this, many, especially Sternorrhyncha, excrete a sugary liquid, **honeydew**. This excess sugar attracts ants (Chapter Nine) and also encourages growth of sooty molds, resulting in cosmetic damage to fruits, automobiles, or whatever else happens to be beneath where Homoptera are feeding.

There are few general references on Homoptera as a group. Britton (1923) is helpful, as are other references noted with each group in the next section.

Suborder Auchenorrhyncha. Within this suborder are two superfamilies. The more "primitive" are **Cicadoidea**, whose members are presumed similar to

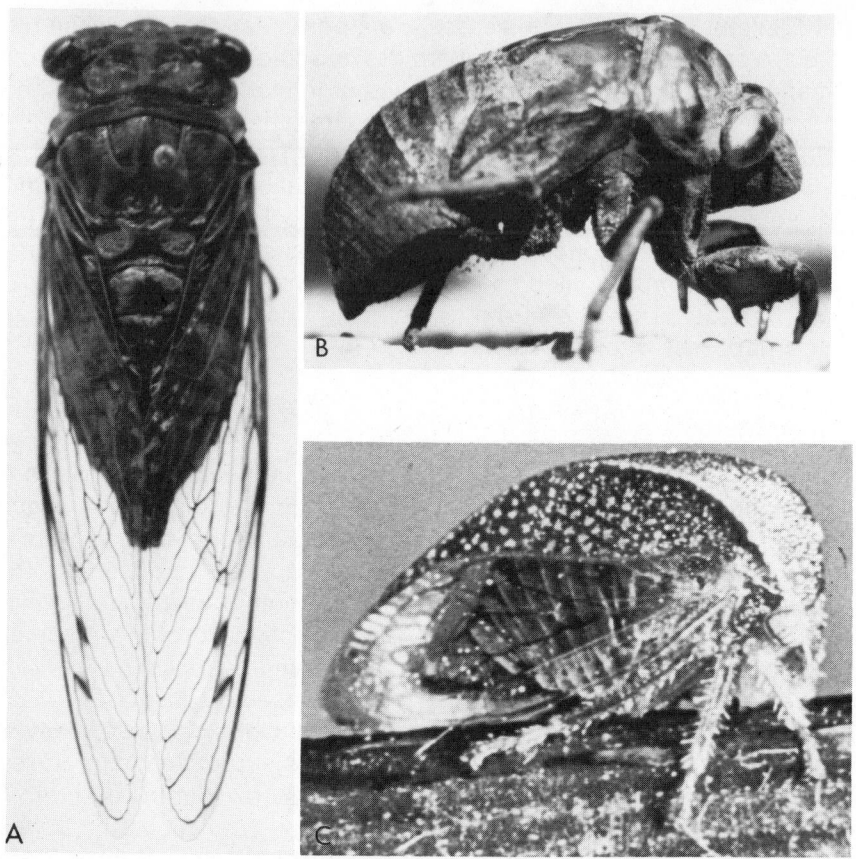

Figure 3–24. Order Homoptera, superfamily Cicadoidea. *A*, Cicada, family Cicadidae, adult. *B*, Cicada, family Cicadidae, cast skin of nymph. *C*, Treehopper, family Membracidae. (USDA photo.)

ancestral Homoptera. **Fulgoroidea** are somewhat more specialized but are superficially very similar to Cicadoidea. The more common families of Cicadoidea follow.

Cicadidae (cicadas, Fig. 3–24*A* and *B*) are large (5 to 50 mm.), black or greenish insects more often heard than seen. Males "sing," producing shrill, loud buzzes or trills on warm summer days. Chapter Five details sound production in cicadas (Fig. 5–34). Eggs are deposited in twigs, and large numbers of ovipositing cicadas may be quite destructive to orchard or woodlot trees. When they hatch, nymphs drop to the ground and burrow in. Most nymphs feed on roots for 2 to 5 years; those of the periodical cicadas *(Magicicada spp.)* remain underground for 13 or 17 years. When emerging, nymphs usually leave a cast skin (Fig. 3–24*B*) on such places as a tree trunk, picnic table, or cabin wall.

Membracidae (treehoppers, Fig. 3–24, *C* and *D*) are mostly small-to-medium (<12 mm.) Homoptera, characterized by a greatly enlarged pronotum often modified into a bizarre shape. Many species resemble thorns; this aids in camouflage, and the pronotum may also be sensory (Wood and Morris, 1974). Most treehoppers feed on sap of woody plants; a few occur on herbs and grasses. They jump when alarmed and most fly well. A few Membracidae harm orchard or ornamental trees by cutting oviposition slits in twigs; most species do no economic damage.

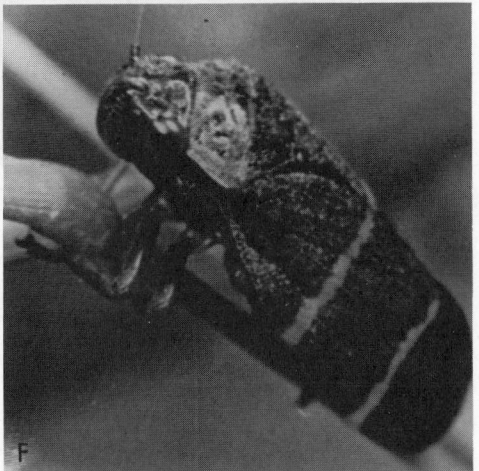

Figure 3–24. *Continued.* D, Treehopper, family Membracidae. (Photo courtesy of T. K. Wood.) E, Leafhopper, family Cicadellidae. (Photo by G. Berkey, courtesy of L. R. Nault and Ohio Agricultural Research and Development Center.) F, Spittlebug, family Cercopidae. (USDA photo.)

Cicadellidae (leafhoppers, Fig. 3–24E) are likewise small (<12 mm.), are slender and tapering, and are very active jumpers. Though their appearance is rather uniform, they represent the major adaptive radiation (5000 species) among the Cicadoidea. Their evolution has paralleled that of their hosts, mostly herbaceous flowering plants; there is thus great diversity of food preferences. Most leafhoppers restrict their feeding to one or a few plant species. Some with broader diets are major pests of crop plants; the potato leafhopper is equally at home on potatoes, alfalfa, or apples, in all of which its feeding causes yellowing and curling of leaves. Several leafhopper species are primary vectors of plant virus and/or mycoplasm diseases (Chapter Eleven). DeLong (1948) and Beirne (1956) are helpful references for further information on this group.

Cercopidae (spittlebugs, or froghoppers, Fig. 3–24F) adults are very similar to leafhoppers but are slightly chubbier and have one or two stout spines, rather than two rows of small spines, on the hind tibia. They are likewise highly active jumping insects as adults. Nymphs are more sedentary, soft-bodied, and slow-moving. They produce a frothy protective secretion (Fig. 9–14B); hence the name spittlebug. Within this, they feed relatively unmolested and breathe via a single pair of posterior spiracles. They feed mostly on sap of grasses and herbs, though some occur on coniferous trees. A few species, notably the meadow spittlebug, *Philaenus leucophthalmus*, are often numerous enough to suck significant sap from crop plants such as alfalfa and strawberries.

Fulgoroidea is a large superfamily of mostly small (10 mm. or less) jumping Homoptera whose antennae arise *below* (rather than before) the compound eyes.

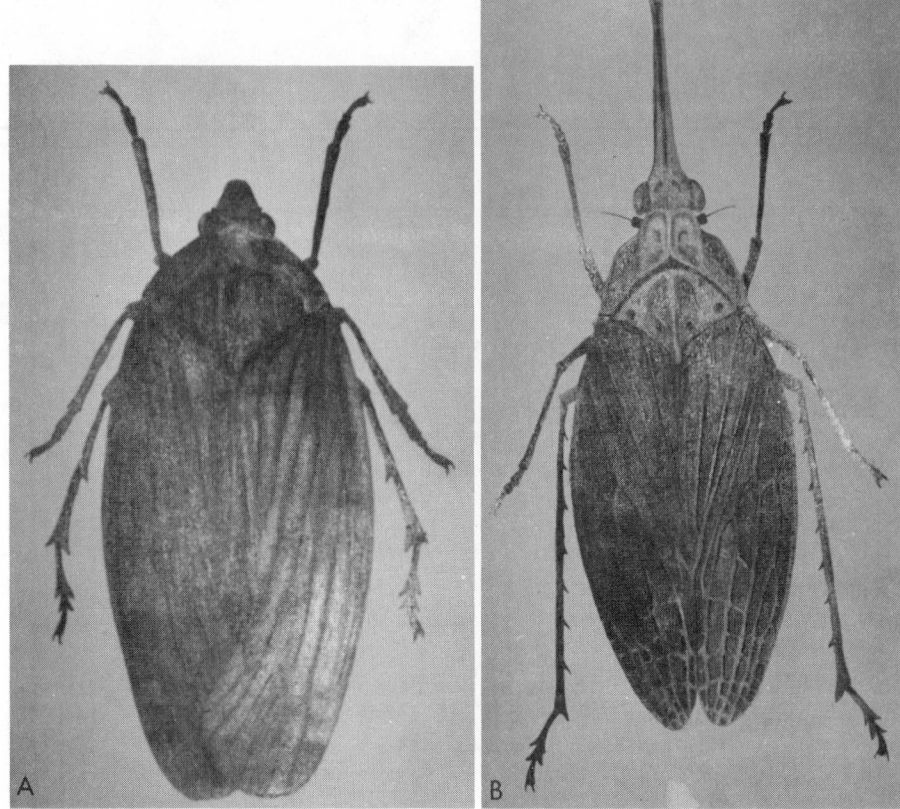

Figure 3–25. Order Homoptera, superfamily Fulgoroidea. *A, Epiptera*, family Achilidae. *B, Scolops*, family Delphacidae.

The eleven United States families show considerable variety in form (Fig. 3–25); like all Homoptera they feed on plant sap and occur most frequently in herbaceous plants or grasses. A few are subterranean as nymphs. Some tropical Fulgoridae are large insects (to 50 mm.) and bear an uncanny and probably protective resemblance to lizard heads.

Suborder Sternorrhyncha. **Psylloidea** contains the single family **Psyllidae** (Fig. 3–26A)–jumping insects that look like tiny (2 to 5 mm.) cicadas with long, 10-segmented antennae. They are called jumping plant lice. Some form galls, which occasionally damage hackberry trees. Nymphs of other species secrete a waxy material and look like tiny puffs of cotton. *Psylla pyricola* is a very serious pest of pears; its population suck enough sap to prevent fruit from ripening and to occasionally kill trees.

Aleyrodoidea is another single-family superfamily; it contains the **Aleyrodidae** (whiteflies, Fig. 3–26B). Adults are up to 3 mm. long, white, and have a scaly powder on the wings; from a distance they look like snowflakes or bits of cigarette ash. Nymphs are white and sessile; they move very little and concentrate on leaf undersides. The last-instar nymph does not feed at all and thus resembles the pupa of endopterygote insects. Aleyrodidae are most often encountered in greenhouses, where the greenhouse whitefly, *Trialeurodes vaporariorum,* is a major crop pest. Its feeding causes wilting, and mold grows in

Figure 3–25. *Continued. C, Otiocerus,* family Derbidae. *D, Laternaria,* family Fulgoridae. (*A–D,* paintings by W. Costello.)

its honeydew secretions, rendering cosmetic damage to greenhouse-grown vegetables and flowers.

Aphidoidea is a large group of small (4 to 8 mm.) insects, the most abundant of which are **Aphididae**, aphids or "plant lice." (Obviously, their relationship to true lice is very distant.) Most aphids (Figs. 3–26C and 7–29) are pear-shaped, with paired abdominal protrusions, **cornicles**. Some are winged and some are not; winged and wingless forms may occur in the same species at different times of year (Chapter Seven). A few aphids feed on roots, but most suck sap from stems, leaves, and buds of green plants. Some are very much restricted to single plant species, whereas others feed on many different hosts. Still others alternate between two (or more) hosts (Chapter Seven, Fig. 7–29). Polyphagous aphids, such as the green peach aphid, *Myzus persicae,* are the most important vectors of plant virus diseases (Chapter Eleven). Aphids also damage plants by their sheer numbers, sucking juices and causing plants to wilt; several species are major pests of vegetable, field, and fruit crops. Some Aphididae form galls, though galls are more prevalent products of the three smaller and more generalized aphidoid families, **Chermidae**, **Eriosomatidae**, and **Phylloxeridae**. Hottes and Frison (1931) is helpful for aphid identification.

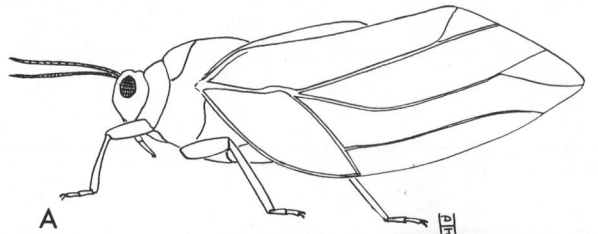

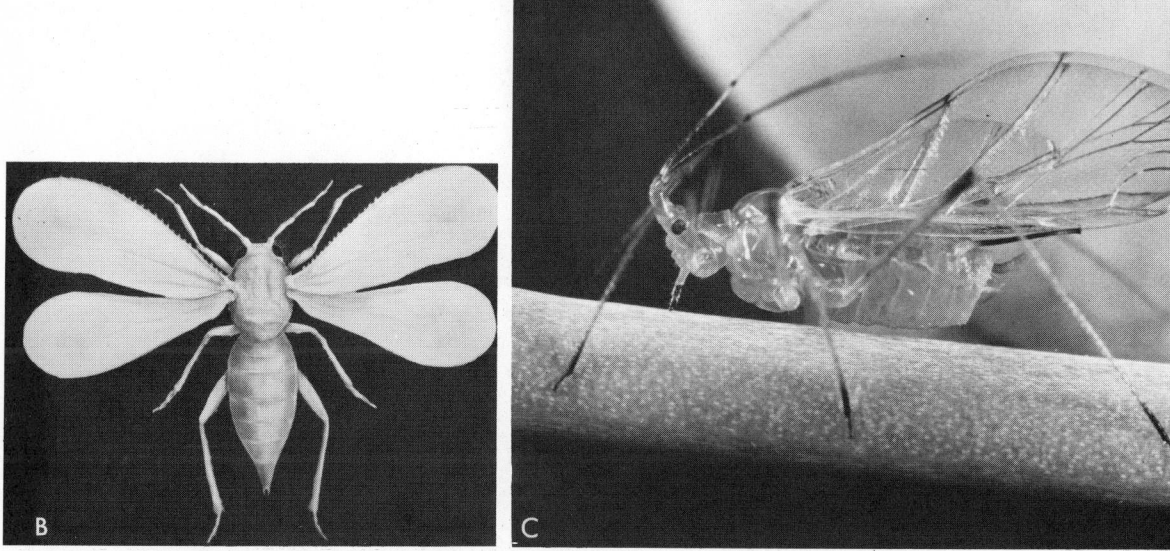

Figure 3–26. Order Homoptera, superfamily Aphidoidea. *A,* Psylla, family Psyllidae. *B,* Whitefly, family Aleyrodidae. (Painting by W. Costello.) *C,* Aphid, family Aphidae. (Photo by G. Berkey, courtesy of L. R. Nault and Ohio Agricultural Research and Development Center.)

Coccoidea is a superfamily comprised of 11 United States families whose members are extremely specialized external parasites of plants; these are the scale insects and mealybugs (Fig. 3–27). There is tremendous variety among scale insects, and most look nothing like insects, at least superficially. Typically, scales and mealybugs are very active "crawlers" as first instars, but within a day or two of hatching they settle down and begin feeding on plant sap. They secrete a waxy covering, a scale, over themselves and pass through subsequent instars beneath this protective scale, which may be hard or soft but is very typical for each species. Female scale insects are larviform and sometimes legless and remain under the scale for their entire lives. Males see more action, for the two-winged, flying, nonfeeding males are produced from quiescent last-instar pupa-like nymphs. Males don't eat, and they live just long enough to mate.

Scale insects predominate on woody plants, while mealybugs are more typical of herbaceous plants, though there are exceptions among both. Several species are severe pests of ornamental and orchard trees, especially apple, citrus, and olive; damage results from sap loss and blemishes of scales on fruit. On the other hand, the lac insect, *Laccifer lacca* (**Lacciferidae**), produces shellac

(Chapter Twelve), and dyes are (or were) made from secretions of other Coccoidea. Ferris (1937–1955) and McKenzie (1967) are detailed guides to scale insects.

Order Hemiptera

Hemiptera is a large (30,000 species) order of small to large insects very diverse in form, habits, and habitats. As the most diverse of Hemimetabola, they are examples of a major adaptive radiation. Hemiptera are "true bugs"; i.e., while many persons call *all* insects "bugs," legitimate use of the term is confined to Hemiptera. Most Hemiptera are somewhat flattened, have antennae with five or fewer segments, and a three- to 5-segmented "beak" or **rostrum**, which is actually a labial sheath containing the stylets and tubes comprising the sucking mouthparts. Winged Hemiptera usually have a forewing that is thickened at its base and membranous over the distal portion; when at rest, the wingtips usually overlap. The triangular **scutellum** between the folded wings is a useful identifying characteristic (Figs. 3–28 to 3–32). Many Hemiptera possess stink-producing glands.

Hemiptera are sometimes called Heteroptera, particularly when the order is enlarged to include Homoptera (discussed previously). Blatchley (1926) and Britton (1923) are comprehensive, although outdated, guides to identification and biology of American Hemiptera. Hemiptera have been divided into two suborders, **Cryptocerata** (antennae small and concealed, usually aquatic) and **Gymnocerata** (antennae prominent, usually terrestrial). These suborders are somewhat artificial, and I prefer to treat bug diversity according to six major superfamilies.

Corixidae (water boatmen, Fig. 3–28A) is the only family in the superfamily **Corixoidea**. Water boatmen are very common in freshwater lakes, ponds, and streams, where most feed on algae and plankton. Their beak is quite short, asymmetrical, and adapted for filtering rather than piercing. Water boatmen are flattened, are up to 12 mm. long, and have dark crosslines on the dorsum and flat-

Figure 3–27. Order Homoptera, superfamily Coccoidea. *A,* Oyster-shell scale, family Diaspididae. (Photo by G. Berkey, courtesy of D. G. Nielsen and Ohio Agricultural Research and Development Center.) *B,* Mealybug, family Pseudococcidae.

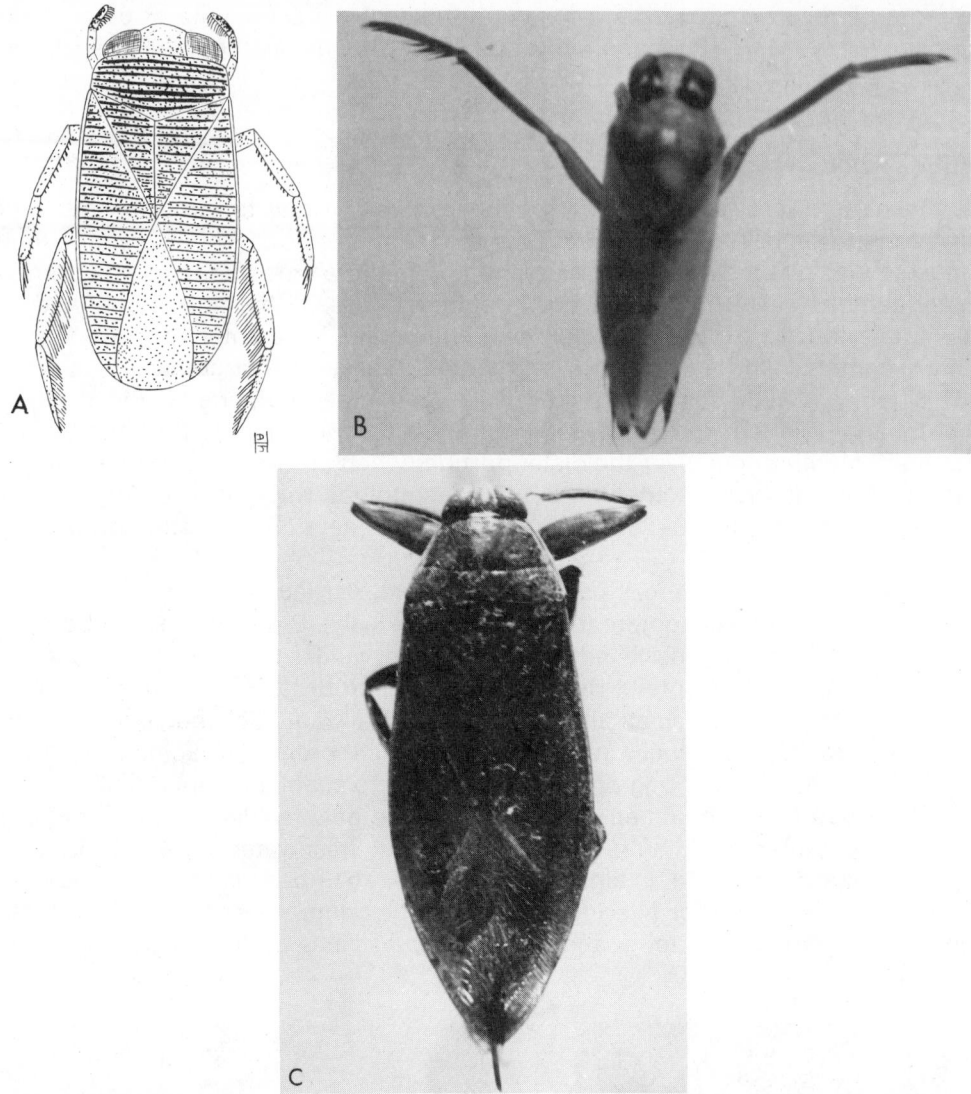

Figure 3–28. Aquatic Hemiptera. *A,* Water boatman, family Corixidae. *B,* Backswimmer, family Notonectidae. *C,* Giant water bug, family Belostomatidae.

tened, oarlike hindlegs. Most are winged, and adults fly to lights at night, sometimes many miles from the nearest fresh water. Like most aquatic yet winged Hemiptera, they often appear in outdoor swimming pools. Adult males stridulate (produce sound) with their forelegs when captured and probably when copulating.

Nepoidea includes the other major families of aquatic Hemiptera. **Notonectidae** (backswimmers, Fig. 3–28*B*) are similar in size (up to 15 mm.) to water boatmen but are convex dorsally. They swim upside down and are patterned accordingly; ventrally dark and dorsally light to blend with the background. Backswimmers prey upon smaller aquatic insects (including one another), into whom they inject powerful digestive enzymes; if handled carelessly they may bite insect-collecting humans, with the usual consequences of pain and profanity.

Larger than backswimmers, and capable of a proportionately stronger bite, are the giant water bugs, **Belostomatidae** (Fig. 3–28*C*). These are oval, flat, 25 to 50 mm. (or longer) brownish bugs with forelegs adapted for grasping and hindlegs adapted for swimming. They prey upon insects, tadpoles, and small fish and hence are said to be pests in fish hatcheries. Adults often are attracted to electric lights and may descend into outdoor swimming pools. Closely related in evolution, appearance, and habits are the **Nepidae**, water scorpions. These bugs have a long breathing tube extending from their posterior (Fig. 4–21*A*). Despite their name, water scorpions do not sting, but they may bite if handled.

　Cimicoidea are entirely terrestrial. The nominate family is **Cimicidae**, bed bugs (Fig. 3–29*A*)—flat, oval, wingless, brown ectoparasites of birds, bats, and people. Apparently, our bed bugs (*Cimex lectolarius* and two other species) were originally bat-biters that acquired a taste for cavepersons and have kept up with us in civilization. Bed bugs feed on blood before each molt and before reproducing but can live several months without food. Unlike many other bloodsucking arthropods, bed bugs do not transmit human diseases, though the irritation of bed bug bites is sufficient to warrant control. The sex life of bed bugs is highly unusual (see Chapter Seven).

　Anthocoridae (minute pirate bugs, Fig. 3–29*B*) are tiny (3 to 5 mm.) black and white bugs that abound on flowers and foliage, where they prey upon other insects and mites, and their eggs. Some are important predators in biological control of phytophagous mites (Holdsworth, 1972a).

　Miridae (plant bugs, Fig. 3–29*C*) is a large (5,000 species) family of small (to 10 mm.) bugs that are abundant on vegetation. This is the most diverse family of Hemiptera. Though Miridae are primarily plant feeders, some supplement their diets with smaller, sedentary insects, especially fly larvae and aphids (Wheeler, 1974). Mirid nymphs sometimes bite people who are sorting through samples of living insects from vegetation. Like leafhoppers, some Miridae are restricted to host plants of a single species, whereas others are quite generalized in food preferences. Among the latter group are several important pests of cultivated plants, notably the tarnished plant bug, *Lygus lineolaris*, whose feeding causes early drop of buds and fruit on such diverse crops as apples, strawberries, cotton, and alfalfa.

　The **Reduvioidea** comprises several families of predaceous Hemiptera. **Gerridae** (water striders, Fig. 3–30*A*) are familiar, long-legged, slender bugs that slide about the surface of slow or still water. They are thus technically not aquatic but feed on smaller insects that fall on the water's surface. They remain on the surface because their weight is widely distributed and their tarsi have water-repellent hairs. The genus *Halobates* contains some of the few marine insects; these water striders occur far at sea, though they are not truly marine in that they breathe air. Adult water striders may be winged or wingless, even within a single species. **Veliidae** is a related family of smaller, similar bugs found in streams.

　Reduviidae (assassin bugs, Fig. 3–30*B*) rival Miridae in diversity (4000 species); they represent the major existing adaptive radiation among predatory bugs. They are usually oval, are 10 to 25 mm. long, and have a long narrow head and thickened fore-femora for grasping prey. The beak has three segments. There is great variation in form among reduviids, and cryptic coloration and protective resemblance are common, especially among those species that feed on other insects. Most assassin bugs stridulate, rubbing the beak against the sternum and squeaking when handled. Most can bite, and they derive their name from the prodigious swelling that accompanies the bite and also from their

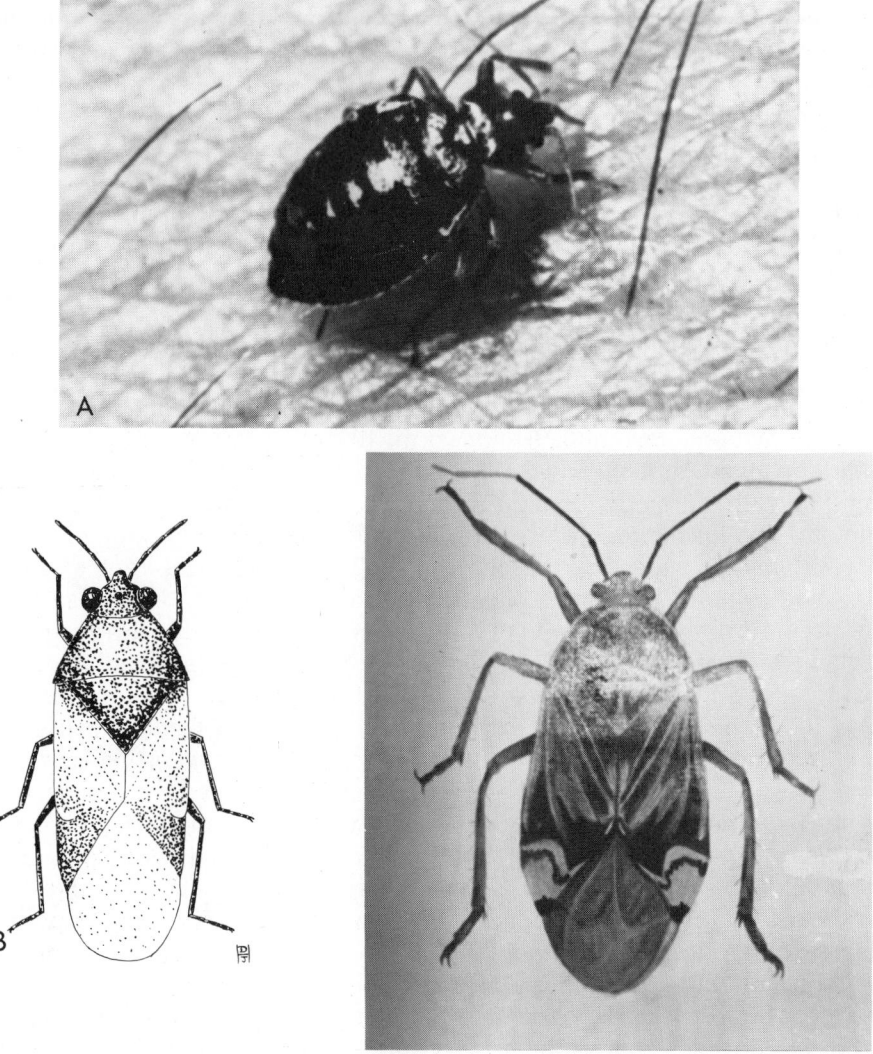

Figure 3–29. Order Hemiptera, superfamily Cimicoidea. *A,* Bed bug, family Cimicidae. *B,* Minute pirate bug, family Anthocoridae. *C,* Plant bug, family Miridae. (Painting by W. Costello.)

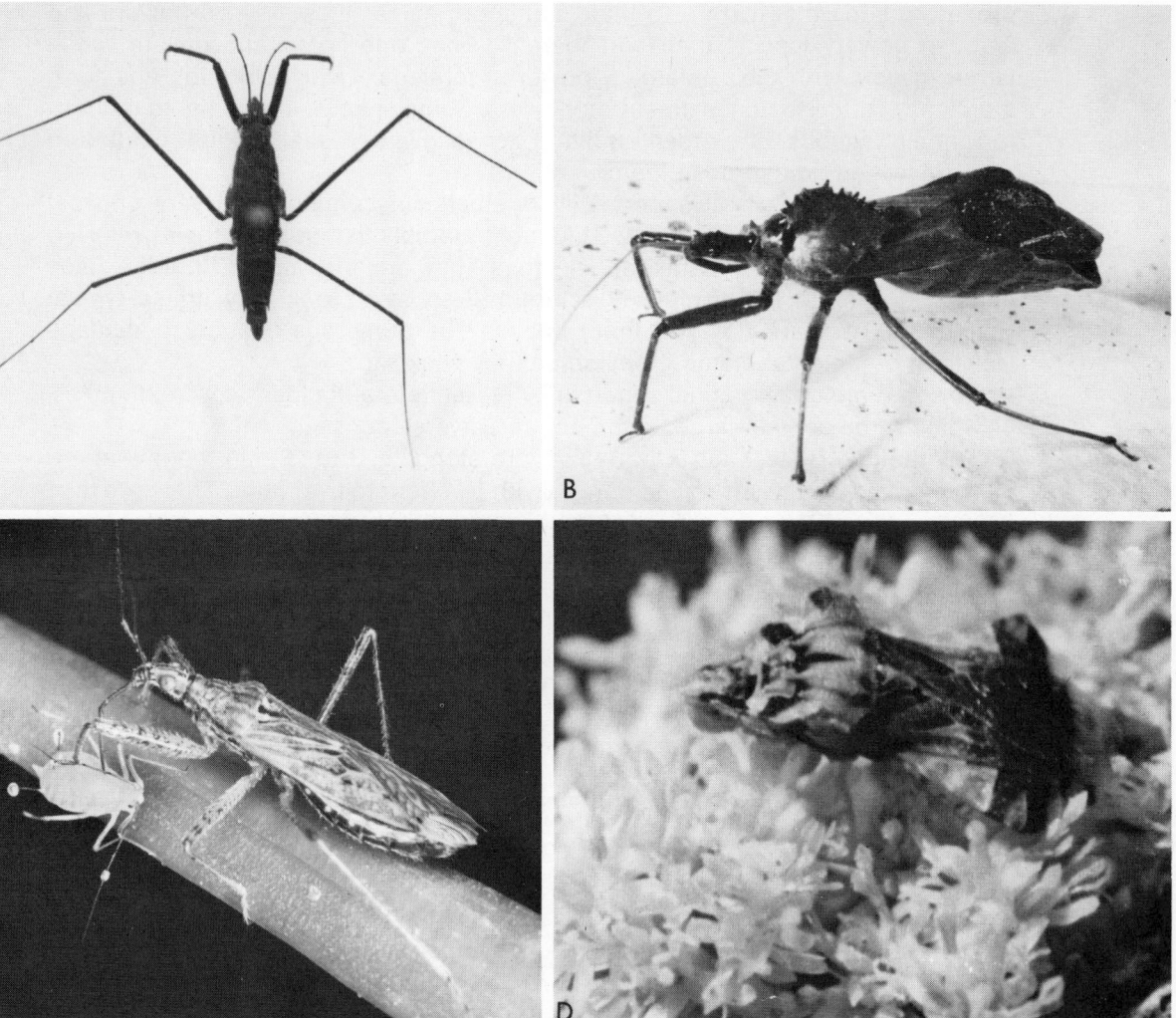

Figure 3–30. Order Hemiptera, superfamily Reduvioidea. *A*, Water strider, family Gerridae. *B*, Assassin bug, family Reduviidae. *C*, Damsel bug, family Nabidae, eating aphid. (Photo by G. Berkey, courtesy of L. R. Nault and Ohio Agricultural Research and Development Center.) *D*, Ambush bug, family Phymatidae.

voracious attacks on smaller insects. A few species routinely feed on the blood of vertebrates. Members of the genus *Triatoma* (conenose bugs) transmit *Trypanosoma cruzi,* a protozoan parasite that causes Chagas' disease in humans in tropical and subtropical regions (Chapter Eleven). Even without introducing Chagas' disease, the bite of an assassin bug is quite irritating. On a positive note, the bloodsucking bug. *Rhodnius prolixus* has proven a very useful experimental animal for studies of physiological processes in insects. Damsel bugs (**Nabidae,** Fig. 3–30*C*) are similar to Reduviidae but smaller (8 to 10 mm.) and are usually gray or brown. They prey on other insects.

Phymatidae (ambush bugs, Fig. 3–30*D*) are unmistakable, small (to 12 mm.), predatory bugs that live up to their (common) name; they hide on flowers and ambush unwary insects that land thereon. They often grab and devour much larger insects with their enlarged, powerful forelegs. Their coloration and form are ideally suited to concealment on flowers. Some species are partial to goldenrod; their nymphs are green, molting to yellow and black adult coloration precisely when goldenrods bloom.

Aradoidea is a small superfamily of small but common and very unusual bugs. **Aradidae** (flat bugs, Fig. 3–31*A*) are incredibly flat, as suits their preferred habitat, crevices under bark and in litter. They are predatory. **Tingidae** (lace bugs, Fig. 3–31*B*) are complexly sculptured so as to look very unlike typical Hemiptera. They are tiny (<3 mm.) but may be numerous enough to damage leaves of ornamental plants, from which they suck sap.

Pentatomoidea, the final superfamily of Hemiptera, includes several families, of which three contain large, common, and diverse bugs.

Lygaeidae (seed bugs, Fig. 3–32*A*) are elongate, 3 to 15 mm. bugs that are characterized by a forewing membrane with few (four to five) veins. There are over 2000 species, showing a variety of habits and habitats. Most prey on plant seeds by injecting potent enzymes, then sucking out the predigested contents. A lesser number of Lygaeidae prey on other insects or suck plant sap. Among the latter is the chinch bug, a tiny but exceedingly destructive pest of grasses, including corn, wheat, oats, and lawns. Milkweed bugs (Fig. 9–18) are Lygaeidae, and because they take readily to laboratory-rearing, are valuable physiological subjects.

Coreidae (Fig. 3–32*B*) are very similar to Lygaeidae but are generally larger (10 mm. or more), with many veins in the forewing membrane. There are likewise

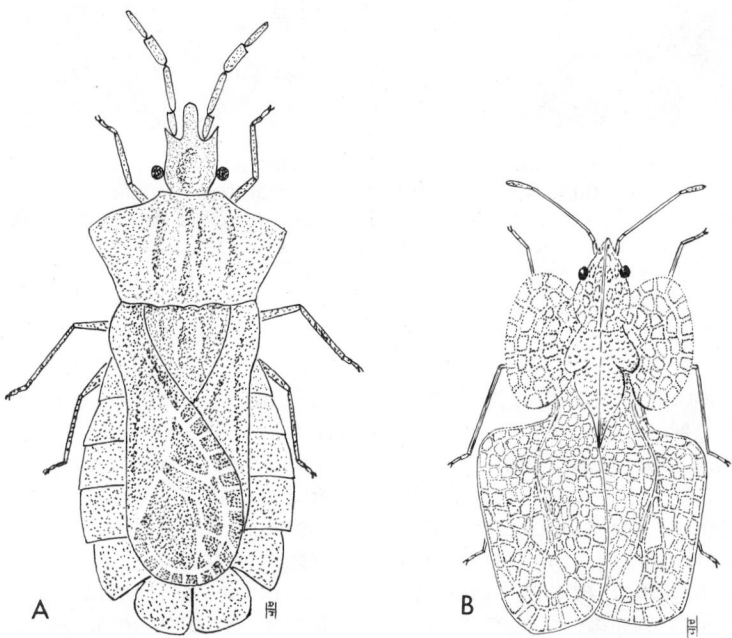

Figure 3–31. Order Hemiptera, superfamily Aradoidea. *A,* Flat bug, family Aradidae. *B,* Lace bug, family Tingidae.

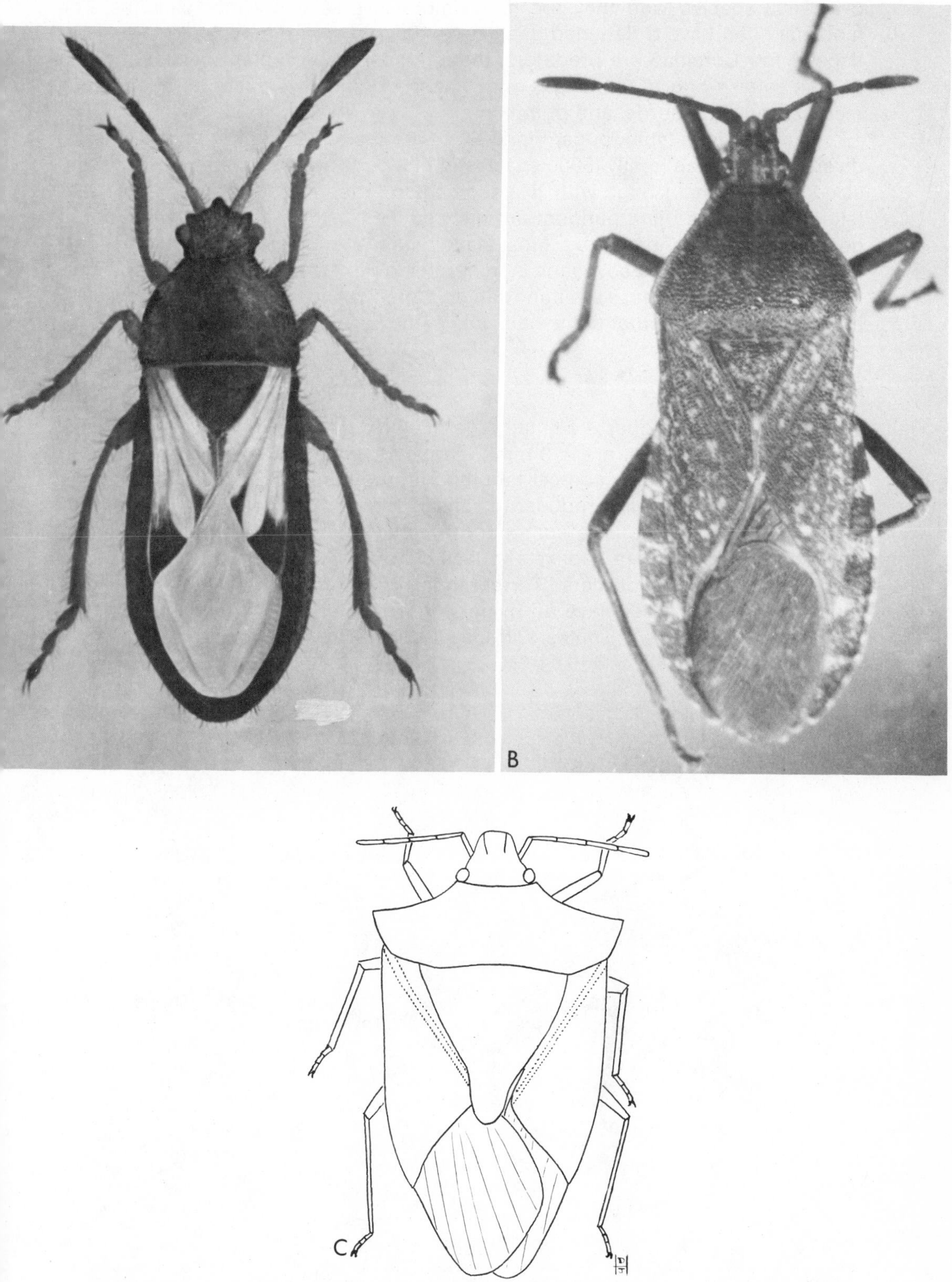

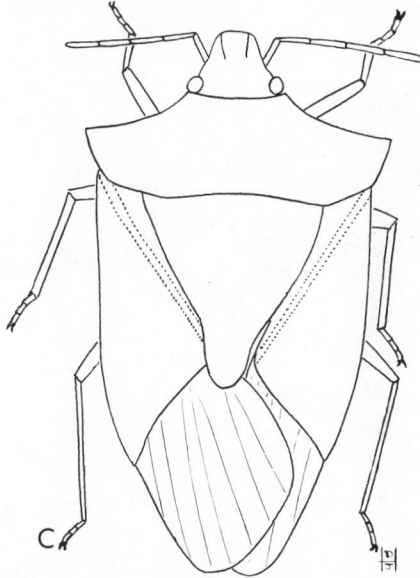

Figure 3–32. Order Hemiptera, superfamily Pentatomoidea. *A,* Chinch bug, family Lygaeidae. (Painting by W. Costello.) *B,* Squash bug, family Coreidae. *C,* Stink bug, family Pentatomidae.

over 2000 species, and they are much more diverse in warmer climates. The hindlegs often have a flattened, leaflike, expanded area that may aid in camouflage. A few Coreidae are predators, though most feed on plant juices; in doing so, the squash bug, *Anasa tristis,* may cause significant damage to cucumbers, melons, squash, gourds, and pumpkins.

Pentatomidae (stink bugs, Fig. 3–32*C*) are the equal of Miridae as the most diverse Hemipteran family (5000 species). Stink bugs are oval, flattened, medium-sized (7 to 20 mm.) bugs with five-segmented antennae and a prominent scutellum. The "stink" is a pungent aroma produced by metasternal glands, and it does repel potential predators. Most stink bugs feed on plants and some damage fruit crops, cotton, and soybeans. A minority are predaceous, especially on caterpillars, and some of these are important in biological control of pests. A few stink bugs are subsocial in that the female guards the eggs and first-instar nymphs.

Order Thysanoptera

Thysanoptera (thrips) is a small order (600 North American species) of small insects (to 6 mm., most are < 3 mm.). Thrips are very slender, dark insects (Fig. 3–33) with very unusual, conical mouthparts; the mouthparts are asymmetrical, the right mandible being reduced or absent. Thrips' wings, when present, are fringed with long setae. The compound eyes have few facets and look like little raspberries. The tarsi are padlike and lack claws.

There are two suborders: Terrebrantia, the more "primitive," are all phytophagous, and females have an ovipositor. Tubulifera lack the ovipositor, and some are predaceous on mites and insect eggs. Phytophagous thrips rasp the

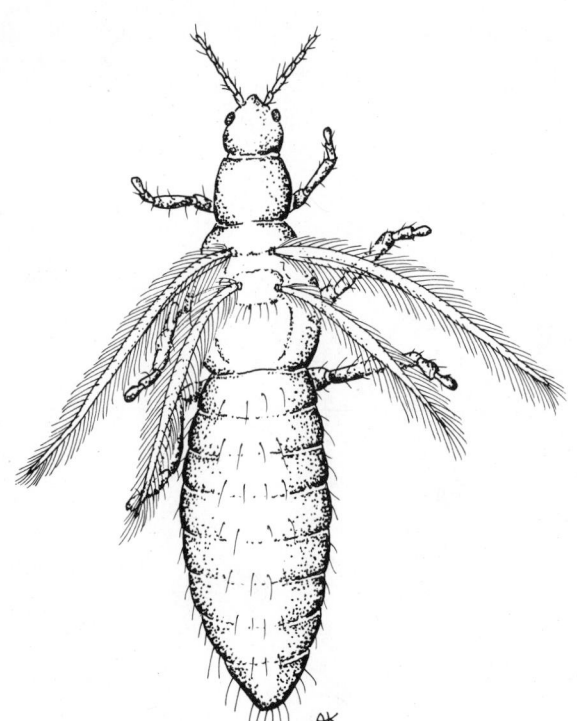

Figure 3–33. Thrips, order Thysanoptera.

surface of leaves and flowers, causing streaks. They also spread some plant diseases. Floral crops, onions, and tobacco are affected significantly by thrips.

Thysanoptera have an unusual life cycle. The final two or three nymphal instars are quiescent, nonfeeding, "resting" stages; a subsoil cocoon may contain the last instar. This occurs despite the nymphs' similarity to adults and is thought to be a forerunner of complex metamorphosis. The thrips, with this "allometabolous" development, thus seem to be developmentally between Hemimetabola and Holometabola.

For more on thrips see Stannard (1968) and T. Lewis (1973).

NEOPTERA: HOLOMETABOLA

Eighty-eight per cent of all living insect species undergo complex (or complete) metamorphosis: egg, larva, pupa, and adult. Complex metamorphosis has obvious advantages, discussed in the previous chapter: larvae have become more specialized for feeding, and adults for dispersal and reproduction; and hostile environmental conditions can be withstood as either egg or pupa. Presumably, holometabolous development evolved in insects (Protorthoptera?) in which the final nymphal instar was a nonfeeding resting stage similar to what we see today in whiteflies and thrips. During evolution of holometabolous development, larvae and adults were subjected to different environmental selection pressures and diverged in habits and appearance. Most presently existing holometabolous larvae are very unlike the corresponding adult forms.

There are three main groups of Holometabola; (Table 3–3) all presumably evolved from a single ancestor. Coleoptera (and Strepsiptera) lack an ovipositor and have greatly modified forewings, so that it is difficult to trace their ancestry. Neuroptera and Mecoptera together comprise a line from which several orders have evolved; only Neuroptera retain the ovipositor. Finally, Hymenoptera have a sawlike ovipositor and reduced venation; their origin is obscure.

Table 3–3. GENERAL CHARACTERISTICS OF HOLOMETABOLA

Order	Wings*	Mouthparts LARVA	Mouthparts ADULT	Larvae†	Pupae†	Comments
Coleoptera	FW thickened	chewing	chewing	variable	exarate	largest order
Strepsiptera	2 wings	chewing	chewing	vermiform	exarate	parasitic on other insects
Neuroptera	FW = HW	chewing	chewing	campodeiform	exarate	some larvae aquatic
Mecoptera	FW = HW	chewing	chewing	eruciform	exarate	
Trichoptera	FW < HW, hairy	chewing	vestigial	eruciform	exarate	aquatic larvae
Lepidoptera	FW > HW	chewing	sucking	eruciform	obtect	most larvae herbivorous
Diptera	2 wings	mouthhooks	sucking	vermiform	coarctate, (some obtect)	diverse
Siphonaptera	none	mouthhooks	sucking	vermiform	exarate	adults parasitize mammals and birds
Hymenoptera	FW > HW	chewing	chewing	vermiform, eruciform (a few)	exarate	some social, many parasitize insects

*FW = HW, forewing and hindwing same size; FW < HW, forewing smaller than hindwing; FW > HW, forewing larger than hindwing.

†See page 276 for definitions of these terms.

Order Coleoptera

Coleoptera, beetles, is collectively one of the outstanding examples of adaptive radiation among any group of animals. One of every three insect species is a member of this, the largest order (250,000 described species). All beetles have the forewings modified into elytra, hardened covers for the thin, membranous hindwings and abdomen. Apparently, evolution of elytra is partially responsible for the beetles' great diversity; elytra are protective, can be cryptically colored, and enable beetles to maneuver in tiny spaces without wrecking the hindwings. Coleoptera contains the largest family (Curculionidae) of insects, as well as the smallest (0.2 mm.) and largest (in bulk) living insect species. Larvae are incredibly varied, much more so than adults. Beetles are successful inhabitants of almost all terrestrial and many aquatic habitats and feed on practically everything. They are of tremendous economic importance, being perhaps the number one order in that regard, too.

Despite their incredible diversity, adult beetles are rather homogeneous in appearance and are easily recognizable. A further limitation to diversity is that there are very few parasitic beetles, as either larvae or adults (and consequently few are of medical importance). Social behavior in beetles is limited too; members of a few families brood offspring or live in loose aggregations.

The origin of Coleoptera is obscure. Some workers suggest a neuropteroid ancestor not unlike some present-day dobsonflies (Fig. 3–50A). Fossil evidence gives few clues to the beetles' ancestry. They apparently diversified rapidly at the start of the Permian period, for they represent 40 per cent of insect fossils from that time. It was once thought that beetles may have evolved from Dermaptera, though the differences are so great that this seems unlikely.

Modern beetles have evolved in three major directions, represented by three suborders. (Some say four.) Within these suborders, in the United States alone, are 20 superfamilies containing 125 families. Table 3–4 lists the major groups discussed here. **Archostemata** is the most primitive, and rarest, of the three suborders and contains the only beetles that retain a suggestion of veins in the elytra. These are rather rare beetles occurring under bark and in rotting logs.

Adephaga is a rather small suborder of common, conspicuous, predatory beetles. The vast majority (85 per cent) of beetles are suborder **Polyphaga,** a very heterogeneous group. Major families of these two suborders are discussed in the following sections, and Arnett (1968), Hatch (1953–1975), Jacques (1951), and Leech and Chandler (1956) are most helpful guides to further identification.

Suborder Adephaga. **Cicindelidae** (tiger beetles, Fig. 3–34A and B) are predaceous, very active beetles, 6 to 40 mm. (most are 10 to 20 mm.), quite commonly found on bare ground or sand, especially in sunny spots. They are wary and hard to catch. If you do catch one (or more), note the long slender legs, large eyes, and narrow pronotum; many are metallic brown, black, or green. Larvae ("doodlebugs," Fig. 3–34B) construct a vertical tunnel within which they await smaller, unsuspecting prey. The doodlebug's flat-topped head is often sculptured and colored precisely to match its local surroundings.

Carabidae (ground beetles, Fig. 3–34C and D) is a large (30,000 species worldwide) family of predatory beetles found everywhere, but most abundantly in moister climates. Adults are diverse in size (3 to 35 mm.; mostly 5 to 15 mm.), form, and coloration, though most are shining black or greenish, with long slender legs and head narrower than the thorax. Most live on or near the ground,

Table 3-4. CLASSIFICATION OF COLEOPTERAN FAMILIES*

Suborder	Superfamily	Families Included†
Archostemata		none
Adephaga		Cicindelidae, Carabidae
		Dytiscidae, Gyrinidae
Polyphaga	Staphylinoidea	Staphylinidae, Silphidae
	Histeroidea	Histeridae
	Hydrophiloidea	Hydrophilidae
	Scarabaeoidea	Lucanidae, Scarabaeidae
	Cantharoidea	Cantharidae, Lampyridae, Lycidae
	Elateroidea	Elateridae, Buprestidae
	Bostrichoidea	Bostrichidae, Anobiidae, Lyctidae
	Cleroidea	Dermestidae, Cleridae
	Cucujoidea	Cucujidae, Nitidulidae, Coccinellidae
	Melooidea	Meloidae
	Mordelloidea	Mordellidae
	Tenebrionoidea	Tenebrionidae, Melandryidae, Alleculidae
	Cerambycoidea	Cerambycidae, Chrysomelidae, Bruchidae
	Curculionoidea	Curculionidae, Scolytidae

*Data from Crowson, R. A. 1967. The natural classification of families of Coleoptera. Rev. ed. E. W. Classey Ltd., Hampton, Middlesex, England.

†This list is limited to those families mentioned in the text; for complete classification of United States families, see Borror et al., 1976.

under rocks, and in similar places; some occur on vegetation, especially in the tropics. Most are nocturnal, and many fly readily to lights, where they may commence feasting on other, smaller insects. Insects, worms, and snails become meals for both adult and larval carabids. Indeed, most are probably beneficial, and *Calosoma calidum,* a large green carabid, has been introduced from Europe to North America to aid in controlling gypsy and brown-tail moth larvae. Carabidae often wander into cellars, where they may be mistaken for cockroaches. The seed corn beetle, *Agonoderus lecontei,* has forsaken its relatives' predatory habits and is occasionally a serious pest of newly seeded corn.

Dytiscidae (predaceous diving beetles, Fig. 3-35A and B) might be considered aquatic carabids. There are many similarities: larvae and adults are predaceous, and diverse in size (2 to 35 mm.); most are shining black or brown; and adults often flock to lights. Dytiscidae have, however, adaptations for aquatic existence: streamlining and flattened, fringed natatorial hindlegs (Fig. 5-27D). Larvae ("water tigers," Fig. 3-35B) possess sickle-shaped jaws with which they inject digestive juices into their prey (water insects, tadpoles, snails, or fish fry). They are sometimes considered pests about fish hatcheries. Three other small families of small aquatic beetles look like, and are closely related to, Dytiscidae.

Gyrinidae (whirligig beetles, Fig. 3-35C) are black, flattened, 3 to 15 mm. long beetles that whirl about in dizzying circles on calm waters. Their compound eyes are completely divided (Fig. 5-6B), giving the impression of four compound eyes. Unlike water striders (Hemiptera:**Gerridae**), whirligig beetles submerge when threatened. Larvae and adults are predaceous on smaller aquatic insects and on terrestrial insects unfortunate enough to fall into a poolful of gyrinids. Gyrinid larvae leave the water to pupate, usually near the water's edge. Adults fly readily and may appear at lights quite some distance from water.

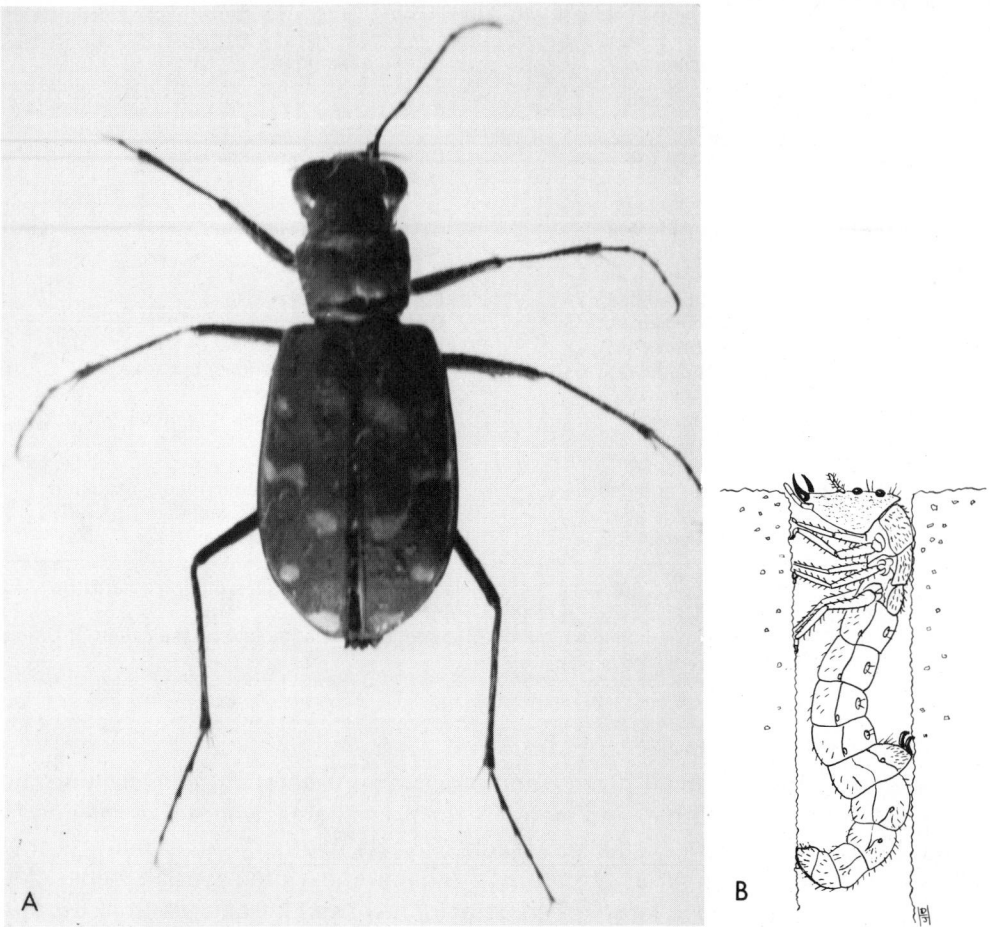

Figure 3–34. Order Coleoptera, suborder Adephaga (terrestrial). *A,* Tiger beetle, family Cicindelidae, adult. *B,* Larva of same.

Suborder Polyphaga. **Silphidae** (carrion beetles, Fig. 3–36*B*) are usually flattened beetles, 2 to 35 mm, with broad elytra and clubbed antennae. They usually occur near decaying meat or vegetation, on which adults feed and oviposit. Developing larvae then continue eating the decaying organic matter. *Necrophorus* species travel in mated pairs, locating and burying carcasses of small vertebrate animals. The female oviposits thereon, and both sexes may help feed the developing larvae (Chapter Six).

Staphylinidae (rove beetles, Fig. 3–36*A*) are abundant and diverse (3000 USA species) beetles that occur in carrion and fungi and on and under ground, bark, dung, and such. They are elongate, with characteristically short elytra reminiscent of those of earwigs (Fig. 3–17*A*). Size varies from 1 to 20 mm. Rove beetles are very active. Most are predaceous as both larvae and adults, feeding on smaller insects, particularly on fly larvae in dung and carrion. A few larvae are parasitic on fly pupae, and some of these are beneficial agents of biological control (Heller 1976).

C

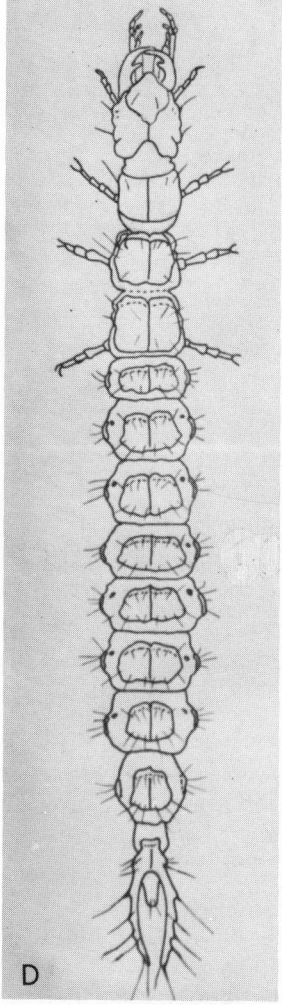

D

Figure 3–34. *Continued.* *C,* Ground beetle, family Carabidae, adult. (USDA photo.) *D*, Larva of same. (Drawing by W. Costello.)

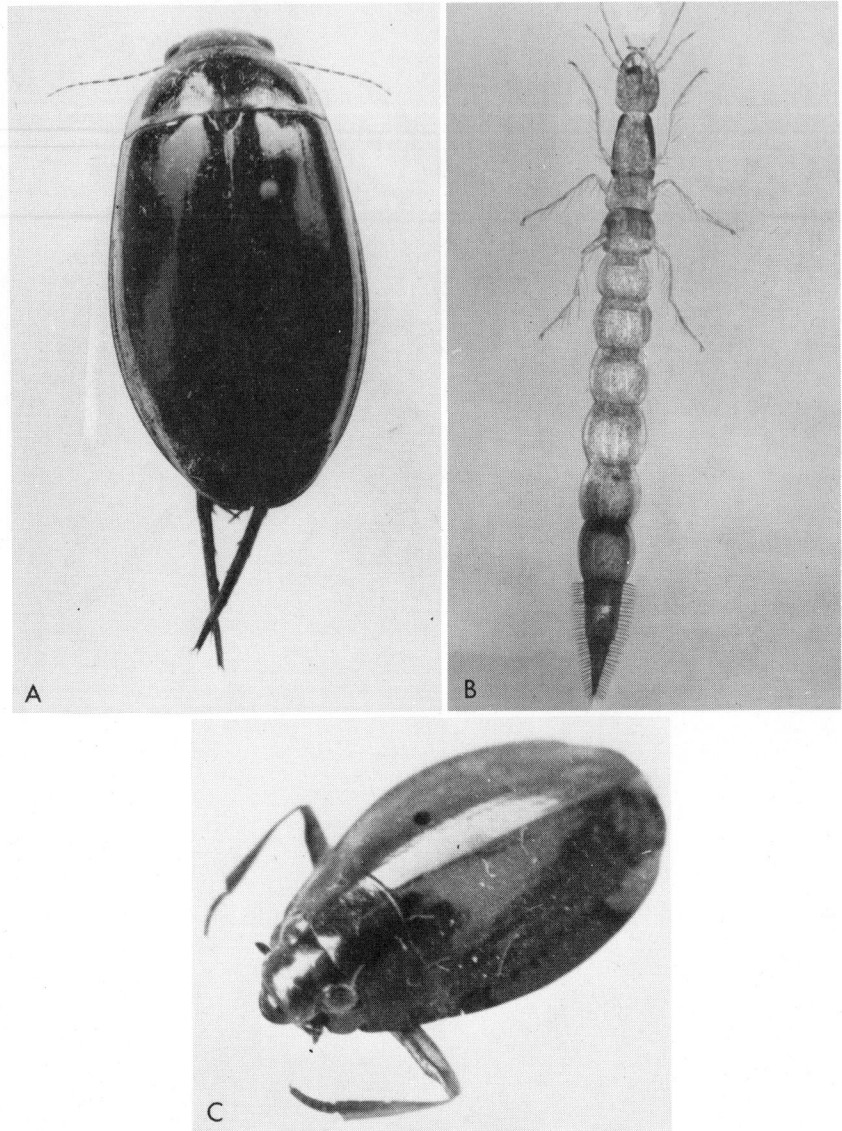

Figure 3–35. Order Coleoptera, suborder Adephaga (aquatic). *A*, Predaceous diving beetle, family Dytiscidae, adult. *B*, Larva of same. (Painting by W. Costello.) *C*, Whirligig beetle, family Gyrinidae.

Histeridae (hister beetles, Fig. 3–37*A*) are shiny, oval, black beetles, 1 to 10 mm. long; the elytra do not entirely cover the abdomen. They are common about carrion, dung, oozing sap, decaying plants and under bark and apparently prey, as larvae and adults, on other insects. Despite their abundance it is not clear exactly what insects they do eat.

Hydrophilidae (water scavenger beetles, Fig. 3–37, *B* and *C*) appear very similar to **Dytiscidae**; they are oval, convex, black or brown, 1 to 40 mm. long aquatic beetles. They may be recognized by their tiny, clubbed antennae. (Dytiscids' antennae are long and filiform.) Their maxillary palpi are usually longer than their

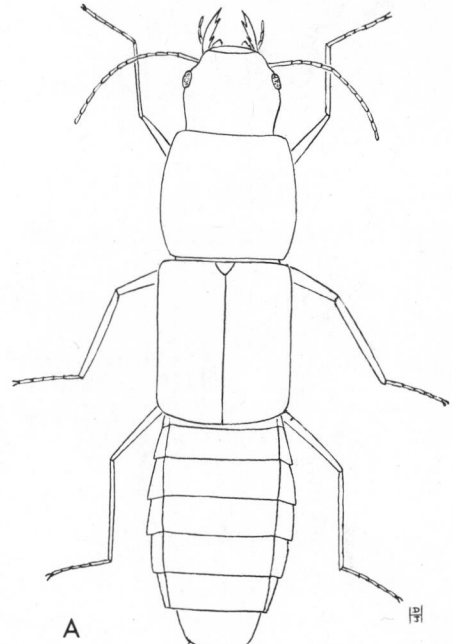

Figure 3–36. Order Coleoptera, superfamily Staphylinoidea. *A,* Rove beetle, family Staphylinidae. *B,* Carrion beetle, family Silphidae.

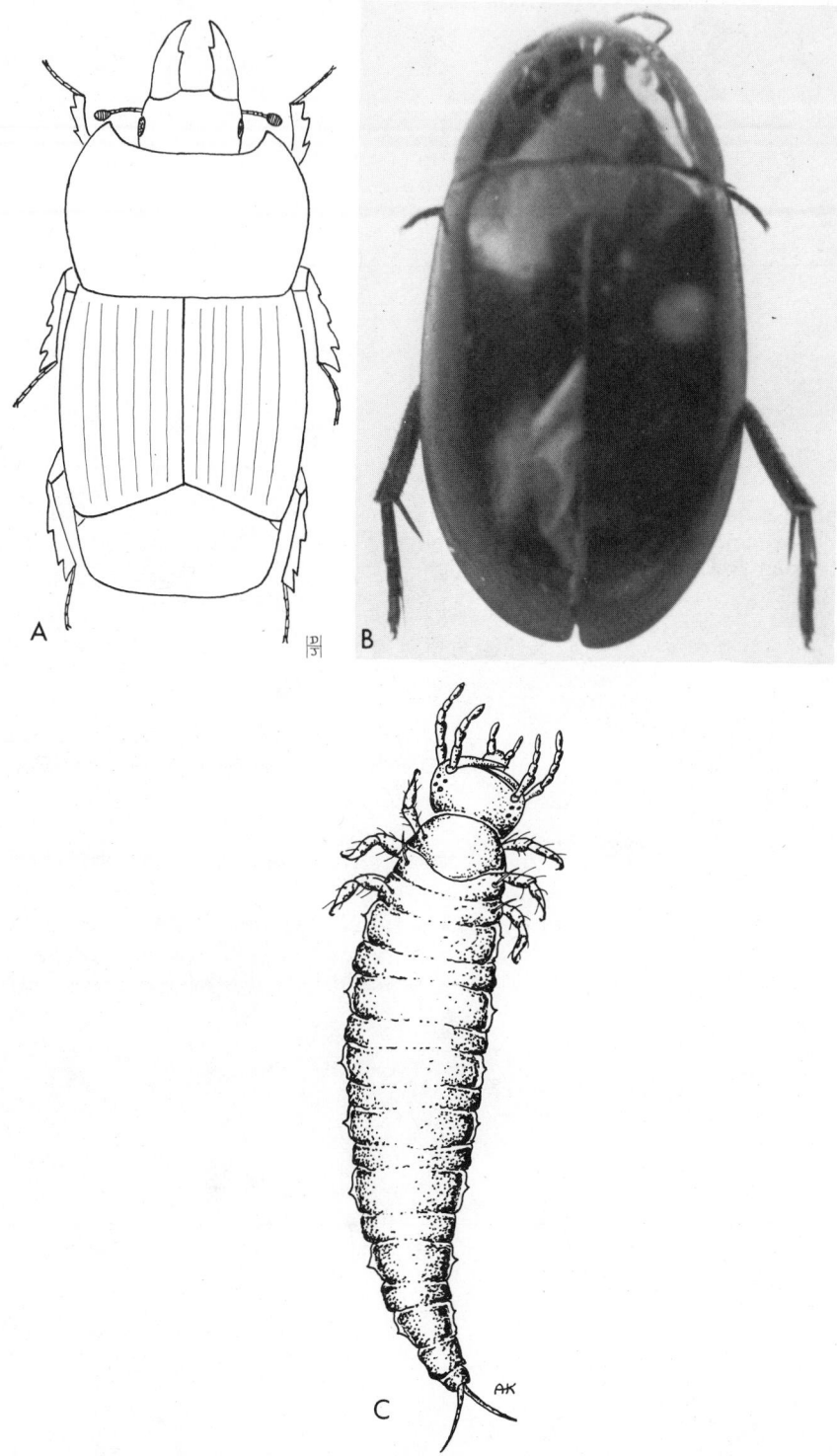

Figure 3–37. Order Coleoptera, superfamilies Histeroidea and Hydrophiloidea. *A,* Hister beetle, family Histeridae. *B,* Water scavenger beetle, family Hydrophilidae, adult. *C,* larva of same.

antennae and seem to function as sensory structures much as antennae. Hydrophilid larvae prey on smaller aquatic creatures, while adults are scavengers and often abound at lights near water.

Lucanidae (stag beetles, Fig. 3–38A) are large (8 to 40 mm.) black or brown beetles with elbowed antennae and greatly enlarged mandibles on males. In the United States they are more common in the East, where there is abundant rotting

Figure 3–38. Order Coleoptera, superfamily Scarabaeoidea. *A,* Stag beetle, family Lucanidae, male. *B,* Scarab, family Scarabaeidae, adult. *C,* White grub, larva of scarab. (USDA photo.)

wood in which larvae feed. Adults eat sap and often are attracted to lights. The enlarged male mandibles are mostly secondary sexual adornments and deliver but a weak pinch; actually, the bite of females is the more painful to humans.

Scarabaeidae (scarabs, Fig. 3–38, *B* and *C*) is a large, diverse, important family (1300 North American species). Most scarabs are stout, oval, or elongate, with lamellate antenna (Fig. 5–16*C*). They vary greatly in size (from 2 to 50 or more millimeters in length) and include the world's largest (bulk) insects, the African goliath beetle and West Indian hercules beetle, each of which can outweigh a mouse.

Larval foods of Scarabaeidae include dung, hide, grass roots, and decaying wood; adults may feed on foliage, pollen, or fruit and may come in numbers to lights. Of particular interest are the dung-rolling beetles or tumblebugs, Scarabaeinae. A mated pair locates a dung pile and rolls from it a ball of dung, which is taken away and buried with the insect's eggs. Developing larvae subsequently consume the dung. Some dung-rollers do not roll their own but parasitize smaller species by stealing their dungball as soon as they have it together. The dung-rolling habit was apparently a basis for the ancient Egyptians' reverence for scarabs; according to their mythology, the sun was rolled through the sky by a giant invisible scarabaeid, who had best not be offended. Several Scarabaeidae (mostly Melolonthinae and Rutelinae) are serious plant pests. Their larvae, "white grubs" or grubworms (Fig. 3–38*C*), eat roots of grasses and often kill grasses in lawns and golf courses. Some of these larvae mature to equally noxious adults, particularly the rose chafer and Japanese beetle (Fig. 10–2), both of which damage a variety of ornamental plants and fruit crops. Other white grubs become May beetles (or June bugs), familiar brown beetles found about lights on warm early summer evenings in most of North America.

Cantharidae (soldier beetles, Fig. 3–39*A*) are of a superfamily (Cantharoidea) whose members have rather soft and pliable elytra. Soldier beetles are elongate, from 1 to 15 mm. long, with a small pronotum and prominent head. Adults are common on foliage and flowers, where they eat pollen; the predaceous larvae live in leaf litter or under bark.

Lampyridae (fireflies or lightning bugs, Fig. 3–39*B*) are very similar to cantharids, but their larger pronotum hides their head from dorsal view. They are best known for their light production (Chapters Four and Six), and males often put on spectacular flashing displays on summer evenings. The flashes are a prelude to mating; many female fireflies are wingless, larviform "glowworms". Not all lampyrids produce light. Lampyrid occur under bark, on the ground, and in other damp situations and are predaceous; apparently most feed on snails.

Lycidae (net-winged beetles, Fig. 3–39*C*) are an unusual family of soft-winged beetles, 5 to 18 mm. long, whose reticulated pronotum and elytra are usually boldly colored in black and yellow, orange, or red. These colors advertise the distastefulness of Lycidae to potential predators (Linsley et al., 1961). Insects of several other orders, particularly Lepidoptera, have evolved great similarity in coloration to lycid beetles, and predators consequently leave these mimics alone too. Lycid adults eat plant juices or small insects; their predaceous larvae occur under bark.

Elateridae (click beetles, Fig. 3–40*A*) are variable in size (3 to 45 mm.) but consistent in form: narrow, oval in cross section, with pointed corners at the hind edge of the pronotum. Most (in the United States) are brown or black, and some larger species have prominent pronotal eyespots. Their most interesting feature is their ability when placed on their back, to bend backward and then vigorously

Figure 3–39. Order Coleoptera, superfamily Cantharoidea. *A,* Soldier beetle, family Cantharidae. *B,* Firefly, family Lampyridae. *C,* Netwinged beetle, family Lycidae.

snap or "click" into the air. Some tropical click beetles (*Pyrophorus* species) produce light. Adult click beetles are common on flowers and foliage, under bark, and at lights. Larvae (wireworms, Fig. 3–40*B*) are omnivorous, living in rotten wood or soils. Some are serious pests of potatoes, corn, wheat, or root crops; they eat both newly planted seeds and roots of older crop plants.

Figure 3–40. Order Coleoptera, superfamily Elateroidea. *A,* Click beetle, family Elateridae. *B,* Wireworm, larva of click beetle. *C,* Metallic wood borer, family Buprestidae, adult. *D,* Flatheaded borer, larva of Buprestidae. (Painting by W. Costello.)

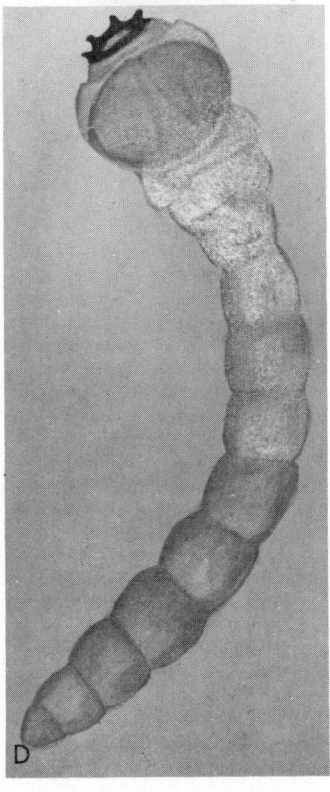

Buprestidae (metallic wood borers, Fig. 3–40C) are active, often brightly colored, metallic beetles, 3 to 40 mm. in length. The first two abdominal sternites are fused; the entire underside often appears metallic. Adults are common day-flying beetles in woodlands; the larvae ("flat-headed borers," Fig. 3–40D) mostly bore in wood. A few feed in stems or form galls. Flat-headed borers are sometimes pests in fruit or ornamental trees, particularly birches. Despite their name, it is the larva's prothorax that is enlarged and flattened—the actual head is small.

Bostrichoidea is a large superfamily of small beetles, some of which do great damage. **Bostrichidae** (Fig. 3–41A), 2 to 20 mm. in length, mostly bore in dead twigs, and one species, quite by accident, also bores in lead sheathing of telephone cables. Closely related to bostrichids are **Lyctidae** (Fig. 3–41B), the powder-post beetles and shot-hole borers. Their larvae riddle standing dead timber or fence posts and beams until nothing but fine sawdust remains. **Anobiidae** (Fig. 3–41C) are tiny beetles (1 to 9 mm.), many of whose larvae also bore in timbers. Most notorious of these is the deathwatch beetle of Europe that habitually raps its head against the walls of its burrow. The consequent monotonous ticking sounds, heard at night, are purported to be the ticking of a watch counting down the seconds before the death of insomniacs in timbered homes. The doom of the infested structure is sometimes more imminent. Other Anobiidae feed on dried plant material, and some are pests: the cigarette beetle on tobacco products and the drugstore beetle in dried herbs and spices.

Dermestidae (carpet and larder beetles, Fig. 3–42A) are small (1 to 12 mm.), scaly, oval beetles, with clubbed antennae. They are best known by their damage, as larvae (and adults) eat dried plant or animal products, especially fur, feathers, skins, and wool products. Several species of carpet beetles are particularly damaging to woolen carpets and clothing and to preserved museum mammal and bird skins and insect collections. These same Dermestidae may be useful in the same museum as biological bone-pickers in preparing skeletons. Other Dermestidae prefer cereals, grains, or dried cheese and are sometimes pantry pests.

Cleridae (checkered beetles, Fig. 3–42B) are elongate beetles with a narrowed pronotum and large head bearing bulging eyes and clubbed antennae. They are 3 to 24 mm. long, and most common species are boldly patterned in combinations of red, orange, yellow, blue and black. Cleridae occur on flowers and leaves and many feed on pollen as adults. Most larvae are predatory, feeding under bark on wood-boring beetles. Some are considered important natural enemies of bark beetles (**Scolytidae**). One clerid, the red-legged ham beetle, feeds as a larva on stored dried meat and was a more important pest before the days of refrigeration.

Cucujidae (flat bark beetles, Fig. 3–43A) are very flat, narrow, red, brown, or black beetles, 2 to 14 mm. long, found usually under bark and more rarely at lights. Larvae and adults of most species prey on small insects and mites. A few Cucujidae depart from this lifestyle by infesting grain and other stored products. The most damaging of these is the sawtoothed grain beetle, whose adults and larvae are equally at home in grain, bread, bird seed, peanuts, candy bars, and dry breakfast cereal.

Nitidulidae (sap beetles, Fig. 3–43B) are small, flat or oval beetles, with clubbed antennae. Most are brown or black, sometimes with yellow or red markings. Their habits are diverse: a few are predaceous; some are inquilines (cohabitants) in bee or ant nests; and most feed on plant sap, decaying fungi, or rotting fruit. One of these, the picnic beetle, is an occasional pest of fruit, particularly

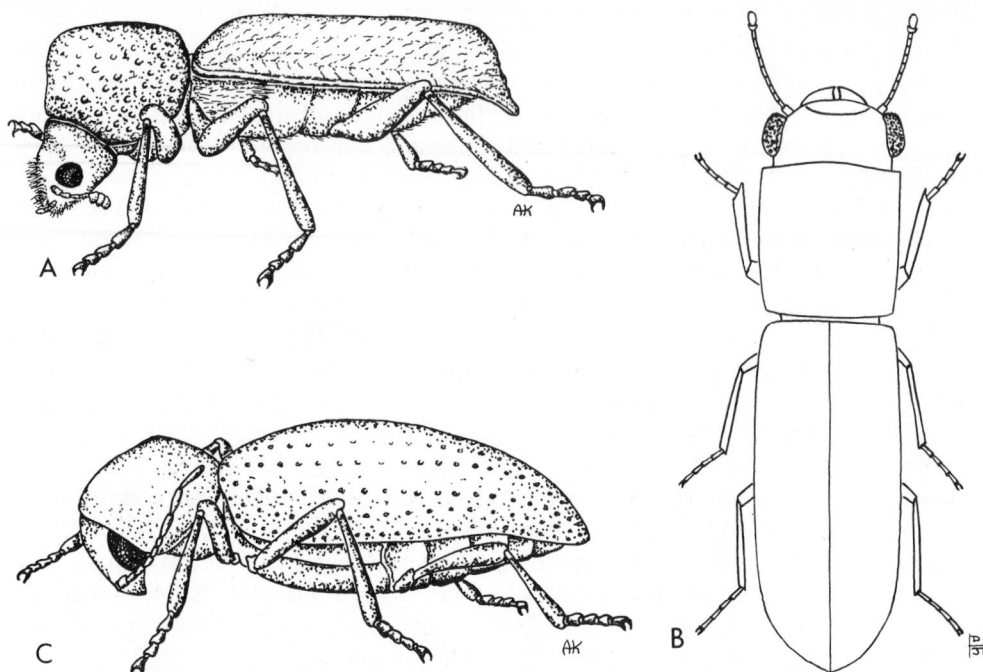

Figure 3–41. Order Coleoptera, superfamily Bostrichoidea. *A,* Family Bostrichidae. *B,* Powder-post beetle, family Lyctidae. *C,* Family Anobiidae.

strawberries. Large numbers are attracted by subtle odors emanating from broken fruit, and they sometimes mob church (and state) picnics when fresh fruit salad is on the menu.

Coccinellidae (lady beetles or ladybugs, Fig. 3–43*C*) are widespread, abundant, familiar, usually orange and black beetles, 1 to 10 mm. long. Adults and larvae (Fig. 3–43*D*) are voracious predators of tiny arthropods, particularly aphids, scale insects, or mites. Many are of great value in control of insect and mite pests (Chapters Eleven and Twelve) and are reared commercially or gathered in the field during huge overwintering aggregations. They disperse readily, so that a bucket of ladybugs may not necessarily rid your yard of aphids overnight. While almost all lady beetles are predaceous, a few eat plants. One such species, the Mexican bean beetle, feeds as larva and adult on leaves of beans, be they bush, pole, lima, or soy.

Meloidae (blister beetles, Fig. 3–44*A*) have long slender legs, a narrow pronotum, and a prominent head. Adults are 3 to 20 mm. long, are blue, black or striped, and feed on foliage, occasionally damaging vegetable and field crops. Their hemolymph contains **cantharidin**, a potent irritant that causes skin blisters on persons who handle these beetles. Larvae are parasitic, on grasshopper eggs or bee brood, and they undergo **hypermetamorphosis** (Fig. 7–30) an unusual developmental pattern related to their parasitic mode of life. Mature larvae may remain underground for two (or more) years before metamorphosing to adults.

Text continued on page 98

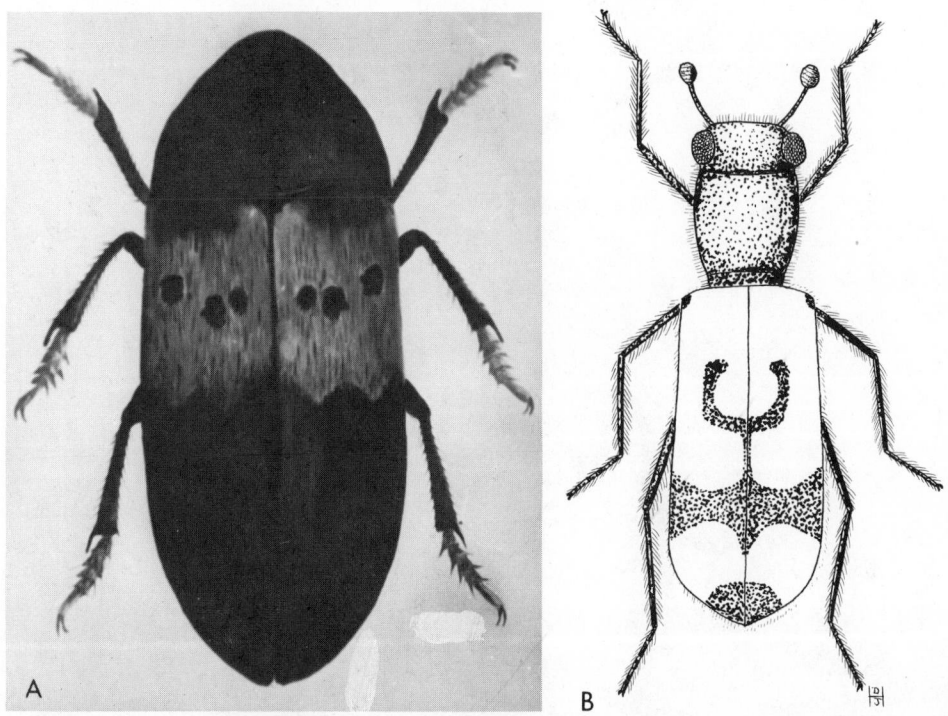

Figure 3–42. Order Coleoptera, superfamily Cleroidea. *A*, Family Dermestidae. *B*, Checkered beetle, family Cleridae.

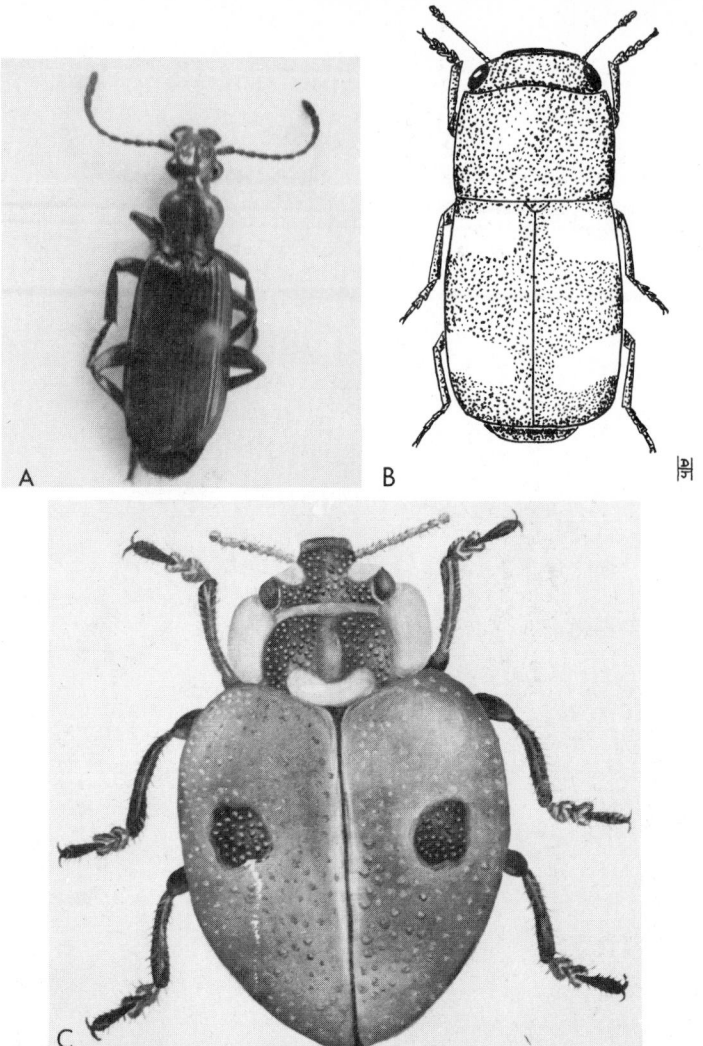

Figure 3–43. Order Coleoptera, superfamily Cucujoidea. *A,* Flat bark beetle, family Cucujidae. *B,* Sap beetle, family Nitidulidae. *C,* Lady beetle, family Coccinellidae. (Painting by W. Costello.) *D,* Lady beetle larva eating aphids. (USDA photo.)

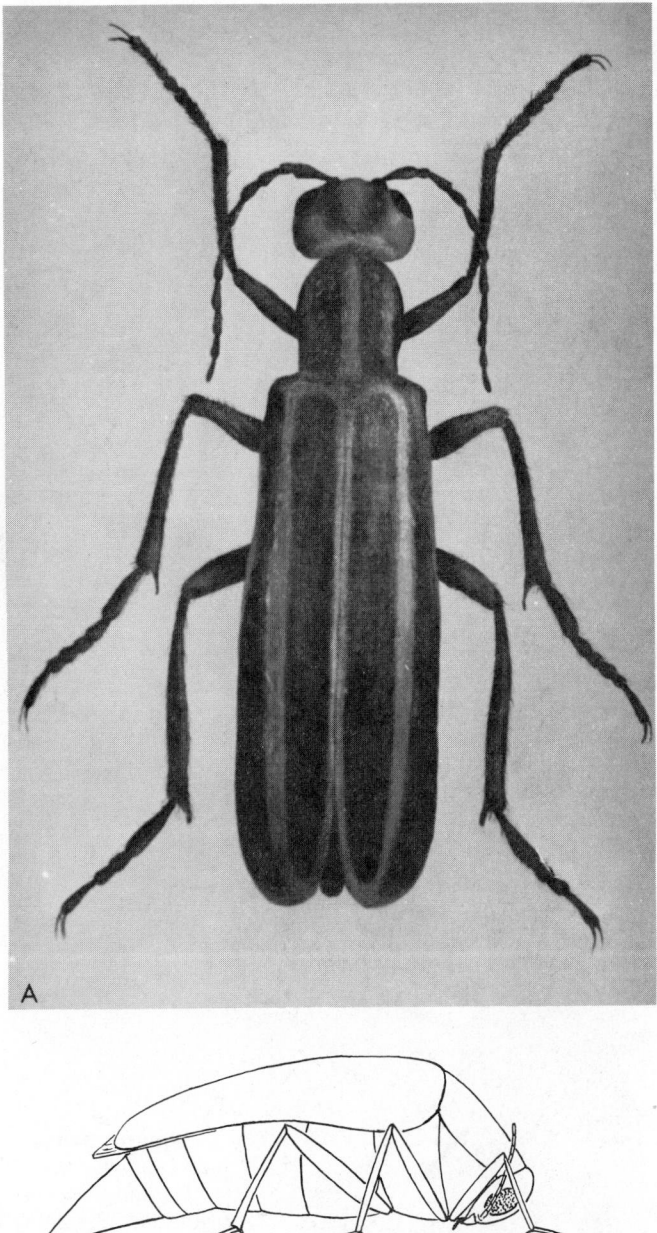

Figure 3–44. Order Coleoptera, superfamilies Melooidea and Mordelloidea. *A*, Blister beetle, family Meloidae. (Painting by W. Costello.) *B*, Tumbling flower beetle, family Mordellidae.

Mordellidae (tumbling flower beetles, Fig. 3–44*B*) are often abundant on flowers, where adults feed on pollen. These very active beetles are humpbacked and have a pointed abdomen. Most larvae tunnel in pith of plant stems, though none are particularly damaging.

Tenebrionidae (darkling beetles, Fig. 3–45*A*) is a large family of varied beetles not easily described in a few words. Most, however, are black or brown, with 11-segmented antennae (sometimes clubbed) and a notch or indentation in the margins of their compound eyes. Sizes range from 2 to 35 mm. These beetles

Figure 3–45. Order Coleoptera, superfamily Tenebrionoidea. *A,* Darkling beetle, family Tenebrionidae. *B,* Family Melandryidae.

are more diverse and numerous in arid regions. Here, some larger (20 to 30 mm.) forms (*Eleodes* species) are called "stinkbugs", and stand on their head shooting spray out their anus when threatened. Tenebrionidae occur commonly in humid areas, too. Most are scavengers, fungivores, or seed-eaters, and among these are some serious pests of stored grain and grain products: mealworms (*Tenebrio*) and flour beetles (*Tribolium* species).

Melandryidae (false darkling beetles, Fig. 3–45*B*) are very similar to **Tenebrionidae** and also remind one of click beetles (**Elateridae,** Fig. 3–40*A*), except that the first tarsal segment is longer than all others combined. Melandryids are 3 to 20 mm. long, are dark brown or black, and occur under bark and at lights. Larvae are carnivores. **Alleculidae** is a very similar family, in which tarsal claws are serrated and comblike.

Cerambycidae (long-horned beetles, Fig. 3–46*A*) are mostly large cylindrical beetles with long (sometimes *very* long) antennae and notched compound eyes (like **Tenebrionidae**). Some are brightly colored with yellow, red, blue, or purple; others are dull gray, brown, or black. Adults are most often seen at lights at night, though some species frequent flowers, particularly in mid- to late summer. Larvae (round-headed borers, Fig. 3–46*B*) bore in wood of trees, living and dead, and some are pests of orchard, ornamental, and shade trees. The boring larvae mature slowly, sometimes taking a few years to complete development; meanwhile, their home may be cut for firewood or incorporated into buildings and furniture. The adult beetles then emerge inside the building.

Chrysomelidae (leaf beetles, Fig. 3–47, *A* and *B*) is a large (1200 North American species), variable family, the members of which all feed on plants. Most are small-to-medium (1 to 20 mm.), oval, and convex, with rather short antennae, rarely longer than half the body. Many are superficially very like ladybugs. Adults occur (and feed) on flowers and foliage; larvae may eat roots, stems, leaves, or flowers. Most Chrysomelidae have narrow food preferences and feed on rather few, usually closely related, host plants. Some are major pests of cultivated plants: these include the asparagus and cucumber beetles, corn rootworms, Colorado potato beetle, and flea beetles (on several crops). This last group are small beetles with greatly enlarged hind femora for jumping.

Bruchidae (seed beetles, Fig. 3–47*C*) are very similar to leaf beetles, but have a somewhat egg-shaped body, are 1 to 10 mm. long, and have a shortened elytra and a head ending in a short, broad snout. They oviposit on seeds or seed pods, usually those of legumes (beans, clover, acacia, etc.), and larvae feed on the developing seeds. Like leaf beetles, most seed beetles are closely tied to specific plant hosts. Two species, the pea and bean weevils, sometimes damage these seeds in storage.

Curculionidae (weevils, Fig. 3–48*A*) are the pinnacle of adaptive radiation within Coleoptera; there are over 50,000 species in 42 subfamilies. Despite such diversity, adults are remarkably constant in appearance, all having an obvious snout bearing clubbed antennae and chewing mouthparts. Almost all weevils feed on plants, and their evolution has paralleled that of their hosts. Adults occur on flowers and foliage, in leafy litter, and at lights. Larvae may feed on leaves, stems, fruit, or seeds. Some are major agricultural pests, including the boll weevil, alfalfa weevil, white-fringed beetle, plum curculio, and billbugs. Others, notably granary and rice weevils, are particularly destructive to stored whole grains.

Scolytidae (bark beetles, Fig. 3–48*B*) are cylindrical, with elbowed and

Figure 3–46. Order Coleoptera, superfamily Cerambycoidea. *A*, Long-horned beetle, family Cerambycidae, camouflaged on bark. *B*, Roundheaded borer, larva of Cerambycidae. (USDA photo.)

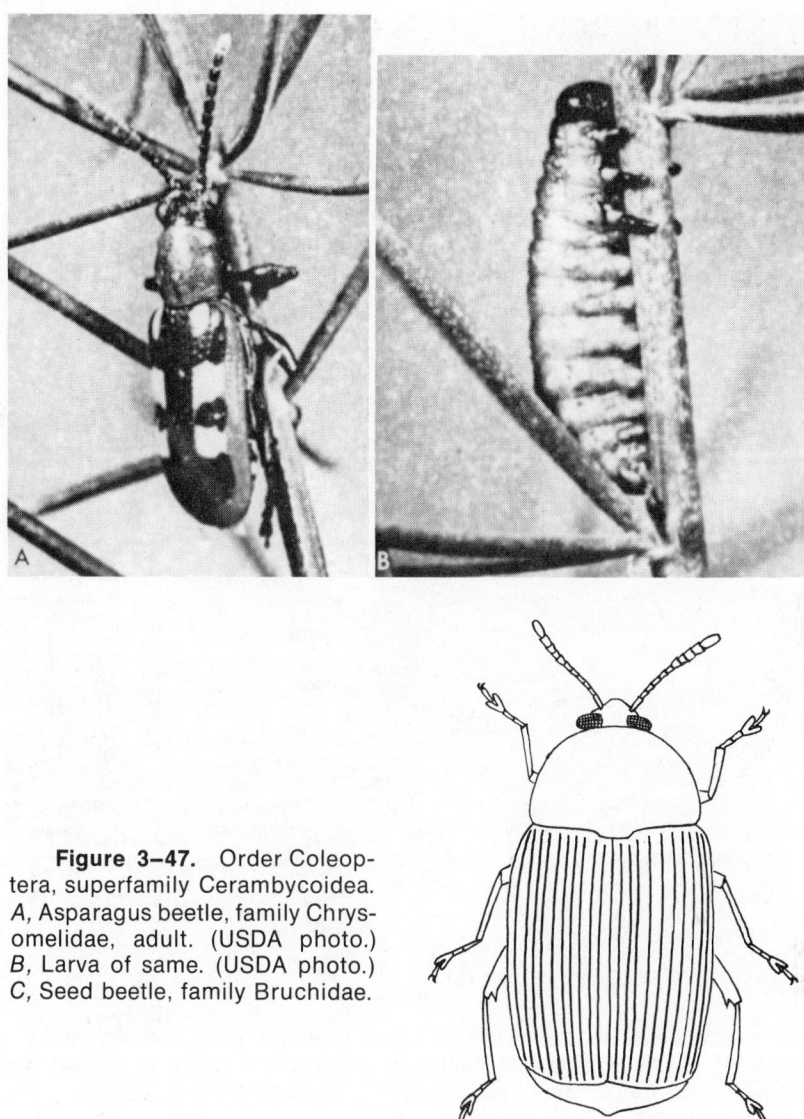

Figure 3–47. Order Coleoptera, superfamily Cerambycoidea. *A,* Asparagus beetle, family Chrysomelidae, adult. (USDA photo.) *B,* Larva of same. (USDA photo.) *C,* Seed beetle, family Bruchidae.

clubbed antennae. Most are quite small (1 to 9 mm.). Larvae bore beneath the bark of living and dead trees, leaving characteristic patterns ("engravings," Fig. 3–48C). In many species, the mated female constructs a gallery under bark of the host and oviposits at intervals along it; the larvae then bore at a right angle to the gallery under the bark. Some bark beetles are considered major pests of timber trees, particularly softwoods (pine and fir) in the southeastern and western United States. Another species transmits Dutch elm disease (Chapter Eleven). Scolytidae are attracted to recently windthrown (or cut) trees, and infestations then move from such foci into healthy trees.

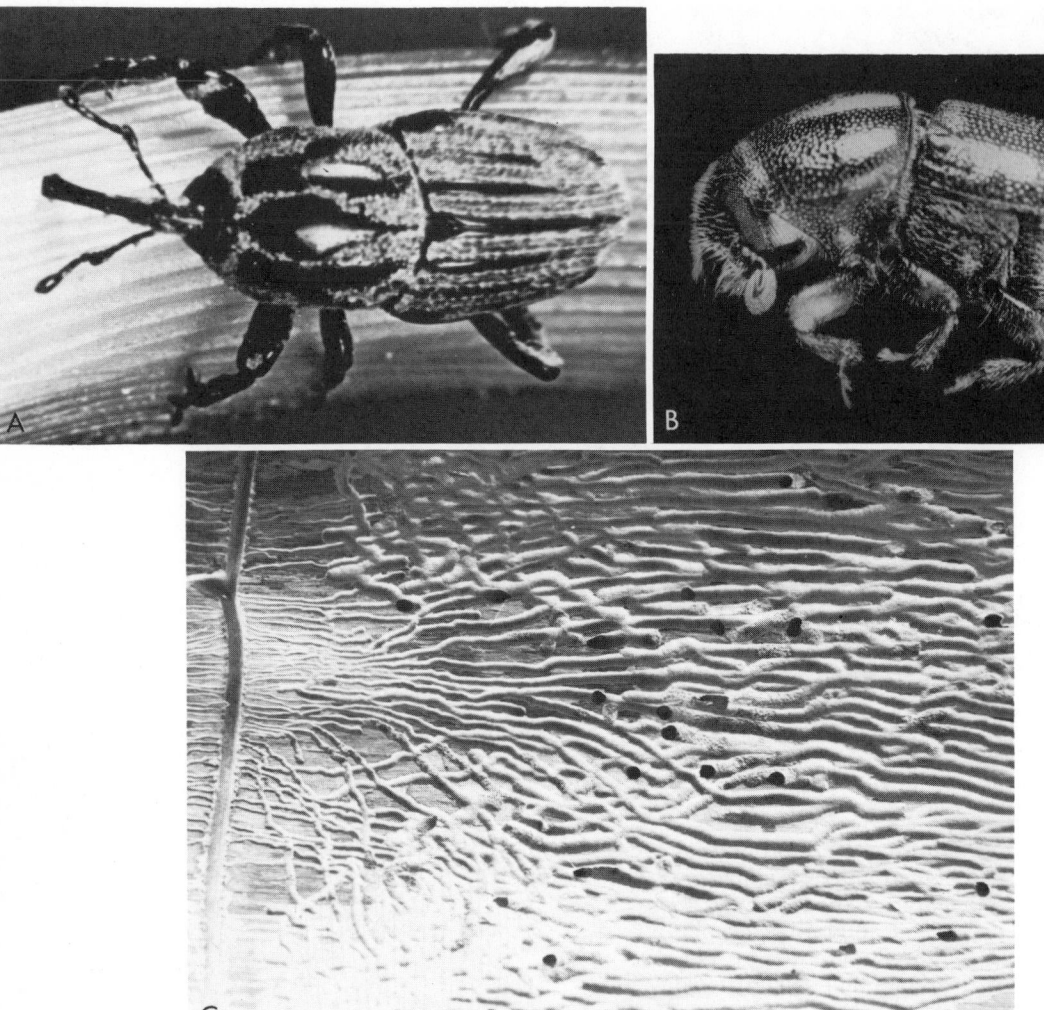

Figure 3–48. Order Coleoptera, superfamily Curculionoidea. *A,* Weevil, family Curculionidae. (USDA photo.) *B,* Bark beetle, family Scolytidae. (Photo courtesy of U.S. Forest Service.) *C,* Engravings of bark beetles (Scolytidae) and emergence holes of shot-hole borers (Lyctidae) on dead limb.

Order Strepsiptera

This is a small order of unusual insects, which very likely evolved from beetles, perhaps ancestral blister beetles (**Meloidae**). Some entomologists (e.g., Ross, 1965) consider Strepsiptera to be Coleoptera that have become greatly specialized for parasitizing other insects. They parasitize Hemiptera, Homoptera, Hymenoptera, Orthoptera, and Thysanura. In many ways, their biology is similar to that of scale insects (Homoptera), though Strepsiptera feed exclusively on insects. Adult males are minute (1 to 3 mm.) two-winged insects with unusual "flabellate" antennae, "raspberry eyes," and tiny, twisted "elytra" (Fig. 3–49A). Most females are wingless and larviform, and do not leave their host but merely protrude through the host's abdomen. Each female produces 2500 to 7000 living, active larvae that attach to a new host and embed themselves in its abdomen. If

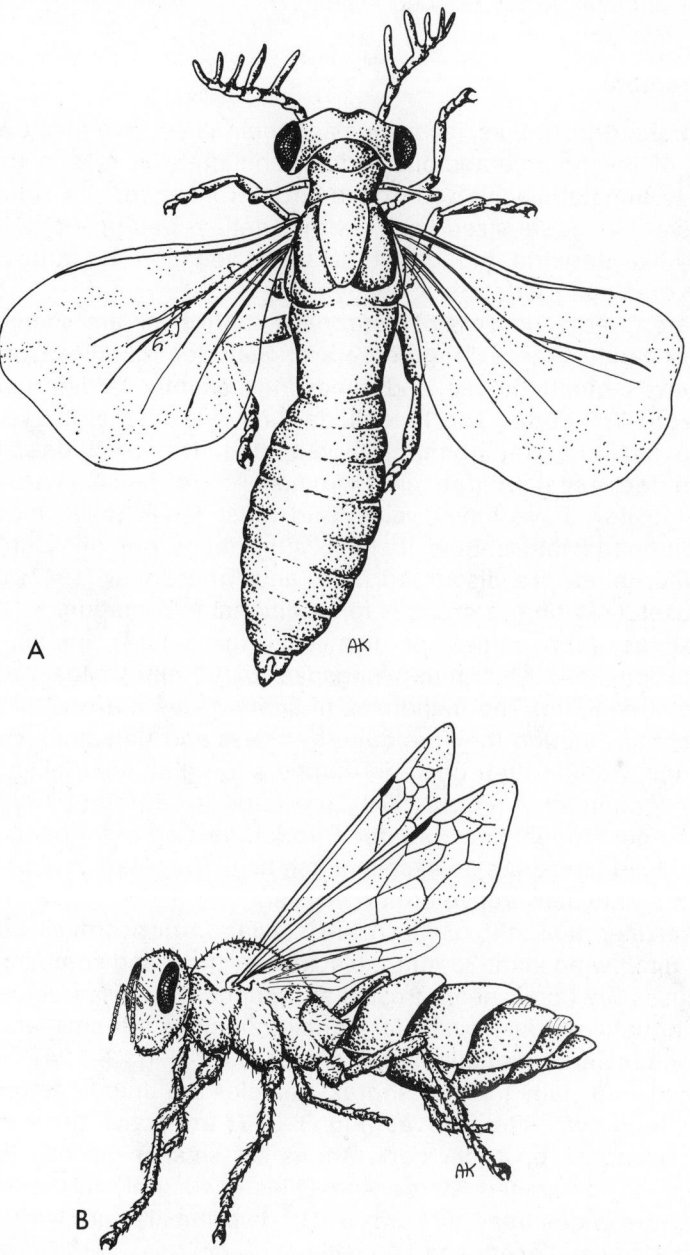

Figure 3–49. Order Strepsiptera. *A*, Adult male. *B*, Females in host protruding through dorsal segments of abdomen.

the host is a bee or wasp, the strepsipteran larva is carried back to the nest, where it parasitizes the host larva. Strepsipterans are true parasites in that the host survives, though often the parasite causes chemical changes within the host that prevent maturation of gonads, leading to sterility. Bohart (1941) tells more about these unusual, rarely noticed insects.

Order Neuroptera

Neuroptera (dobsonflies, lacewings and their allies) is in many ways the most "primitive" of the holometabolous orders, and there is reason to believe that most other Holometabola evolved from neuropteroid ancestors. Adult Neuroptera typically have four equal-sized wings with a netlike pattern of many crossveins superficially like Odonata, though the details of venation are quite different. Larvae are all voracious predators of smaller insects.

There are three suborders of Neuroptera, and these are sometimes considered to be separate orders. **Megaloptera** or **Sialodea** (families **Corydalidae** and **Sialidae**) have aquatic larvae and hindwings slightly larger than forewings. **Raphidiodea** (**Raphidiidae** and **Inocelliidae**) have terrestrial larvae, but retain a very long ovipositor. **Planipennia** (**Chrysopidae, Hemerobiidae, Mantispidae, Myrmeleontidae, Ascalaphidae,** and six smaller, rarer families) are all terrestrial, lack an ovipositor, have many veins, and most larvae have modified sickle-shaped mouthparts that enable them to suck fluids out of victims. The more common Neuroptera are discussed here, and Froeschner (1947) and Chandler (1956) are useful starting references for additional information.

Corydalidae (dobsonflies or fishflies, Fig. 3–50A) contain the largest Neuroptera (body length, 30 mm.; wingspan to 100 mm.). Most are gray, with a fluttery, mothlike flight. The mandibles of some males are greatly enlarged and appear fearsome, though they are quite harmless and only hold the female during copulation. Adults often come in numbers to lights near lakes and streams. Larvae, "hellgrammites" (Fig. 3–50B), are large (to 80 mm.) aquatic predators that occur under stones. They breathe through gills on eight pairs of lateral filaments. Corydalid larvae are an excellent fish bait. They leave the water to pupate; the pupae are unusually active but do not eat.

Sialidae (alderflies, Fig. 3–50C) are similar to dobsonflies but are smaller (length, 10 mm.; wingspan, 30 mm.), blackish or gray, and sometimes have spots on the wings. They occur near streams and ponds and, less frequently, at lights. Larvae are aquatic predators, similar to hellgrammites but smaller.

Raphidiidae (and **Inocelliidae**) are snakeflies (Fig. 3–51A), so named because of their unusually long prothorax. Females are unique among Neuroptera in having a long ovipositor. Larvae (Fig. 3–51B) are active terrestrial predators, most often found on or under bark. Adults eat smaller insects, too, on foliage and in grass. In the United States, snakeflies occur only in the western states, though they are widespread in Eurasia. The two families are very similar except that Raphidiidae have ocelli and Inocelliidae do not.

Chrysopidae (green lacewings, Fig. 3–52A) are common, usually green, delicate insects with golden or coppery eyes. They occur on most plants and are often attracted to lights. Larvae (Fig. 3–52B) occur on foliage and are active, with sickle-shaped "sucking mandibles" (Fig. 4–3E). Both adults and larvae prey on other insects and are particularly fond of aphids and scale insects (Homoptera). Some are of great value in controlling pest aphids biologically. So voracious are

Figure 3–50. Order Neuroptera, suborder Sialodea. *A,* Dobsonfly, family Corydalidae, male. *B,* Hellgrammite, larva of dobsonfly. *C,* Alderfly, family Sialidae.

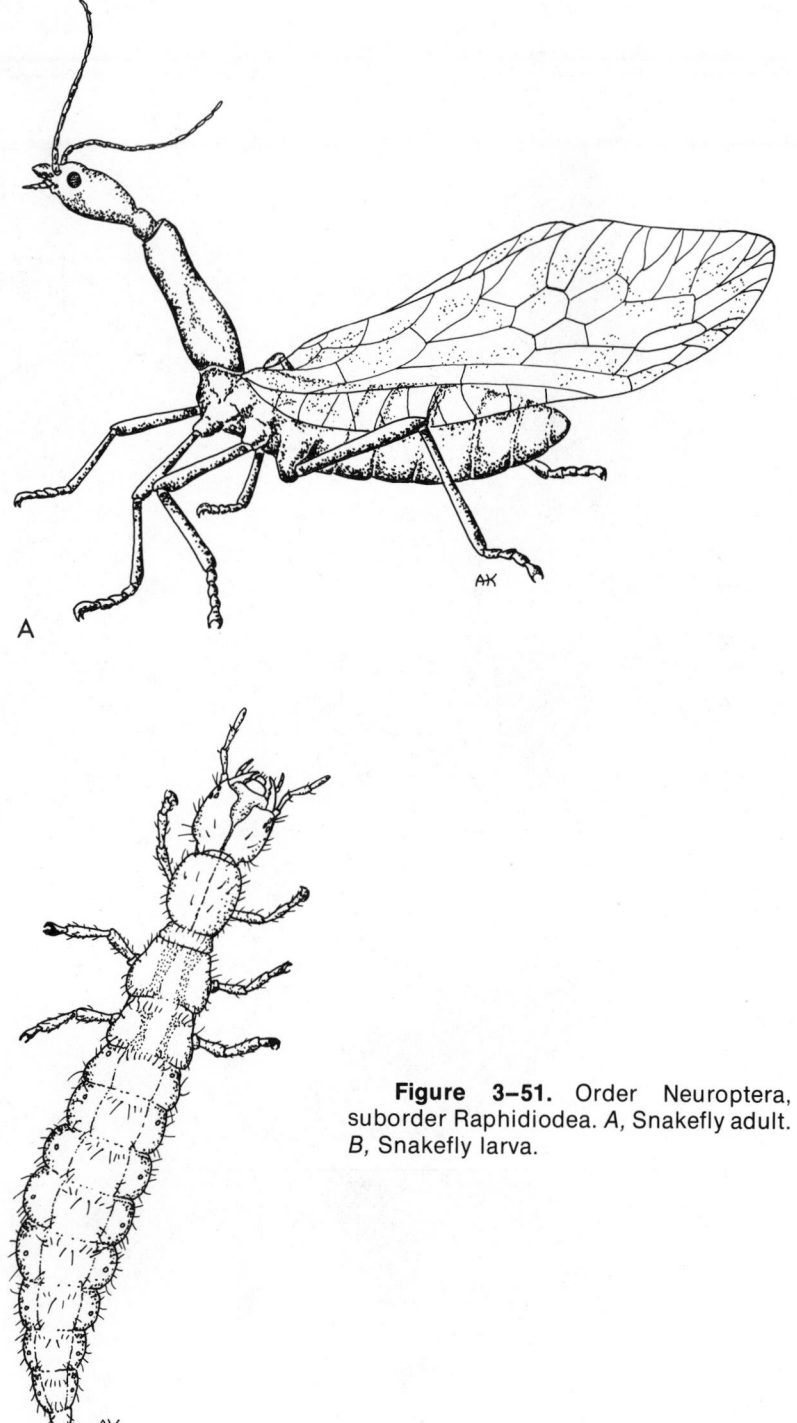

Figure 3–51. Order Neuroptera, suborder Raphidiodea. *A*, Snakefly adult. *B*, Snakefly larva.

the larvae that lacewings oviposit on slender silken stalks (Fig. 7–9D), thus preventing sibling cannibalism by the first larva hatched. **Hemerobiidae** (brown lacewings, Fig. 3–52C) are very similar to Chrysopidae but are smaller, brown or gray insects more common in woodlands.

Mantispidae (Fig. 2–2B) are a remarkable example of convergent evolution, for they look like, and act like, mantids (Orthoptera). There are obvious differences in wing venation, placement of forelegs, and size. (Most mantispids are less than 25 cm. long.) Adult mantispids occur on flowers, foliage, and at lights, primarily in the southern United States and southward. Some mimic wasps. Larvae are predators of ground spider eggs and undergo hypermetamorphosis (Chapter Seven). The highly active first instar attaches to a female ground spider and enters her egg case when it is deposited. Subsequent larval instars lose their legs and become grublike.

Myrmeleontidae (antlions, Fig. 3–52D) are long-winged, delicate looking insects resembling damselflies (Fig. 3–11C), but wing venation and other structural details are very different, and antlions have longer antennae. Their name derives from the fact that their larvae dig pits in sand (Fig. 4–1B) and lie in wait at the bottom to eat unwary ants. Not all antlions make pits; some are terrestrial predators of insects in leaf litter. A closely related family, **Ascalaphidae** (owlflies) occurs in the southeastern United States. They look like dragonflies with very long, clubbed antennae.

Order Mecoptera

Mecoptera (scorpionflies) are a small (< 400 species) remnant of a once (Permian) large and diverse order. Characteristically, they have a long-faced look (Fig. 3–53), with a rostrum (beak) bearing mandibulate mouthparts. Wings, if present, are equal-sized, often spotted or banded, with many cross-veins. Larvae look like caterpillars and scavenge in moss or mud. There are three major families. **Panorpidae** (Fig. 3–53A) are 15 to 20 mm. long. Males bear genitalia on an enlarged terminal bulb that looks vaguely like a scorpion's sting, though Mecoptera are quite harmless. **Bittacidae** (Fig. 3–53B), 20 to 25 mm. long, look like four-winged craneflies (Diptera: **Tipulidae**), and in fact, extinct Mecoptera very likely were ancestors of Diptera. Bittacids frequent long grass and protected greenery where they hang by their forelegs and snag insect victims (especially craneflies) with their hindlegs. **Boreidae** (Fig. 3–53C) occur on snow or nearby moss in northern areas. They are wingless; wings of males are modified into hooks that hold the female during mating. Among fossil Mecoptera are two important genera, **Belmontia** and **Parabelmontia,** with wing venation and other characteristics very similar to Trichoptera and Hymenoptera respectively. They may well be the ancestors of those two orders.

Order Trichoptera

Trichoptera (caddisflies, Fig. 3–54) are fairly uniform insects, apparently derived from Mecoptera. The adults are similar to moths, having hairy wings held rooflike over the abdomen at rest. Most have long antennae, and some are large (40 mm. maximum). Adult mouthparts are nonfunctional. The 16 United States families differ by details in wing venation, thoracic structure, and legs. H. Ross (1944) and Denning (1956) present these details.

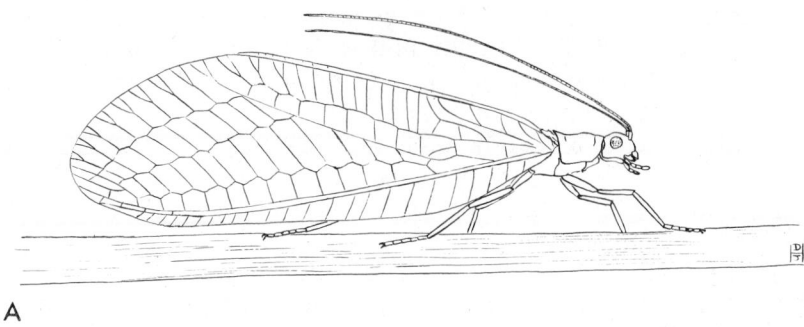

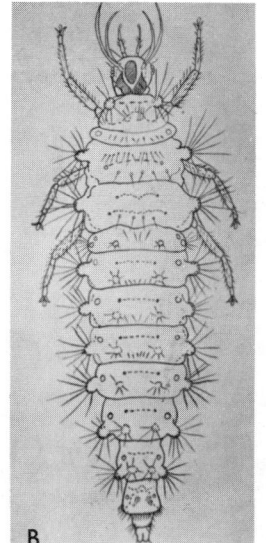

Figure 3–52. Order Neuroptera, suborder Planipennia. *A,* Green lacewing, family Chrysopidae. *B,* Lacewing larva. (Drawing by W. Costello.) *C,* Brown lacewing, family Hemerobiidae.

Caddisfly larvae are aquatic in lakes and streams, and many are important components of stream ecosystems. Some are scavengers, while others are predaceous on fly larvae. Larvae of many caddisflies build protective cases of sand, pebbles, or bits of wood and leaves (Fig. 9–14*A*). These cases are very distinctive, and one can recognize many species from the cases they build. Some caddis larvae spin threads or nets of silk with which they "fish" streams for detritus. A few live in silken tubes in sand. Caddis larvae pupate within an underwater cocoon. Pupae have functional mandibles, and when the teneral adult is fully formed within, the pupa chews its way out of the cocoon and swims to the surface.

Order Lepidoptera

This order, moths and butterflies, is the second largest (150,000 species), and some of its more showy members are among the most familiar of all insects. Adult Lepidoptera characteristically have four large wings, whose surfaces are covered with scales, often brightly colored. With few exceptions, mouthparts of

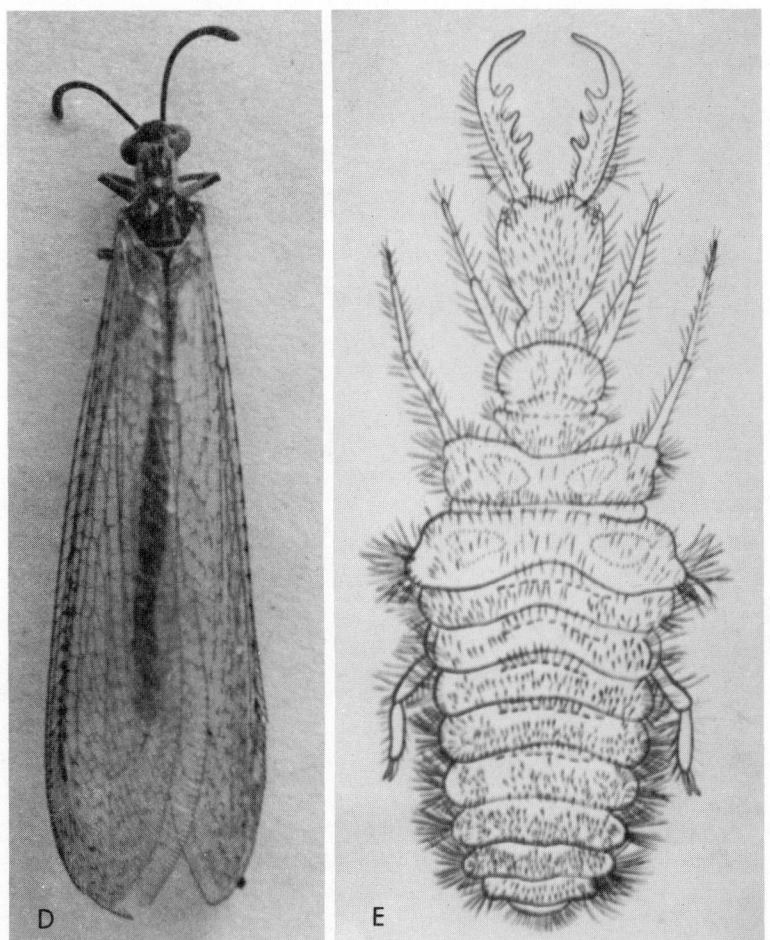

Figure 3–52. *Continued.* *D,* Antlion, family Myrmeleontidae. *E,* Larva of same. (Drawing by W. Costello.)

Lepidoptera adults form a coiled tube (Fig. 4–5C), which is unrolled by blood pressure. They eat fluids: mostly nectar but sometimes fermenting fruit juices, excrement, or sap.

Larvae of Lepidoptera are quite diverse, though most have obvious mandibulate mouthparts and fleshy abdominal prolegs which bear sets of hooks or crochets. Most larvae eat leaves, though some bore in stems or eat seeds, furs, woolen goods, aphids, or other things. A few are aquatic. All produce silk from labial glands, and many spin a protective cocoon in which they pupate.

Lepidoptera presumably evolved from trichopteralike ancestors in which the wing hairs became progressively more scalelike. Sex determination is similar in both orders and is reversed from the "usual" (i.e., human) procedures; in Trichoptera and Lepidoptera, males are homozygous XX and females have XY chromosomes. The most primitive moths, **Micropterygidae,** are a further link with the Trichoptera, because these moths bear functional mandibles.

Traditionally, and popularly, Lepidoptera are divided into two "suborders," moths (Heterocera) and butterflies (Rhopalocera). Table 3–5 lists differences between the two. A more natural, phylogenetic classification (Table 3–6) considers

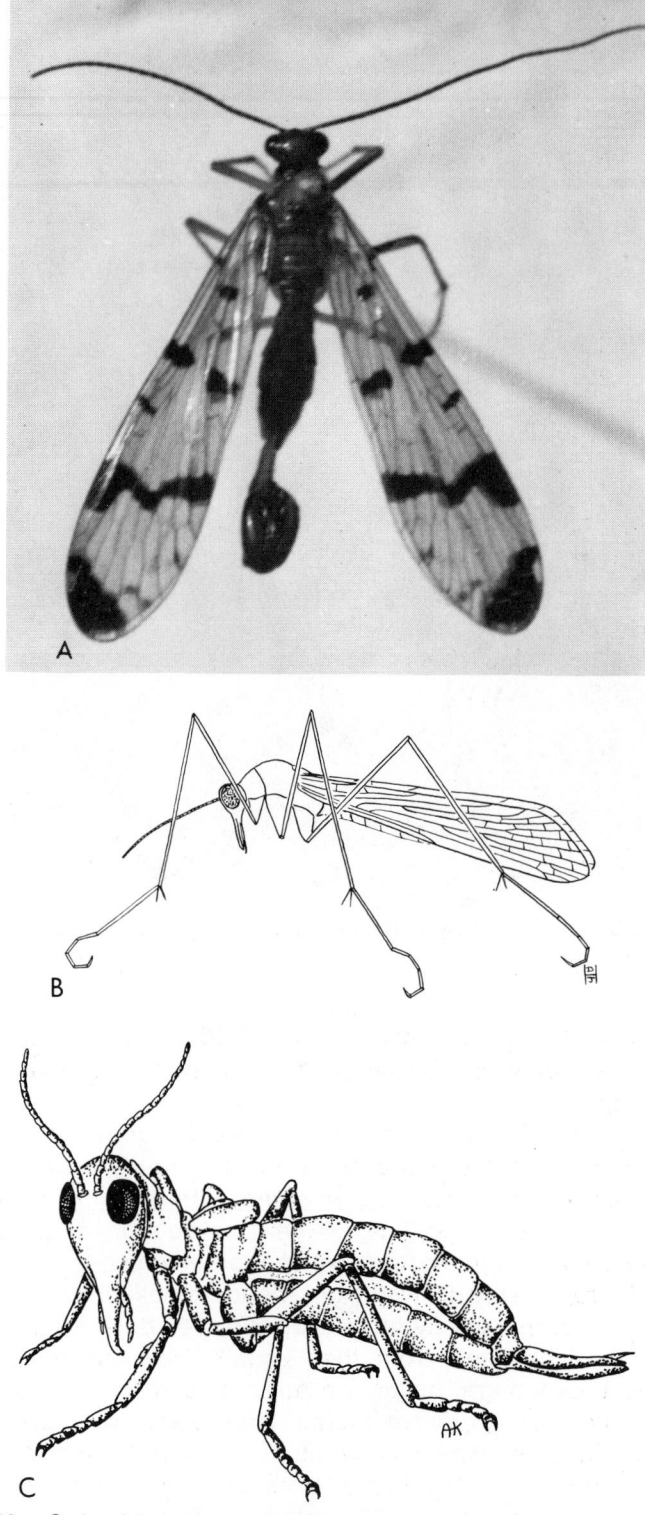

Figure 3–53. Order Mecoptera. *A,* Scorpionfly, family Panorpidae. *B,* Hangingfly, family Bittacidae. *C,* Snow scorpionfly, Boreidae.

Figure 3–54. Caddisfly, order Trichoptera.

Table 3–5. DISTINGUISHING CHARACTERISTICS OF BUTTERFLIES AND MOTHS*

Characteristic	Butterflies	Moths
Antennae	Clubbed	Feathery or threadlike
Body	Slender	Stout
Wings at rest	Vertical over body	Outstretched or flexed downward over back
Coloration	Brightly colored	Many dull-colored
Activity	Primarily diurnal	Primarily nocturnal
Pupa	Naked chrysalis	Enclosed in cocoon or concealed under debris, rocks, etc.

*These are general characteristics; there are exceptions for each.

Table 3–6. CLASSIFICATION OF LEPIDOPTERAN FAMILIES

Suborder	Superfamily	Families Included*
Jugatae		Micropterygidae
Frenatae (Microlepidoptera)	Tineoidea	Tineidae, Psychidae
	Gelechoidea	Gelechiidae
	Yponomeutoidea	Sesiidae
	Tortricoidea	Tortricidae, Olethreutidae
	Pyraloidea	Pyralidae, Pterophoridae
Frenatae (Macrolepidoptera)	Sphingoidea	Sphingidae
	Geometroidea	Geometridae
	Bombycoidea	Saturniidae, Citheroniidae, Lasiocampidae, Bombycidae
	Noctuoidea	Noctuidae, Liparidae, Arctiidae
	Hesperioidea (skippers)	Hesperiidae
	Papilionoidea (butterflies)	Papilionidae, Pieridae, Lycaenidae, Nymphalidae, Heliconiidae, Danaidae, Satyridae

*This list is limited to those families mentioned in the text; for complete classification of United States families, see Borror et al., 1976.

11 superfamilies of moths and 2 of butterflies, within 2 suborders. The suborder Jugatae is the smaller and is composed of rare and primitive moths. The aforementioned **Micropterygidae** belong here. (If indeed they are moths at all—some authors erect a separate order, Zeugloptera, for them). The remaining Jugatae (or Monotrysia) have mandibulate pupae; adults have all four wings similar in venation (12 veins) and a **jugum,** a lobe of the forewing, to connect the wings during flight. Frenatae (or Ditrysia), on the other hand, bear on the hindwing a **frenulum,** a stout spine (or two), for wing coupling. Hindwings of Frenatae have fewer veins (eight or fewer reaching margin) than forewings. Most Lepidoptera are Frenatae, and this suborder is further divided into two groups: Microlepidoptera (five superfamilies), mostly small moths (span < 25 mm.) with narrow, often fringed wings; and Macrolepidoptera (five superfamilies of moths, two of butterflies), which are mostly larger (span > 25 mm.) with broader wings. There are further, more technical, differences.

Many guidebooks have been written for butterflies and moths. Comprehensive references include, for moths, Dominick and Edwards (1970) and Holland (1913), and for butterflies, Ehrlich and Ehrlich (1961) and Klots (1951). Several regional or local guides exist, especially for butterflies.

Microlepidoptera.   The vast majority of Microlepidoptera are small moths, difficult to identify even as to family without detailed knowledge of wing venation and very well prepared specimens. Much remains to be learned of this group; Opler (1974) discovered several new species of microlepidopterous leaf miners in California oak woodlands where entomologists had thoroughly collected for a hundred years. What follows, therefore, is merely an overview of the major groups.

Tineidae (Fig. 3–55) are clothes moths and their relatives. Adults are small, plain, brown or tan moths with narrow, lanceolate wings, spanning to 15 mm. They are best known from the damage that larvae of three species do in feeding on woolens, furs, feathers, and so forth. Ecologically, these tineids are part of the scavenging crew that keeps us from being buried in old feathers and fur, but this is not appreciated by those whose pile rugs or teddy bears have been riddled with holes. Larvae of many Tineidae, including some clothes moths, construct protective silken bags or cases around themselves.

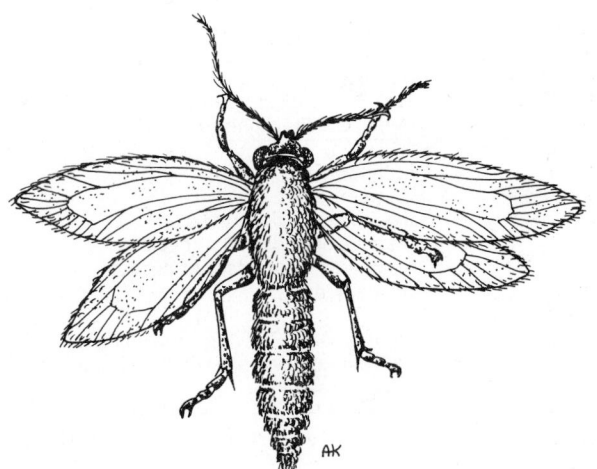

Figure 3–55. Clothes moth, family Tineidae.

Figure 3–56. Bagworm moth, family Psychidae, male. (See also Figure 9–14D.)

Psychidae (bagworms, Fig. 3–56) are large for Microlepidoptera (30 mm. span). Many males have clear wings and look (and act) more like flies than moths. Bagworms are so named because each larva builds a silk-and-debris bag for protection and enlarges the bag as it grows (Fig. 9–14D). Adult females are wingless and larviform; they mate and oviposit without leaving their bag, then wriggle out to die. One bagworm species in the eastern United States is a pest of ornamental plants, especially conifers.

Gelechiidae (Fig. 3–57) is a large (600 North American species, 20,000 worldwide) family of small or minute moths that may, when all moths are described, become the largest family of Lepidoptera. Most adults have long, curving palpi and pointed wings, the hindwing having a sharply pointed apex. The larvae are a diverse lot; leaf miners, rollers, and folders; flower, fruit, stem, and root eaters; gallmakers. Three major pests are the Angoumois grain moth (particularly on stored corn), potato tuberworm, and pink bollworm (on cotton in the southwestern United States and tropical America).

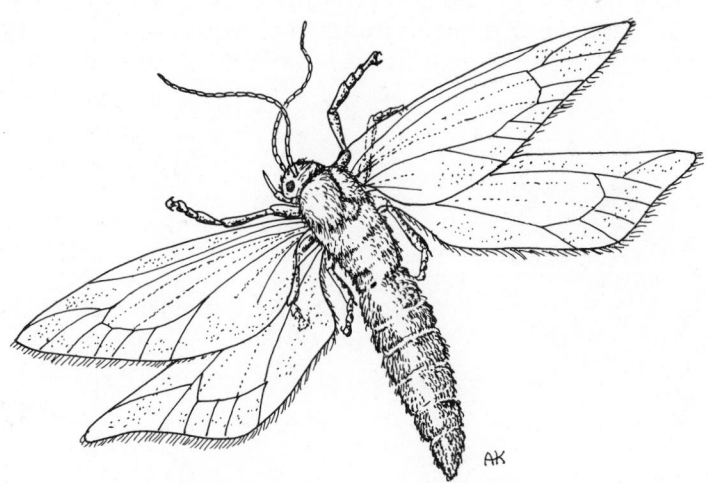

Figure 3–57. Family Gelechiidae.

Figure 3–58. Clearwing moth, family Sesiidae. (See also Figure 6–12.)

Sesiidae (formerly **Aegeriidae**) (clearwing moths, Fig. 3–58) are diurnal, fast-flying moths that mimic wasps. Large areas of their wings lack scales; these develop within the pupa but are rubbed off on eclosion. Coloration of male and female often differs. Sesiid larvae bore within stems of woody and herbaceous plants. A few are major pests, boring in stems of ash, lilac, peach, or squash.

Tortricidae (leafroller moths, Fig. 3–59) is a large family of small (span, 15 mm.) common moths normally with an enlarged, projecting front edge of the forewing. Some adults are very colorful. They fly to lights by night and remain on vegetation during the day. Most tortricid larvae eat leaves and roll or tie leaves together with silk for a protective covering. (Caterpillars of other families do this too). Others feed on seeds or bore in twigs. Some Tortricidae are serious pests; the spruce budworm periodically defoliates extensive areas of potential pulpwood in northern North America. Among fruit pests are the grape berry moth, Oriental fruit moth (peaches), and several other leafroller species. The codling moth, that denizen of wormy apples, is from a very similar family, **Olethreutidae,** as is the European pine shoot moth.

Pyralidae (Fig. 3–60A) is a large (1100 North American species) family of moderately sized moths with characteristics of both Micro- and Macrolepidoptera. Many adults have enlarged, projecting palpi, and some have an abdominal tympanum (ear) capable of detecting ultrasonic squeaks of bats (Chapters Five

Figure 3–59. Leafroller moth, family Tortricidae.

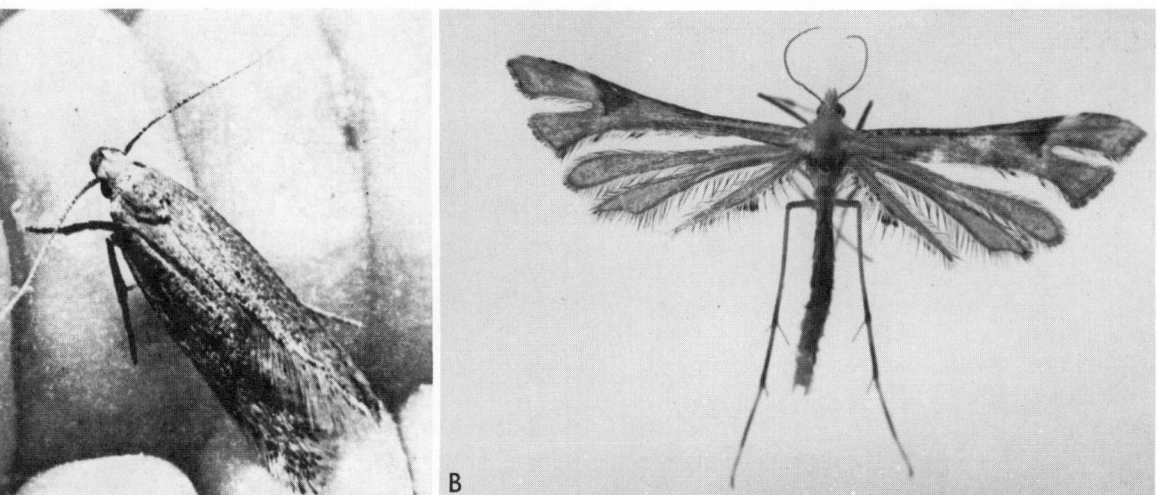

Figure 3–60. Superfamily Pyraloidea. *A,* Indian meal moth, family Pyralidae. *B,* Plume moth, family Pterophoridae.

and Nine.) There is great diversity in larval foods, including leaves, stems, fruits, seeds, grain, and even beeswax. A few species feed underwater on aquatic plants. Again, some important plant pests are included here. Three are the European corn borer, grape leaf tier, and sod webworm (on turfgrass). The Indian meal moth larva eats grain, bran, and other cereal products. Wax moths eat beeswax and can cause problems in weak honeybee hives. Both meal and wax moths are easily reared in laboratories and so are useful research animals. Another beneficial pyralid is the cactus moth, *Cactoblastis cactorum,* introduced from South America to Australia to control prickly-pear cactus (Chapter Twelve).

Pterophoridae (plume moths, Fig. 3–60*B*) are close relatives of **Pyralidae.** Adults have delicate wings divided into fringed lobes, and though small (< 20 mm.), are among the most beautiful of insects.

Macrolepidoptera. **Sphingidae** (sphinx or hawk moths, Fig. 3–61*A*) are large (span 65 mm. +) distinctive moths with a stout, tapered body and narrow wings. The mouthparts uncoil into a very long tube (often longer than the body), enabling the moth to feed on nectar from long, cone-shaped flowers. Sphingidae are strong, fast fliers and resemble hummingbirds when flying. Larvae (hornworms, Fig. 3–61*B*) are common foliage feeders, and some damage tobacco or tomato plants. They rear up when disturbed, resembling (supposedly) the sphinx of mythology. Most species bear an entirely harmless horn at their hind end.

Geometridae (Fig. 3–62) is a large family (1200 North American species) of delicate moths with slender bodies and broad wings usually held outstretched at rest. Some females are wingless and present a challenge in identification. Adults are often highly camouflaged, resting on bark or leaves during the day. Larvae (inchworms) typically lack several pairs of abdominal prolegs and "loop" or "inch" along rather than strolling in the more normal caterpillar gait. Inchworms occur in some other families, too. A few species, spanworms and cankerworms, sometimes damage orchard and shade trees. Cankerworm adults (two species) mate in late fall or early spring, and males may fly about among snowflakes in early December.

Saturniidae (giant silkworm moths, Fig. 3–63) are very large, showy moths with broad wings usually bearing either large eyespots or crescent-shaped

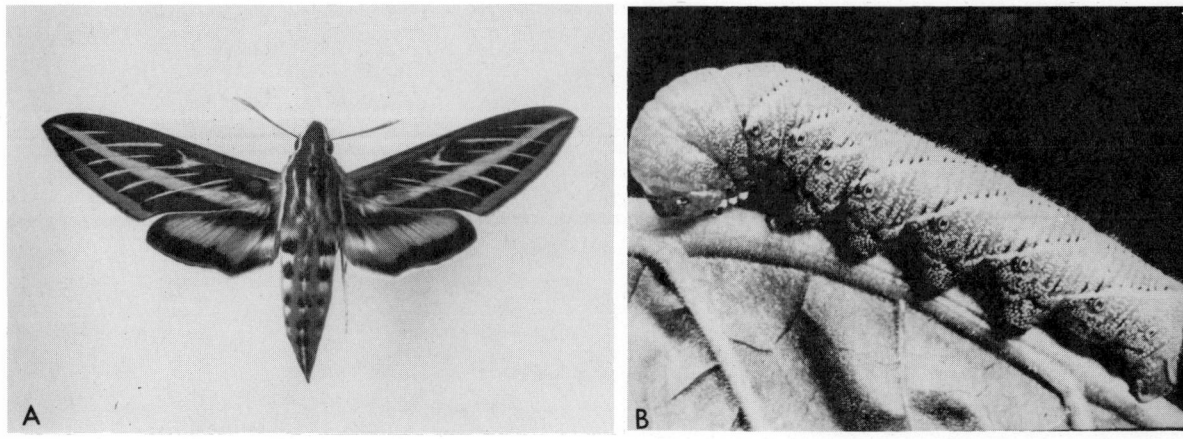

Figure 3–61. Sphinx moths, family Sphingidae. *A*, Adult. *B*, Larva, or hornworm. (USDA photo.)

lunules. The wings lack a frenulum. Saturniidae includes the world's largest moth, the Southeast Asian *Attacus atlas,* with a wingspan of more than 30 cm. Saturniid larvae are likewise large (to 10 cm.), robust caterpillars, usually bearing tubercules or spines (Fig. 11–4). These spines may be poisonous, causing an irritating rash. Most species feed on tree foliage. Adult Saturniidae have reduced, nonfunctional mouthparts and do not feed. **Citheroniidae** (Fig. 3–64) is a closely related family (sometimes considered a subfamily of Saturniidae) of large moths similar to Saturniidae.

Lasiocampidae (tent caterpillar moths, Fig. 3–65) are smaller (span to 30 mm. except in larger southwestern genera), stout, fuzzy, brown or grayish moths. They overwinter as eggs, and the hairy larvae of many species construct a silken communal tent, a familiar sight on shade and forest trees in early spring. Larvae of several species are periodically destructive to trees; cherry, crabapple, and aspen seem to be favorites.

Bombycidae deserves brief mention for containing the commercial silkworm, *Bombyx mori* (Fig. 12–2). This insect is of great commercial value (Chapter Twelve) and also presents an interesting case of retrogressive evolution.

Figure 3–62. Family Geometridae.

Figure 3–63. Family Saturniidae. *A*, Luna moth, *Tropaea luna*. *B*, Polyphemus moth, *Anthraea polyphemus*.

Figure 3–64. Family Citheroniidae.

Figure 3–65. Tent caterpillar, family Lasiocampidae, adult.

Larvae feed on mulberry leaves, but after centuries of domestication in the Orient, they have lost functional use of prolegs to the point that they cannot climb or hold onto the food plant in nature. Silkworms no longer exist in the wild and are dependent on people for their survival as a species, the only insect so domesticated.

Noctuidae (owlet moths, Fig. 3–66) is a very large (3000 North American species) family of small-to-large moths. Most are dark brown or grayish and have extensive mottling, especially on the forewings. Some are more brightly colored; underwings (genus *Catocala* Fig. 3–66*B*) have bright concentric bands of black and red, orange, yellow or white on the hindwings. Adult Noctuidae possess a thoracic tympanum with which they detect bat squeaks (Chapters Five and Nine). Larval Noctuidae feed on plant material: leaves, stems, or roots. Some, called cutworms (Fig. 3–66*C*) down whole plants and are among the most serious of plant-feeding insect pests. Seedling vegetables and grains are particular cutworm targets. Armyworms are cutworms that travel in large groups and are occasionally injurious to corn and wheat. The corn earworm, familiar to anyone who regularly eats fresh corn off the cob, is a noctuid that also damages cotton bolls and green tomatoes.

Liparidae (or **Lymantriidae,** Fig. 3–67) includes the tussock and gypsy moths. Adults are medium-sized (20 to 40 mm. span), drab, brown or whitish moths, with broad wings. Some females are wingless. The hairy larvae feed mostly on tree foliage, and some are considered serious forest pests, periodically defoliating extensive coniferous or deciduous forest areas. Chief among these are the gypsy moth of Eurasia and the northeastern United States and tussock moths (several species), a recent (1974) problem in Douglas fir forests of the Pacific Northwest.

Arctiidae (tiger moths, Fig. 3–68, *A* and *B*) look very much like **Noctuidae** but are generally more brightly colored or patterned in red, orange, yellow, or black. Some are all white, and all are very fuzzy. Adults are apparently distasteful to predators, and a tiger moth, on hearing a bat, may emit a return squeak that prompts the bat to avoid this potential meal. Arctiid larvae (Fig. 3–68*C*) are among the hairiest of caterpillars and have thereby earned the name woolly bears. Some species are alleged weather prophets, the severity of winter being correlated with the amount of brown hairs, or overall hairiness, or other things. This has not been scientifically verified, and in any event, the woolly bears in Ohio do not heed their prophecy, for I have found them wandering aimlessly over the snow in January.

B

Figure 3-66. Family Noctuidae. *A,* Armyworm adult, or miller moth, *Pseudaletia unipunctata. B,* Underwing moth, *Catocala* spp. *C,* Cutworm in action. (USDA photo.)

Figure 3-67. Gypsy moth, *Lymantria dispar,* family Liparidae, male.

Figure 3–68. Family Arctiidae. *A* and *B*, Tiger moths. *C*, Tiger moth larva, or woolly bear.

RHOPALOCERA: BUTTERFLIES. Superfamilies **Hesperioidea** (skippers) and **Papilionoidea** (butterflies) differ from moths by the characteristics listed in Table 3–5. Skippers and butterflies apparently represent independent evolutionary lines that have converged owing to similar, diurnal, habits. Both are favorite collectors' items.

Hesperiidae (common skippers, Fig. 3–69) is a diverse family of medium-sized Lepidoptera (span to 30 mm.) that combine the stout body and rapid flight of typical moths with the diurnal habits and bright coloration of typical butterflies. The antennal club has a hook on the end. Many species are orange or yellow and brown. There is sometimes sexual dimorphism, so that females look more like those of another species than males of their own species (and vice versa). Larvae (Fig. 3–69*B*) usually have a necklike constriction and hide in a loose cocoon. Most feed on grasses; a few eat leaves of broadleaved plants and rarely damage crops.

Papilionidae (swallowtails, Fig. 3–70) are large (to 150 mm. wingspan) showy butterflies, often (but not always) having a pair of slender projections on the hindwings. They are strong fliers, and are among the largest butterflies. Larvae feed mostly on leaves of shrubs and trees. They are large caterpillars and bear a forked, orange stink gland, or **osmeterium**, that they evert when disturbed. This emits a pungent, supposedly defensive, odor. Some Papilionidae are occasional pests of carrots, celery, parsley, and, in Florida and Mexico, citrus fruits. Like most butterflies (and other insects), they are more diverse in warmer climates; Florida has 11 species, whereas Maine has only 4.

Pieridae (whites and sulfurs, Fig. 3–71) are common white, yellow or orange butterflies (wingspan, 25 to 75 mm.). Most have characteristic dark markings on the wings. Larvae are green and feed mostly on herbaceous plants, particularly Cruciferae (mustards, cabbages, etc.) or Leguminosae (pea and bean family, clovers, etc.). A few are pests, notably the imported cabbageworm, *Pieris rapae,*

Figure 3–69. Skippers, family Hesperiidae. *A,* Adult. *B,* Larva. (USDA photo.)

Figure 3–70. Swallowtail, family Papilionidae.

and, in the southwestern United States, the alfalfa butterfly, *Colias eurytheme*. Adults of the latter occur in huge numbers in central California in September, and their collective squashed bodies sometimes accumulate on automobile radiators in sufficient numbers to cause boilover.

Lycaenidae (gossamer-winged butterflies, Fig. 3–72) are usually small (span to 30 mm.), delicate, brightly colored butterflies that fly rapidly despite their thin, fragile wings. Some are brilliant metallic blue, purple, or copper. They are among the earliest butterflies to emerge from overwintering pupae. Larvae look like slugs and feed mostly on low-growing plants, though a few feed on leaves of trees and shrubs. Larvae of one species, the harvester, eat aphids on alder bushes; they are among the very few predatory Lepidoptera.

Nymphalidae (brush-footed butterflies, Fig. 3–73) is the largest butterfly family, many members of which are very common. All have very small brushlike forelegs and appear to have only four feet. Most are brightly colored; orange or

Figure 3–71. Orange-tip, family Pieridae.

Figure 3–72. Family Lycaenidae. *A,* Silvery blue, *Glaucopsyche lygdamus. B,* Bronze copper, *Lycaena thoe.*

black predominate in North American species, and many are brilliantly spotted, banded, or otherwise patterned. Some (e.g., the mourning cloak, Fig. 3–73A) overwinter as adults and may fly about over the snow on sunny, late winter days. Nymphalid larvae are diverse in appearance and utilize food plants of all sorts. Each genus seems to have a food preference: *Speyeria* and *Boloria* for violets, *Phyciodes* for asters, *Polygonia* for elms and nettles, *Limenitis* for willows, *Asterocampa* for hackberries, and so forth. Despite this broad feeding diversity, none are really serious pests. The painted lady larva occasionally damages soybeans.

The following three families also have small forelegs, and some lepidopterists consider them subfamilies of Nymphalidae:

Heliconiidae (Fig. 3–74) are narrow-winged, brilliantly colored, mostly tropical butterflies, only two species of which occur very far into the United States. Most are distasteful to vertebrate predators, particularly birds, and they therefore

Figure 3–73. Family Nymphalidae. *A*, Mourning cloak, *Nymphalis antiopa*. *B*, California sister, *Limenitis bredowii*.

Figure 3–74. Zebra, family Heliconiidae.

Figure 3–75. Monarch, family Danaidae.

serve as models for imitators in some incredibly diverse tropical mimicry complexes (Chapter Nine). **Danaidae** (Fig. 3–75) show a similar tendency; adults are usually bright orange and black, and birds avoid them. Figure 9–19 illustrates a familiar case of mimicry involving the distasteful monarch (**Danaidae**) and tasty viceroy (**Nymphalidae**).

Satyridae (Fig. 3–76) gain some protection from their brown, drab coloration, usually featuring eyelike spots, and their dodging flight through grass and brush. They are common in meadows, marshes, and woods, where the larvae feed mostly on grasses. Some (called Arctics) are limited to arctic tundra and occur southward only in bogs or on alpine mountaintops where their food plants grow.

Figure 3–76. Wood nymph, family Satyridae.

Order Diptera

Diptera (flies) is the fourth largest insect order, and a very diverse group it is. All have in common two wings with few crossveins. The hindwings have evolved into balancing organs, the **halteres** (Fig. 3–77). Dipteran mouthparts display the widest range of any insect order, from piercing-sucking (e.g., mosquitoes, Fig. 4–4) to sponging-lapping (e.g., houseflies, Fig. 4–5B). Nearly all adults feed on liquids, especially plant juices and blood; some of the blood-feeders are important medical and veterinary pests. Accompanying the wide diversity in adult foods is wide diversity in larval foods and habitat (mostly in moist and unexposed situations). Most larvae of more "primitive" Diptera (Nematocera and Brachycera) are aquatic scavengers, while in the "advanced" Cyclorrhapha (and in some others) there is a greater tendency to feeding on decaying plant and animal matter, including rotten fruit, dung, meat, fungi, and so forth. Some also infest living plant and animal tissue, and obviously these can be serious pests. Diptera is the only insect order having members that parasitize vertebrate animals internally (Askew, 1971).

Flies are divided into three suborders: Nematocera, Brachycera, and Cyclorrhapha (or "Athericera") (Table 3–7). Each is successively more diverse in numbers, biology, and food eaten. Nematocera share a number of characteristics with Mecoptera; this and fossil evidence (*Permotipula,* page 29) suggest that flies evolved from Mecoptera like ancestors. Within Diptera, evolutionary trends have been toward compactness, with reduction in antennal and body segments, reduced wing venation, and fusion of the central nervous system and mouthparts. (Compare, for instance, the crane fly, Fig. 3–78, with the house fly, Fig. 3–96). Perhaps the major adaptation permitting adaptive radiation among flies was loss of all larval spiracles except the posterior pair, an adaptation to survival in mud or shallow water. This tendency (present in most Nematocera and all

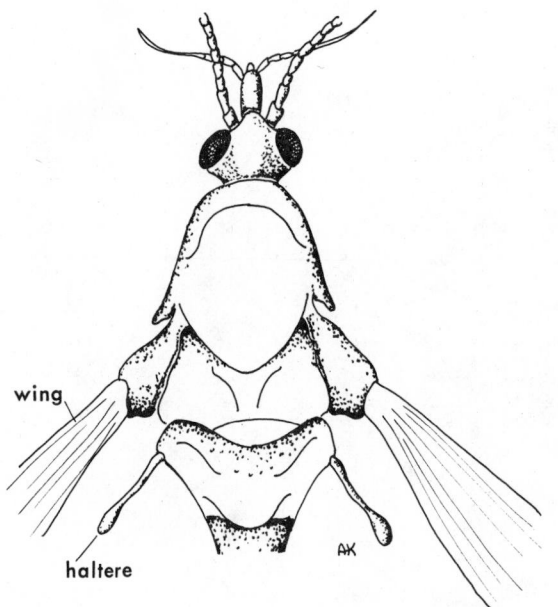

Figure 3–77. Thorax of crane fly, order Diptera.

wing

haltere

Table 3–7. CHARACTERISTICS OF DIPTERAN SUBORDERS

Suborder	♀ Mandibles	Antennae	Larval Mandibles	Larval Tagmosis	Pupa
Nematocera (crane flies, mosquitoes, etc.)	present in some	filamentous, many segments	typical mandibulate	head, thorax, abdomen, distinct	head, thorax, abdomen distinct
Brachycera (horse flies, etc.)	present in some	3-segmented, 3rd segment ringed	tilted mandibles	head distinct, thorax=abdomen	tagmata indistinct
Cyclorrhapha (house flies, etc.)	none	3-segmented, 3rd segment aristate	mouthhooks	undifferentiated	"puparium" in last larval skin

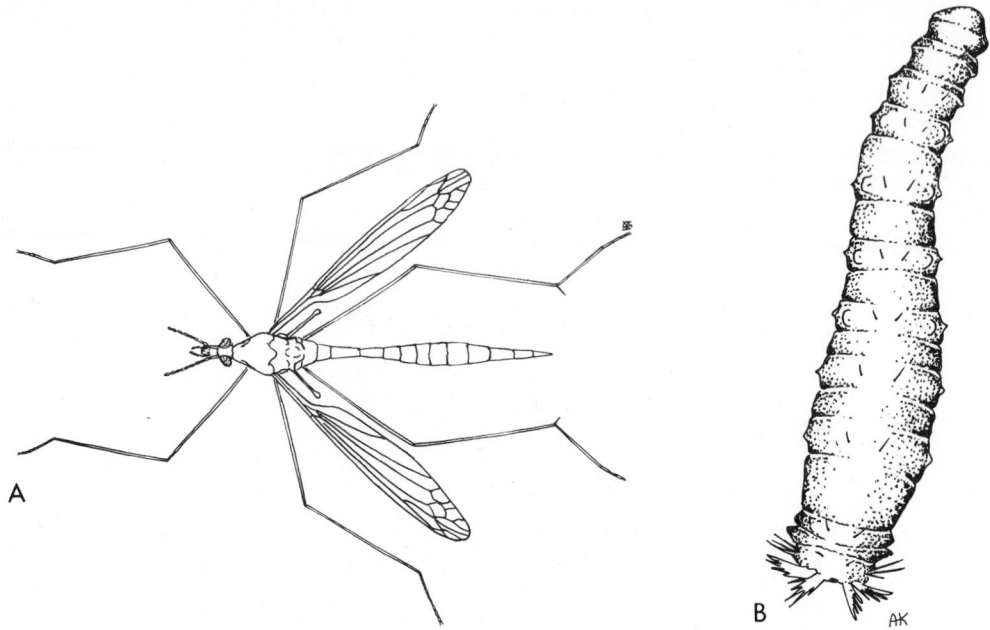

Figure 3–78. Crane flies, family Tipulidae. *A*, Adult. *B*, Larva.

"higher" flies) permitted subsequent radiation into the great range of moist environments—mud, humus, dung, flesh, fruit, stems—in which we find Diptera larvae today, feeding head down with their posterior at or near the surface. Some have become completely aspiracular: midge larvae are totally aquatic, and some of the bots are anaerobic internal parasites.

For identification of flies, useful references are Curran (1934), Cole (1971), and Usinger (1956). Oldroyd (1964) discusses biology and evolution of flies in considerable detail. Identification of Diptera depends greatly on wing venation and the placement of bristles, especially among the "higher" Diptera.

Suborder Nematocera. Nematocera are the most "primitive" of flies and are the only flies with antennae of more than three segments. Within this group, however, is a variety of larval types, and some have been exceedingly successful ecologically. Adult male Nematocera have no mandibles, but females in some families have retained their mandibles and some are among our most serious medical pests. Important families are the following:

Tipulidae (crane flies, Fig. 3–78) include some of the largest flies (up to 30 mm. long), which have extremely long legs (that break off very easily). They occur most commonly where dense plant growth restricts wind movement, usually near water or where moist decaying vegetation provides scavenge for the large, wormlike larvae ("leather-jackets," Fig. 3–78*B*). Adults are often attracted to lights and enter buildings, where they may be mistaken for giant mosquitoes. They do not bite; most have nonfunctional mouthparts. A few other less common families look and act superficially like Tipulidae.

Psychodidae (moth flies, drain flies, sand flies, Fig. 3–79) are minute (usually 3 mm.) hairy flies that would hardly be noticed except the female sand flies (genus *Phlebotomus*) bite, causing great discomfort to bathers in the southern United States in these days of scanty bathing apparel. In the tropics, *Phlebotomus*

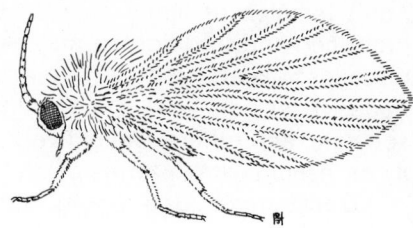

Figure 3–79. Moth fly, family Psychodidae.

bites can cause more than temporary discomfort; there they are carriers of leishmaniasis, a severe and debilitating protozoan disease. Closer to home, the drain fly occasionally appears about my sink drain, in which the larva feeds on decaying material — whiskers, toothpaste, soap, grease, and shampoo. Psychodid larvae generally feed on decaying materials.

Culicidae (mosquitoes, Fig. 3–80) are familiar to all and may be differentiated from similar families (**Tipulidae, Tendepedidae,** etc.) by having scales on wing veins and margin. Only females take blood; males lack mandibles and feed on plant juices. Not all mosquitoes bite. Eggs are deposited in or near water, and aquatic larvae (''wrigglers,'' Fig. 3–80B) feed mostly on algae and organic debris. A few prey on other mosquito larvae. The aquatic pupae are unusually active.

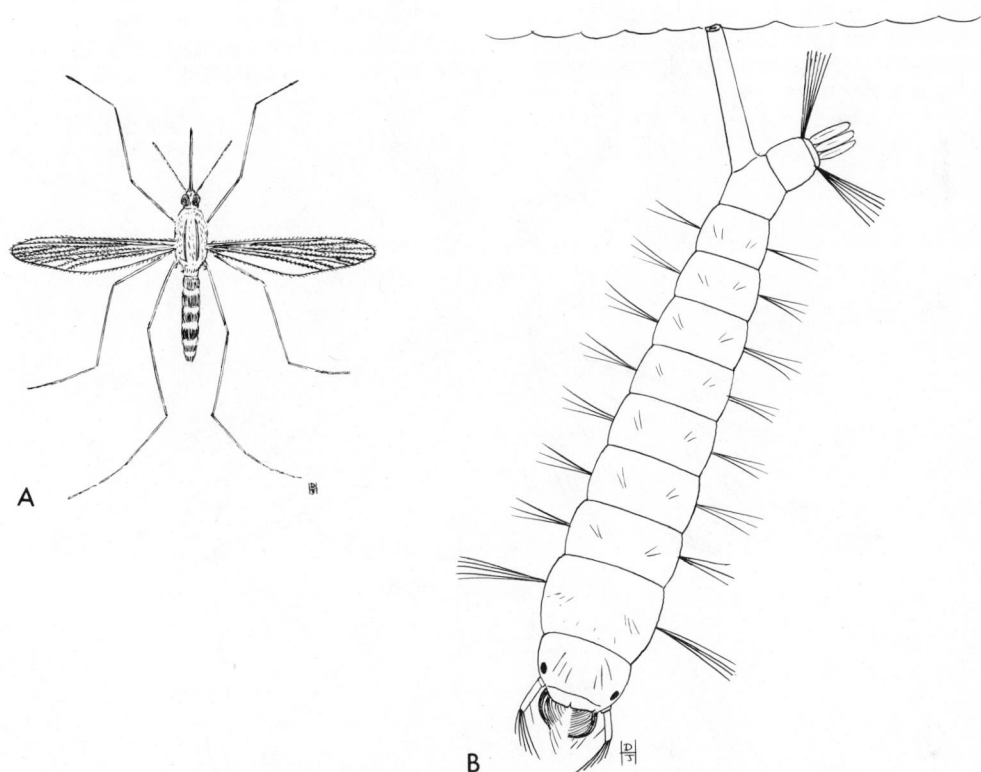

Figure 3–80. Mosquito. *A,* Adult. *B,* Larva.

Adult females of many species take one blood meal for each batch of eggs produced and in doing so may introduce the causative agent for one of several diseases: malaria (spread by *Anopheles* mosquitoes), yellow fever (spread by *Aedes* species), viral encephalitis and filariasis (spread by *Aedes* or *Culex* species), and others. Collectively, mosquitoes are probably the most serious family of insect pests in terms of damage and effort expended in control.

Ceratopogonidae (biting midges, or punkies) are tiny (<3 mm.) biting flies, more often felt than seen, particularly on the shores of lakes and rivers near sunset. Their simultaneous attacks have forced an early end to more than one fishing trip. Some parasitize insects by taking blood from, among others, crane flies and mosquitoes. Larvae are aquatic scavengers about which little is known.

Tendepedidae, or **Chironomidae** (midges, Fig. 3–81), are similar to mosquitoes but lack wing scales. Most midge larvae are aquatic scavengers and have completely lost their spiracles. As a consequence, midge larvae are among the most diverse of aquatic insects. Some inhabit mud of extremely low oxygen content. Others occur in very hot springs or in high arctic regions; midges are among the very few terrestrial organisms on Antarctica. Chironomidae also boast some of the very few marine insects and occur even in the extremely salty Great Salt Lake. In the evening, midge adults swarm, often in great numbers, and are attracted to lights. Such swarms may be particularly huge near shallow lakes and may therefore be considered pestiferous around lakeside resort areas.

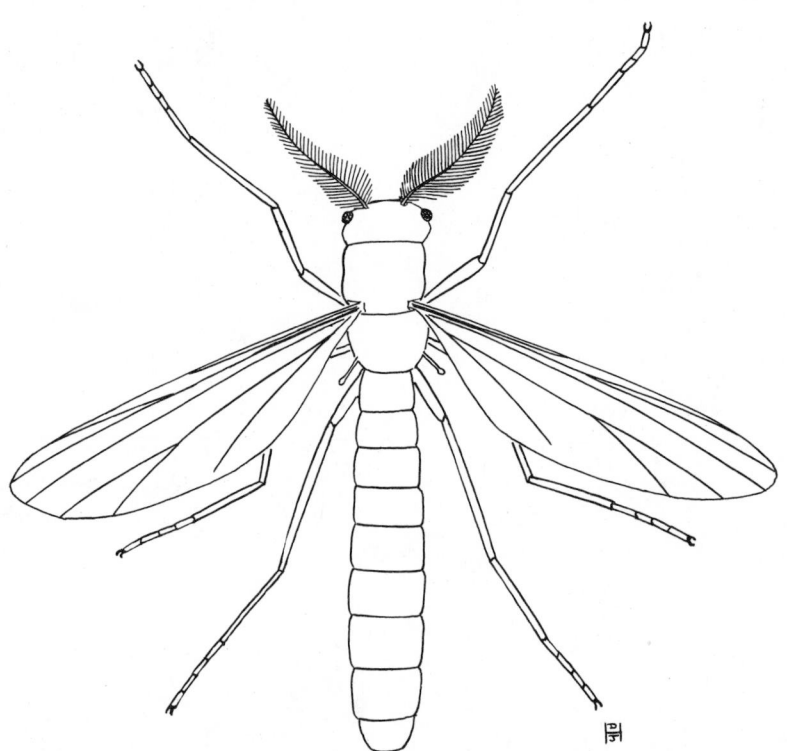

Figure 3–81. Midge, family Tendepedidae or Chironomidae.

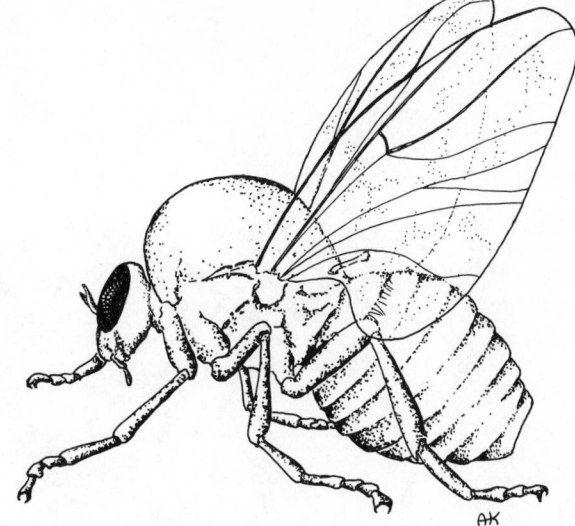

Figure 3–82. Black fly, family Simuliidae.

Simuliidae (black flies, Fig. 3–82) are another family of small (to 4 mm.) biters; females, often in large numbers, suck blood from livestock and humans, causing painful swelling. Some tropical species transmit disease. They do not transmit diseases in the United States but are most unwelcome anyway to those who venture into the woods of northern states or Canada in June. Larvae are scavengers in fast-moving streams, in which they attach themselves by holdfasts. During pupation, the pupal shell becomes filled with air. Later, this air is released as a bubble containing the adult fly, thus permitting the delicate adult to escape from the rushing deluge (Lutz, 1936).

Bibionidae (march flies, Fig. 3–83) range in length to about 10 mm. Most are dark flies that occur on flowers and vegetation in spring and early summer. They may be incredibly numerous; in 1968, my wife and I drove through a swarm of march flies for 50 miles in south Florida, and the flies were so numerous that we had to turn on our windshield wipers. In Florida, roadside rest areas are equipped to aid in cleaning the flies from automobiles. Such swarms often contain many mating pairs, and these bibionids are popularly called "love bugs." Larvae feed on plant roots and decaying vegetation.

Figure 3–83. March fly, family Bibionidae.

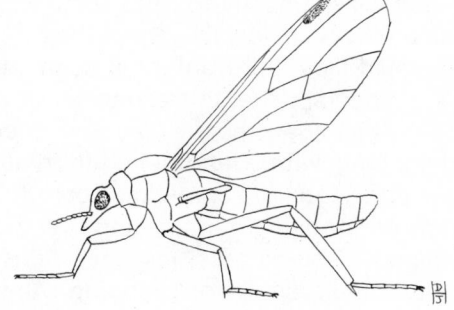

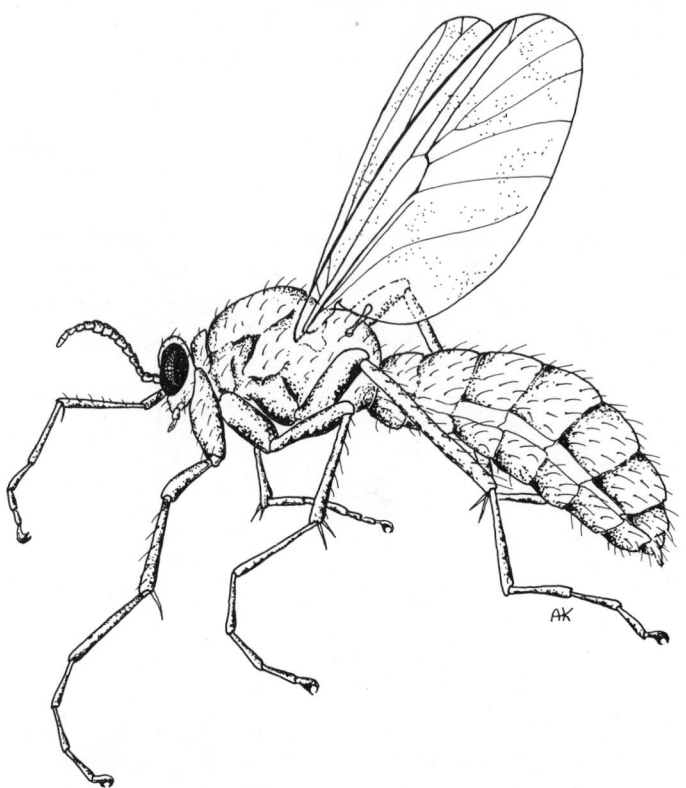

Figure 3–84. Fungus gnat, family Mycetophilidae.

Mycetophilidae (fungus gnats, Fig. 3–84) and **Sciaridae** are two closely related families whose larvae feed on fungi in soil and decaying vegetation. They occasionally damage commercial mushroom crops. Adults occur most abundantly in moist and densely vegetated places and look very like mosquitoes but for their lengthened coxae. There are a few minor families of fungivorous mosquitolike gnats similar to these.

Cecidomyiidae (gall midges, Fig. 3–85) are minute (<3 mm.) flies, most of whose larvae inhabit plant stems and cause development of distinctive galls (Chapter Nine). Infestation by gall midges usually has a negligible effect on the plant (other than the gall), but the Hessian fly, *Myaetiola destructor,* is potentially a severe pest of wheat; larvae feed in the whorls at leaf bases and weaken the stalk so that it cannot support the ripening grain head.

Suborder Brachycera. **Stratiomyidae** (soldier flies, Fig. 3–86) are medium-sized (mostly 10 to 15 mm.) wasplike flies often found on flowers or vegetation. They are very like **Syrphidae** (Fig. 3–92), but wing venation differs and stratiomyid flies' third antennal segment is either elongate or rounded. Larvae are scavengers, either in fresh water or decaying plant matter.

Tabanidae (horse flies and deer flies, Fig. 3–87) are stocky flies, 10 to 30 mm. long, with a lengthened third antennal segment and characteristically large, multifaceted (and sometimes colorful) compound eyes. Female tabanids are best known for biting humans and livestock. Bites are painful and livestock may be affected by blood loss; moreover, the buzzing is maddening as the fly circles almost endlessly before landing. American tabanids come in two editions. The

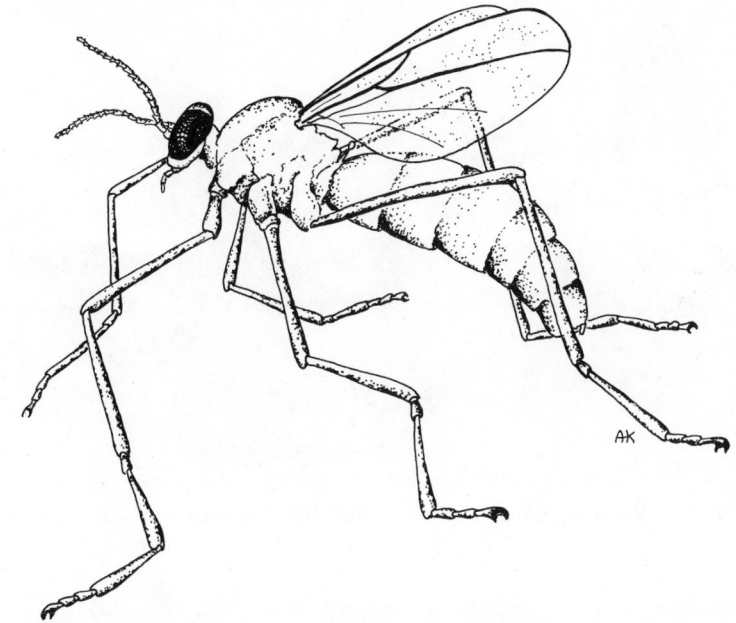

Figure 3–85. Gall midge, Cecidomyiidae. (Redrawn from USDA photo.)

larger horse flies (mostly *Tabanus* species, Fig. 3–87A) have uniformly colored wings and bite humans on the lower part of the body, on legs and posterior. Smaller deer flies (mostly *Chrysops* species, Fig. 3–87B), with bicolored wings, bite about the shoulders and head. In the United States, Tabanidae do not transmit diseases. Larvae are scavengers in water or mud.

Figure 3–86. Soldier fly, family Stratiomyidae. (Painting by W. Costello.)

Figure 3–87. Family Tabanidae. *A,* Horse fly, *Tabanus* spp. *B,* Deer fly, *Chrysops* spp.

Rhagionidae (snipe flies, Fig. 3–88) are more delicate, mostly 8 to 15 mm., black or gray flies with spotted wings. The third antennal segment is rounded and bears a terminal projection. They are common in woods, especially near water, where they often rest on leaves. A few species bite humans and livestock. Most larvae, like those of **Tabanidae,** occur in water or decaying vegetation. *Vermileo,* of the southwestern United States and adjacent Mexico, is unusual in that its larva is a terrestrial predator, digging a pit remarkably like those of antlions (Fig. 4–1*B*). Their predatory habits are an unusual example of behavioral convergence.

Asilidae (robber flies, Fig. 3–89) are usually slender flies (5 to 30 mm.) that have a bearded face and an indentation atop the head between the eyes. Some are very hairy and are effective mimics of bumblebees (Fig. 3–89*B*). Robber flies are active predators. One will wait on vegetation, flowers, or exposed ground for

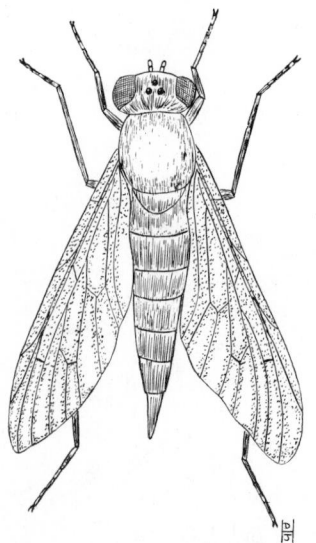

Figure 3–88. Snipe fly, family Rhagionidae.

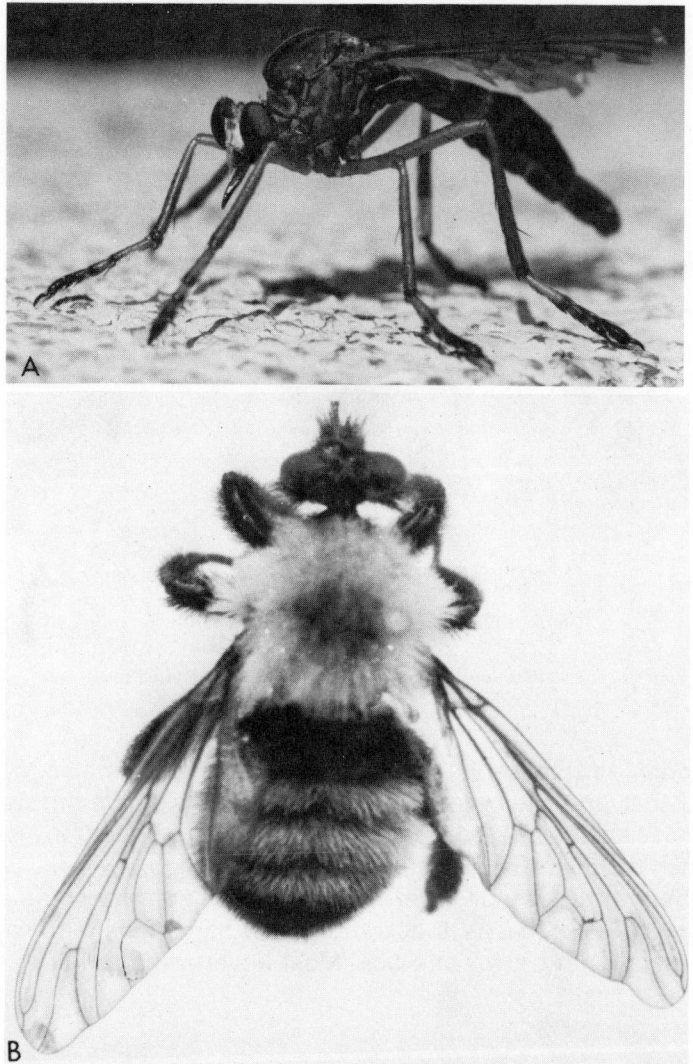

Figure 3–89. Robber flies, family Asilidae. *A,* Typical robber fly. *B, Bombomima,* mimic of bumble bee.

another insect to fly by, then dart out and snatch its quarry out of the air. I have chased more than one butterfly into the waiting legs of a robber fly, who robbed me. Asilid larvae occur in decaying wood or soil and are scavengers or predators. Two less common families of similar appearance and habits are **Mydaidae** and **Therevidae.**

Bombyliidae (bee flies, Fig. 3–90) are stout, hairy, medium-to-large flies, often having a long proboscis. Many mimic bees; others have dark areas on their wings and look rather like deer flies (Fig. 3–87*B*). Adults often hover in one spot just above flowers or bare earth. Larvae of Bombyliidae parasitize other insects or insect eggs, and some undergo hypermetamorphosis (Fig. 7–30). Those that parasitize bees oviposit on flowers from which the active first instar larva rides a bee to its nest and commences feeding, first on pollen and later on a bee larva.

Figure 3–90.   Bee fly, family Bombyliidae.

Dolichopodidae (Fig. 3–91) are small, long-legged, metallic, coppery green or gold flies that one often sees running about on vegetation. Adults prey on smaller insects. Larvae are scavengers in decaying vegetation, mud, or fresh water or under bark.

Syrphidae (flower flies, or hover flies, Fig. 3–92) are very common flies, most of which mimic bees or wasps. Black and yellow banding is a prevailing pattern, though some are plain brown or black. Most hover rather like bee flies, usually

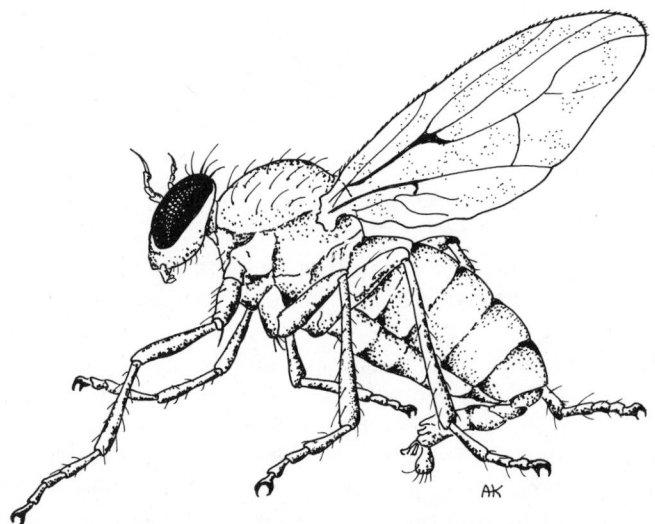

Figure 3–91.   Long-legged fly, family Dolichopodidae.

Figure 3–92. Flower fly, family Syrphidae.

near flowers. Adults eat pollen and nectar; larval habits vary. Some larvae are active predators of aphids and other small insects and are among the relatively few dipteran larvae that crawl about exposed on vegetation. These larvae are often green. Others (e.g., *Eristalis* species) are scavengers in the bottom mud of stagnant, shallow ponds and streams. A few inhabit ant colonies.

Suborder Cyclorrhapha. Cyclorrhapha (also called Athericera) represent the culmination of dipteran evolution. All these flies are compact, inside and out. They have adaptively radiated to include very diverse habitats and habits, especially in regard to larval foods. As with many such actively evolving groups, familial and specific differences are sometimes obscure. This is especially true within the **Acalyptrata** (**Otitidae** through **Agromyzidae,** discussed in the next section), a vast group of small flies identified by subtleties in wing venation (see Cole, 1971). **Calyptrata** (**Anthomyiidae** through **Oestridae**) are, on the average, larger and bear an enlarged lobe, or **calypter**, on the hind edge of each wing (Figs. 3–96 to 3–100).

Acalyptrate cyclorrhapha. **Tephritidae** (fruit flies, Fig. 3–93) are small- to medium-sized (3 to 8 mm.) flies with spotted or banded wings. Adults often are found on flowers, and some are said to mimic spiders, the wing banding appearing like spider legs when the insect is at rest. Larvae feed on plant matter and some are pests of fruit crops. The apple maggot and cherry fruit fly infest the obvious hosts; the Mediterranean fruit fly is a serious pest of citrus fruits in tropical countries but so far has not become permanently established in the United States (Chapter Ten). *Eurosta* species form galls on goldenrod. **Otitidae** is a closely related family of similar habits and very similar appearance.

Sciomyzidae (Fig. 3–94) have forward-projecting antennae and occur on vegetation near ponds and slow-moving streams. Larvae are predaceous or parasitic, eating freshwater snails.

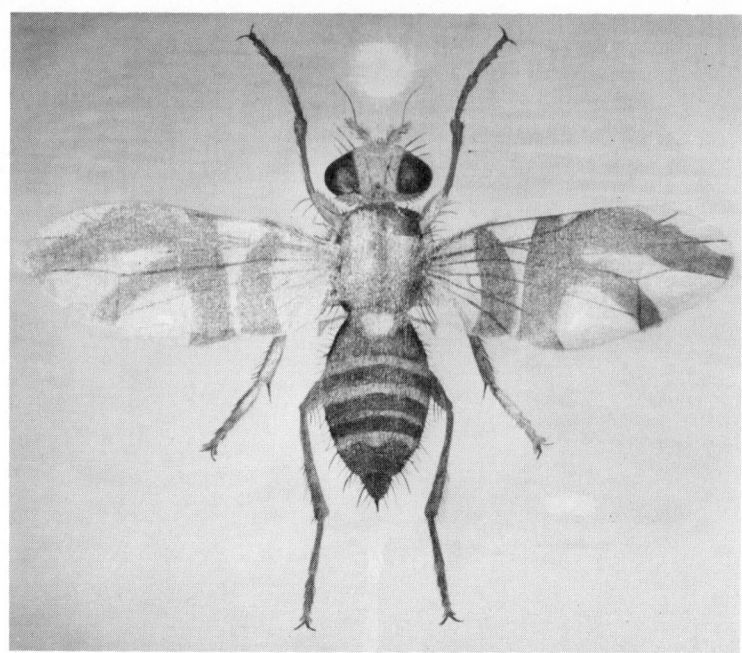

Figure 3–93. Fruit fly, family Tephritidae. (Painting by W. Costello.)

Piophilidae (skipper flies, Fig. 3–95*A*) are small (<5 mm.) metallic flies, of interest because some of their larvae "jump" by bending until the mouthhooks grab the rear, then rapidly releasing to snap into the air. The cheese skipper is a jumping piophilid that is less familiar now that refrigeration has all but eliminated dry cheese. Most piophilid larvae eat decaying animal matter, and a few species

Figure 3–94. Marsh fly, family Sciomyzidae.

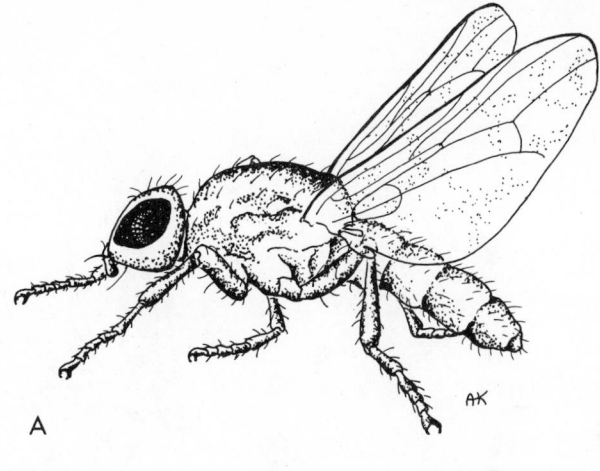

Figure 3–95. Acalyptrate Cyclorrhapha. *A,* Family Piophilidae. *B,* Family Ephydridae.

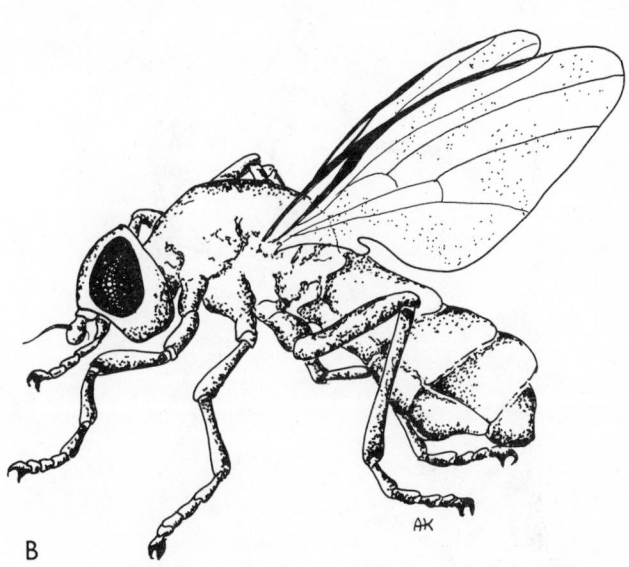

Figure 3–95 continued on the following page.

have a gruesome knack of wending their way into apparently sealed coffins and feeding on the embalmed remains of the occupant.

Ephydridae (shore flies, Fig. 3–95*B*) are small, blackish flies that are common on vegetation along shores of lakes, streams, and salt water. Most of their larvae are aquatic scavengers, though one species scavenges in pools of crude oil.

Drosophilidae (vinegar or pomace flies, Fig. 3–95*C*) are small (3 to 4 mm.), brown or yellowish, obscure flies whose larvae occur in decaying fruit and fungi. Rather than feeding on the fruit itself, they apparently eat yeasts that develop in the rotting fruit. Nonetheless, they are considered pests in homes and especially in fruit canneries and processing plants, for fly fragments are not legally allowable ingredients in prepared foods (in the United States). *Drosophila* species, especially *D. melanogaster,* have been invaluable laboratory animals to scientists trying to unlock the secrets of heredity.

Chloropidae (Fig. 3–95*D*) are tiny flies, colored black, black and yellow, or gray, most commonly found in grassy places. Most larvae feed in plant stems;

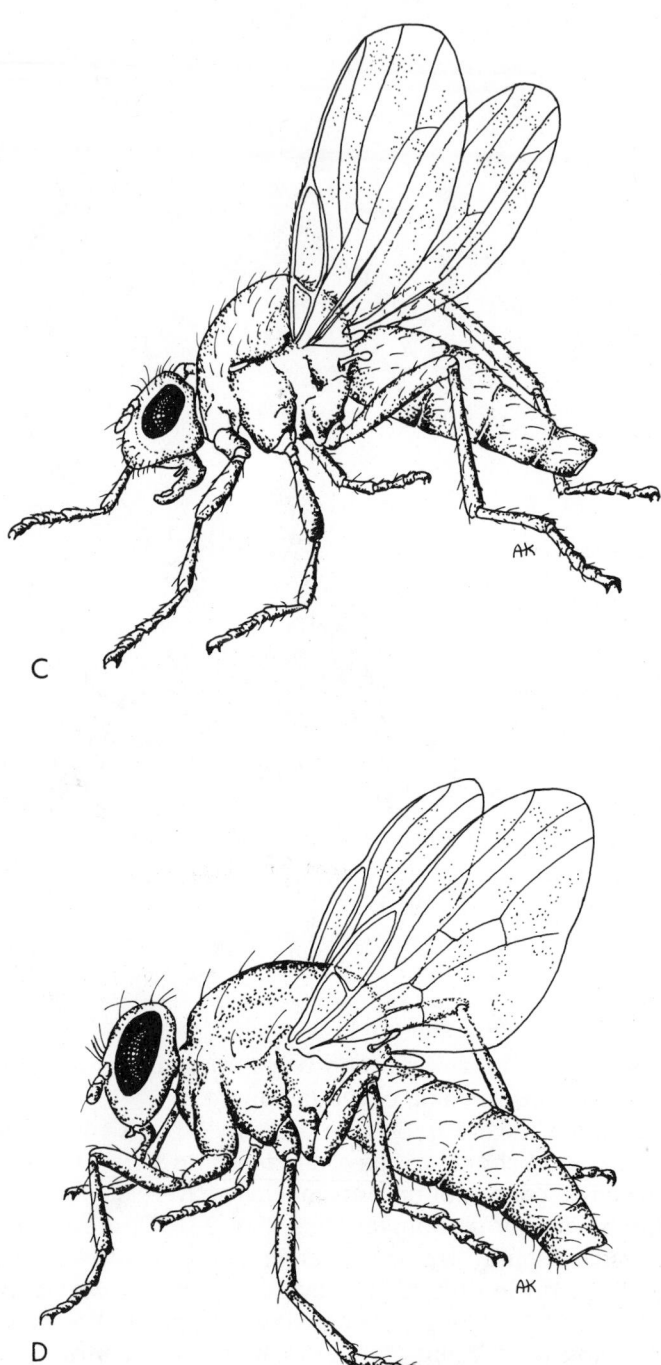

C

D

Figure 3–95. *Continued.* Acalyptrate Cyclorrhapha. *C,* Family Drosophilidae. *D,* Family Chloropidae.

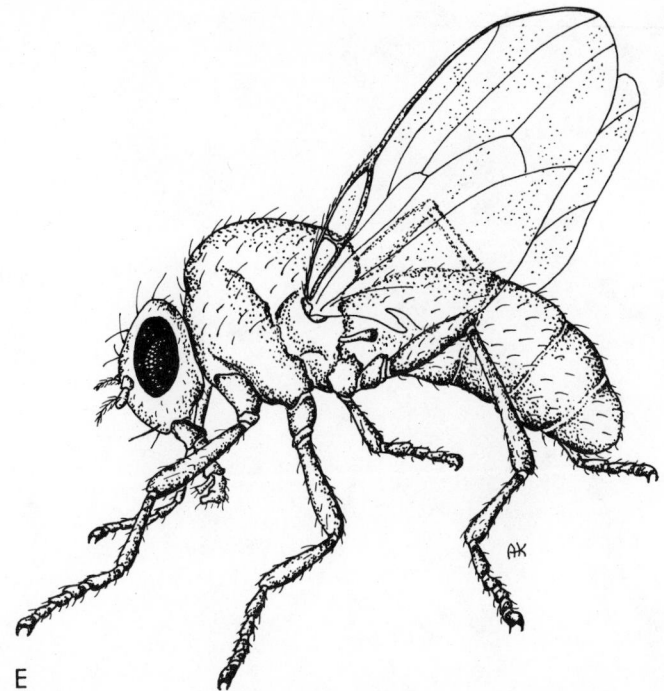

Figure 3–95. *Continued.*   Acalyptrate Cyclorrhapha. *E,* Family Agromyzidae.

some scavenge in decaying vegetation. A few species (mostly *Hippelates* species) are attracted to secretions from eyes, noses, or open sores of humans and livestock; these eye gnats do not bite but do cause restlessness and irritation, especially if one gets trapped on an eyeball.

Agromyzidae (Fig. 3–95*E*) are small yellowish or black flies. Larvae are mostly leaf miners, characteristically constructing a tortuous mine in a leaf of a herbaceous plant. Some, called serpentine leaf miners, are a problem in greenhouse crops and also on vegetables outdoors, particularly when there has been great reliance on chemical insecticide treatments to reduce infestations of other pests. Apparently the leaf miners have evolved resistance to insecticides.

CALYPTRATE CYCLORRHAPHA.   **Muscidae** (house flies and relatives, Fig. 3–96) are small to medium (6 mm.), usually brown or gray flies, some of whom need little introduction. Most familiar is the ubiquitous house fly, *Musca domestica*, a constant companion of humans throughout the world. It has lapping mouthparts and so confines its damage to (potentially) spreading disease. The face fly, *Musca autumnalis,* does not bite but irritates livestock considerably anyway by sitting on the animal's face and lapping secretions from eyes, nose, and mouth. Not so, however, with its biting cousins, the stable fly, horn fly, and African tsetse flies. Both sexes of these flies readily bite both humans and livestock (though the horn fly greatly prefers cows); the tsetses in addition transmit serious protozoan blood diseases (Chapter Eleven). Tsetse larval development is very unusual; larvae develop to maturity within the female parent. Chapter Seven details more of this peculiar developmental pattern. Other muscid larvae thrive in dung or decaying vegetation (which often are the same thing).

Figure 3–96. Family Muscidae. House fly, *Musca domestica.* (Painting by W. Costello.)

Anthomyiidae are medium-sized grayish or blackish flies, very similar to **Muscidae** (with which they are sometimes included) but for a few details of wing venation and bristle placement. Adults occur on vegetation, at lights, or near larval food sources, which are diverse; larvae consume dung, decaying plant or animal matter, or living insects. Of considerable economic importance are species that feed in stems or roots of cultivated plants: the spinach leaf miner, and cabbage, onion, and seed-corn maggots.

Hippoboscidae (louse flies, Fig. 3–97A) are winged or wingless, flattened flies, which are ectoparasitic on birds and mammals (but not people). Both sexes suck blood. Like tsetse flies, larvae of Hippoboscidae develop within their mother. The sheep ked (Fig. 3–97A) is a major pest of sheep but is controllable by application of insecticide after shearing. Two other families of rare parasitic flies, **Streblidae** and **Nycteribiidae** (Fig. 3–97B), represent extreme specializations. They parasitize bats, and, like Hippoboscidae, their larvae develop internally; for this reason, they are sometimes combined with Hippoboscidae into a separate group, **Pupipara.** It is likely that this "uterine" development evolved independently at least three times among bloodsucking muscoid flies (Oldroyd, 1964).

One of the most unusual of flies is the bee louse, *Braula coeca* (**Braulidae,** Fig. 3–97C). This wingless fly, 1 to 1 1/2 mm. long, clings to hairs of honeybees and steals food from their mouths. Its tiny larvae feed on pollen, nectar, and wax at the bases of honeycombs. For many years, it was considered to be pupiparous; now its closest relatives are thought to be acalyptrate Cyclorrhapha (Oldroyd, 1964).

Calliphoridae (blow flies, Fig. 3–98) are medium-sized, usually metallic green, blue, or gray flies, often found in numbers about homes, barns, and garbage pails. Most are scavengers on decaying meat, though Evans (1966) suggests that they may feed primarily on bacteria within the rotting flesh. Adults

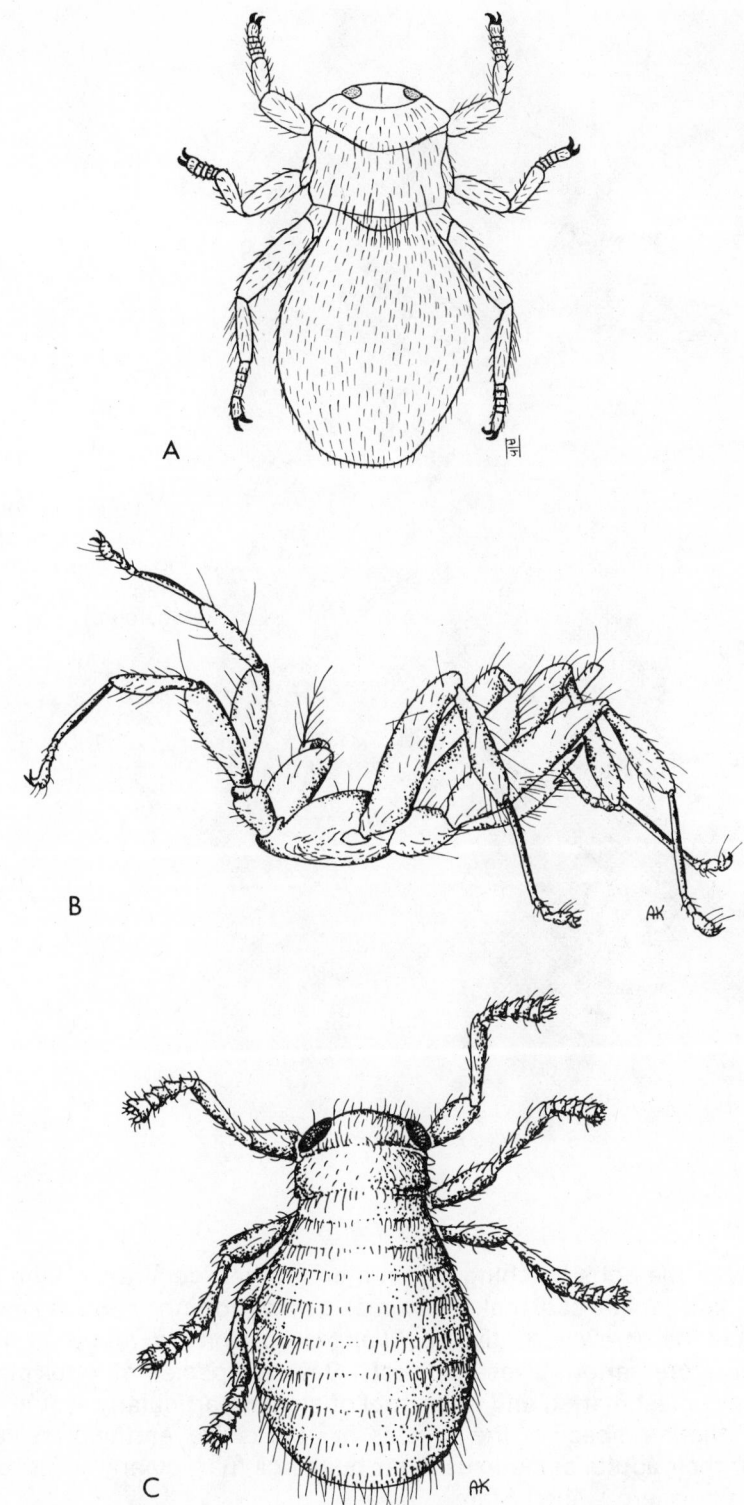

Figure 3–97. Parasitic flies. *A*, Sheep ked, family Hippoboscidae. *B*, Bat fly, family Nycteribiidae. *C*, Bee louse, family Braulidae. (*B* redrawn from Askew, R. R. 1971. Parasitic Insects. American Elsevier Publishing Co., Inc., New York. *C* redrawn from Theodor, O. 1967. An illustrated catalogue of the Rothschild collection of Nycteribiidae. British Museum [Natural History], London.)

Figure 3–98. A, Blow fly, family Calliphoridae. *B,* Flesh fly, family Sarcophagidae. (Painting by W. Costello.)

are viviparous, the eggs hatching within their mother; generation time is thereby shortened, and larvae can make maximal use of rotting meat. A few species, most notably the screwworm fly, *Cochliomyia hominivorax,* feed on living flesh and are therefore serious livestock pests. Several species of wool maggots, or fleeceworms, infest matted and dirty wool of sheep, particularly around the anus. Larvae of another species, the cluster fly, parasitize earthworms, and huge numbers of their adults sometimes enter buildings, particularly attics, during autumn in the northern United States.

Sarcophagidae (flesh flies, Fig. 3–98*B*) are similar to **Calliphoridae,** and some authorities combine both into a single family (**Metopiidae**). Sarcophagids are blackish with gray thoracic stripes. Larvae of most eat decaying flesh, though some are parasites of snails, earthworms, or insects, particularly pupae of Lepidoptera.

Tachinidae (Fig. 3–99) are similar to flesh flies but are very bristly. Some mimic wasps; larvae of all parasitize other insects. There are 1500 species worldwide. Adults usually occur on flowers or foliage, where they search for oviposition sites on or near hosts. Having no ovipositor, they are limited to exposed hosts, usually larvae of Lepidoptera, Hymenoptera, or Coleoptera. The range of hosts is wide; *Compsilura concinnata* has been reared from over 200 species of Lepidoptera. Some Tachinidae oviposit on foliage and depend upon the host larva to eat the egg, which then hatches inside its victim. Exotic Tachinidae have been imported for biological control of gypsy moth, Mexican bean beetle, and other plant pests; their value is sometimes minimal owing to their wide range of alternate hosts.

Oestridae (bot and warble flies, Fig. 3–100) are stout, fuzzy, beelike flies with greatly reduced mouthparts. Larvae are encountered more often than adults. Larvae, or bots, are internal parasites of wild and domestic animals. The sheep bot adult larviposits about the nostrils of sheep, and the spiny larvae feed within the nasal cavity, irritating the animal and paving the way for infections. Two species of ox warble oviposit on legs of cattle. Their larvae tunnel through the skin and worm their way via connective tissue to the back, where they form a boil, or warble, in which they feed (Fig. 4–21*E*). Other species form warbles on deer or rodents. The related family **Gasterophilidae** contains four species of horse bots, which are stomach and intestinal parasites of horses. **Cuterebridae** are uncommon flies whose larvae (in the United States) form warbles on rabbits and rodents. Of interest here is the tropical torsalo, or human bot fly, *Dermatobia hominis,* that forms warbles on people (Chapter Eleven).

Figure 3–99. Family Tachinidae.

Figure 3–100. Warble fly, family Oestridae. (Painting by W. Costello.)

Order Siphonaptera

Siphonaptera (fleas, Fig. 3–101) are specialized intermittent ectoparasites of mammals and birds. The bilaterally flattened, active, wingless adults are familiar to most persons who have cared for dogs or cats. Winglessness, flattening, and hideaway antennae are adaptations for moving with ease through the hairy forest on the victim. Flea mouthparts resemble those of primitive Diptera, from which fleas presumably evolved. Flea larvae (Fig. 3–102) are rarely seen. They eat organic debris and their parents' droppings in nests and lairs of wild and domestic animals. Adults, of course, suck blood, usually from a preferred host species, but many fleas can subsist on a variety of hosts. Adults may live a few months without food, especially as pre-emergent adults within the cocoon. These pre-emergent adults are sensitive to warmth and vibration and emerge to tear into the flesh of the first warm and vibrant mammal who walks by, as some cat-lovers discover to their chagrin on returning to an unopened home after vacation. Fleas usually bite people on the ankles. The breeding cycle of some fleas is very closely attuned to that of the host; the hormones that circulate within a pregnant rabbit also induce ovary maturation in rabbit fleas (Chapter Seven).

Of the seven flea families in the United States, two are particularly important. **Pulicidae** contains the irritating dog, cat, and human fleas, and the potentially much more serious Oriental rat flea. The rat flea is a primary vector spreading plague from rats to people (Chapter Eleven). **Tungidae** are unusual fleas that at-

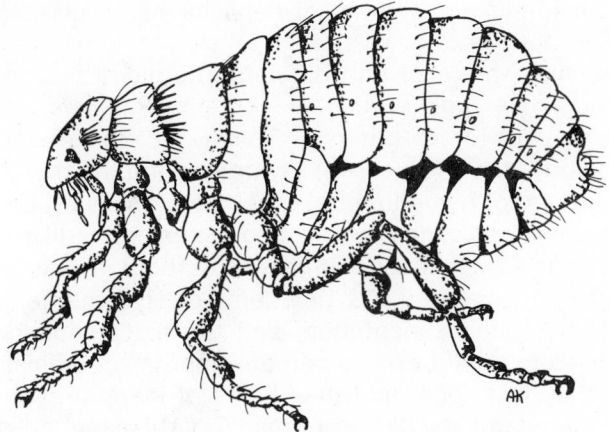

Figure 3–101.   Flea, order Siphonaptera.

tach semipermanently to vertebrate hosts. Sticktights attach to the head of poultry, causing irritation and debilitation. Chigoes (which are *not* chiggers) attach under the toenails of humans and evidently cause the skin to envelop them. Subsequently, they swell to the size of a pea, causing tremendous pain and a wish, sometimes fulfilled, that the offending toe be chopped off. Chigoes occur mostly in tropical climates, but this includes some beaches in Florida.

Fox (1940) and Hubbard (1947) contain much additional information and guides to identification of North American fleas.

Order Hymenoptera

This, the last insect order, rivals Lepidoptera in diversity; there are an estimated 105,000 species of ants, bees, and wasps. Hymenoptera typically bear four translucent membranous wings with relatively few veins, and the forewings are larger than the hindwings. A series of hooks (hamuli) on the anterior margin of each hindwing engages a vein at the rear of the forewing to attach the wings together; they act as a functional unit. Some (e.g., worker ants) lack wings. Hymenoptera retain an ovipositor, though in several groups it no longer functions as such but rather has become an offensive and defensive stinger. (Therefore, only females sting.) A final characteristic is the method of sex determination: in Hymenoptera, fertilized eggs develop into females, whereas unfertilized eggs normally become males. This is obviously a handy adaptation to generate

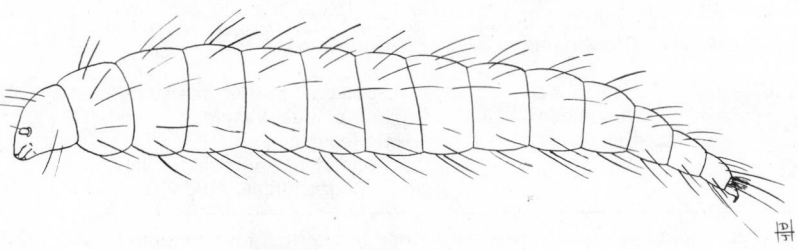

Figure 3–102.   Flea larva.

sperm and may also explain why social behavior has evolved among "higher" Hymenoptera (see Chapter Six).

Hymenoptera may have evolved from neuropteroid or mecopteran ancestors, perhaps something like the Permian mecopteran *Parabelmontia.* Their evolutionary relationship with other orders is somewhat obscure. Hymenoptera are divided into two suborders (Table 3–8). **Symphyta** are the more "primitive" and less diverse (5 per cent of Hymenoptera). They possess a sawlike ovipositor, their abdomen is broadly joined to the thorax, and the caterpillarlike larvae have functional legs and mandibles; most eat leaves or bore in stems. The suborder **Apocrita** contains the majority (95 per cent) of Hymenoptera. These have a "wasp-waisted" abdominal constriction, and the first abdominal segment (the propodium) is fused to the thorax. Larvae of Apocrita superficially resemble dipteran maggots; they lack legs, and mandibles of many are very tiny. Apocrita contains eleven superfamilies. Larvae of many, particularly the more "primitive" forms, parasitize other insects. In the "advanced" Apocrita, called **Aculeata,** the ovipositor has become a stinger and eggs are deposited directly. This group includes social ants, wasps, and bees.

There are few reference works on the entire order Hymenoptera; identification is difficult, being dependent on details of thoracic sclerotization and wing venation. Viereck et al. (1916) is an older, comprehensive guide. Townes and Townes (1959–1962) presents keys to **Ichneumonidae.** Creighton (1950) discusses ants, and Michener (1944), bees. Askew (1971) covers the biology of parasitic Hymenoptera in interesting detail, and Wilson (1971) is an eminently worthwhile discussion of social Hymenoptera and the biology of their unique societies.

Suborder Symphyta. **Tenthredinidae** (sawflies, Fig. 3–103*A*) are 5 to 20 mm. long, usually black or brown insects commonly found on flowers or in sweep-net samples from vegetation. There is no abdominal constriction, and females bear a short, sawlike ovipositor. Their larvae (Fig. 3–103*B*) look very much like caterpillars, except that they have only one pair of lateral ocelli (caterpillars have several) and their abdominal prolegs bear no hooks. Most sawfly lar-

Table 3–8. CLASSIFICATION OF HYMENOPTERAN SUPERFAMILIES

Suborder	Superfamily	Families Included*
Symphyta	Tenthredinoidea	Tenthredinidae, Diprionidae
	Siricoidea	Siricidae, Orussidae
Apocrita (parasitic)	Ichneumonoidea	Ichneumonidae, Braconidae, Aphidiidae
	Chalcidoidea	none
	Cynipoidea	none
	Evanioidea	none
	Pelecinoidea	Pelecinidae
	Proctotrupoidea	none
	Bethyloidea	Chrysididae
Apocrita (Aculeata)	Scolioidea	Scoliidae, Formicidae, Mutillidae
	Vespoidea	Pompilidae, Vespidae
	Sphecoidea	Sphecidae
	Apoidea	Colletidae, Andrenidae, Halictidae, Megachilidae, Apidae

*This list is limited to those families mentioned in the text; for complete classification of United States families, see Borror et al., 1976.

Figure 3–103. Order Hymenoptera, suborder Symphyta. *A*, Sawfly, family Tenthredinidae. (Painting by W. Costello.) *B*, Sawfly larvae. (USDA photo.) *C*, Horntail, family Siricidae.

vae eat leaves and often are gregarious. Some bore in plant stems, where they may form galls.

There are 800 species of Tenthredinidae in North America; seven other smaller families of sawflies are closely related to Tenthredinidae. Of these, **Diprionidae** includes spruce and pine sawflies, which may be very destructive to coniferous forests, ornamental plantings, or Christmas trees. Some **Cephidae** bore in stems of wheat. **Siricidae** (Fig. 3–103C) are large (20 to 25 mm.) and are called horntails because of a (harmless) spine at the apex of their abdomen. Larvae bore in sapwood of deciduous trees. **Orussidae** are uncommon but deserve mention for being the only parasitic Symphyta; they parasitize wood-boring larvae of buprestid beetles. Perhaps Apocrita evolved from similar parasitic Symphyta.

Suborder Apocrita. **Ichneumonidae** (Fig. 3–104) are slender, wasplike insects with long antennae (often 1/2 the body length) and often a long (sometimes *very* long) slender ovipositor. Sizes vary from 3 to 40 mm., excluding ovipositor. Most are black but some are brightly colored with blue, red, or yellow. The trochanter appears two-segmented. A few species are wingless and look very much like ants but for the threadlike antennae and absence of nodes on the petiole (p. 154). Ichneumonidae is a large family with over 3000 described North American species. Many species remain to be described, and it may end up being the largest insect family (Borror and White, 1970). Ichneumonidae, and all the parasitic Hymenoptera, are actively evolving, and there is great, and often confusing, similarity among related forms. Ichneumonid adults are most common on

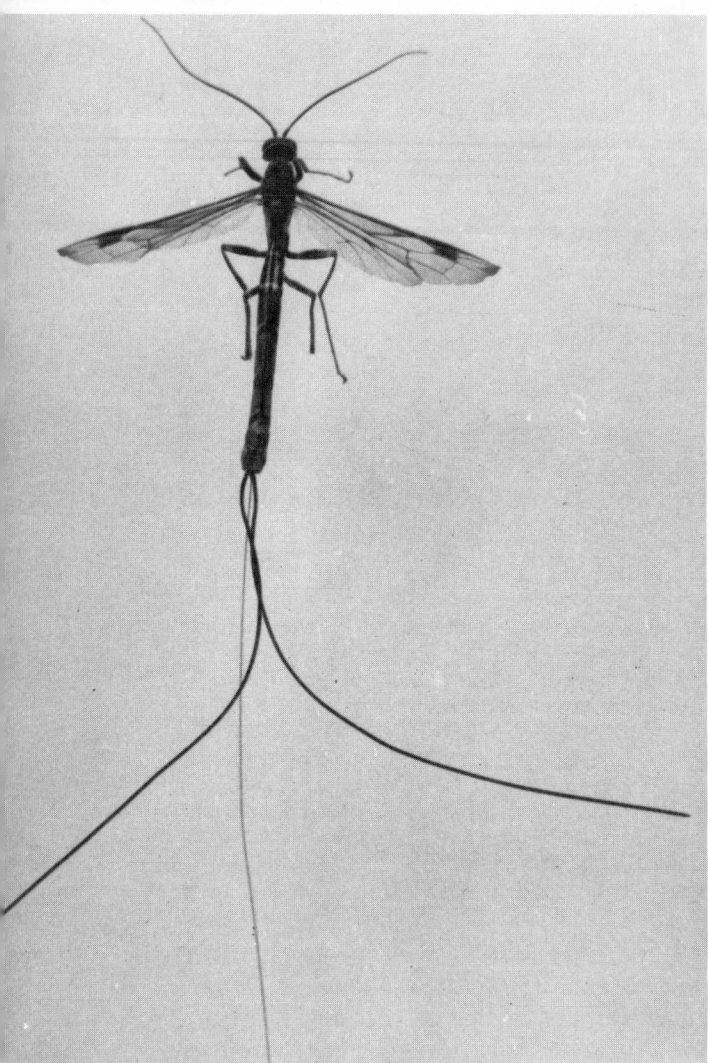

Figure 3–104. Ichneumon, family Ichneumonidae. *Megarhyssa* spp., parasitoid of horntails (shown in Figure 3–103C). (Ovipositor valves, separated in this figure, are normally held together; cf. Figure 7–10.)

vegetation, flowers, or at lights. Their larvae are internal parasites, or parasitoids, (see Chapter Nine) of other insects, including other Ichneumonidae. The adult female selects a host, oviposits therein, and the larva (or larvae) feed within the host, consuming it and ultimately killing it. Insect larvae and pupae, especially Lepidoptera, are favored hosts, and Ichneumonidae are sometimes highly host-specific, attacking but a single host species. They are generally considered beneficial, and many species have been imported into the United States and other countries to assist in contol of noxious insect pests, particularly the alfalfa weevil, gypsy moth, sawflies, and European corn borer.

Braconidae (Fig. 3–105) are very similar to **Ichneumonidae,** though they are smaller on the average (2 to 15 mm.). Differentiation between the two depends on details of wing venation. Most Braconidae are brown or black, and like Ichneumonidae, they are common about vegetation. They are parasitoids of other insects, and from one to over 100 may develop within a single host. Dying caterpillars frequently are covered with cocoons of braconid wasps that have completed feeding on the host (Fig. 3–105B). Some Braconidae are of value in biological control; e.g., *Apanteles* parasitize the imported cabbageworm, and *Microctonus* species parasitize the alfalfa weevil. **Aphidiidae,** a related family (sometimes considered a Braconid subfamily), parasitize aphids, and when done, leave a ''mummy'' aphid with a neat round emergence hole.

The preceding are **Ichneumonoidea**; the following parasitic wasps I discuss at the superfamily level. Identification to families depends on details of wing venation and location of thoracic sclerites and is left to more advanced books (such as Borror et al., 1976).

Chalcidoidea is a huge array (18 families) of tiny or very small (<5 mm.), metallic wasps with very few wing veins and (usually) elbowed antennae. Most parasitize other insects or insect eggs, and several are valuable in biological

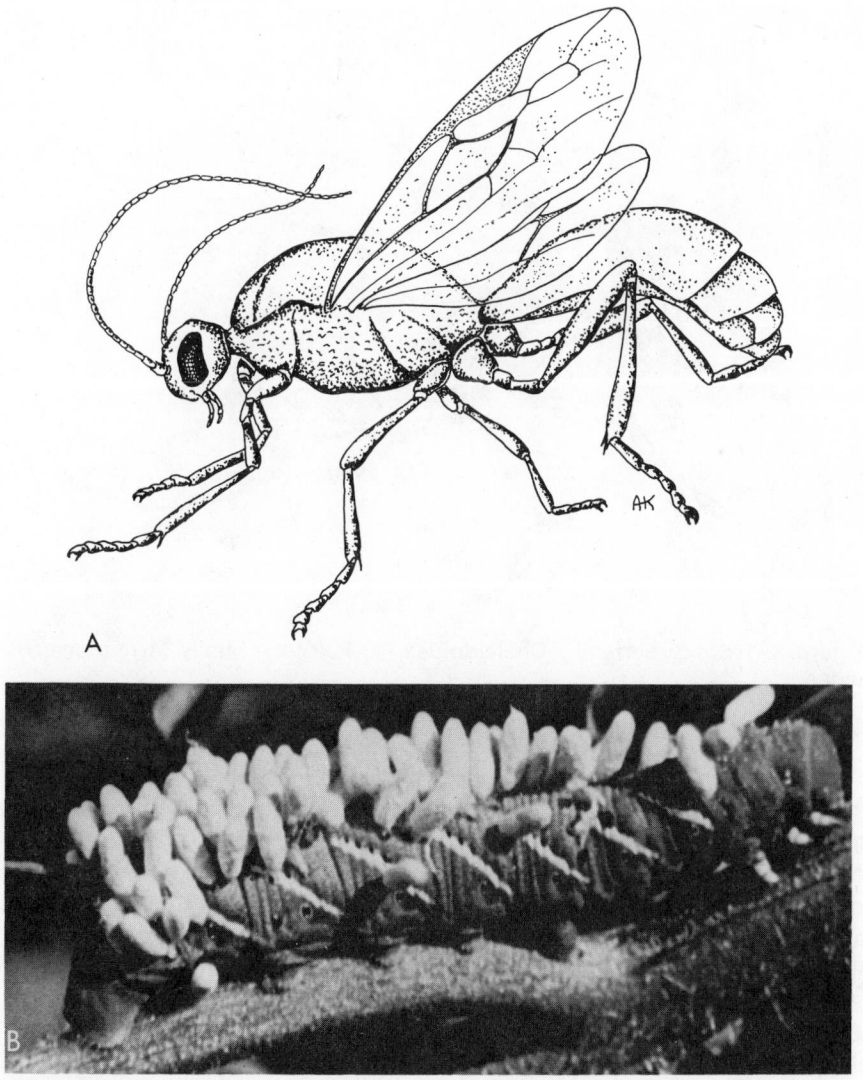

Figure 3–105. Family Braconidae. *A*, Adult. *B*, Cocoons on host (tomato hornworm). (USDA photo.)

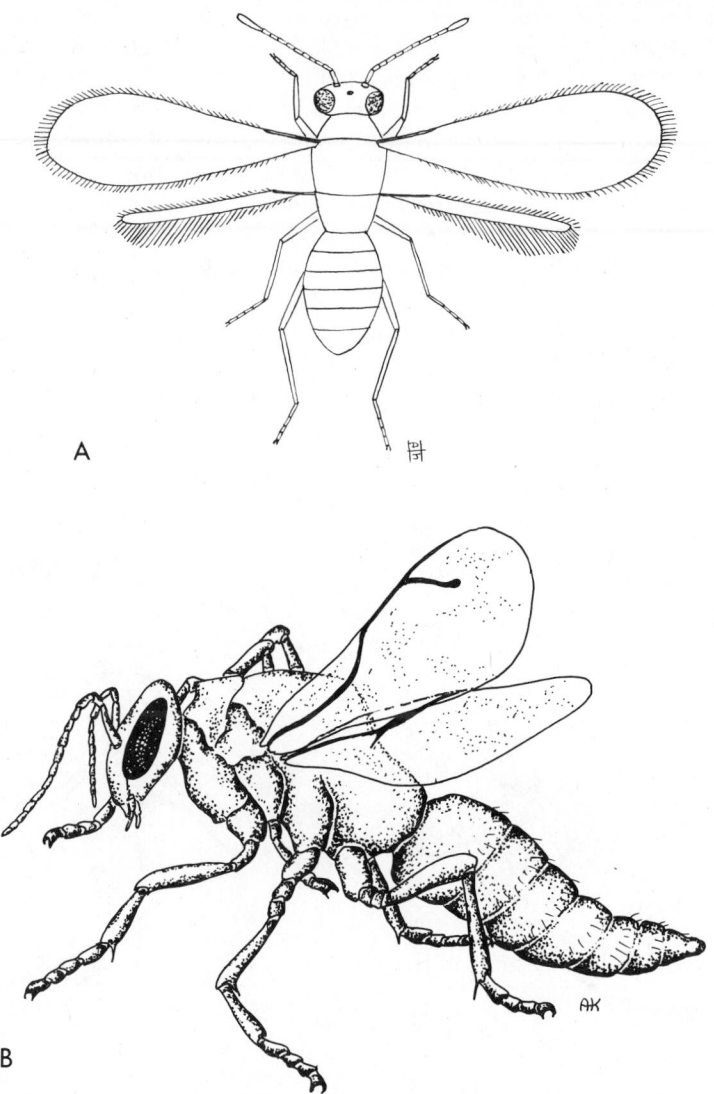

Figure 3–106. Superfamily Chalcidoidea. *A,* Fairy-fly, family Mymaridae. *B,* Family Chalcidae.

control, particularly of scale insects. Many species are hyperparasitoids. **Trichogrammatidae** and **Mymaridae** parasitize insect eggs, and some of the latter, called fairy-flies (Fig. 3–106), are among the smallest of insects: 0.2 mm. long when full-grown. Some parasitize damselfly eggs and use their wings as oars to swim underwater. A few Chalcidoidea are leaf miners as larvae, and still fewer develop in seeds, sometimes damaging alfalfa seed or wheat. They do not reinfest seeds in storage, as grain-eating beetles do.

Cynipoidea (Fig. 3–107) consists of four United States families with 800 species; **Cynipidae** (gall wasps) are most common. They are small (2 to 8 mm.) metallic wasps with a round, dorsolaterally flattened discoidal abdomen. A few are parasitic; larvae of most feed on plants and form galls thereon.

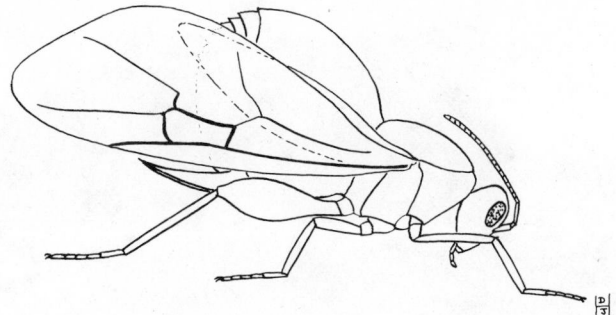

Figure 3–107. Superfamily Cynipoidea. Gall wasp, family Cynipidae.

Evanioidea, Pelecinoidea, and **Proctotrupoidea** are less common parasitic wasps. They include an array of families, and their hosts likewise vary: some parasitize cockroach eggs, others parasitize wasps, bees, or insect larvae. Most noticeable are **Pelecinidae** (Fig. 3–108), whose extended abdomen compensates for the lacking ovipositor length when females bore through sod to their hosts, larvae of **Scarabaeidae** (Coleoptera).

Bethyloidea includes five families of parasitic wasps. The commonest and largest (6 to 12 mm.) are **Chrysididae,** cuckoo wasps (Fig. 3–109). These oviposit within nests of other wasps and bees, whose larvae the chrysidid larva eats. Cuckoo wasps are metallic blue or green with a roughened body surface. Most curl into a ball when disturbed, but they also may sting. The other four bethyloid families are rare and parasitize other insects.

Suborder Aculeata.   Scoliidae (Fig. 3–110*A*) are robust, hairy, dark wasps, 20 to 30 mm. long, with wrinkled wingtips. Some (like many other wasps) are banded with black and yellow. Adults feed on nectar and pollen, hence are common on flowers. They oviposit on white grubs (scarabaeid larvae), which they then sting; the scoliid larva then feeds upon the paralyzed host. Members of a related family, **Tiphiidae** (Fig. 3–110*B*) are smaller (10 to 20 mm.), less common parasites of larval beetles, bees, or wasps.

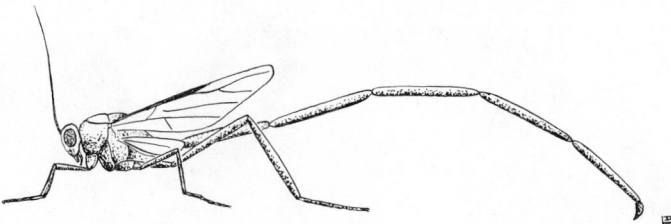

Figure 3–108. Family Pelecinidae.

Figure 3–109. Cuckoo wasp, family Chrysididae.

Formicidae (Fig. 3–111) are ants—a familiar, abundant, diverse, and extremely important group economically and ecologically. Adults have elbowed antennae and a lump or **node** (sometimes two) on the narrowed abdominal petiole. Reproductive males and females are winged (at least until mating); the more frequently encountered workers are wingless. All species are social (Chapter Six), and colonies may number up to several hundred thousand individuals. Ants are everywhere; most species are scavengers (especially in temperate climates), though some are carnivorous and others only herbivorous. There is fascinating diversity in ant societies; Chapter Six discusses some of these, and Goetsch (1957) further recounts the fascinating biology of ants. Most ants are beneficial, for their scavenging disposes quickly of dead insects and small vertebrates that otherwise might pile up. Unfortunately (for us, and them) their scavenging activities may bring them into homes or other food storage and food handling places.

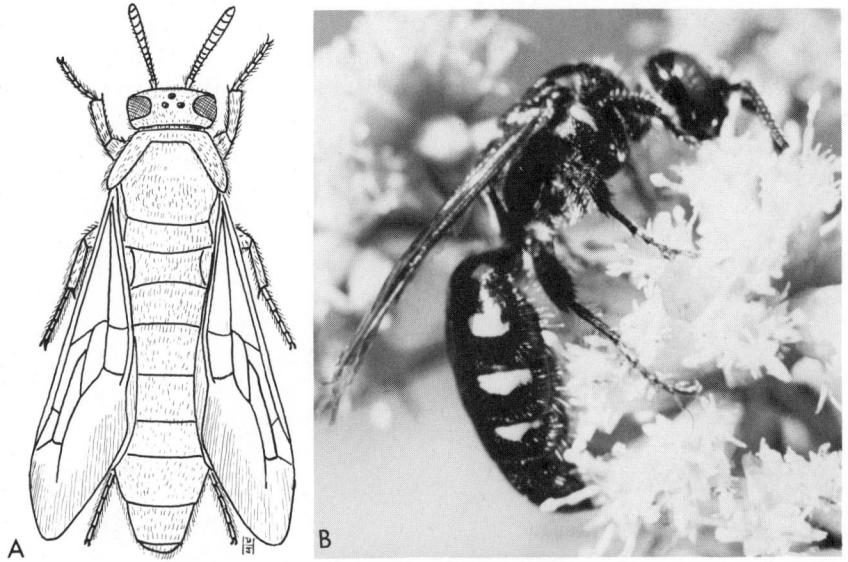

Figure 3–110. Superfamily Scolioidea. *A,* Family Scoliidae. *B,* Family Tiphiidae.

Figure 3–111. Carpenter ant, family Formicidae. (USDA photo.)

They take some food, but often their mere, massed presence is sufficient irritation to a homeowner. Their ability to scavenge outdoor picnics is legendary. Most ants nest underground or in foundations of buildings. Carpenter ants are large species that hollow out wood for nesting cavities and may thereby destroy beams, fence posts, and the like. Many ants bite or sting, but few do so en masse. One exception is the fire ant of the southeastern United States and tropical America; these swarm from their nests and sting hapless bystanders. These stings are very painful; poultry and livestock have allegedly been killed by fire ants. In contrast, the threat from army ants in tropical countries is generally oversold.

Mutillidae (velvet ants, Fig. 3–112) are superficially similar to **Formicidae** but are larger (6 to 20 mm.), hairy, and often banded with black and bright red.

Figure 3–112. Velvet ant, family Mutillidae.

Males are winged, and females wingless. Velvet ants parasitize larvae of ground-nesting solitary bees and wasps. Females are most common in sandy areas, such as beaches and golf course sand traps, where they run rapidly over the ground searching for potential hosts. They sting people if disturbed, and the sting of a velvet ant can be most painful.

Pompilidae (spider wasps, Fig. 3–113) are medium-to-large wasps (10 to 40 mm.) usually having blue or red wings and hind femora longer than the abdomen. Some are the world's largest wasps. They prey on spiders: A female pompilid excavates a burrow, then hunts spiders, which she paralyzes by stinging, and brings into the burrow. She then oviposits on them and plugs the burrow. Spider wasps are more abundant and diverse in the arid western United States. There one finds the "tarantula hawks" (*Pepsis* species), huge wasps that specialize in killing tarantulas. Each species of tarantula is parasitized by a specific *Pepsis,* and tarantulas will fight off other species but become submissive in the presence of their "own" predator (Williams, 1956).

Vespidae (Fig. 3–114) are common wasps, 10 to 30 mm., banded with black and yellow or white. Characteristically, the forewings fold lengthwise when the insect is not flying. Vespid wasps are insect and spider eaters. Solitary species, the potter wasps, construct little mud jugs which they provision with paralyzed caterpillars before ovipositing in and sealing them. Social species, such as hornets, paper wasps, and yellow jackets, make nests of finely chewed wood mixed with saliva to form paper. Within the nest, larvae are reared in honeycomblike cells, provisioned with insect, spider, carrion, or picnic fragments gathered by adults. Adults of social species are sometimes a nuisance in late summer. Hornets (*Vespula* and *Vespa* species) become belligerent about the nest, which is sometimes built near or on habitations or outbuildings. A run-in with a nest can result in multiple stinging with serious consequences.

Sphecidae (Fig. 3–115) closely resemble vespids (and other wasps) but bear a short, collarlike pronotum and do not fold the forewings longitudinally when at

Figure 3–113.   Spider wasp, family Pompilidae.

Figure 3–114. Family Vespidae. *A,* Paper wasp, *Polistes* spp. *B,* Yellow jacket, *Vespula* spp.

rest. Adults are 8 to 30 mm. long. They eat spiders and insects, especially crickets and caterpillars, and feed these to their larvae either in underground burrows or in mud nests on cliffs, trees, or buildings. The most familiar of these are the mud daubers, black and yellow or steely blue wasps numerous about mud puddles, barns, and vacation homes in humid areas. The largest American sphecid, the cicada killer, specializes in parasitizing cicadas (Fig. 3–24A). The female will sting and paralyze several cicadas and drag them to the wasp's burrow. She then stuffs the burrow with cicadas, lays an egg, and seals the chamber. The emerging larva later eats the cicadas.

Apoidea, bees, are in many respects simply hairy, pollen-eating wasps. In the United States, there are six families, which, like other Hymenoptera, differ mainly

Figure 3–115. Family Sphecidae. Cicada killer, *Sphecius speciosus.*

in details of wing venation. Most bees eat pollen and nectar and provision their larvae with these. **Colletidae** and **Andrenidae** are brownish bees that nest in burrows, often in small groups. **Halictidae** have similar habits and are small (5 to 15 mm.), often metallic, black or bright green bees. Some halictids are attracted to perspiration and have thus earned the nickname "sweat bees." **Megachilidae** (Fig. 3–116) are moderate-sized (10 to 20 mm.), big-headed bees that chew out very neat sections of leaves to line and partition their nesting burrows. Seldom are they common enough to seriously damage plants.

Apidae (Fig. 3–117) are the most common bees. They are very hairy, black and yellow or orange, with the maxillae modified to a long, slender tongue (Fig. 4–5A). They are very diverse in habit and include both solitary and social forms. There are three subfamilies (considered full families by some authorities). **Anthophorinae** includes cuckoo bees, which oviposit in nests of other bees, who then raise the intruder's larva as if it were their own. Carpenter bees, **Xylocopinae,** resemble bumble bees superficially. They excavate a nesting bur-

Figure 3–116. Superfamily Apoidea, bees. *A,* Sweat bee, family Halictidae. *B,* Leafcutting bee, family Megachilidae.

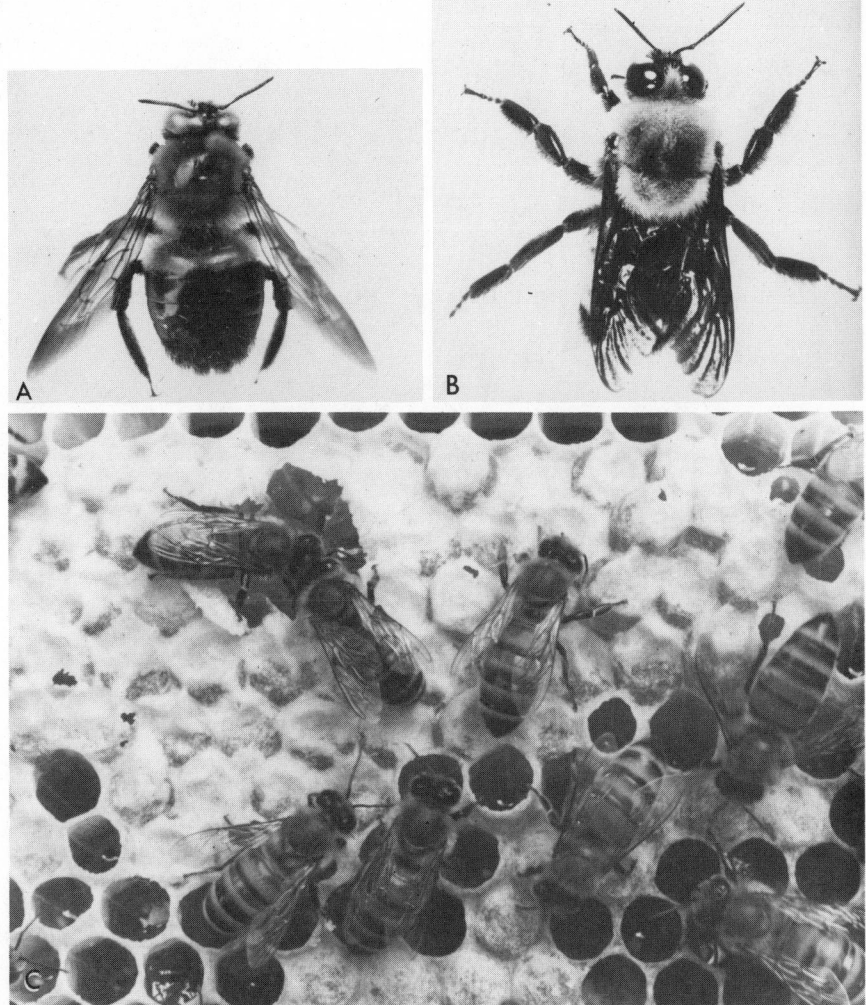

Figure 3–117. Family Apidae. *A*, Carpenter bee, *Xylocopa* spp. *B*, Bumble bee, *Bombus* spp. (Photo by G. Berkey, courtesy of D. G. Nielsen and Ohio Agricultural Research and Development Center.) *C*, Honey bee, *Apis mellifera.* (Photo courtesy of L. J. Connor.)

row in wood and occasionally thereby damage unpainted porch railings, outside rafters, and the like. The robust adults often hover about the eaves of farm and camp buildings. **Apinae** are truly social bees, including two familiar groups, bumble bees and honey bees. Bumble bees (mostly *Bombus* species) are abundant, rotund, black and yellow (or orange) bees that nest in or on the ground (Chapter Six). A colony lasts but a single season and contains a maximum of several hundred bees. In the Americas, honey bees are a single species. *Apis mellifera.* Other species of *Apis* occur in Eurasia. Honey bees are familiar orange and brown insects about 10 mm. long. They have perennial colonies, usually located in cavities, either natural or manmade. Honey bee society has been carefully studied and Chapter Six recounts some of this work. The economic importance of this one insect is tremendous, for honey bees provide most pollination of fruit, vegetable, and seed crops, as well as all our honey. Their services not only compensate for a few unfortunate stinging incidents but also, perhaps, for all the economic damage done by all noxious insects combined.

Part Two

Insect Biology

Chapter Four

Maintenance Functions

INTRODUCTION

Insects, like all living things, derive energy for growth and maintenance from oxidation (cellular respiration, or metabolism) of organic molecules. I leave the details of cellular respiration to a modern biology text such as Keeton (1972) or Wilson et al. (1973); Gilmour (1965) treats insect metabolism. Here, it is sufficient to say that respiration is an intracellular process, requiring organic molecules and oxygen in an aqueous medium of appropriate temperature and chemical composition. Respiration yields by-products: water, carbon dioxide, amines (containing nitrogen), and heat. Each living cell in an insect's body must therefore be provided food, water, oxygen, and minerals, while excess carbon dioxide and nitrogen must be eliminated. An insect may therefore be regarded as an interacting system: eating, drinking, disseminating organic molecules and oxygen within itself, and excreting excess chemicals while maintaining appropriate temperature, salt, and water balance. These functions are the subjects for this chapter, and although they are discussed as separate systems here, keep in mind that these activities interact simultaneously in a living insect.

NUTRITION

Nearly every conceivable food source is utilized by one or more insect species. Plant-feeding, or phytophagous, insects may eat whole plants or parts: leaves, stems, roots, flowers, fruit, seeds, pollen, nectar, sap, or wood. Carnivorous insects eat animals (whole or in part), blood, fur, or feathers. Saprophagous insects eat decaying vegetable and/or animal material, or dung, and mycetophagous species eat fungi. An insect may be monophagous (restricting its diet to a single source), oligophagous (feeding on relatively few items), or polyphagous (feeding on a wide variety of foods). Some insects do not feed at all as adults, obtaining all their food when immature. The degree of dietary diversity has important consequences for insect ecology (Chapter Nine) and control (Chapter Ten), as we shall see.

Despite the great dietary diversity among insects, there are certain basic necessities for growth, development, and maintenance. Dadd (1973) has reviewed these requirements in detail. All insects need sources of chemical energy, usually carbohydrates (sugars, starches, or cellulose) but sometimes proteins or fats. Proteins also provide amino acids, basic chemicals for structural growth and enzyme synthesis. Insects can synthesize some amino acids, but other *essential* amino acids are required in the diet. For example, Srivastava and Auclair (1974) demonstrated the importance of amino acids in survival and growth of aphids fed sugar solutions (Table 4–1). All insects need sterols, such as cholesterol, for hormone synthesis and normal growth and development (Robbins et al., 1971).

The preceding are macronutrients, required in relatively large amounts. Insects also need micronutrients in rather small quantities. Vitamins, especially several water-soluble B vitamins, are vital for normal metabolism (Gilmour, 1961) and vitamin A is necessary for effective vision in some insects (Brammer and White, 1969; see also Chapter Five). Small amounts of mineral ions, such as calcium, chloride, copper, iron, potassium, sodium, and zinc, are necessary for most insects (Trager, 1953). Water, of course, is required, though the amount may vary; insects inhabiting extremely dry environments, from deserts to flour sacks, may never drink, obtaining all their water from their food.

The amounts and proportions of various food substances can have important consequences beyond the obvious effects of deficiency or surplus (well-fed insects often being larger in size). For instance, egg production in parasitic Hymenoptera and Diptera increases when more flowers are available for increased feeding on nectar (carbohydrate) and pollen (protein) (Leius, 1967). Addition of "royal jelly" to the routine diet of a larval honeybee produces a fertile reproductive queen rather than a sterile worker. Mitsuhashi and Koyama (1974) found that planthoppers developed shortened wings only when folic acid (a B vitamin) concentration was between 0.5 and 0.7 mg./liter of diet; otherwise their wings grew to full length. Interrelation of diet and development is discussed further in Chapter Seven.

OBTAINING NUTRIENTS

Location, recognition, and capture of food involve interactions among several adaptations within the receptor-coordinator-effector systems, discussed in

Table 4–1.   EFFECT OF AMINO ACIDS ON SURVIVAL AND GROWTH OF PEA APHIDS*

Per Cent Amino Acids in Diet	12-Day Weight Gain (Mean)	12-Day Survival Rate (Per Cent)	Days to Adult Stage (Range)
0	0.09 mg.	3	†
1	0.42 mg.	56	12–15
2	0.83 mg.	74	8–10
4	1.19 mg.	62	10

*Modified from Srivastava, P. N., and J. L. Auclair. 1974. Effect of amino acid concentration on diet uptake and performance by the pea aphid, *Acyrthosiphon pisum* (Homoptera:Aphididae). Canad. Entomol. *106*:149–156.
†No adults produced.

more detail in Chapter Five. Briefly, when sensory structures are appropriately stimulated, a feeding response may result. Many insects initiate search for food when stimulated by sensory receptors in the digestive system; i.e., they are hungry. Initial orientation toward food is visual in many predators; dragonflies fly (briefly) toward pebbles or bits of paper tossed in the air, and mantids turn to face any unusual movements. Other insects rely on both visual and chemical stimuli. Winged aphids are attracted to yellow-green color, and once they land on a plant, locate phloem vessels tactilely and chemically by probing with mouthparts. A great many, perhaps most, insects sense food at close range by contact chemoreceptors on tarsi and mouthparts. Cicada killer wasps evidently locate their victims by sound, while ladybird larvae (Coccinellidae) apparently blunder into their aphid prey and only sense food by contact.

Structures other than mouthparts may be adapted for food-getting. Raptorial forelegs of mantids, mantispids, and many Hemiptera are most familiar (Fig. 5–27), while bristly limbs of Odonata make an efficient mosquito-catching basket (Fig. 4–1A). Most wasps possess a sting whose venom subdues reluctant prey: spiders, caterpillars, or other insects. Some insects construct traps for catching prey. In soft sand, antlion larvae dig a conical pit and lie in wait at the base of it for ants or other small insects that may tumble in (Fig. 4–1B). In running water, certain caddis larvae spin a silken web that traps very small crustacea and insects, which the caddis larva eats when periodically checking its net.

STRUCTURE AND FUNCTION OF CHEWING MOUTHPARTS

Many insects, including Odonata, Orthoptera, Neuroptera, Coleoptera, most Hymenoptera, and larval Trichoptera and Lepidoptera, have chewing, or **mandibulate**, mouthparts, formed from greatly modified appendages that collectively form a basketlike container, the preoral cavity or cibarium, for holding, tasting, and chewing food. Technically, the mouthparts are external and the true mouth lies at the base of the preoral cavity. Mandibulate mouthparts take, and chew, discrete bites of living or dead plant or animal material. As an example, we may view mouthparts of a cricket, a polyphagous insect (Fig. 4–2; see also Fig. 2–9).

The **labrum** functions as a hinged upper lip, holding in food and covering the paired **mandibles**, which in turn articulate with the head and function as both jaws and teeth. Cusps on the distal portion of the mandibles often form a cutting edge, while the proximal portion is more of a grinding surface. Mandibles are generally very heavily sclerotized, or hardened. Powerful muscles for opening and closing the mandibles are anchored to internal processes within the head. Mandibular form varies according to diet (Fig. 4–3). Mandibles of predators, such as tiger beetles and dragonflies, have well-developed cutting edges, while those of leaf-feeding insects have more of a grinding edge. In honeybee workers, the mandibles are flattened and are used mostly for packing wax and pollen.

Behind the mandibles lies a pair of **maxillae,** segmented structures forming the sides of the preoral cavity. They manipulate and taste food, keeping it pressed against the mandibular cutting edges. Maxillae may also bear a cutting edge on the **lacinia** and (usually) bear **palpi**, fingerlike projections having many chemical and tactile receptors. Maxillae are often used to clean antennae and legs.

Beneath the maxillae is the **labium**, or lower lip, forming the base of the

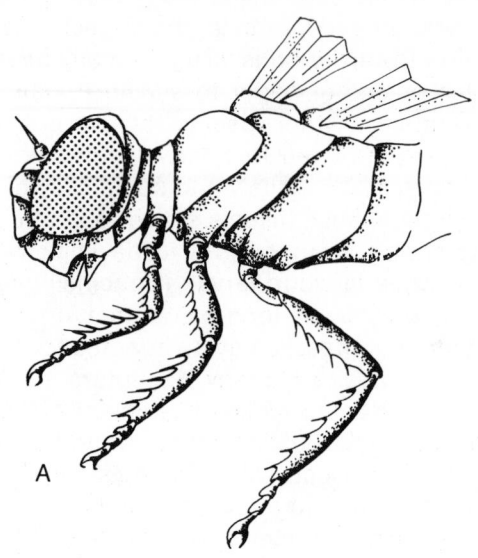

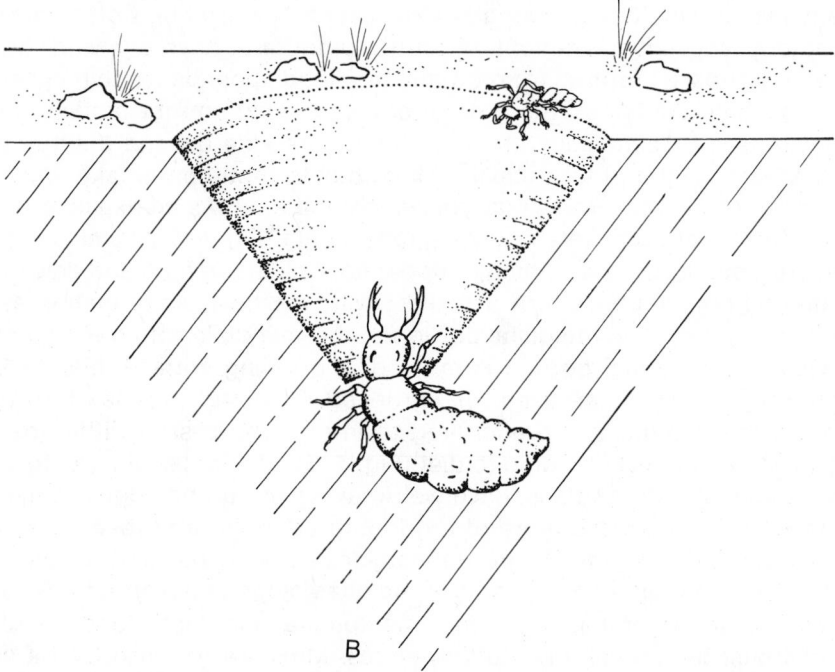

Figure 4–1. Adaptations for procuring food. *A*, Dragonfly legs, showing spines. *B*, Antlion larva in pit.

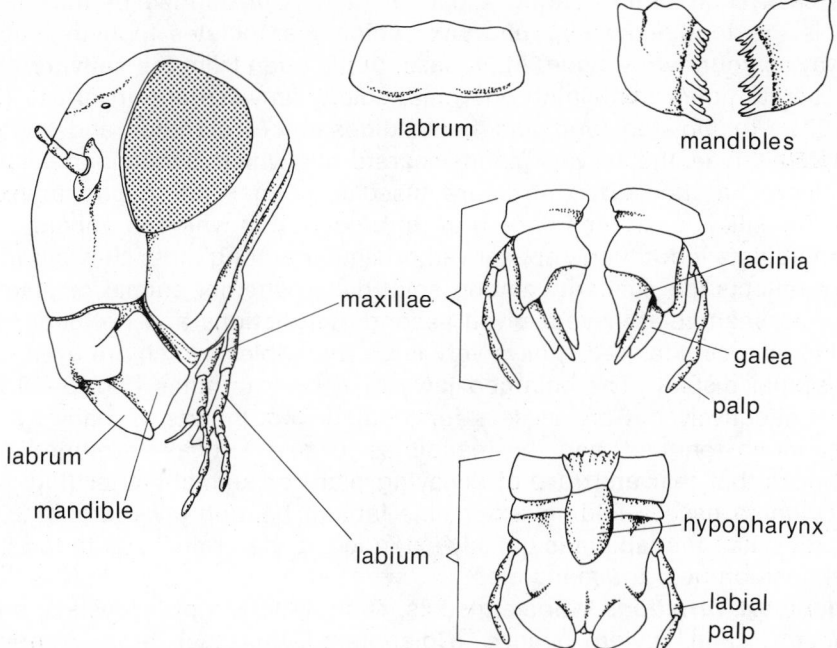

Figure 4-2. Mandibulate mouthparts of grasshopper, together (side view) and separated (front view).

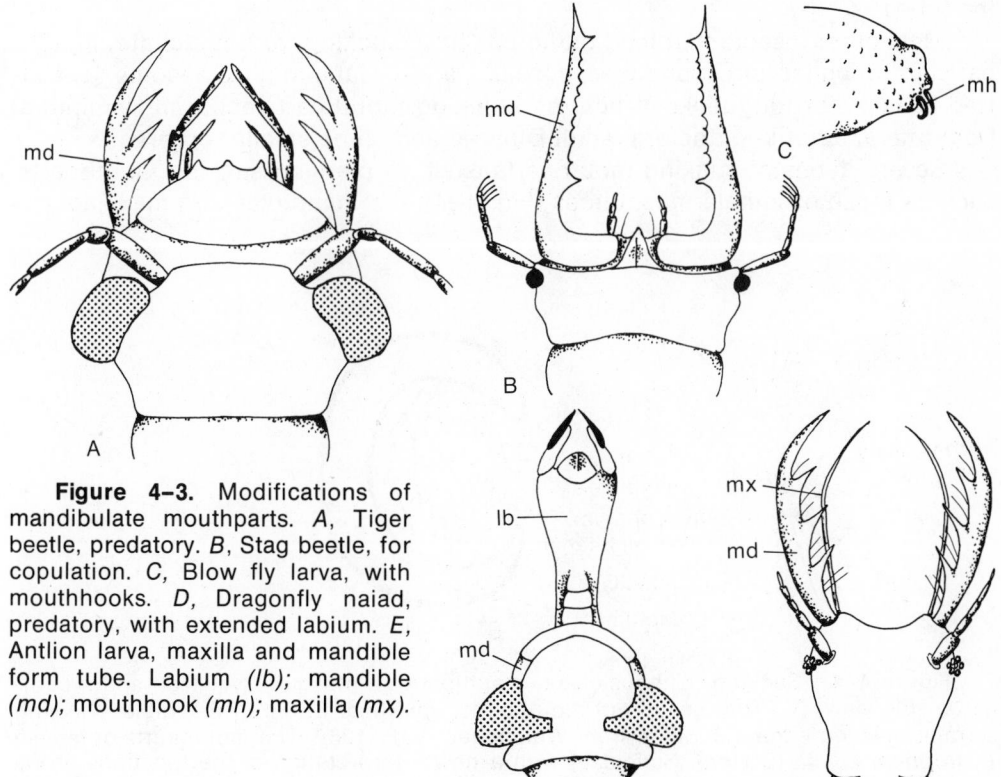

Figure 4-3. Modifications of mandibulate mouthparts. *A,* Tiger beetle, predatory. *B,* Stag beetle, for copulation. *C,* Blow fly larva, with mouthhooks. *D,* Dragonfly naiad, predatory, with extended labium. *E,* Antlion larva, maxilla and mandible form tube. Labium *(lb);* mandible *(md);* mouthhook *(mh);* maxilla *(mx).*

preoral cavity and often bearing a pair of palpi. Surrounded by maxillae and labium is the tonguelike **hypopharynx**, which manipulates food in much the same way as your own tongue. At its base, ducts open from the **salivary glands,** which secrete liquid containing enzymes, chiefly amylase and invertase (Chapman, 1971), to moisten food and begin digestion of starches and sugars. In Lepidoptera larvae, the salivary glands secrete silk, which is then manipulated by the spinneret, a specialized structure fused from maxillae, hypopharynx, and labium. The silk is used for webbing or for a cocoon in which to pupate.

Mandibulate mouthparts appear rather similar among most chewing insects, and this reflects the similarity among solid diets, whether animal or plant. In a few insects, mandibles have evolved secondary functions and no longer chew. Male stag beetles (Fig. 4–3B) have very large mandibles, which are used as part of the sexual display. The enlarged jaws of soldier termites (Fig. 6–18B) bite intruders effectively but are useless for feeding. Mouthparts of many fly larvae are very much reduced, and the mandibles form a vertically arranged pair of mouthhooks that tear and rasp at decaying plant or animal matter (Fig. 4–3C). Naiad Odonata have a folding, extensible labium bearing jaws (Fig. 4–3D) that grasp prey when the labium is quickly extended. It then returns, with food, to its original position near the mandibles.

Mouthpart Variations.   Some insects, such as larvae of lacewings, antlions (Neuroptera), and diving beetles (Coleoptera:Dytiscidae) have mandibulate mouthparts but effectively feed on liquid diets. In these insects, mandible and maxillae fit together to form a tube (Fig. 4–3E). When they bite a smaller insect (occasionally, a dytiscid will take on a fish or tadpole), they inject powerful salivary enzymes that digest the victim's innards, which are then sucked through the tubes.

Most other insects that feed on liquids have sucking, or **haustellate,** mouthparts, in which labrum, mandibles, maxillae, and/or labium have become specialized beaklike or tonguelike structures. Sucking mouthparts occur in Hemiptera, Homoptera, adult Lepidoptera, adult Diptera, and some smaller orders.

Several types of sucking mouthparts exist. In piercing-sucking mouthparts, such as those of female mosquitoes (Fig. 4–4), the mandibles and maxillae (ex-

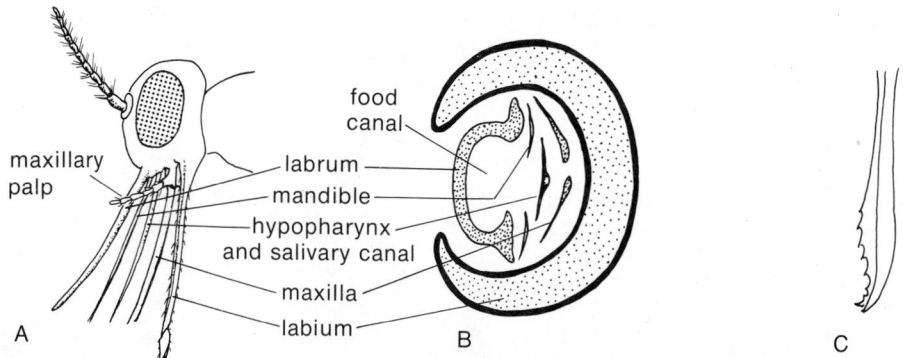

Figure 4–4. Sucking, or haustellate, mouthparts of mosquito. *A*, Head and mouthparts, side view. *B*, Cross section of mouthparts, enlarged. *C*, Tip of mandible, showing serrated rasping edge. (Modified from Waldbauer, G. P. 1962. The mouthparts of female *Psorophora ciliata* (Diptera, Culicidae) with a new interpretation of the functions of the labral muscles. J. Morphol. *111*:201–215.)

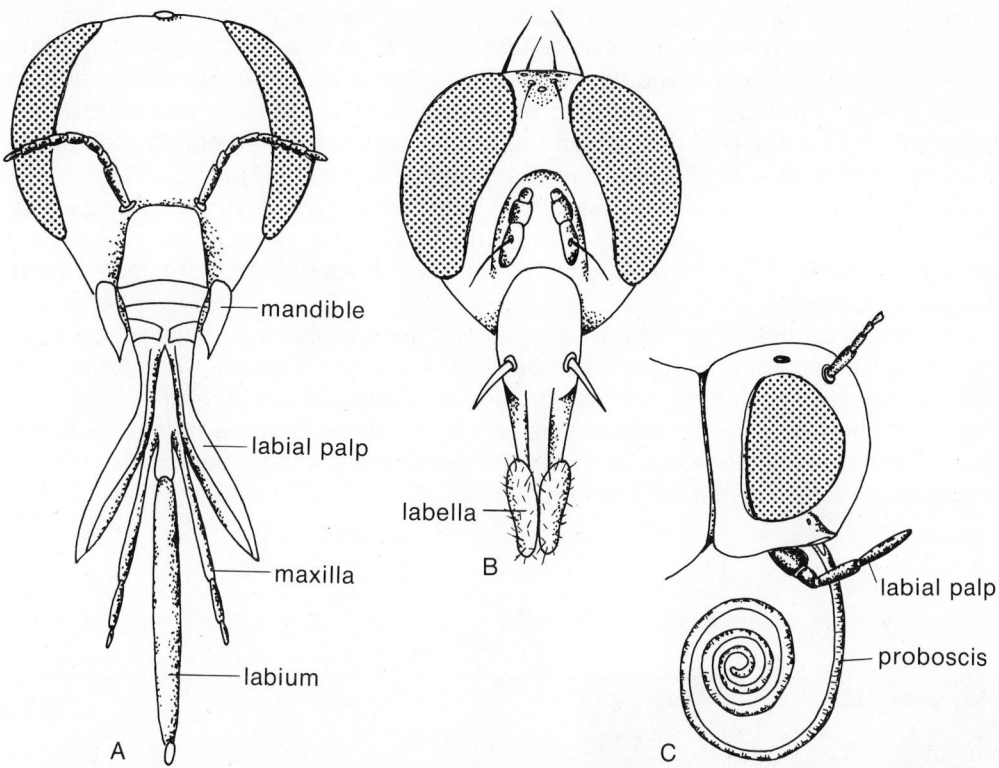

Figure 4–5. Modifications of haustellate mouthparts. *A,* Honey bee. *B,* House fly. *C,* Moth. (Modified from Snodgrass, R. E. 1935. Principles of Insect Morphology. Copyright © 1935 by McGraw-Hill, Inc. Used by permission of McGraw-Hill Book Co.)

cept the palpi) form sharp stylets that rasp up and down, rather like tiny chisels, to cut a hole in which the hypopharynx and labrum are also inserted. The hypopharynx contains a tube through which is injected saliva containing anticoagulant (to keep the blood flowing) and anaesthetic (to keep the victim unaware of the bite). With the saliva may also be introduced causative pathogens of disease (Chapter Eleven). The labrum likewise forms a tube through which blood is sucked. The labium forms a sheath, a "tool box," for the mouthparts when not in use. In mosquitoes, maxillary palpi retain their ancestral sensory function (Waldbauer, 1962).

Piercing-sucking mouthparts occur in many biting flies and in nearly all Hemiptera and Homoptera, though there is some variety in structures involved with piercing, salivation, and feeding. Figure 4–5 illustrates additional modifications for liquid diets. The honey bee has lapping mouthparts, formed from maxillae and labium, that enable it to reach into flowers to obtain nectar. It also has recognizable mandibles for chewing pollen and for comb construction and cleaning around the hive (Chapter Six). The house fly and many other "higher" Diptera have sponging-lapping mouthparts. At their tip is a fleshy **labella** bearing many tiny holes, entrances to tubules that lead to a central food channel. These flies lap or sponge liquids and often spit enzyme-containing saliva onto solid foods such as sugar or bread crumbs to liquefy them. In almost all adult Lepidoptera, mandibles are completely lacking, and the galeae (parts of the maxillae) are "zippered" together forming a proboscis, or "tongue," which is coiled at rest and which uncoils to form a tube for sucking liquids—nectar, water, fruit juices, plant exudates, and, occasionally in some Malaysian moths, blood. Electron microscopy and field observations have revealed that *Heliconius* butterflies feed also on pollen, which they manipulate with their coiled proboscis, causing release of amino acids from the pollen (Gilbert, 1972) (Fig. 4–6).

Finally, some insects (mayflies, most caddisflies, and many moths) do not feed at all as adults and bear only nonfunctional vestiges of mouthparts. Such insects rely totally on food stored when immature and, as one might expect, do not live long as adults.

Specialized mouthparts reflect specialized diets, which may have particularly important ecological and economic consequences. For instance, winged insects which feed discontinuously on nectar, pollen, blood, or sap are also dispersal agents for pollen and microorganisms and in doing so become intimately coinvolved with plant ecology and evolution (Chapter Nine) and transmission of plant and animal disease (Chapter Eleven).

Figure 4–6. Scanning electron micrograph of proboscis of *Heliconius,* with pollen grains attached. (From Gilbert, 1972.)

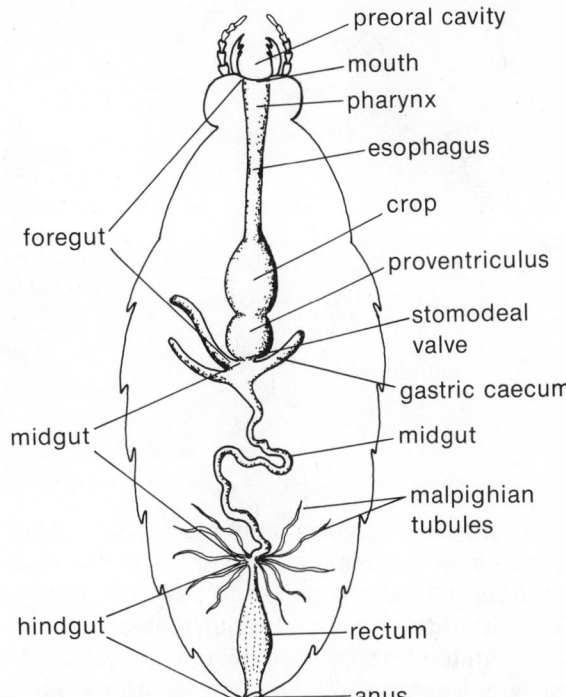

Figure 4-7. Digestive system of cockroach (dorsal view).

Labels on figure: preoral cavity, mouth, pharynx, esophagus, crop, proventriculus, stomodeal valve, gastric caecum, midgut, malpighian tubules, rectum, anus, foregut, midgut, hindgut

INTERNAL DIGESTION

After food enters the insect, it must be further broken down physically and chemically before it can be utilized by individual cells. Digestion is accomplished by the alimentary system, a compartmentalized tube that (usually) runs from mouth to anus. The great diversity in insect diets and mouthparts is reflected in diversity among digestive systems. Figure 4-7 illustrates diagrammatically the digestive system of a cockroach as an example of an insect with chewing mouthparts and a varied diet. In all insects three distinct regions can be recognized: foregut (stomodaeum), midgut (mesenteron), and hindgut (proctodeum). In general, insects that feed on relatively indigestible materials (such as leaves or wood) have relatively longer digestive tracts for longer, slower digestion.

In many insects, digestion begins in the oral cavity as salivary enzymes begin to break down sugars and starches. In this sense, liquid food is already partly digested. Food that passes through the mouth enters the **foregut**, which is lined with cuticle continuous with the exoskeleton. The region of the foregut immediately adjoining the mouth is the **pharynx**. In sucking insects, powerful pumping muscles (Fig. 4-8) aid in sucking liquids through the cibarium and pharynx. Food is moved through the foregut, and through the entire tract, by peristalsis, wavelike contraction of muscles. In cockroaches and some other insects, the foregut enlarges posteriorly to form a **crop**, a storage sac, leading to the **proventriculus**, or "gizzard," a muscular chamber bearing sclerotized protrusions, or "teeth," that aid in further grinding food. Snodgrass (1935) suggested that, functionally, the proventriculus is part of the mouth, continuing the grinding process that began with the mandibles. Proventricular "teeth" are often very character-

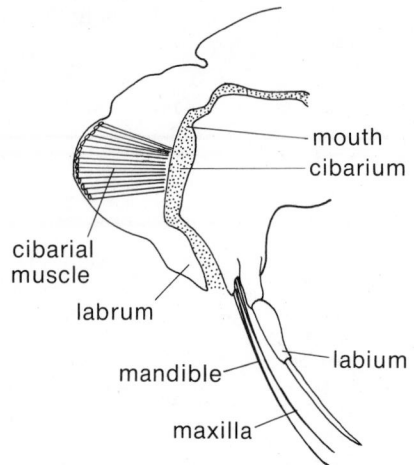

mouth
cibarium

cibarial
muscle

labrum

mandible

maxilla

labium

Figure 4–8. Diagrammatic cross section of cicada head, showing cibarial muscle. (Modified from Snodgrass, R. E. 1944. The feeding apparatus of biting and sucking insects affecting men and animals. Smithsonian Institution Miscellaneous Collections *104*:1–113. Used by permission of the Smithsonian Institution, Washington, D.C.)

istic within a species and have been used as characters to differentiate ant species in systematic studies. Proventricular spines in honey bees act as a strainer, permitting pollen to pass through while retaining nectar, which is then converted to honey and regurgitated.

Limited enzymatic digestion may occur in the foregut by means of midgut enzymes passed forward through the **stomodeal valve**, a sphincter muscle that regulates passage of food from the proventriculus to the midgut. At the juncture of foregut and midgut are (often) several sacs, **gastric caeca.** Their function is uncertain, though perhaps they hold food away from the mainstream of peristalsis for a time, allowing additional, slower digestion.

In the midgut there is no cuticular lining, though food particles are often surrounded with a **peritrophic membrane**, a thin chitinous layer apparently secreted by epithelial cells around the foregut-midgut connection. In chewing insects, this is thought to protect the delicate epithelial lining of the midgut from damaging abrasion, though some liquid-feeding insects, such as mosquitoes, have a peritrophic membrane too. It is in the midgut that most enzymatic digestion and absorption of nutrients into the blood takes place. Investigators have identified a number of enzymes in the midgut by exposing food substances to midgut contents removed from hundreds of insects (Table 4–2). These enzymes are generally correlated with diet; that is, predators have proteinases (enzymes that digest proteins) in abundance, while insects that eat starch have mostly carbohydrases. Midgut enzymes are apparently secreted by epithelial cells, a single layer of which lines the midgut. These cells also have fingerlike projections, brush borders, that increase the surface area of the midgut for absorption (Fig. 4–9). Amino acids, simple sugars, and lipids probably move through the midgut epithelium by simple diffusion, from the area of greater to lesser concentration. Mineral salts, especially sodium and potassium, are probably actively transported or ''pumped'' across the epithelium.

From the midgut, indigestible food material and water, together with excretory products from malpighian tubules, enter the **hindgut**, which, like the foregut, is lined with cuticle. Here, water and salts are absorbed through the epithelial lining (see the sections ''Excretions'' and ''Water Balance,''), and in most insects, very dry fecal pellets are formed here and eliminated through the anus with the aid of powerful rectal muscles.

In all insects we find microorganisms within the digestive tract. These assume special importance in insects that feed on wood and wood products, such as wood-borers and termites. In termites, flagellate protozoa are found in sacs in the hindgut, where they produce enzymes that digest cellulose to simple sugars, enabling termites to subsist on a diet of wood. Since the hindgut lining is shed along with the cuticle at molting time, termites would rapidly lose their ability to digest cellulose, and consequently die, were it not for their habit of eating one another's cast skins and fecal pellets. Wood-boring beetles have cellulose-digesting bacteria or fungi. Some bloodsucking bugs possess alimentary bacteria that synthesize vital B vitamins that these insects do not normally receive in their diet (Wigglesworth, 1972). The digestive system is the first point of entry for a number of bacterial and viral diseases of insects.

Many insects' digestive systems differ considerably from this pattern, and Figure 4–9 illustrates some of these modifications. A female mosquito has a foregut sac, or **diverticulum**, that fills only when she feeds on nectar or water; when she drinks blood, it moves directly into the midgut. Eisner et al. (1974) reported that a sawfly has foregut diverticula in which it stores gummy pine resins until attacked by a predator, whereupon it spits the resin onto its tormentor. Aphids and plant-feeding Hemiptera feed on very watery plant fluids and have a midgut bypass by which excess liquid can pass directly to the hindgut (Goodchild, 1966). In larval honey bees, and many other Hymenoptera, the midgut does not connect with the hindgut at all until maturity; fecal matter collects at the blind end of the midgut throughout larval life, and a single fecal pellet is deposited immediately before pupation. This is only possible because the bees' food, honey and "beebread," is almost completely digestible, contributing immeasurably to overall cleanliness in a beehive.

CONTROL OF FEEDING AND DIGESTION

Control of insect feeding and digestion is not yet well understood. Insects seek food and commence feeding in response to both internal and external stim-

Table 4–2. MIDGUT ENZYMES OF INSECTS*

Insect	Diet	Protease[†] (Digests Proteins)	Lipase (Digests Fats)	Amylase (Digests Starches)	Invertase (Digests Sugars)
Cockroach	omnivorous	XX	XX	XX	XX
Lepidoptera					
larva	phytophagous	XX	XX	XX	XX
adult	nectar	O	O	O	XX
Blowfly					
larva	meat	XX	XX	O	O
adult	sugars	X	O	XX	XX
Tsetse fly	blood	XX	?	X	O

*From Wigglesworth, V. B. 1972. The Principles of Insect Physiology. 7th ed. Chapman & Hall Ltd., London.

[†]XX = strong enzyme; X = weak enzyme; O = no enzyme.

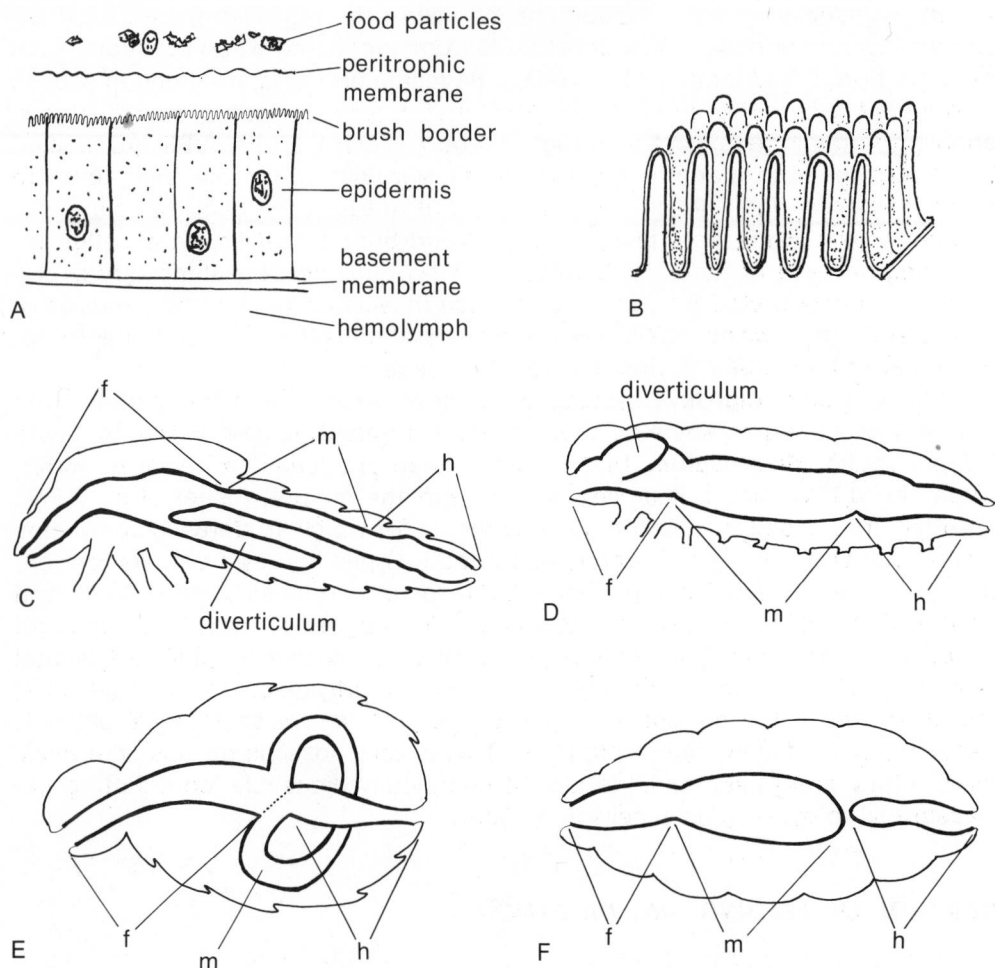

Figure 4–9. Diagrammatic representation of insect digestive systems. *A,* Midgut lining. *B,* Close-up of single cell brush border. *C,* Mosquito digestive system, foregut diverticulum for fluid storage. *D,* Sawfly larva, diverticulum for resin storage. (Modified from Eisner, T., J. S. Johnessee, J. Carrel, L. B. Hendry, and J. Meinwald. 1974. Defensive use by an insect of a plant resin. Science *184*:996–999. Copyright 1974 by the American Association for the Advancement of Science.) *E,* Aphid, with bypass filter for liquids. *F,* Honey bee larva, midgut not connected to hindgut. Foregut *(F)*; midgut *(M)*; hindgut *(H).*

uli. Stretch and chemical receptors within the gut detect lack of food, and a hungry insect thus conditioned seeks food by visual, tactile, or chemical means, as mentioned previously. Once food is located and "recognized," locomotion is inhibited (Thorsteinson, 1960), and the insect eats as long as chemical receptors on mouthparts and tarsi "taste" certain chemicals, **phagostimulants**, or until receptors in the gut detect enough stretching to inhibit feeding (Dadd, 1963). A number of chemicals are phagostimulants; for example, sugar stimulates blow flies to feed (Dethier, 1963) and amino acids in plant sap stimulate some aphids to feed (Srivastava and Auclair, 1974). Sinigrin, an alkaloid in cruciferous plants (cabbages, mustards, and relatives), is a phagostimulant for the cabbage aphid; these aphids feed on any leaves if sinigrin is added (Fig. 4–10). An insect may

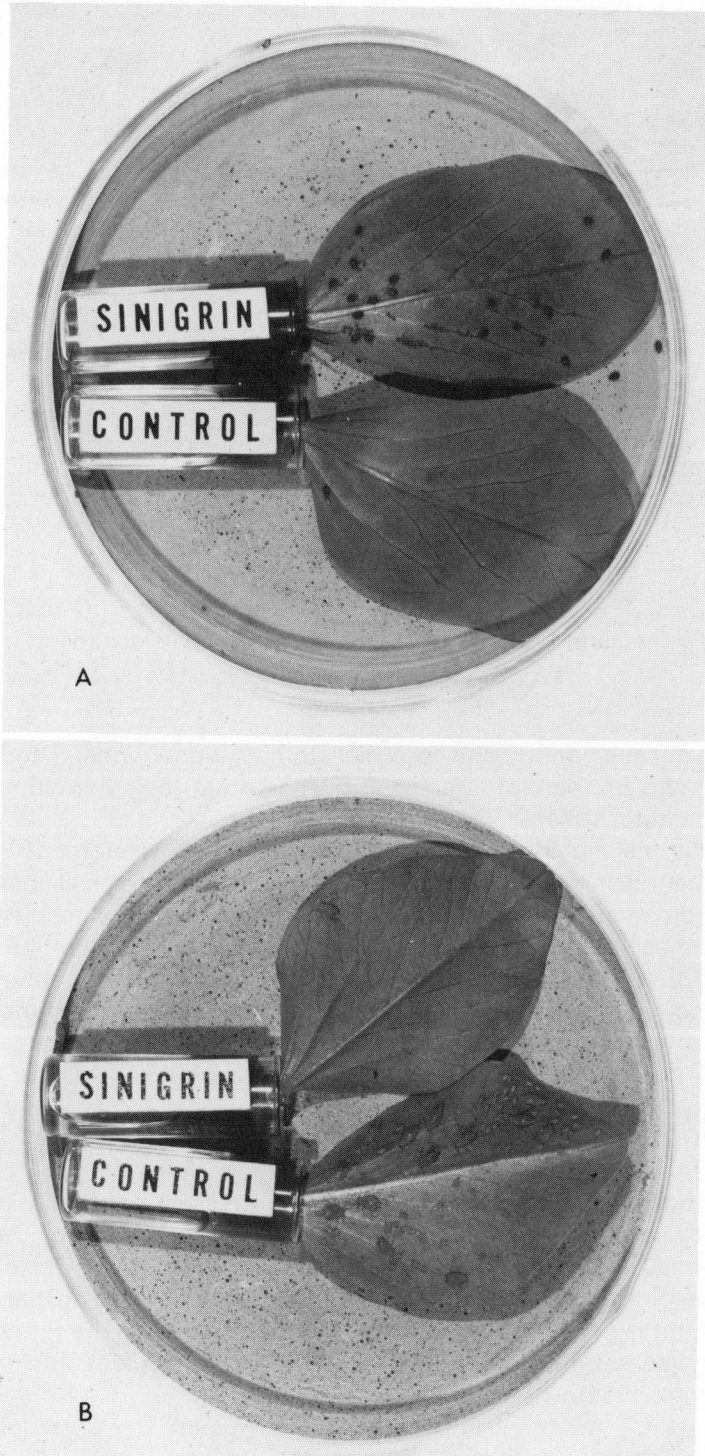

Figure 4–10. Sinigrin as a phagostimulant on broadbean leaves. *A,* Cabbage aphids feed only on sinigrin-treated leaves. *B,* Pea aphids feed on untreated leaves and avoid sinigrin. (Photo by G. Berkey, courtesy of L. R. Nault and Ohio Agricultural Research and Development Center.)

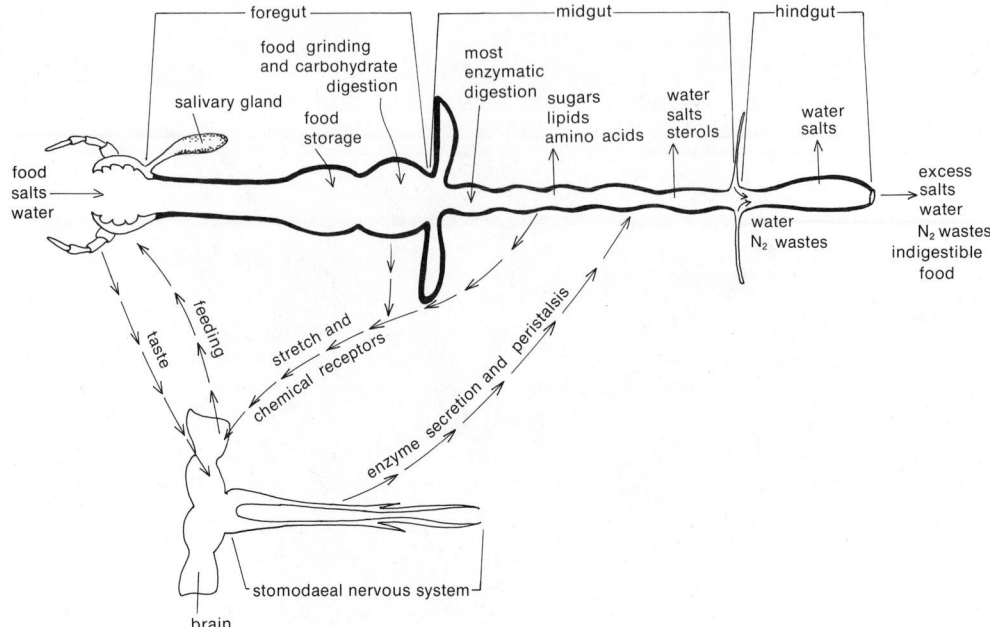

Figure 4–11. Summary of digestion and its control.

become chemically conditioned to a diet; tomato hornworms, if fed a synthetic diet in early instars, cannot later be induced to eat their normal food, tomato leaves (Yamamoto, 1974).

Internally, the digestive system is innervated by the stomodeal or visceral nervous system (Chapter 5) and contains stretch and chemical receptors. Sensory input from mouthparts and the foregut apparently stimulates nerve impulses and hormone secretion, in turn controlling peristalsis and secretion of enzymes (Bignell, 1973). Hormone concentrations may also determine whether an insect is hungry or not (Chapter Seven). Figure 4–11 summarizes the functioning and control of an insect digestive tract.

THE FAT BODY

The **fat body** is a vaguely defined mass (or masses) not found in all insects. The fat body is a chemical storage reservoir for food (Dadd, 1963), and in honeybee larvae and some cockroaches, for uric acid wastes. Up to 33 per cent of the dry weight of a mature honeybee larva may be fat body (Chapman, 1971). In fireflies, light is produced in the fat body (Chapter Five). The fat body of many insects contains enzymes that detoxify synthetic insecticides and natural plant poisons (Smith, 1955).

CIRCULATION

Materials absorbed through the gut wall pass directly into the insect's blood, or **hemolymph**, which circulates within the body cavity, or **hemocoel.** Unlike humans, insects have an open circulatory system, with no blood vessels save the dorsal vessel or heart, a pulsating tube that keeps the hemolymph in motion. Hemolymph has several vital functions performed by both its liquid portion and its blood cells, **hemocytes.**

COMPOSITION AND FUNCTION OF HEMOLYMPH

Entomologists have withdrawn hemolymph from many insect species, and after it is spun at high speed in a centrifuge, it is free of cells and can be analyzed chemically. Water is, of course, dominant; up to 92 per cent of hemolymph is water (Buck, 1953; Chapman, 1971), making hemolymph the major storage reservoir for fluid in most insects. In addition to thus providing an aqueous medium for cellular respiration, this liquid is an important hydraulic substance; for example, it is forced into insect wings as they expand after molting. Liquids are relatively incompressible, so that if an insect exerts internal pressure on hemolymph in one place, a bulge is likely to appear elsewhere. This is important in larval locomotion (Chapter Five, Fig. 5–24) and in shedding of old cuticle when molting (Chapter Seven).

Besides water, hemolymph contains various chemical substances absorbed from the midgut: carbohydrates, amino acids, lipids, salts, vitamins. Some of these are converted to new chemical arrangements in hemolymph. Most insect blood sugar is α-trehalose, a unique disaccharide found in few other organisms. The concentration of free amino acids is remarkably high (Table 4–3), and some of these are probably synthesized internally by the insect. Some are combined to form proteins, lipoproteins (protein and lipid), and glycoproteins (protein and sugars). In addition, hemolymph contains hormones (Chapter Seven), enzymes, and pigments. Insectoverdin is a common pigment that imparts a green color to the blood of many insects (Nickerson, 1956); other insects absorb pigments from

Table 4–3. CHEMICAL COMPOSITION OF INSECT HEMOLYMPH AND HUMAN BLOOD*

Chemical	Average Concentration in mg./100 ml.	
	HEMOLYMPH	BLOOD
Protein	4375–5625	6500–8200
Amino acids	200–300	5–8
Urea	1–10	10–15
Uric acid	12–24	2–3.5
Glycogen	24	5.5
Trehalose	700–800	—
Lipids	398	652
Sodium	20–300	330
Potassium	20–180	178
Calcium	35–150	9–11.5
Magnesium	10–25	1–3
Phosphorus	64–245	34.9
Chloride	50–100	450–500

*From Patton, R. L. 1963. Introductory Insect Physiology. W. B. Saunders Co., Philadelphia.

their food (Chapter Five). A very few insects have red hemoglobin, an oxygen-carrying pigment (discussed subsequently). In all insects, hemolymph carries wastes of cellular metabolism: carbon dioxide and nitrogenous waste, usually as uric acid, though occasionally as ammonia or allantoin. Chemical composition of hemolymph varies according to diet and the physiological and developmental state of the insect (e.g., whether the insect has recently eaten or is about to molt).

Two major functions of hemolymph are transport and storage. Up to half the body weight of a caterpillar may be stored food (Wigglesworth, 1964). Hemolymph takes nutritive materials, hormones, and other substances to cells, carries away wastes, and bathes tissues in a fluid of optimal chemical consistency for normal metabolic processes. Except for rare instances, however, insect blood does *not* carry oxygen, that being the function of the tracheal system, as will be discussed.

The liquid portion of hemolymph may also have a defensive function. Blister beetles (Meloidae) have a strong irritant, **cantharidin,** in their hemolymph, which they expel through their leg joints when attacked. Some insect blood also carries antibodies that are at least partly effective against bacterial invasion (Hink and Briggs, 1968), though antibody reactions among insects are not as effective as those of most vertebrates. Tissue rejection, reaction to implanted tissues of another insect of the same species, is not known in insects (Miller, 1973). This facilitates experiments involving transplantation of tissues and organs from one insect to another (Chapter Seven).

Several blood cell types have been recognized in insects (Jones, 1964; Gupta, 1969) (Fig. 4–12). These cells differ somewhat in form and in reaction to

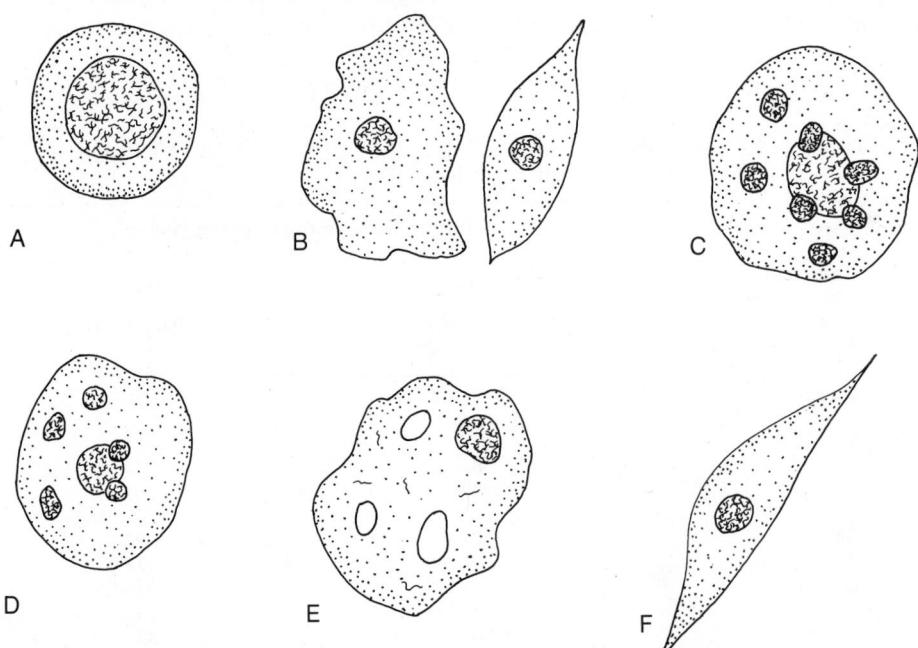

Figure 4–12. Representative insect blood cells. *A,* Prohemocyte. *B,* Plasmatocyte. *C,* Spherule cell. *D,* Granular hemocyte. *E,* Oenocyte. *F,* Vermiform cell.

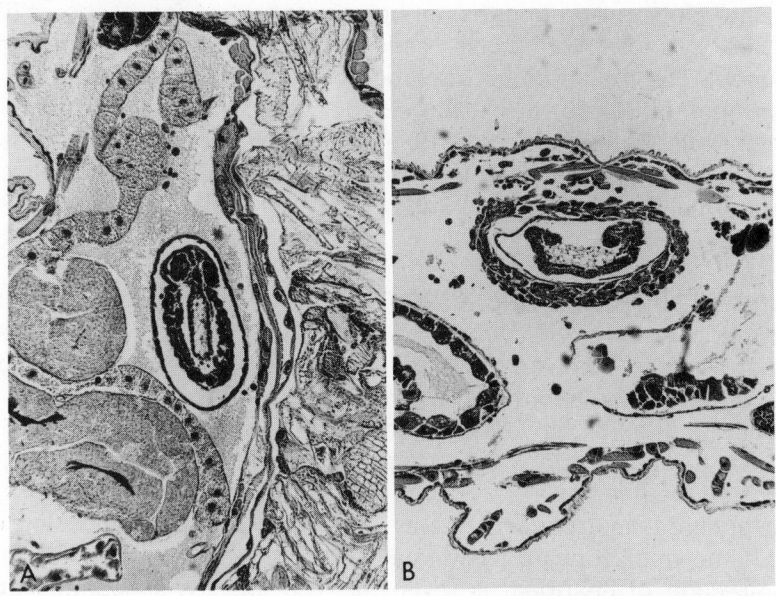

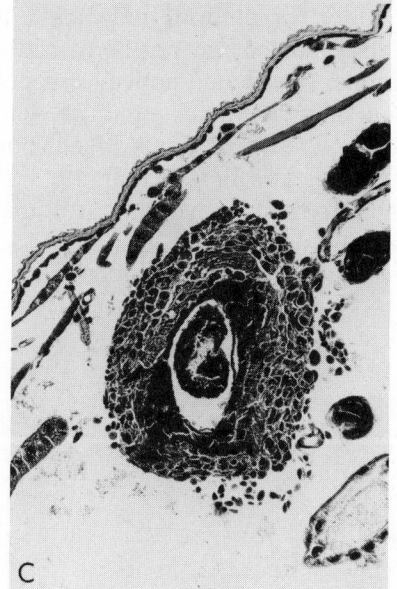

Figure 4–13. Encapsulation of eggs of parasitoid *Bathyplectes curculionis* by hemocytes of alfalfa weevil larva. *A,* Unencapsulated egg, newly laid. *B,* Encapsulation in progress. *C,* Completely encapsulated egg. (*A, B,* and *C* from Gibson, W. P., and R. C. Berberet. 1974. Histological studies on encapsulation of *Bathyplectes curculionis* eggs by larvae of the alfalfa weevil. Ann. Entomol. Soc. Amer. *67:*588–590.)

chemical stains; they are probably all derived from prohemocytes or plasmatocytes, and many undergo active cell division (Arnold and Sohi, 1974). Specific functions are unknown for some cell types, but plasmatocytes and granular hemocytes engulf and destroy foreign particles, bacteria, and cell fragments. Blood cells may encapsulate foreign objects too large to be engulfed. Physical and chemical properties of eggs of parasitic wasps or nematode worms induce hemocytes to surround the invader and cut off its oxygen supply (Salt, 1965) (Fig. 4–13). Hemocytes of alfalfa weevil larvae sometimes encapsulate enough eggs of the parasitoid *Bathyplectes curculionis* to hinder the success of the parasitoid as an agent of biological control (Puttler, 1967). Other hemocytes coalesce into clots, preventing loss of hemolymph when injury occurs (Grégoire, 1964). Hemocytes form connective tissue both around wounds and elsewhere in the hemocoel. The total number of blood cells varies; Tauber and Yeager (1936) found averages of 30,000 to 50,000 cells per cubic millimeter in hemolymph of immature insects. Patton and Flint (1959) found that in cockroaches, this number dropped precipitously (to 10,000/mm.[3]) directly before a molt. Cell count returned to normal shortly after molting.

PULSATING STRUCTURES AND CIRCULATION

Though insects have an open circulatory system, hemolymph does not merely slosh about the hemocoel; it circulates in more or less defined patterns and is kept in motion by movements and by the pumping of the dorsal vessel, or heart. This is a tube, ringed with muscle, lying dorsally immediately beneath the tergum. When the heart relaxes, hemolymph is drawn inward through 3 (in flies) to 12 (in cockroaches) pairs of valves, the ostia. Then the muscles contract, pumping hemolymph forward by peristalsis into the thorax and head. (Occasionally the direction of heartbeat is reversed.) The heart is suspended by several pairs of alary (or aliform) muscles (Fig. 4–14), whose function is otherwise unclear; they may or may not be partially responsible for heartbeat (Miller, 1973).

Heartbeat varies with activity, temperature, and physiological state. Housefly hearts beat 60 to 400 times a minute, while cockroach hearts beat 60 to 200 times a minute (Fig. 4–15). In some insect pupae, heartbeat may cease altogether for several minutes at a time (Miller, 1973). It is not clear precisely how heartbeat is controlled; the beat is myogenic (originating within the heart muscle), and an insect heart often will continue to beat for a while after being removed intact from its owner if it is kept in an appropriate solution. Nerves of the visceral nervous

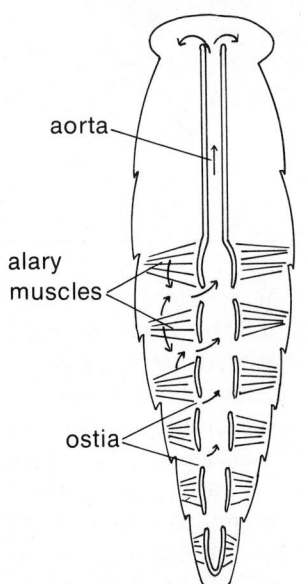

aorta

alary muscles

ostia

Figure 4–14. Cockroach heart (dorsal view). Arrows indicate direction of normal hemolymph circulation.

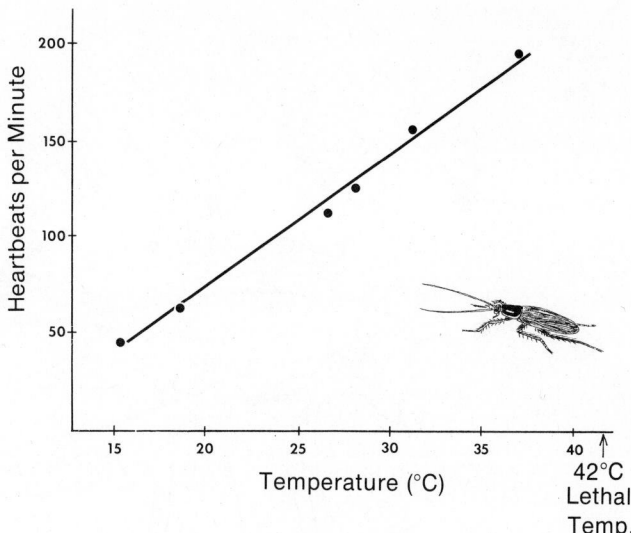

Figure 4–15. Relationship between heart rate and temperature in American cockroach. (Data of D. J. Horn and C. G. Summers.)

system connect with the heart and may regulate the beat, as may hormones secreted by corpora allata (Novák, 1966).

Besides the heart, many insects have small accessory pulsating organs at bases of wings, legs, and antennae (Fig. 4–16). Directional flow of hemolymph is further aided by diaphragms and septa (connective tissue layers), solid or fenestrated (Fig. 4–17). Thus blood flows down one side of an insect's leg and back the other. A dorsal diaphragm partially separates the area surrounding the heart (the pericardial cavity) from the rest of the hemocoel. A ventral diaphragm may also be present in insects having abdominal nerve ganglia. Movement of diaphragms is thought to speed circulation.

Overall, the open circulatory system is rather inefficient. By injecting dye into a cockroach, you will find that it takes up to five minutes for dye to permeate the entire insect, whereas a single human blood cell can make the trip from heart to toe and return in less than a minute. There is less necessity for speed in insects because, with rare exceptions, they do not depend on hemolymph for oxygen transport.

Figure 4–16. Accessory pulsatile organ in dragonfly metathorax, sagittal section. (Redrawn from Whedon, A. D. 1938. The aortic diverticula of the Odonata. J. Morphol. *63*:229–261.)

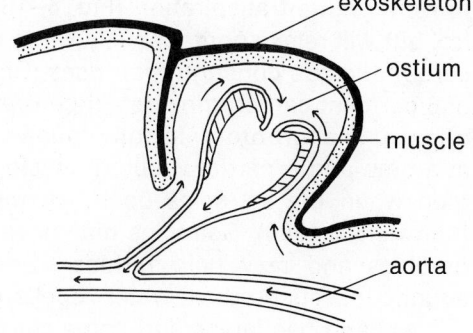

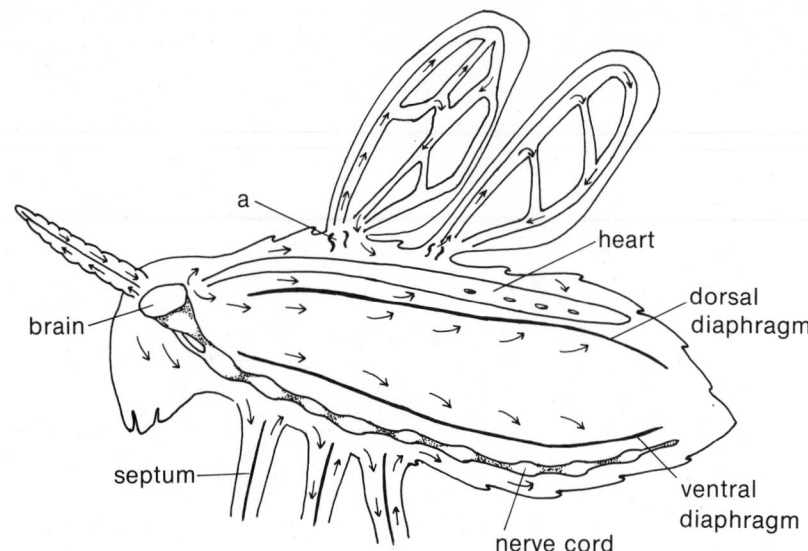

Figure 4–17. Sagittal section of insect showing hemolymph circulation and function of heart, diaphragms, and septa. Accessory pulsatile organ *(a)*.

GAS EXCHANGE

Cellular respiration in insects depends on an adequate oxygen supply, which must be obtained from the insect's surroundings. Respiration also produces carbon dioxide as a waste product, which must be eliminated. Oxygen diffuses through a membrane only if it is moist, presenting a problem for terrestrial insects (and all other air-breathing organisms) in that adaptations for assimilating oxygen expose tissues to water loss. Very small organisms, including insects, have not much water to begin with, and a little water loss to air (transpiration) can be fatal.

SPIRACLES AND TRACHEAE

Air is inhaled through ten (or fewer) pairs of spiracles, small portholes on the sides of the thorax (two pairs) and abdomen (up to eight pairs). Most spiracles have a valve operated by muscles that close the spiracle when necessary to prevent undue transpiration (Fig. 4–18). These muscles are under nervous control but will relax spontaneously when their oxygen content lowers sufficiently or carbon dioxide concentration rises (Chapman, 1971). If an insect is placed in air of 5 per cent carbon dioxide concentration, spiracles remain open and the insect dries up in short order. In some pupae, spiracles remain closed for several hours at a time and a partial vacuum develops within the insect as oxygen is utilized; then when the spiracles open, air moves in and relatively little water is lost (Kanwisher, 1966). Spiracles may have comblike filters that apparently keep out particles and may help reduce transpiration. Tiny glands near spiracles of aquatic insects produce water-repellent chemicals that keep the opening dry.

Ant and bee larvae and some springtails live in moist environments and obtain oxygen and lose carbon dioxide directly through the integument. Most insects, however, possess a system of air tubes, **tracheae**, that open at the spiracles and branch throughout the insect interior. The tracheae originate as invaginations of the epidermis and ramify into continually finer branches, ending in tiny tracheoles from 0.2 to 1μ in diameter (approximately 1/1000th the diameter of a human hair) (Fig. 4–18). The tracheal system brings oxygen-containing air directly to cells and at the same time removes carbon dioxide. Some carbon dioxide is also given off from the body surface because it diffuses through hemolymph 35 times more readily than does oxygen.

Tracheae are lined with cuticle, which is shed when molting occurs, and this cuticle is reinforced with stiffening rings, the **taenidia** (Fig. 4–18). These permit tracheae to stretch while preventing their collapse, rather like the stiffening wire spiral on a vacuum cleaner hose. Tracheoles are similar though smaller; they have tiny taenidia (Whitten, 1972) and their cuticle is not shed with that of the tracheae at molting. Tracheoles are usually generated from a tracheal end cell

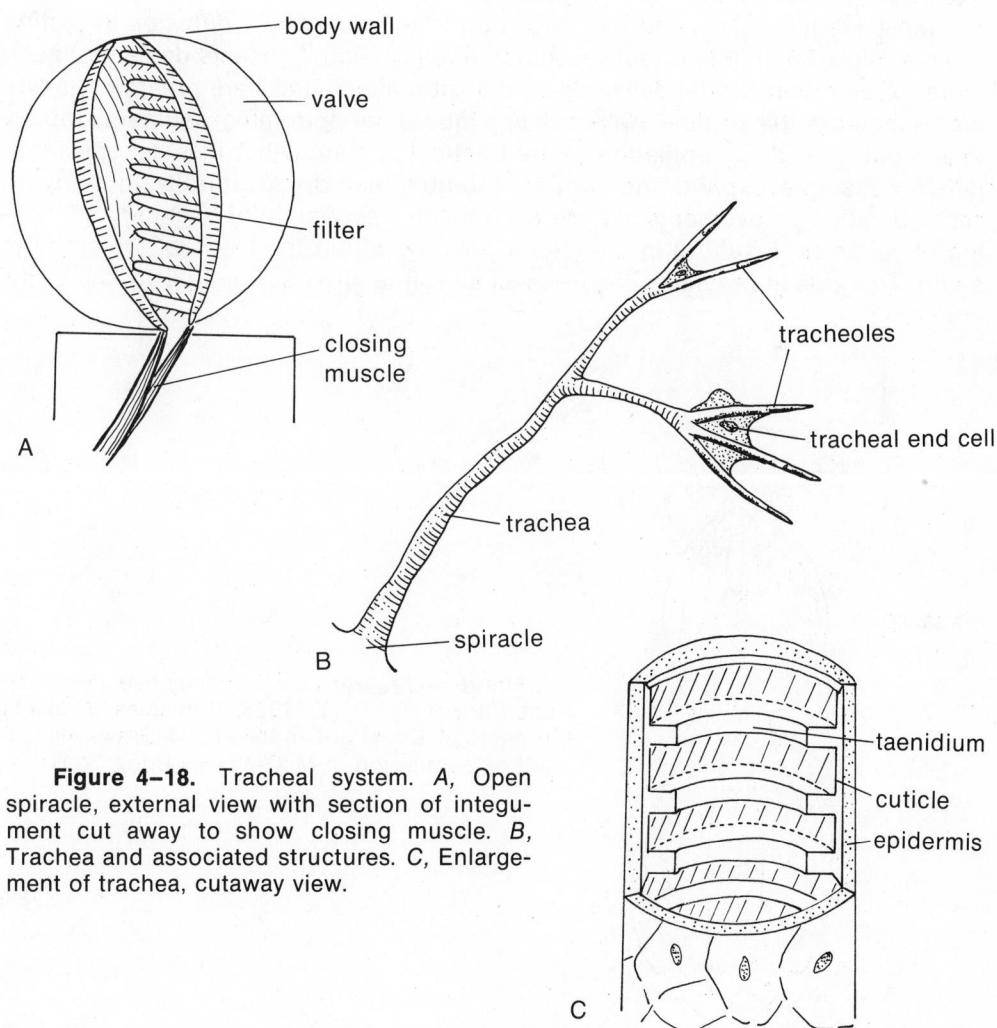

Figure 4–18. Tracheal system. *A,* Open spiracle, external view with section of integument cut away to show closing muscle. *B,* Trachea and associated structures. *C,* Enlargement of trachea, cutaway view.

(Fig. 4–18), and their distal end often contains fluid that is gradually withdrawn if the underlying tissue is deprived of air for some time. Apparently this fluid withdrawal increases the potential oxygen supply (Miller, 1964). If tracheae and tracheoles are destroyed locally, adjacent tracheae will move into the area at the next molt.

In some insects, the tracheal system of each segment is discrete and there are no interconnections; in most, however, the tracheae are interconnected by a series of tracheal **trunks**, making it possible for oxygen to be obtained while some spiracles are clogged or closed. In addition, many flying insects contain **air sacs** (Fig. 4–19), areas of the tracheal system that have no taenidia and may expand or contract as the need arises. This provides stability in flight and perhaps some buoyancy. (Much of the head of stag beetles [Fig. 4–3] is filled by air sacs.) More importantly, since the exoskeleton of insects is rather inflexible, the air sacs provide compressibility as eggs grow, as food is taken in, or as internal structures enlarge. Up to 80 per cent of the volume of a newly molted insect may be air, and this may decrease to 5 per cent as internal structures enlarge before the next molt (Whitehead, 1973). Air sacs also increase the volume of air that is inspired and expired with each breath.

Most oxygen enters and moves through the tracheae by diffusion in resting insects (Weis-Fogh, 1964), but muscular action in active insects demands much more oxygen than can be delivered by diffusion alone, and here breathing movements increase the air flow. An active bee moves her abdominal segments rapidly in and out, providing ventilation to the tracheal system. Other insects, grasshoppers for example, expand and contract the abdomen dorsoventrally. In many insects, breathing movements are correlated with a sequence of opening and closing of spiracles, resulting in directional air flow within the tracheal system (Fig. 4–20). This aids in providing the freshest air to the most active areas of the body.

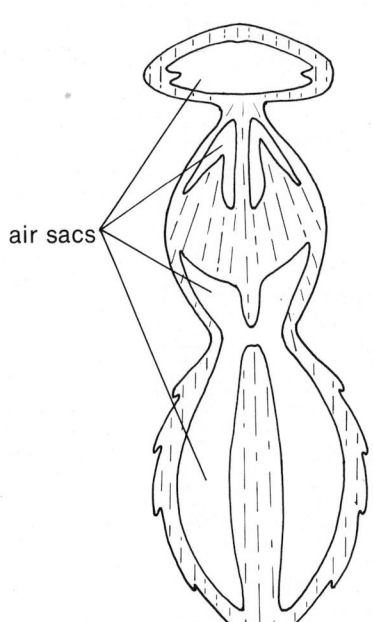

air sacs

Figure 4–19. Air sacs in honey bee. (Modified from Snodgrass, R. E. 1935. Principles of Insect Morphology. Copyright © 1935 by McGraw-Hill, Inc. Used by permission of McGraw-Hill Book Co.)

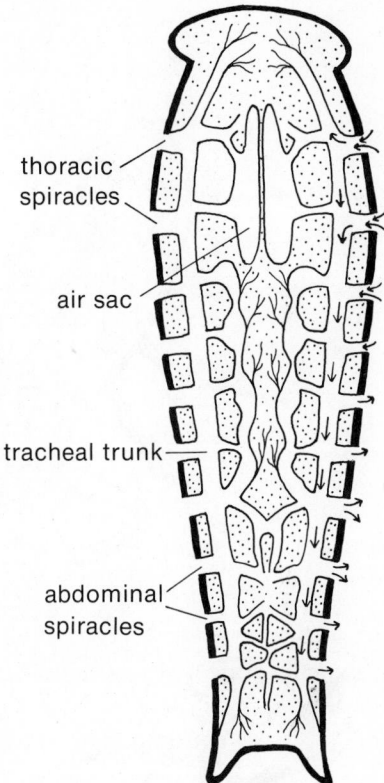

thoracic
spiracles

air sac

Figure 4–20. Diagrammatic representation of
tracheal system of grasshopper. Arrows indicate direction of air flow.

tracheal trunk

abdominal
spiracles

A secondary function of the tracheal system is connective, holding internal
organs in place (Edwards, 1960).

SPECIALIZATIONS FOR GAS EXCHANGE

Insects are abundant in fresh water and as internal parasites of many
animals, and they have evolved specializations for obtaining oxygen in these environments. Large numbers of aquatic insects, including many water bugs,
beetles, mosquito larvae, and the like, are not totally aquatic and must periodically return to the surface for a breath of fresh air. Some, like water bugs, the rat-
tailed maggot *Eristalis,* and mosquito larvae, have tubes opening to air at the
water surface and connecting with the tracheal system (Fig. 4–21). Others,
especially some beetles, trap a bubble under partially opened elytra, and their
spiracles open into this bubble. Such a bubble may function as a gill, for as
oxygen in the bubble is used up, the oxygen pressure within the bubble decreases
to that of dissolved oxygen in the water, and then oxygen begins to diffuse from
the water into the bubble. Because oxygen diffuses in faster than nitrogen diffuses
out (and air is 78 per cent nitrogen, 21 per cent oxygen), the bubble remains.
Most aquatic insects that breathe air have wet-resistant **hydrofuge hairs** associated with spiracles, and these hairs can break surface tension of water to expose spiracles to the air. Underwater, they keep water out of the spiracles.

Other aquatic insects, especially naiads of Ephemeroptera, Odonata, and
Plecoptera, possess tracheal gills. Internally, their tracheal system is air-filled.

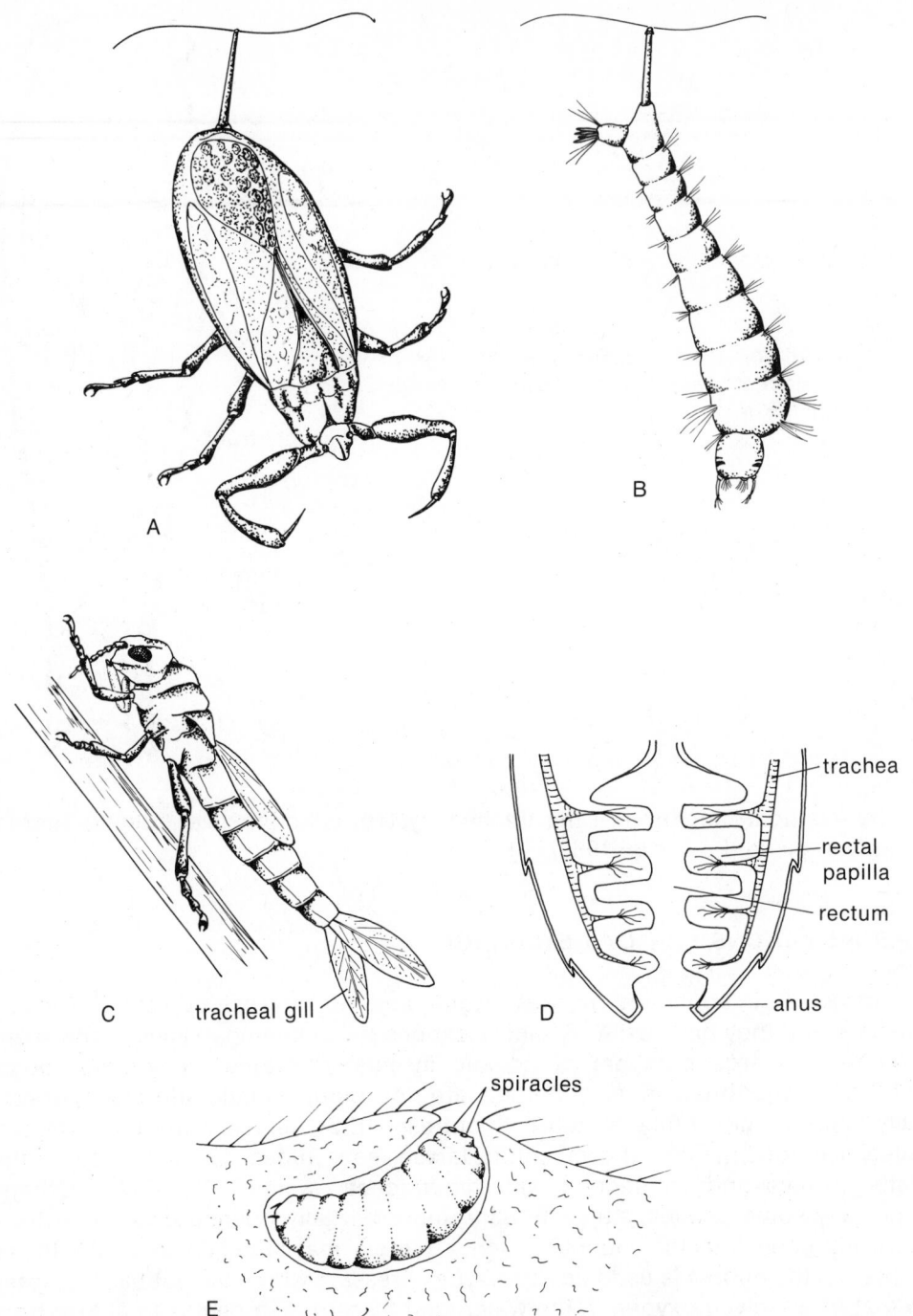

Figure 4-21. Specializations for obtaining oxygen. *A*, Water scorpion (Hemiptera), air tube. *B*, Mosquito larva, air tube. *C*, Damselfly naiad, tracheal gill. *D*, Cross section of rectal gills of dragon fly naiad. *E*, Cattle grub, posterior spiracles.

Their tracheae interface closely with the surrounding water inside thin-walled external structures (Fig. 4–21C) through which oxygen diffuses inward from the water. Gills of dragonfly naiads, **rectal papillae**, are in the hindgut (Fig. 4–21D), and these insects inhale and exhale water through the anus.

Unusual respiratory adaptations occur in insects that inhabit environments with very little oxygen. The bloodworm, *Chironomus,* lives in bottom mud of stagnant streams and ponds. It lacks tracheae, but its blood contains hemoglobin, a red pigment very similar to that which carries oxygen in vertebrates like ourselves. Bloodworm hemoglobin takes up and transports oxygen at much lower concentrations than does ours.

Internal parasites also may live under low oxygen conditions. Sometimes they, like aquatic insects, get oxygen directly from the air. The cattle grub larva, which forms boils, or warbles, under the backs of cows, has but one pair of spiracles that open at the posterior end (Fig. 4–21E), which penetrates the cow's skin to reach air. Larvae of parasitic Hymenoptera may absorb oxygen directly from the tracheal system of their host, or, when very small, may lack tracheae entirely and depend on cutaneous gas exchange. The horse bot, living in the digestive system of horses, can live by completely anaerobic (no oxygen) respiration for periods of time. It also has hemoglobin that can load and store oxygen when an air bubble happens by (Chapman, 1971).

EXCRETION

Cellular metabolism, particularly oxidation of amino acids, results in excess nitrogenous wastes, especially amines and ammonium. Because these are poisonous when concentrated, all multicellular animals, including insects, have means of excreting them. Insects that feed on protein-rich foods have to excrete more nitrogen than do other species.

Hemolymph carries excess nitrogen until it is absorbed by **malpighian tubules**, found at the junction of midgut and hindgut (Fig. 4–7). Malpighian tubules are unique to insects and vary in number from 2 to 200, except in aphids and Collembola, which have none. In Collembola, labial glands excrete nitrogen.

Each malpighian tubule is one cell layer thick, with a brush border inside and strands of muscle outside that move the distal portion of the tubule around within the hemocoel (Fig. 4–23A). The distal end of the tubule is closed off, and the proximal end empties at the junction of midgut and hindgut. In most insect orders, tubule ends are free in the hemolymph, while in Coleoptera and Lepidoptera, the distal ends of the tubules are cryptonephridial (closely associated with the rectum) (Fig. 4–22). In Orthoptera, tubules are filled with uniformly clear fluid, whereas Ramsay (1964) and others, taking small samples of liquid from malpighian tubules of Hemiptera and Coleoptera, have demonstrated qualitative fluid differences in successive portions of the tubules. In the distal region (Fig. 4–23), water and salts, including ammonium, are absorbed into the tubule, and as this fluid passes through the proximal portions, uric acid (containing amines) sometimes precipitates, while water and salts are reabsorbed. How this occurs is not yet clear (Schmidt-Nielsen, 1973).

Terrestrial insects face severe problems in water conservation, and one way in which water is conserved is by excretion of nitrogenous wastes as uric acid crystals, which involves little or no water. This is one significant adaptation permitting insects' survival in the terrestrial environment. In contrast, we mammals

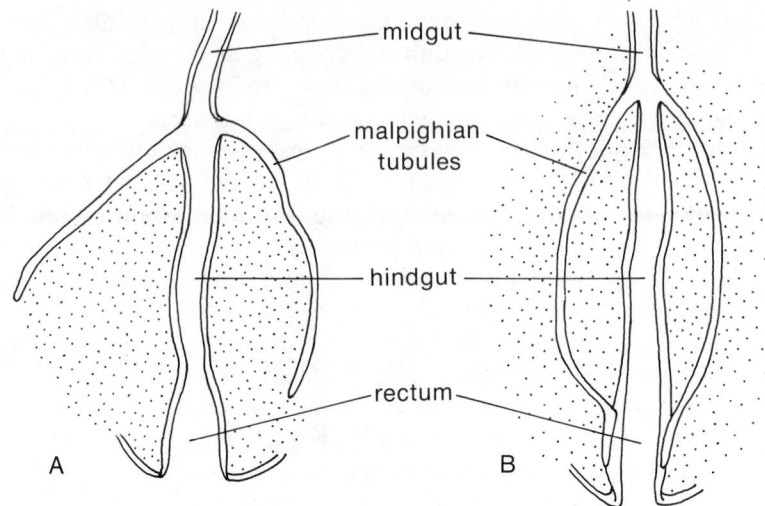

Figure 4–22. Excretory systems. *A,* Normal. *B,* Cryptonephridial.

excrete urea through urination, which involves moderate amounts of water. Aquatic insects, and some fly larvae that live in aqueous media, need not conserve water and consequently excrete nitrogenous wastes as ammonia in urine that contains a large amount of water (Table 4–4). Some insects, notably most pupae and adult cockroaches, retain uric acid, storing it in the fat body.

In terrestrial insects, the water-salt-uric acid solution released into the hindgut is still rather liquid, and major reabsorption of water and salt occurs here (Berridge and Oschman, 1972). The reabsorption of water varies with osmotic concentration of urine and with the need of the insect to conserve water; insects inhabiting the desert environments have extremely dry, concentrated urine

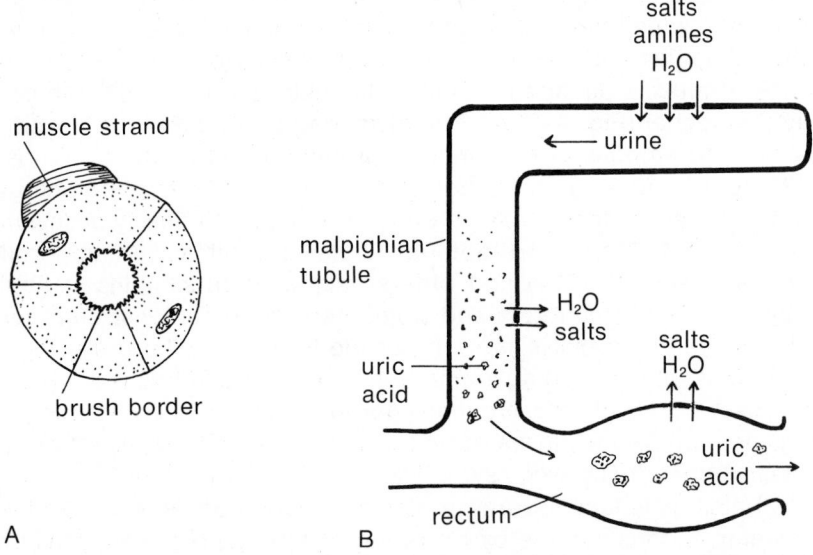

Figure 4–23. Malpighian tubules. *A,* Cross section of tubule. *B,* Diagram of excretory function.

Table 4–4. EXCRETORY PRODUCTS OF SELECTED INSECTS*

Insect	Per Cent of Nitrogen Excreted as:		
	Uric Acid	Urea	Ammonia
Rhodnius (bloodsucking bug)	90	trace	0
Silkworm larva	86	0	0
Culex mosquito	47	8	10
Blow fly larva	0	0	90
Dragonfly naiad	8	0	74
Alderfly larva (aquatic)	0	0	90

*From Chapman, R. F. 1969. The Insects: Structure and Function. American Elsevier Publishing Co., New York.

(Edney, 1967). Because water is reabsorbed against an osmotic (concentration) gradient, active transport (expending chemical energy) doubtless occurs, as the extensive tracheal supply to the rectum attests. Precisely how water is reabsorbed is unclear. In cryptonephridial systems, malpighian tubules may aid in reabsorbing water and needed salts at their distal end.

Urine production and water reabsorption apparently are partially under hormonal control. For instance, the bloodsucking bug *Rhodnius* excretes excess water only after a blood meal; its feeding on blood stimulates production of a diuretic (urine-producing) hormone, increasing malpighian tubule function. In contrast, the walkingstick *Corestus* feeds (on leaves) more or less continually, producing diuretic hormone continually, and urinating more or less regularly (Maddrell, 1971).

WATER BALANCE

For maximum metabolic efficiency, insects must regulate water, temperature, salt, and chemical balance within rather narrow limits, and the excretion-reabsorption process is an important aspect of this process. Transpiration increases as the ratio of body surface to body volume increases, and thus because of their small size, insects are exceedingly sensitive to water loss. I have already discussed the role of spiracles and the rectum in retaining water; the waterproofing waxy layer over the insect's cuticle (Fig. 5–22) also serves an important function, keeping water in as well as out.

Usually, water is taken in along with food or drink. Water is also produced as a by-product of cellular respiration, and the amount of this "metabolic water" varies according to the energy source utilized: carbohydrates yield about 55 grams H_2O/100 grams carbohydrate used; proteins yield 70 grams/100 grams; and fats have the highest yield, 107 grams H_2O/100 grams fat. This, incidentally, permits migratory locusts (and some other insects) to fly for long periods in semiarid climates without losing water; by utilizing fats for energy, locusts can replace water lost through the spiracles. A few insects, notably flea pupae, the firebrat *Thermobia,* and the desert cockroach *Arenivega,* take on water directly from the air; it is uncertain whether this is done through cuticle or rectum.

Insects inhabiting environments with extreme conditions of dryness or freezing have evolved adaptations that overcome such environmental rigors. Aquatic larvae of an African midge, *Polypedilum,* lose much water, shrivel, and remain desiccated for years when their temporary desert pools dry up. Hinton (1960b) kept some at −190° C for three days and heated others to 102° C (boiling water) for one minute; both groups survived. Resistance to freezing apparently involves removal of hemolymph particles around which ice could form, and many over-wintering insects, such as cecropia moth pupae, also contain glycerol as "an-tifreeze" in their hemolymph, which may lower its freezing point slightly (Salt, R. W., 1961).

TEMPERATURE REGULATION

A common fallacy is that insects are "cold-blooded," assuming the ambient temperature (that of their surroundings). Whereas this is true of many resting in-sects, microthermometers implanted into active insects indicate temperatures of 30° to 35°C, not much different from our own, even at ambient temperatures as low as 2°C (Heinrich, 1972). There are two sources of heat for most insects: me-tabolic heat generated by release of chemical energy in respiration, and direct or indirect solar radiation.

Of the chemical energy released by respiration, 50 per cent is given off as heat. Metabolic activity is highest in active muscles, so by contracting flight muscles in rapid sequence, a sphinx moth or bumblebee can raise thoracic tem-perature 10°C over that of the abdomen (Heinrich, 1972). Figure 4–24 illustrates the speed with which an insect can heat up by muscular action. Once warm, in-sects with dense "hair" or scale coverings are somewhat insulated and heat loss is slowed; a shaved bumblebee cools more quickly than does a hairy one. Air sacs of dragonflies (Fig. 4–25) apparently insulate their flight muscles (Church, 1960). Muscular activity among social wasps, ants, and bees is used to raise tem-perature in the nest (Chapter Six) to the optimum temperature for development of brood (Gibo et al., 1974).

Insects rely also on solar radiation for heat gain, and many possess morpho-logical and/or behavioral adaptations for heat gain. *Colias* butterflies are darker at higher (and therefore cooler) altitudes, and Watt (1968) has shown that darker coloration speeds heat absorption (Fig. 4–26). Locusts orient themselves perpen-

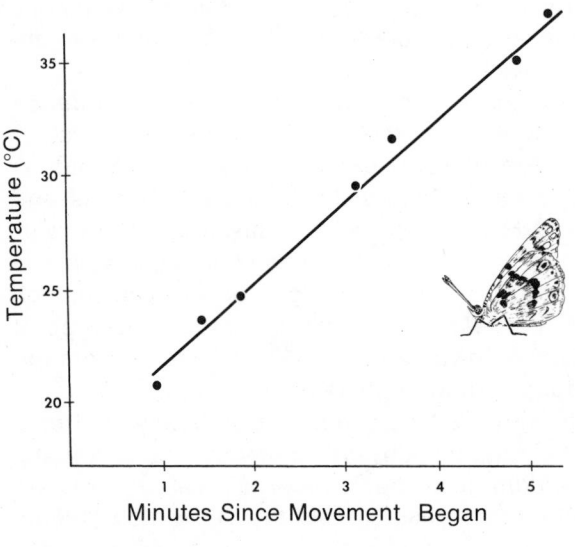

Figure 4–24. Relationship be-tween muscular activity and thoracic temperature in *Vanessa* butterfly. (Redrawn from Krogh, A., and E. Zeuthen. 1941. The mecha-nism of flight preparation in some insects. J. Exp. Biol. *18*:1–10.)

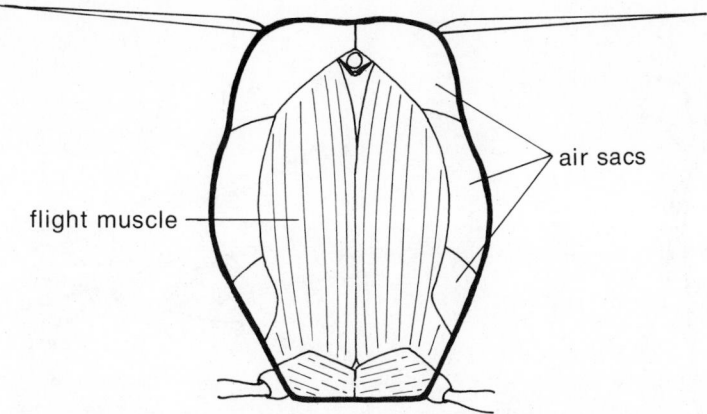

Figure 4–25. Cross section of dragonfly thorax, with air sacs.

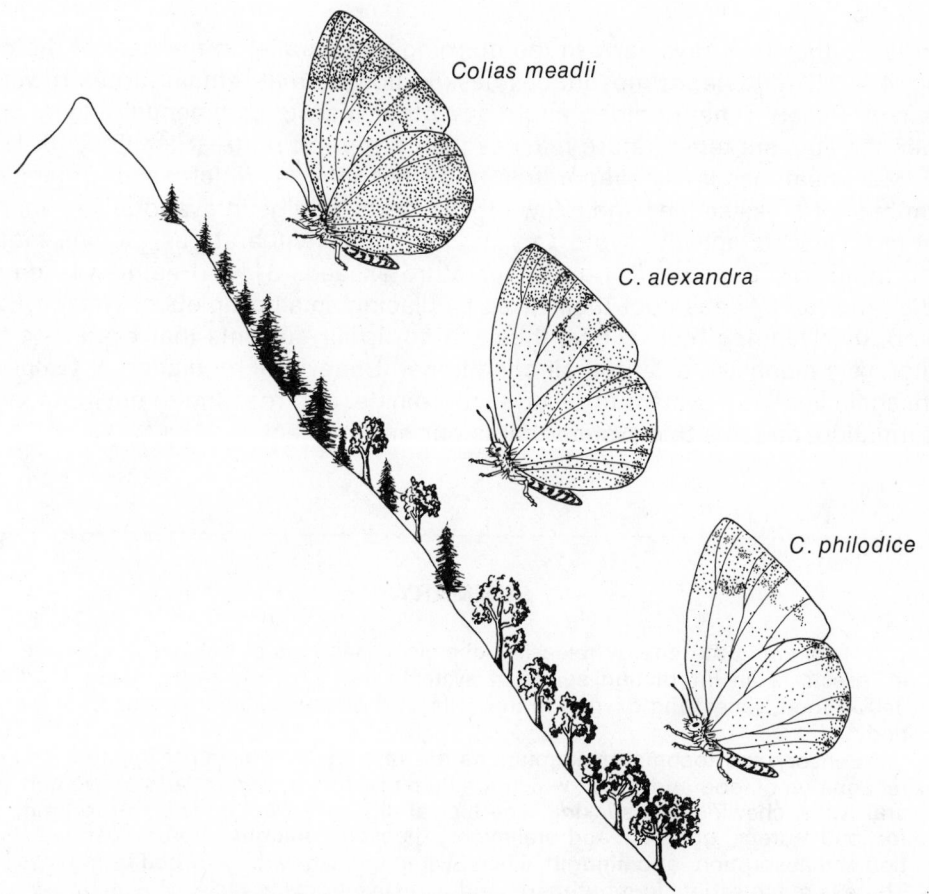

Figure 4–26. Increase of dark pigments on wings of *Colias* butterflies with increasing altitude and lower temperatures in Rocky Mountains. *Colias meadii,* alpine. *C. alexandra,* montane coniferous forests. *C. philodice,* lower forests and plains. (Data from Watt, 1968.)

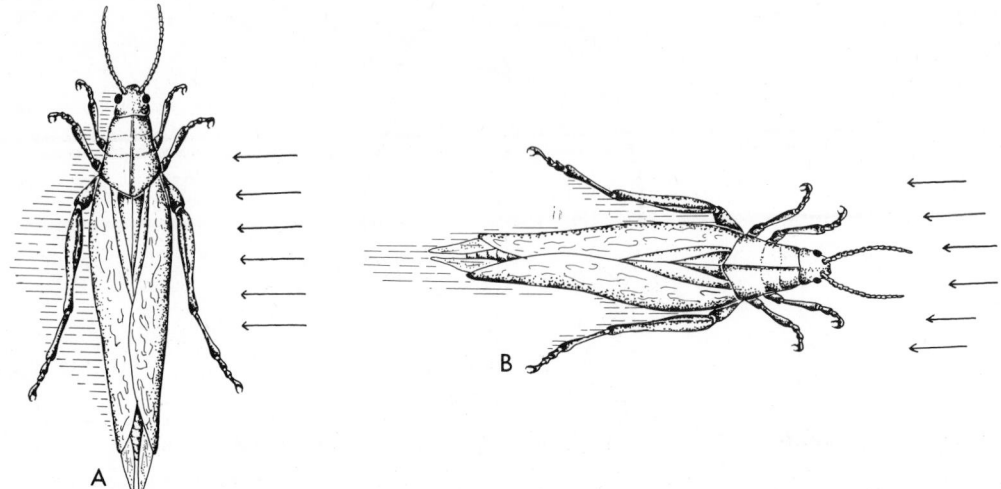

Figure 4–27. Behavioral thermoregulation of grasshopper. *A,* Early morning, when cool. *B,* Midday, when warm. Arrows indicate direction of solar radiation.

dicular to the sun's rays early in the morning and parallel in the heat of the day (Fig. 4–27). Arctic *Aedes* mosquitoes bask in flowers that remain turned towards the sun. Desert Tenebrionidae and many other insects commence activity only when the ambient temperature reaches their preferred range (Hamilton, 1971).

Most heat loss is via evaporation and transpiration, which small organisms cannot afford. Tsetse flies and a few other insects indulge in evaporative cooling, but most insects actively avoid very high ambient temperatures. Sphinx moths land frequently to cool off if air temperature exceeds 31°C (Heath and Adams, 1965) and honey bees cool their hives by placing small droplets of water on the comb, then fanning their wings, thus setting up air currents that evaporate the water, very much like a central air conditioner. Behavioral regulation of temperature again implies a system to receive, coordinate, and respond to environmental information, and it is this system that is our next subject.

SUMMARY

Maintaining the energy-releasing chemical reactions of cellular metabolism in insects is an interacting series of systems that procure and process food, deliver food, water, and oxygen to the cells, and remove cellular wastes from the body.

Sensory and locomotor adaptations are responsible for initial location and recognition of food and water, which are then taken in by mouthparts of two general types, chewing and sucking. The typical digestive tract consists of **foregut,** for food storage, grinding, and preliminary digestion; **midgut,** site of most digestion and absorption; and **hindgut,** where water and salts are absorbed from feces. There is much variety in mouthparts and digestive tracts.

From the gut, digested nutrients, salts, and water enter **hemolymph,** a fluid containing cells, nutrients and water, kept in motion by a pulsating dorsal heart.

Hemolymph distributes nutrients about the body, stores food, carries wastes, and possesses defensive systems.

Oxygen is taken in through openings, **spiracles**, leading into a system of tubes, **tracheae**, that carry oxygen (and some carbon dioxide) to and from tissues of most insects. There are specialized tracheal systems in aquatic and parasitic insects.

Malpighian tubules remove nitrogenous wastes from hemolymph, depositing them in the hindgut as uric acid (in most terrestrial insects). Water and needed salts are then reabsorbed in the hindgut, resulting in extremely efficient water conservation, necessary in very tiny animals exposed to drying conditions.

Cellular metabolism and muscular action are most efficient at warm temperatures, and the chapter ends with consideration of behavioral and morphological adaptations for regulating body temperature.

Chapter Five

Coordination and Locomotion

INTRODUCTION

An insect is an amazingly specialized and integrated machine capable of receiving information and responding to it in characteristic ways that, usually, enable its continued survival and reproduction. Essential to the function of an insect as a machine are two coordinating systems: one is the hormonal (or endocrine) system, which regulates slow responses like growth and development; and the other is a fast-acting system capable of receiving a stimulus and producing a coordinated response within a fraction of a second. To convince yourself of the speed and efficiency with which an insect responds to stimuli you need but try to snatch a fly between your thumb and forefinger. Sense receptors receive both visual and mechanical stimuli as your digits approach the fly; effectors (muscles and exoskeleton) are responsible for the response, and, very likely, escape. Coordination between stimulus and response is accomplished by the nervous system. In this chapter, beginning with the nervous system, we shall take the stimulus-transmission-response system apart to better understand how it works. In the next chapter, we shall reassemble the parts to discover how the insect operates as a coordinated unit—that is, how it behaves.

NERVOUS SYSTEM

NERVE CELLS AND NERVES

The entire nervous system is composed of nerve cells, or neurons, very similar to those found in our own bodies and in nearly all multicellular animals. The way in which impulses are transmitted seems to be nearly universal among animals, including insects. Each neuron typically consists of a cell body and a long projection, the axon, that terminates in a series of branches or dendrites (Fig. 5–1). At rest, there is a greater concentration of positive sodium ions out-

194

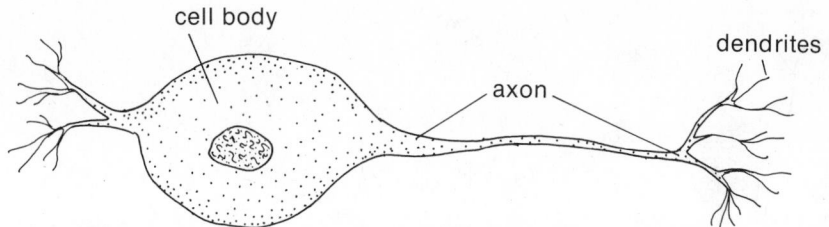

Figure 5–1. A typical neuron.

side the cell and a greater concentration of positive potassium ions and nondiffusible organic negative ions within the cell, so that a potential difference, or electrical charge, of about 70 millivolts exists across the cell membrane. Stimulation of the nerve by a sense organ or by a chemical secreted by another nerve (discussed subsequently) causes a momentary increase in permeability to Na^+, which rushes into the cell, changing the permeability to K^+, which shortly rushes out of the cell, reestablishing the original electrical charge. The change in electrical charge stimulates adjacent areas of the nerve cell membrane to alter permeability to sodium, which rushes inward as before. Thus an impulse "flows" along the nerve axon.

With the advent of microelectronic techniques (and with extreme patience), investigators have been able to insert microelectrodes onto or into a single axon and measure the minute voltage changes accompanying transmission of a nerve impulse; thus they can discover which nerve cells are transmitting impulses at any given moment. Moreover, electrodes can stimulate nerve fibers, since a tiny electrical current will increase permeability to sodium just as will more normal stimuli.

Transmission of impulses between nerve cells is accomplished chemically. Between one dendrite and a neighboring cell is a gap, or synapse. The arrival of a nerve impulse at a synapse triggers secretion of acetylcholine*. This chemical diffuses across the synapse and stimulates a change in Na^+ permeability, an impulse, in the neighboring nerve cell. Acetylcholine is then inactivated by the enzyme acetylcholinesterase. Some insecticides kill insects by acting on this "chemical messenger" system. Nicotine, for instance, imitates acetylcholine, causing nerves to fire impulses indiscriminately. Organophosphorous insecticides, including parathion, malathion, and others, inhibit the enzyme acetylcholinesterase, so that acetylcholine builds up at synapses and the receiving nerve cells continue to produce impulses. In both cases, the insect is overstimulated, goes into tremors, and dies.

Neurons are of three basic morphological types (Fig. 5–2): unipolar, having a single axon leading from the cell body; bipolar, having the cell body located along the axon (in effect, having two axons); and multipolar, having several axons radiating from the cell body. **Sensory** neurons, those that transmit impulses from a sensory structure such as the eye or ear, are usually bipolar, and **motor** neurons, which transmit impulses to effectors (muscles and some glands) are usually monopolar. **Association** neurons, as befits their function of integrat-

---

* Other chemicals have recently been identified as chemical transmitter substances in insect neurons.

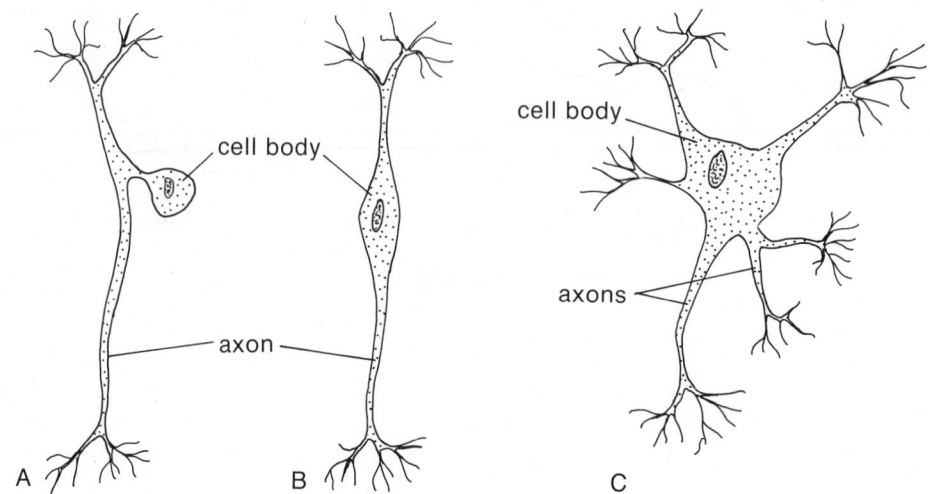

Figure 5–2. Types of neurons. *A,* Unipolar. *B,* Bipolar. *C,* Multipolar.

ing information from and coordinating responses to many other neurons, are often multipolar.

In the ventral nerve cord of dragonfly nymphs, locusts, cockroaches, and perhaps most insects (and some mollusks) are found giant fibers, unique nerve cells whose axons are much larger (20 to 60μ in diameter) than those of other neurons. Single giant fibers run the length of the nerve cord and conduct impulses much faster than do smaller neurons. They are responsible for the speed with which some insects take evasive action when threatened; giant fibers in cockroaches conduct impulses from vibration receptors to the brain and legs, enabling the insect to move rapidly away when threatened by a fast-falling foot.

Most insect nerves are made up of many neurons and companion cells responsible for support, nutrition, and salt balance. The nerve of a grasshopper leg, for example, contains 2000 axons bundled together rather like a telephone cable (Hughes, 1965). Because of their small size, insects generally have far fewer neurons than do vertebrates, and it is not fully understood how insects, with few nerve cells, are sometimes capable of very complex behavior.

THE CENTRAL NERVOUS SYSTEM

In insects, as in other arthropods and annelid worms, the central nervous system consists of an anterior mass (brain) and a double-stranded ventral nerve cord connecting a series of masses, or ganglia. There is one ganglion per body segment in more "primitive" insects such as Thysanura, while in the "higher" insects, especially Diptera and Hymenoptera, ganglia are often fused anteriorly (Fig. 5–3). Each ganglion is a mass of nerve cells that has (usually) three pairs of nerves radiating outward, which apparently receive sensory input and control muscular response within that segment. All association neurons and the cell bodies of motor neurons are located within the central nervous system.

Ganglia within the head are of central importance in coordinating the activity of segmental ganglia so that the insect functions as a unit. The most anterior ganglion we dignify by the term "brain." Like our own brain, it is a center of coordination, association, and inhibition, though it is unlikely, given the relatively small quantity of neurons present, that conscious thought occurs in insects. The insect brain consists of three paired parts (Fig. 5–4): the protocerebrum, from which nerves connect to (innervate) the compound eyes and ocelli; the deutocerebrum, which innervates the antennae; and the tritocerebrum, innervating the labrum and the visceral nervous system. Two nerve cords (commissures) extend posteriorly from the tritocerebrum around the esophagus, where they connect with the **subesophageal ganglion,** which innervates the mouthparts directly and coordinates impulses to segmental ganglia in thorax and abdomen.

There are relatively few motor neurons (transmitting impulses to muscles) in the insect brain; its major functions are apparently association and inhibition. The inhibitory function may be demonstrated when the head is removed from an adult male mantis (Roeder, 1967). He immediately begins precopulatory behavior with a curious rotary walk not seen in intact mantises. He will copulate with anything remotely resembling a female, depositing sperm with abandon until the supply is exhausted. This unusual adaptation continues mantid species, for in the normal course of mantis-love, the female seizes her mate shortly after he comes within reach. Then she devours him headfirst, and as soon as she munches beyond his brain, his genitalia move into action. Operations on other insects have shown a similar importance of the head as a center of inhibition. For example, removal of the head of a mature female silkworm moth results in immediate egg laying. A cockroach with the head removed is hyperactive, running aimlessly and without pause until exhausted.

Extending forward within the protocerebrum in many insects are the corpora pedunculata, or "mushroom bodies," which are enlarged in insects having very

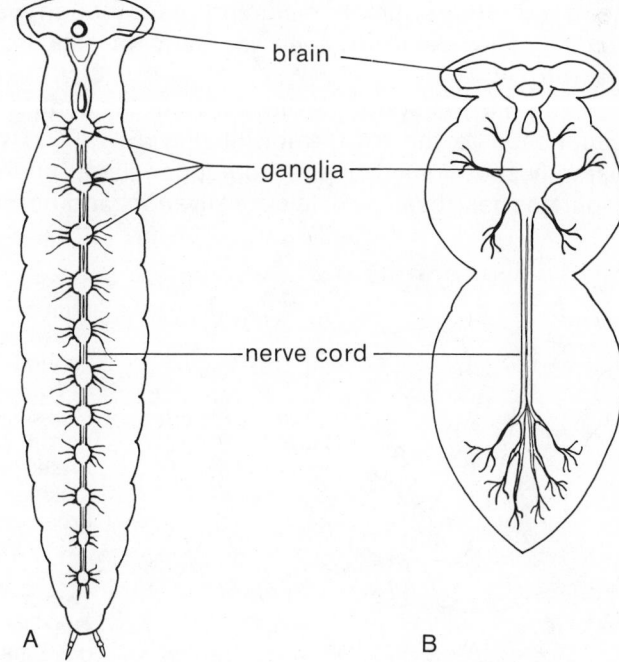

brain

ganglia

Figure 5–3. Central nervous system of mantid (*A*) and fly (*B*).

nerve cord

A   B

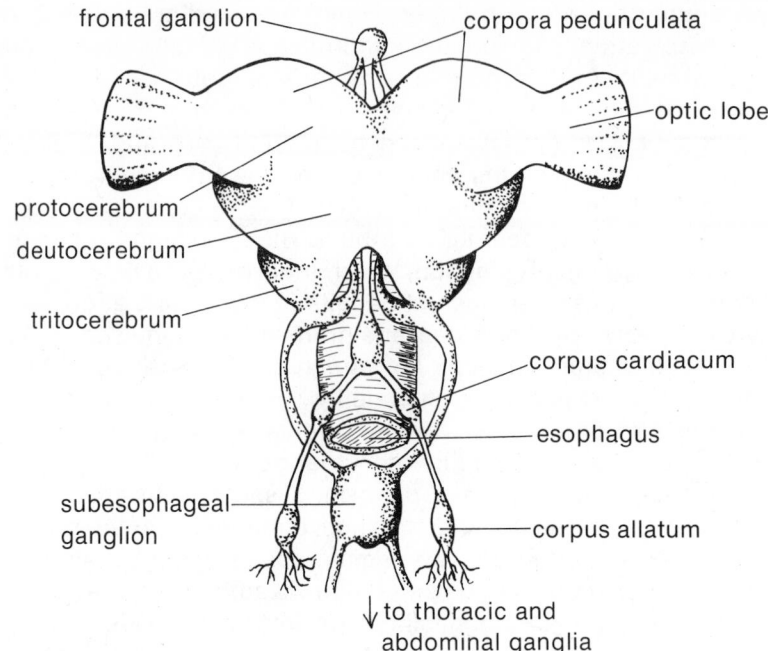

Figure 5–4. Diagram of grasshopper brain (dorsal view).

complex behavior (e.g., ants and bees). The corpora pedunculata may therefore be centers of coding and storing information as "memory," because insects do indeed learn (Chapter Six). By electrically stimulating areas of the cricket brain, Huber (Horridge, 1965) elicited several behavioral responses and thereby "mapped" locations in which these behaviors originated (Fig. 5–5). Such techniques have revolutionized the study of neural association and response in insects and other animals including man, though we still know very little of how the complex behavior seen in many insects is controlled by relatively few neurons.

The visceral system is distinct from the central nervous system except for its connection to the tritocerebrum (Fig. 5–4). The visceral system, which is apparently coordinated by the frontal ganglion, innervates the internal organs and regulates heartbeat, peristalsis, salivation, and hormone secretion. This last func-

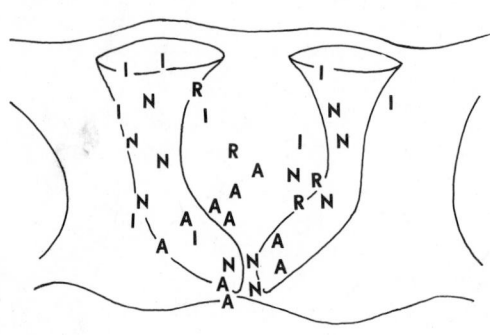

Figure 5–5. Corpora pedunculata ("mushroom bodies") of cricket brain, showing points of stimulation for various "songs." Abnormal song (A); inhibition of song (I); normal song (N); rivalry song (R). (Modified from Structure and Function in the Nervous Systems of Invertebrates, Vol. II, by Theodore Holmes Bullock and G. Adrian Horridge. W. H. Freeman and Company. Copyright © 1965; and from Huber, F. 1960. Untersuchungen über die Funktion des Zentralnervensystems und insbesondere des Gehirnes bei der Fortbewegung und der Lauterzeugung der Grillen. Z. Vergl. Physiol. *44*:60–132.)

tion of the nervous system, secretion of hormones by the corpora cardiaca and corpora allata, is discussed in Chapter Seven.

SENSORY RECEPTION

Like humans, insects are sensitive to several forms of environmental input, these being radiation (light and heat), movement and pressure (including sound), and chemicals (taste and smell). There is great variety in the sensory organs of insects; in general, sense receptors are more developed in very active forms which need very efficient systems of sensory input. Receptors of some sort are found everywhere on the surface of most insects. All involve a cuticular structure whereby an incipient stimulus causes a local physical or chemical change, which in turn initiates a nerve impulse. Most insects are much more sensitive to chemicals (taste and smell) than they are to sound and light, which makes it difficult for us to imagine the world in which they live.

Since most of the information to which insects respond is environmental input, most of the sense receptors are located on the body surface. The head is usually the part of the body that meets the environment first, so as we might expect, specialized sensory structures, particularly the eyes and antennae, are located here. Chemical sense and sound receptors (when present) are often found elsewhere on the body, however, and this is partly why the insect central nervous system is not so concentrated into a brain, as it is in vertebrates.

Much research on the identity of insect sense receptors has involved bioassay, a technique in which a sensory structure is stimulated so that if a behavioral response results, that sensory structure's function is thereby revealed. For example, Dethier (1963) tethered blow flies by attaching their thorax to a stick with paraffin and touched their tarsi with a successive series of dilute sugar solutions. Stimulation of chemical receptors by a sugar solution resulted (usually) in extension of the mouthparts, and Dethier was thus able to demonstrate the minimum threshold for response. (The flies' taste was exceedingly more sensitive than ours.) He showed further that stimulation of a single hair receptor in the blow fly "tongue" was responsible for sensing sugar, salt, water, and pressure (Dethier, 1963).

Bioassay techniques have limitations, among which are the inevitable variability among individual insects' behaviors and the uncertainty that a particular behavior is necessarily a response to the stimulus involved. Removal of receptors has been tried; if its antennae are removed, the bloodsucking bug *Rhodnius* will not orient toward a potential victim (Wigglesworth, 1972), but again one is not always certain that behavioral changes are a result of loss of the receptor itself and not a result of the trauma of operation. Recently, therefore, researchers in insect sensory physiology have been employing the technique (referred to earlier) of implanting microelectrodes in neurons leading from presumed sensory receptors in intact, living insects. They then stimulate the sensory structure and record the impulses produced in the nerve. Roeder (1967) was among the pioneers in this area; he implanted electrodes in neurons leading from the "ear" (tympanum) of an otherwise intact moth and could thereby not only demonstrate the hearing function of the tympanum and its range of response (Fig. 5–15) but could also trace the sensory impulses within the thoracic ganglia. Progress is continuing in identifying the function(s) of many sensilla on insects' cuticles. For other structures (eyes, for instance), the function is obvious.

EYES AND LIGHT

Most insects, except some that are parasitic or found in other dark environments (caves, soil), have specialized light-sensitive structures. A major feature of the head of many insects is a pair of large compound eyes (Fig. 5–6) consisting of a few to many thousand closely packed facets, or lenses. Characteristically, the eyes bulge, increasing the field of vision. Microscopic examination of a cross section of the compound eye reveals a series of units, the **ommatidia.** Each ommatidium consists of a lens and pigment cells grouped around a central core of retinula (nerve) cells, which in turn surround a light-sensitive core, the rhabdom (Fig. 5–7). Retinene, a chemical pigment similar to vitamin A, has been isolated from insect rhabdoms, and it is presumed to operate similarly to pigments in the vertebrate eye; i.e., light coming through the lens strikes the rhabdom and causes a chemical change in retinene (Goldsmith and Warner, 1964). This altered form of retinene stimulates a nerve impulse to the insect's brain.

There is some variation in the structure of ommatidia in different insect groups. In particular, compound eyes can be classified into two groups according to the location of the pigment cells. In the **apposition** eye (Fig. 5–7A), each ommatidium is completely separated from its neighbor by pigment cells, preventing the entry of light from neighboring lenses. In the **superposition** eye (Fig. 5–7B), the pigment is capable of movement. In the light, the pigment completely screens each ommatidium, as in the apposition eye; whereas in the dark, the pig-

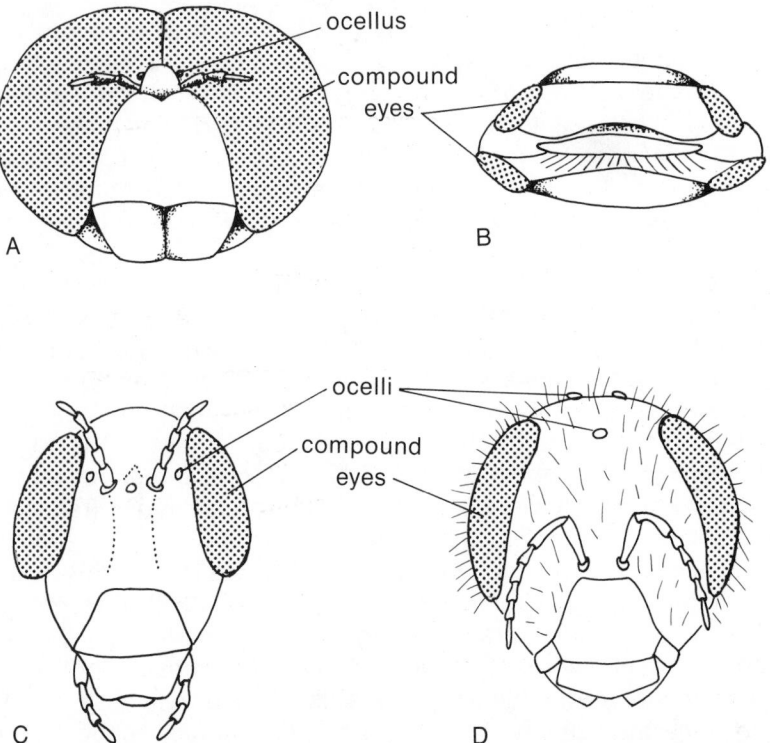

Figure 5–6. Anterior views of insect heads. *A*, Dragonfly. *B*, Whirligig beetle (Gyrinidae). *C*, Grasshopper. *D*, Honey bee.

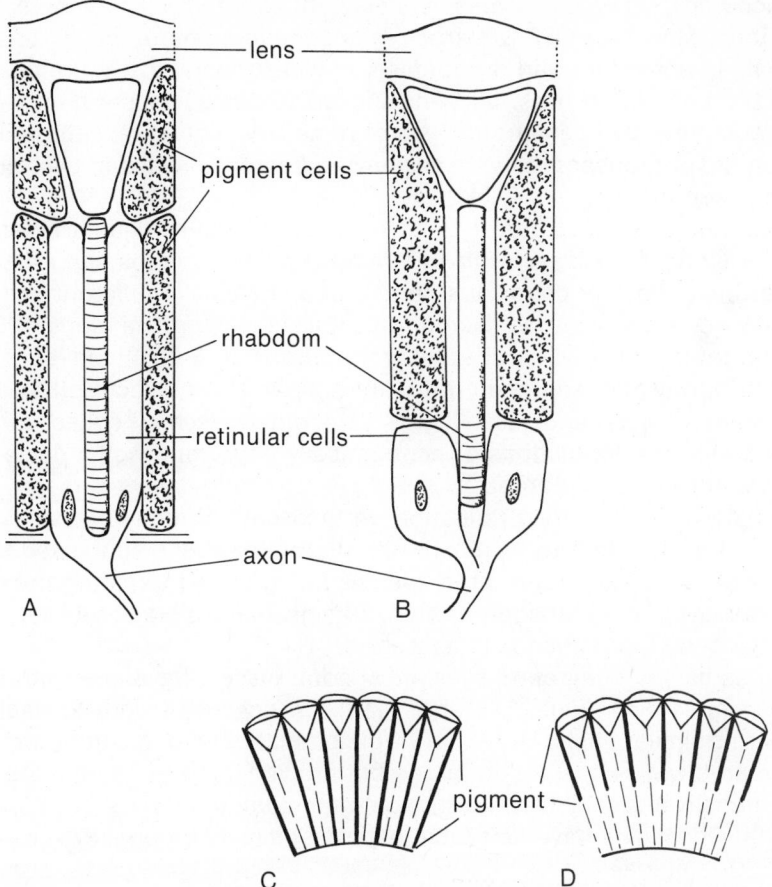

Figure 5–7. Structure of compound eyes. *A*, Ommatidium of apposition eye. *B*, Ommatidium of superposition eye. *C*, Superposition eye, light-adapted. *D*, Superposition eye, dark-adapted.

ment moves toward the lens, so that each rhabdom receives light from both its own and neighboring lenses. Presumably, this increases light input but clouds the picture. In addition, the bases of the ommatidia are rather heavily endowed with tracheae from which light may be reflected. This reflection concentrates light, and is popularly believed to cause the "eyeshine" that we see in the eyes of some moths at night in the glare of an electric flashlight. Recently, however, Swihart et al. (1974) showed that, instead, the reflection is caused by changes in optical characteristics of contracted retinular cells.

Muller (1839) first proposed the current concept of insect vision: Each ommatidium forms a small image of the light it receives, and the composite of many single images is somehow integrated within the insect brain. Photographs have been taken through insect compound eyes, but these indicated nothing more than that the insect eye makes a rather blurry camera filter. We do not know precisely how the insect perceives visual stimuli, though we suspect that it is with rather high acuity. Wasps and bees locate their nests partly by visual cues from the surroundings and can be taught to distinguish forms (Chapter Six). Dragonflies quickly distinguish mosquitoes from bits of paper tossed in the air. Mantids, and probably all predatory insects, judge distance and size of prey with deadly accuracy. The insect eye is very efficient at judging movements. In general, the more active insects have larger eyes containing more facets; this reaches its extreme in some flies and dragonflies, in which nearly the entire head is covered by the compound eyes, each having up to 50,000 facets (Fig. 5–6). Most adult insects have two compound eyes or none. The whirligig beetles (Gyrinidae) have four, the original compound eyes having become divided in two for efficient vision in water and air.

Unlike humans, insects do not have morphologically distinct receptor cells for color vision. Many insects obviously do see colors (bees can be trained to feed at artificial flowers of various colors) and chemically different sensory pigments may be responsible, but beyond this little is known. The range of color distinguished by insect eyes is different from ours (Fig. 5–8); their range extends further into ultraviolet, and deep red is invisible to most insects. Ultraviolet light attracts many insects, and "blacklights" are widely used to collect night-flying insects, to monitor populations of economically important moth species, and as attractants in electric grid traps.

The pattern of ultraviolet reflection on the wings of many insects is very different from the visible patterns (Fig. 5–9). Silberglied (1973) suggested that these ultraviolet patterns are important in species recognition for mating because they give these insects a visual code of flashing signals invisible to vertebrate predators—a "closed-circuit channel," as it were.

Besides having compound eyes, most adult insects have one to three dorsal ocelli, or simple eyes (Figs. 5–6 and 5–10). An ocellus, except for lacking pigment cells, is similar in structure to a single ommatidium of a compound eye. The ocelli apparently do not form an image but are very sensitive to minute changes in light intensity and may thereby stimulate the compound eyes or regulate input from them. Ocelli may have no visible external lens, as Eaton (1971) has demonstrated in Sphingidae.

Some, maybe most, insects are also capable of distinguishing the plane of light polarization. The manner in which they do so is not known, though compound eyes and ocelli are probably involved. The significance is clear, however: scattered sunlight in a blue sky is polarized (convince yourself by rotating polaroid sunglasses), and the plane of polarization changes as the sun moves through the sky. Thus, a bee orients with reference to the sun's direction even on cloudy days. Wellington (1974) showed that bumble bees orient with respect to light polarization, especially when foraging at dusk with a clear sky overhead.

The visual organs of insect larvae are one or more lateral ocelli, or stemmata, located on the sides of the head. These are similar to dorsal ocelli in form and

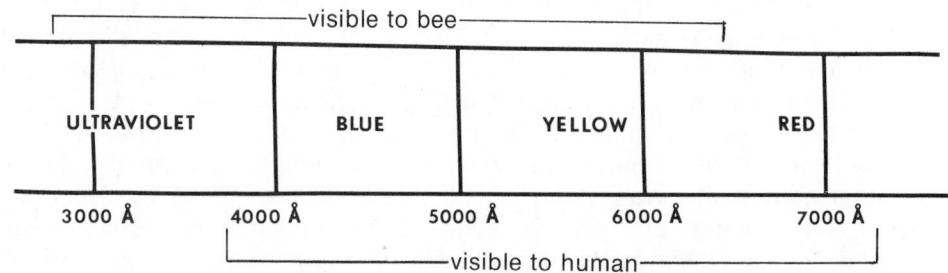

Figure 5–8. Spectra visible to bees and humans.

Figure 5–9. Ultraviolet reflection from butterfly wings (male, top; female, bottom). *A*, As seen by ultraviolet-sensitive film or insect eye. *B*, As seen in visible light. (From Ghiradella, H., D. Aneshansley, T. Eisner, R. E. Silberglied, and H. E. Hinton. Ultraviolet reflection of a male butterfly: interference color caused by thin-layer elaboration of wing scales. Science *178*:1214–1217, 1972. Copyright 1972 by the American Association for the Advancement of Science.)

function. With them, some larvae can perceive sufficient detail to distinguish upright forms to climb; they do this by moving their head to and fro, gradually accumulating a composite impression of their surrounding (Wigglesworth, 1972).

There are evidently light receptors elsewhere on the surface of some insects, for mealworm larvae respond to light even when blinded, and diving beetle larvae point their posterior tracheal openings toward a light source (Chapman, 1969). These surface light receptors have not yet been identified as such.

Finally, some insects, particularly as immatures, are sensitive to changes in daylength (photoperiod), and this regulates their development (Chapter Seven). In sightless insects (e.g. many pupae), photoperiod may be perceived directly by the brain. (The cuticle of many insects is thin enough to transmit light.)

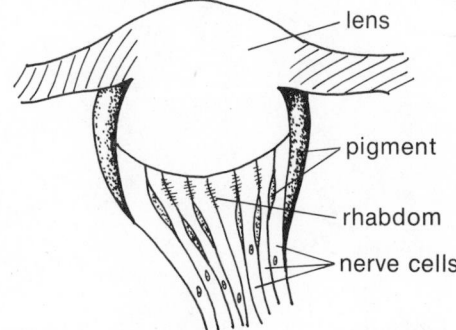

Figure 5–10. Diagrammatic cross section of dorsal ocellus. (Modified from Imms, A. D. 1957. A General Textbook of Entomology. 9th ed., revised by Professor O. W. Richards and R. G. Davies. Methuen & Co. Ltd. London.)

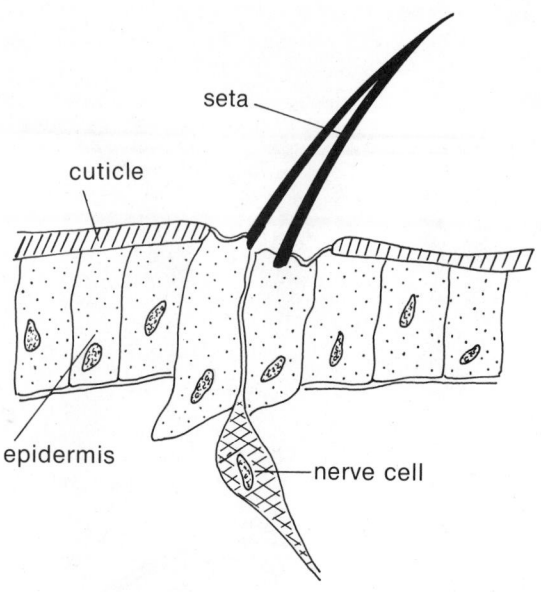

Figure 5–11. Structure of simple hair sensillum.

PRESSURE AND SOUND

Covering the cuticle of many insects, and most concentrated on the antennae, mouthparts, legs, and cerci, are receptors that respond to pressures ranging from light movements of air and water to contact with solid objects. Typically, the simplest pressure receptors consist of an articulating "hair" or **seta,** epidermal cells, and a nerve cell ending (Fig. 5–11). Clearly, any movement of the seta stimulates a nerve impulse to the central nervous system. There is much variation on this basic pattern (Figs. 5–12 and 5–13), and the practical difficulty of recording impulses from a single nerve fiber sometimes precludes our knowing whether a given sensillum responds to movement alone or to chemical changes as well.

Most insects have no specific sound receptors, but we do find auditory receptors in those insects (Orthoptera and cicadas) among which sound plays a major part in social life (Chapter Six). "Ears" are also found on some moths (Noctuidae, Pyralidae, Geometridae, Arctiidae) that use them to hear the ultrasonic squeaks of bats (Chapter Nine). The auditory receptors are located on the forelegs of crickets and long-horned grasshoppers, on the rear of the thorax in noctuid moths, and on the first abdominal segment in short-horned grasshoppers, cicadas and geometrid moths (Fig. 5–14). The several locations reflect sep-

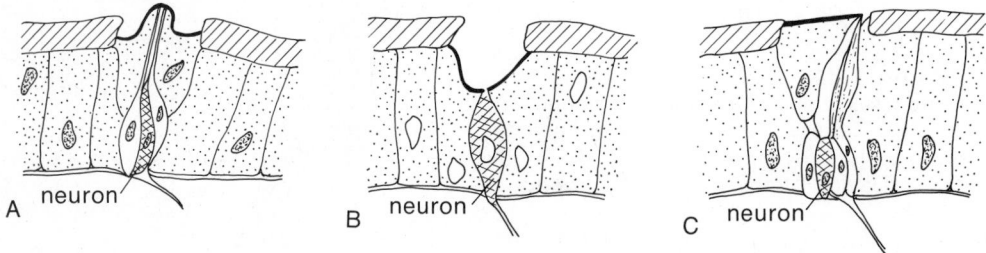

Figure 5–12. Cross sections of sensilla. *A*, Peg sensillum. *B*, Pit sensillum. *C*, Plate sensillum.

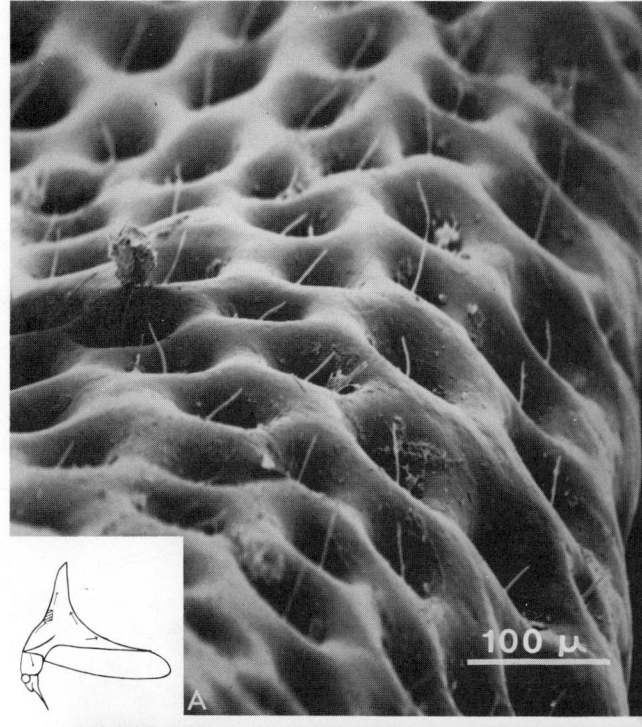

Figure 5–13. Scanning electron micrographs showing sensilla on insect surfaces. *A*, Pronotum of treehopper. (Courtesy of T. K. Wood.) *B*, Leg of honey bee. (Courtesy of Eastman Kodak Co.)

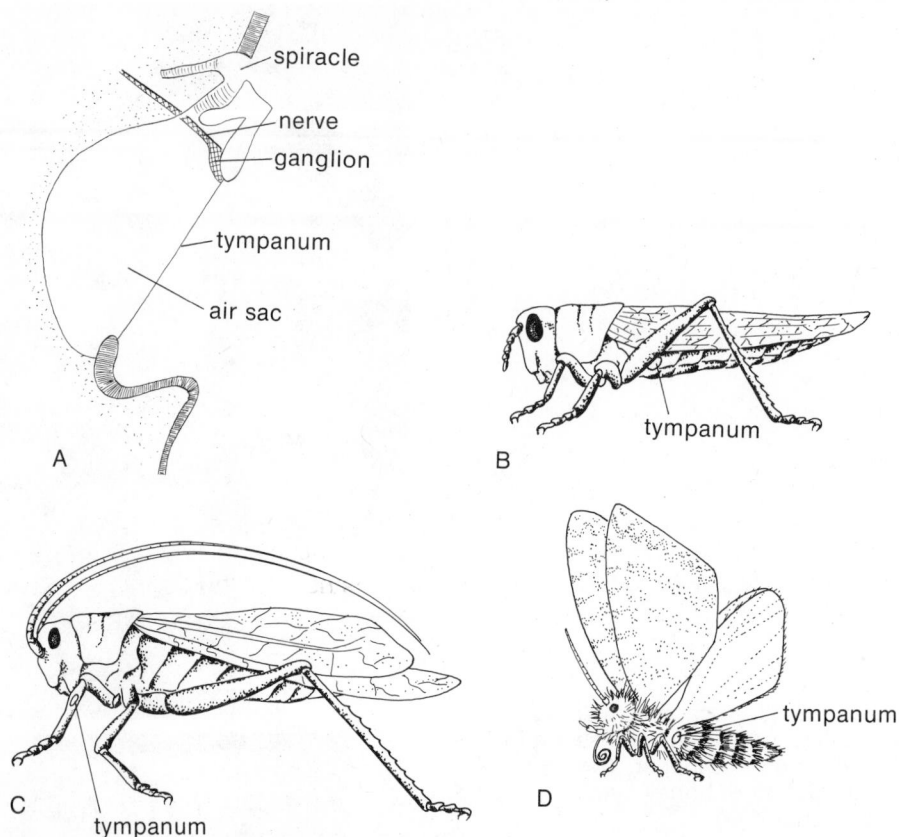

Figure 5–14. Tympani ("ears"). *A*, Structure of locust tympanum. *B*, Location of tympanum on locust (Acrididae). *C*, Tympanum of Tettigoniidae. *D*, Tympanum of Noctuidae.

arate origins of the auditory organs, probably from chordotonal organs (discussed subsequently). The most obvious structure is the **tympanum,** a "drumhead" of cuticle covering an air sac. Pressure waves at certain frequencies, usually those produced by that species, cause vibration of the tympanum, which in turn sets in motion a sensillum connected to a nerve. Movement again causes an impulse. There are two sensilla in some moth tympani as opposed to over 1500 in cicadas.

Insects apparently are not able to discriminate among sounds of different frequencies but are more sensitive to high than to low frequencies (Fig. 5–15). They can distinguish intensity: increasing amplitude of a sound causes greater tympanal vibration, stimulating more nerves. Sensitivity is greatest to sounds approaching at a right angle to the plane of the tympanum, and insects with hearing can thus locate, or avoid, the source of a sound.

Sound waves are simply air (or water) pressure waves, and therefore their presence can be detected by some tactile hair sensilla as movements in the air. Thus, some "deaf" insects receive sounds. In some flies, particularly male mosquitoes (Culicidae) and midges (Chironomidae), the second segment of the antennae is very much enlarged and contains a sound receptor (Johnston's organ). It is sensitive to vibrations of the antenna, which in these insects is

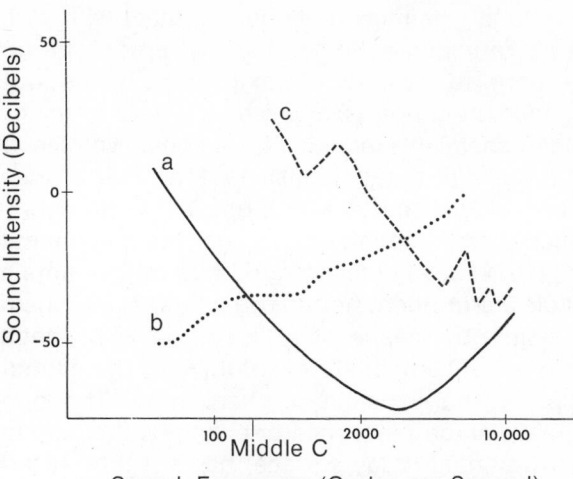

Figure 5–15. Thresholds of hearing response. Human (*a*); cricket cercus (*b*); locust tympanum (*c*). (Redrawn from Wigglesworth, V. B. 1972. The Principles of Insect Physiology. 7th ed. Chapman & Hall Ltd., London. After Pumphrey and Rawson-Smith.)

plumose. The hairs vibrate at the same frequency as the wingbeat of the female, and thus the males can locate mates. Lacewings have sound receptors in the radial veins of the forewings. These detect ultrasonic squeaks from bats (Miller, 1975).

CHEMICAL SENSE

It is difficult to discuss "taste" (gustation) and "smell" (olfaction) in insects as we know these senses, for both olfactory and gustatory receptors are found all over the insect's body, particularly on antennae, mouthparts, feet, and ovipositor. Figure 5–16 shows variations in structure of antennae. Often it is difficult to know precisely what receptors are specifically for chemicals. Some are similar to the hair sensilla discussed previously and there are a variety of other chemical receptors (Fig. 5–13).

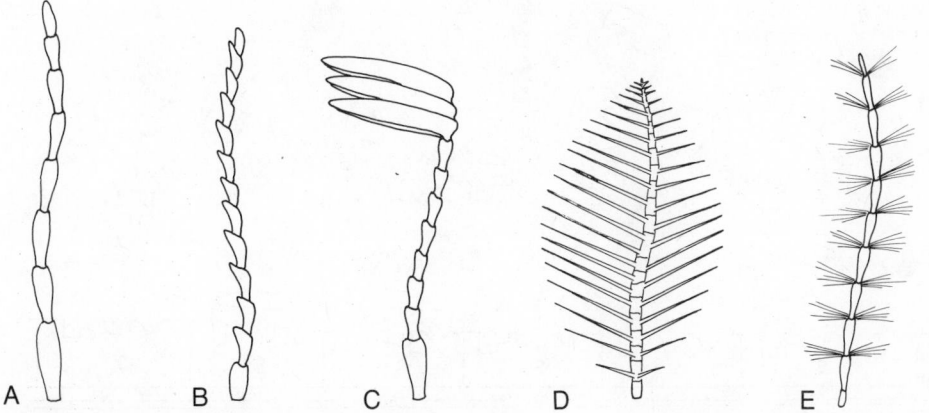

Figure 5–16. Types of insect antennae. Outgrowths increase receptive surface. *A*, Filiform, ground beetle. *B*, Serrate, long-horn beetle. *C*, Lamellate, scarab beetle. *D*, Plumose, saturniid moth. *E*, Plumose, male midge.

In all chemical reception, contact with a chemical by a sense cell stimulates a nerve impulse. Some chemoreceptors, particularly those on the body surface, respond to a variety of noxious chemicals; others, particularly some on the antennae, mouthparts, and feet, are very specific, responding to a single chemical. Such chemicals include pheromones, volatile chemicals from food plants or from the hosts of parasitic insects. (The role of these chemicals in reproduction and survival is discussed in subsequent chapters.) We do not yet know exactly how such discrimination occurs, but the discrimination may be very precise; Riley et al. (1974) have demonstrated that fungus ants may respond to a single isomer of their alarm pheromone. Perhaps specific chemicals may stimulate only specific sensilla, by means of a "lock and key" mechanism (Fig. 5–17). In some male moths, *all* antennal receptors may be stimulated by a single chemical substance, the female sex pheromone. The number of chemical sensilla differs greatly among insects. For example, the human louse, living in a rather constant environment (body surface) has but 9 or 10 antennal olfactory sensilla. By contrast, the male honey bee has 30,000 antennal receptors, necessitated by the wider variety of situations it encounters (Larsen, 1973).

HEAT, HUMIDITY, AND MAGNETISM

Heat, cold, and humidity receptors have not been specifically identified in most insects (an exception being the human louse, Fig. 5–18), but many insects do respond to humidity and temperature gradients in field and lab. Some parasitic wasps locate wood-boring hosts by the heat they generate, and the blood-sucking bug *Rhodnius* does likewise for mammals until its antennae are removed. Removal of mealworm antennae destroys the insect's capacity to orient in a humidity gradient, suggesting that receptor sites may be concentrated there.

Lindauer and Martin (1972) demonstrated that honey bees, at least, perceive earth's magnetic field. Honey bees build a comb oriented in a north-south direction under normal circumstances but produce a circular comb when the magnetic field is experimentally increased 10 times. The location and structure of the bees' "magneto-receptors" have yet to be discovered.

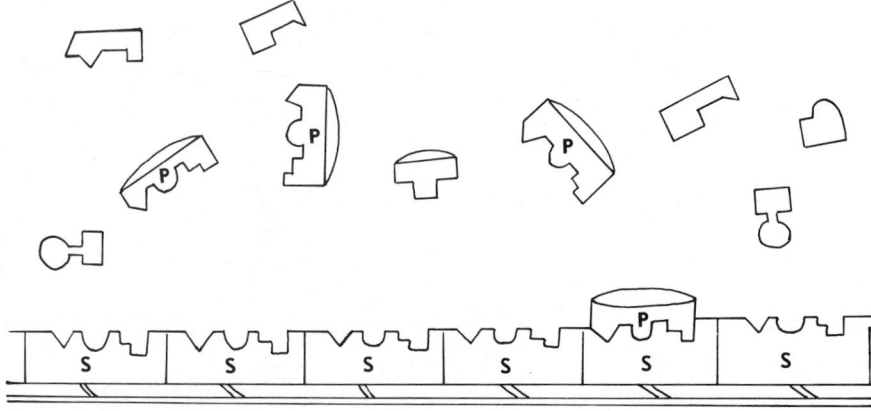

Figure 5–17. Diagrammatic representation of "lock-and-key" hypothesis of pheromone reception. Only specific pheromones (*P*) fit specialized chemical receptor sites (*S*) to generate a nerve impulse.

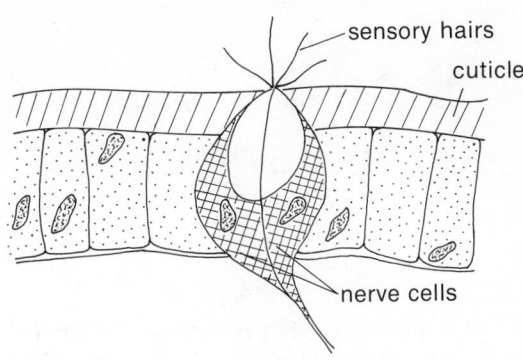

Figure 5–18. Cross section of humidity-sensing organ of human body louse. (Modified from Carthy, J. D. 1958. An Introduction to the Behaviour of Invertebrates. George Allen & Unwin Ltd., London.)

ORIENTATION

To this point, we have discussed reception of environmental inputs. The insect also receives impulses from sensors that determine the relative orientation of the parts of the body (proprioception). Johnston's organ, on the second antennal segment, is one such sensor, being stimulated by the orientation of the antenna. This is particularly important in insect flight and swimming. As an example, the whirligig beetles that speed around the water surface avoid collisions because of the change in antennal orientation that occurs when they hit a wave. Throughout the surface of the insect body are **campaniform sensilla,** and inside one often finds **chordotonal organs** (Fig. 5–19). Both are sensitive to stresses in the cuticle. In addition, there are some stretch receptors in muscles and connective tissue (Dethier, 1963).

Some hair sensilla double as proprioceptors. In particular, on the prothorax of bees, Orthoptera, and other insects are hairs that are stimulated when the head is turned to one side or downward (Fig. 5–20). The downward pull of gravity on the bee's head enables it to orient to gravity in the darkness of the hive, and this is vital to the success of the bee "dance" (Chapter Six). Pressure-sensitive hairs on the forewings of many insects are moved when the insect is in flight, and these "airspeed indicators" provide input enabling a fly or bee to compensate for wind velocity and to remain hovering in one spot.

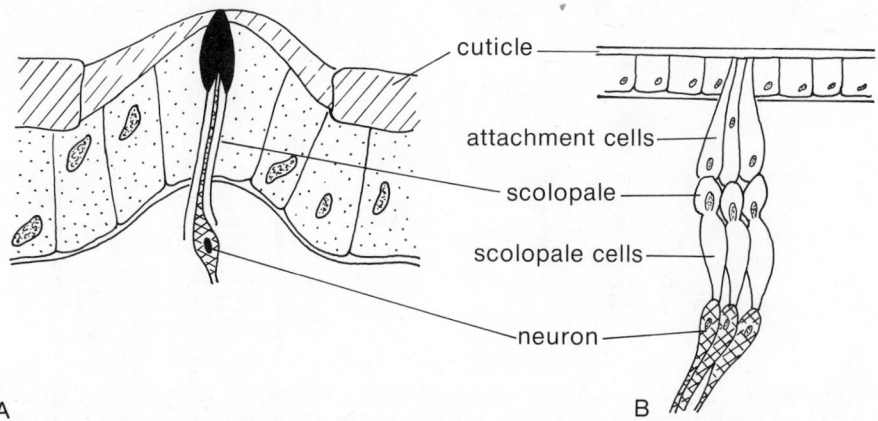

Figure 5–19. More sensilla. *A*, Campaniform sensillum. *B*, Chordotonal organ.

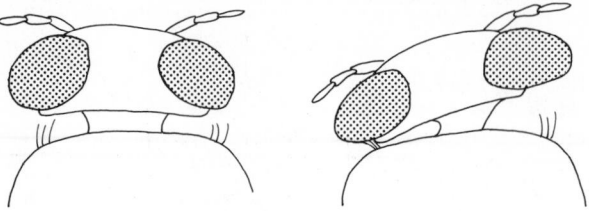

Figure 5–20. Function of hair sensilla in orientation of head.

Having now seen how insects receive stimuli, we are ready to discuss what they do with them, first in terms of isolated structures and then as an integrated unit.

EFFECTOR SYSTEMS

MUSCLE

An effector system is one that does something active; in insects there are effectors for light and sound production and for movement. In movement, a nerve impulse stimulates a muscle to contract, and this contraction moves that to which the muscle is attached, usually a portion of the insect exoskeleton. Observable insect activity is composed of many coordinated effectors acting in this way. In insects, we find muscles most prevalent where movement is concentrated, especially in the thorax and legs.

All insect muscles are made of striated fibers, with bands appearing under the microscope (Fig. 5–21), though the visceral muscles, controlling slow movements of the digestive, circulatory, reproductive, and excretory systems, are more branched than the compact "skeletal" muscles that move segments and ap-

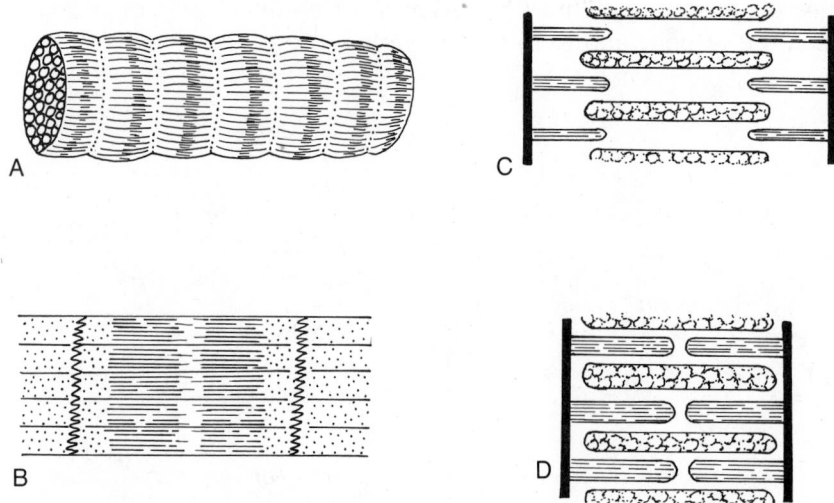

Figure 5–21. Insect muscle. *A*, Muscle fiber composed of many fibrils. *B*, Enlargement of single fiber, showing bands. *C*, Position of bands in relaxed muscle fiber. *D*, Position of bands in contracted muscle fiber.

pendages. A single muscle is composed of many fibers. The physiology of contraction, studied mostly in vertebrates, is similar in insects (Hoyle, 1973). Arrival of a nerve impulse at a neuromuscular junction induces the secretion of a chemical at the nerve ending. This chemical, not yet identified, causes a change in permeability of the muscle cells to calcium ions, which then rush into the cell. The chemical change evidently then causes the filaments to slide together, shortening the muscle (Fig. 5–21). The chemical reaction has not been fully worked out but involves energy and oxygen consumption.

Typically, insect muscles are innervated by two motor neurons: a "fast" neuron, whose impulse elicits a rapid twitch, and a "slow" neuron, eliciting a slower "tonic" contraction. For instance, the femoral muscle of a grasshopper leg produces slow responses for walking and fast ones for jumping (Smith, 1965). Striated muscle will also contract spontaneously if stretched suddenly in insects (*and* in humans, as the physician discovers when tapping your knee with his hammer). This tendency of muscle to contract automatically is of importance in maintaining the extremely rapid wingbeats of many insects, as we shall see. A few visceral muscles (e.g., the heart of larval *Anopheles*) are not innervated and may be controlled exclusively by hormones. Blood pressure is important in some arthropod movements, particularly the unfolding of the beak in Hemiptera and the extension of legs in spiders and centipedes.

INTEGUMENT

The insect exoskeleton, a protective covering for internal organs and an attachment for muscles, consists of a layer of epidermal cells over which lies an external cuticle, a light but exceedingly strong covering that extends over the entire body and lines the foregut, hindgut, tracheae, and genital tract. The epidermis secretes the cuticle, in which three layers are recognizable: endocuticle, exocuticle, and epicuticle (Fig. 5–22).

Endocuticle and exocuticle are composed of a flexible polysaccharide, **chitin,** and (often) a tanned protein, **sclerotin,** chemically rather like hard plastic. Sclero-

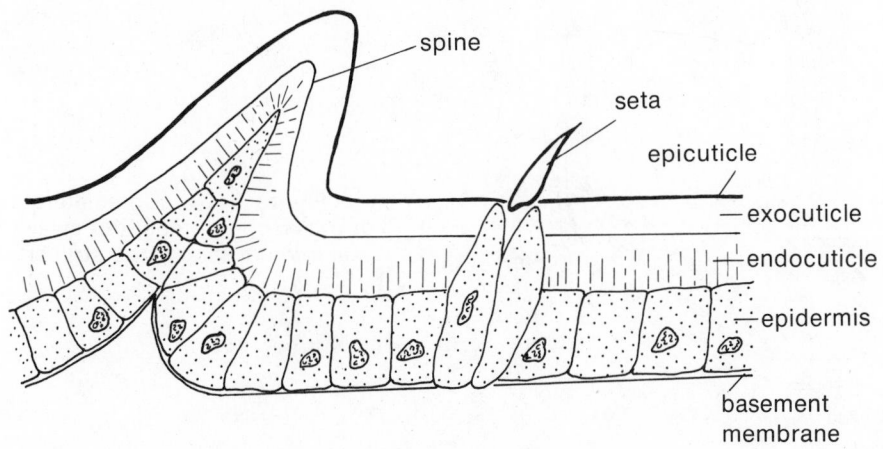

Figure 5–22.   Cross section of insect integument.

tin is responsible for the hardness of many insects; their cuticle is sclerotized. The amount of sclerotized cuticle varies greatly in insects; in larvae of many Diptera, Lepidoptera, and Hymenoptera, only the mandibles are sclerotized, whereas the extreme hardness of some fleas and beetles is legendary.* Thinner sclerotized cuticle is flexible enough to be distorted slightly, thereby storing energy and snapping back into place when released. This is important in flight (discussed subsequently), though greater freedom of movement between sclerotized parts is afforded by thin, unsclerotized membranes at joints of moveable body parts (Fig. 2–8).

Overlying sclerotized endocuticle and exocuticle is the very thin epicuticle, composed of a waterproof wax layer and cuticulin, a cementing substance similar to shellac. Both cuticulin and wax impart the shiny reflective surface characteristic of many insects. More important to the insect's survival, the epicuticle is almost impermeable to water, and we have seen (Chapter Four) the necessity of water conservation to very small animals. A small scratch through the epicuticle of a caterpillar will cause it to dry out in short order. Wigglesworth (1964) relates the North African practice of mixing a bit of road dust with stored flour; the resulting abrasion to cuticles of grain pests kills them quickly, preventing further infestation.

The exoskeleton provides both a light but strong support for an insect externally and rigid attachments for muscles internally. Particularly within the head and thorax but in every place where there are moving parts are ridges and spines (**apodemes**), sometimes amounting to a rudimentary internal skeleton (Figs. 5–23 and 5–29). Within the head, mouthpart and neck muscles attach to a rigid skeletal structure, the **tentorium** (Fig. 5–23). Locations of such internal attachments are externally evidenced by sutures and pits. The external integument may be modified, forming spines, sculpturing, scales, or hairs that may aid an insect

---

* Certain Tenebrionidae have earned the name "ironclad beetles," having tried the patience of many a collector by causing insect pins to bend.

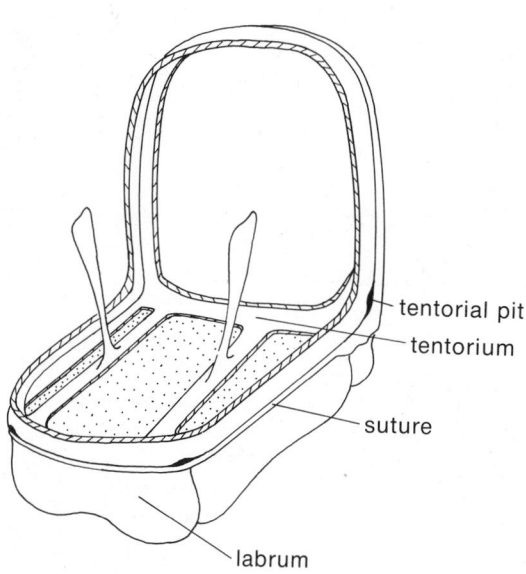

tentorial pit
tentorium

suture

labrum

Figure 5–23. Dorsolateral view of grasshopper head, cut away to reveal internal sclerotized structures.

in blending with its background or, conversely, may advertise an insect's presence to potential mates or would-be predators. External sensory structures, discussed previously, are almost all outgrowths of the integument and therefore are secreted originally by the epidermis.

Colors of insects are of two types: pigments and structural colors. Pigments are organic chemicals (usually proteins) deposited in the epicuticle or present in hemolymph and visible through thin, transparent, unsclerotized cuticle, as in many larvae. Pigments absorb light of certain wavelengths and reflect others; we see the reflected wavelengths as color. Some pigments like melanins, which are responsible for most dark browns and blacks, are synthesized internally, while others, particularly many yellows, oranges, and reds, are pigments taken unchanged from plant food and incorporated directly into the integument. The bright orange of many milkweed-feeding insects (Chapter Nine) is exemplary. Hemoglobin, discussed earlier (Chapter Four), is a red pigment. In the days before synthetic dyes, quinone pigments from scale insects were widely used; cochineal is perhaps the best-remembered of these. Structural colors, including most blue, purple, or metallic hues, are caused by interference, or "breaking-up", of reflected white light into several wavelengths by very fine striations or several very thin cuticular layers. This same process causes color reflection from an exceedingly thin layer of oil on wet pavement or water.

The exoskeleton is ideal for the movements of a very small organism but sets limitations on the maximum size of insects. The strength of a muscle is proportional to its area in cross section; as an animal doubles in weight, its muscles must double in cross-sectional size to maintain efficiency. In the terrestrial environment, there comes a point at which an animal with an external skeleton can no longer encase the muscles necessary to hold itself up, and an internal skeleton then becomes more efficient. This point is reached approximately at the mass of a mouse; very few insects are larger, and few terrestrial vertebrates are smaller.

Another problem is that, though cuticle is secreted by epidermal cells, it is nonliving and hence cannot grow or even stretch after sclerotin hardens. Periodically, therefore, as internal tissues enlarge, epidermal cells must secrete a newer, larger cuticle and shed the old exoskeleton. We shall return to this subject when considering insect development (Chapter Seven).

MOVEMENT

Insect activity results from contraction of skeletal muscle, which pulls on the exoskeleton to which it is attached by tendons. Muscles usually occur in antagonistic pairs; when one contracts, the other relaxes and vice versa, so that a part may be moved back and forth. Some insects, including many larvae, have little hardened cuticle and depend on muscle pressure on the internal hemolymph for form and movement. A caterpillar, for instance, moves each segment forward by first retracting its legs, then contracting muscles to change the shape of the segment, then extending the legs and relaxing the body muscles. Waves of such motions moving forward between segments enable the caterpillar to move forward (Fig. 5–24).

Nearly all adult insects and most larvae possess legs. Leg segments are articulated by **condyles** (Fig. 5–25), attachments about which the segments move.

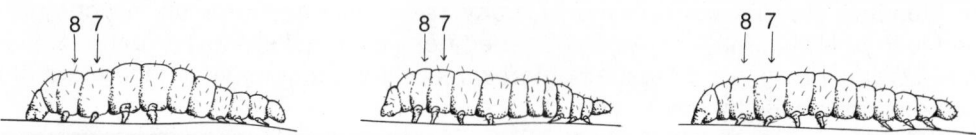

Figure 5–24. Walking caterpillar, alternately shortening and lengthening segments (note segments 7 and 8).

Two dicondylic joints at right angles permit the distal segments of the leg to rotate in any direction (Fig. 5–25 C and D). Movements occur when leg muscles are stimulated to contract by nerve impulses. Constant input from campaniform sensilla and other proprioceptors is integrated by the central nervous system to control the motion of the legs. High-speed photography reveals that in normal walking, cockroaches (and probably most insects) move the legs in sequence: L1 L3 R2 and R1 R3 L2 (Fig. 5–26A). Thus three legs are constantly in contact with the ground, and this tripod arrangement is very stable; a walking insect does not wobble and can stop and turn in its tracks. Legs are arranged so that the insect is suspended from its own "knees," lowering the center of gravity which also provides stability (Fig. 5–26B).

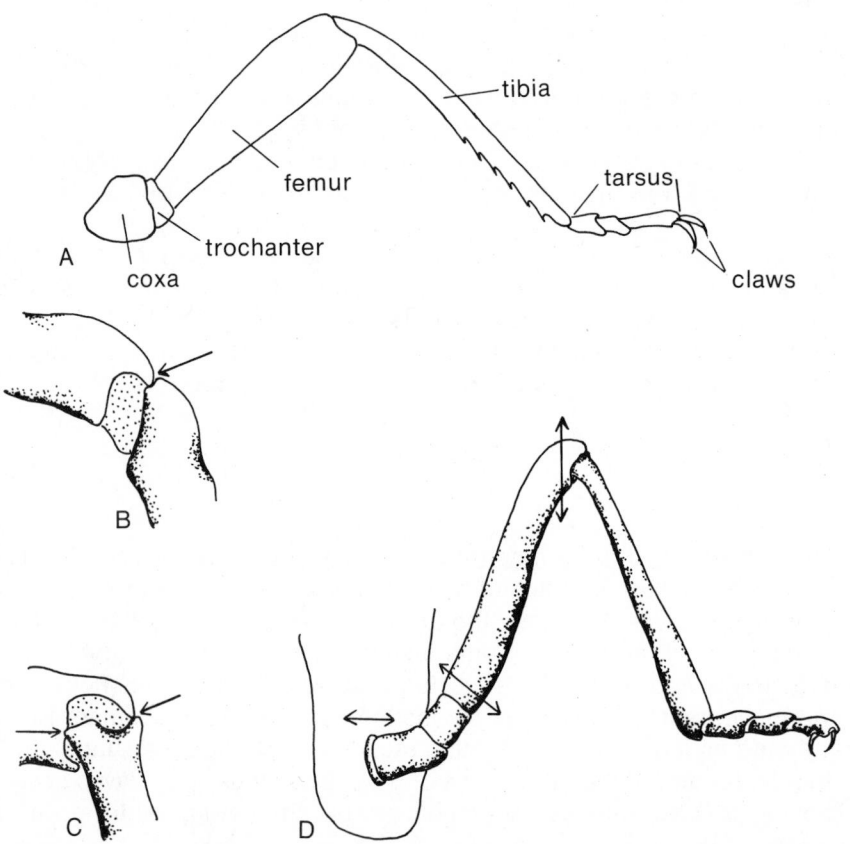

Figure 5–25. Insect legs. *A*, Parts of leg. *B*, Monocondylic joint; condyle (*arrow*). *C*, Dicondylic joint; condyles (*arrows*). *D*, Leg movements. Arrows indicate directions of movement at each of three dicondylic joints.

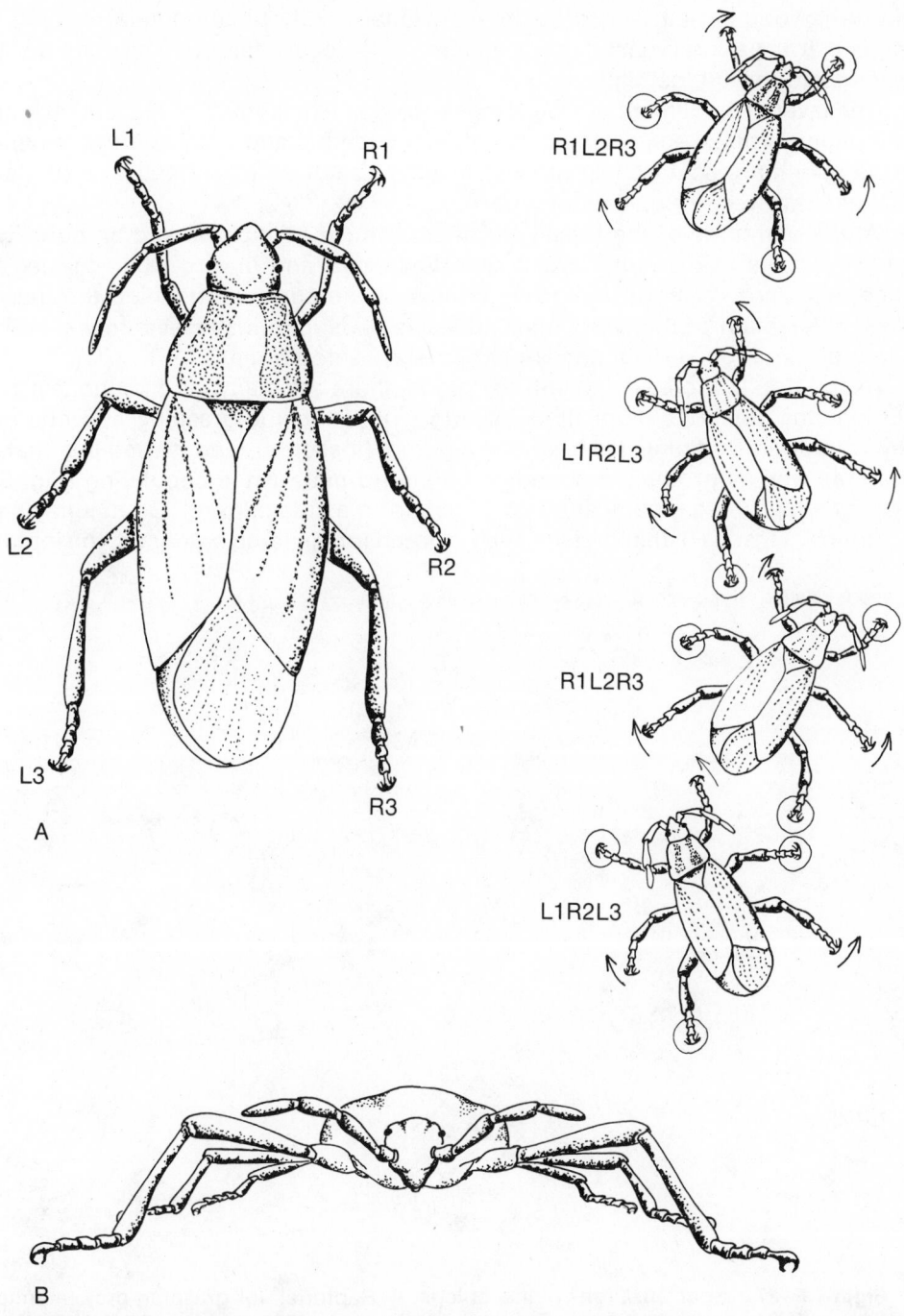

Figure 5–26. Insect walking. *A*, Sequence of leg movements in normal movement. Circled legs are in contact with substrate. *B*, Anterior view of insect showing center of gravity suspended between legs.

The nervous control of walking is not thoroughly understood, though it appears that walking movements are reflex movements inhibited or modified by the central nervous system and probably controlled by thoracic ganglia. If a leg is removed from a cockroach, the remaining five legs alter their movements to compensate for the lost limb.

The lever arrangement of insect legs provides a maximum of movement from a minimum of muscle shortening. Additional speed is added by additional joints and lengthening, so that fast-moving insects,* such as tiger beetles and cockroaches, have very long, slender legs.

At the extremity of the tarsus are often one (or two) claws and an adhesive pad. The claws in particular are drawn downward and inward when the leg is flexed, and they catch on tiny irregularities of the surface on which the insect walks. This action of the claws, plus adhesive pads, permits insects to walk on a ceiling or perch on vertical panes of apparently smooth glass.

In addition to increased length for speed, there are many modifications of insect legs for functions other than walking. These include grasping and holding prey (raptorial), jumping (saltatorial), digging (fossorial), and swimming (natatorial), as well as producing sound or holding a mate while copulating (Fig. 5–27). A number of leg modifications may occur on a single insect. On a honey bee (Fig. 5–27*F, G,* and *H*), the forelegs carry a notch for cleaning antennae; the middle

---

* Speed is relative; at top speed, a cockroach moves 4.6 kph.

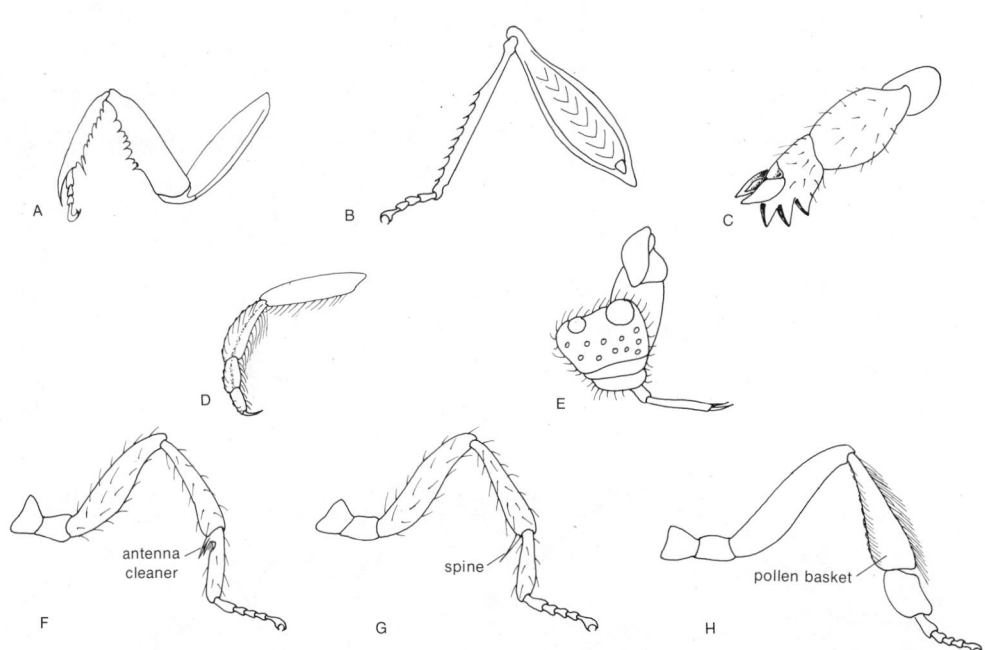

Figure 5–27. Specializations of insect legs. *A,* Raptorial, for grasping prey (mantid). *B,* Saltatorial, for jumping (locust). *C,* Fossorial, for digging (mole cricket). *D,* Natatorial, for swimming (water bug). *E,* For holding female during copulation (predaceous diving beetle). *F,* Foreleg of honey bee, with antenna cleaner on first tarsal segment. *G,* Midleg of honey bee, with spine for cleaning spiracles. *H,* Hindleg of honey bee, with pollen basket on tibia. (*F, G,* and H redrawn from Snodgrass, R. E. 1925. Anatomy and Physiology of the Honeybee. Copyright © 1925 by McGraw-Hill, Inc. Used by permission of McGraw-Hill Book Co.)

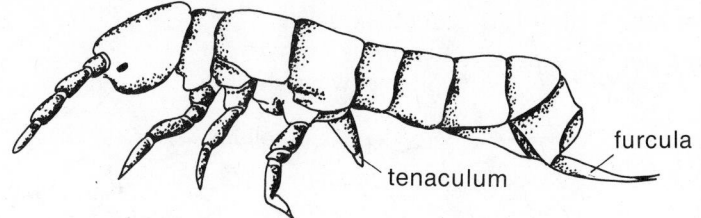

Figure 5–28. Springtail, order Collembola.

legs, a spur to clean spiracles; and the hindlegs, an enlarged tarsus with long hairs forming a "pollen basket" for carrying pollen. The first two are inevitable adaptations to getting pollen plastered all over their bodies.

Swimming insects have unusual orientation problems in that they are often not in contact with anything but water. Apparently, those that carry an air bubble (Chapter Four) can orient with reference to gravity owing to the action of the air bubble on the antennae. Some swim by rowing, others by undulating, and dragonfly nymphs swim by jet propulsion; the hindgut is filled with water, which is then suddenly expelled, propelling the insect forward. Some insects, because of their light weight and waxy cuticle, can make use of the surface film of water by moving about on it; the hindlegs of *Gyrinus* move 50 strokes per second, propelling the beetle along at speeds up to 3.6 kph (Chapman, 1969).

There are other ways to get about on land. The springtails have at their hind end a furcula, which is normally tucked under their body and held in place by a tenaculum (Fig. 5–28). Muscular tension builds up, and when the tenaculum is released, up hops the springtail. Some fly larvae, notably that of the cheese skipper, grasp their rear end by their mouthhooks, then suddenly release, and jump about in this way. The Mexican jumping bean, the larva of a Tortricid moth, infests seeds; sudden movements of the larva cause the frijole to leap. Some parasitic Hymenoptera do this in their cocoon. When placed on their backs, click beetles (Elateridae) (Chapter Three) bend the anterior portion of their body backward, then straighten suddenly, snapping into the air. Sometimes they land right side up and sometimes they don't.

THE THORAX AND FLIGHT

Perhaps the most important adaptation leading to the phenomenal diversity of insects is their wings. Insects are the only invertebrates to possess wings, and most adult insects have them. Consideration of flight must begin with a look at the thorax, three segments more or less fused and specialized as an attachment for legs and wings and as a housing for the muscles responsible for locomotion. In insects having no wings (Thysanura, Diplura, Protura, and many larvae) the thoracic segments are relatively distinct and somewhat moveable with respect to one another. In the winged insects (and in those wingless insects, such as Anoplura and Mallophaga, whose ancestors were winged), the thoracic segments have been modified by being fused into a reinforced box with an internal structure for attachment of the wing muscles and external sclerites responsible for wing orientation and wing-folding (Fig. 5–29).

In terms of evolution, winged insects can be divided into two groups on the basis of wing-folding (Chapter Three). In terms of function, they can be divided

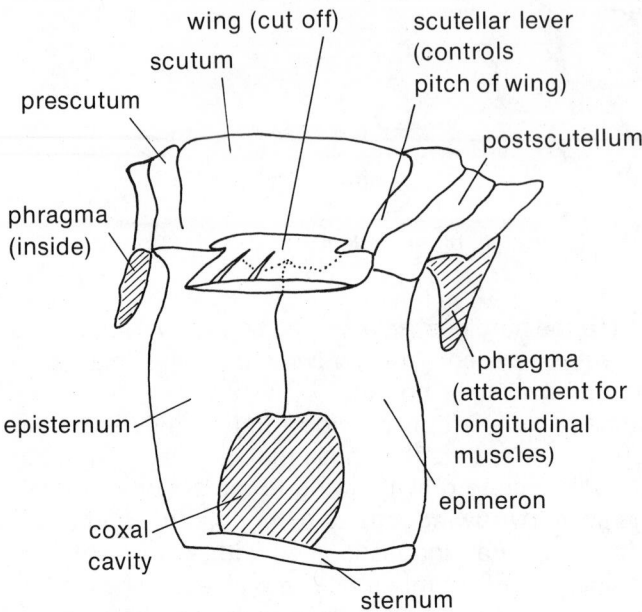

Figure 5–29. Diagrammatic side view of mesothorax of winged insect (wing and leg removed). (Modified from Snodgrass, R. E. 1935. Principles of Insect Morphology. Copyright © 1935 by McGraw-Hill, Inc. Used by permission of McGraw-Hill Book Co.)

into two groups based on the attachment and function of the wing muscles. In Ephemeroptera, Odonata, Orthoptera and relatives, and Lepidoptera, the wings are moved up and down by direct, or **synchronous,** flight muscles, attached to the wing bases and the thorax (Fig. 5–30). Such muscles are directly innervated, and a single nerve impulse elicits a single muscle twitch. Such musculature contracts only as fast as single nerve impulses reach it, and most Odonata, Orthoptera, and Lepidoptera average 25 wing beats or less per second (Table 5–1). Other insects, particularly beetles, Hymenoptera, and Diptera, have wingbeat frequencies from 100 to 600 times per second (or more), and these depend on indirect, or **asynchronous,** flight muscles (Fig. 5–31), both ends of which attach directly to the thorax.

To understand the action of indirect flight muscles one must view the thorax as a resilient box capable of being changed in shape by muscular action. When wings are extended, the thorax is "stable" in two positions: with wings up and with wings down. Elasticity renders the thorax unstable when wings are level.

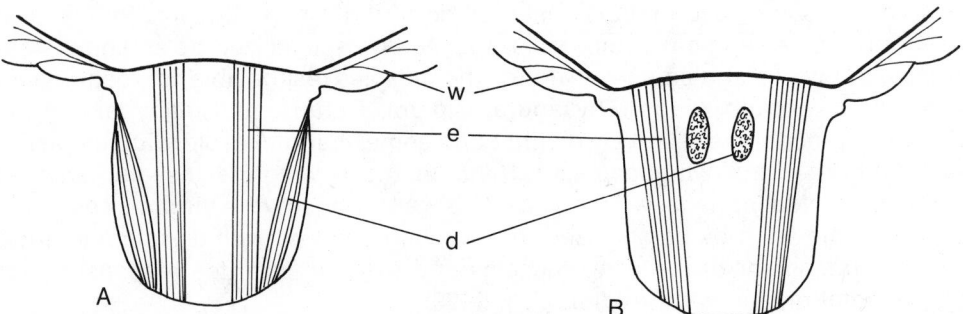

Figure 5–30. Attachment of direct (*A*) and indirect (*B*) flight muscles. Wing depressor muscle (*d*); wing elevator muscle (*e*); wing (*w*).

Table 5–1. MAXIMUM WINGBEAT FREQUENCIES OF SELECTED INSECTS*

Insect	Wingbeats per Second
Coleoptera	
Coccinella (ladybird)	91
Melolontha (chafer)	46
Diptera	
Culex (mosquito)	307
Forcipomyia (midge)	1047
Musca (house fly)	190
Tabanus (horse fly)	96
Hymenoptera	
Apis (honey bee)	250
Bombus (bumble bee)	240
Vespa (hornet)	110
Lepidoptera	
Colias (sulfur butterfly)	8
Papilio (swallowtail)	9
Odonata	
Aeshna (dragonfly)	28
Hummingbird (for comparison)	50

*From Wigglesworth, V. B. 1972. The Principles of Insect Physiology. 7th ed. Chapman & Hall Ltd., London.

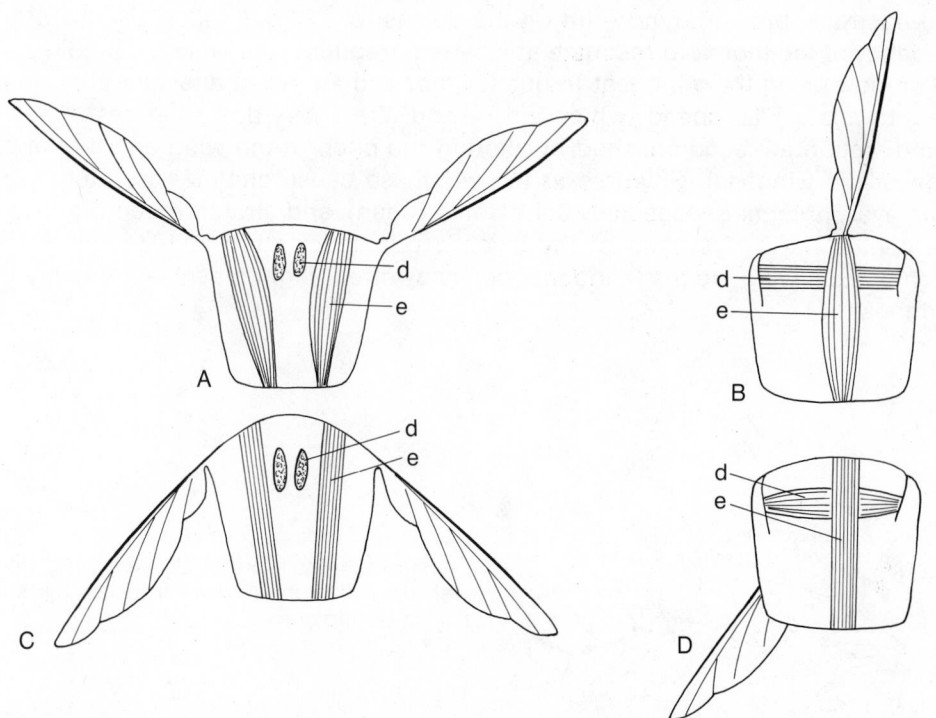

Figure 5–31. Action of indirect flight muscles. *A*, Cross section; wings raised, elevator muscles (*e*) contracted, depressor muscles (*d*) relaxed. *B*, Side view of *A*. *C*, Cross section; wings depressed, elevators (*e*) relaxed, depressors (*d*) contracted. *D*, Side view of *C*.

The process of flight is set in motion by arrival of a nerve impulse causing contraction of the longitudinal muscles (Fig. 5–31A). Because the cuticle is flexible, the contraction distorts the thorax, with the following results: (1) A lever arrangement of sclerites forces the wings downward and (2) the thorax is distorted until elastic forces snap, or "click," it into the "wings down" stability, (3) stretching the vertical muscles. As mentioned previously, momentary stretching of a muscle causes it to contract spontaneously, and the vertical muscles do so, distorting the thorax in such a way as to (4) force the wings upward and (5) stretch the longitudinal muscles. Thus stretched, the longitudinal muscles then contract, beginning the cycle over again without (necessarily) the arrival of another nerve impulse. In this way the thorax may distort, and wings flap, several times for each arriving nerve impulse (Pringle, 1957).

As we have seen, there is great variation among insect wings, and it is likely that our knowledge of insect flight, gleaned mostly from studies of tethered locusts, bees, and flies, may not hold true for all insects. All winged insects except flies (and a few scale insects and mayflies) have four wings, but in Hymenoptera and Lepidoptera the forewings and hindwings are often coupled and in Coleoptera the forewings are protective structures, so that in all major orders the wings function as a two-winged unit.

With high-speed cinematography or strobe lights, entomologists have investigated movements of insect wings (e.g., Dalton, 1975). It is possible to adjust the timing of light flashes to "slow" or even "stop" the apparent wing motions. With such techniques, we can analyze positions of wings and thoracic sclerites and measure wingbeat frequency (see Table 5–1). For instance, in normal fly flight, the wingtips describe a figure 8, and the wing changes in pitch on downstroke and upstroke, providing more lift on the downstroke (Fig. 5–32). Because of the tendency of the thorax to resonate at a certain frequency, an insect cannot speed up or slow down the wingbeat frequency, nor can an insect alter the area of the wing to change air speed (which birds—and airplanes—do). Changes in speed and direction are accomplished by altering the pitch of the wing and the amplitude of the wingbeat. Sclerites at the wingbase cause changes in pitch. Input from eyes, antennae (especially Johnston's organ), and stretch receptors inform the central nervous system of the insect's orientation, and adjustments in the pitch of each wing are made independently by direct flight muscles to modify the wingbeat.

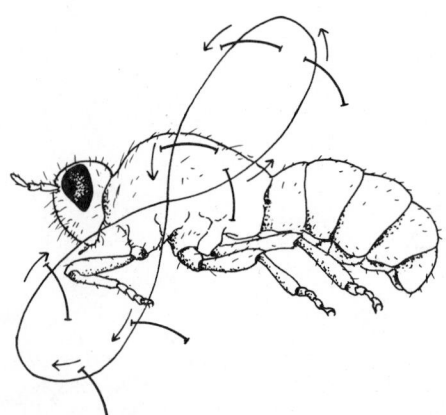

Figure 5–32. Orientation of wing tip in level forward flight. Arrows indicate direction of wing tip movement.

Table 5–2. MAXIMUM SPEED OF INSECTS IN FLIGHT*

Insect	Maximum Speed	
	METERS/SECOND	MPH
Coleoptera		
Melolontha	3	6.75
Diptera		
Musca	2	4.5
Tabanus	4	9
Hymenoptera		
Apis	3.7	8.5
Bombus	5	11.2
Lepidoptera		
Pieris	2.5	5.6
Sphingidae	15	33.7
Neuroptera		
Chrysopa (lacewing)	0.6	1.3
Odonata		
Anax	8	18
Libellula	10	22.4

*From Wigglesworth, V. B. 1972. The Principles of Insect Physiology. 7th ed. Chapman & Hall Ltd., London.

Flies and bees are unique in their ability to hover, which they do by fixing visually on an object and constantly compensating for windspeed by changing their airspeed. Either a high wingbeat frequency, as seen in most flies and bees, or a long tail, as in dragonflies, will control the tendency to pitch forward.

There are many wing modifications which affect insect flight. In Coleoptera, Hemiptera, and Orthoptera, the forewing is partly or completely hardened and serves as a covering, though the latter two do flap their elytra. The elytra of beetles are usually spread during flight, and since they cannot fly without the elytra, it is presumed that the elytra contribute to the stability of the resonating thorax and perhaps provide some lift. Tiny insects of several orders have fringed wings and apparently can alter their wingbeat frequency, moving the wings faster on the downstroke and slower on the upstroke (Benett, 1973). Another interesting modification is the hindwing, or haltere, of the Diptera, modified into a highly developed chordotonal sense organ (Fig. 3–77) for maintaining stability. When the fly is under way, these halteres vibrate up and down, usually at the same frequency as the wingbeats. Having their center of gravity located distally, the halteres are exceedingly sensitive to twisting forces that occur when the insect changes orientation. Nerve impulses are sent to the brain, which may then correct the course with impulses to the appropriate direct flight muscles. A fly with the halteres removed is unstable and simply pitches head over heels. Stability can be restored by gluing a small thread to the fly's rear end, like the tail of a kite or of a dragonfly.

All this produces a maxium speed of perhaps 15 meters per second (33 mph) in some sphinx moths (Table 5–2). (The 818 mph deerfly of a generation ago has been debunked). Most insects fly more slowly. The stimuli for initiating flight may be exceedingly varied—food, sex, wind, and so forth. In flies, flying is a reflex reaction to drawing the tarsi against the body; if the tarsi are removed, a tethered fly will buzz until dead. Landing is less complex; as the fly approaches an object, sudden changes in visual stimuli lead to extension of the legs and cessation of the wingbeat.

Wings are used for activities other than flying. The protective function of forewings has been mentioned. In some insects, notably many butterflies, flashing of bright-colored wings may function as a sexual or territorial display or as a warning of foul taste to potential predators. Wing coloration may also aid in camouflage; sometimes the same species will be brightly colored on one side and camouflaged on the other. Some tiny parasitic wasps use the wings as oars, swimming underwater. Many Orthoptera use the wings to produce sounds.

SOUND PRODUCTION

All flying insects produce sound when beating their wings, and a great variety of insects produce sounds of other sorts. These sounds can be produced in many ways, from the deathwatch beetle tapping its head against the wood of its burrow to the hissing cockroach *Gromphadorhina* that emits air through the tracheae when disturbed. **Stridulation** is a general term for any production of insect sound made by rubbing surfaces together. When disturbed, many beetles rub the abdomen against the wings and some Hemiptera rub the beak along a roughened surface on the prosternum. The study of insect sounds, however, has centered chiefly on those insects, Cicadidae and Orthoptera, in which the sound has a major social significance.

Orthoptera produced sound by rubbing together a "file" and "scraper" (Fig. 5–33*A*). In the acridoid grasshoppers, the file is on the inner surface of the hind femur and the scraper is a thickened vein in the forewing. Rapid movement of the femur along the forewing produces characteristic sounds, the frequencies of which are species-specific. In male Gryllidae (crickets) and Tettigoniidae (long-horned grasshoppers and katydids), the file and scraper are on the forewings (Fig. 5–33*B*), which in stridulation are rapidly rubbed together, producing characteristic sounds. The morphology of file and scraper differ slightly among species, so that the songs differ, and high-speed photography shows that indi-

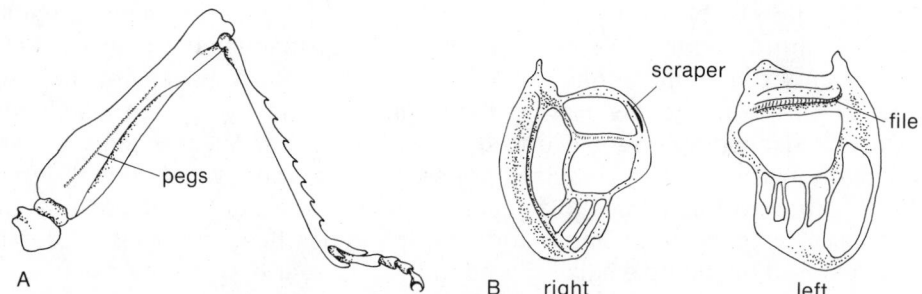

Figure 5–33. Stridulatory organs. *A*, Acridid grasshopper, femur. *B*, Cricket forewings. (Modified from Chapman, R. F. 1969. The Insects: Structure and Function. American Elsevier Publishing Co., Inc., New York.)

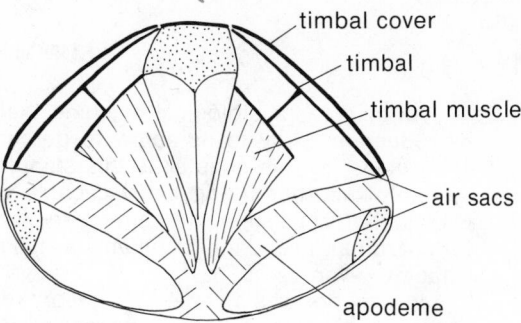

Figure 5–34. Cross section of first abdominal segment of cicada. (Redrawn from Pringle, J. W. S. 1954. A physiological analysis of cicada song. J. Exp. Biol. *31*:525–560.)

viduals of a single species may alter their songs by changing the frequency and manner of stridulations (Walker and Dew, 1972).

Some acridid grasshoppers and a few cicadas produce sounds by **crepitating**, snapping their wings against one another. Most cicadas produce sounds by **timballing,** which involves specialized structures, the timbals (Fig. 5–34). These are paired, sclerotized structures to which are attached muscles that contract alternately, "popping" the timbal inward. It snaps back by itself. Sound is produced when the timbal pops inward and it reverberates within the air sac, which thus amplifies the sound. The whole assembly functions rather like the metal "snappers" or "clickers" sometimes used as favors at little children's parties. In the case of cicadas, the individual "pops" occur so rapidly that we perceive them as a buzz or whistle.

LIGHT PRODUCTION

Several insect orders, notably Collembola, Homoptera, Diptera, and Coleoptera, contain members capable of producing light, but the production and significance of light has been studied only in the tropical click beetle *Pyrophorus* and in the most famous and familiar group, fireflies or lightning bugs (Lampyridae). The light-producing organs are on the ventral surface of the sixth and seventh abdominal segments in males of North American fireflies. They are composed of large cells, photocytes, and are well-endowed with tracheae. The photocytes contain quantities of the chemical luciferin (Smith, 1963). Nerve impulses from the last two abdominal ganglia release an as yet unidentified chemical which stimulates the oxidation of luciferin, catalyzed by the enzyme luciferase. The oxidation releases light in a reaction that is very efficient in that almost no heat is generated. The duration and sequence of the flashes vary according to the species involved, and this has behavioral and ecological significance. How insects act as complete and integrated organisms, that is, how they behave is the subject of the next chapter.

SUMMARY

An insect is a biological machine that, like ourselves, owes its survival and reproduction partly to its ability to perceive stimuli and respond appropriately. The subject of this chapter is this stimulus-response system, coordinated by a system of neurons (nerve cells) capable of conducting impulses. A central nervous system consisting of a paired nerve cord and a series of ganglia is the center for coordination and inhibition and is also responsible for hormone secretion (see Chapter Seven).

Insects possess a variety of sensory receptors, and there is great variation in the stimuli to which insects can respond. All sense reception involves an external stimulus generating a nerve impulse. Most (not all) insects have compound or simple eyes or both; relatively few insects have ears. Chemical (taste, smell) and mechanical receptors, though concentrated on feet, mouthparts, antennae, and ovipositor, are found on many places on insects. Many insects also possess heat and humidity receptors.

Active response to stimuli usually involves muscular action; a nerve impulse arrives at a muscle and causes it to shorten. Muscles pull on the exoskeleton, resulting in movement. Most insect locomotion involves legs (which in many insects have other uses as well) and, when present, wings; this chapter discusses the function of both. Other responses, particularly sound and light production, are briefly surveyed here.

Chapter Six

Behavior

INTRODUCTION

The receptor-coordinator-effector systems discussed in the previous chapter are inextricably linked with maintenance functions (Chapter Four) and reproduction and development (Chapter Seven) to produce integrated behavioral responses in whole, living insects. Insect behavior ranges from extremely simple movements, perhaps a twitch of a single leg or antenna, to extremely complex phenomena, such as nest-provisioning by sand wasps or the waggle dance of honeybees (discussed subsequently). Regardless of how simple or complex they are, most insect behaviors are functions of the stimulus-response system: sense receptors receive environmental input and nerves communicate this input to coordinating centers that transmit the impulses to effectors, resulting in a response. Some insect behavior is endogenous, originating within the insect as a response to hormonal or other chemical changes; an example is feeding behavior emanating from hunger.

Insect behavior, unlike that of many vertebrates, is normally rather predictable, stereotyped, and unmodifiable. Insects are capable of minimal learning, though much insect behavior seems intrinsic, perhaps "programmed" into the nervous system. This limitation is a result of insects' small size and consequent low number of association neurons. Also, since most insects have a rather short life span, they are not as likely to encounter experiences as diverse as those of longer-lived vertebrates (Mayr, 1974).

Despite intellectual limitations, insects in their great diversity are exceedingly interesting to watch, and we have been watching insects at least throughout recorded history and probably for a long time before. **Ethology,** the objective study of animal behavior, is, however, quite recent, and much remains to be done. An objective approach to behavior can best be built on a solid understanding of sensory-effector physiology, and this in turn often depends on application of appropriate instrumentation. Until rather recently, therefore, study of insect behavior was largely descriptive. Description is still the basis for study of behavior, but description introduces a difficulty: human language may not precisely describe the behavior we see, and explanations for behaviors may erroneously introduce subjective criteria. Two common pitfalls are **anthropomorphism,** attributing human characteristics to insects, and **teleology,** suggesting that natural events purposefully occur to fulfill a goal. Thus, the female earwig broods her young "because she loves them" (anthropomorphism) or "so that they will grow up" (teleology). Note that we cannot test these hypotheses by experiment (See Chapter One); they could be true, but they are unscientific. An objective ethological explanation is that brooding increases the probability of survival of offspring. This can be tested simply by comparing survival of young with and without brooding females. Knabke and Grigarick (1971) did this and found that when brooding female *Euboriella* earwigs were removed, mold became established and destroyed the eggs.

TYPES OF BEHAVIOR

Not all insect ethologists agree as yet on a uniform terminology. This is symptomatic of the relative youth of the field. For this discussion, I have divided insect behavior into four broad categories, ranging from simple to complex: reflexes, kineses, taxes, and learning. The first three are innate, "built-in", and probably largely genetically determined, though, obviously, modifiable by environmental circumstances. Learning does occur in many insects but is much more limited than in vertebrates.

REFLEXES

The simplest stimulus-response system is the **reflex arc** (Fig. 6–1), in which a sensory structure (in this case, a hair on a bee's tarsus), is moved very slightly, generating a nerve impulse along a sensory neuron to an association neuron in a thoracic ganglion. The association neuron transmits the impulse to motor neurons, which in turn synapse with muscles that extrude the stinger and release poison. (If *you* are being stung, your own reflexes cause you to withdraw your hand a few milliseconds before association neurons in your brain perceive the sting as painful and direct your vocal structures to form appropriate phrases.) Stinging is thus a reflex action involving relatively few neurons. Most reflexes are more complex and involve hundreds or thousands of sense receptors, neurons, and muscles; for example, normal insect walking (p. 214) is a series of reflexes. Much insect activity is ultimately the result of many simultaneous integrated reflexes, though it is currently impossible to trace the thousands of individual reflex arcs involved.

KINESES (NONDIRECTED ORIENTATION)

A **kinesis** is an undirected locomotor reaction to a stimulus; kineses are general movements in response to external stimuli. In addition to providing specific environmental input, impulses from sensory neurons also increase overall excitability of the central nervous system, "turning on" the insect, as it were. We have seen examples of kineses in previous chapters: e.g., increasing temperature above the preferred range for an insect generates increased locomotor activity, resulting ultimately in the insect's moving into a cooler area (Chapter Four). This kinesis may appear to be directed movement; the insect seems to avoid the heat by remaining in motion and turning until in a cooler place (Wigglesworth, 1972).

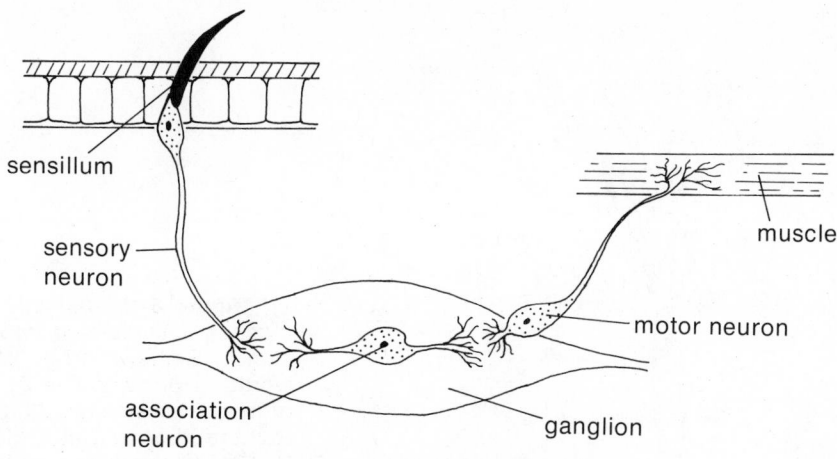

Figure 6–1. Simplified reflex arc.

The flight reaction of flies (and other insects) is a kinesis wherein tactile receptors on tarsi are not stimulated by contact with a surface. Fraenkel (1932) found that a fly tethered by the thorax attempted flight unless tarsi were extended and in contact with a tiny ball of cotton. He noted too that the intensity of flight kinesis was partially dependent upon sensory input from halteres, for when these were removed, tethered flies "flew" much less. Lice orient to optimum temperature and humidity merely by increasing their rate of turning and remaining in motion until they reach their preferred range (Fig. 6–2).

Akinesis, an overall lack of movement, is likewise controlled by sensory input, normally by tarsal contact with a surface. Tarsal contact combined with other stimuli (for a dragonfly, lowered temperature and reduced light intensity in the evening) inhibits central nervous system function in most insects (Wigglesworth, 1972). Conversely, in some insects, especially many beetles and Orthoptera, akinesis is induced by sudden loss of contact with a surface, causing **thanatosis,** or feigning death. This inhibits sensory input and locomotor reflexes; an

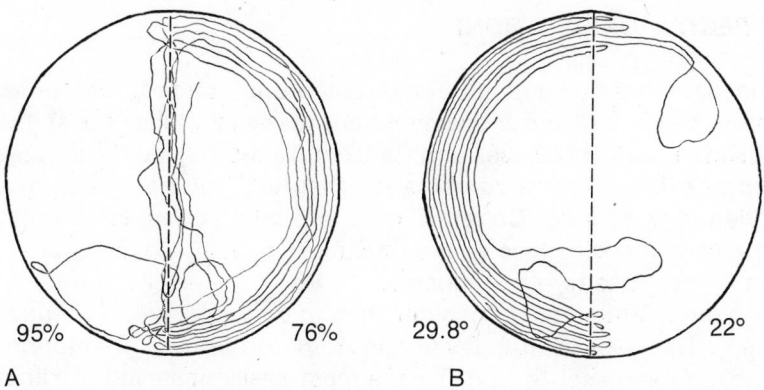

Figure 6–2. Tracks followed by human body louse. *A*, Eight minutes at 76 per cent and 95 per cent relative humidity. *B*, Five minutes at surface temperatures of 29.8°C and 22°C. (Redrawn from Wigglesworth, V. B. 1972. The Principles of Insect Physiology. Chapman & Hall Ltd., London.)

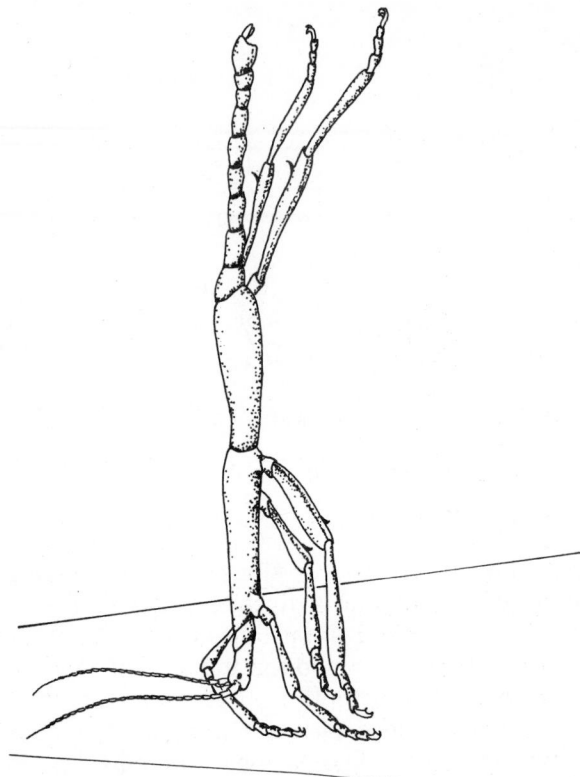

Figure 6–3. Akinetic walkingstick, manipulated into headstand. (Redrawn from Wigglesworth, V. B. 1972. The Principles of Insect Physiology. Chapman & Hall Ltd., London, after Schmidt, P. 1913. Katalepsie der Phasmiden. Biol. Zentralblatt *33*:193–207.)

insect thus immobilized can sometimes be arranged into almost any position (Fig. 6–3). Akinesis is apparently controlled by the brain, as Schmidt (1913) demonstrated by slicing through the thorax of an akinetic walkingstick; the tail end recovered its reflex activity, but the anterior portion remained immobile.

TAXES (DIRECTED ORIENTATION)

Most insect movements result in a directed orientation to one or several external stimuli. These directed movements are **taxes** (singular: taxis), movements superimposed on simpler kineses and reflexes. Taxes may be responses to physical or biological factors (or a combination thereof). You have seen examples of taxes in orientation to food (Chapter Four), and later I consider orientation to insects of the same species (see Communication, p. 234). Chapter Nine considers orientation in response to other species.

Fraenkel and Gunn (1961) consider that, in general, taxes are superimposed on reflexes and kineses in that deviations from "preferred" orientation increase the tendency of the insect to turn. This is most easily observed in klinotaxis, the simplest of taxes, in which an insect moves alternately right and left, sequentially comparing the intensity of a stimulus on each side of the body. When maggots move away from a light source (negative phototaxis), they turn their heads successively right and left. If two light sources are used, maggots move away along a line at equal angles between them (Fig. 6–4). In many, perhaps most, insects, unequal stimuli on each side of the body are compared simultaneously by integrating them within the insect brain. This integration, tropotaxis, is more efficient than klinotaxis and shows the selective advantage of having paired sensory structures: eyes, cerci, antennae. If an antenna is removed or an eye is painted over, the insect will not orient properly. If antennae are crossed and then glued in their new positions, an insect will turn toward the "wrong" side when orienting to an odor source.

Finally, there is telotaxis, in which the insect fixes the position of a stimulus and then moves directly toward (or away from) it. An example of telotaxis that has fascinated researchers is **light-compass orientation.** Here, an insect moves in a straight line by fixing the position of the sun in the sky (or of another light source) and then walking or flying at a constant angle to the light source (Fig. 6–5). Light-compass orientation was first noted in social insects, ants and bees, but it is now clear that many insects rely on it for direction. Insects' ability to perceive the plane of light polarization (Chapter Five) may also be involved in light-compass orientation. Apparently, night-flying insects are attracted to lights because of the light-compass reaction; by flying at a constant angle to a fixed light source, a moth spirals inward to a light (Fig. 6–6). Moth fanciers have long known that the best collecting can be done on cloudy nights when moon and stars do not compete with moths' orientation to artificial lights.

Taxes are also classified according to the environmental stimulus involved and are qualified as being positive or negative. Thus, moths' attraction to light is positive phototaxis, while maggots are negatively phototactic. Negative geotaxis is orientation away from the pull of gravity, which occurs in nymphs of cicadas as they emerge from under ground and climb vegetation prior to metamorphosing into adults. Many aquatic naiads also display negative geotaxis when emerging from under water prior to adult emergence (eclosion). Other sorts of taxes include anemotaxis (wind direction), chemotaxis (chemicals), hygrotaxis (humidity), menotaxis (constant visual pattern, such as that fixed by hovering flies; Chapter Five), skototaxis (darkness), and thigmotaxis (contact).

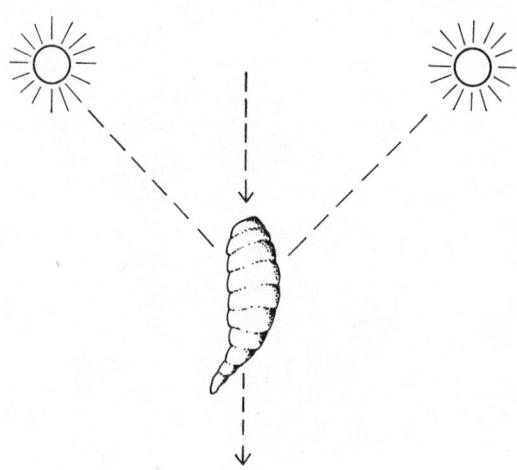

Figure 6–4. Negative phototaxis of maggot. Larva moves along dashed line by maintaining equal incidence of two lights.

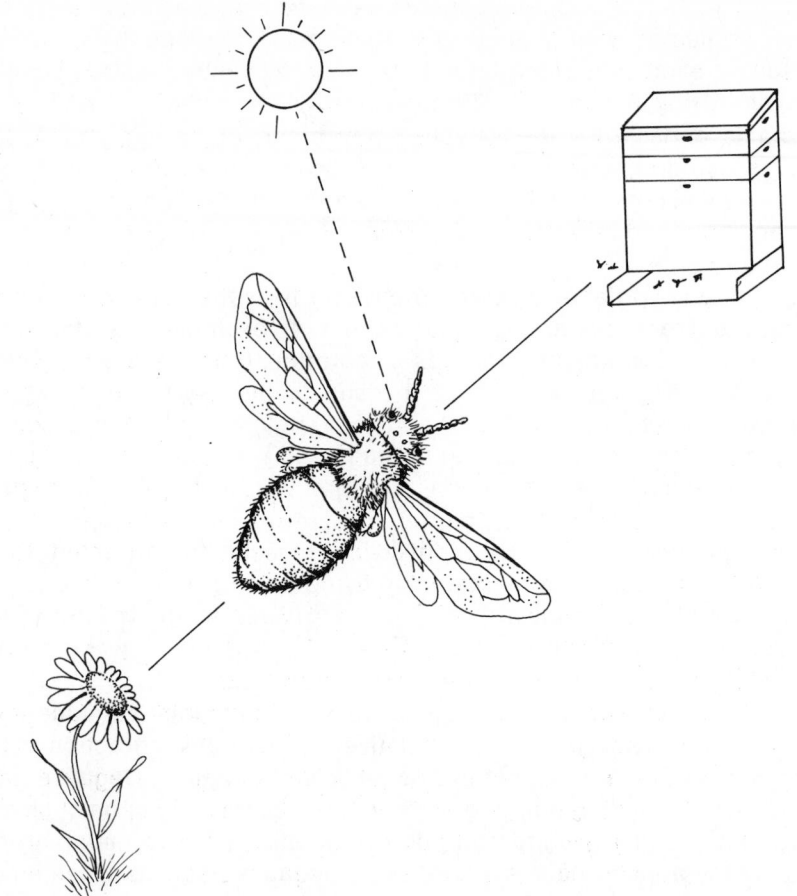

Figure 6–5. Light-compass orientation. Loaded bee flies in direct ''beeline'' by maintaining constant angle between flight direction and sun position.

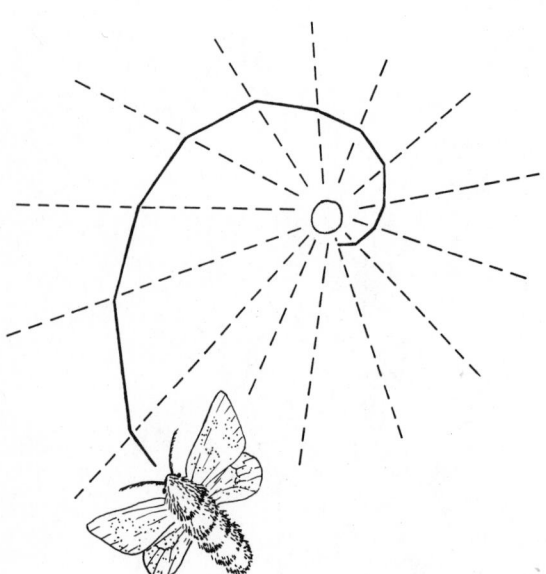

Figure 6–6. Light-compass orientation. Moth maintains constant angle between light source and flight path and thus follows spiral path inward toward light.

PATTERNS OF BEHAVIOR

Except in the ethologist's laboratory (and even there, usually) insects are simultaneously accosted by a variety of varying environmental stimuli and consequently often react simultaneously to more than one stimulus. The thermoregulatory behavior of locusts (Fig. 4–27) involves orientation to both light and temperature. Anemotaxis in male moths is often initiated by a chemical stimulus (female sex pheromone) and is modified by visual cues from the ground (Kennedy and Marsh, 1974). A taxis may be reversed, depending upon an insect's internal state; alfalfa weevil adults are normally negatively phototactic but become positively phototactic when starved (Armbrust and Gyrisco, 1968).

Reflexes, kineses, taxes, and the more complex behaviors derived from them usually require two things: an external stimulus, or **releaser,** and a state of internal readiness, or motivation (not to be anthropomorphically confused with conscious motivation in humans). The various environmental stimuli mentioned previously can be releasers; or, alternatively, a behavior itself may be a releaser for a subsequent behavior. For example, a female *Ammophila* digger wasp, upon capturing a caterpillar, carries it to the nest site, puts it down, digs open the nest entrance, turns around, drags the caterpillar in, and temporarily closes the nest again. Each act in the sequence serves as a releaser for the next, as the wasp never performs the tasks in any order but this (Baerends, 1941). Such stereotyped, rigid patterns are evidently instinctive, genetically programmed in the insect, subject to slight modification but basically unchanging.

The motivation for a behavioral act is dependent on the physiological state of the insect. Truman (1973) determined that in the moth *Anthraea pernyi* (Saturniidae), flight of adults was mediated by a hormone secreted by the brain. Prior to hormone secretion, the insects did not fly even though fully capable. Truman removed brains from newly emerged moths and replaced them with brains from older moths. Moths began flight activity only after receiving a brain from a moth that had already flown.

BEHAVIORAL MODIFICATION: PERIODICITY

Some insect behavior occurs intrinsically at regular intervals, timed to variations in the external environment. (We shall see intrinsic rhythms again when considering insect development.) Intrinsic activity patterns of the American cockroach, *Periplaneta americana,* have been extensively studied. The cockroaches' major activity period occurs every 24 hours, under normal circumstances, beginning just at dark (Fig. 6–7). If the roaches are reared in total darkness, they still adhere to the 24-hour activity rhythm, becoming active in the early evening. If the cockroaches are reared in a chamber in which "lights out" occurs earlier in the day (Fig. 6–7), their time of maximum activity moves up accordingly but maintains its 24-hour rhythm. If they are reared in continuous light, their activity eventually loses its rhythm (Beck, 1973). Cockroaches, and many other insects, apparently have an internal "clock," probably in the brain, that is "set" by external stimuli (in this case, the onset of darkness) and once "set," it maintains a 24-hour cycle. This "clock" may have a biochemical basis; to slow this presumed chemical reaction, Harker (1961) cooled a cockroach head, and then transplanted its brain to a cockroach whose activity rhythms had ceased owing

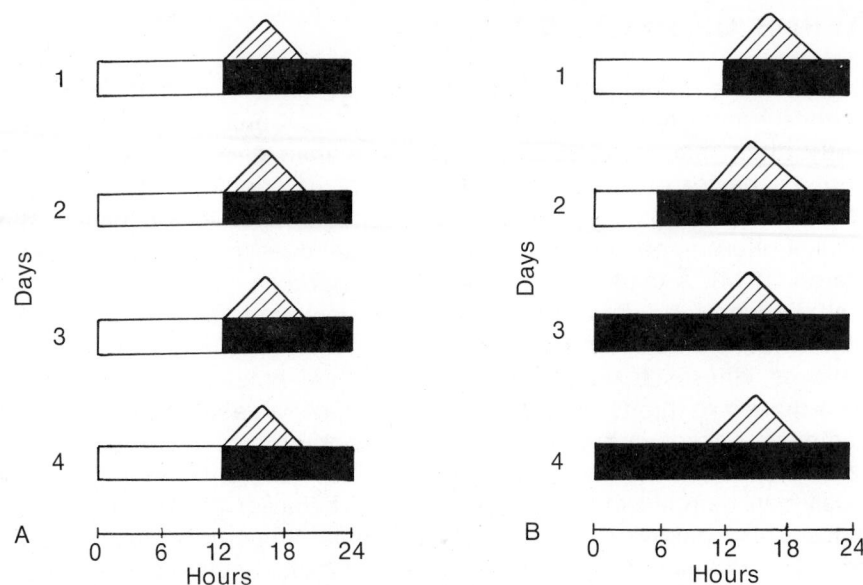

Figure 6-7. Circadian activity of American cockroaches in laboratory chamber. Light area of graph indicates lights on (photophase). Dark area indicates lights off (scotophase). Peak indicates major period of cockroach activity. *A*, Twelve-hour photophase: activity peaks after lights off. *B*, Lights turned off earlier on day 2, then left off: activity peaks earlier but maintains 24-hour rhythm. (Redrawn from Beck, S. D. 1963. Physiology and ecology of photoperiodism. Bull. Entomol. Soc. Amer. *9*:8–16.)

to continuous light exposure. The recipient then displayed an activity rhythm like that of the donor but which was advanced by the number of hours that the brain had been chilled.

Many insects display such internal activity rhythms and are active at specific, limited times during a 24-hour period. Such rhythms are called **circadian** (''about a day''), or **diel,** rhythms. Diurnal species, such as most bees, wasps, dragonflies, and butterflies, are those whose activites are limited principally to daylight hours; while nocturnal insects—most moths and the aforementioned cockroaches, for example—are active during darkness. A third group, crepuscular insects, are most active around dusk and dawn. There may be considerable overlap among these classifications for a given insect, as anyone who has slapped mosquitoes for 24 hours straight in northern New England will readily attest!

Circadian activity rhythms, though internally controlled, are subject to external modification, particularly by temperature. Truman (1973) compared the flight and ''calling'' (see page 238) rhythms of male and female moths reared at 12° C and 25° C; moths raised at 12° C ''called'' and flew earlier in the dark period than those raised at 25° C, even though both groups were observed at 25° C. Similarly, Cardé and Roelofs (1973) showed that male *Holomelina* moths (Arctiidae) respond to female sex pheromone after darkness on warm evenings and two hours before darkness on cool evenings. Females begin ''calling'' in response to either ''lights off'' or a drop in temperature.

Behavioral periodicity has important implications for control of pest insects (Chapter Ten) as well as for the number of insects that can utilize a single environmental resource. For instance, restricted foraging periods of *Andrena* bees reduce competition for pollen and nectar of *Oenothera* flowers (Table 6–1) (Linsley et al., 1964).

BEHAVIORAL MODIFICATION: LEARNING

At the outset of this chapter, I stated that most insect behavior is highly stereotyped, rigid, and predictable. Though such "innate" behavior is very important and perhaps most of what insects do is instinctual, nonetheless, limited learning does play a vital role in the survival of many insects. Learning experiments are particularly difficult to perform because one must make certain that an observed "improvement" in behavior is actually a result of learning and not merely a behavioral change at a particular point in an insect's life cycle. Some parasitic wasps *(Bathyplectes curculionis,* for one) search for hosts much more efficiently when one day old (when their eggs have matured) than when newly eclosed, regardless of previous experience (Dowell, 1976).

Alloway (1972) defined learning as a modifiable, relatively permanent change in behavior as a result of practice. The simplest form of learning, habituation ("getting used to"), is common among insects. For example, Lindauer (1965) reported that 500 training flights were necessary before a honey bee could ascertain the speed and angle of the sun's apparent movement through the sky. Repeated exposures condition the bee's nervous system (in a way not understood) to recognize movement of the sun and thus to compensate its light-compass orientation to the small apparent change in solar position that occurs between the time the bee leaves the hive and the time she returns.

Extensive studies of ants in mazes have shown that ants can learn a maze by trial and error and become more efficient in negotiating a maze after repeated trials. Such learning in one context may not carry over to another context, however. Having learned a maze, the trained ant does not learn the same maze backwards any faster (on the average) than a naive ant, and a maze that has been learned in order to locate food is not as quickly negotiated to find the nest (Weiss and Schneirla, 1967). Maze-learning in ants may therefore be a combination of conditioning and associative learning. Incidentally, Schneirla and associates have found that individual ants differ greatly in their speed of learning.

Table 6–1. NUMBERS OF INDIVIDUAL BEES (*Andrena*) VISITING FLOWERS OF *Oenothera clavaeformis* IN NEVADA AT DIFFERENT TIMES OF THE DAY*

Time	Bee Species		
	A. chylismiae	*A. raveni*	*A. rozeni*
5:40–6:40 AM	22	1	0
6:41–7:40	9	16	0
7:41–8:40	7	3	0
4:10–5:10 PM	0	18	6
5:11–6:10	0	13	6

*From Linsley, E. G., MacSwain, J. W., and Raven, P. H. 1964. Comparative behavior of bees and Onagraceae. Univ. Calif. Publ. Entomol. *33*:1–92. Published in 1964 by The Regents of the University of California; reprinted by permission of the University of California Press.

Other insects, cockroaches and flour beetles, for instance, learn mazes. Bees have been trained to associate colors with food, and some parasitic Hymenoptera associate odors or tactile stimuli with the presence of their hosts, thus increasing ovipositional efficiency (Arthur, 1966). Sand wasps orient to visual cues (menotaxis) and can "remember" the location of their nests by the visual cues of the surroundings, as can be neatly demonstrated by placing a ring of pine cones about the nest entrance, and then, after the wasp has made several visits, moving the circle to a nearby point while she is away (Fig. 6–8). On her return, she goes directly to the center of the circle (Tinbergen and Kruyt, 1938). Such learning in insects is doubtless under the control of association neurons in the central nervous system, probably the brain itself. Eisenstein and Cohen (1965) have shown that limited learning is also possible in single thoracic ganglia; they removed a cockroach leg and its associated ganglion and trained the leg to avoid electric shock. Learning as a behavioral modifier is probably most important in those insects that have rather long life cycles during which they encounter a great variety of environmental circumstances. These same insects often have the most enlarged "mushroom bodies" in the brain (Chapter Five). Despite ability to learn, no insect has been demonstrated to reason, to apply "knowledge" from one context to a completely different context (though it is tempting to view the "waggle dance" of the honeybee in this regard). This alone sets major limitations on what insects can do and is another major behavioral difference between insects and vertebrates.

COMMUNICATION

In this section, I consider behavioral interactions between individuals of the same species in which a stimulus from one individual evokes a behavioral

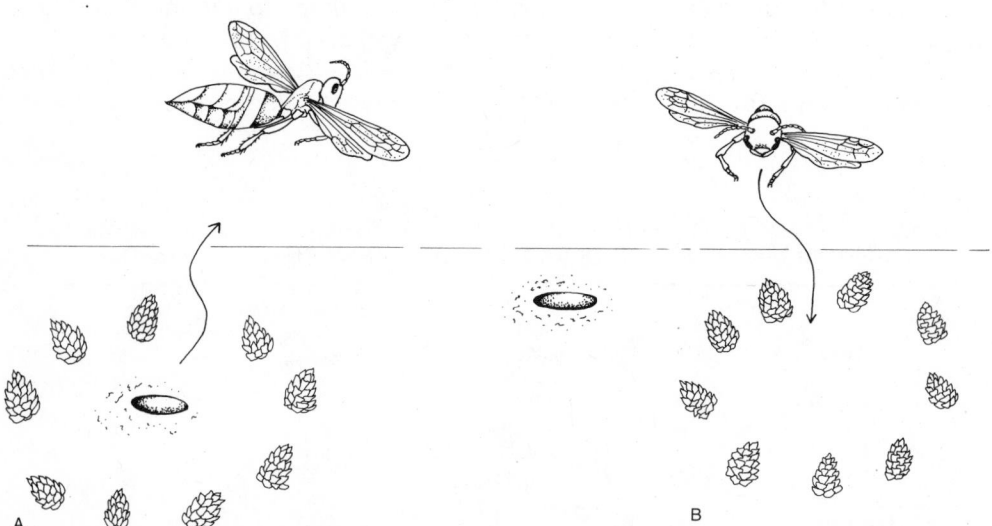

Figure 6–8. Visual orientation of sand wasp to nest. *A*, Ring of pine cones placed around nest before wasp leaves. *B*, Pine cone ring moved while wasp was away; returning, wasp goes to center of pine cone ring.

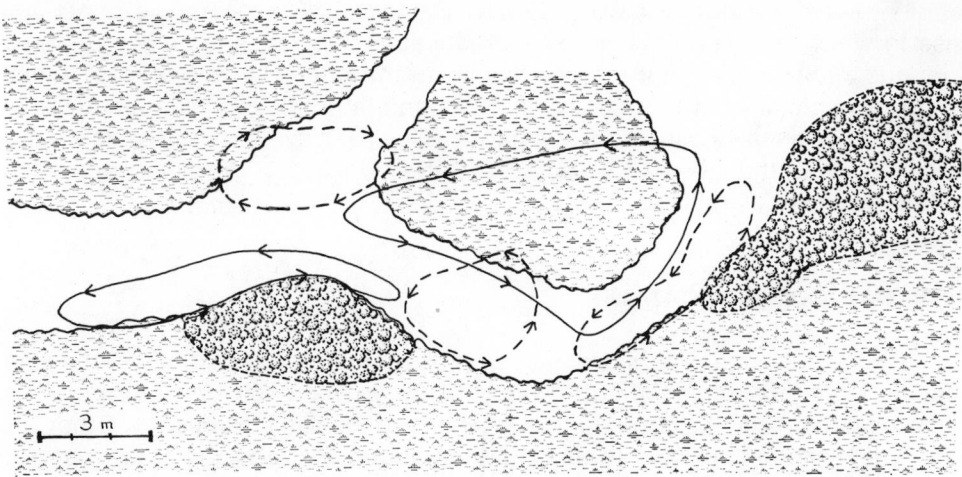

Figure 6–9. Dragonfly territories in Massachusetts marsh. Arrows show direction of travel over regular "beats" patrolled by male *Plathemis lydia* (solid lines) and *Libellula pulchella* (dashed lines). (Unpublished data of Horn, Horn, Horn, and Horn.)

response in another. This narrow view of communication ignores interspecific communications, chiefly defense and symbioses, which are discussed in Chapter Nine. In addition, following Lloyd (1971), I consider communication to have been acted on by natural selection, transmission and reception having a coevolved genetic basis and being "tuned" to one another (Hoy and Paul, 1973). A communication system is as much an adaptation as any morphological feature. Communication can occur through any of the sense receptors discussed in Chapter Five: visual, auditory, tactile, or chemical, or a combination of these.

VISUAL COMMUNICATION

Among visual communication systems exists a great variety of patterns and colorations which, when combined with appropriate behavioral display, elicit a response. Representative is the territorial behavior of dragonflies, some male butterflies, and other insects in which males patrol a "beat" (Fig. 6–9), flying a regular pattern and resting occasionally on a prominent perch. If another individual of the same species enters the "territory," the local male will give chase. Kaiser (1974) demonstrated that a visual display stimulates the chasing response; he built model dragonflies and found that dragonflies respond most quickly to pattern of their own species. Many insects use visual communication, sometimes combined with tactile and chemical communication, in location and recognition of mates. In some, such as the Colorado potato beetle, sex may not be discriminated and males may mount either sex.

Perhaps the most aesthetically appealing (to us) visual communication system is that of luminous insects, particularly fireflies (Lampyridae). These produce light flashes (see Chapter Five) that are species-specific mating "codes." Timing and pattern of flashes bring the sexes together; on warm summer evenings (in eastern North America), we see cruising males, each flashing species-specific code to which females respond. If she responds in the appropriate code, he orients toward its source (Lloyd, 1971). J. E. Lloyd (1965) recounts a remarkable case in which females of *Photuris,* a predaceous species, lure smaller males of *Photinus* to dinner by mimicking the flashes of the latter's code. Moreover, female *Photuris* mimic at least four smaller fireflies and thus can vary their menu (Lloyd, 1975). Arboreal males of southeast Asian fireflies flash synchronously, lighting up whole trees as though they were huge Christmas trees. These are apparently mating aggregations (Lloyd, 1973).

AUDITORY COMMUNICATION

Insects of several orders produce sounds that attract individuals of the same species. Male mosquitoes orient toward the sound of the female's buzzing wings and are attacted also by a tuning fork vibrating at the same frequency. Other Diptera, and Hymenoptera, are attracted by the sound of the wings of the opposite sex. Many beetles produce sound by stridulation (see Chapter Five); these sounds are species-specific and apparently serve for sexual recognition, at least in Scolytidae. Queen honey bees make a curious "piping" sound whose function is unclear.

The most obvious insect sounds, and therefore the most studied from a behavioral standpoint, are the "song" of Cicadidae (Homoptera) and jumping Orthoptera. In both groups, it is predominately males that "sing," and these sounds are long-distance attractants for females. Both the songs and the response (phonotaxis) to them are species-specific and function as isolating mechanisms, congregating individuals of one species and assuring reproductive isolation from others. Female grasshoppers and katydids rarely make mistakes in locating mates of the appropriate species.

In many Orthoptera and in Cicadidae, singing males aggregate and produce synchronous "choruses" capable of attracting females over a much longer distance than could the "song" of an individual. Apparently, a "leader" sets the initial pace and others nearby respond when he calls (Moore, 1973). The resulting chorus ranges in size from antiphonally stridulating pairs in male katydids to groups of several thousand in periodical cicadas. Aggregation probably increases the frequency of mating by drawing more females, though experimental evidence for this is lacking.

Singing Orthoptera and cicadas are capable of a variety of sounds, not all of which are sexual. In particular, there are alarm sounds that cause receivers to cease singing and to move away from the alarm caller. Male crickets and long-horned grasshoppers are moderately territorial, as discussed later, and produce a "rivalry song" when challenged by another male.

Control of singing is genetic in that each song is species-specific, though environmental input modifies singing. Many sound-producing insects have a circadian rhythm of song production, commencing at sundown (many tree crickets and Tettigoniidae) or singing only in daylight hours (cicadas).

TACTILE COMMUNICATION

In tactile communication pressure-sensitive sensilla are stimulated and a response is thereby elicited. It occurs to a limited extent in all bisexual insects, at least at mating time, and together with chemical and visual communication, is a major link in sexual recognition. Often, female acceptance or rejection of a courting male occurs only after contact; the courtship-cum-feeding behavior of female mantids (Chapter Five) is an extreme example of acceptance. In most cases of precopulatory behavior, tactile cues are apparently secondary to chemical stimuli in releasing behavior.

Social insects often stroke and groom one another with antennae and mouthparts, and termite "soldiers" alarm a colony to the presence of intruders by unison tapping of mandibles against the walls of the termite nest. Termites throughout the nest perceive these taps tactilely through their tarsi. Perhaps the most involved tactile communication system is the waggle dance of the honey bee. A "scout" bee that has located a new food source (newly bloomed flowers —or the ethologist's bee-feeding tray) returns to the hive and performs a figure-eight dance on the vertical comb inside (Fig. 6–10), during which she waggles her abdomen while walking upward. Because the bees are crowded together on the comb, nearby bees can feel the direction of the dance. Von Frisch (1974) demonstrated that the departure from vertical of the angle of the dance is equal to the angle of departure of the food source from the sun (Fig. 6–10) and that the length of time spent per waggle-walk is proportional to the distance of the food source. Most remarkable is the fact that the bee may do a marathon dance for over three hours on the comb (Von Frisch, 1967), during which she compensates for the apparent movement of the sun through the sky by changing the waggle angle on the comb. This adjustment is done in the total darkness of the hive, without a peek at the sky; it is probably a function of the bee's internal clock and its conditioning to the movement of the sun (Lindauer, 1965). Hive bees, perceiving duration and direction of the dance, leave the hive at the appropriate angle and fly the correct distance directly (more or less) to the food source! Source odors on the dancer's body apparently are of lesser importance to other bees' response to the dance, though Gould (1975) varied the concentration of food odors and discovered that bees preferentially gathered at the stronger odor source. He demonstrated the importance of tactile communication by covering ocelli of dancing scouts in outdoor swarms. Unable to correctly determine the sun's position, blinded scouts "lied" about the location of food, and workers predictably flew to the wrong place.

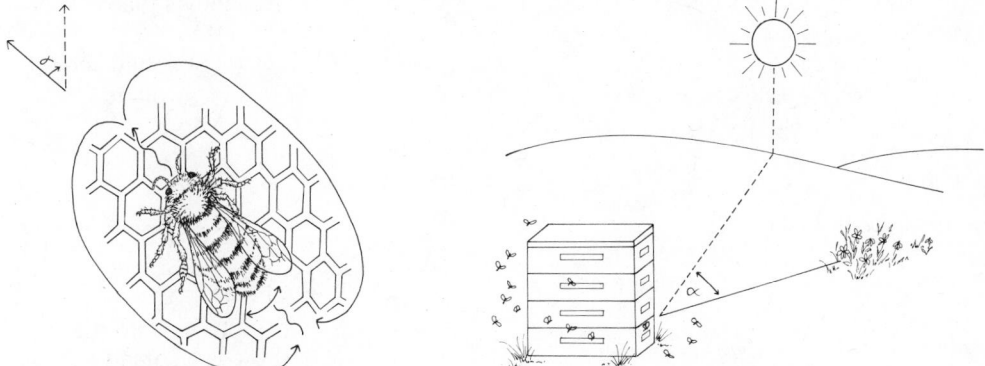

Figure 6–10. "Waggle dance" of honey bee. Angle α between "waggle" and vertical in hive (left) equals angle between incident rays of sun and food supply (right). Duration of each waggle is proportional to the distance of food from the hive.

CHEMICAL COMMUNICATION

Much of insect behavior is mediated by **pheromones,** chemicals secreted by other insects of the same species. Pheromones are secreted into the environment by exocrine glands (Fig. 6–11) or by other structures, such as specialized scent scales or wings, and are perceived by chemoreceptors on antennae, tarsi, or mouthparts of a recipient. Such chemical messengers usually volatilize, or disperse, rapidly in the atmosphere, serving as either releasers for an immediate behavioral response (like the sex pheromones of female moths that induce males to fly upwind) or as primers for longer lasting physiological changes in recipients (like the pheromones that determine caste in social insects [see Chapter Seven]). Pheromones in incredibly small quantities stimulate activity over amazingly long distances. They have been chemically extracted from abdomens of female gypsy moths and applied to antennae of males, who respond to amounts as low as 10^{-7} μg. In experiments, marked moths have been attracted to an upwind pheromone source almost five miles away, though not with great regularity. An attractant this powerful is a potentially valuable tool for insect control in which normal orientation of a pest species can be disrupted without harm to beneficial species (Chapter Ten). Because of this, insect chemical communication is now receiving much-needed attention. Although uniform terminology (among other things), has yet to be agreed upon, short-term pheromones may be broadly categorized into orienting compounds, exciters (releasers of sexual behavior), and aphrodisiacs (usually produced by males to inhibit female locomotor activity). I discuss these types by function:

The existence of sex pheromones, or attractants, was suspected for many years, and recently many have been extracted and synthesized for potential pest control. Those of Lepidoptera have been studied most, though sex pheromones apparently occur in most insect orders. In Lepidoptera, the female assumes "calling" behavior shortly after eclosion (Fig. 6–12), releasing pheromone from exocrine glands under the intersegmental membrane. The pheromone releases anemotaxis in males, which then fly upwind until they reach an

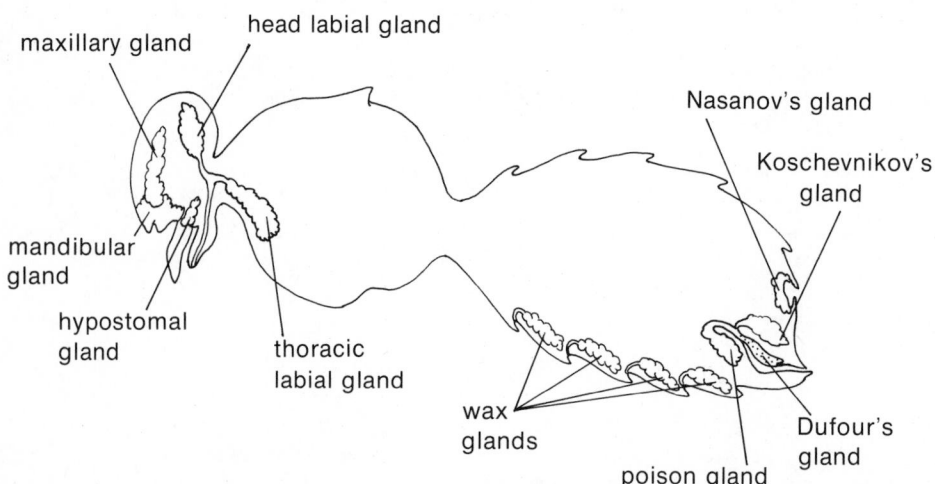

Figure 6–11.   Exocrine glands of honey bee. (Redrawn from Wilson, E. O. 1971. The Insect Societies. Harvard University Press, Cambridge, Mass. Copyright © 1971 Harvard University Press.)

Figure 6–12. Female sesiid moth "calling." Pheromone issues from everted gland at abdominal tip. (Photo by G. Berkey, courtesy of D. G. Neilsen and Ohio Agricultural Research and Development Center.)

area of greater concentration where their turning movements increase and, in diurnal species, visual contact is made. There is normally a circadian rhythm to pheromone release—"calling hours," as it were. Sex pheromones secreted by virgin queen bees attract drones on the mating flight. Females of some parasitic wasps emit pheromone while still within the cocoon and are greeted by expectant males before their wings dry out.

Aggregation pheromones draw more than two individuals together. Virgin bark beetle females (Scolytidae) release pheromones that attract both sexes to mating and oviposition sites, thus aggregating large numbers of beetles to recently damaged timber (Furniss et al., 1972). The "queen substance" of the queen honey bee is instrumental in attracting a swarm outside the hive when colonies divide. Aggregation pheromones have also been demonstrated in ants and may occur in many insects that habitually form clusters. Social insect colonies circulate pheromones also by **trophallaxis,** feeding exchanges of liquid that occur when two individuals meet head-on. (It looks like they are kissing.) Wilson and Eisner (1957) fed radioactive honey to foraging ants and found that it took but 27 hours for radioactivity to be passed to all ants in the colony. Obviously, pheromones are passed around in the same way for organization of the insect society and control of caste production (Chapter Seven).

Alarm pheromones are released when an intrusion or other disruptive and potentially threatening event occurs. When their nest is disturbed, ants seem at once to scurry rapidly about whether or not they have been at the disturbance site. This increased activity is a response to an alarm chemical dispersed into the air, which is effective on ants up to 10 cm. away (Regnier and Wilson, 1968). Many alarm pheromones are not species-specific (Wilson, 1971). Alarm pheromones have recently been demonstrated in aphids (Bowers et al., 1972); when an

aphid is bitten, it often emits droplets containing a pheromone that releases escape behavior in nearby individuals (Fig. 6–13). Alarm pheromones of one aphid
may elicit fleeing in several different species and may elicit defensive behavior in
ants that attend aphids.

Trail pheromones occur in ants, parasitic Hymenoptera, and probably other
foraging insects. As ants forage, they periodically touch their abdomen to the
substrate and deposit a pheromone droplet that other ants orient to when following. The greater the number of ants that move to a food source, the greater the
amount of pheromone deposited, but as the food is removed, fewer ants return
and the pheromone trail evaporates. The pheromone trail is directional, as you can
demonstrate by permitting an ant column to march across a piece of paper for a
while. Then rotate the paper 180°; the ants rush about in "confusion" for a few
minutes but eventually reestablish the trail. Some parasitic wasps deposit trail
pheromones and thus avoid searching for hosts in an area in which they have
previously searched (Price, 1970a).

Death pheromones constitute another chemical messenger in social insects.
Dead bees or ants emit a pheromone (which may be oleic acid), that stimulates
workers to remove their corpses from the nest. It matters not whether the body is
moving; if oleic acid is smeared on a living ant, it will be bodily hauled from the
nest and deposited upon the trash heap regardless of how many times it returns
to the nest alive and well.

RESULTS OF COMMUNICATION: COURTSHIP AND MATING

Location of mates may be visual, chemical, tactile, or auditory, as explained
previously. Once mates have been located through orientation (in insects, males
usually orient toward females), courtship and mating behavior begins. Many sex
attractants also are releasers for mating behavior.

Courtship behavior may be simple or extremely complex. In many insects,
the sexes quickly copulate after mate location with no preliminary courtship maneuvers. A lovemaking session in the parasitic wasp *Microctonus aethiops* lasts
about one second (Lewis, D. R. 1973). Copulation in many other insects may last
longer but with few or no specialized behavioral patterns evident. Beetles, flies,
and butterflies are often seen walking or flying in tandem; some treehoppers
remain coupled for days.

More complex courtships occur in many Orthoptera (and other insects);
male and female engage in a sequence of precopulatory activities, each of which
apparently is a releaser for the activity that follows. For instance, Kerr (1974)
noted that when a Carolina locust male approaches a receptive female, he raises
his femora, sometimes stridulating in the process, inducing the female to assume
a similar posture. If receptive, she then adopts a raised-abdomen "presentation"
posture, and the male mounts. Sounds made by males in this courtship are
rather different from attraction, alarm, or rivalry sounds.

Some of the most elaborate mating rituals occur among predatory insects, in
which courtship behavior must be not only a releaser for copulation but also an
inhibitor of predatory behavior. An example is the predatory balloon flies (Em-
pididae). In "primitive" empidids, the male obtains a small dead insect prior to
copulation. He then presents it to the female and mounts her and copulates while
she is occupied with the meal. In more "advanced" balloon-flies, males wrap a
small insect or other object in a ball of silk (Fig. 6–14), which the female unwraps

Figure 6–13. Aphid emitting droplet of alarm pheromone when attacked by predaceous damsel bug. (Photo by G. Berkey, courtesy of L. R. Nault and Ohio Agricultural Research and Development Center.)

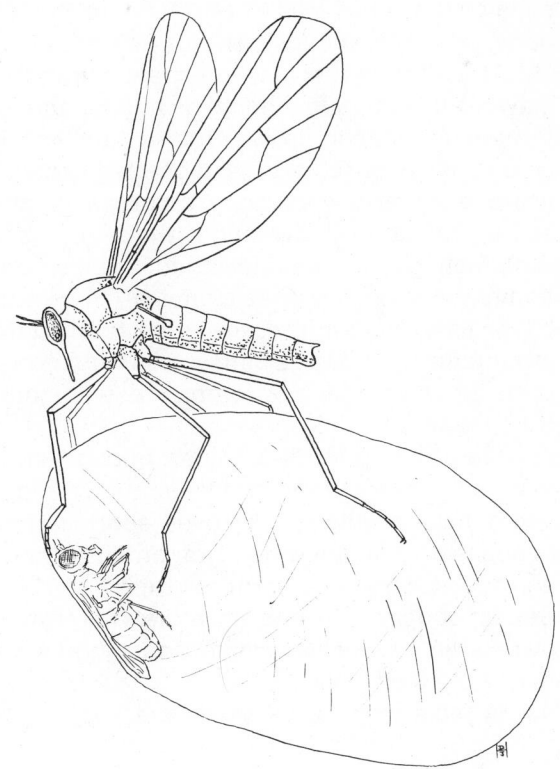

Figure 6–14. Male balloon fly carrying balloon containing dead insect. (Modified from Aldrich, J. M., and L. A. Turley. 1899. A balloon-making fly. Amer. Nat. *33*:809–12. Copyright © The University of Chicago.)

during mating. Evolutionary development of this behavior culminates in those species that present the female with an empty ball of silk, which she unwraps during copulation. The praying mantis (Chapter Five), on the other hand, has evolved another way; being eaten is essentially a releaser for sexual behavior in male mantids.

TERRITORIALITY

Territorial behavior, in which a particular area is defended against intrusion by other insects (usually of the same species), occurs in several insect orders, particularly in insects that utilize energy-rich but scattered and ephemeral resources (carrion and dung beetles, temporary-pool dragonflies, or social insects) (Wilson, 1971). Aggressive encounters may occur between courting males in the presence of a single female (Kerr, 1974). Crickets and long-horned grasshoppers are notorious for territoriality. Males stridulate in a particular area, and when encountering another male, alter their chirping to a "rivalry" song, which is usually enough to release flight behavior in the intruder. On occasion, however, physical combat involving kicking and biting will ensue, particularly if the contestants are confined. Cricket fighting has been a betting sport for centuries in the Orient, with many thousand yen often being wagered on the life-or-death outcome of grylloid pugilistics.

OVIPOSITION AND BROODING

In most insects, the adult is the active dispersal stage, and females distribute eggs or larvae, usually in areas where the latter will find favorable living conditions. In short-lived insects, females deposit eggs wherever they may happen to be. The shorter the life, the greater the chances that food is close by; some mayflies live but a few hours as adults, and large numbers do not get far beyond the pond or stream in which they hatched. In other circumstances, particularly among those insects with restricted tastes in food, adult females will locate nymphal or larval food supplies by visual, chemical, and/or tactile stimuli, much as they locate their own food (which may be quite different from that of the larvae). Mating may be a releaser for ovipositional behavior. In many insects, attraction to oviposition sites is chemical, the source being either an attractant chemical or an **arrestant,** present in the food source, which inhibits locomotion. Fruit attractants have been synthesized in quantity and have been used successfully in traps in Hawaii and elsewhere to eliminate populations of tropical fruit flies (Chambers et al., 1974).

Male insects rarely take part in oviposition activity. An exception is Odonata, in which males and females fly about in tandem. In dragonflies the male leads and the female alternately removes spermatophores from the male abdomen and deposits eggs in the water. Dragonflies orient visually to reflected light from water and therefore also attempt to oviposit on the roofs of shiny green automobiles. Sexual cooperation is even more vital in damselflies. The female submerges to oviposit in underwater plants, and a joint effort by both sexes is needed to get her out of the water.

In most insects, parental care ceases with oviposition in a favored spot. A relative minority continue association with their offspring, protecting or caring for eggs and immatures. In some giant water bugs (Belostomatidae), the female oviposits on the dorsum of the male, which carries the eggs about until they hatch (Fig. 6–15). Presumably this has survival value in that a predator is less likely to take on father water bug than the defenseless eggs. Wood (1974) has shown that the female of some Membracidae remains with her egg mass until it hatches, and then she slices the bark of the host tree with her ovipositor, presumably to make it easier for nymphs to obtain plant juices. The nymphs stay in a cluster with their mother nearby, and if a nymph wanders down the stem, mother membracid gently shoves it back to the group (Fig. 6–16). She also defends the aggregation against predators. A group of bark beetles, the ambrosia beetles, carry fungi in a specialized structure, the **mycangium** (usually on the thorax or maxillae). After ovipositing under bark, the female ambrosia beetle deposits

Figure 6–15. Giant water bug, male, with eggs on back.

Figure 6–16. Female treehoppers (Membracidae) brooding nymphs on twig. (Photo courtesy of T. K. Wood.)

some of the fungus, which thrives on decaying wood and grows while the beetle's eggs develop. When larvae hatch, they feed on the fungus. Some Scolytidae go beyond this; the female remains behind and feeds larvae with fungus and removes feces from the excavation (Schedl, 1956). Burying beetles (*Necrophorus,* family Silphidae), working in pairs, locate a vertebrate corpse (mouse-sized) and excavate beneath it, eventually burying it. After ovipositing, the female, sometimes accompanied by her mate, remains to feed the young larvae with partially digested food until they are old enough (six hours) to feed on the rotting meat. Occasionally, they will be fed by their parent throughout their larval life.

By laying eggs in a mass, many insects unwittingly cause aggregation of their offspring, and in some cases, these aggregations have definite survival value. Many lepidopterous larvae aggregate, most notably those that construct large communal webs in which they can gather with some protection from predators and parasitoids (Fig. 6–17). Wellington (1957) has shown that behavior of western tent caterpillars differs among individuals. Some larvae are "leaders," moving out to new sources of leaves; others are "followers," going only where silken trails have already been deposited. After hatching from eggs, sawfly larvae (Hymenoptera: Tenthredinidae) are attracted to feeding sites by odors emanating from breaks in the food plant. Thus, they gather where the leaves are already broken through and are easier to chew.

SOCIAL INSECTS

The ultimate in aggregation and brood care is seen in the insect societies. Michener (1969) offers the following classification of social behaviors based on the degree of involvement: subsocial, in which adults care for young; communal,

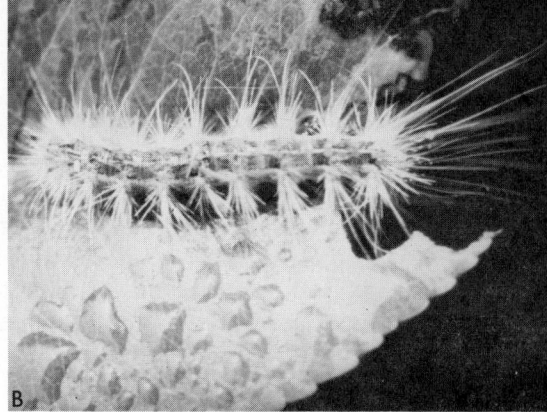

Figure 6–17. Communal web of fall webworm. *A*, Web. *B*, Single larva.

in which members of the same generation use a composite nest; quasisocial, which is like communal but in which adults cooperate in brood care; semisocial, which is like quasisocial but in which workers care for young of reproductives; and eusocial, in which truly social insects are found in overlapping generations and offspring assist their parents (or grandparents, etc.) in maintenance of the colony. We have already seen examples of subsocial (brooding) and communal (aggregating) behavior. The "higher" forms of sociality are restricted to Isoptera and Hymenoptera; in the latter order, eusociality is thought to have evolved independently 11 times (Wilson, 1971), whereas termite society is probably monophyletic. Eusocial insects are typified by long-lasting colonies (lasting several generations and often more than a single growing season) and by specialized **castes,** including nonreproductive forms responsible for the maintenance of the colony. The physiological bases of caste determination are discussed more fully in Chapter Seven.

SOCIAL ISOPTERA

Termites are unique among insect orders in that all species are eusocial. Typically, a mated pair initiates a colony. After a short reproductive flight, they shed their wings and seek out a favorable area (underground in most species, though some infest wood directly). Here the female lays eggs that hatch into tiny blind nymphs, which are the first workers. As these grow, they take up the tasks of foraging, feeding the reproductives and the younger nymphs. All termites feed on cellulose-containing foods; most United States species concentrate on wood, but tropical termites, which are far more diverse, also eat seeds and grasses for which they forage in the open air. Some Asian and African termites feed primarily on fungi, which they grow and carefully tend in "gardens" within the colony. Cellulose, the major part of their diet, is evidently digested by symbiotic protozoa in the hindgut; termites eat one another's cast skins and feces, thus conserving hindgut protozoa. They also eat excess eggs and dead termites, and thereby conserve protein which is in short supply in a cellulose diet.

A reproductive female soon becomes distended with eggs in her undergound chamber and thereafter is totally dependent on workers for food, grooming, and removal of feces and eggs. As nymphs grow, they become specialized to one of several morphological castes (forms) (Fig. 6–18). Workers are primarily foragers and cleaners. A specialized soldier caste, often having enlarged mandibles, defends the colony against intruders when a colony is broken open. The soldiers are incapable of feeding themselves and must be fed by the workers. Throughout the colony, there is constant exchange of liquid (trophallaxis), which aids in circulation of pheromones regulating caste determination.

Termites reach their greatest behavioral and morphological diversity in the tropics, where huge, perennial colonies may construct elaborate nests of soil particles cemented together to produce towers up to 20 feet high. Skaife (1961) discusses some interesting adaptations among tropical termites. A **nasute** caste (Fig. 6–18D) of "soldiers" that specialize in chemical warfare is sometimes found among these termites. A nasute has an enlarged head with a long snout. At the end of this snout, a duct opens that leads from a gland that contains a defensive secretion. This chemical coagulates in air, turning into a sticky goo that entraps small-sized enemies. (Ants are major predators of tropical termites.) The nasute's

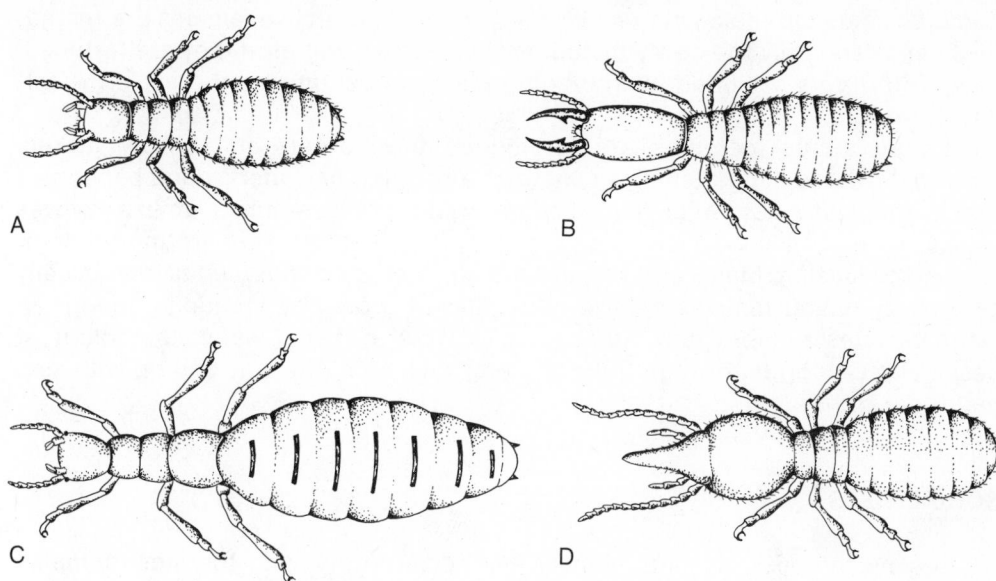

Figure 6–18. Termite castes. *A*, Worker. *B*, Soldier. *C*, Female reproductive, or "queen," gravid with eggs. *D*, Nasute.

aim is accurate over several centimeters despite its being totally blind. How it locates the target remains a mystery.

SOCIAL WASPS

In the social Hymenoptera, and particularly in the eusocial wasps, caste determination is more behavioral than morphological (as in termites). Furthermore, Hymenoptera have a unique mechanism for sex determination: unfertilized eggs develop into males, while fertilized eggs become females. In Hymenoptera, the "worker" caste is made up entirely of sterile, nonreproductive females.

Most wasps are subsocial: they provision nests (sometimes communally) and occasionally guard the young but usually do not feed them and do not have a worker caste. The mud wasps often seen about mud puddles are an example: Each mated female builds a mud nest and provisions it with the paralyzed bodies of spiders, caterpillars, and such before laying her eggs and sealing the nest. The sand wasp, *Ammophila,* mentioned previously, is another subsocial wasp. The truly eusocial wasps are all of the family Vespidae and (in the United States) construct seasonal colonies. An example is the large, brown paper wasp, *Polistes,* often seen about the eaves of unpainted wooden buildings. A single mated overwintering female starts a nest in spring. She chews wood into a pulp which dries into a papery substance, and in this open nest she rears a brood by feeding the developing larvae pieces of caterpillars, flies, and spiders. Usually other females join her, and in these females, the ovaries gradually atrophy, which renders them sterile workers that assist the foundress "queen" in rearing her brood (Eberhard, 1969). Likewise the first offspring are workers; females that are morphologically similar to the foundress but have reduced ovaries. The colony continues thus until fall, when males and virgin reproductive females are reared; these mate and only the newly mated females survive winter (if they are fortunate enough to find a secluded, warm hiding place) to commence the cycle the following year.

Larger annual colonies are formed by the hornets and yellow jackets (*Vespula*), whose mated females construct a hanging or underground paper nest that is gradually enlarged as the brood grows during the summer. Unlike *Polistes* wasps, no other females join the *Vespula* queen, and workers are morphologically much smaller. Males and females are again produced in the fall, and usually only newly mated females survive the winter in protected locations, though in warm climates a colony may survive a mild winter or two. I watched a colony of *Vespula* in California through three winters; such a colony may end up with several thousand workers.

SOCIAL BEES

Among the bees are both solitary and social forms, with the most complex societies in the family Apidae (bumble bees and honey bees). The complexities of communication and social behavior are perhaps best understood in that most-studied of all insects, the honey bee, *Apis mellifera.* The honey bee is one of rather few bee species whose colonies are perennial, lasting through winter.

A honey bee colony consists of several thousand individuals of three castes: a single female reproductive (queen); nonreproductive females (workers); and, in season, reproductive males (drones). The seasonal life of a colony begins in spring with a number of overwintered workers and a mated queen laying eggs. Developing larvae are fed a mixture of pollen and honey (beebread) from winter stores in the hive. With spring begins the honey flow, when flowers bloom in profusion and the bees busy themselves in foraging for nectar and pollen, provisioning the comb, and increasing numbers of brood. As the colony enlarges, the bees become more active within the hive; they jostle the queen, preventing her from ovipositing and slimming her down for a swarming flight. At this time, the alert beekeeper may add a box onto his hive to increase the interior size to prevent swarming. When the queen is capable of flight, she leaves the hive, accompanied by many (but not all) workers and drones. Responding to a pheromone secreted by the queen, the swarm assembles nearby, and some workers "scout" for suitable nest sites, then return and communicate nest site location to the swarm by the "waggle dance" (p. 237). It is not fully understood how the swarm "decides" on a location (and an alert beekeeper makes that "decision" for them by dumping them into a hive), but they usually fly off to a hollow tree, an attic, or another suitable location and set up shop. The workers build new comb from wax that is secreted by the abdominal glands, then chewed and mashed into place with the flattened mandibles (Fig. 4–5A).

Meanwhile, back at the old hive, there is no queen and therefore no queen pheromone. Honey bees engage in trophallaxis, and within a day, the remaining workers, free of the tyranny and conformity of queen pheromone, construct specialized peanut-shaped comb cells (Fig. 6–19) in which developing larvae are fed a nutritive glandular secretion, **royal jelly**, in addition to their normal rations of beebread. When fed to larvae over their entire larval life, royal jelly induces larger

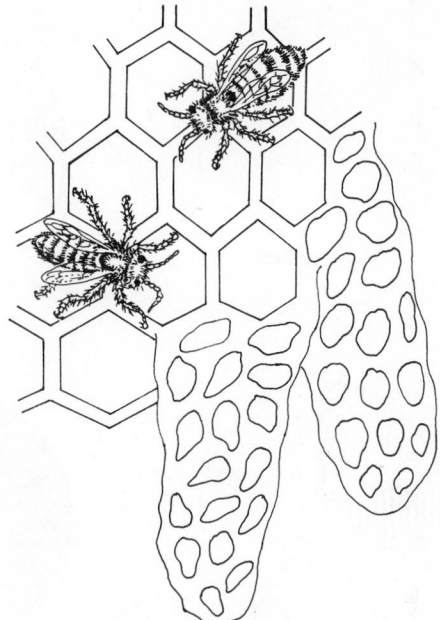

Figure 6–19. Queen cells of honey bee.

size and maturation of ovaries (Chapter Seven), resulting in queens. The first queen to emerge promptly rips open other queen cells, and the workers then dispose of the contents. Sometimes she may sting developing queens, but the much-publicized "fight to the death" between queens is rare indeed.

Emergence of a queen inhibits production of additional queen cells, and now comes the moment the drones have awaited. The queen departs on a mating flight, the drones chase after her, attracted by a pheromone, and several males mate with her. (Today, most commercial beekeepers buy artificially inseminated queens.) Thereafter she returns to the hive to live out her life (up to six or seven years). She does not mate again but fertilizes her eggs with stored sperm. Her major functions thereafter are laying eggs, one every 30 seconds, and secreting pheromones. Workers feed and groom both queen and drones, though the latter are forcibly ejected from the hive when cold weather ends the honey flow.

In contrast to the long life of the queen, the average worker may live but a month during honey flow. During their adult lifetime, morphologically identical worker bees go through a series of behavioral patterns that, in sum, ensure continuance of the hive (Fig. 6–20). The worker commences as a housecleaning and nurse bee, cleaning out old brood cells, exporting bee droppings, and feeding developing larvae with pollen and nectar brought in by foraging field bees. After a few days thus domestically employed, she may participate in comb construction or guard duty at the hive entrance. Hive bees also regulate temperature within the hive (see Chapter Four). Eventually, she progresses to being a field worker and makes several trips a day to collect pollen and nectar. If she survives predation, bad weather, and insecticides, she spends her old age as a scout bee, exploring for new food sources at great distances from the hive and, if successful, returning to do the waggle dance. Despite honeybees' precise orienta-

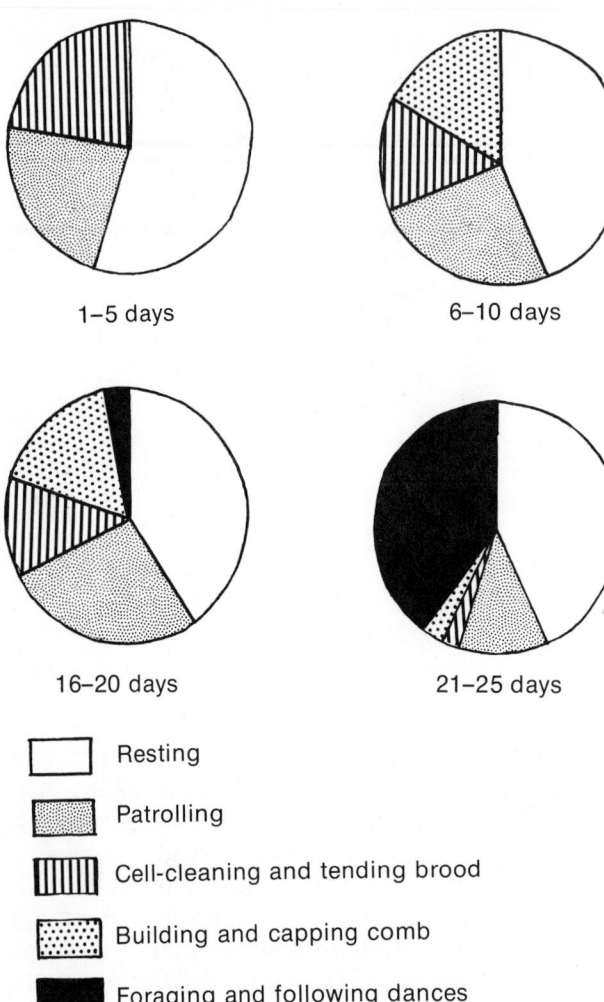

1–5 days   6–10 days

16–20 days   21–25 days

Figure 6–20. Proportion of total time spent in various activities by worker honey bee in first 25 days of adult life. (Data from Lindauer. *In* Ribbands, C. R. 1953. The Behavior and Social Life of Honeybees. Bee Research Association Ltd., London.)

☐ Resting

▦ Patrolling

▥ Cell-cleaning and tending brood

▨ Building and capping comb

■ Foraging and following dances

tion, great mortality occurs among scout bees, as they literally wear themselves out.

Exemplary of seasonal bee colonies are those of bumble bees, *Bombus* and related genera. In bumble bees, a mated queen overwinters and in spring locates a suitable subterranean nesting site. The oversized bumble bees that blunder into buildings in April and May are queens seeking nesting sites. In an underground chamber, she constructs waxen brood cells, lays eggs, and forages for nectar and pollen herself, rearing the brood to maturity. This brood is made up of small, sterile females that then take up the task of foraging while the queen settles down to full-time oviposition. Later broods contain large and small workers, and generally the larger bees forage while their smaller sisters keep house (Free and Butler, 1959). In late summer, males and reproductive females are produced; they mate and the latter then seek out protected hibernation sites. The remainder of the colony dies shortly after early frosts, though in warmer areas where flowers bloom the year round, some colonies may survive the winter, whereupon the queen may run out of stored sperm.

ANTS

The greatest diversity among hymenopterous (and all other insect) societies is found among the ants (Formicidae), all of which are eusocial. Sociality among ants may have evolved twice (Wilson, 1971). Like termites, ants are most diverse in the tropics, though most temperate-zone species maintain year-round colonies. Initial colony formation is rather like that in termites; i.e., after a mating flight, male and female construct their nest. Goetsch (1957) and Wilson (1971) discuss the diversity of ant societies in great detail.

Many temperate zone species are scavengers. They are among the most important scavengers of dead animal matter and, with earthworms, are major soil movers. Other species, the harvester ants of arid areas, feed primarily on seeds, which they gather to the nest and open, discarding the inedible seed coats on a refuse pile outsde the nest hole. Among ants with a more specialized diet are the fungus-growing ants, tribe Attini, from warm-temperate and tropical America. These ants cut small pieces of leaves and carry them into underground chambers (Fig. 6–21) where the leaves are used as mulch in "gardens" to grow fungi on which the ants feed (Weber, 1966). Workers maintain a scrupulously pure culture of the appropriate fungus by removing all other fungal growth from the mulch pile. (One can demonstrate this by barring the entrance to a "garden"—other fungi soon take over.) Moreover, the food-fungus produces no spores, so it cannot reproduce without the ants, nor can it be cultured outside attine ant nests (Weber, 1966). This suggests that coevolution between ants and their fungi has been going on for quite some time. Coevolution between ants and other plants and between ants and other insects (discussed in greater detail in Chapter Nine) has also occurred. An example of the latter is the well-known interrelationship

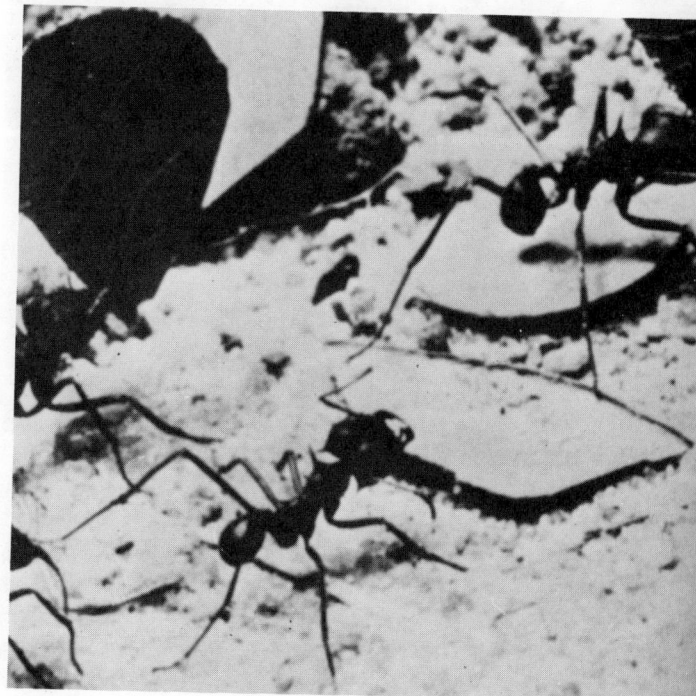

Figure 6–21. Leafcutting ants carrying bits of leaves in procession. (From the book *Insects* by Ross E. Hutchins. © 1966 by Ross E. Hutchins. Published by Prentice-Hall, Inc., Englewood Cliffs, New Jersey.)

between ants and aphids (Homoptera). The ants receive sweet-tasting honeydew from the aphids and, in return, protect aphid aggregations from predators and inclement weather. Among some ants one finds unusual workers, **repletes**, which are specialized for storage of honeydew and plant exudates (Fig. 6–22). These ants remain underground, hanging from the ceiling, where they are fed to repleteness by incoming workers. These living storage tanks are then emptied when aphids or plant sap are out of season.

Temperate-zone ants occupy relatively permanent, protected nest sites underground or within trees, hollow logs, or other protected places. Some tropical rainforest species nest in the open. Probably the most famous of these are the driver, or army, ants, colonies of which may contain up to a million workers. Driver ants form an assemblage, or "bivouac," nightly, and during the day, columns of many thousands forage on the surrounding forest floor. Often the whole colony will move to a new bivouac, with workers carrying eggs, larvae, and

Figure 6–22. Replete ant filled with honeydew and hanging from ceiling of underground colony. (From the book *Insects* by Ross E. Hutchins. © 1966 by Ross E. Hutchins. Published by Prentice-Hall, Inc., Englewood Cliffs, New Jersey.)

pupae. The forays are primarily scavenging trips, though the ants will attempt to subdue live insects and young or injured small vertebrates (Rettenmeyer, 1963). However, since the column moves at about 20 meters/hr., larger vertebrates, including humans, can merely step out of the way. The lurid tales of army ants subduing healthy adult human beings are unjustified and originate mostly in Hollywood.

EVOLUTION OF EUSOCIALITY

The adaptive significance of much insect behavior is relatively easy to understand. We can understand why dragonflies orient toward small flying objects, why flies quickly take flight at the near approach of a large object, or why lice seek an area of optimal temperature. According to natural selection theory, if these behaviors are genetically based and contribute to survival, they will be passed on to offspring. A difficult question arises when one considers the eusocial insects: How has natural selection produced *sterile* castes and their behavior, since they produce no offspring?

Hamilton (1964) and others have advanced a hypothesis based on the observation that insect eusociality is limited to Isoptera and Hymenoptera, two groups that are only very distantly related. Subsocial behaviors occur among many other insect orders, but there is no evidence that eusociality has ever occurred among any but these two orders. According to Hamilton, the closer the relationship between individuals, the greater the number of genes shared (obviously) and the greater the likelihood that siblings will share identical genes. Because of the unique sex-determination mechanism in Hymenoptera (an unfertilized egg develops into a male, and a fertilized egg into a female), the degree of relationship between siblings is even greater than in other orders, and thus there is a greater likelihood that one individual's genes could be passed via her sister to the next generation (see box). All sterile workers in a social insect colony are siblings if only one queen is present.

Hamilton's (1964) hypothesis, in outline, is as follows: Consider the offspring of parents having genotypes* AB and CD:

```
              AB  ×  CD
            /    / \    \
          AC    AD  BC    BD
```

---

*If you are unfamiliar with these terms, consult a general biology text.

Since each offspring gets one set of chromosomes* from its father and one set from its mother, four combinations are possible: AC, AD, BC, and BD. In this simplified system, each offspring has both genes in common with 25 per cent of all offspring and one gene in common with 67 per cent of the remaining offspring.

Now consider Hymenoptera, in which the male is haploid.* Parents are now AB (female) and C (male).

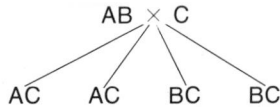

Only two combinations are possible, AC and BC, and each offspring has both genes in common with 50 per cent of all offspring and one gene in common with the other 50 per cent. The degree of relationship among siblings is closer than that between parent and offspring. Genetically, it pays more to help your mother raise a queen who is your sister than to raise a baby princess of your own (H. Horn, personal communication).

---

*If you are unfamiliar with this term, consult a general biology text.

This hypothesis suggests that eusociality was much more *likely* to develop in Hymenoptera, particularly if related individuals tended to aggregate, thus fostering inbreeding. Selective pressures leading to evolution of a sterile worker caste remain a mystery, though some clues may be had from bees, in which eusociality may have evolved eight times. Existing bees show every degree of aggregation from solitary to eusocial (Michener, 1969). In solitary bees, females provision a nest and may stay around to guard it. The next steps are aggregations of solitary bees, then a communal nest used by several females. Next there are quasisocial tropical bees, *Euglossa,* which use a common nest and cooperatively feed one another's larvae; and semisocial bees, *Augochloropsis,* in which several females use a common nest and in which some females gradually become sterile and subordinate, a development reminiscent of *Polistes* wasps (p. 247). Because bees feed on nectar and pollen, which are very concentrated but short-lived resources, it was (and is) selectively advantageous for large numbers of individuals to locate and utilize flowers quickly. This is partly true of ants and social wasps, which likewise feed on scattered, ephemeral resources.

Termite societies may have evolved because termites feed on cellulose and consequently must eat one another's cast skins and fecal pellets to conserve cellulose-digesting microorganisms. Had these aggregations been very local, sibling matings might have increased the degree of relationship (Hamilton, 1964) and thus the likelihood of there being a worker caste. Cockroaches aggregate in response to pheromones and eat each other's cast skins, and a remarkable subsocial roach, *Cryptocercus,* forms loose colonies and eats wood (McKittrick, 1964). Termites, which are similar to roaches in several ways (Chapter Three), may have evolved from such subsocial roaches.

SUMMARY

This chapter discusses insect **ethology,** the scientific study of insect behavior. Behaviors are classified into a hierarchy of increasingly complex patterns: **reflexes,** simple stimulus response patterns; **kineses,** undirected (random) movements; and **taxes,** directed or oriented responses to environmental events, These relatively straightforward behaviors are modified by **releasers** (external or internal stimuli that generate a response), by behavioral rhythms, or by learning, though learning is a minor influence in insect behavior.

A central function of insect behavior is communication, wherein a behavioral act by one insect evokes a response in another individual (or a group) of the same species. (Communication *between* species is discussed in Chapter Nine). Communication may be visual, auditory, tactile, chemical, or (most often) a combination of these.

Results of communication discussed here are courtship and mating, territorial behavior, aggregation, and brooding and protection of offspring. Such subsocial behavior has evolved into truly social (**eusocial**) behavior in Isoptera (termites) and Hymenoptera (ants, bees, and wasps). The chapter ends with an examination of insect societies from a behavioral standpoint.

Chapter Seven

Reproduction and Development

INTRODUCTION

Like most other organisms, insects develop from a single cell, which in turn most often results from fusion of two cells—sperm and egg. Most insect species are bisexual (male and female), and fertilization of eggs with sperm occurs before development continues. Sexual reproduction thereby provides recombination of somewhat dissimilar genes (unless parents are identical twins), producing in a species the variation necessary for survival and change in a changing environment (Chapter Two). This advantage that sexual reproduction provides to the entire species usually outweighs whatever disadvantage may accrue to the individual. The vast majority of insects (and of all organisms) are normally bisexual, though a few reproduce parthenogenetically (without males), as discussed later.

As they develop from fertilized egg (zygote) to adulthood, most insects undergo metamorphosis, a change in form that may be very great and that may enable the insect to utilize two (or more) very different ecological situations. In addition, many insect inhabitants of seasonal environments undergo diapause (physiological inactivity), which permits survival in harsh temperatures or drought conditions. Metamorphosis and diapause occur to a lesser extent in other animal groups, but they are major adaptations in insect biology and are yet another reason why insects have successfully invaded and diversified in numerous terrestrial habitats.

ENDOCRINE SYSTEM

Insect reproduction, growth, and development depend on numerous extrinsic and intrinsic factors. Among the most important of these are hormones, internally secreted chemicals that elicit a physiological response (usually at a specific site). Insect hormones are secreted by groups of specialized cells, particularly the structures shown in Figure 7–1. The corpus cardiacum secretes several hormones that regulate physiological functions: heartbeat, excretion (Chapter Four)

256

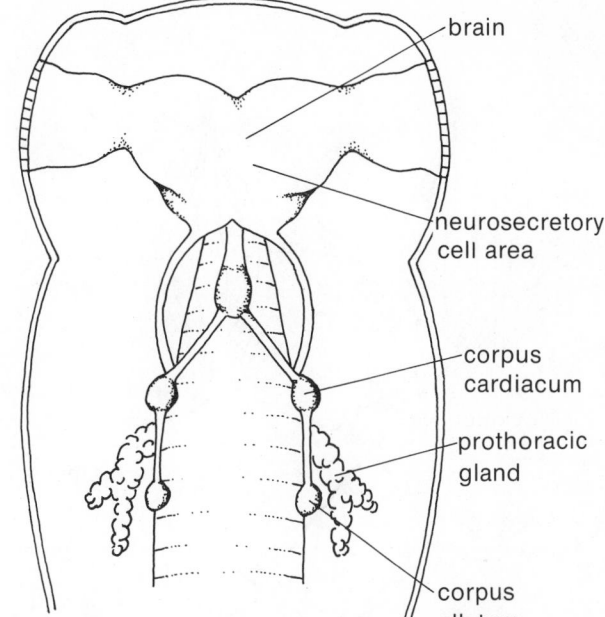

Figure 7–1. Major endocrine structures of an insect.

- brain
- neurosecretory cell area
- corpus cardiacum
- prothoracic gland
- corpus allatum

and fat body metabolism (Gilbert and King, 1973). The corpus allatum secretes juvenile hormone (JH), and the prothoracic glands secrete α-ecdysone, which other tissues (including oenocytes) convert to β-ecdysone, or molting hormone (MH). Ecdysones are also produced by ovaries, at least in mosquitoes (Hagedorn, 1974). JH and MH are most vital to control of reproduction and development, as we shall see. Insect neurosecretory cells are similar to nervous tissue, and these secretory cells might be thought of as specialized neurons. (Recall from Chapter Five that all neurons secrete chemical transmitters at synapses.) Hormones seem to be secreted directly into hemolymph, though they may be transmitted by connective tissue or neurons as well (Whitten, 1964).

REPRODUCTIVE SYSTEM

FEMALE

One location acted upon by insect hormones is the female reproductive system, where the new insect begins its development. Figure 7–2 depicts a female reproductive system. The paired ovaries end in a terminal filament, which in turn attaches to the dorsal diaphragm (see Fig. 4–17). Eggs (oocytes) are formed in functional units, **ovarioles,** ranging in number from one per ovary (in aphids, some scarab beetles, and pupiparous Diptera) to over 2000 (in queen termites). The number of ovarioles per ovary sets a maximum upper limit on fecundity, the number of eggs that an insect can produce (see Table 8–4). Fecundity is important in determining how rapidly an insect population grows (Chapters Eight and Ten).

Each ovariole consists of (1) a germarium, a region of actively dividing cells that give rise to oocytes and "nurse cells"; and (2) a vitellarium in which yolk is

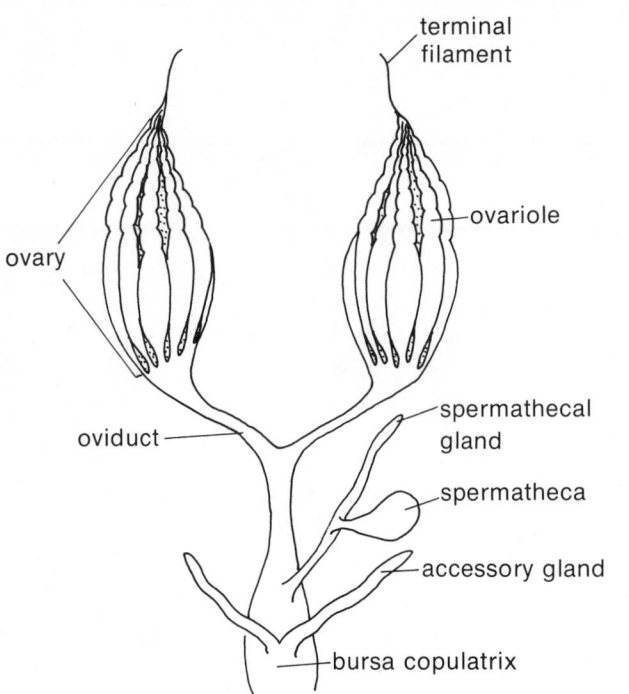

terminal
filament

ovariole

ovary

oviduct

spermathecal
gland

spermatheca

accessory gland

bursa copulatrix

Figure 7–2. Female reproductive system.

added to the developing oocyte. There are three major types of ovarioles (Fig. 7–3). **Panoistic** ovarioles are typical of more "primitive" Apterygota, Orthoptera, and Odonata. Here follicle cells surround the oocyte in the vitellarium and deposit yolk and chorion (eggshell) until the egg is fully formed; then they are reabsorbed (Fig. 7–3A). In **polytrophic** ovarioles (in most Endopterygota), a group of nurse cells moves down the vitellarium with the egg (Fig. 7–3B), while in **telotrophic** ovarioles (Hemiptera and some Coleoptera) the nurse cell bodies remain in the germarium while attached by a cytoplasmic strand to the oocyte (Fig. 7–3C). In all cases, yolk and chorion are deposited in the vitellarium, during which time the egg (of a cockroach, at least) may increase up to 2½ million times in volume (Bonhag, 1959).

On the basis of many experiments by Wigglesworth and associates, especially on the bloodsucking bug *Rhodnius* (Hemiptera:Reduviidae), hormonal control of oogenesis is quite well understood. Wigglesworth (1936) found that when a decapitated, mature, ovary-ripened female was surgically attached (parabiosed) to one in which oogenesis had not yet begun, the recipient half of the resulting monster then commenced oogenesis. Implantation of the corpus allatum from an active female also induced oogenesis in the recipient. Subsequent experiments showed that in *Rhodnius* impulses from receptors in a blood-filled crop stimulated the brain to induce secretion of JH (juvenile hormone) from the corpus allatum into the hemolymph, and this JH stimulated deposition of yolk by follicle cells (Melius and Telfer, 1969). Mating may also stimulate oogenesis; the presence of male spermatophores (or anything, even a small glass bead) in the spermatheca of a female cockroach activates the JH–oogenesis cycle (Davey, 1965). MH (β-ecdysone) is also necessary for oogenesis in some Lepidoptera (Sahota, 1969) and may be the primary oogenetic hormone in short-lived insects, whose ovaries begin producing eggs before adult eclosion (deWilde and deLoof, 1973a). Hagedorn (1974) found that mosquito ovaries produced MH, which stimulated fat body activity after the adult female fed. Oogenesis in the rabbit flea is initiated by hormones ingested with host blood; the flea's ovaries ripen when she feeds on a pregnant rabbit and her breeding cycle is thus timed to that of her host (Rothschild, 1965). The method by which oogenesis is turned off is less clear, though many insects will cease oogenesis and will reabsorb eggs if starved or unable to mate. Among some mosquitoes, the ovary itself secretes an inhibitory hormone that turns off oogenesis whether or not the mosquito feeds again (Hagedorn, 1974). Hormonal control of oogenesis is summarized in Figure 7–4.

Following yolk deposition, follicle cells secrete a thin vitelline membrane and a thicker, hardened chorion (see p. 264). The egg then passes through an oviduct and past a pouch, the **spermatheca,** in which sperm are stored after mating. Sperm are released as the egg passes by, and they move through one or several funnel-shaped pores, micropyles, in the chorion. The mechanism of sperm release is not clear, though females of some parasitic wasps apparently have some muscular control over the spermathecal entrance and deposit fertilized or unfertilized eggs, depending on environmental factors (Flanders, 1956). Accessory glands may also be involved; Leopold and Degrullier (1973) have noted that removal of accessory glands from flies results in fewer inseminations. Accessory glands are also a source of secretions that are helpful in oviposition; cement, to glue eggs to a substrate; ootheca, the "egg case" material of mantids and cockroaches (see Fig. 7–9); and lubricating fluid to aid the eggs' passage down

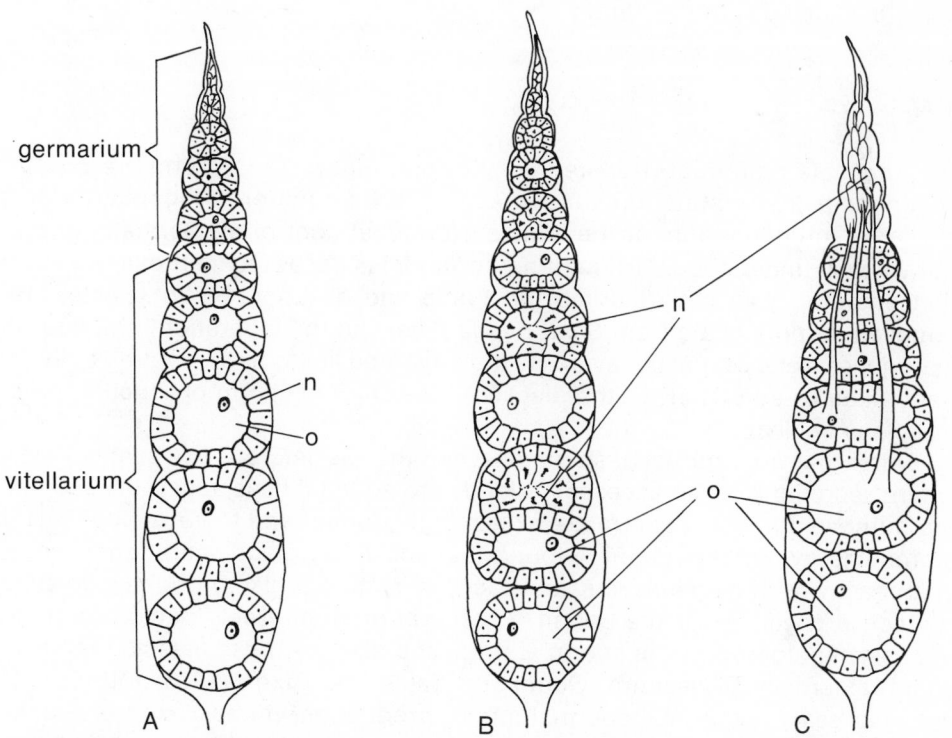

Figure 7–3. Types of ovarioles. *A,* Panoistic. *B,* Polytrophic. *C,* Telotrophic. Nurse cells (*n*); oocyte (egg) (*o*).

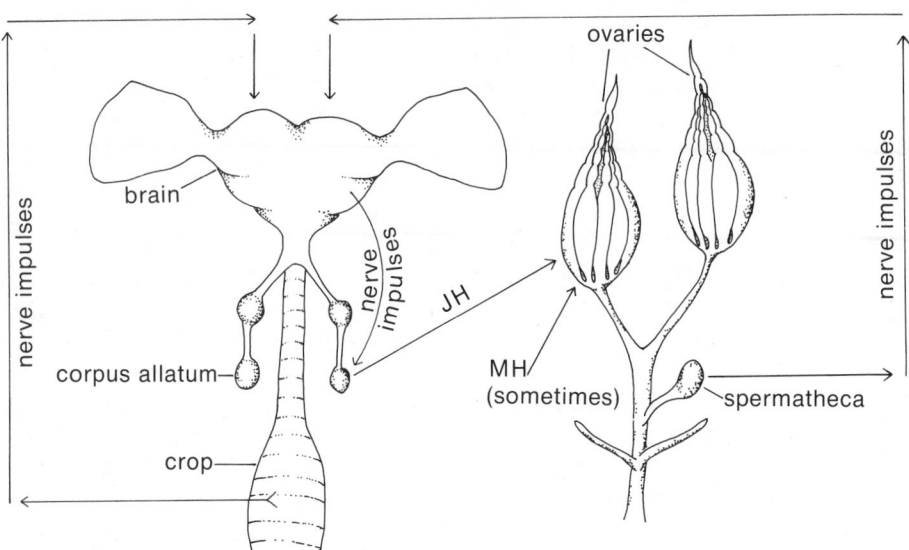

Figure 7–4. Nervous and hormonal control of oogenesis in cockroach or *Rhodnius.* Nerve impulses from stretch receptors in crop or spermatheca stimulate brain to send impulses to corpus allatum. This secretes juvenile hormone (*JH*), which acts on ovarioles to initiate yolk deposition. Molting hormone (*MH*) is sometimes involved, as are oogenic hormones secreted by the ovaries themselves.

the ovipositor. In ants, bees, and wasps, accessory glands are the source of poisons injected with the sting.

MALE

The male reproductive system is shown in Figure 7–5. Sperm are produced within the paired **testes** from among actively dividing **spermatogonia,** which are similar to the germarium of the female. Hormonal control of spermatogenesis is not yet well understood. MH (molting hormone) is necessary in those few species that entomologists have studied (de Wilde and de Loof, 1973b). Foster (1967) removed corpora allata from *Scatophaga* flies, and this operation inhibited spermatogenesis and sexual behavior. He then restored libido by implanting active corpora allata or adding JH to the diet. The role of JH in sperm production of most insects is unclear.

After they are produced, sperm descend the vas deferens to a seminal vesicle, where secretions of the accessory glands are added. These accessory secretions are nutritive, for insect sperm are exceedingly slender and therefore contain little stored energy. Shepherd (1975) found that accessory gland secretions increased sperm activity. In many insects, male accessory glands also produce a gelatinous protective covering for the sperm. These **spermatophores,** "packaged sperm," are essential for long-term sperm storage and also for those insects that deposit sperm externally (Thysanura, Odonata). Blaine and Dixon (1973) found that JH was necessary for normal spermatophore production in cockroaches. Some insects do not form spermatophores but store sperm and accessory gland secretions together as semiliquid semen.

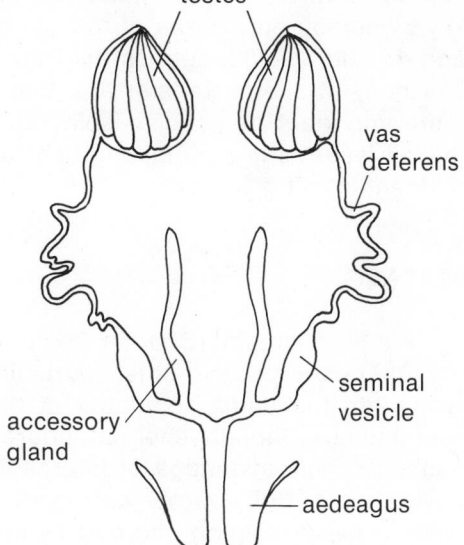

Figure 7–5. Male reproductive system.

In most insects, semen or spermatophores are deposited directly into the bursa copulatrix of the female by the male's **aedeagus,** a fleshy protrusion of the ninth abdominal segment that is everted by hydrostatic pressure from hemolymph. Associated with the aedeagus are often a pair of claspers having a rather involved morphology (Fig. 7–6). These external male genitalia often are morphologically very typical within a species and very different between species, and as such, systematists find them useful characteristics for differentiating otherwise nearly identical species. It has been suggested (Rentz, 1972, and others) that the

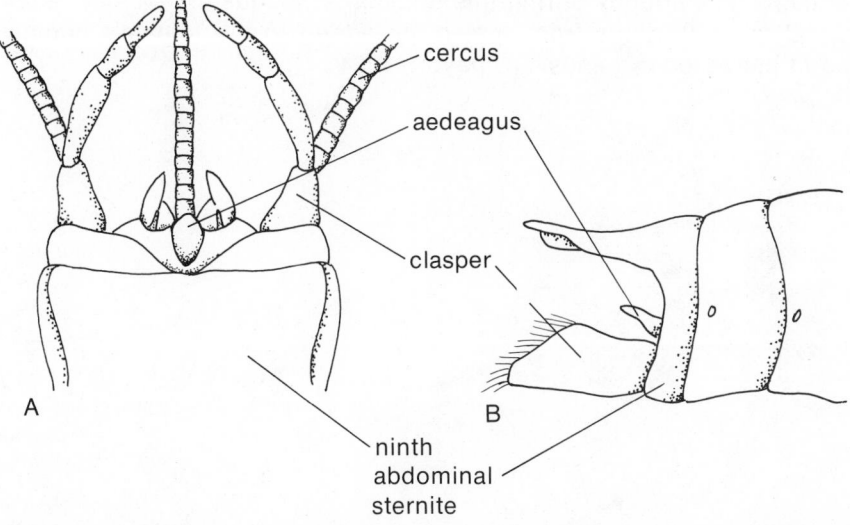

Figure 7–6. External male genitalia. *A*, Mayfly (ventral view). *B*, Cabbage butterfly (lateral view). (Redrawn from Imms, A. D. 1957. A General Textbook of Entomology. 9th ed., revised by Professor O. W. Richards and R. G. Davies. Methuen & Co. Ltd. London.)

unique structure of male (and female) external genitalia serve as a "lock and key" whereby only sexes of the same species can mate. Alternatively, de Wilde and de Loof (1973a) suggest that the "lock and key" mechanism only increases efficiency of sperm transfer and that ecological and behavioral differences are more important as species-isolating mechanisms. The importance of morphological features in maintaining species' integrity probably varies greatly among different insect groups.

MATING

We have already (Chapter Six) considered behavioral aspects of insect mating. After appropriate mutual courtship (in most insects), sperm are deposited directly into the bursa copulatrix of the female, from whence they move to the spermatheca (though spermatophores may be deposited directly in the spermatheca). The advantage of internal fertilization is considerable in a terrestrial environment. Both oocyte and sperm are aquatic and would quickly dry in air without the protection afforded by internal fertilization. External fertilization, in which males deposit spermatophores that females then pick up and insert, occurs quite commonly among soil arthropods, including Collembola and Thysanura (Schaller, 1971). Soil is, of course, a damp environment. External fertilization may have been practiced by the wingless ancestors of modern insects.

Odonata, dragonflies and damselflies, have retained external fertilization. Male and female fly about in tandem (Fig. 7–7), and the male deposits spermatophores on a specialized structure on his second abdominal sternite. The female, held by the neck between his claspers, then bends her abdomen underneath his to pick up the spermatophores.

A most deviant mating activity occurs among bedbugs. Rather than going the "normal" route, the male pierces the female's abdomen with his aedeagus (at a specialized location) and deposits semen within her body cavity. The spermatozoa (some of them) make their way through the hemolymph and thence into the spermatheca. Evidently during this unusual sensuous experience, additional protein and micronutrients from semen are added to the female's hemolymph, resulting in increased oogenesis (Carayon, 1964).

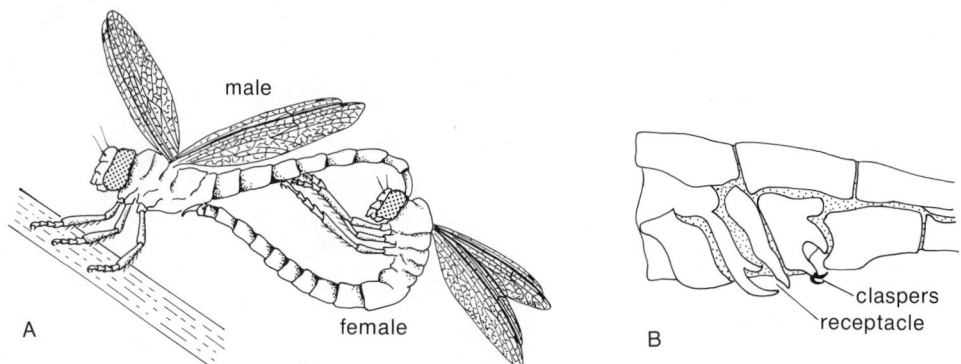

Figure 7–7. External fertilization in dragonflies. *A*, Male and female in tandem. *B*, Close-up of anterior portion of male abdomen showing claspers for holding female and receptacle for spermatophores.

PARTHENOGENESIS

Parthenogenesis, reproduction without fertilization, occurs rather commonly in certain insect groups, especially walkingsticks, weevils, and some parasitic wasps (Suomalainen, 1962). The unfertilized oocyte simply commences embryonic development (see further on), and eventually produces a complete adult, usually female. White (1964) suggests that all insects are potentially parthenogenetic because unfertilized eggs of many normally heterosexual species have been induced to commence embryonic development. Parthenogenesis has the selective advantage of producing offspring immediately and concentrating food resources on procreative females rather than nonbearing males. This short-term advantage is a compromise with lack of recombination; such offspring are genetically identical (excepting mutations) to parents. In the long (evolutionary) run, parthenogenetic species are therefore less capable of change in response to a changing environment. Some insects procure the environmental advantages of both parthenogenesis and bisexuality by alternating generations. Aphids (and some midges) are parthenogenetic during the growing season when food conditions are favorable and then produce bisexual forms that mate, assuring recombination, and lay overwintering eggs (see Fig. 7–29).

INSECT EGGS

With the exception of a few species that produce active young, most insects lay eggs. The mature insect egg consists of the oocyte, covered by a thin vitelline membrane, and an even thinner waxy layer overlaid by the thickened chorion, or eggshell. From the time it leaves the female parent, the egg is a free-living individual faced with problems of survival similar to those of terrestrial adults: avoiding desiccation while obtaining oxygen, and procuring nutrients. Fortunately for the developing insect, most of the oocyte is yolk, consisting mostly of protein, carbohydrates, and lipid, the amounts depending on how long the insect remains in the egg. The thickened chorion protects the oocyte from desiccation and has tiny exterior pores on its outer surface that lead to a spongy inner area from which the developing embryo takes oxygen (Fig. 7–8). The aquatic water scavenger beetles (Hydrophilidae) construct an egg cocoon with a breathing tube leading to the water's surface (Fig. 7–9A). Terrestrial whiteflies (Homoptera:Aleyrodidae) solve the water-conservation problem by inserting or "planting" eggs endwise in leaves; the eggs absorb water from the leaf (Fig. 7–9B). Many insect eggs absorb water readily but will become dormant if they get dry.

Insects usually lay their eggs (oviposit) near the larval food supply. We have already seen the sensory (Chapter Five) and behavioral (Chapter Six) mechanisms of oviposition site location. Oviposition is facilitated in many insect orders by the **ovipositor,** consisting of six **valvulae,** two on the eighth and four on the ninth abdominal sternite. These function as a unit, depositing eggs in protected places that otherwise could not be reached. Figure 7–10 depicts variety in ovipositors, some of which may be used to cut into twigs (katydids, Fig. 7–10A), to bore through wood (Fig. 7–10B), or to insert eggs into an insect host (Fig. 7–10C). In ants, bees, and wasps, the ovipositor is modified into a sting (hence, only females sting), which in the worker honey bee is barbed (Fig. 7–11). On attempted withdrawal, it is torn from the bee with fatal consequences. Ovipositors occur in

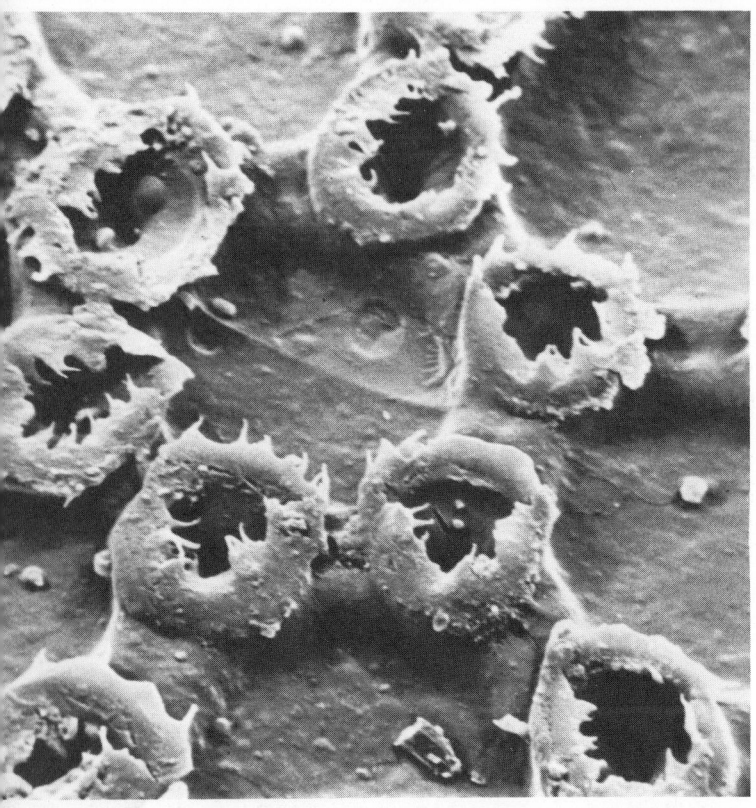

Figure 7–8. Chorion of egg of *Anthraea pernyi;* magnification × 1500. (From Insect Eggshells, by H. E. Hinton. Sci. Amer. *223*(2): 84–91, 1968. Copyright © 1968 by Scientific American, Inc. All rights reserved.)

Figure 7–9. Variety in insect eggs. *A,* Egg case of water scavenger beetle attached to floating leaf. *B,* Egg of whitefly inserted into leaf for moisture. *C,* Ootheca of mantid. *D,* Stalked eggs of lacewing. *E,* Eggs of *Culex* mosquito in floating raft. *F,* Eggs of alfalfa weevil inserted into stem. (*A* and *B* redrawn from Wigglesworth, V. B. 1964. The Life of Insects. World Publishing Co., Cleveland.)

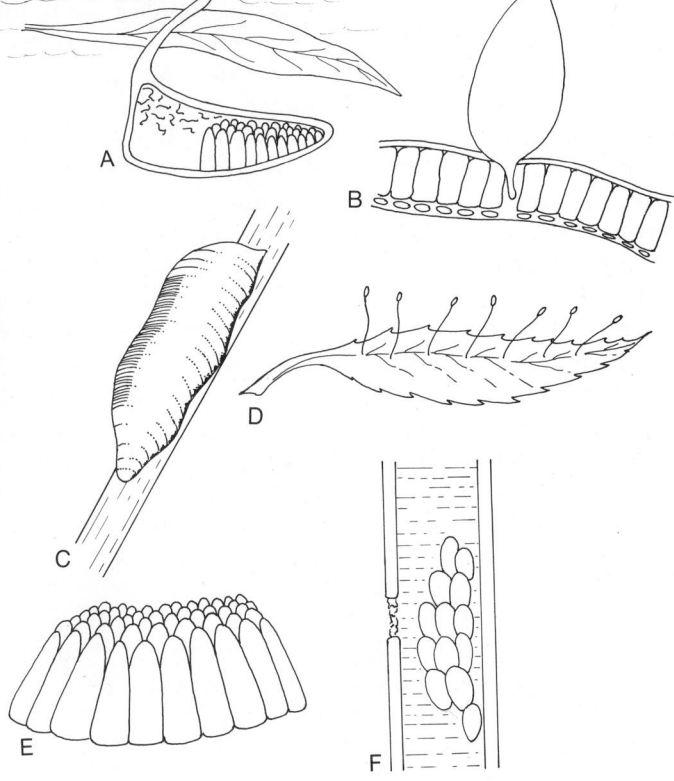

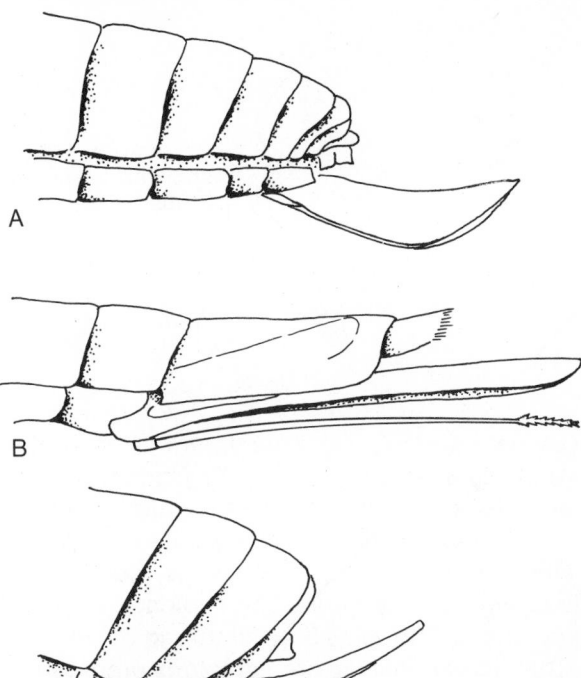

Figure 7–10. Ovipositors. *A*, Katydid, which inserts eggs into twigs (see also Figure 10–3). *B*, Horntail (Hymenoptera: Siricidae), which bores into wood. *C*, Ichneumon, a wasp parasitic on insect larvae.

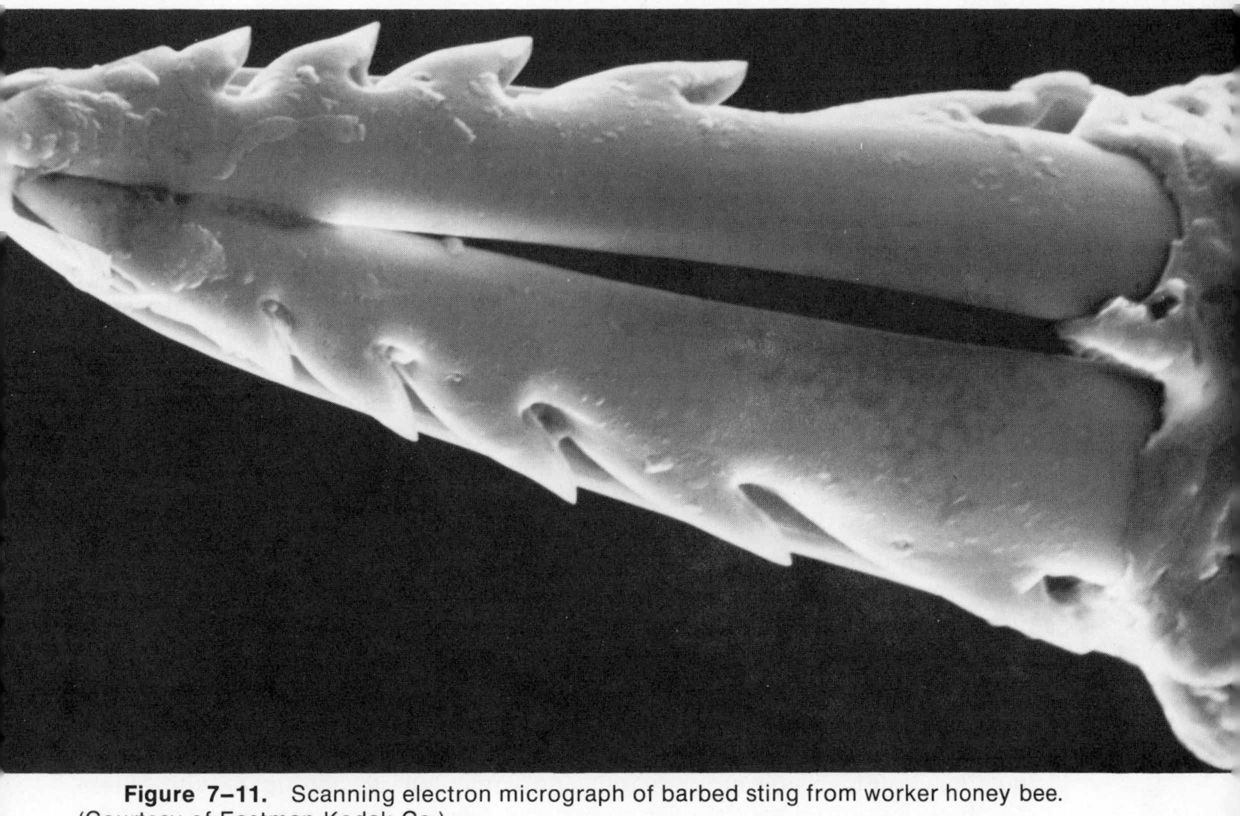

Figure 7–11. Scanning electron micrograph of barbed sting from worker honey bee. (Courtesy of Eastman Kodak Co.)

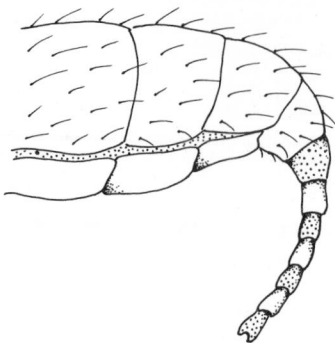

Figure 7–12. Terminal segments of fly abdomen, showing telescoping segments that extend to form ovitubus.

Orthoptera, Odonata, Hemiptera, Hymenoptera, and some Homoptera and Neuroptera. In Diptera and Thysanoptera, the terminal abdominal segment is lengthened into an "ovitubus," which functions as an ovipositor (Fig. 7–12).

Insect eggs may be laid singly or in groups (Fig. 7–9) and may be covered with a frothy secretion (**ootheca,** see Fig. 7–9C) in addition to the chorion. Lacewings (Neuroptera:Chrysopidae) display interesting oviposition; for each egg, the female spins a small thread of silk atop which the egg is laid (see Fig. 7–9D). Lacewing larvae are voracious predators, and the first one out would doubtless devour its defenseless brethren were they not elevated on silken towers that can be climbed down but not up.

SEX DETERMINATION

Egg and sperm cells are both haploid, receiving a single set of chromosomes from each parent. Among these chromosomes (which may vary from 8 to 40 depending on the species) are one set, sex chromosomes, which determine the sex of the future insect. In most insects (and in all humans), females are the homozygous sex, having a matched pair of sex chromosomes (XX), whereas males are heterozygous, having an unmatched pair (XY). An oocyte can therefore have only an X chromosome (because the female is homozygous XX), but a spermatozoan may carry either X or Y and the sex of the offspring thus depends on the first sperm through. In Lepidoptera and Trichoptera, sex determination is reversed; males are XX and females, XY. In Hymenoptera, Thysanoptera, and some Homoptera, there is no Y chromosome; all sperm carry the X and all fertilized eggs become females, XX. In these orders, unfertilized eggs remain haploid, X, and develop into males (see p. 253). Eggs of most parthenogenetic insects apparently produce an extra chromosome set, becoming XX (female) when commencing division.

In most heterosexual insect species, the sex ratio, males to females, is about equal, though this may change in response to the external environment, nutrition, or behavior (Bergerard, 1972). For instance, walkingsticks (Orthoptera) raised at 23°C all become female, while those raised at 30°C become male. Apparently temperature here affects the movement of sex chromosomes. An additional anomaly may occur at an early cell division following fertilization; sex chromosomes may fail to divide properly, causing some cells to end up XX and others, X. Such an individual may survive to become a **gynandromorph,** with characteristics of both male and female. Gynandromorphs may be bilateral (Fig. 7–13) or a mosaic, a patchwork of male and female. Gynandromorph parasitic wasps (*Habrobracon*) that are anteriorly male and posteriorly female also behave gynandromorphically; the male (head) end courts hosts, while the female (tail) end attempts to sting potential mates!

EMBRYONIC DEVELOPMENT

After entering the egg through the micropyle, the sperm loses its tail and fuses with the egg nucleus, forming a zygote, the initial stage of embryonic development. Morphological changes during subsequent development are well-described (Johannsen and Butt, 1941; Hagan, 1951), but very little is known of chemical regulation in insect embryology. This is a very fertile field for future research. One controversy that has persisted since the days of Aristotle is whether or not insect larvae are actually free-living embryos in a state of arrested development, which is then completed in the pupa. The present trend among entomologists is to classify as "embryonic" only those developmental changes occurring within the insect egg prior to hatching.

After fusion of egg and sperm into a zygote (Fig. 7–14), the nucleus divides.

Figure 7–13. Bilateral gynandromorph of tiger swallowtail butterfly. Left half is female; right half, male. (Specimen from Fairfield County, Ohio.)

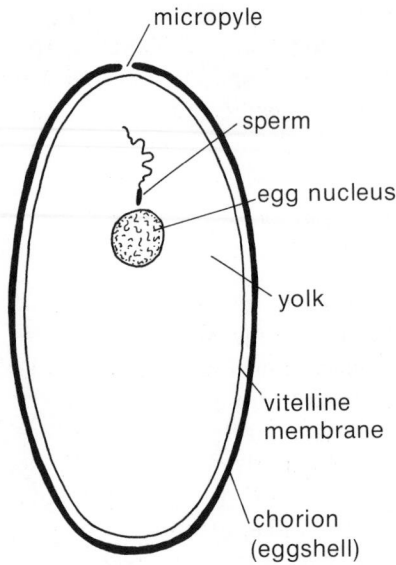

Figure 7–14. Cross section of insect egg after penetration of sperm.

The resulting "daughter" nuclei divide again, and successive cleavages, most prevalent near the future head (cleavage center) continue until many nuclei are present. In eggs with little yolk (parasitic wasps, for example), cleavage may be total (Fig. 7–15A), involving the entire egg. More often, insect eggs contain a relatively large yolk mass that does not divide; instead, nuclei migrate to the periphery of the yolk (Fig. 7–15B), leaving behind a few **yolk cells** that apparently speed utilization of yolk (Youssef, 1973). This is superficial (or mèroblastic) cleavage. Each peripheral cell forms a membrane about itself, whereupon these cells are collectively termed blastoderm (Fig. 7–16A). At this time, a few ventral

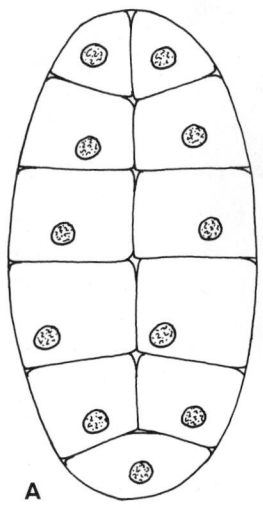

Figure 7–15. Types of initial cleavage in insect eggs (chorion omitted). *A,* Total cleavage. *B,* Superficial cleavage.

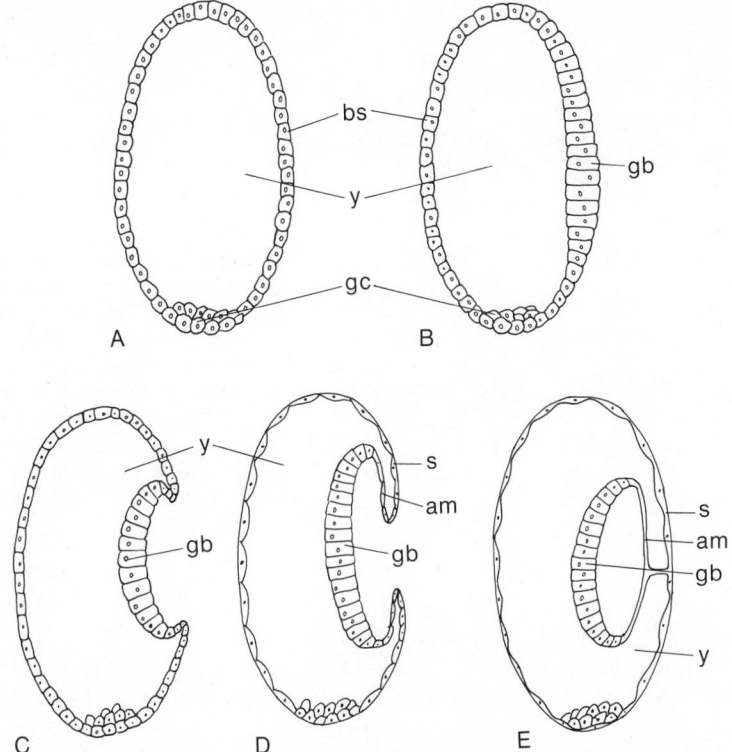

Figure 7–16. Sagittal sections of developing insect embryos in time sequence. *A*, Formation of blastoderm and germ cells. *B*, Formation of germ band. *C*, *D*, and *E*, Formation of embryonic membranes. Amnion (*am*); blastoderm (*bs*); germ band (*gb*); germ cells (*gc*); serosa (*s*); yolk (*y*).

cells differentiate to become **germ cells** (which ultimately form eggs or sperm in the adult insect) and part of the blastoderm enlarges, forming a **germ band** (Fig. 7–16*B*). This germ band will differentiate into the embryo. The remainder of the blastoderm cells become flattened and form the embryonic membranes, the amnion and serosa, (usually) after inward movement of the germ band (Fig. 7–16*C*, *D* and *E*). Amnion and serosa apparently help cushion the embryo. In some insects, a second set of membranes, the inner and outer **indusium,** develop from invagination of blastoderm opposite the germ band.

As cell cleavages continue, germ band cells move inward by either invagination or inward divisions of germ band cells (Fig. 7–17). This is gastrulation, and it results in the formation of a second, inner cell layer, the **mesentoderm.** The outer layer is then termed **ectoderm.** Cell division continues as segmentation becomes visible, first in mesentoderm and then as furrows and appendage buds in ectoderm (Fig. 7–18). At this stage, differentiation of tissues commences and future tagmatization becomes evident; the **protocephalon** (primitive head) and next three segments become the head, the next three become the thorax, and the rest (never more than twelve), become the abdomen (Fig. 7–18). Most insect embryos have abdominal appendages; this reflects the insects' early, multilegged ancestry (Chapter Two).

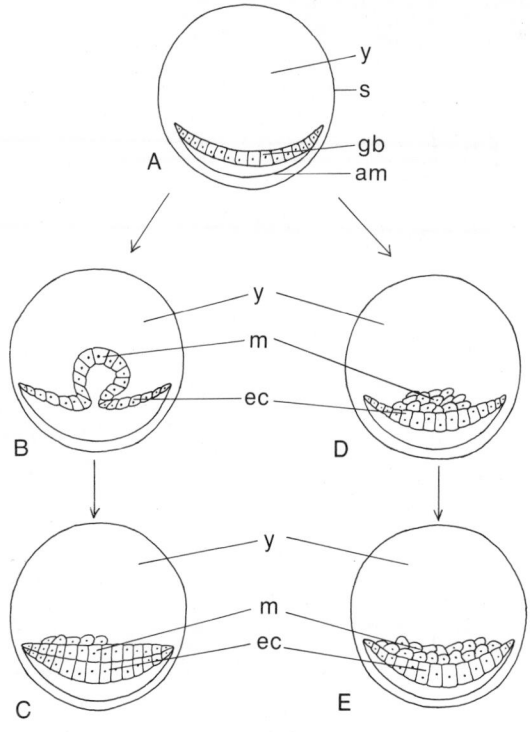

Figure 7–17. Cross section of developing insect embryo showing development of mesentoderm. *A*, Germ band stage (same as that shown in Figure 7–16*E*). *B* and *C*, Invagination of ectoderm to form mesentoderm. *D* and *E*, Inward division of ectoderm to form mesentoderm. Amnion(*am*); ectoderm(*ec*); germ band (*gb*); mesentoderm(*m*); serosa(*s*); yolk(*y*).

By dyeing certain areas of ecto- or mesentoderm and then noting the presence of the dye in the resulting insect, experimenters have discerned the embryonic origin of insect organ systems. The ectoderm forms the epidermis, including all cuticular structures: exoskeleton, wings, and linings of foregut, hindgut, tracheae, and genital ducts. Nerve and glandular tissue is also of ectodermal origin. Mesentoderm becomes fat body, blood cells, gonads, and the midgut. As tissue differentiation proceeds, fueled by yolk, the embryo grows and spreads over the yolk, which eventually absorbs the embryonic membranes.

Embryos of "primitive" insects, especially Odonata and Orthoptera, undergo **blastokinesis,** movements that reverse the position of the embryo and pull it further into the yolk for a time. This may increase efficiency of yolk usage and provide additional protection (Sharov, 1966), though what causes it is questionable. Blastokinesis also occurs in a few "higher" orders, especially Lepidoptera.

Control of embryonic development in insects is not well understood. In dragonflies, at least, embryogenesis is initiated by an "activation center" in the future head; Seidel (1929) removed this area from dragonfly eggs, and they failed to develop embryos. Seidel (1963) also reported a "differentiation center" in the future prothorax; this area is often more advanced in development than other embryonic areas. How, or even whether, this center "directs" development of undifferentiated ectodermal cells is not at all clear. Current evidence suggests that ectoderm may differentiate automatically, while mesentoderm differentiation is controlled by chemicals (yet unknown) that diffuse from overlying ectoderm. Another puzzle is the extent to which embryogenesis is predetermined. Some parasitic wasps undergo **polyembryony,** in which each of many cells resulting

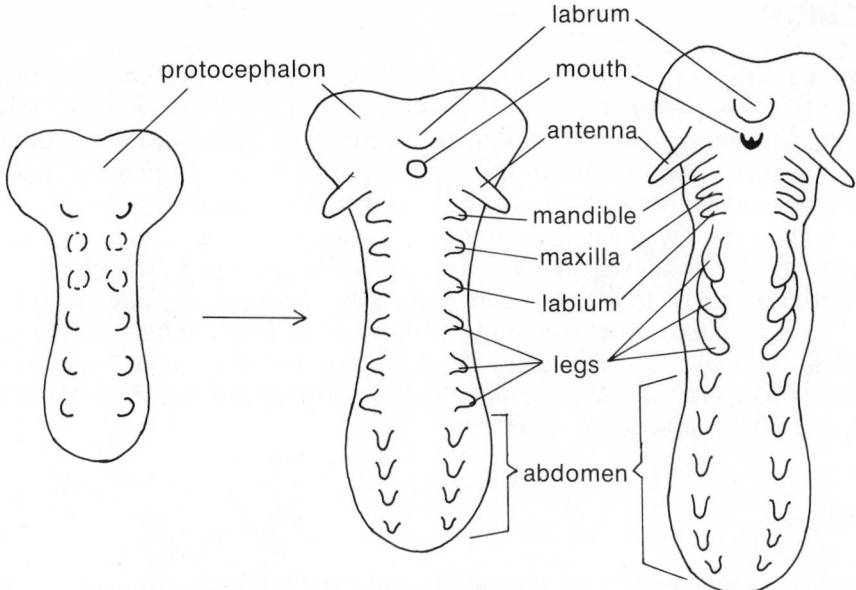

Figure 7–18. Sequential development of segments and appendages in insect embryo.

from early cleavages can, and does, develop independently into an entire wasp. On the other hand, embryonic fates are determined well before first cleavages in Diptera, as Yajima (1960) demonstrated by centrifuging *Chironomus* eggs, thereby scrambling their chemical contents and generating the monsters shown in Figure 7–19. Epidermal cells retain ability to differentiate even after the insect hatches, permitting, for instance, the regeneration of lost limbs at times.

Figure 7–19. Malformations of *Chironomus* larvae formed by centrifugation of eggs (germ cells included in eggs). Direction of centrifugation (*g*). *A,* Normal larva. *B,* Two-headed larva. *C,* Double abdomen. (Redrawn from Yajima, H. 1960. Studies on embryonic determination of the harlequin-fly, *Chironomus dorsalis.* I. Effects of centrifugation and of its combination with constriction and puncturing. J. Embryol. Exp. Morphol. 8:198–215.)

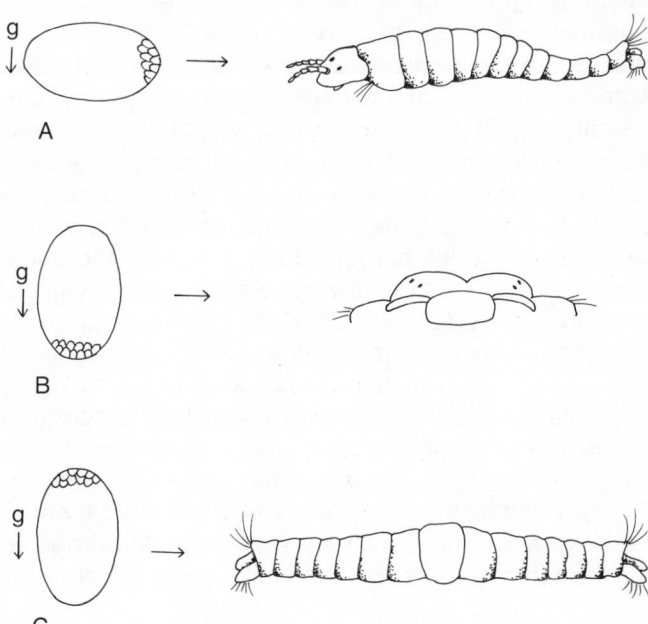

ECLOSION

Shortly after the yolk is completely used up, the young insect emerges from the egg; this is **eclosion.** Details of eclosion vary, but most insects swallow amniotic fluid, which causes air to diffuse through the egg. The insect then may press against the chorion, which breaks along predetermined lines of weakness. Alternatively, many lepidopterous and dipterous larvae use mandibles or mouthhooks to chew their way out. Mosquito and flea larvae possess a sclerotized spine, which they use rather like an awl to punch an escape hole. The spine is shed shortly after eclosion. In a few insects (e.g., aphids, flesh flies), eggs are retained within the female reproductive tract until they hatch, whereupon living young are larviposited, usually directly onto the food supply. This trend culminates in pupiparous Diptera, whose unusual development is discussed in the section "Developmental Patterns" (p. 281).

GROWTH

As the young insect feeds, it enlarges and soon begins to press on its cuticle. Because the sclerotized exoskeleton is made of hardened, nonliving tissue, it does not grow along with the insect and must therefore be periodically molted, or shed, and replaced by newer, larger cuticle. In preparation for molting, or **ecdysis,** epidermal cells first pull away from the old cuticle and secrete into the resulting space a molting fluid containing chitinase, which digests up to 90 per cent of the old endocuticle. Meanwhile, epidermal cells also begin to secrete new cuticle (Fig. 7–20)—epicuticle first, then exo- and endocuticle. This new cuticle is often pleated or wrinkled to accommodate the larger sized insect that will soon be inside. Abdominal muscles become larger. Immediately preceding ecdysis, epidermal glands produce waterproofing wax and cement layers over the new epicuticle, and the fluid between old and new cuticle is reabsorbed, conserving needed water and nutrients. (An insect thus ready to emerge is termed a pharate.) Then the abdominal muscles contract, forcing hemolymph into the thorax and head; this causes the old cuticle to break open, usually along ecdysial sutures, the lines of weakness where the old cuticle is thinnest. The insect then literally steps out of its skin (Fig. 7–21), leaving behind the old cuticle including linings of tracheae, foregut, hindgut, and reproductive tract. The insect expands to fit its new suit by swallowing air while the new cuticle is still pliable and soft. (Some flies that pupate within the last larval skin possess a specialized structure, the ptilinum, which is everted to push apart the pupal integument when the adult emerges [Fig. 7–22].). In winged adults, hemolymph is pumped into wing veins to expand them (Fig. 7–21). Insects that have just molted (called teneral) are exceedingly vulnerable to predation, and ecdysis usually occurs in protected times and places. Sclerotization, the hardening and darkening of the cuticle, begins immediately upon exposure to air, and more sclerotin is added to new cuticle between molts (Wigglesworth, 1959). Insects with mandibulate mouthparts often eat the old skin, or **exuvia,** which again conserves nutrients.

How the insect "decides" when to molt depends on several factors. In *Rhodnius* nymphs, a nutritious meal of vertebrate blood stretches the abdomen, causing stretch receptors to send impulses to the brain which induce secretion of MH

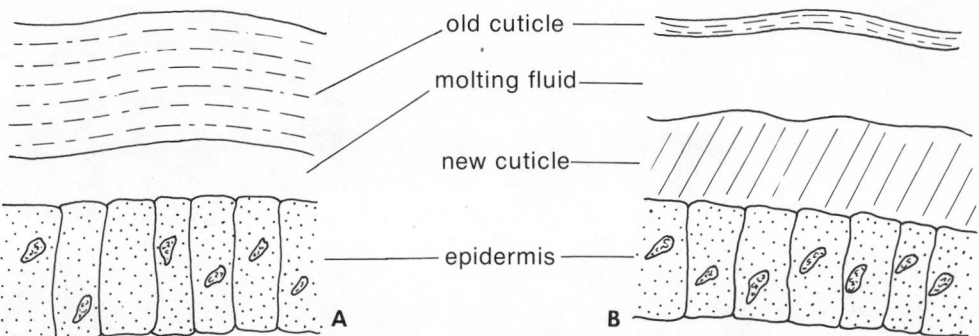

Figure 7-20. Cross sections of insect integument before ecdysis. *A,* Before secretion of new cuticle. *B,* New cuticle secreted before shedding of old.

(molting hormone). MH apparently acts directly on nuclei of epidermal cells (Wigglesworth; 1959, Gilbert and King, 1973) to begin the molting process. Juvenile hormone (JH) interacts with MH in metamorphosis, as described in the next section. Precisely why MH acts selectively on epidermal cells or what mechanism turns glandular secretions off is not yet certain.

Thysanura molt up to 60 times and are the only insect order whose members continue to molt after reaching sexual maturity. Ephemeroptera naiads may molt 20 to 30 times before adulthood. All other insects molt less frequently—usually 5 to 10 times between egg and adult. Each stage between molts is termed an **instar,** and the length of time spent within an instar is a **stadium.** The length of each stadium is partially dependent on environmental variables, such as temperature, moisture, and food, and this is important in determining how rapidly an insect develops from egg to adult and, consequently, how rapidly a population may increase in numbers to economic pest status (Chapter Ten). Cotter (1974) has recently shown when flour moth larvae have optimum living space their rate of development increases when food supply is held constant.

Epidermal cells not only can form new cuticle, spines, or tracheal linings just like the old, but also have limited regenerative capacity. If a leg is removed from an early-instar nymph or larva, nearby epidermis can regenerate a completely new (though smaller) leg, including nervous and muscular tissue, by the next molt.

METAMORPHOSIS

Metamorphosis (in Greek literally "change in form") is a major adaptation of Insecta that has permitted efficient utilization of different environments for immature and mature forms, with immature forms specializing largely in growth, and adults, in reproduction and dispersal. Metamorphosis may be gradual (incomplete, hemimetabolous) or complex (complete, holometabolous).

In gradual metamorphosis, nymphs (immature forms) look rather like small adults (see Fig. 2-13), except that they lack wings and mature reproductive organs. Their mouthparts are similar to adults', and they usually utilize similar habitats in similar ways. Exceptions are orders (Ephemeroptera, Odonata, Ple-

Figure 7–21. Molting of cuticle and metamorphosis in monarch butterfly. *A*, Larva before pupating. *B*, Pupa wriggling free of larval cuticle. *C*, Pupa. *D*, Adult cuticle visible through thin pupal cuticle.

Figure 7–21 *Continued.* *E,* Teneral adult emerging from pupal cuticle. *F,* Fully expanded adult. (Photos by and courtesy of George and Zelda Glasser.)

Figure 7–22. Emerging house fly using ptilinum to push puparium open. (From Brown, L. R. 1973. Postembryonic development. *In* Tipton, V. J. (ed.). Syllabus/Introductory Entomology. Brigham Young University Press, Provo, Utah, pp. 125–156. Photo by L. R. Brown, used with permission.)

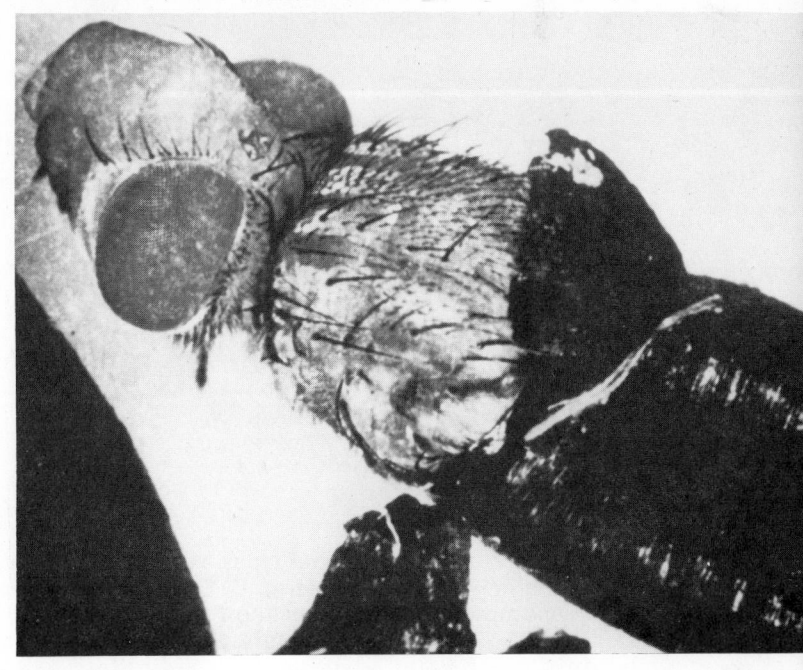

coptera) having aquatic nymphs (or naiads) and terrestrial adults. In these orders, adults and young may appear quite different, in response to different selective pressures in terrestrial and aquatic environments. Whether terrestrial or aquatic, however, Hemimetabola are best characterized by external development of wings, the wing buds gradually appearing in late nymphal instars. However, this is not so in those Hemimetabola (Mallophaga, Anoplura, some Hemiptera and Orthoptera) whose adults have no wings. Apterygota (Thysanura) likewise have no wings and are said to be **ametabolous** (having no metamorphosis), their only change (other than increasing size) being sexual maturity.

In complex metamorphosis, eggs hatch into larvae, which are almost always very different from the adult. Larvae are often wormlike, do not have compound eyes, and are mandibulate whether or not the corresponding adults are. Most importantly, there is no external manifestation of wings or wing buds. Larvae usually occur in different environmental situations and utilize different resources from those of their corresponding adults. This may reduce competition between adults and offspring, and it certainly has subjected larval insects to different, and varied, evolutionary pressures. There is consequently great variety in larval form, and the order to which a given larva belongs may not always be readily discernible. Larvae have been classified according to form, and Figure 7–23 illustrates these various larval types. In one order, or even in one species, one may find several of these types (Fig. 7–30).

Following the last larval instar in Holometabola is the pupa, a "resting stage" during which gonads mature, mouthparts and digestive system may be reorganized, and wings (in most) form. Hinton (1964) states that the pupal stage may have evolved in response to the necessity for restructuring the larva into a winged insect and that larvae and adults have subsequently diverged evolutionarily, each having become successively more specialized. A few Hemimetabola (thrips, whiteflies, and scale insects) have a nonfeeding "pupa" as well. Pupae are usually quiescent, though some (e.g., mosquitoes) are very active but

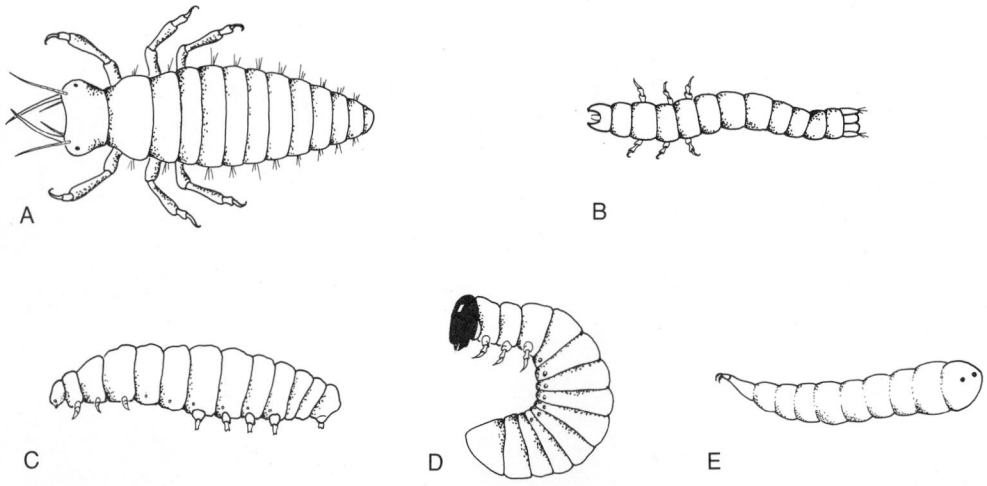

Figure 7–23. Major larval types. *A,* Campodeiform (Neuroptera, some Coleoptera). *B,* Elateriform (some Coleoptera). *C,* Eruciform (Lepidoptera, Mecoptera, Trichoptera, a few Hymenoptera). *D,* Scarabaeiform (some Coleoptera). *E,* Vermiform (most Hymenoptera and Diptera, also Siphonaptera, Strepsiptera).

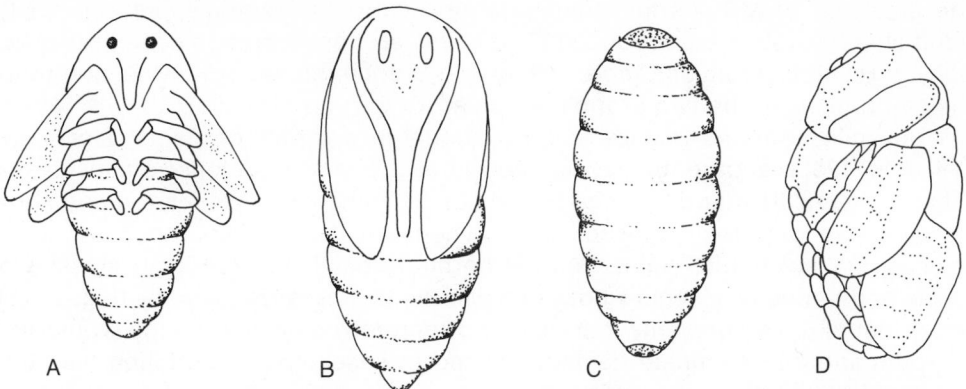

Figure 7-24. Types of insect pupae. *A*, Exarate (most orders). *B*, Obtect (Lepidoptera). *C*, Coarctate, pupa in puparium (Diptera:Cyclorrhapha). *D*, Coarctate pupa as in *C*, but with larval integument removed.

do not feed. The pupa is a vulnerable stage, and often the larva constructs a protective cocoon or cell in a sheltered place before pupating. **Exarate** pupae have free legs, antennae, and wing buds (Fig. 7-24*A*); this type is typical of Coleoptera, Hymenoptera, Neuroptera, Trichoptera, some Diptera, and minor holometabolous orders. **Obtect** pupae have appendages that are tightly fused to the body (Fig. 7-24*B*) these are typical of most Lepidoptera. Some flies pupate within the last larval skin; such a pupa is **coarctate** (also called a puparium) (Fig. 7-24*C*).

CONTROL OF METAMORPHOSIS

Control of metamorphosis has been one of the more exciting areas of entomological research in the last several years. The work of Wigglesworth, Williams, Piepho, Gilbert, and others has given us a fairly clear picture of how insects change form, though many of the specific details, particularly the intracellular biochemical action of hormones, remain to be discerned.

Metamorphosis is apparently controlled by juvenile hormone (JH), which acts as a modulator or regulator of molting hormone (MH) (Gilbert and King, 1973). In a way not yet fully understood, the brain directs the corpus allatum to secrete JH throughout larval (or nymphal) life. Within insect larvae, under the epidermis, are **imaginal discs,** pockets of undifferentiated epidermal cells that eventually become wings, antennae, and other structures of the adult insect. JH apparently suppresses development of the imaginal discs. When MH is present, JH influences active epidermal cells to produce larval cuticular structures; if the corpus allatum is removed from an early-instar nymph of *Rhodnius,* a tiny adult is produced at the next molt. Piepho and coworkers (1951) in a series of experiments transplanted epidermis and cuticle of wax moths from one individual to another. When adult epidermis was transplanted into a larva, it formed pupal cuticle at the next molt, then larval cuticle at subsequent molts under the influence of JH in the recipient. The transplanted cuticle again formed normal pupal cuticle when the recipient metamorphosed. Apparently, JH acts as a "genetic switch" in the presence of MH. As the concentration of JH decreases, pupal and finally adult characteristics are produced (Fig. 7–25). JH concentration decreases gradually in Hemimetabola and more abruptly in Holometabola; otherwise, control of metamorphosis in the two groups is similar (Gilbert and King, 1973).

Juvenile hormone mimics occur naturally in a variety of plants (Sláma and Williams, 1966), apparently having evolved as a chemical defense against insect attack. Chemicals that mimic the actions of JH have been synthesized and show considerable promise as insecticides. When applied to immature insects, JH mimics, or "juvenoids," upset normal hormone balance, producing mosaics of larvae and pupae or insects whose cuticle fails to sclerotize properly (Fig. 7–26). JH, of course, also prevents maturity, and therefore a JH insecticide would halt reproduction and eliminate damage caused by insects such as biting flies that are pestiferous only in the adult stage.

DIAPAUSE

A part of metamorphosis, and likewise under hormonal control, is diapause, a time of slowing or stopping of development, feeding, and all but a few maintenance functions. Heartbeat, breathing, and activity are nearly halted, and major changes often take place in hemolymph concentration. In some pupae, water

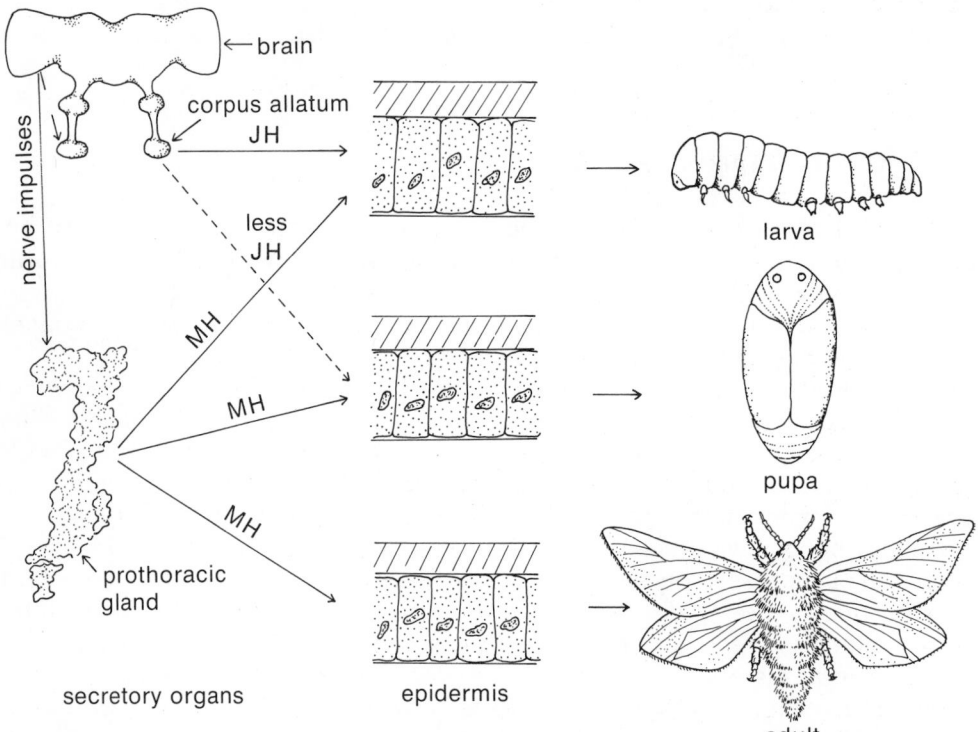

Figure 7–25. Hormonal control of development. High concentrations of juvenile hormone (*JH*) in hemolymph stimulate development of larval characteristics. Lower JH concentration leads to pupal formation. Adult characteristics develop in absence of JH. Molting hormone (*MH*).

Figure 7-26. Effect of juvenile hormone (JH) mimics on mealworm beetle. *A*, Normal beetle. *B*, Beetle that received JH as pupa. (Courtesy of W. T. Anderson.)

content is reduced and glycerol concentration increases, permitting the diapausing insect to resist freezing (Salt, R. W., 1961). Mansingh (1971) argues for delineating several types of insect dormancy and diapause; however, for this discussion it is sufficient to separate dormancy into quiescence (simple inactivity) and diapause (an actual physiological shutdown). Quiescence may occur in response to cool or warm temperatures, reduced humidity, and other environmental changes, though the quiescent insect may resume activity immediately when the environment again becomes favorable. Diapause, on the other hand, may be initiated by quite different environmental factors and requires special circumstances for termination (Mansingh, 1971).

Diapause may occur in egg, larval, pupal, or adult stages, though most commonly it occurs in the egg or pupa. In immature insects, diapause involves arrest of development; in adults, it prevents maturation of gonads. Insects that diapause in every generation are said to have obligate diapause and a **univoltine** life cycle. The eggs of most temperate-zone grasshoppers diapause over winter; they are univoltine. Other species have a facultative diapause, occurring only at certain seasons, and are therefore **multivoltine.** The European corn borer pupa over much of its United States range alternates diapausing (overwintering) with nondiapausing generations; it is **bivoltine.** Still other insects, particularly those in equable climates, may exhibit no diapause at all.

Diapause has evolved in response to deleterious environmental conditions, such as seasonal low temperatures, freezing, and lack of food, that occur over most of the temperate climate zones. Were insects to wait for the onset of bitter weather before diapausing they would likely not survive, and diapause is usually initiated by secondary, predictable factors that precede rather unpredictable inclement weather. Change in daylength, photoperiod, is probably the most important initiator of diapause. Steadily decreasing photoperiod in late summer and autumn is perceived by the brain of the Colorado potato beetle (one of the best-understood diapausers), and the brain then inhibits secretion of JH by the corpus allatum (de Wilde and de Boer, 1969). In the laboratory, diapause can be induced in Colorado potato beetles either by rearing them under a short photoperiod or by removing the corpus allatum. Development of internal parasitoid larvae is arrested by absence of JH in the host; host and parasitoid diapause together. The parent female may (somehow) determine whether or not her offspring undergo diapause; the parasitic wasp, *Tetrastichus incertus,* produces diapausing offspring when hosts are scarce, permitting their survival until hosts are more abundant again (Horn, 1971).

Once initiated, diapause usually can be terminated or "broken" only by a specific environmental stimulus. In many insects that overwinter in diapause, exposure to low temperatures for several days or weeks is sufficient to break diapause. Development of insects that diapause during seasonal droughts (e.g., some Australian grasshopper eggs) commences after exposure to high humidity brought on by drenching rains. Evidently, low temperature or high humidity induces renewed secretion of JH, for diapause ceases and development begins anew if an active corpus allatum is implanted in a Colorado potato beetle (de Wilde and de Boer, 1969). Application of a JH mimic to diapausing alfalfa weevils breaks both their own diapause and that of their internal parasitoid, *Microctonus aethiops* (Bowers and Blickenstaff, 1966; Neal and Bickley, 1971). In some other insect larvae, JH induces diapause that experimenters can terminate by removing the corpora allata.

AGING AND LIFE SPAN

Once an insect becomes a reproductive adult, no further molts occur (except for Thysanura) and there is no increase in size. Occasionally, wings may be shed (e.g., in reproductive termites and ants [Chapter Six]), and female *Ascodipteron* flies shed their legs after mating (Askew, 1971). The life span of adult insects varies widely (Table 7–1), depending on a number of genetic and environmental factors. Measurements of life span are crude at best, but reproductive adults may live for a few hours (mayflies) up to an alleged maximum of 50 years for a queen termite (Brown, 1973). Rockstein and Miquel (1973) review entomological geriatrics; old age in postreproductive insects is accompanied by wing fraying and, in mosquitoes at least, a gradual deterioration of flight muscles (Hylton, 1966). Haydak (1957) noted accumulation of pigments in hemolymph of honey bees and suggested that aging and tissue degeneration may be due to chemical imbalance. In adult insects, there is little or no cell and tissue replacement with the exception of gonads.

Table 7–1. AVERAGE ADULT LIFE SPAN OF SELECTED INSECTS*

Species	Mean Laboratory Life Span (days)	
	FEMALE	MALE
Diptera		
house fly	29	17.5
Aedes mosquito	15	–
Lepidoptera		
silkworm (unmated)	11.9	11.9
luna moth	5.9	6
Hymenoptera		
honey bee (summer)	35	–
honey bee (winter)	350	–
Orthoptera		
Oriental cockroach	43.5	40.2
American cockroach	225	200
Coleoptera		
flour beetle	195	178
stag beetle	32	19
dung beetle	642	700

*Data from Rockstein, M. (ed.) 1973. The Physiology of Insecta, Vol. I. 2nd ed. Academic Press, Inc., Washington, D.C.

Total generation life span for an insect species, from oviposition to the eggs of the next generation, again varies greatly depending on circumstances of developmental time (p. 300), duration of diapause (if any), and preovipositional adult life span. House flies may complete a generation in less than two weeks in summer, or it may take six months before adults from the last autumnal larval generation lay eggs in spring. In general, temperate-zone insects have at least one generation per year; aphids may have nine or ten. The shorter the generation life span, the greater the population's potential to produce large numbers in a short time (Chapters Eight and Ten). Exceptions to the "rule" of one or more generations per year include some mayflies and many wood-boring beetle and moth larvae that may take two to four years (or even more) to complete development. Sometimes borer-infested wood is cut, cured, milled, and incorporated into structures and furniture, which then contain the borer larvae; and more than one homeowner has been terrorized by the sight of a quite large beetle suddenly and inexplicably stepping out of the wall. Insect champions of long life span are the periodical cicadas (Homoptera), whose nymphs feed on roots for 13 or 17 years (depending on species and geographical location) and then emerge en masse as adults for a brief (they don't feed) adult life of mating and dispersal. Lloyd and Dybas (1966) suggest that concentrated predation is avoided by this long generation time. The hormonal control of developmental synchrony in periodical cicadas would be worth investigating by someone with job security.

DIVERSITY IN DEVELOPMENTAL PATTERNS

As in other aspects of their physiology, insects display a large variety of developmental patterns, the most general of which are the two major kinds of metamorphosis already discussed. In addition, you have read of parthenogenesis (reproduction without fertilization) and polyembryony (production of several individuals from a single egg or zygote). Viviparity is birth of living young, circumventing the egg stage.

The extremes of viviparity occur in Diptera, particularly the pupiparous Diptera (Chapter Three), including the African tsetse flies, *Glossina* species, that transmit African sleeping sickness. Tsetse fly females produce a single egg at a time, and after fertilization, this egg hatches within the adult female (Fig. 7–27). The ensuing larva attaches itself to a nipple-like structure through which is secreted a nutritive liquid formed by glands from hemolymph contents (which in turn come ultimately from a meal of mammal blood ingested by the female). The larva grows to full size within its mother's body. When fully grown, the larva is expelled and within a few hours forms a puparium; tsetses and other Pupipara have eliminated a free-living larval stage almost completely. Presence of but a single set of posterior spiracles (in all "higher" Diptera) was a critical preadaptation for evolution of pupipary.

Other Diptera occasionally skip the adult stage. *Miastor,* a midge that inhabits decaying vegetation, alternates between rather normal development involving bisexual winged adults and production of parthenogenetic female larvae in which ovaries mature and eggs hatch. The young larvae then become parasitic, devouring the insides of their mother (Fig. 7–28) before moving into surrounding decaying vegetation. Several generations may be produced in this manner before bisexual winged adults are again produced (Went, 1971). This production of offspring by morphologically immature forms is termed **paedogenesis.**

Production of offspring by wingless forms of "normally" winged Hemimetabola may be considered paedogenesis, and many aphids seasonally alternate paedogenesis with production of sexual winged reproductives. For example, the rosy apple aphid (Fig. 7–29) overwinters in eggs that hatch in early spring. Nymphs feed on the new growth and metamorphose into winged adult females

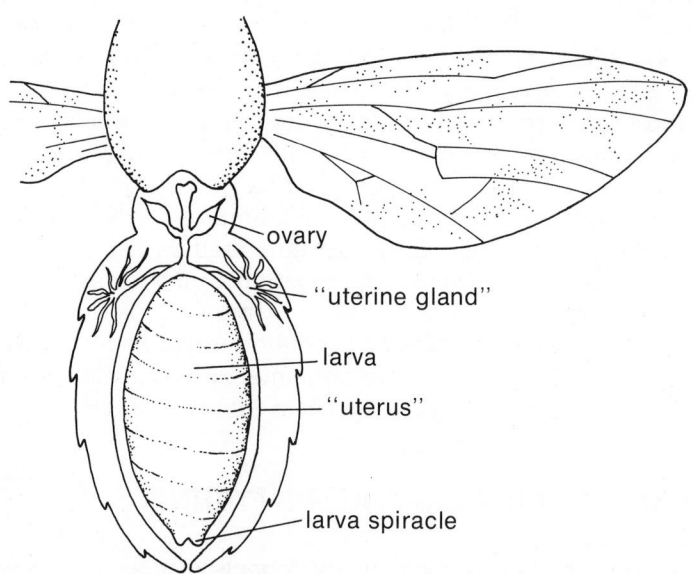

Figure 7–27. Larva of tsetse fly developing within female parent.

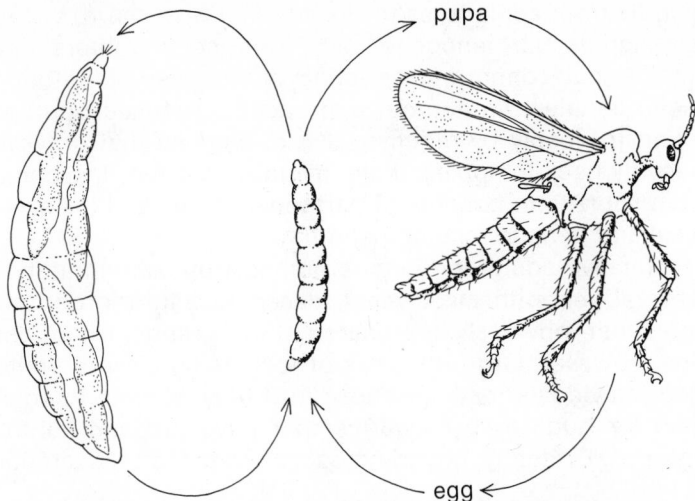

Figure 7–28. Paedogenesis in *Miastor* midge. *Left,* Ovaries mature and larvae hatch inside female; they eventually consume her. *Right,* Alternate, "normal," development. (Redrawn from Wigglesworth, V. B. 1964. The Life of Insects. World Publishing Co., Cleveland.)

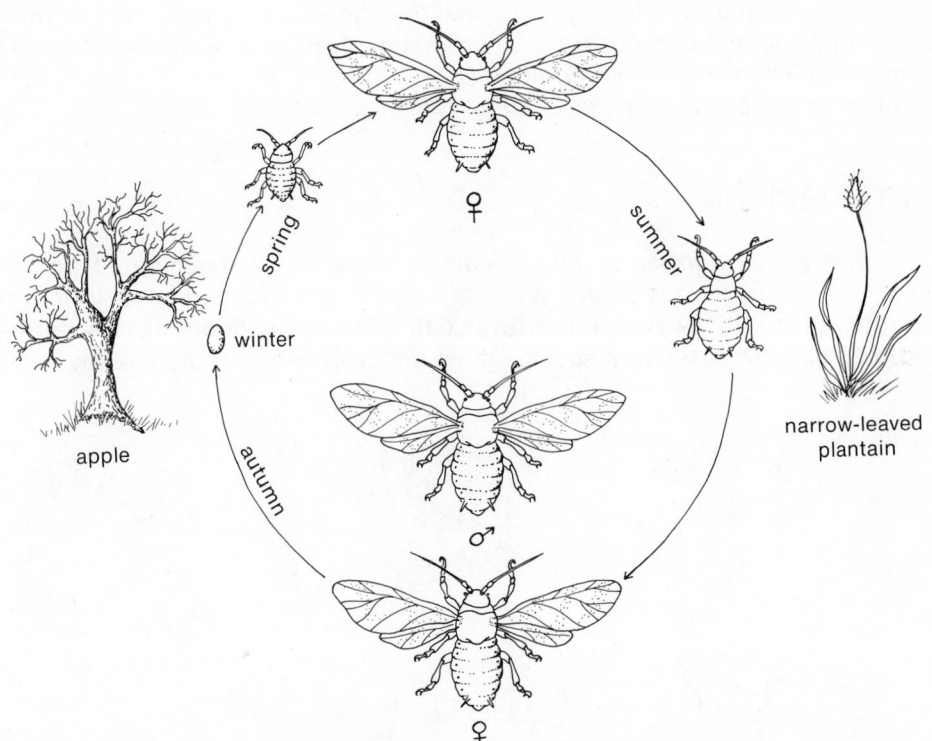

Figure 7–29. Alternation of generations in rosy apple aphid. Eggs overwinter and hatch on apple; spring generation flies to a narrow-leaved plantain, the summer host. Parthenogenetic, wingless populations reproduce on plantain until short photophase induces development of winged sexual morphs, which move back to apple, mate, and oviposit in autumn.

(**alates**), which fly from apple trees to the summer host, narrow-leaved plantain. There, female aphids parthenogenetically produce daughters that grow into wingless females that continue production of wingless (therefore "immature") parthenogenetic females. As autumn approaches, reduced photoperiod stimulates production (probably by reducing JH) of nymphs that grow into alates of each sex; these fly back to apples, mate, oviposit, and die. The aphid population thus enjoys the short-term benefits of parthenogenesis and the long-term benefits of dispersal and genetic recombination.

Similar facultative adulthood occurs among tropical migratory locusts over periods of several years. In most years, desert locusts reproduce as wingless "solitary" forms that, obviously, are limited in their range. Under optimal breeding conditions, however, large numbers of locusts hatch in a limited area, and these crowded individuals metamorphose into fully winged "gregarious" forms that comprise the huge locust swarms that have plagued subtropical Africa for many centuries. Evidently, crowding causes reduced JH secretion in gregarious forms.

Hypermetamorphosis is a developmental form that occurs in some Diptera (Bombyliidae), Coleoptera (Meloidae), Neuroptera (Mantispidae), and most Strepsiptera—groups in which larvae are usually parasitic on other insects or spiders. Eggs hatch into a tiny, very active campodeiform larva (Fig. 7–30) that attaches itself to the appropriate host. Once established on (or in) the host, the larva commences feeding and molts; it subsequently becomes more sluggish, scarabaeiform, or even vermiform, losing functional legs and moving very little. Hormonal control of hypermetamorphosis is another unsolved puzzle, though it may be regulated by changing concentrations of MH. JH does not seem to exert any effect other than keeping the insect larval (Willis, 1974).

POLYMORPHISM

Hypermetamorphosis, or any metamorphosis, is an example of polymorphism, the simultaneous appearance of several genetically based forms in a single population. However, a narrower definition of polymorphism is normally used: one or both sexes of a species must occur in two or more sharply distinct

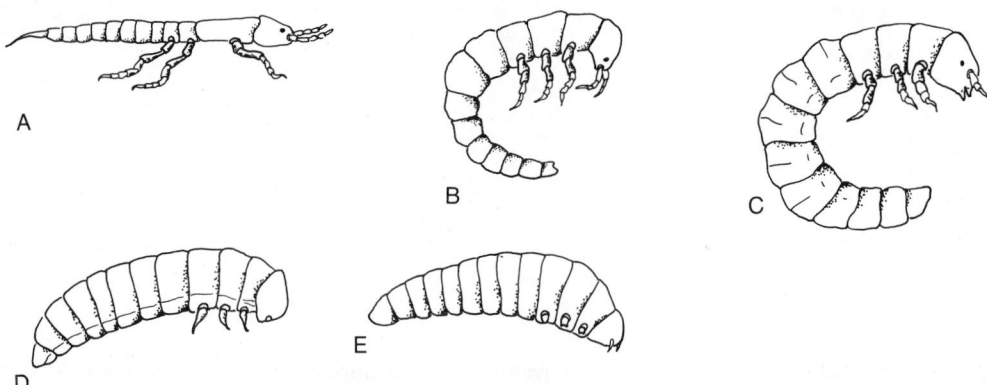

Figure 7–30. Hypermetamorphosis of blister beetle. Each successive larval instar is less active than the one preceding. First instar (*A*) locates host, and subsequent stages are parasitic.

forms (Richards, 1953). According to this definition, sexual or metamorphic differences are not polymorphism, though the occurrence of winged and wingless aphids or locusts, described previously, is. Polymorphism occurs in many insect orders and is strikingly evident in some tropical mimetic butterflies.

Social insects provide some fine examples of polymorphism. In termites, ants, and bees, we find **castes,** individuals of the same sex that are specialized morphologically and behaviorally for differing functions (Chapter Six; Fig. 6–18). In all species studied, caste is chemically determined, though the hormonal mechanisms involved are not always understood (Wilson, 1971). For instance, in honeybees, female larvae whose diet is supplemented with royal jelly secreted by hypopharyngeal and mandibular glands of workers, develop into fully fertile queens. Larvae not fed royal jelly become sterile workers; evidently royal jelly stimulates maturation of ovaries. In ants (*Myrmica* species), a number of secondary factors, such as winter and spring temperature, egg size, age of old queen, and larval nutrition, influence the proportion of queens produced. In bees and ants, secretion of a pheromone by the queen inhibits ovarian development in maturing larvae and adults (Brian and Blum, 1969). Removal of a queen honeybee from a hive stimulates secretion of royal jelly by workers; furthermore, ovaries of a few workers may mature and they may lay a few (infertile) eggs. In *Kalotermes* (Isoptera), production of workers, soldiers, or reproductives is hormonally controlled (Luscher, 1969). If JH concentration is high, soldiers are produced; if JH is less but MH concentration is high, a reproductive results; and if both JH and MH are present at low concentrations, workers result. Balance among the three castes is evidently maintained by constant pheromone communication within a nest.

SUMMARY

Sexual reproduction in insects, as in most living things, ensures the genetic variability necessary for change in response to changing environments. Development of eggs in ovaries of females is controlled by hormones whose secretion is in turn directed by a variety of internal or external stimuli. Sperm are produced by testes in males; the role of hormones here is unclear. Most insects are bisexual and fertilization is required, though a few reproduce parthenogenetically, without fertilization.

Female insects usually oviposit in or near the larval food supply. A hardened eggshell protects the developing embryo from desiccation while providing for gas exchange, and the yolk within the egg supplies nourishment. Development of a multicellular free-living nymph or larva from a single undifferentiated zygote in insects is well documented, but is not as well understood as embryology in vertebrates.

After hatching (eclosion), insects undergo further growth and development in a series of molts when new cuticle is produced and old cuticle is shed. Metamorphosis is a major adaptation that has permitted insects to occupy diverse ecological habitats. Metamorphosis may be gradual or complex and is controlled by hormones. Once insects reach sexual maturity they do not (with rare exceptions) molt or grow again, and generally they do not live very long as adults. This chapter concludes with a discussion of several rather unusual developmental adaptations.

Chapter Eight

Population Ecology

INTRODUCTION

Under natural conditions, insect species exist in populations, groups of individuals that interbreed among themselves but do not exchange genes with other such interbreeding groups. Insect populations may be small and localized, as those of isolated *Oeneis* and *Boloria* butterflies, found on mountaintops in New England; or large and widespread, as those of house flies, found throughout the world. Distribution and density of insect populations are determined by interactions between the populations and the environment; population ecology (sometimes called **autecology**) is the study of these interactions.

Many ecological concepts are based on studies made in allied areas of biology: physiology, biochemistry, morphology, genetics. Some of this dependence on allied disciplines is necessary because of the difficulty in controlling environmental variables and in obtaining adequate samples of naturally occurring populations. In addition, experimental ecology is a rather new discipline, having developed within the last 50 years. Because of these factors and because of the difficulties in studying field populations, many of the theories and concepts of population ecology are not as clear-cut as those of other disciplines. Population ecology is nonetheless a vitally important area of entomology from the standpoint of insect pest management. Our understanding of how populations are regulated naturally is of immeasurable help when we apply control measures to noxious species. General references for population ecology are Krebs (1972), Pianka (1973), and Price (1975).

STUDYING INSECT POPULATIONS

In the field, interactions among environmental factors are enormously complex. For this reason, entomologists often have studied laboratory populations under controlled conditions. Many insects are small, have short generation times and plenteous offspring, and feed readily on artificial media, so that significant changes in density or gene frequency can be observed over time spans as short as several weeks. Fruit flies, house flies, flesh flies, cockroaches, mites, and,

286

especially, grain beetles have long been favored by insect population ecologists as well as by geneticists, physiologists, and toxicologists. Laboratory population studies have a few advantages over field studies: (1) Environmental conditions such as temperature, photoperiod, and humidity can be carefully controlled within narrow limits and can be manipulated individually, so that population changes are measurable in response to each. (2) Confinement sets distributional limits on the population, and often all insects therein can be observed at once, so that sampling problems are minimal. (3) The investigator does not get as wet, cold, or hungry as he or she might in the field. On the other hand, laboratory conditions are artificial; dispersal is limited and environmental conditions are artificially and unusually constant. Over several generations, small inbred laboratory populations may change genetically, altering the "normal" response to the very factors under investigation. Insects often behave differently in the laboratory from in the field.

SAMPLING INSECT POPULATIONS

In the field, it is difficult to determine accurately which insect groups are interbreeding among themselves but with no others. In practice, therefore, field entomologists usually define a population operationally as an arbitrarily delineated local group of interbreeding insects. Pea aphids or spittlebugs in a single alfalfa field disperse regularly to other fields, but an entomologist usually considers only that population in the field under study. It is, moreover, infeasible to study all members of a population within a single field, so entomologists sample a proportion of the local population under study, and with the help of statistical analyses of the samples, they draw inferences about the whole population.

A wide variety of sampling methods are available to the field entomologist, and Southwood (1966) discusses many of these at some length. Figure 8–1 illustrates some of the more widely used methods for sampling insect populations; the number of different sampling techniques is limited only by the ingenuity of entomologists. A sampling technique may determine merely the presence of an insect, or it may give a quantitative estimate of population density. Estimates of population density may be **absolute** or **relative.** Absolute estimates seek to relate a number of insects to a standard unit of area or of habitat, as, for example, the number of cloverworms per row-foot of soybeans or the number of red mites per leaf in an apple orchard. Relative estimates relate insect numbers to a unit of effort; grasshoppers per net sweep or moths per light trap are examples. A population **index** (Southwood, 1966) is also a relative estimate; the amount of droppings falling on a forest floor is an index of the caterpillar population density in the treetops.

Relative estimates and population indices often are more easily measured (in terms of time and money) than absolute estimates, but their use is more limited unless they can be validly converted to absolute estimates. A relative estimate, such as larvae per net sweep, can be compared to another relative estimate to indicate a population trend: this is often adequate in studies of insect pests, whose numbers may change vastly over time. Absolute estimates are more useful in detailed studies of insect population dynamics, such as life table investigations (discussed subsequently). A truism is that the sampling method used depends on the objectives of the study, though in all cases, a sampling method produces but

Figure 8–1. Apparati for sampling insects. *A.* Berlese (or Tullgren) funnel. Litter or soil samples are placed on screen in funnel, then heat from above drives arthropods down into jar. *B,* Ultraviolet light trap. Insects attracted to light fall down funnel into collecting chamber. *C,* Vacuum insect net. Insects are sucked into net bag by air currents generated by gasoline-powered fan. *D,* Malaise trap. Insects are attracted into tent by CO_2 source at peak. (Courtesy of Insect Museum Supply, Lake City, Minnesota.)

a sample, a portion, of the whole population. Because the whole insect population cannot be observed simultaneously, investigators must rely on these somewhat variable estimates of population events to draw inferences about the entire population. Consequently, results of field population studies may be subject to variable interpretations. Conclusions based on field samples are only as valid as the sampling method employed, and introduction of a systematic bias into a sampling scheme may lead to false conclusions. For example, bagworms often are most numerous at the tops of arborvitae trees; an investigator who samples the reachable portion of 12-foot trees will underestimate the bagworm population density. Morris (1960) and Southwood (1966) comprehensively discuss some of the problems with and limitations of field sampling methods.

POPULATION GROWTH AND REGULATION

An oft-repeated "astounding fact" is that if all the potential progeny of a mated female house fly in March were to survive and reproduce to the maximum limit of their capability, by October we should be up to our necks in flies. This legendary reproductive potential of insects is, thankfully, not realized, because one factor or another acts as a "brake" on population numbers to limit density. A generalized, admittedly oversimplified, mathematical description of population regulation is (Clark et al., 1967):

$$N_t = N_0 e^{(b - d)t} + I - E$$

where N_t = population density after an interval of time, t
        N_0 = starting population density
        e = base of natural logarithms (2.71828), reflecting that population growth is exponential, or "compounded"
        b = birth rate
        d = death rate
        I = immigration during time interval t
        E = emigration during time interval t

A graph of this expression is shown in Figure 8–2A, which suggests that when a population is introduced into a favorable environment, its growth is uninhibited for a time, and then as regulatory factors exert their effect, the numbers level off at an upper limit K, the environmental **carrying capacity.** Results of laboratory studies (Figs. 8–2, B and C) in which populations were grown under controlled conditions sometimes approximate the theoretical growth curve rather closely (Crombie, 1945; Lloyd, M. 1965; Varley et al., 1973), though rarely in field or laboratory populations is K a constant—too many variables are involved.

LIFE SYSTEMS

As is obvious from the foregoing equation, population presence and density are functions of primary events, births, deaths, immigration, and emigration; and these in turn are affected, directly or indirectly, by various secondary events (Clark et al., 1967). For instance, birth rate, a primary event, is directly influenced by food supply, which in turn is often related to weather. Is population size therefore determined by birth rate, by food supply, or by weather? Clark and co-workers (1967) point out that insect populations cannot be considered apart from their environments, that observed ecological events (such as changes in density) are a consequence of both intrinsic (genetic) factors (e.g., fecundity, sex ratio) and external, environmental factors (e.g., food, predation, weather). Therefore, they propose a **life system** concept, a life system being a population plus its effective environment (that portion of the total environment that exerts some effect on the population under study). Clark and co-workers consider genetic and environmental factors to be co-determinants of abundance because they act in concert rather than singly and produce both short-term alterations in distribution and

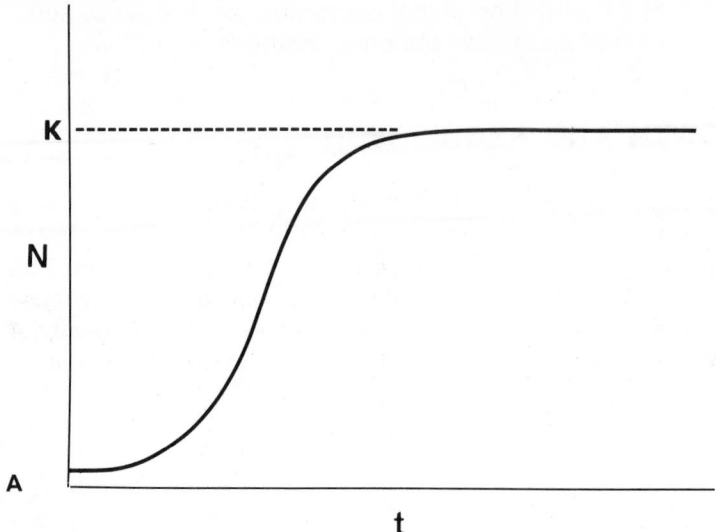

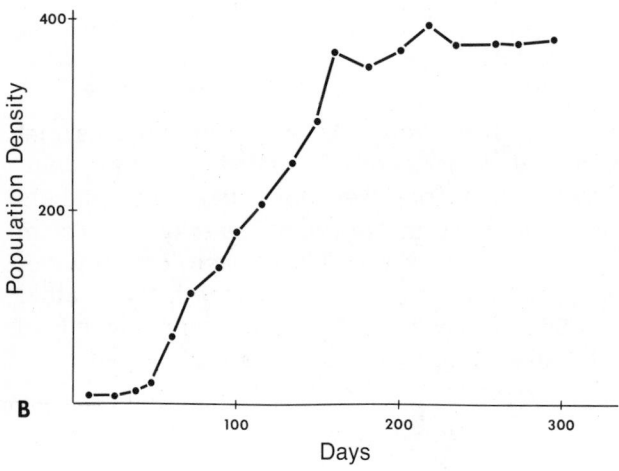

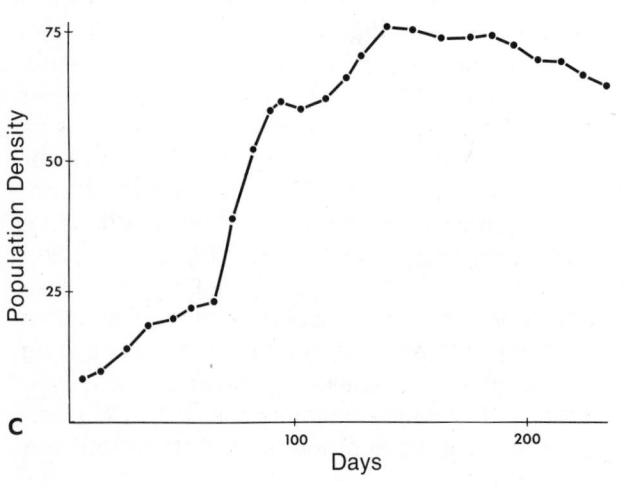

Figure 8-2. Logistic population growth stabilizing at carrying capacity K. *A,* Theoretical curve: N = numbers; t = time; K = carrying capacity. *B,* Population curve for *Rhizopertha* adults in lab cultures. (Data from Crombie, A. C. 1945. On competition between different species of graminivorous insects. Proc. Roy. Entomol. Soc. (Ser. B.) *132*:362–395.) Used by permission of The Royal Society, London. *C,* Population curve for Tribolium adults in lab culture. (Data from Lloyd, M. 1965. Laboratory studies with confined cannibalistic populations of flour beetles (*Tribolium castaneum*) in a cold-dry environment. I. Data for 24 unmanipulated populations. Tribolium Info. Bull. *8*:88–123.)

Table 8–1. FACTORS REGULATING INSECT POPULATIONS AS DETERMINED
BY EXTENSIVE LIFE SYSTEM STUDIES*

Insect	Major Limiting Factors
Brevicoryne brassicae (cabbage aphid)	emigration lower fecundity
Cydia pomonella (codling moth)	competition for feeding space and pupating sites
Diprion hercyniae (European spruce sawfly)	weather disease parasitoids
Perga affinis (sawfly)	emigration parasitism
Phaulacridium vittatum (locust)	emigration competition for food
Zeiraphera griseana (larch budmoth)	parasitoids disease

*From Clark, L. R., P. W. Geier, R. D. Hughes, and R. F. Morris. 1967. The Ecology of
Insect Populations in Theory and Practice. Methuen & Co . Ltd., London.

density and longer-term evolutionary changes in genetic material. The life system
concept is useful to summarize the extremely complex interactions among co-
determinants of abundance that produce population changes. Accordingly, each
life system is unique, and even a single widespread species may have very different life systems in different portions of its range. In practice, life systems are
often delineated by purpose and convenience; Clark and co-workers (1967) give
several examples (Table 8–1).

POPULATION STRUCTURE AND LIFE TABLES

To determine the relative importance of the co-determinants of abundance
in an insect population, insect population ecologists undertake detailed and extensive sampling, using as accurate methods as possible, to census density, age,
and mortality in several locations. The data thus obtained are organized into a
life table, a summary of vital statistics (mortality and survival, or suvivorship) for
a population (Table 8–2). The age-structure of a population is far more meaning-
ful than a simple, single estimate of density. A life table is a summary of population changes within a generation.

Life tables are of two kinds: **age-specific,** in which a cohort of 1000 insects
of a single generation is followed throughout its existence; and **time-specific,** in
which a field population is sampled and individuals are grouped according to
age, survival being inferred from shrinkage between successive age classes. In
both cases, mortality is either directly measured or inferred from field samples.
For insects, age-specific life tables are very difficult to construct outside the laboratory, owing to the difficulty of finding and marking 1000 specific individuals;

Table 8–2. LIFE TABLE FOR THIRD GENERATION DIAMONDBACK MOTH, OTTAWA, ONTARIO*

Age Interval	Density per 100 Plants	Mortality Factor	Number Dying	Per Cent Mortality
Eggs	1154	infertility	14	1.2
Larvae, period I	1140	rainfall	536	47
Larvae, period II	604	parasitism	140	23.2
		rainfall	77	12.7
Prepupae	387	parasitism	198	51.2
Pupae	189	parasitism	53	28.2
Emerging moths	136	sex ratio 40% ♀♀†	27	19.9
		photoperiod	52.4	48.1
		adult mortality	48.1	85.0
Reproducing females‡	8.5	aging	8.5	100

*Modified from Harcourt, D. G. 1969. The development and use of life tables in the study of natural insect populations. Ann. Rev. Entomol. *14*:175–196.

†Sex ratio favoring males is treated as mortality; i.e., with fewer than 50 per cent females (as here), the number surviving is adjusted downward (here by 27) to give a sex ratio of 1:1.

‡Estimates based on egg populations in subsequent generation. This assumes 8.5 females at maximum fertility. It is more likely that a larger female population averaged fewer eggs each.

hence, most insect life tables are time-specific. Time-specific life tables are necessary for each of several generations in several locations if one is to draw valid conclusions concerning a life system. Sampling problems associated with life tables studies are acute, and much time and money must be invested for accurate sampling (Ives, 1964; Harcourt, 1969, 1970).

A life table approach has the advantage that, if either age structure or mortality alone is known, missing values can be calculated. For instance, Table 8–3 depicts a partial life table for alfalfa weevils. Adult female alfalfa weevils lay eggs in growing alfalfa stems from March through May (in central Ohio), and resulting larvae crawl to stem tips and feed on new growth during May and June. From January to July, my students and I sampled eggs and larvae regularly from several fields, and we also reared field-collected specimens to determine viability and parasitization. Observed mortality factors (sterility, parasitization, cannibalism, disease, low vitality) did not fully cover shrinkage between age classes, and "other" mortality is therefore inferred between egg and first instar larvae (probably due to larvae getting lost before finding the stem tip) and between first and fourth instar larvae (probably due to cutting the field, which occurred before all larvae had pupated). Furthermore, if the population numbers remain more or less stable and a female weevil averages 1000 eggs, only two reproductive adults (male and female) are necessary to replace the population, and therefore significant mortality must have occurred between fourth instar larva and reproductive adult (Horn, 1975).

KEY FACTORS

A series of life tables for several generations and several locations may be analyzed (Morris, 1959, 1963; Varley and Gradwell, 1970) to reveal **key factors,** environmental variables that show greatest correlation with generation-to-generation population trends. Southwood (1966) and Luck (1971) detail methods of identifying key factors. It is sufficient here to say that while variation in a particular key factor may not cause observed population density changes, it is closely correlated with density. Once key factors are identified, they can be used to predict population densities, often with great accuracy.

In England, Varley and Gradwell (1968, 1970) intensively sampled winter moth populations on and under oak trees for 18 years. From the resulting life tables, they found that winter disappearance, probably due to predation by shrews and beetles, was the key factor influencing year-to-year population trends. They formulated mathematical models that predicted winter moth population densities under certain management schemes; in particular, they predicted that insecticides directed at eggs or adult moths would not interfere with the action of winter disappearance. Parasitization, particularly that by a tachinid fly, *Cyzenis albicans,* was a minor factor in England, but Varley and Gradwell's model predicted that it could stabilize winter moth populations at low densities if pupal mortality was low enough. The population model proved invaluable when the winter moth was accidentally introduced into eastern Canada, where it promptly set about defoliating deciduous trees. Pupal mortality was low; *C.*

Table 8–3. PARTIAL LIFE TABLE FOR ALFALFA WEEVILS, WOOSTER, OHIO, APRIL TO JUNE, 1973*

Age Interval	Survivors of Initial 1000	Mortality Factor	Number Dying	Per cent Mortality
Eggs	1000	parasitism	130	13
		infertility	90	9
		unknown†	280	28
Larvae (first instar)	500	parasitism	70	14
		cannibalism	20	4
		disease?	15	3
		low vitality	25	5
		unknown†	50	10
Larvae (fourth instar) and prepupae	320	desiccation as pupa	16	5
		molting problems	45	14
Prereproductive adults	259‡	parasitism	6	2
		unknown†	251	99
1974 adults	2§	aging	2	100

*From Horn, D. J. 1975. Life tables for the alfalfa weevil in Ohio. Proc. North Centr. Branch Entomol. Soc. Amer. *30*:98.

†Unknown mortality inferred from shrinkage between successive age intervals. Disappearance probably due to weather (rain) and predation.

‡Maximum estimate based on observed mortality of pupae.

§Estimate based on 1:1 sex ratio and 1974 egg data.

albicans was introduced, and within six years, winter moth populations were reduced substantially and their numbers have remained low (Embree, 1965).

CO-DETERMINANTS OF ABUNDANCE

Clark and co-workers' (1967) consideration that populations are inseparable from their effective environment implies that density and distribution are functions of intrinsic (genetically determined) and extrinsic (environmental) influences. The operation of these co-determinants of abundance is simultaneous and complex, analogous, perhaps, to the simultaneous interactive physiological processes of maintenance, growth, and development. In the sections to follow, I discuss co-determinants of abundance separately, but it should be remembered that many factors act together on populations, even though one or two key factors may appear primarily responsible for observed changes in density and distribution.

Our simple model of population regulation (p. 289) suggested that population density is determined by a relationship between **additive** (birth and immigration) and **subtractive** factors (deaths and emigration) (Nicholson, 1933, 1954). Among insects, additive factors include births and immigration as mentioned. Weather, food supply, predation, and vitality are predominately subtractive factors that interact closely with birth rates and movements. In fact, co-determinants of abundance usually have both additive and subtractive components. The ecological factors discussed in the next sections may also be selective factors (Chapter Two), alone or in combination, if they cause differential survival and, consequently, differential reproduction.

Additive Factors

Births. The reproductive capabilities of insects were discussed in some detail in Chapter Seven. **Fecundity** is the potential number of offspring that an insect is capable of producing, and its maximum is determined by the number of ovarioles (see Fig. 7–2). Fecundity is important in determining how rapidly insects may reach pest status or, alternatively, how rapidly an agent of biological control may bring its host under control. Of even greater concern is **fertility**, the actual number of viable offspring produced (Table 8–4), which is dependent on a number of factors. Nutrition is most important: Most bloodsucking insects (e.g., mosquitoes, bedbugs) need a blood meal to produce each batch of eggs (Wigglesworth, 1972). Starving insects generally reabsorb eggs. The proportion of eggs fertilized depends on the proportion of male insects in the population. With the exception of parthenogenetic forms, most insects' sex ratio is near 1:1 (females:males) at eclosion, though male longevity is often less than that of females. If males are artificially sterilized and then released (as with screwworm flies, Chapter Ten), population fertility declines sharply.

Fertility also depends, of course, upon the average longevity of breeding females, which is a function of one or several subtractive factors, discussed subsequently. **Underpopulation** may reduce fertility when population density is so low that a significant proportion of males and females cannot locate one another to reproduce and continue the population. Andrewartha and Birch (1954) demonstrated this for Milne's (1952) data on sheep tick populations. Sheep ticks

Table 8–4. AVERAGE AND MAXIMUM FERTILITY OF SELECTED INSECTS*

Insect	Eggs Laid During Lifetime	
	Average	Maximum
Orthoptera		
Acheta (house cricket)	1060	
Periplaneta (American cockroach)	938	
Schistocerca (migratory locust)	697	
Hemiptera		
Cimex (bed bug)		541
Triatoma (assassin bug)	711	1166
Neuroptera		
Lacewing *(Chrysopa)*	477	1022
Lepidoptera		
Galleria (wax moth)	1550	1900
Pseudaletia (armyworm)	1451	1756
Diptera		
Anopheles (mosquito)	450	1145
Drosophila (fruit fly)	1532	
Glossina (tsetse fly)	9	14
Musca (house fly)	920	1278
Coleoptera		
Coccinella (ladybird)	814	3765
Sitona (clover root curculio)	1800	4500
Tenebrio (mealworm)	83	178
Hymenoptera		
Apanteles (braconid wasp)	120	142
Apis (honey bee)	120,000/year	

*Modified from Engelmann, F. 1970. The Physiology of Insect Reproduction. Pergamon Press Ltd., Oxford.

mate on their host, and a local population becomes extinct when sheep do not pick up at least two ticks of opposite sex.

Movement. Movement of insects may be either additive (immigration) or subtractive (emigration) in a local population. Movements may be directed, in response to specific environmental stimuli (food, mating, escape), or may simply result from random activity. Clark and co-workers (1967) suggest three sorts of movement: **spread,** local movements within a region of favorable environment; **dispersal,** movement of individuals away from a favorable area to other locations, which may or may not be favorable to survival; and **migration,** directed (usually) movement from one favorable area to another. Spread occurs in all insect species (Clark et al., 1967) and ensures, among most sexual species, sufficient local genetic recombination to maintain a relatively diverse population. Dispersal reduces competition for local resources and sometimes leads to establishment of a portion of the population in a new, favorable area that is relatively free from competition. The cost of dispersal to a population is the loss of many propagules (dispersing insects) that do not locate, or happen to land in, favorable locations. Dispersal is nevertheless vital to long-term survival of a species because all local environments are, in the long run, likely to change. Dispersal is especially vital to insects that inhabit ephemeral resources: carrion, dung, temporary pools, or annual plants. This last category includes a number of crop plants, and many agricultural pests are highly efficient and active dispersers. A general positive correlation exists between dispersal tendency and fertility. The stage at which individuals disperse is important: A fertilized, gravid female propagule has a better chance to establish a new population than does a first-instar nymph or larva (MacArthur and Wilson, 1967). Dispersal tendency may be genetically controlled, as Wellington (1964) showed for populations of western tent caterpillar. These populations consist of active individuals that move out to found new colonies or replenish old ones and passive caterpillars that remain in a local area until food runs out and many starve.

Means of spread, dispersal, and migration in insects are as diverse as the insects themselves. Much movement is active and directed, involving adaptations for walking, swimming, and flying discussed previously (Chapter Five). Other insects disperse passively, by either drifting with air or water currents or hitching a ride (phoresy) on a larger animal. Many tinier insects, particularly aphids, leafhoppers, thrips, parasitic wasps, and small beetles, cannot make headway in winds over 1 k.p.h., and they usually float passively in the air, riding drafts until they are deposited, occasionally in favorable areas. After dragging a net behind an airplane, Coad (1931) estimated that 25 million insects were airborne above a square mile of Louisiana. A surprising number of arthropods thus collected were wingless (Table 8–5). Spiders, mites and caterpillars often disperse by "ballooning"—spinning out small silken strands that catch the wind, thereby allowing these wingless animals to float aloft.

Many insects that hitchhike are parasitic on their phoretic host (the advantages of this are obvious). Others use the host for riding only, as is the case with mites that travel between flowers on the bills of hummingbirds (Colwell, 1973). The human bot fly attaches its egg to a mosquito (or other biting fly), and when the mosquito reaches a human, the warmth of the human's body causes the bot fly egg to hatch, whereupon the resulting larva bores its way beneath the (human) host's skin. Man has been an unwitting (and sometimes witting) indirect

Table 8–5. NUMBERS OF SPECIMENS FROM REPRESENTATIVE ORDERS OF ARTHROPODS COLLECTED IN APPROXIMATELY 150 HOURS OF AIR-NETTING OVER LOUISIANA*

	Altitude in Feet			
	200	1000	2000	5000
Arachnida†	653	375	228	36
Diptera	5172	1979	1024	279
Coleoptera	2225	519	161	51
Hymenoptera	1646	508	235	62
Homoptera	1493	571	361	100
Hemiptera	550	214	106	22
Collembola†	6	5	4	5
Thysanura†	11	15	4	0

*From Glick, P. A. 1939. The distribution of insects, spiders, and mites in the air. USDA Tech. Bull. No. 673.
†Wingless.

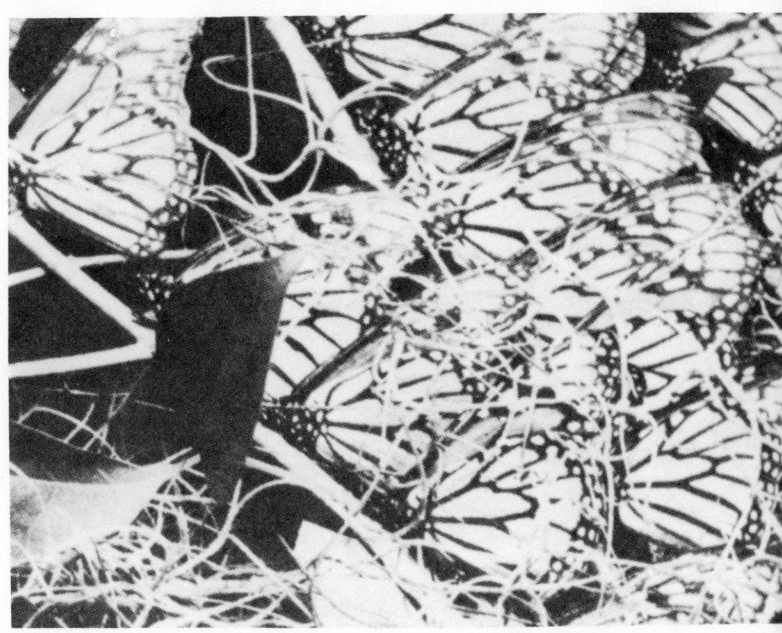

Figure 8–3. Display of migrating monarch butterflies on branches of California "butterfly trees." (From the book Insects by Ross E. Hutchins: © 1966 by Ross E. Hutchins. Published by Prentice-Hall, Inc., Englewood Cliffs, New Jersey.)

host for the spread of many insects, beginning, perhaps, with the introduction of ground beetles from Europe to North America in ballast of sailing ships (Lindroth, 1957). The Japanese beetle was introduced into New Jersey in nursery stock (azalea or iris roots). Many other pest insects were accidentally spread from one area to another by means yet unknown. At present, egg masses of the gypsy moth are being dispersed southward and westward from the northeastern United States on the undersides of recreational vehicles, despite quarantine efforts by the United States Department of Agriculture. On a more positive note, many predator and parasitoid populations have been successfully dispersed by humans to new favorable homes in successful biological control efforts (see Chapter Ten).

Migration, which is directed movement from one favorable area to another, does not occur in many insects, though the migrations of those that do migrate are often spectacular. Two of the most studied migrators are the monarch butterfly, *Danaus plexippus* (Fig. 8–3), and the plague locusts *Schistocerca gregaria* and *S. migratoria* (Fig. 8–4). Urquhart (1960) has devoted much effort to studying the monarch and its migrations. In Ontario, he tagged thousands of butterflies, a few of which have been recovered up to 3000 miles away in San Luis Potosí, Mexico, and Pacific Grove, California. The latter locality has for years hosted thousands of overwintering monarchs in groves of pine trees (locally called "butterfly trees"). In spring, these insects or their offspring move northward and eastward to lay eggs on milkweed, their food plant. A new generation then returns to overwintering sites.

Plague locusts periodically undergo a phase change from "solitary" to "migratory" form (Chapter Seven), apparently partly in response to local crowding. The migratory form is a longer winged, stronger flyer that forms huge swarms up to several kilometers in length and breadth. Such locust swarms fly primarily with prevailing winds, which in their semiarid subtropical homeland eventually bring

Figure 8–4. Part of a large (400 square mile) immature swarm of desert locusts *Schistocerca gregaria* near Gigiga, Ethiopia, September, 1958. This swarm caused extensive damage to maize and millet cultivations in the area. (Photo by C. Ashall, courtesy of Centre for Overseas Pest Research, London.)

the swarm to a convergence (frontal) area where rain falls in sufficient quantity to provide plant growth for the next generation of locusts (Rainey, 1963; Baron, 1972). Migration is thus an adaptation ensuring population survival in a semiarid region where rainfall is irregular and localized. On their way to oviposition sites, however, locust swarms often descend on agricultural crops and inflict incredible damage.

Most migrating insects are young, prereproductive adults of insect species that are characteristic of ephemeral, localized habitats (Johnson, 1969). Dingle (1972) states that migration is part of a reproductive diapause, in which ovarian development is delayed but flight and (often) feeding continue normally. Caldwell and Rankin (1972) demonstrated that topical application of juvenile hormone stimulated migratory flight in the milkweed bug *Oncopeltus;* this is consistent with current notions on hormonal control of diapause (Chapter Seven).

Subtractive Factors

Subtractive factors are co-determinants of abundance that, directly or indirectly, remove individuals from local populations, either by death or by emigration. They include physical factors (weather, in a broad sense), food supply and food quality, predation, disease, accidents, vitality, and old age. Any subtractive factor is a potential insect control tool, and the basic strategy in management of insect pests is to adjust co-determinants of abundance so that insect density is reduced (Chapter Ten).

Any subtractive factor that varies continuously (for example, temperature) will be tolerable within a certain range and lethal outside that range. Within those limits of tolerance (which may vary between individuals of the same species) is a narrower limit within which activity occurs, and an even narrower limit determining development and growth and reproduction (Fig. 8–5). Limits of tolerance vary with age and condition of an insect; in general, older or weaker insects have narrower ranges of tolerance for almost all subtractive factors.

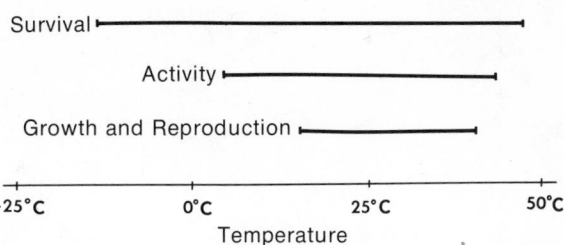

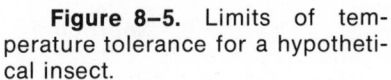

Figure 8–5. Limits of temperature tolerance for a hypothetical insect.

Weather and Microclimate. Weather, in its broad sense, includes all aspects of the physical environment: temperature, moisture, light, air and water currents, oxygen, and so forth. In studying effects of weather on insects, laboratory investigators attempt to hold constant all conditions except that being studied, though in air it is difficult to alter temperature independently of humidity, since warmer air retains more moisture. Moreover, in some insects, development is apparently speeded by rearing at fluctuating temperatures rather than a constant temperature of the same average (Table 8–6).

Entomologists often correlate events in insect populations with weather data measured in standard, ventilated, wooden boxes placed 2 m. above ground surface. This may do when no other data are available, but the actual weather to which insects are exposed may be radically different (Fig. 8–6). This microclimate (the weather conditions where insects live) should be considered when one attempts to explain effects of the physical environment on insects. On a sunny midwinter day near Columbus, Ohio, air temperature at 2 m. may be 4°C and the snow temperature 0°C, but near a tree trunk and 3 mm. above the snow, the air temperature of 24°C is well within the range of activity for the snowflea *Achorutes* (Collembola). On even a dry day, relative humidity approaches 100 per

Table 8–6. EFFECTS OF FLUCTUATING TEMPERATURES ON INSECT DEVELOPMENT*

Insect	Temperature Range (°C)	Per cent Increase in Development Time Over Constant Temperature
Aedes aegypti (yellow fever mosquito)	10–27	27
Anthonomus grandis (boll weevil) eggs	20–40	23
Bathyplectes curculionis (parasitic wasp)	15–25	18
Drosophila melanogaster (fruit fly) pupae	10–20	12
Locusta migratoria (migratory locust)	5–32	4
Melanoplus mexicanus (locust)	12–27	58

*Data from Hagstrum, D. W., and W. R. Hagstrum. 1970. A simple device for producing fluctuating temperatures, with an evaluation of the ecological significance of fluctuating temperatures. Ann. Entomol. Soc. Amer. *63*:1385–1389.

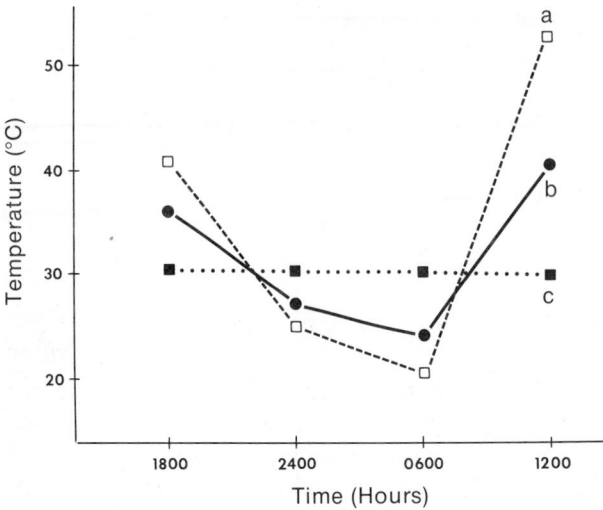

Figure 8–6. Microclimatic temperature differences, Mojave Desert, California, 7–8 July, 1972. *A,* Temperature on ground in sun. *B,* Air temperature in shade 1 meter above ground. *C,* Soil temperature 30 cm. below surface. (Data courtesy of S. McGinnis and desert biology class, California State University, Hayward, California.)

cent on undersides of transpiring leaves, and aphids feeding there run less risk of desiccation. Geiger (1965) and Chauvin (1967) stress the importance of microclimate and the methods of studying it.

Temperature. Insects are poikilothermal ("cold-blooded"), and though many can regulate their body temperature behaviorally (Chapter Four), they are still very dependent on the environmental, or ambient, temperature. Since speed of chemical reactions is partially a function of temperature, insect growth and development proceed faster at high temperatures. I have already discussed in Chapter Seven the relationship between temperature and developmental time. One implication of this relationship is that generation time is shorter in warmer weather, and insect populations therefore increase faster in warm weather. Mite populations in particular increase to damaging levels much more quickly in hot, dry August weather than in the cooler weather of June. Table 8–7 shows the relationship between temperature and growth rates for alfalfa weevils.

Because development, and therefore population growth, is temperature-dependent, it is well to think of population density changes in relation to physiological time rather than calendar time. In alfalfa weevil population studies, I

Table 8–7. RELATIONSHIP BETWEEN TEMPERATURE AND DEVELOPMENTAL TIME OF IMMATURE ALFALFA WEEVILS*

Temperature (°C)	Developmental Time (Days)			
	LARVAE	PREPUPAE	PUPAE	TOTAL
18.3	22.6	5.2	12.3	40.1
22.2	15.9	2.1	6.7	24.7
26.1	12.1	2.3	4.5	18.9
30	10.1	1.4	2.9	14.3

*Data from Hsieh, F., S. J. Roberts, and E. J. Armbrust. 1974. Developmental rate and population dynamics of alfalfa weevil larvae. Envir. Entomol. *3*:593–597.

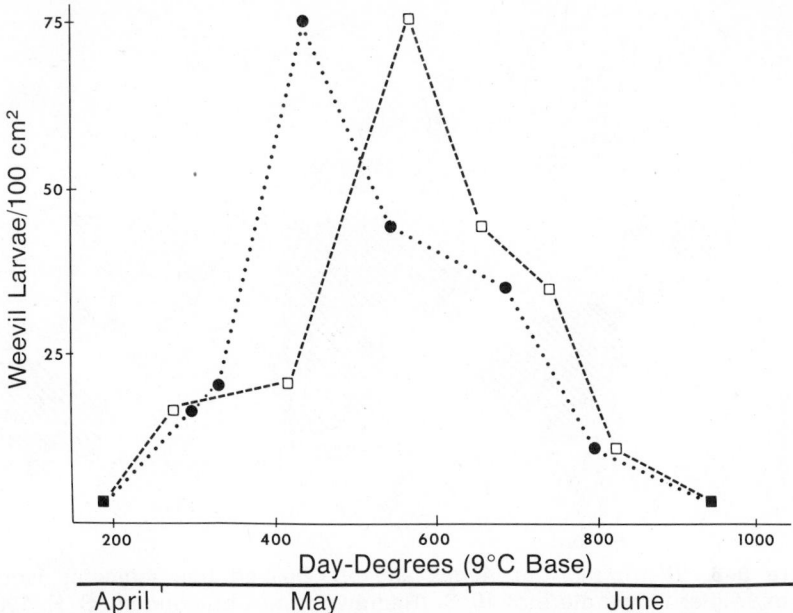

Figure 8–7. Population curves for alfalfa weevil larvae, Wooster, Ohio, 1974. Circles and dotted line indicate calendar time. Squares and dashed line indicate physiological time (day-degrees).

sample at intervals of 44 day-degrees* where 9°C is considered a threshold temperature for development of weevil larvae. Figure 8–7 shows the relationship between physiological and calendar time. Because of this intimate relationship between temperature and developmental rates of alfalfa weevil eggs and larvae, a computer population model can be made that predicts the onset of damaging populations from data on accumulated temperatures (Giese et al., 1975).

The range of temperatures an insect tolerates may be relatively narrow or rather wide, depending on its physiology. Tsetse flies reproduce only within very narrow limits because at high temperatures they consume fats faster than their larvae develop, while at lower temperatures fat deposition is retarded and not enough is stored (Bursell, 1970). Tolerable temperature varies with the stage of the insect; most insects that overwinter in temperate areas can stand much lower temperatures when in diapause, and low temperature is sometimes necessary to terminate diapause (Chapter Seven). Insects can be acclimated to extreme temperatures; *Aedes* mosquito larvae reared at 30°C are killed by a temperature of −5°C for 17 hours unless they are previously conditioned by being reared at 20°C for a day (Bursell, 1970). Severe temperatures, high or low, kill most insects, particularly subtropical and tropical forms. The yellow fever mosquito *Aedes aegypti* is roughly limited in its northern and southern distribution by average winter temperatures of 10°C (Christophers, 1960) (Fig. 8–8). Populations of corn earworm and potato leafhopper in the northern and central United States are killed by cold weather each winter, so these pests reinvade from southern states the following crop season. Severe temperatures are used to control grain pests;

---

*A day-degree is roughly calculated by subtracting a threshold temperature (here, 9°C) from the mean daily temperature if this exceeds the threshold. Thus, a day of mean temperature 20° is 11 day-degrees; four such days equal 44 day-degrees. The idea is to reflect the obvious fact that insect populations grow faster at higher temperatures (until the optimal temperature is exceeded).

Figure 8–8. Distribution of *Aedes aegypti*. Dashed line indicates isotherms of average midwinter temperature of 10°C. (Redrawn from Christophers, S. R. 1960. *Aedes aegypti* (L.), The Yellow Fever Mosquito: Its Life, History, Bionomics, and Structure. Cambridge University Press, New York.)

temperatures of either 54°C for ½ hour or −18°C for 4 days eliminate grain pests from elevators, mills, or flour bags. Some insects are very tolerant of high or low temperatures. Ephydrid flies live on algae in hot springs (40°C) in Yellowstone National Park (Mitchell, 1974), while not far away the unusual orthopteroid *Grylloblatta* exists at edges of snowfields where temperatures are near 0°C.

Moisture. Because of their size, insects are susceptible to water loss, and I have already discussed certain adaptations to conserve water: tracheae, water reabsorption (Chapter Four), diapause during drought (Chapter Seven), and migration to rainfall zones. Most insects acquire the water they need through drinking (dew, water from pools, honeydew, sap, etc.) and humidity, the atmospheric moisture content, is thus critical for insects' survival. As with temperature and other factors, there are ranges of tolerance and optimum limits for insect activity, development, and reproduction, but these are not as well understood, owing to the difficulty of maintaining (and measuring) constant humidities in the laboratory. Most grain insects cannot survive in less than 10 per cent humidity (Wilbur, 1971). Increased rainfall is at least partially correlated with swarming of the Australian plague locust (Key, 1945) (Fig. 8–9). Humidity interacts with other mortality factors, most notably with temperature but also with biotic factors. Ullyet (1947) showed that heavy rainfall in South Africa increased the incidence of fungal infestation in *Plutella,* but decreased parasitization by Hymenoptera. Very high humidity often increases dispersal and reproduction of microorganisms; consequently, more insects may succumb to bacterial or viral infections in damp surroundings (Stairs, 1972). Beirne (1970) stressed that while rainfall may be very important in determining insect numbers, it is less predictable than temperature and hence less useful in predictive population models.

The form of precipitation may be important. Very heavy rainfall knocks stem-feeding aphids from plants (Dixon, 1973), and flooding kills many insects. Snow cover during winter in temperate regions is well known for its insulating capability and may protect significant numbers of overwintering insects from freezing.

Light. Light seldom, if ever, directly causes insect mortality, though its secondary effects are certainly important in regulating insect activity and development. Photoperiod (daylength) is an important regulator of diapause (Chapter Seven), and it enables some insects to "predict" and respond to rigorous temperatures and lack of food that might otherwise kill them. Flight (or other) activity is often modulated by light intensity, as explained in Chapter Six. Particular wavelengths of light are used for orientation to host plants, and the sun's position in the sky and the plane of polarized light are both used by insects for navigation.

Green plants depend on light for photosynthesis, and insects (like all animals) depend ultimately on this photosynthesis for food and, in water, for oxygen. In deeper ponds or lakes and in caves, plant material is limited and thus incapable of supporting large populations of insects or anything else. Oxygen is often in short supply in deep or turbid waters into which adequate light cannot penetrate.

Currents. Currents, either of air or water, limit insect populations by dispersal and mortality. I have already mentioned wind as a dispersal agent of caterpillars and locusts. Richter and colleagues (1973) have shown by radar that insect distributions within the atmosphere are closely correlated with air currents. Southerly winds are largely responsible for annual reinfestation of northern states by potato leafhoppers and corn earworms.

Water currents limit such insects as mosquito and midge larvae to calm areas; only insects such as black fly larvae, which have specialized holdfasts (Fig. 8–10), can survive in swift water without being swept away. Cummins (1964)

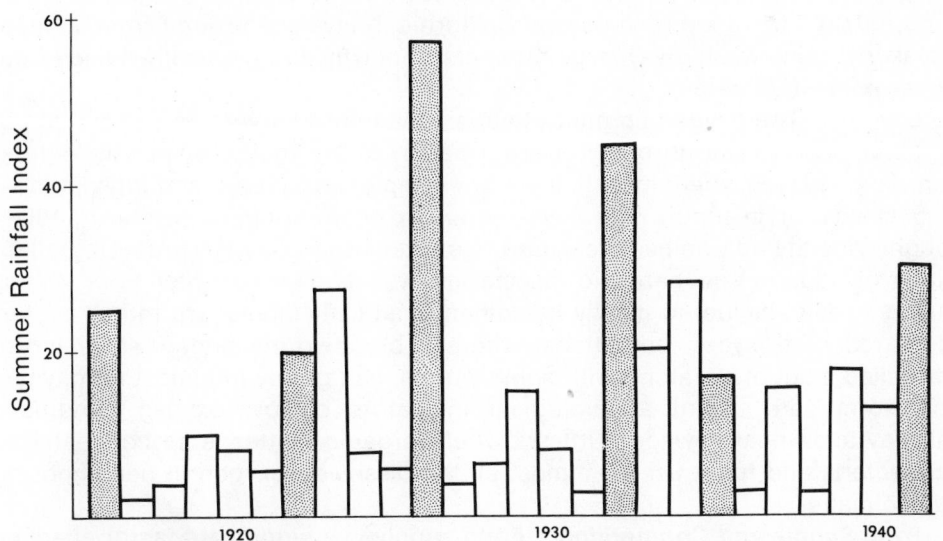

Figure 8–9. Relationship between rainfall index and swarming in Australian plague locust. Shaded bars indicate years of locust swarms. (From Varley, G. C., G. R. Gradwell, and M. P. Hassell. 1973. Insect population ecology: an analytical approach. University of California Press, Berkeley. Data from Key, K. H. L. 1945. The general ecological characteristics of the outbreak areas and outbreak years of the Australian plague locust (*Chortoicetes terminifera* Walk.). Bull. C.S.I.R.O. *186*:1–127.)

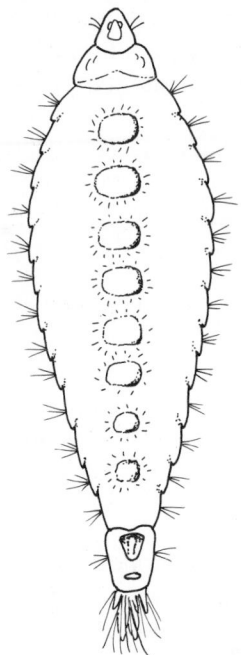

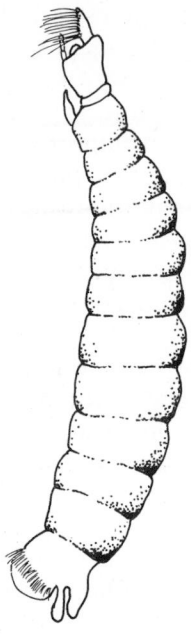

Figure 8-10. Adaptations of aquatic Diptera for holding on in fast water. Left, *Pericoma* (Psychodidae) with ventral sucking discs. Right, *Simulium* (Simuliidae) with single posterior sucking disc. (Redrawn from Hesse, R., W. C. Allee, and K. P. Schmidt. 1937. Ecological Animal Geography. © 1937 by John Wiley & Sons, Inc. Used by permission of John Wiley & Sons, Inc.)

found that two caddisfly species segregated themselves in water of different speeds and constructed cases (Chapter Three) of either gravel (in swift water) or sticks (in slow, silty areas).

Extreme currents are lethal to many insects. Putnam (1970) showed that high winds in peach orchards removed large numbers of European red mites when leaves rubbed against one another. Most insects cannot make headway in winds of more than 3 to 10 k.p.h. In coastal California, I have seen runoff from sudden, unseasonal rains wash away large numbers of mayfly and damselfly naiads from quieter pools in streams.

Oxygen. The oxygen content of air is very uniform, averaging about 20 per cent, and insects living in open air are probably rarely limited by insufficient oxygen. Some places where insects live (for example, under bark and logs, in flowers or seeds, or in fungi) may have reduced oxygen supplies (Chauvin, 1967), though evidently no one has measured this extensively. Oxygen-procuring adaptations of aquatic and parasitic insects are well known (Chapter Four). Many aquatic insects, including mayfly naiads and caddisfly larvae, are rather intolerant of reduced-oxygen conditions, whereas bloodworms and *Eristalis* larvae ("rat-tailed maggots"), along with some worms, can get by in almost no oxygen. Bloodworms are useful as biological indicators of low oxygen conditions that may arise near sewage outflows where organic matter is so concentrated that bacteria and fungi use up almost all the dissolved oxygen in decomposing organic matter.

Food Supply and Competition. Food supply is a significant factor affecting both birth and death rates in many insect populations. A supply of nutrients is a major ultimate limiting factor preventing continuous population growth. In many populations food is responsible for the levelling-off of the population at its carrying capacity (see Fig. 8-2), though the nature of the action of food supply on a population is variable. Andrewartha (1961) and others distinguish between absolute and relative shortages of food. In absolute food shortage, insects find and consume every bit of available food, and mass starvation results; such a situation may occur among maggots on a decaying carcass who are involved in scramble competition (p. 306). Instead of starving, many maggots may mature into flies of smaller-than-average size with lower than normal fecundity, but either way, population density in the subsequent generation is less (Varley et al., 1973).

In relative food shortage, food may be present but unavailable to an insect population for one or several reasons. Tsetse flies (*Glossina* species) die off if a proportion of their mammal hosts are removed from an area; not all the hosts need be removed—just enough so that the flies will utilize completely one blood meal before finding the next (Potts and Jackson, 1953). Many insects, both phytophagous and parasitic, are very host-specific, feeding on but one or two host species. Chrysomelid beetles that feed on Klamath weed, *Hypericum* species, are limited in their distribution by their host; moreover, as the beetles destroy Klamath weed in one location, large numbers of them may perish searching for other weed infestations (Huffaker and Kennett, 1959). Feeny (1970) showed that as oak leaves mature, they produce tannins which render protein indigestible to winter moth caterpillars. Most winter moth larvae eat early oak leaves; those that feed later may die of a relative shortage of protein even with a full stomach.

Cannibalism is an important factor for many insect species when food shortages occur (Fox, 1975). Cannibalism is particularly prevalent among grain-feeding insects: Adults of the flour beetle *Tribolium* eat their own eggs, larvae, and pupae, and cannibalism increases as the population becomes more crowded (Chapman, 1928). Larvae of the codling moth and corn earworm are cannibalistic, and an apple or an ear of sweet corn will rarely contain more than one. Larvae of parasitic wasps very often eat smaller larvae of the same or other species that they encounter within their host (Salt, G., 1961).

Cannibalism is perhaps the most visible manifestation of competition in which "two or more organisms exert a disadvantageous influence upon each other because their . . . active demands exceed the immediate supply of their common resources" (Bakker, 1969). Implied in this definition is the fact that if the population density increases but the resource supply does not also increase, the severity of competition will increase. Competition is thus a density-dependent factor (p. 310) and can occur for any resource—food, water, oviposition or nesting sites—that is in limited supply. Since all insect populations are *potentially* capable of infinite growth, competition is a potential limiting factor, in all insect populations, though many, and perhaps most, remain at densities below that at which measurable competition occurs. Competition may occur between members of the same (**intraspecific** competition) or different species (**interspecific** competition). Some of the important evolutionary consequences of interspecific competition are explored in Chapter Nine.

Nicholson (1954) distinguished between contest (or interference) and scramble (or exploitation) competition. In **contest** competition, insects vie for a particular environmental requisite, and "successful" individuals procure all they need for survival and reproduction. Territorial behavior (Chapter Six) is an example: Dragonflies (and crickets) actively and physically "compete" for territories which (presumably) are sufficiently large to assure survival of offspring. "Losers" fail to reproduce, and thus contest competition serves to limit a population below the density at which food shortage would occur. There is good evidence that contest competition limits many vertebrate populations (Errington,

1963; Lack, 1966; Wynne-Edwards, 1962), but experimental proof of the role of contest competition in limiting insect populations is lacking.

Scramble competition occurs when all individuals have equal access to a resource. Such competition occurs only after insects have located a resource and are using it. This may occur on a corpse, as mentioned before, or in laboratory cultures. To a culture containing 1 gram of bullock's brain are added differing numbers of blow fly larvae (Fig. 8–11). When very large numbers of larvae (200 or more) are added, all starve before adulthood, and therefore in scramble competition an unpredictable proportion of the population survives. Varley and coworkers (1973) point out that a range of competition types exists, and many examples are not easily categorized definitively as either contest or scramble; they (and others) suggest, however, that contest competition is more typical of those insects that utilize rather long-lasting and stable resources (such as nesting sites or ponds), whereas scramble competitors are found in temporary, ephemeral resources (such as carrion or annual plants).

Predation and Disease. Predators, parasites, or pathogens are a direct cause of death in most insect populations. As with competition, so the severity of predation (including disease) varies with population density of the prey. In general, the denser the prey population, the greater the proportion of the insect population that is preyed upon. Solomon (1949) suggested that the responses of predators to prey density are of two types: **functional** and **numerical.** Each has subsequently been studied in detail by Holling (1959, 1965) and others. In the functional response, the number of prey taken per individual predator increases with prey density (Figs. 8–12 and 8–13). The functional response of a predator varies not only with respect to prey density but also with respect to density and kinds of associated prey. A numerical response represents an increase in predator population density (through either immigration or births) in response to prey density (Fig. 8–14). Both types of response occur in the same species. For instance, mantids will show a functional response to increased prey density, and thus being well fed, will produce more eggs, a numerical response. Functional and numerical responses combine to form a total response of a predator popula-

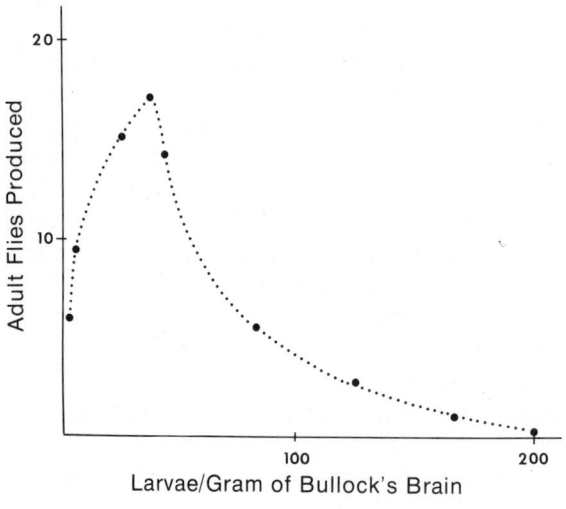

Figure 8–11. Adult flies produced at different densities of young larvae applied to 1 gram of bullock's brain. (From Nicholson, A. J. 1954. An outline of the dynamics of animal populations. Austr. J. Zool. 2:9–95.)

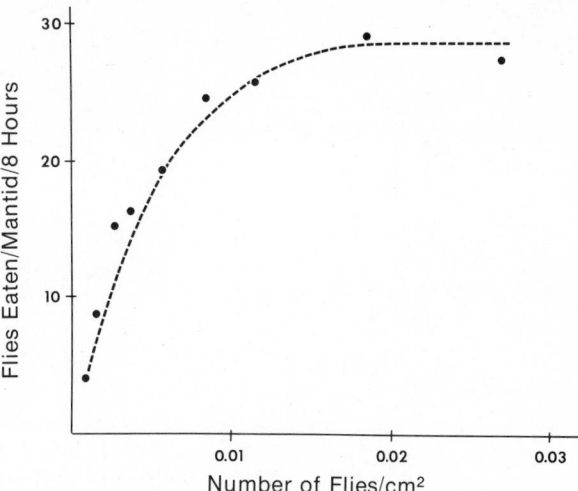

Figure 8–12. Functional response of mantids to fly density; number of flies eaten per mantid during 8 hours. (From Holling, C. S. 1965. The functional response of predators to prey density and its role in mimicry and population regulation. Mem. Entomol. Soc. Can. *45*:1–60.)

tion to a prey species (Fig. 8–15). At high densities of prey, the total response of a predator may level off or even decline, indicating that predation, though a subtractive factor, may not regulate prey populations at high densities. This has important implications for biological control of pest insects (Chapter Ten).

The numerical response implies that reproduction of predators (or parasitoids) is regulated by availability of prey. Predators need abundant food to produce large numbers of offspring, so there is a time lag between consumption of prey at high density and production of predatory offspring. If in the meantime numbers of prey have been reduced through predation, not enough will be present to support a large predator population and many of them will subsequently starve (or at least emigrate or lay fewer or no eggs). This reduces predation pressure on the remnant of prey, whose population then increases, starting the cycle over again.

Utida (1957) (Fig. 8–16) demonstrated this cyclic relationship in laboratory cultures of azuki bean weevil and its parasitoid over several generations, as did Huffaker (1958) using a two-mite predator-prey system. As discussed subsequently in the section "Cycles and Stability," some naturally occurring population cycles may result partly from this cyclic predator-prey interrelationship.

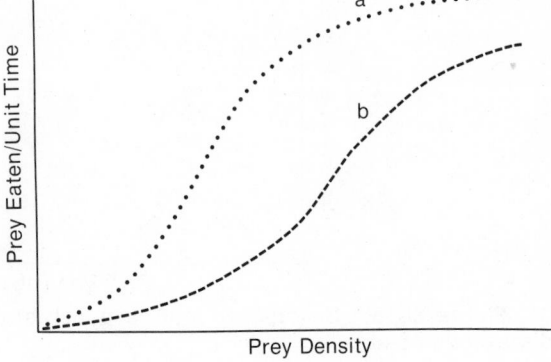

Figure 8–13. Sigmoid-type functional responses typical of vertebrate predator. *A,* No alternate prey. *B,* Other prey species available. (From Price, P. W. 1975. Insect Ecology. © 1975 by John Wiley & Sons, Inc. Used by permission of John Wiley & Sons, Inc.)

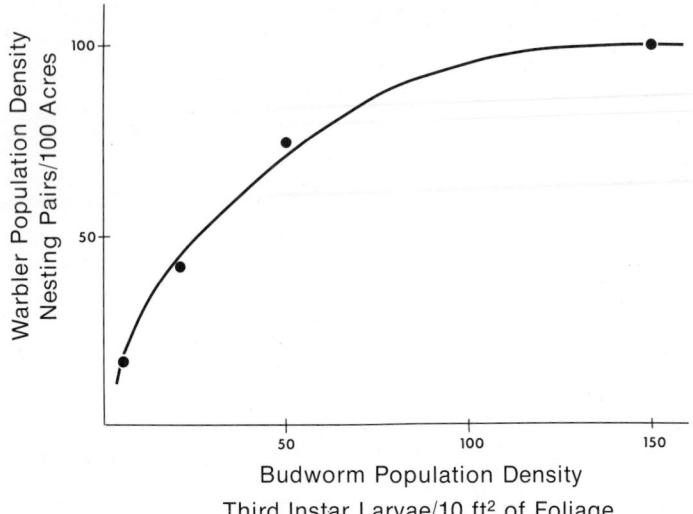

Figure 8–14. Numerical response of bay-breasted warblers to density of spruce budworm larvae. (From Mook, L. J. 1963. Birds and the spruce budworm. *In* Morris, R. F. (ed.). The dynamics of epidemic spruce budworm populations. Mem. Entomol. Soc. Can. *31*:268–271.)

Pimentel and co-workers (1963) demonstrated genetic changes in cyclic host-parasitoid populations (blow fly-*Nasonia*) in laboratory cultures and suggested that such genetic changes may also regulate population density. Chapter Nine explores more evolutionary results of predator-prey and host-parasite interactions.

Insects are subject to a variety of viral, bacterial, fungal, protozoan, and nematode infections. Epizootics* of such diseases often produce great mortality, particularly in dense host populations, whose members are close together and are often physiologically stressed by deteriorating food supply (Tanada, 1965). Once an epizootic commences, it reduces host numbers more quickly than do predators or parasitoids because the life cycle of most pathogens is very short

---

* An epizootic is a disease outbreak among animals; it is analogous to an epidemic among humans or an epiphytotic disease in a plant population.

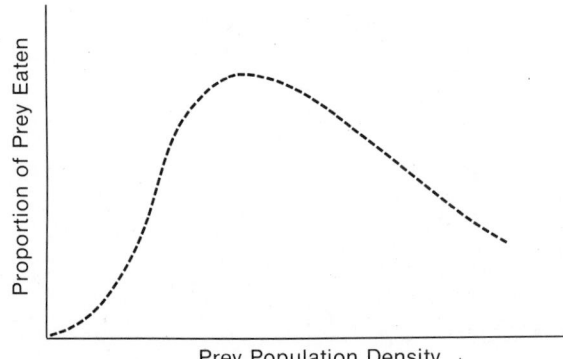

Figure 8–15. Generalized total response of predator population to prey population, discussed in text.

and they multiply quickly. American foulbrood, a bacterial disease of honey bees, can destroy a hive in a few days. Pathogens often interact with other environmental factors, particularly moisture. Protozoan and fungal epizootics particularly are much more severe in damp weather, which increases survival and dispersal of the pathogens.

Accidents and Vitality. Insect deaths may be due to a variety of accidental causes, not all of which fit neatly into the preceding categories. Molting malfunctions have killed up to 5 per cent of alfalfa weevil adults in my laboratory cultures. Flying insects may be blown over and into water, where they drown; predators are injured and sometimes killed by defensive actions of their intended prey (Chapter Nine); and, from an insect's standpoint, death from insecticide poisoning is accidental.

Some insects seem inherently weaker and less able to survive environmental stresses than others of the same species. Wellington (1960) exhaustively studied tent caterpillar populations and determined that in a given locality overall vitality decreased from year to year and that this decrease was at least partially due to genetic (evolutionary) changes: Active and hardy individuals tended to disperse away from an infestation, leaving behind a successively more sluggish population. A small but consistent proportion (5 per cent) of alfalfa weevil larvae apparently have low vitality and die in our rearings of field samples (see Table 8–3). All insects lose vitality after having reproduced, and adults of tsetse flies (Saunders, 1962), and perhaps of many other insects, die of "old age" rather often. Note that differential mortality following reproduction has no selective genetic effects on the population.

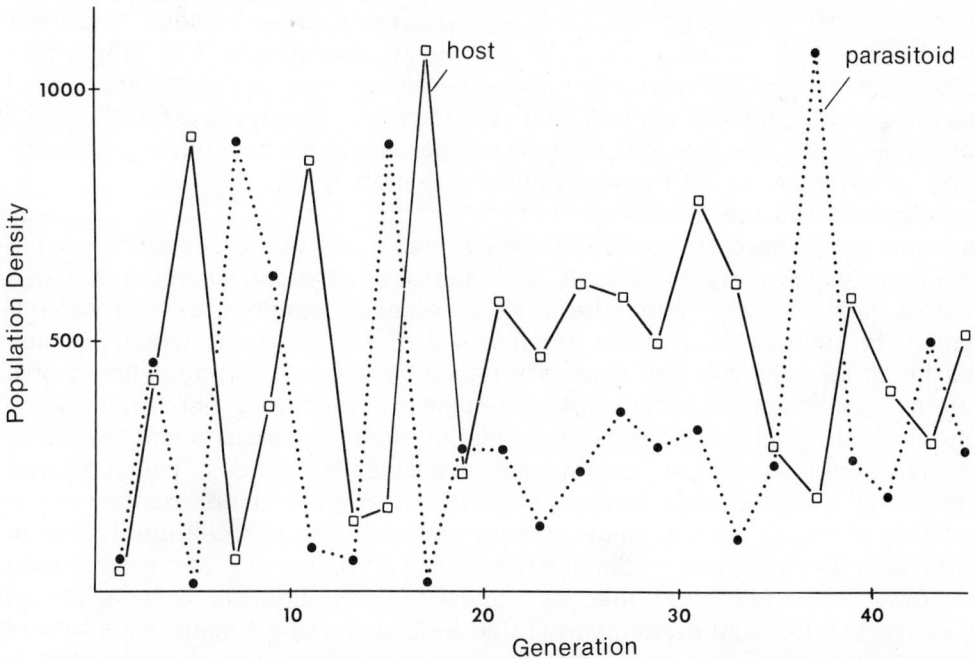

Figure 8–16. Fluctuations in population density of laboratory host-parasitoid system. Host, azuki bean weevil (*Callosobruchus chinensis*), represented by squares and solid line. Parasitoid (*Neocatolaccus mamezophagus*), represented by circles and dotted line. (From Utida, S. 1957. Cyclic fluctuations of population density intrinsic to the host-parasite system. Ecology *38*:442–449.)

DENSITY DEPENDENCE AND POPULATION REGULATION

For many years, debate over regulation of insect numbers has generated many investigations and much heated debate. A central theme has been whether environmental factors are largely density-independent or density-dependent in their effects on insect numbers. Clark and co-workers (1967) reviewed this debate in some detail. Andrewartha and Birch (1954) contended that insect abundance was largely determined by factors (chiefly weather) operating independently of population density. Others, notably Nicholson (1954) and Lack (1966), suggested that most animal populations are regulated by factors such as predation, competition, and available food, whose effects vary with population density. In fact, most environmental factors have both density-independent and density dependent effects (Horn, 1968), and a single, simple, all-inclusive theory of insect population density regulation is probably unattainable (and perhaps undesirable). It is sufficient to agree with Varley and colleagues (1973) that while density-independence may affect density, it is (by definition) insensitive to changes in density. Only density-dependent effects tend to stabilize, a fact that should not be ignored by those who wish to manage insect pest populations.

ADAPTIVE STRATEGY

All environmental factors can cause differential reproduction resulting in evolutionary changes, and therefore, adaptations (detailed in Chapters Four through Seven) are results of selective environmental factors acting on populations. The population ecology of insects as a group is perhaps as diverse as their morphological adaptations. To generalize about population ecology, MacArthur and Wilson (1967), Pianka (1970), Force (1972), Price (1975), and others have suggested the concept of adaptive strategy—the result of concurrent action of all adaptations to promote survival and reproduction. They propose that insects (and other organisms) can be generally compared along a continuum whose theoretical extremes are the r-strategy and the K-strategy.

According to the hypothesis, r-strategists live in ephemeral, unpredictable environments. These environments are not stable enough to support a population density near carrying capacity, or the local populations' attendant competition or carrying capacity may be quickly exceeded, resulting in their extermination. In such environments, organisms evolve adaptations which promote maximum reproduction and dispersal; hence there is a high population growth rate (r), perhaps at the expense of wastefulness in food utilization. K-strategists, on the other hand, are considered typical of more equable and stable environments where resources are continuously available. Populations in such environments may exist at or near carrying capacity (K), and this favors adaptations that increase efficiency and competitive ability and, perhaps, reduce reproductive effort. Table 8–8 lists some additional theoretical attributes of r- and K-strategists.

Data from studies on real, as opposed to hypothetical, insects do not precisely fit into r- and K-strategies (Table 8–9), and a single species may exhibit attributes of either type depending on local conditions. The adaptive strategy approach has value as a tool for comparison of similar insects in a particular environment (Chapter Nine). Moreover, adaptive strategy is a helpful generality for economic entomologists. Most agricultural crops are ephemeral and unpredictable environments in which tomorrow may bring harvesting, plowing, insecticide

POPULATION ECOLOGY   **311**

Table 8–8. THEORETICAL EXTREMES BETWEEN r- AND K-STRATEGISTS*

	r-strategist	K-strategist
Environmental qualities exerting selection		
environmental variability	unpredictable	more certain
mortality	density-independent	density-dependent
competition	variable, often lax	keen
Adaptations responding to selection		
life span	shorter	longer
reproductive rate	higher†	lower‡
body size	smaller	larger

*Modified from Pianka, E. R.: On r- and K-selection. Amer. Nat. *104*:592–597, 1970. The University of Chicago Press, © 1970 The University of Chicago.
†Therefore, greater egg production and shorter generation time.
‡Therefore, lower egg production and longer generation time.

applications or replacement by another crop. Just as blow flies must reproduce rapidly so that offspring can move on to find another fresh carcass, so most crop pests exhibit many attributes of r-strategists, dispersing quickly and reproducing rapidly to maintain a breeding population. The speed with which these insects disperse and reproduce contributes markedly to their pest status (Chapter Ten). Knowledge of adaptive strategy of parasitic insects is important for biological control (Force, 1972).

CYCLES AND STABILITY

Nicholson (1954) cultured blow flies in the laboratory and allowed them a limited amount (50 grams) of bullock's brain on which to oviposit. He then

Table 8–9. BIOLOGICAL CHARACTERISTICS OF PARASITOIDS ATTACKING THE GALL MIDGE *Rhopalomyia californica* (DIPTERA:CECIDOMYIIDAE)

	r-strategist	K-strategists	
	Tetrastichus sp.	*Torymus baccharicidis*	*Platygaster californica*
Locality	commoner in unstable areas	dominant in stable habitats	
Competitive ability	inferior	superior	?
Mean life span (as adult)	21 days	30 days	6 days
Mean fecundity	117.5	94.2	194.8
Body length†	1–3 mm.	2–4 mm.	1–2 mm.

*Data from Force, D. C. 1970. Competition among four hymenopterous parasites of an endemic insect host. Ann. Entomol. Soc. Amer. *63*:1675–1688.
†Based on specimens of each genus in The Ohio State University collection.

counted viable puparia and adult flies over several generations, during which population densities fluctuated through a wide range (Fig. 8–17). Other workers have obtained similar cycles in single-species laboratory cultures of grain insects, mites, and other insects. It is generally (though not universally) thought that such cycles result from a delay in the action of competition on the death rate; that is, undernourished adults may go right on reproducing as the population "overshoots" carrying capacity, until mass starvation occurs, reducing the population to a mere remnant, which, in the midst of again plenteous food, maximizes reproduction.

Many insect populations fluctuate quite widely in nature, and explaining these cycles is a much more complex problem. Forest defoliators—sawflies, tussock and gypsy moths, loopers, spanworms, webworms, and tent caterpillars—are all notorious for periodic mass outbreaks followed by spectacular "crashes," with little activity between (Fig. 8–18). Forests are very complex systems, and very likely a variety of factors acts in concert to produce periodically favorable conditions. Several studies (reviewed by Ives [1973]) have demonstrated a correlation between weather conditions and subsequent insect outbreaks. Ives suggested that outbreaks of forest tent caterpillars are directly related to favorable weather conditions occurring in the preceding two or three years. Recently, White (1974) theorized that when rainfall is adequate, New Zealand pine looper larvae often die of nitrogen deficiency but that pines become a richer source of nitrogen when water-stressed in dry years. More loopers then survive, leading to a population outbreak. The "crash" phase of particular forest insect outbreaks has been variously attributed to weather (Ives, 1973), parasitoids (Klomp, 1966; Horn, 1974), deteriorating food quality (Wellington, 1960; Baltensweiler, 1968), and epizootics (Stairs, 1972). Perhaps all these and more may be involved in a single case; longer-term experiments are sorely needed in this area, though Leonard (1974) has pointed out that financial support for study of cyclic insects is not

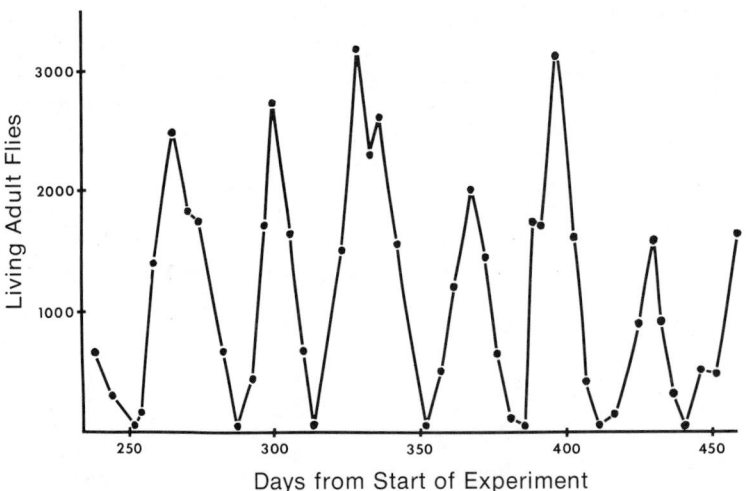

Figure 8–17. Cyclic density changes in laboratory culture of blow flies. (Data from Nicholson, A. J. 1954. An outline of the dynamics of animal populations. J. Anim. Ecol. 2:132–178.)

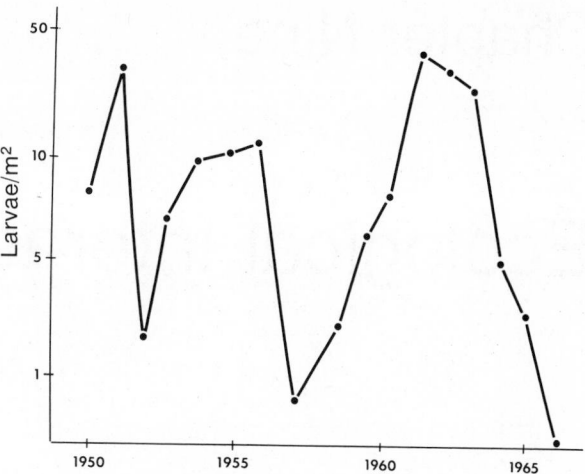

Figure 8–18. Cyclic density changes in field populations of pine looper, *Bupalus piniarius,* in the Netherlands. (From Klomp, H. 1968. A seventeen-year study of the abundance of the pine looper, *Bupalus pinarius* L. (Lepidoptera: Geometridae). *In* Southwood, T. R. E. (ed.). Insect Abundance. Roy. Entomol. Soc. Symp. No. 4. Royal Entomological Society, London.)

prevalent during periods when they are not causing damage. Even correlations are useful, for they may predict when outbreaks are likely. The relationship between population stability and ecological diversity is explored further in Chapter Nine.

SUMMARY

Populations are interbreeding groups of insects (or any other organism), and this chapter discusses regulation of numbers in and distribution of insect populations. Conclusions concerning insect populations are only as valid as the sampling methods employed, and these are briefly discussed along with the interrelationship between field and laboratory studies.

Generally, population density is determined by interactions between births and immigration and deaths and emigration. These in turn are determined by the population age-structure and life system, which consists of the population and its effective environment, the **co-determinants of abundance.** Among these co-determinants are **additive** factors (fecundity, fertility, and dispersal) and **subtractive** factors (weather—in a broad sense, food, competition, predation, disease, and viability). The short-term cyclic and long-term adaptive responses of insect populations to these environmental factors are also examined.

Chapter Nine

Ecological Interactions

INTRODUCTION

Insect populations are intimately associated with those of other animals and plants in **communities,** assemblages of organisms living within a prescribed area. The study of interrelationships among organisms in communities is **synecology.** This field is an appropriate culmination of the study of insect biology, for here we consider insects within the environmental context in which their adaptations evolve. A community and its nonliving, physical environmental components constitute an ecosystem. Communities characteristically have trophic structure (feeding relationships), with resulting interspecific interactions and patterns of diversity. Though these interactions are measurable within communities, the boundaries of natural communities are not distinct. A pond community may seem clearly distinct from that of a surrounding forest, but even there, boundaries are diffuse. Dragonflies and salamanders, for instance, spend their immature lives in the pond. Some then move into the forest, returning to the pond to mate and oviposit. As one moves northward in the northern United States or southern Canada, one generally passes from deciduous to coniferous forest communities, but the boundary again is obscure. Whittaker (1962) reviews the debate over boundaries in detail. Perhaps the best operational definition of community is simply: those organisms located within an area of interest. This is an adequate definition for entomologists dealing with insects on a particular crop plant. Beyond this, all biotic communities on earth are at least partially interrelated through food chains and chemical cycles, though the boundaries of any given local community are more or less arbitrary.

TROPHIC STRUCTURE — INTERRELATIONSHIPS

All communities consist of organisms more or less interrelated through **trophic** (feeding) interactions. Energy is required by all living things for growth, maintenance, and reproduction (Fig. 9–1). In obtaining this energy, animals and plants in a natural community interact in **food webs** (Fig. 9–2), which represent extremely complex feeding relationships. Actual analysis of who eats whom is

314

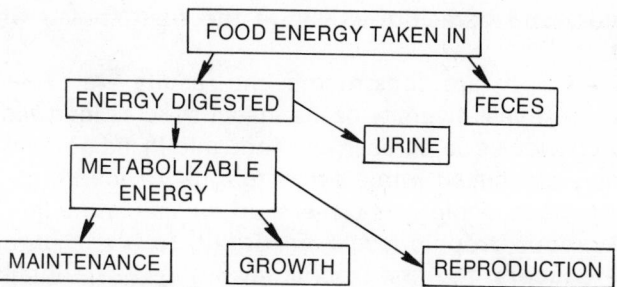

Figure 9–1. Energy budget of an insect. Arrows indicate directions of energy flow.

very tedious and not always possible. Vertebrate animals have been killed and their stomachs analyzed for insect contents, and insect remains in spiderwebs are often identifiable. Hosts of many parasitic Diptera and Hymenoptera are reared for emergence of parasitoids. Recently, radioactive tracers have been used successfully to delineate food webs; radioactive phosphorus is incorporated into plants, and after several days, insects and other members of the local community are collected and examined for radioactivity (Patten, 1971). A time-consuming but interesting method for working out partial food webs is merely to

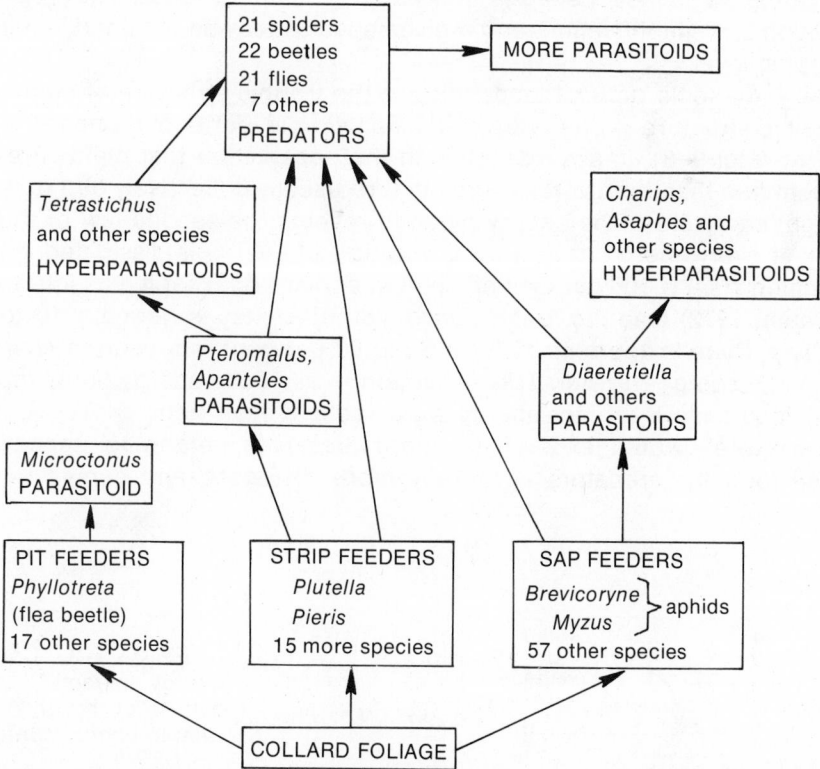

Figure 9–2. Food web on collards, Ithaca, New York. Arrows indicate directions of energy flow. (From Root, R. B. 1973. Organization of a plant-arthropod association in simple and diverse habitats: The fauna of collards *(Brassica oleracea)*. Ecol. Monogr. 43:95–124.)

observe predatory and parasitic insects in the field to see what they do and whom they eat.

However food webs are constructed, the results are exceedingly complex, partly because of the vast diversity of the insect species involved. Wheeler (1971) found 800 insect species in three New York alfalfa fields, while Powell (1971) noted 160 species associated with a single fungus (*Cronartium*). To impose order on this potential chaos, ecologists classify organisms into admittedly oversimplified functional groups, trophic levels, according to where an organism gets its food energy. **Producers,** the first trophic level (Fig. 9–3), obtain energy directly from the sun by using light to convert carbon dioxide and water into energy-rich sugars. With a few minor exceptions, producers are green plants, and organisms on all other trophic levels obtain their energy directly or indirectly from green plants. **Consumers** are one group of organisms that derive energy from producers; they may do so directly (as do herbivores, or **primary** consumers) or indirectly by eating herbivores or each other (as do carnivores, or **secondary** and **tertiary** consumers). Completing the community are **decomposers,** a group that contains mostly bacteria and fungi but also includes many insects. These decomposers obtain energy from partial or whole dead bodies of producers and consumers. Most insects are either primary or secondary consumers, though many do not fit neatly into any category. Cockroaches, for instance, eat whatever is available and palatable, be it of animal or plant origin. Flour beetles are normally herbivores, eating flour, but sometimes they eat one another. Larvae and adults of the same insect species may eat very different foods. The trophic-level description is a simplification, and a given species may be included in more than one trophic level.

There are some general tendencies in the trophic structure of communities. The trophic structure is often depicted as a pyramid, either of numbers, biomass, or energy (Fig. 9–3), in accordance with the observation that plants are usually more common than herbivores, which in turn usually collectively outnumber (and outweigh) carnivores. The energy pyramid reflects the second law of thermodynamics: at every energy transfer, a proportion of energy is dissipated. No insect (or anything else) is 100 per cent efficient at converting what it eats into living tissue (Odum, 1972) (see Fig. 9–1); conversion efficiency is normally 10 to 20 per cent. Thus, there is approximately an 80 to 90 per cent reduction in energy content at each energy transfer. This reduction in available energy limits the length of most food chains, for less energy is available at each trophic level. A potential "top carnivore" would expend its energy reserves getting to its next meal. Because food for predators is thereby more dispersed and comes in smaller

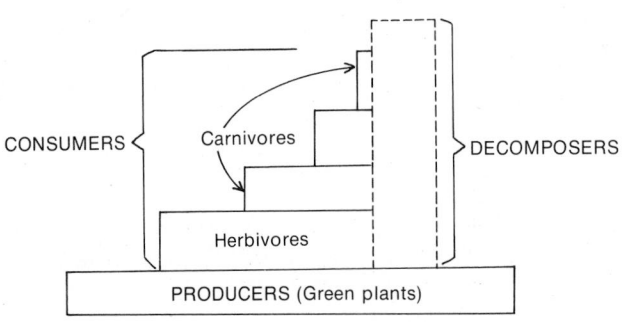

Figure 9–3. Community "energy pyramid." Size of each level roughly proportional to energy content.

packages than green plants, insect predators often have a generalized diet and eat more or less whatever is available (Root, 1973). Insect herbivores are more likely to feed on one or a few host plant species. There are indeed rather few insect (or any other) **tertiary** consumers (those that feed only on other predators). However, parasites and parasitoids are an exception, as many are specialized to eat predators.

Each trophic level is limited ultimately by the energy available on the preceding level, and green plants on the average convert only 1 to 5 per cent of incipient sunlight to usable energy. Temperature, light, water, and micronutrients are perhaps the most important limiting factors in photosynthesis, as one can demonstrate by fertilizing mineral-poor farmland to increase yields or by dumping phosphates or warm water into lakes, thereby stimulating growth of algae.

INTERSPECIFIC INTERACTIONS

Insects and other animals and plants in ecological communities interact with one another in several ways. Some of these interactions, such as those involving predation, disease, and food supply, cause short-term density changes (discussed in Chapter 8). Interspecific interactions also lead to long-term evolutionary changes as adaptations evolve in each species in response to another species. This is coevolution, and one result is the great diversity in the class Insecta. Very generally, four interactions, or symbioses, are possible (Table 9–1): (1) **commensalism,** an interaction advantageous* to one species and of no consequence to the other; (2) **mutualism,** interactions advantageous to both; (3) **parasitism** (in a broad sense), interaction advantageous to one (parasite or predator) and deleterious to another (host or prey); and (4) **competition,** mutually deleterious interaction. As in the case of trophic levels, classification of symbioses is a simplification, and subtle interactions that may well cause an overlap of categories are disregarded. For instance, caterpillars' eating the leaves of forest trees is parasitism in the short run. However, minor defoliation (to 20 per cent) may ultimately stimulate plant growth, so that the final result of light defoliation is mutualism (Mattson and Addy, 1975). More examples of such interactions will be discussed.

Advantage here is simply increased survivorship.

Table 9–1. TYPES OF INTERSPECIFIC INTERACTIONS

Interaction	Species A	Species B
Commensalism	+*	0
Mutualism	+	+
Parasitism	+	−
Competition	−	−

*Plus sign indicates advantage and minus sign, disadvantage.

COMMENSALISM

In commensalism, one species presumably benefits while the second is unaffected by the interaction, though very few experimenters have compared the effects of the presence or absence of a commensal on its host. Phoresy, or "hitchhiking" by smaller insects on larger insects or other organisms is a common form of commensalism (see p. 296); a louse hitching a phoretic ride on a hippoboscid fly does not weigh it down much. Some parasitic wasps (Scelionidae) lose their wings after mating and ride about on female mantids (Fig. 9–4) until the mantid oviposits, whereupon the interaction becomes parasitic as the wasp oviposits within the freshly laid mantid ootheca.

Perhaps the best-documented commensals are *inquilines,* cohabitants of social insect colonies. Wilson (1971) lists members of 12 arthropod orders, with beetles and mites predominating, that have been collected from colonies, primarily those of army ants and termites. Most inquilines are tropical, perhaps because colonies of social insects reach very large sizes there. By living with ants or termites, inquilines gain some protection from predators. Many steal food from the jaws of their hosts, and some are even fed by their hosts. Most inquilines are obligate (totally dependent on the host), having never been collected away from host colonies. Many secrete appeasement pheromones with which they suppress the "normal" aggressive response of the host to foreign organisms (Wilson, 1971). This attests to a long evolutionary relationship between inquilines and their hosts, and it is of definite adaptive advantage for insects living in raiding columns of army ants, for instance. Commensal association with social insects is not limited to arthropods; some antbirds (Formicariidae) of tropical American rainforests habitually follow raiding army ants and feed on insects stirred up by the ants.

MUTUALISM

Mutualism (symbiosis, in its oft-used narrow sense) imparts advantage to two (or more) interacting organisms. You have read already of several examples: recall the hindgut protozoa in termites (Chapter Four) that digest cellulose. Neither these protozoa nor termites can survive without the other. Recall also mutualism between fungus ants and the fungi they grow for food (Chapter Six); again you can't have one without the other. Female ambrosia beetles (Scolytidae) have a specialized structure, the mycangium, in which they carry a culture of fungus. When infesting a log, the beetle tunnels under the bark, oviposits, and then "plants" the fungus, which grows, hastening decay under the bark. When beetle larvae hatch, they commence feeding on the fungus. Ambrosia fungi are species-specific, which suggests a long coevolution with the beetles.

One of the most celebrated of insect-insect mutualisms is that between Homoptera (primarily aphids) and ants. Aphids feed on plant sap, which is rich in sugar but low in protein and micronutrients, so aphids (and most other Homoptera) secrete large amounts of **honeydew,** a sugary, energy-rich liquid, as they drink enough sap to obtain requisite micronutrients. Mittler (1958) calculated that in one hour, an aphid produces up to 133 per cent of her body weight in honeydew. Ants feed on secreted honeydew and actively "milk" aphids to obtain honeydew (Fig. 9–5A). Wickler (1968) suggested that this mutualism may have

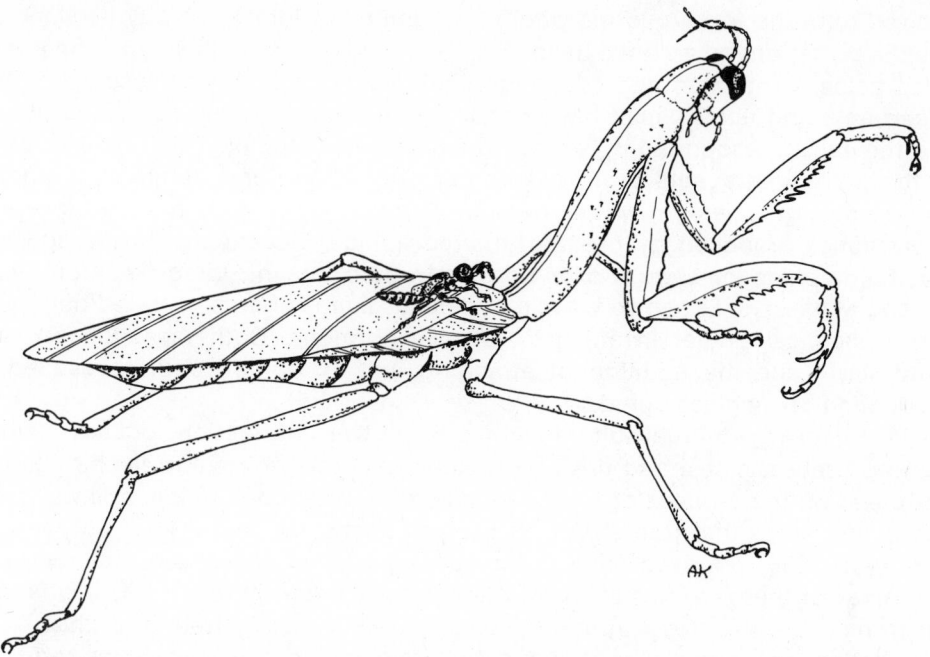

Figure 9–4. Female scelionid wasp riding on wings of female mantid.

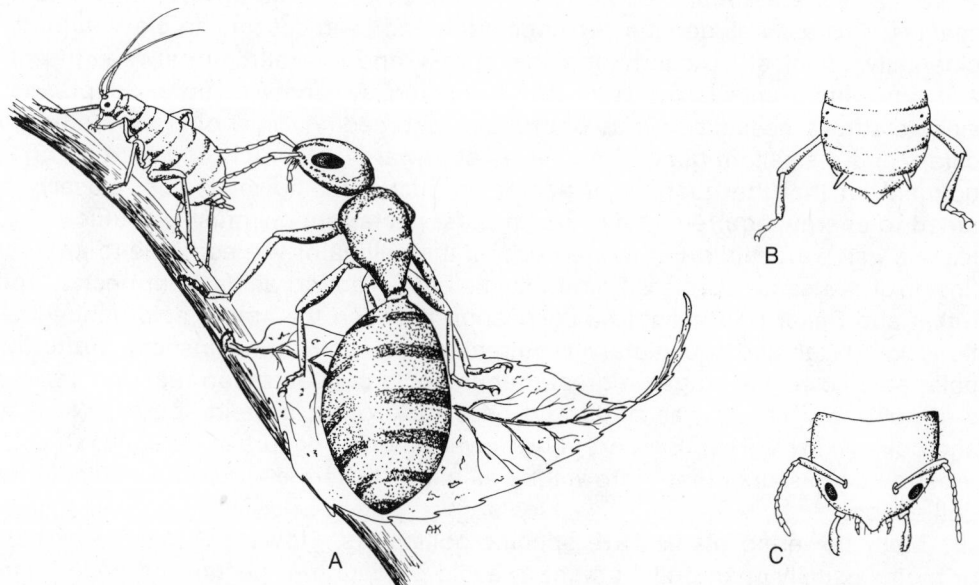

Figure 9–5. Mutualism between ants and aphids. *A,* Ant ''milking'' aphid to get honeydew. *B,* Aphid rear. *C,* Ant head. Note morphological similarity between *B* and *C.* (Redrawn From Wickler, W. 1968. Mimicry in Plants and Animals. © 1968 by McGraw-Hill, Inc. Used by permission of McGraw-Hill Book Co.)

evolved from the fortuitous morphological and behavioral similarity between an aphid's posterior and an ant's head (Fig. 9–5, B and C). When two ants meet they often palpate antennae and exchange liquid (Chapter Six). The association between ants and aphids may have begun when ants palpated aphids' cornicles and the aphids responded by secreting a honeydew droplet. This has developed to the point where ants that tend aphids sometimes tend aphid eggs underground during inclement winter weather (Forbes, 1906). Ants respond to alarm pheromones produced by predator-injured aphids. Depending on the species, ants herd aphids to safety and/or vigorously attack the intruding predator. Kleinjan and Mittler (1975) showed that mandibular glands of ants secreted dendrolasin, a chemical similar in effect to juvenile hormone. Both the application of dendrolasin and the addition of attending ants to aphid cultures resulted in production of wingless aphids.

A three-way mutualistic-parasitic-competitive interaction occurs among burying beetles, mites, and flesh flies. Burying beetle larvae and flesh fly larvae both feed on the corpses of freshly killed small vertebrates (mice, shrews, sparrows), and mites that ride about on burying beetle adults eat young fly larvae. Springett (1968) removed mites from burying beetles and noted that relatively few larvae of these beetles survived the competitive onslaught of flesh fly larvae. Offspring of beetles carrying mites found themselves on fly-free food; thus burying beetles with mites gain a competitive advantage over flesh flies, and the mites get transportation to a new food source.

Insect-Plant Mutualism

The evolutionary history of "higher" insects, particularly Lepidoptera, Diptera, and Hymenoptera, closely parallels that of flowering plants. Most flowers attract insects that are essential for transferring pollen to female flowers of the same species. This assures genetic recombination and seed set for the plant (and, incidentally, for most fruit and vegetable crops), and coevolution between insects and flowering plants is therefore not surprising. A variety of floral adaptations exist to attract insects and thus promote crossbreeding. Most obvious are bright colors and a small amount of nectar as a "reward." Heinrich and Raven (1972) pointed out that the quantity of nectar produced per flower is very closely attuned to energy requirements of pollinators; nectar supply must be sufficient to make a visit worthwhile, yet limited so that the pollinator will continue to another flower of the same species. Some insects obtain amino acids from nectar, and Baker and Baker (1973) noted a correlation between the amino acid concentrations in nectar and the dietary requirements of pollinating insects. Butterfly-pollinated flowers averaged a greater amino acid concentration than did bee- or bird-pollinated flowers, as birds and bees have other protein sources (insects and pollen) (Table 9–2). Synchronous flowering often occurs in response to photoperiod and assures that there will be as many flowers as possible available for pollination.

Many flowering plants have specific pollinators. Flowers pollinated by bats or moths usually open only at night to avoid predation of nectar and pollen during the day (Heinrich and Raven, 1972). *Ophrys* orchids look like, and smell like, female bees, and thereby attract males, which, in their futile attempts to copulate with the blossom, end up wearing two pollenia, which they then transfer to the next blossom (Fig. 9–6). Yucca plants of the American southwest and Mexico are

Table 9–2. AMOUNTS OF AMINO ACIDS IN NECTAR FROM FLOWERS POLLINATED
BY INSECTS OR BIRDS*

Pollinator	Mean of Histidine Scale†
Carrion-feeding fly	9.25
Butterfly	6.68
Moth	5.60
Hummingbird	5.22
Bee	4.76
Unspecialized flies	3.77

*From Baker, H. G., and I. Baker. 1973. Amino-acids in nectar and their evolutionary
significance. Nature *241*:543–545.

†Histidine scale is proportional to amino acid concentration.

pollinated by several species of yucca moths (Fig. 9–7) whose females have unusual mouthparts with which they gather pollen and place it directly on pistils
(the female portion of the flower). A specific moth pollinates each species of
yucca (Powell and Mackie, 1966); without the moths the plants could not survive.
Each female yucca moth oviposits in some (but not all) flowers and her larvae
feed on developing seeds, though enough are left over to assure the next yucca
generation.

Other mutualism occurs between insects and plants. Janzen (1966, 1967) has
experimentally verified mutualistic interactions between ants and acacia trees in

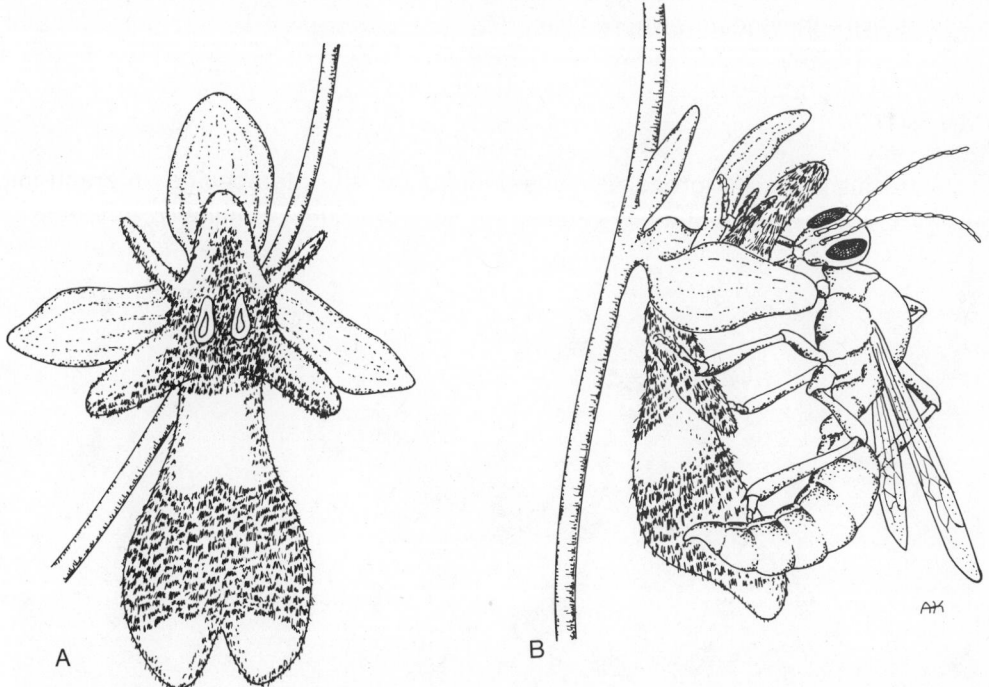

Figure 9–6. Pollination of *Ophrys* orchids. *A*, Flower resembling female bee. *B*, Male
bee attempting to copulate with blossom. (Redrawn from Wickler, W. 1968. Mimicry in
Plants and Animals.©1968 by McGraw-Hill, Inc. Used by permission of McGraw-Hill Book
Co.)

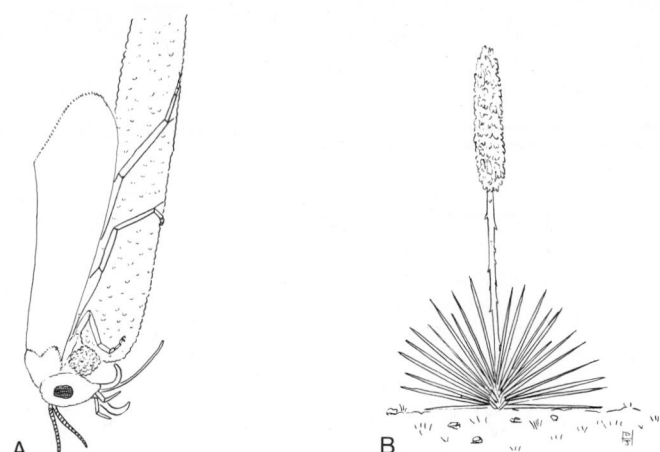

Figure 9–7. Yucca moth and yucca. *A,* Moth gathering pollen from stamen. *B,* Yucca plant in flower.

Central America. These acacias have large, hollow thorns (Fig. 9–8) in which small colonies of aggressive ants nest. The ants feed on sweet secretions produced by **beltian bodies** (small nodules on the leaves) and patrol the plant; woe to the herbivore (or investigator) that disturbs them. By spraying insecticide or clipping thorns, Janzen removed ants and noted significant loss of leaves and sap to insect herbivores as compared to untreated acacias. The mutualistic advantage to the ants is, of course, having food, from the beltian bodies, and a place to live—they nest nowhere else.

PARASITISM

Parasitism, in its broadest sense, includes all interspecific interactions whereby one species benefits at the expense of another. Ultimately, this means

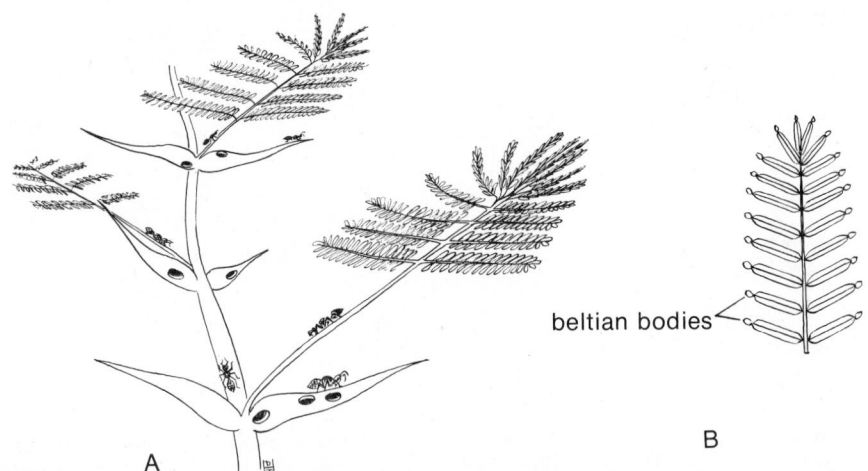

Figure 9–8. Mutualism between ants and acacias. *A,* Bull's horn acacia with ant nests in thorns. *B,* Close-up of leaf with beltian bodies at leaflet tips.

Table 9-3. COMPARISON OF INSECT PARASITES, PARASITOIDS, AND PREDATORS

	Parasite	Parasitoid	Predator
Terminology of food	host	host	prey
Free-living	sometimes	larva, no; adult, yes	yes
Host range	narrow	variable, often narrow	broad
Number of individual hosts used	one	one	several
Effect on host	not killed*	killed	killed
Fecundity	high	variable	low
Size compared with host	smaller	similar	usually larger
Carnivorous example	body louse	ichneumon wasp	mantid
Herbivorous example	aphid	bean weevil	cutworm

*Usually; this ignores virulent disease.

that all insects that eat living plant or animal material engage in parasitism. Food habits of parasitic and predaceous insects may be thought of as a continuum between "true" parasites and predators (Table 9–3). Truly parasitic insects are a relative minority; they include lice and some fleas (on bird and mammal hosts), and the unique order Strepsiptera (Chapter Three), together with a few members of other orders. More prevalent are **facultative** parasites, such as biting flies and bloodsucking Hemiptera, whose females parasitize vertebrates before reproducing. Homoptera, Hemiptera, and other sap-feeding insects may be considered parasites in that their life histories and effect on the host are similar to those of animal parasites (Table 9–3). The most effective parasites are those that obtain energy from the host without being noticed, and these parasites could therefore be considered commensals. Chances are better than 50-50 that parasitic mites are living in the skin pores of your face.

At the other end of the "parasitism spectrum" are predators, whose nutrient-procuring activities result directly in the death of their prey. Predatory insects occur in almost all orders, and most predaceous insects feed upon other insects. Adaptations that facilitate prey location and capture have been detailed earlier in Chapters Four, Five, and Six.

Included also is a third major category, **parasitoids,** with some characteristics of both typical parasites and predators (Table 9–3). Parasitoids are mostly Hymenoptera (many families) and Diptera (especially Tachinidae), but there are a few in other orders. All characteristically have free-living adults that oviposit in, on, or near potential hosts, and the resulting larvae feed within (or sometimes outside) the host, which almost always is killed before the parasitoid pupates. These characteristics, especially host specificity and killing of the host, make parasitoids quite suitable to biological control of pest insects. Some herbivores, particularly Coleoptera, Hymenoptera, and Lepidoptera whose larvae feed within seeds, function much like parasitoids. In the literature these are often called seed predators (e. g., Janzen, 1971).

Within the Hymenoptera are many parasitoids whose hosts are themselves parasitic. Any extensive study in which one rears field-collected parasitoids is sure to reveal these **hyperparasitoids.** (Their hosts are then called primary parasitoids.) Hyperparasitoids may be secondary, tertiary, or even quaternary parasitoids, depending on what they eat. Hyperparasitoids generally have a greater diversity of hosts than do primary parasitoids, as one might expect from their higher position on the trophic pyramid, just as many insect predators take more different prey species than do herbivores. Hyperparasitism therefore contributes to complexity of food webs (see Fig. 9–2).

Social parasitism occurs among social insects, mostly commonly among ants (Wilson, 1971). A few ant species are "slave-makers." Being incapable of rearing larvae of their own species, they raid colonies of other species, carrying off eggs, larvae, pupae, and sometimes the queen. The "slaves" then attend to both their own brood and that of their parasites. Bumblebees of the genus *Psithyrus* are parasitic on *Bombus* bumblebees; fertile queens of the former simply move into *Bombus* nests and set up shop. *Bombus* workers do all the foraging and brood rearing, and a female *Psithyrus* may kill the *Bombus* queen (Lutz, 1936). The steely-blue mud wasp *Chalybion,* often seen about buildings in the eastern United States and California, does not forage for food (caterpillars and spiders) for its brood but rather pirates nearby mud wasps of other species in order to stock its own brood cells.

Insects themselves are a concentrated energy source from the viewpoint of a hungry animal. Because they are so abundant and diverse, insects are subject to attack from a wide array of parasites and predators and are a major source of energy for higher levels on terrestrial and aquatic food chains. Their major predators are often other insects, though huge numbers are consumed by small birds, small mammals, and lizards in terrestrial ecosystems, and by fish and amphibians in fresh water. A variety of mites and nematodes are parasitic on insects (Welch, 1965).

Predation in its broad definition includes disease-causing pathogens. Over 1000 microbial diseases (reviewed by Steinhaus, 1963, and Burges and Hussey, 1971) have been found in insects. Economically, the most important are two bacterial diseases: *Bacillus thuringiensis* is lethal to most larval Lepidoptera but to little else (some Diptera and earthworms), and *B. popillae* causes "milky disease," which kills larvae of Japanese beetles and other Scarabaeidae. Both bacteria form spores, which are formulated as commercial insecticides. Viral diseases (Fig. 9–9), particularly nuclear polyhedrosis virus (NPV) of caterpillars, are under intensive study for potential development as insecticides. Naturally occurring virus epizootics are apparently partially responsible for a number of spectacular declines in densities of defoliating caterpillars (Stairs, 1972). NPV has been used successfully in control of cotton bollworm. A microsporidian (protozoan) disease, caused by *Nosema* and several bacterial and viral diseases affect honey bees and may cause significant losses. Insects themselves transmit numerous diseases of other organisms (Chapter Eleven).

Escape

Active Defense. Predation by other animals on insects is ubiquitous and potentially decimating so it is not surprising that an interesting variety of adapta-

Figure 9–9. Forest tent caterpillar larva dead of virus; note liquefied body contents running down tree trunk. (Photo courtesy of G. R. Stairs.)

tions for avoiding predation have evolved. Perhaps the most obvious is the ability to run, to crawl, or fly away. Most insects take flight at any sudden movements of large objects nearby. Noctuid, Geometrid, and Pyralid moths have on their thorax or abdomen "ears" (see Fig. 5–14) with which they hear ultrasonic squeaks of bats (Roeder and Treat, 1961). While insectivorous bats attempt to locate moths by the pattern of echoes, moths take evasive action by flying in spins or loops or by dropping to the ground (Fig. 9–10). The wildly gyrating flights of bats we see on warm summer evenings are sometimes attempts to follow the insects' evasive maneuvers.

Chemical defense is practiced by insects of most orders. Stinging, the insertion of chemical poisons either by a modified ovipositor (in Hymenoptera) or through a mandibular bite, is effective against even large vertebrates such as you or me. Some insects secrete digestive juices or gut contents when handled (see Fig. 4–9) and this may deter predators. Reflex bleeding occurs in insects of several orders, notably Coleoptera and Plecoptera (Benfield, 1974). The blood is squeezed out, usually through leg joints, when the insect is handled. Hemolymph of Meloidae and Coccinellidae contains a toxic irritant, cantharidin. Happ and Eisner (1961) demonstrated that cantharidin in hemolymph of the Mexican bean beetle is significantly repellent to ants. There are numerous other primarily defensive chemical secretions, which are detailed by Eisner and Meinwald (1966). Glands that produce irritating or noxious substances occur within the thorax of stinkbugs (Pentatomidae and related families) and at the abdominal tip in some Tenebrionidae (often called "stinkbugs" in some parts of the Western United States). Many ants,

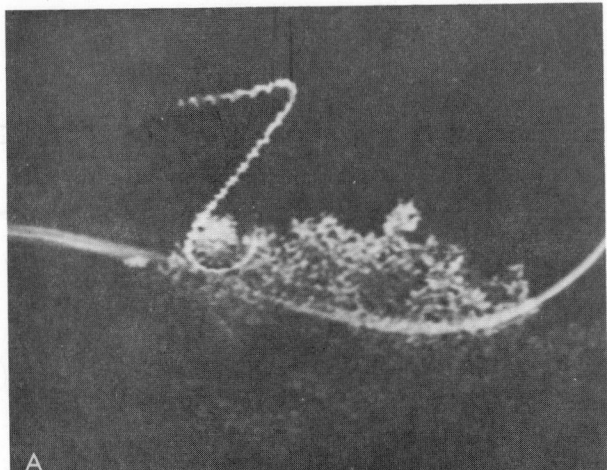

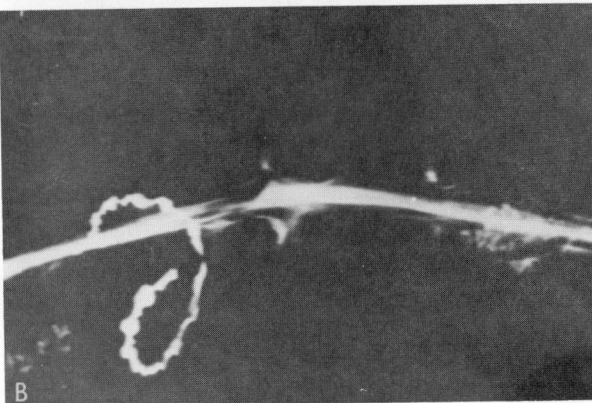

Figure 9–10. Tracks of bats and moths at night. *A,* Moth escapes. *B,* Bat captures moth. (*A* and *B* from Roeder, K. D. 1967. Nerve Cells and Insect Behavior. Harvard University Press, Cambridge, Massachusetts. ©1967 by Harvard University Press. Photos by Frederic A. Webster, Cambridge, Massachusetts.)

cockroaches, Carabidae, and Staphylinidae also possess defensive "stink" glands, and nasute termites (Fig. 6–18) spray attackers with a gluey resin. One of the more unusual chemical defenses is that of the bombardier beetle (Fig. 9–11). When disturbed, the beetle ejects a mist of volatile irritant with an audible "pop" and with an aim that is accurate over 25 cm. Moreover, the chemical is hot (100° C!), and woe to the toad that tries eating the beetle. The inevitable distraction and irritation caused by chemical defenses permits the "sender" more than enough time to run away. The beetle produces the hot, irritating chemical without apparent damage to itself by mixing two separate and innocuous precursors together at the last possible moment to form the active, volatile ingredient (Fig. 9–12), (Eisner and Meinwald, 1966).

Insects that lack chemical defenses may resort to physical defense; biting, kicking, and scratching ward off attackers throughout the animal kingdom. Many insect predators are apt to bite when handled. Beetle pupae of several species have an unusual structure, a **gin trap** (Fig. 9–13), whose function is obscure, though Askew (1971) suggests that it might be used to chop off ovipositors of those parasitic wasps that attempt to probe therein. Blood cells of many insects encapsulate eggs or small larvae of parasitic wasps (Chapter Four). The hardened integument of some insects discourages would-be predators, and soft-

Figure 9–11. Bombardier beetle releasing defensive chemical spray. (From Eisner, T. 1970. Chemical defense against predation in arthropods. *In* Sondheimer, E., and J. B. Simeone (eds.). Chemical Ecology. Academic Press, Inc., New York. Photo by T. Eisner and D. Aneshansley.)

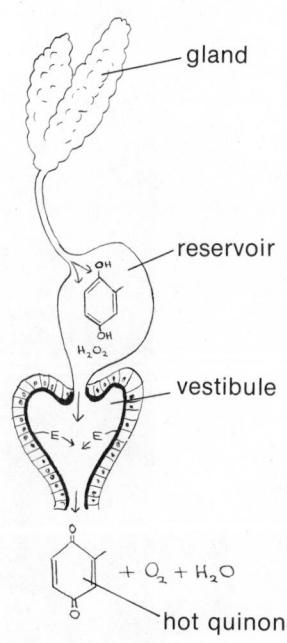

Figure 9–12. Mechanism of bombardier beetle spray. Precursor from reservoir is mixed with enzyme E at last moment in vestibule. Oxygen forces hot spray out. (Redrawn from Schildknecht, H., and K. Holoubek. 1961. Die Bombardierkafer und ihre Explosionschemie, V. Mitteilung uber insekten Abwehrstoffe. Angew, Chem. *73*:1–6.)

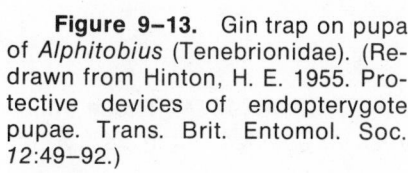

Figure 9–13. Gin trap on pupa of *Alphitobius* (Tenebrionidae). (Redrawn from Hinton, H. E. 1955. Protective devices of endopterygote pupae. Trans. Brit. Entomol. Soc. *12*:49–92.)

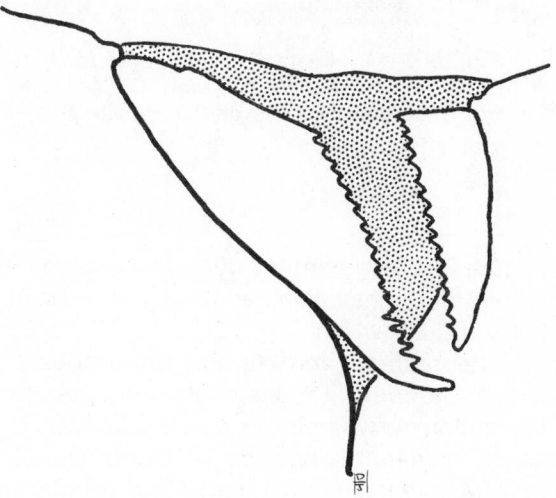

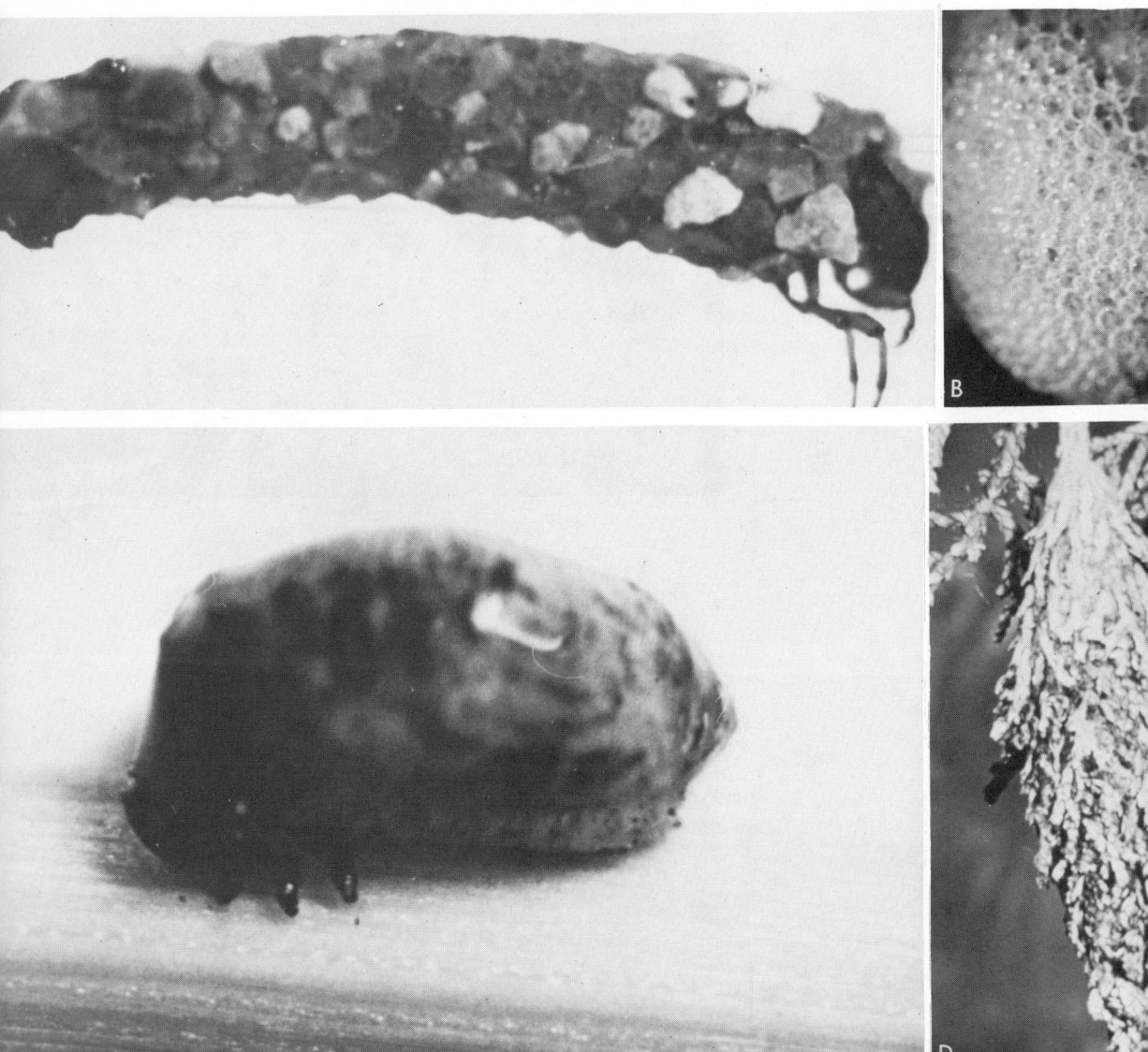

Figure 9–14. Protective structures for immature insects. *A*, Caddisfly larva in case. *B*, Froth covering spittlebug nymph. *C*, Cereal leaf beetle larva covered with excrement. *D*, Bagworm (Lepidoptera: Psychidae) in silk-and-leaf bag. (USDA photo.)

bodied forms sometimes construct protective structures (Fig. 9–14). These adaptations doubtless also reduce water loss in terrestrial species, such as spittlebugs and bagworms.

Camouflage and Warning Coloration.   In addition to its hardness, the form and coloration of the insect cuticle offers protection to many insects. Protective resemblance, wherein an insect's coloration and/or appearance apparently deceives predators, abounds in the class Insecta. Insects have evolved similarities to leaves, twigs, stones, bark, bird droppings, flowers, and a host of other inedible items. Presumably, such resemblances have evolved by natural selection, in much the same way that melanic moths have become more common in Britain and North America since the advent of widespread air pollution (see Chapter Two). Cryptic coloration, or camouflage, is enhanced by appropriate behavior, and there is evidence (Rettenmeyer, 1970) that camouflaged moths select appropriate backgrounds and align themselves to match local patterns. Akinesis (Chapter Six) is very common in insects that resemble inanimate objects, especially in Phasmidae. I have seen lizards walk right past rigid "twig" caterpillars and even step on them.

Deceptive coloration is likewise a common adaptation for deceiving visually orienting predators. Many insects have eyelike spots and antennalike extensions near their hind end (Fig. 9–15), while the true head is rather inconspicuous. This draws predators' attention to the insect's rear, a deception furthered by appropriate behavior. When at rest, most hairstreak butterflies (Fig. 9–15, C and D) move their hind wings alternately up and down, which moves the hairlike tips. That this deception is at least partially effective is attested to by the fact that their wings frequently bear V-shaped wedges that are precisely the size and shape of beaks of insectivorous birds (Shapiro, 1974). Some insects (and many other animals) have large eye spots that bear remarkable similarity to a pair of vertebrate eyes (Fig. 9–16), and for generations naturalists have suggested that these may frighten potential predators. Blest (1957) provided experimental support for this view by training birds to eat mealworms and then suddenly projecting spots of various sorts (Fig. 9–17) beside the worms just as the birds were picking them up. The birds withdrew most vigorously when confronted with a pair of spots closely resembling vertebrate eyes, and Blest concluded that sudden exposure of insect eyespots may frighten birds (and perhaps lizards) into seeking food elsewhere. Blest provided corroborating field data by carefully removing eyespots from wings of butterflies and then releasing them; those with eyespots removed were preferred by predators over normal butterflies. Behavior is important; io moths (and others) normally rest with wings closed, but when touched (or pecked) they instantly raise the front wings, exposing hindwing eyespots (Fig. 9–16, C and D).

Some insects "deliberately" draw predators' attention to themselves by "warning", or **aposematic,** coloration, usually a bold pattern of black and yellow, orange, or red. Perhaps the most familiar and obvious example is the black and yellow banding on stinging bees and wasps; birds, lizards, and curious children very quickly learn to associate these colors with insects that are best left alone. Many brightly colored insects are bad-tasting, or even poisonous to vertebrate predators by virtue of toxic chemicals obtained from their plant food. In the United States, insects of several orders feed on milkweed (*Asclepias*), several species of which contain cardiac glycosides, which are poisonous and bad-tasting to most vertebrate predators. The milkweed eaters, however, are unharmed by the poisons, and all are brightly colored and patterned in black and orange, yellow, or white, advertising their unpalatability to would-be predators (Fig. 9–18). Such warning coloration is very prevalent in the tropics, though many temperate-zone and arctic insects are aposematically colored too.

Mimicry. Mimicry, in its narrow sense, is the resemblance of an otherwise unprotected insect species to another insect that predators avoid. Wickler (1968) and others extend this definition to include *all* kinds of protective resemblance, including camouflage. A classic and familiar example is the resemblance be-

Figure 9–15. Protective resemblance wherein rear end looks like front end. *A*, Fulgorid, Thailand. (Redrawn from Wickler, W. 1968. Mimicry in Plants and Animals. © 1968 by McGraw-Hill, Inc. Used by permission of McGraw-Hill Book Co.) *B*, Caterpillar, California. *C*, Hairstreak butterfly. *D*, Same as *C*, with V-shaped gap made by beak of insectivorous bird.

Figure 9–16. Eye spots. *A*, Owl. *B*, Owl butterfly (Nymphalidae), showing underside resembling owl. *C*, Io moth (Saturniidae) resting on tree trunk. *D*, Same moth as *C* but with forewings raised after being disturbed by a 5-year-old child.

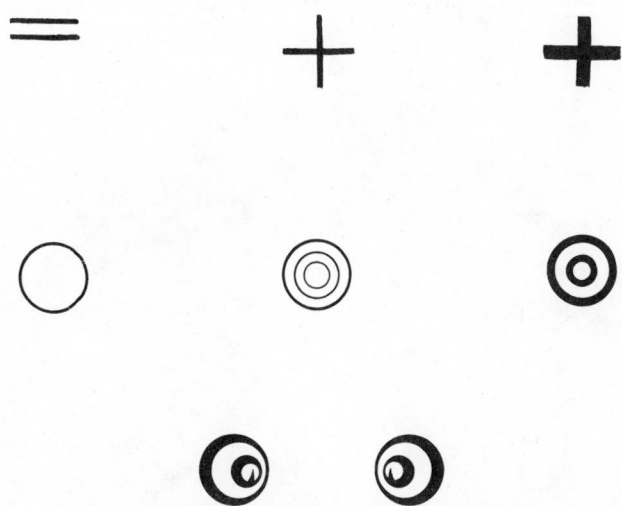

Figure 9–17. Patterns that Blest projected alongside mealworms fed to caged birds. The pair at the bottom evoked the most consistent startle response. (From Blest, A. D. 1957. The function of eyespot patterns in the Lepidoptera. Behaviour *11*:209–256.)

Figure 9–18. Insects that feed on milkweed. Clockwise, from lower left: longhorn beetle (*Tetraopes*); leaf beetle (*Labidomera*); monarch butterfly; larva of monarch; seed bug (*Lygaeus*).

tween the monarch and viceroy butterflies (Fig. 9–19, *A* and *B*). The monarch is bad-tasting by virtue of the poisonous glycosides it receives from its food plant, milkweed. Birds leave both it and the rather palatable and similar viceroy alone. This simplest form of mimicry is **Batesian** mimicry, in which a single protected model (here, the monarch) is imitated by one or several species of otherwise

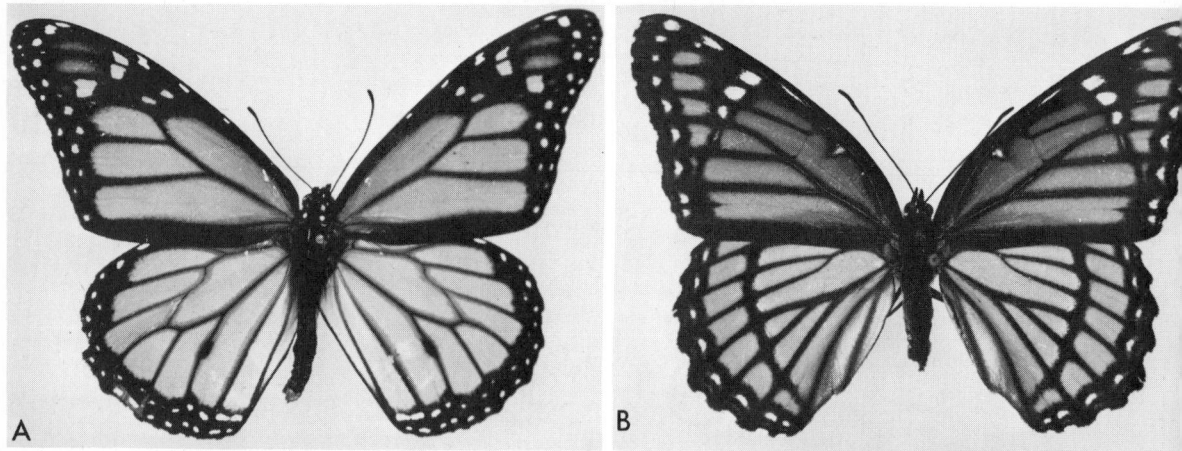

Figure 9–19. Mimicry. *A*, Monarch butterfly, model. *B*, Viceroy, mimic.

unprotected mimics. **Müllerian** mimicry, by contrast, occurs when several distasteful (or otherwise noxious) models all are similar and gain a degree of protection by their collective resemblance. Such mimicry exists among wasps and bees; a predator need be stung but once to learn to avoid all black and yellow banded insects. The categories of Batesian and Müllerian mimicry overlap, as there are many flies, moths, and other insects that are banded black and yellow and look and act like wasps. Batesian and Müllerian mimicry systems are more prevalent and varied among tropical insects, perhaps partly because of the greater diversity of visually oriented diurnal predators, notably lizards and arboreal mammals.

In the tropics we also find **Wasmannian** mimicry, commonly among inquilines of ant colonies; these house guests look very much like their ant hosts (Fig. 9–20). Initially, Wasmann (1925) and others thought that the inquilines thereby

Figure 9–19 *Continued.* *C,* Wasp, model. *D,* Sesiid moth, mimic. *E,* Syrphid fly, mimic. (*C* and *D*, photos by G. Berkey, courtesy of D. G. Nielsen and Ohio Agricultural Research and Development Center.)

Figure 9–20. Wasmannian mimicry: *Ecitosus* (Staphylinidae), a beetle that travels within foraging columns of army ants. (Modified from Seevers, C. H. 1965. The systematics, evolution, and zoogeography of staphylinid beetles associated with army ants (Coleoptera: Staphylinidae). Fieldiana-Zoology *47*:137–351.)

deceived their ant hosts into accepting them as ants. We now know that most ant communication is chemical and tactile and that ant mimicry is probably more likely an adaptation to deceive vertebrate predators (Rettenmeyer, 1970). **Aggressive,** or **Peckhammian** mimicry occurs among tropical mantids, some of which resemble flowers (Fig. 9–21) and presumably lure flies and bees to their doom. Female *Photuris* fireflies that attract males of other species to eat them (Chapter Six) are likewise aggressive mimics.

For many years, there was little experimental verification of the adaptive value of mimicry in deceiving predators. However, a series of experiments by Brower (1958a and b, 1960) clarified and documented mimicry. Initially, she used hand-reared, inexperienced scrub jays, which ate viceroys with alacrity until they bit into their first monarch, which they normally spat out or vomited. Thereafter the jays, with few exceptions, avoided monarch and viceroy alike. However, Brower (1958b) noted that some jays could in fact visually distinguish between the bad-tasting pipevine swallowtail (*Battus philenor*) and its mimic, the female black swallowtail (*Papilio polyxenes*). In another experiment, Brower (1960) showed that some conditioned jays that avoided both monarch and viceroy also rejected a very dark brown colored form of the viceroy. These findings suggest that slight resemblance is more protective than no resemblance at all and that the greater the resemblance, the greater the survival rate, at least in regard to attacks by visually oriented vertebrate predators.

Plant Defenses. Parasitism, defined broadly, includes the actions of the herbivorous insects that "parasitize" plants by sucking, chewing, boring, mining, and so forth. Plants have been subject to attack from insect herbivores for several hundred million years, and it is not surprising that plants, being unable to run away* have evolved an array of physical and chemical defensive adaptations. Hair on leaves and stems deters attack by small insects, such as aphids or leafhoppers. Gilbert (1971) found that tiny trichomes (hairs) on leaves of *Passiflora adenopoda* impaled larvae of *Heliconius melopomene,* which then became dehydrated (Fig. 9–22). (However, Rathcke and Poole (1975) noted that caterpillars of *Mechanitis isthmia* avoided spines of *Solanum* plants by spinning a communal web over them.) Gummy resins of coniferous trees trap and suffocate many larvae of bark beetles and wood borers.

Chemical defenses reach their greatest diversity among flowering plants, and this has been an active area of recent research by both basic and applied insect ecologists. It has long been known that green plants contain a variety of "secondary substances," such as alkaloids, quinones, and glycosides, whose

---

*Not quite: Plants may "escape" insect attack by spreading seeds over long distances and by setting seed only in specific years during which seeds may be so abundant that not all can be found and eaten by insects (Janzen, 1971).

Figure 9–21. Aggressive mimicry: the African mantid, *Idolum diabolicum,* hangs motionless, upside down, mimicking a flower. (Redrawn from Wickler, W. 1968. Mimicry in Plants and Animals. ©1968 by McGraw-Hill, Inc. Used by permission of McGraw-Hill Book Co.)

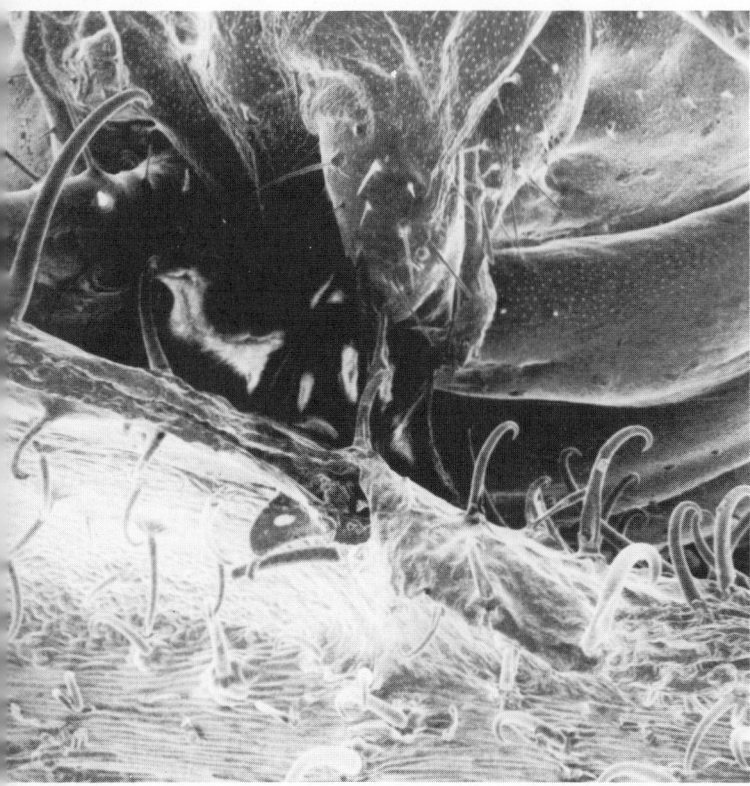

Figure 9–22. Larva of *Heliconius melopomene* caught on trichomes of *Passiflora adenopoda* leaves. (Photo courtesy of L. R. Gilbert.)

function was initially unclear, since they were not required for normal growth and maintenance (Whittaker and Feeny, 1971). Some of these substances were, and are, of considerable economic importance: caffeine, nicotine, marijuana, and peyote are alkaloids, and pyrethrum (extracted from chrysanthemums) is a quinone. Both nicotine and pyrethrum have been used commercially as insecticides for many years, and it now seems likely that most secondary substances have evolved in response to insect feeding (Ehrlich and Raven, 1964, 1967; Whittaker and Feeny, 1971). Further evidence comes from experiments wherein secondary substances were removed from cucumbers by selective breeding: phytophagous mites decimated deficient plants (DaCosta and Jones, 1971).

Insects have not stood still evolutionarily, and many species have developed a resistance to the toxic chemicals of particular plants. Krieger and co-workers (1971) demonstrated a correlation between the range of caterpillars' diets and the activity of detoxifying enzymes in their digestive systems. "Broad-spectrum" feeders not only are more likely to overcome plant chemical defenses but also are more likely to evolve resistance to chemical insecticides (Chapter Two). Insects such as the monarch butterfly incorporate noxious chemicals from food plants into their hemolymph; monarchs lab-reared on cabbages are quite tasty to birds. Pierid butterflies not only have overcome the toxic mustard oils of the plant family Cruciferae (mustard, cabbage, radish, etc.) but also orient toward these same chemicals when locating oviposition sites (Ehrlich and Raven, 1964). Plant alkaloids and glycosides are arrestants (Chapter Five) for some aphids (Dixon, 1973).

The insect that overcomes plant defenses may sometimes become exceedingly specialized. *Drosophila pachea* resists alkaloids produced by senita cactus and consequently is the only *Drosophila* species that parasitizes senita. This relationship has continued long enough that *D. pachea,* alone among insects so far studied, cannot utilize cholesterol as a hormone precursor but requires a unique sterol, schottenol, in its diet (Heed and Kircher, 1965). Senita cactus is its only source of schottenol. This and similar instances of insects' being "hooked" on specific plants may explain the extreme specificity of host plants for many phytophagous insects. Levins and MacArthur (1969) suggested that monophagous insects might be able to survive on a wider variety of plants but that insect evolution has favored adaptations for choosing a single "safe" plant rather than distinguishing a range of harmless plants from the majority of unacceptable foods.

The chemical warfare between plants and insects has further effects on plants. Many insects, particularly sap feeders, inject into their hosts saliva that induces abnormal growth; Hori (1974) isolated a plant growth hormone from salivary glands of *Lygus disponsi* (Hemiptera: Miridae). It is thought that salivary chemicals speed sap flow and prevent clogging of phloem vessels, and saliva, often together with excreta, induces abnormal tissue growth around the insect. These growths, or galls, are formed by members of several orders, most notably Homoptera, Diptera, and Hymenoptera, and are very characteristic for each insect and host plant species (Fig. 9–23). The galls protect the occupants from severe weather and at least some predation and, in small numbers, do not harm the plant on which they occur, though many people consider them unsightly on ornamental or house plants. However, a severe infestation of galls, like an unusually large amount of almost anything, can be disastrous for the host plant.

Finally, a discussion of insect-plant relationships must also include the insectivorous plants. (Three types are illustrated in Figure 9–24.) These plants are typical of acidic, boggy environments in which nitrogen supply to herbaceous plants is very limited. The insectivorous plants therefore supplement their nitrogen by capturing insects and digesting their protein with strong enzymes. The most widespread of these are pitcher plants (*Sarracenia* species are the most common in the United States), whose fragrance and color attract small insects to their vase-shaped, water-filled leaves. The unsuspecting insects fall into the leaves and drown; they slowly decompose and are utilized by the plant. *Wyeomyia* mosquito larvae, however, swim with impunity in the water of *Sarracenia* pitcher plants but nowhere else. Sundews are widespread but very tiny; they trap insects on sticky pads, which slowly envelop the victim. Among insectivorous plants, the Venus' flytrap has the greatest reputation for ferocity, and woe to the unsuspecting fly who treads on the bright red inner surface and triggers the leaf to snap shut. (The sensory mechanism is not yet clearly understood.) The leaf reopens when the insect is mostly consumed. In nature, Venus' flytraps are limited to a few localities in North Carolina, though they are widely sold as unique house plants (or pets).

INTERSPECIFIC COMPETITION

The fourth interspecific interaction is competition, a negative interaction between species. Park (1954) established laboratory cultures containing *Tribolium castaneum* and *T. confusum* and a limited quantity of flour for which, presum-

Figure 9–23. Common galls. *A*, Gouty gall on oak (Cynipidae). *B*, Rough oak bullet gall (Cynipidae).

ably, both species would compete. Park found that after several generations, *T. confusum* was eliminated from cultures above 29°C, but below 29°C it was usually the winner, eliminating *T. castaneum*. Birch (1953) performed similar experiments on the grain beetles *Calandra oryzae* and *Rhizopertha dominica* (Fig. 9–25). Park (1954) also found that other variables, such as moisture, food supply, and parasitism, affected the outcome of competition. Results of these experiments and earlier ones on protozoa (Gause, 1934) have led to the competitive exclusion principle: no two species can occupy the same functional role indefinitely, because one will displace the other through competition.

The validity of the competitive exclusion principle has been debated because of a general lack of unequivocal evidence for competition between species in nature. On the one hand, insects that apparently have identical ecological requirements appear to coexist in nature. Ross (1957) noted that six species of leafhoppers (*Erythroneura* sp.) appeared to coexist on sycamore trees and displayed no apparent differences in feeding, breeding, hibernation, and so forth. However, McClure and Price (1975) found that each of the species existed most

Figure 9–23 *Continued.* *C,* Willow pinecone gall (Cecidomyiidae). *D,* Goldenrod gall (Tephritidae). *E,* Cooley spruce gall (Adelgidae). (Family of gall-maker noted in parenthesis.)

abundantly at a different latitude. There are other examples of apparent coexistence without competition (Southwood, 1961). On the other hand, supporters of the universality of competitive exclusion suggest that these apparent cases of peaceful coexistence simply mean that we have not as yet found differences but that differences will eventually turn up after further study. Istock (1973) noted

Figure 9–24. Insectivorous plants. *A*, Sundew. (From the book Insects by Ross E. Hutchins. ©1966 by Ross E. Hutchins. Published by Prentice-Hall, Inc., Englewood Cliffs, New Jersey.) *B*, Pitcher plant. *C*, Venus' flytrap. (*B* and *C* from Gleason, H. A., and Cronquist, A. 1964. The Natural Geography of Plants. Columbia University Press, New York.)

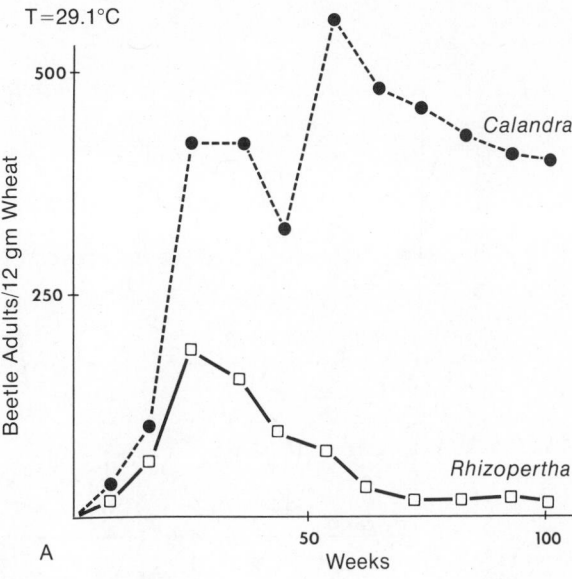

Figure 9-25. Results of culturing *Calandra oryzae* and *Rhizopertha dominica* together in wheat of 14 per cent moisture. *Calandra* indicated by circles and dashed lines. *Rhizopertha* indicated by squares and solid lines. *A*, At 29.1°C, *Calandra* wins. *B*, At 32.3°C, *Rhizopertha* wins. (From Birch, L. C. 1953. Experimental background to the study of the distribution and abundance of insects. III. The relations between innate capacity for increase and survival of different species of beetles living together on the same food. Evolution 7:136–144.)

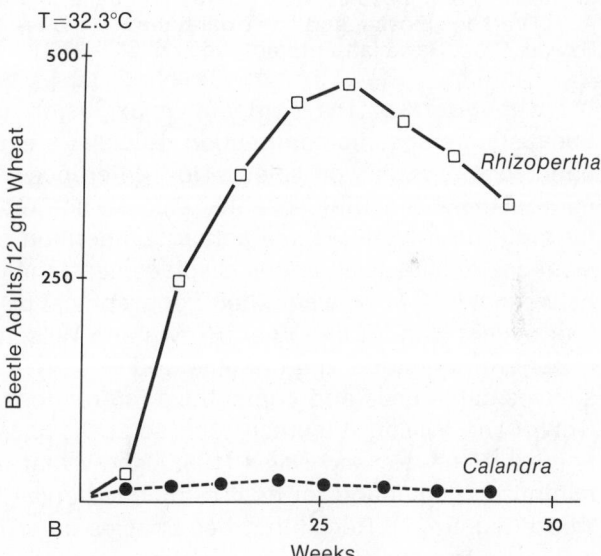

that naturally coexisting Corixidae compete when caged to prevent dispersal. Actual competitive displacement in the field has rarely been observed; two rather well-documented cases are from biological control programs. DeBach and Sundby (1963) reported results of successive release of three species of Aphytis parasitic on California red scale (a pest of oranges). Each successive species introduced apparently displaced the previous one, incidentally controlling the host more successfuly. In Hawaii, Bess and co-workers (1961) reported a similar case in which three *Opius* species, parasitoids of the Oriental fruit fly, sequentially replaced one another (Fig. 9–26).

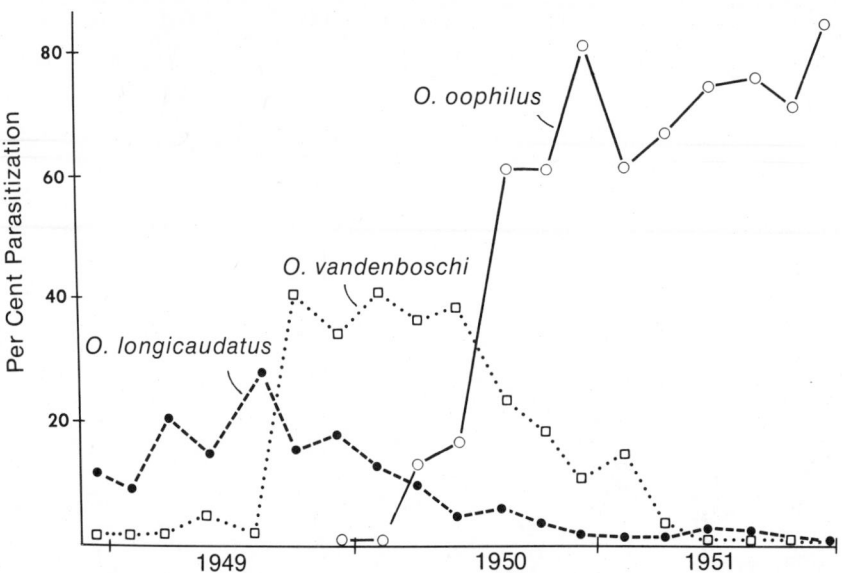

Figure 9-26. Competitive displacement among parasitoids of *Dacus oleae* fruit fly in Hawaii. Dots and dashed line indicate *Opius longicaudatus*. Squares and dotted line indicate *O. vandenboschi*. Open circles and solid line indicate *O. oophilus*. (From Bess H. A., R. Van den Bosch, and F. H. Haramoto, 1961. Fruit fly parasites and their activities in Hawaii. Proc. Hawaiian Entomol. Soc. *17*:367–378.)

Supporters of the competitive exclusion principle further point out that because interspecific competition quickly (in evolutionary terms) either exterminates one species or selects for differences in foods, preferred habitat or microclimate, breeding seasons, etc., we see results of interspecific competition far more often than we see actual competition occurring. Strong circumstantial evidence for this is character displacement, the existence of a greater difference between two species when their geographical distributions overlap than when either occurs without the other (Brown and Wilson, 1958). Character displacement is better understood and documented in vertebrates, particularly birds, in which species differences and competitive interactions are not so subtle as in insects. Brown and Wilson document character displacement in some ants and scarab beetles. Heatwole and Davis (1965) show that ichneumon wasps (*Megarhyssa*) minimize competition for host (Siricidae) larvae by drilling to different depths in wood (Fig. 9-27). Recall that bee species differ in pollen preferences (see Table 6-1), and this likely minimizes competition.

Further evidence for competitive exclusion exists from studies on parasitic Hymenoptera. Price (1970b) noted that the parasitoid *Pleolophus basizonus* displaced the similar *P. indistinctus* at high host (Swaine jack pine sawfly) densities but that at low host densities, *P. indistinctus* prevailed because the searching efficiency of *P. basizonus* was not suited to host location at low densities. Meanwhile, *Mastrus aciculatus* dominated host cocoons in drier areas, where both *Pleolophus* species were less abundant. Where it occurs alone, *Bathyplectes curculionis* parasitizes alfalfa weevil larvae throughout spring and early summer, but where it co-occurs with the similar *B. anurus,* the latter species predominates in midseason (Dowell and Horn, 1976). In this case, interspecific competition seems directly implicated, since early-instar larvae of *B. anurus* kill those of *B. curculionis* if both occur in the same host larva.

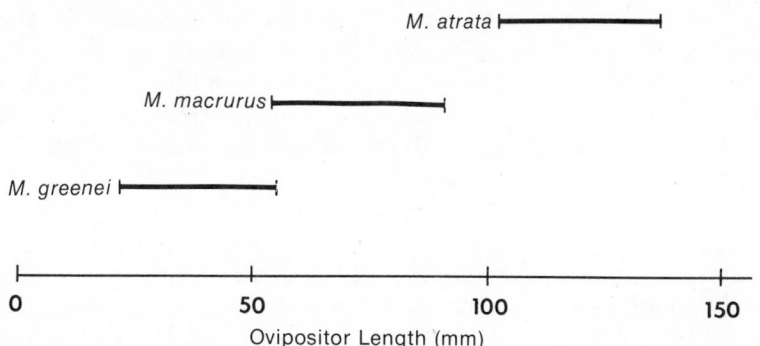

Figure 9–27. Comparative lengths of ovipositors among three sympatric *Megarhyssa* (Ichneumonidae) species. (Modified from Heatwole, H., and D. M. Davis, 1965. Ecology of three sympatric species of parasitic insects of the genus *Megarhyssa* (Hymenoptera: Ichneumonidae). Ecology *46*:140–150.)

DOMINANCE AND DIVERSITY

Besides trophic structure and its attendant coevolutionary interactions between species, communities are characterized by dominance and diversity. Ecological dominance occurs when one or several species have major influence on distribution and density of the remaining species in a community. This may result from dominant species' numbers, size, or strategic position in food webs. Dominance reflects the observation that in most communities, one finds relatively few common species and rather a lot of rare ones. For one and one-half years, I collected moths nightly at an ultraviolet light, and of 164 species collected, I found more than 200 individuals of only 12 species and less than 10 individuals each of the 80 rarest species (Table 9–4). Some of the more common species were well-known pests and are dominant in some agricultural ecosystems.

Organisms need not be common to be dominant. Paine (1966) demonstrated that relatively uncommon starfish, carnivores at the top of the trophic pyramid, were a major determinant of community diversity in tide pools. When he removed starfish, the mussel population increased dramatically, crowding out other species. Such experimental studies on the role of insect dominance in communities have yet to be done, though Fager (1968), in a study of decaying oak logs, noted that 46 of 108 invertebrate species were dominant at least once and that a dominant species in one log could be absent in adjacent logs. Fager proposed that

Table 9–4. FREQUENCY DISTRIBUTION OF MOTH SPECIES COLLECTED IN BLACKLIGHT TRAP, HAYWARD, CALIFORNIA, 1971–1972

Number of Individuals Collected	Number of Species
1–10	80
11–20	20
21–30	16
31–40	6
41–50	8
51–100	14
101–150	7
150–200	6
200 or more	12

dominance in decaying logs was largely a question of which species arrived first. Whatever their individual dominance, insects as a class are dominant in most terrestrial and aquatic ecosystems by virtue of their sheer abundance and diversity; 147 insect species inhabit a single fungus, *Fomes,* (Matthewman and Pielou 1971), while Evans and Murdoch (1968) found 1584 species in sweep-net samples from abandoned pastures in Michigan.

Related to dominance is **species diversity,** a measure of the number of species and their relative abundance in a community. There are several ways to measure diversity (reviewed by Hurlbert, 1971), all of which take species number and individual abundance into account and are therefore dependent on adequate sampling methods. The greater the number of species, the higher the species diversity in a community.

Much has been made of a supposed relationship between diversity and stability. Presumably, in the most diverse and complex communities, there is a general absence of major fluctuations in population densities, whereas in simpler, less diverse systems, population densities fluctuate between greater extremes (Pimentel, 1961). Certainly, more insect pest problems occur in monocultures (large plantings of a single crop variety) than in mixed plantings involving several plant species. Root (1973) planted collards in several fields, partly in pure stands and partly in rows surrounded by diverse old-field vegetation (Fig. 9–28). He then, over three growing seasons, "bagged" and counted all insects on sample collards in both areas. He found that herbivores, particularly herbivores specific to Cruciferae, attained higher population densities in the pure collard stands than in the mixed plantings, despite predators' being more diverse in the pure stands. Root suggested a **resource concentration hypothesis:** herbivores are more likely to find and remain on hosts in dense or nearly pure stands, leading to higher relative densities of herbivores in "simpler" (monoculture) environments.

Seeming to contradict the diversity-stability hypothesis is the fact that populations of many forest insects, particularly defoliating caterpillars, have notoriously unstable, cyclic populations despite their occurrence in diverse ecosystems. The fall webworm, tent caterpillar, forest tent caterpillar, spruce budworm, and gypsy moth each is host to a diverse array of over 50 parasitoid species, yet populations of each periodically increase spectacularly and defoliate many square miles of forest. Loucks (1970) suggested that such outbreaks are a normal part of forest ecosystem dynamics and that forests, allegedly "stable," are in fact cyclic, unstable systems. Southwood and Way (1970) suggested that each ecological system is unique and therefore a generalization such as "diversity leads to stability" is not likely to hold true in all, or even most, cases. May (1974) demonstrated mathematically that models describing community interactions actually become less stable as complexity is added. There may indeed be a relationship between diversity and stability in some ecological communities, but nobody has proved that diversity causes stability (Van Emden and Williams, 1974).

DIVERSITY PATTERNS; SUCCESSION

Succession is a more or less orderly sequence of replacement of communities by other communities over time. In most of the eastern United States, when ground is bared and then left undisturbed, succession commences with annual plants, grasses, and forbs coming in first. Shrubs soon follow, and then, after several years, come sun-tolerant trees: cherry, birch, and pine. Eventually, a

Figure 9-28. Root's garden. Collards planted in solid planting, center, and perimeter row in abandoned field. (Food web shown in Figure 9-2 concerns this collard patch.) (Redrawn from Root, R. B. 1973. Organization of a plant-arthropod association in simple and diverse habitats: The fauna of collards (*Brassica oleracea*). Ecol. Monogr. *43*:95–124.)

climax forest usually occurs, with shade-tolerant species predominating. (There is great local variation in succession, however, as Krebs [1972], Odum [1972], and Price [1975] point out.) Succession of insects closely follows that of plants: tiger beetles (or bare ground) give way to grasshoppers, while Cerambycidae, wood borers, are not likely to be abundant until later stages in succession. Plant species diversity often increases toward the middle stages of succession, and insect species diversity is correlated with plant species diversity, at least in abandoned fields in Michigan (Murdoch et al., 1972). Succession can and does occur on a very small scale: Mohr (1943) observed insect succession in cow dung in Illinois pastures (Fig. 9-29). A series of flies arrive in sequence and oviposit. Their larvae feed as

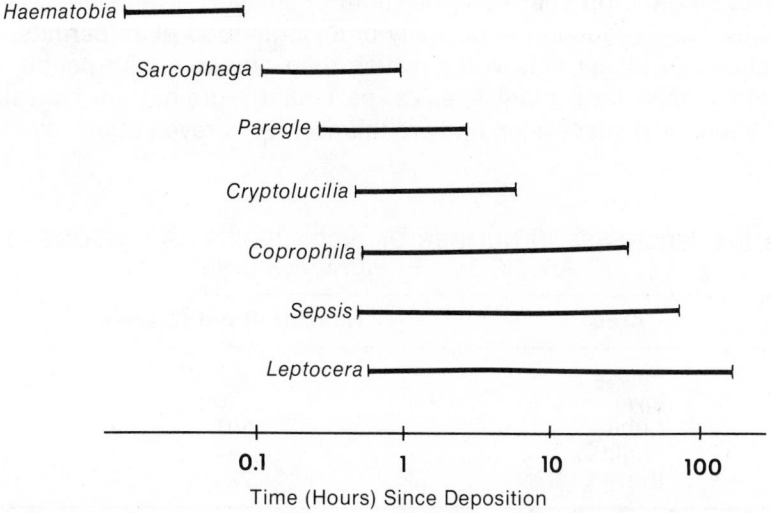

Figure 9-29. Succession of adult flies feeding and ovipositing on fresh cow dung. (From Mohr, C. O. 1943. Cattle droppings as ecological units. *13*:275–298.)

the dung dries out, even as predatory beetles and parasitic wasps arrive to feed on fly larvae. As the dung dries further, more arthropod species are attracted, but after about a month, the dung is too dry for insects and succession ends.

GEOGRAPHICAL DIVERSITY PATTERNS

Tropical ecosystems are unquestionably more diverse than those of temperate or arctic areas, regardless of what group of animals is considered. Insects, in particular, reach a diversity in the tropics that consistently amazes and befuddles investigators from temperate areas (Table 9–5). Current explanations for this observed geographical diversity gradient are less than satisfying. Among the more popular hypotheses are: (1) that long-term climatic stability in the tropics has permitted evolution of more specialized, inflexible species (Sanders, 1968); (2) that increased tropical plant diversity and intense selection by herbivores have led to many specific insect-plant associations (Ehrlich and Raven, 1967); and (3) that severe interspecific competition in the absence of harsh physical conditions has led to successively narrower niches, permitting coexistence of more species (Dobzhansky, 1950). These hypotheses, and others, are reviewed by Price (1975). As questionable as the foregoing hypotheses is whether tropical ecosystems are really that much more stable than those of temperate climates. Careful, long-term studies documenting relative stability in tropical ecosystems remain to be done.

NATURAL AND ARTIFICIAL COMMUNITIES

Homo sapiens is a most dominant organism, altering natural communities for economic or aesthetic reasons. Our ecological alterations, which have been the subject of many recent and long-overdue treatises, have several broad effects that particularly concern entomologists. The most important of these are:

1. Modern agriculture is most efficient (usually) when crops are grown in large plantings of single crop species rather than in smaller, diversified systems. This concentration and reduction in diversity of a single food plant permits increases of populations of insect herbivores, which then compete with people for food. Furthermore, many crop plant species, particularly grains, are typical of early stages in ecological succession and are themselves "preyed upon" by insect her-

Table 9–5. INCREASE IN NUMBER OF ANT SPECIES AS ONE GOES FROM ARCTIC TO TROPICAL REGIONS*

Area	Number of Ant Species
Alaska	7
Iowa	73
Cuba	101
Trinidad	134
Brazil	222

*Data from Fischer, A. G. 1960. Latitudinal variations in organic diversity. Evolution *14*: 64–81.

bivores typical of early succession: grasshoppers, cutworms, and the like. Many of these pests are monstrously efficient at dispersal, growth, and reproduction, further exacerbating the problem.

2. From natural, coevolved communities, we have removed certain crop and ornamental plants (and animals) and transported them to new locations and artificial communities wherein a new host of selective pressures are assembled. The crops may not withstand the onslaught of totally alien herbivores. Alternatively, herbivorous insects may be accidentally carried to a new location where, in the absence of significant natural controls, populations may increase to abnormal densities (see Chapter Ten). In breeding plants for higher yields, we may unwittingly breed out resistance to insect attack.

3. To control imbalances generated by the first and second factors, we often resort to chemical treatments that further reduce diversity. Moreover, some of these, like DDT, are long lasting and are transferred through some natural food chains to become concentrated in certain "top carnivores" like eagles, pelicans, and predatory fish. Paine (1966) suggested that predators maintain diversity in ecosystems generally. If this is so, we may expect further reduction in diversity, and perhaps stability, in ecosystems after reduction or elimination of predators.

SUMMARY

Insect populations exist together with those of other animals and plants in **communities**. Communities are characterized by **trophic** (feeding) relationships among green plants, herbivores, carnivores, and decomposers. These interspecific interactions are broadly divisible into four kinds: commensalism, mutualism, parasitism, and competition. **Commensalism** is advantageous to one organism and has no effect on the other. **Mutualism** is advantageous to both species involved. **Parasitism** is advantageous to one species and deleterious to another, while interspecific **competition** is mutually deleterious. This chapter discusses examples of each type of interaction and some of the evolutionary consequences for insect populations.

Communities are also characterized by **dominance** and **diversity** patterns; these vary both regionally and temporarily. Human influences on dominance and diversity relationships have important consequences for insect pest management.

Part Three

Insects and Human Affairs

Chapter Ten

Pest Management

INTRODUCTION

The vast majority of insect species are not detrimental to the interests of humanity but rather are beneficial in maintaining energy flow in natural communities. However, a few thousand species are considered pests because they interfere with comfort, health, convenience, or profits. How these insects become pests and how they can be controlled are concerns of economic entomology, or **pest management.**

Pest management is "reduction of pest problems by actions selected after the life systems of the pests are understood and the ecologic as well as economic consequences of these actions have been predicted, as accurately as possible, to the best interests of mankind" (Rabb and Guthrie, 1970), and that is what this chapter is about.

Economic entomology in a broad sense also includes beneficial insects, which are discussed in Chapter Twelve. The relationships between insects and disease organisms will be explored in Chapter Eleven.

HOW INSECTS BECOME PESTS

The density of an insect population (or that of any other organism) is determined by the life system of that population (Chapter Eight). Figure 10–1A depicts this density limitation, where K is the carrying capacity, or maximum possible density. Variation in K reflects the variability of most insect populations, whose numbers are not constant for long.

For all pest insects there exists another level E (Fig. 10–1B), the **economic injury level.** This is determined by economic, psychological, or political factors. When insect density (N) exceeds the economic injury level (E), the insect is a pest. The basis for all insect control or management strategies is to alter the relationship so that N is less than E, and this usually is done by reducing N rather than raising E. Ideally, controls are applied when the insect population density reaches an economic **threshold,** T, (Fig. 10–1B), a level lower than the economic injury level.

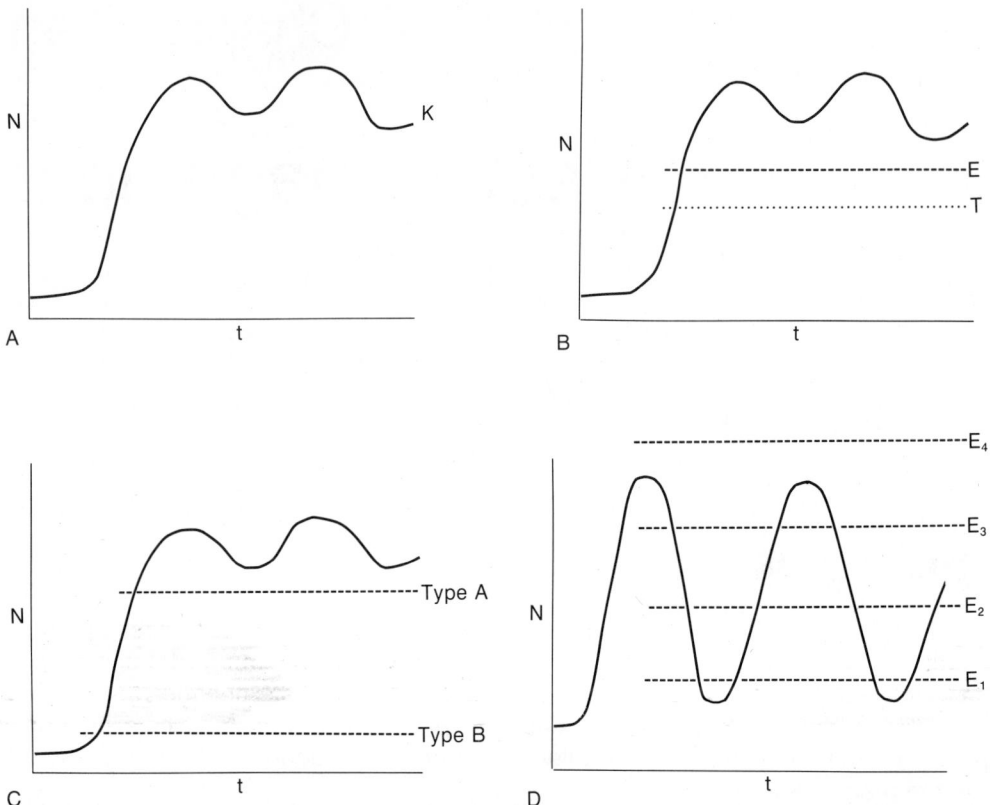

Figure 10–1. Economic injury levels. *A*, Population growth curve. *B*, Same, with economic injury level, *E*, and economic threshold, T (see text). *C*, Economic injury levels for Type A and Type B pest situations. *D*, Complex of economic injury levels for insect with fluctuating population density (see text for explanation).

There is great variation in economic injury levels and thresholds for even a single commodity. A grower of "organic" apples may not mind if up to 30 per cent of his crop have worms, whereas a commercial grower of fresh produce for supermarkets might be intolerant of a rate of more than 2 to 4 per cent. Generally, there are two extremes of economic injury levels (Fig. 10–1*C*). "Type A" (Subcommittee on Insect Pests, 1969) is typical of many low value-per-acre field crops and forests, where light-to-moderate insect infestations may be tolerated. It matters not whether forest trees lose 5 per cent or 10 per cent of their leaves to caterpillars—tree survival and lumber yield are unaffected (Kulman, 1971). Likewise, it is unprofitable to apply insecticide for control of alfalfa weevils when fewer than 50 per cent of plant tips show injury (Cothran and Summers, 1974).

In contrast is the "Type B" injury level (Fig. 10–1*C*), in which little or no damage is tolerated and the presence of even one insect (or insect fragment) may cause economic loss to a producer. In the United States, this is true of most fruits and vegetables, greenhouse flowers, and nursery stock transported in interstate commerce (Pfadt, 1971). These low injury-level pest situations require that insect population densities be artificially maintained at levels far lower than densities determined by the life systems of the species involved. Normally, an insecticide is necessary to control a Type B pest. Type A situations are more amenable to management by a wider variety of methods, including biological, physical, and cultural controls.

Obviously, the key to successful insect pest management is an accurate estimation of the economic injury level, together with a thorough understanding of the co-determinants of abundance (Chapter Nine) that determine insect numbers. Unfortunately, these are well understood for only a very few insect pests because both insect life systems and human economic systems are exceedingly complex and changeable. Figure 10–1D illustrates some of the difficulties involved in determining these factors for a cyclic forest defoliator such as the gypsy moth. In undisturbed forests, gypsy moth numbers fluctuate over periods of 10 to 20 years. There may be several years of comparative rarity, followed by spectacular outbreaks during which many square miles of forests are totally defoliated and hordes of starving caterpillars chew paint off buildings. The causes of such outbreaks are unclear; the gypsy moth life system is not well understood (Leonard, 1974). As caterpillar numbers vary greatly, so does the economic threshold. For instance, a campground owner loses customers at rather low caterpillar densities (E_1, Fig. 10–1D), as soon as large, hairy caterpillars or their excrement appears on tops of picnic tables. A lumber company tolerates higher infestations up to the point (E_2) at which defoliation reduces wood deposition and future timber yield. A municipality that has wooded watersheds above its reservoir may well tolerate even greater infestations (E_3), for until trees are actually killed, water runoff will not change appreciably, and insecticides must be used selectively and carefully. Finally, there are wilderness areas into which people do not go, and thus there is an injury level (E_4) that the pest population never reaches. Economic injury levels for gypsy moths therefore depend on who you are and where you are. Headley (1972) details further complexities in estimating economic injury levels.

Because density is determined by the life system of a population, a change in any co-determinant of abundance potentially can result in insect numbers increasing above the economic injury level. In particular, there are three changes that are involved in generating a pest situation.

Entry Into Previously Uninhabited Regions. Many insect species have been transported from their natural "homeland" to a new location. There they may find conditions favorable to population increase, including an abundance of food and an absence of predation and disease, which remain behind in their homeland (Elton, 1958). The Japanese beetle (Fig. 10–2A), European corn borer, cabbage butterfly, gypsy moth, and a host of others have been introduced from Europe or the Orient to North America, where they have reached much higher population densities than in their respective homelands, where many are not considered pests. Such dispersal goes in both directions: North America has given the Colorado potato beetle to Europe and the fall webworm to Europe and Japan.

Changes in an Insect's Biology. The Colorado potato beetle (Fig. 10–2B) was originally limited to the southern Rocky Mountains, where it fed on wild Solanaceae (potato relatives) until the cultivated potato was brought to Colorado in the late nineteenth century. Soon thereafter, the potato beetle included the cultivated potato in its diet and subsequently spread across North America and thence to Europe (Elton, 1958). Bush (1969) suggests a similar history for the apple maggot, *Rhagoletis pomonella,* whose ancestors apparently fed on wild hawthorns until apples were introduced into colonial New York; only then did

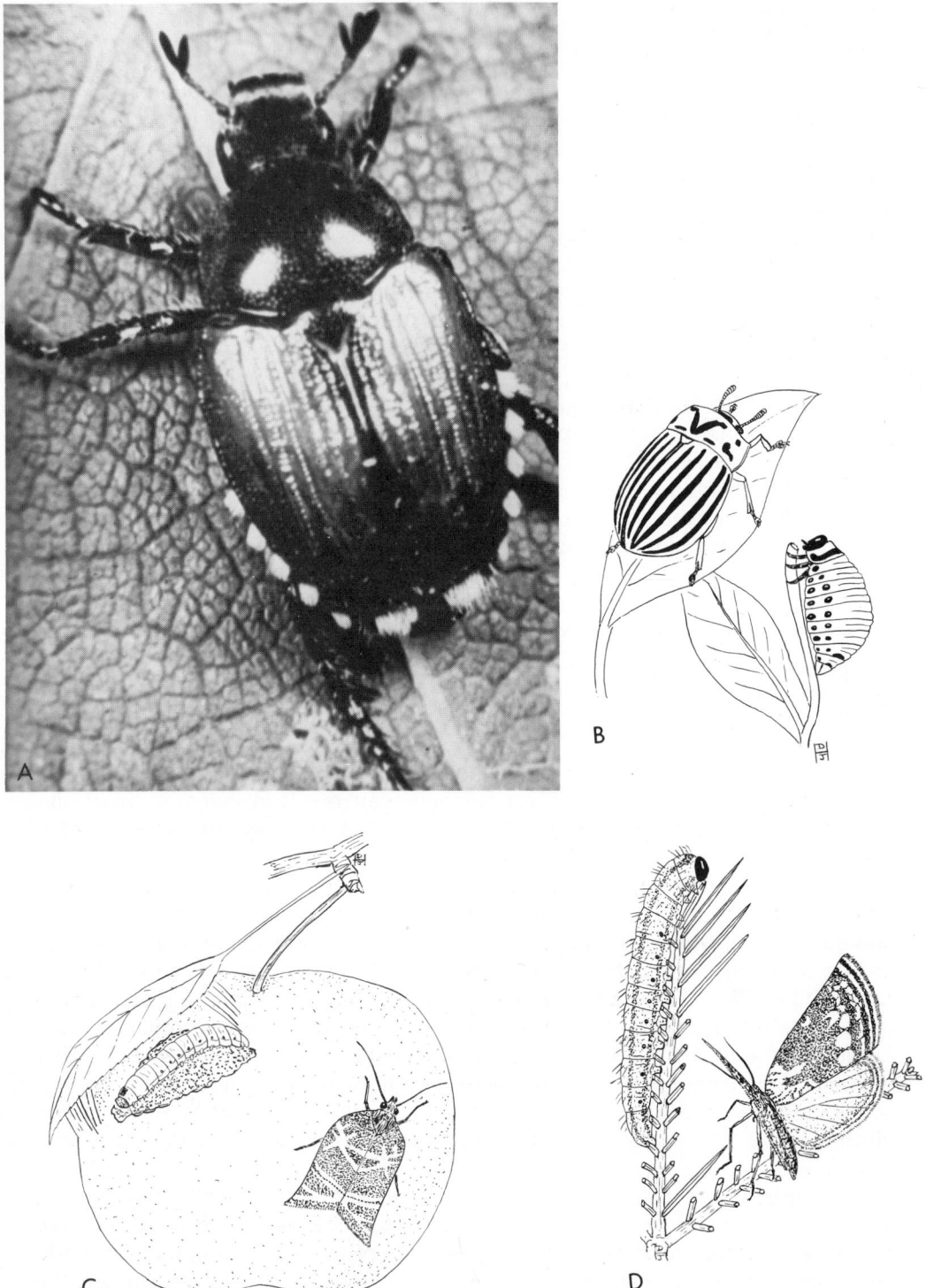

Figure 10–2.   Some insect pests. *A*, Japanese beetle. (USDA photo.) *B*, Colorado potato beetle. *C*, Red-banded leafroller. *D*, Spruce budworm.

apple maggots commence feeding on apples. More recently, other *Rhagoletis* species have switched from wild to cultivated cherry and walnut.

Extensive Monocultures of Crop Plants. Increased mechanization of agriculture demands large acreages planted to single crop species, rather than small diversified plots. This concentration of resources and reduction in plant diversity leads to proliferation of herbivorous insects (Chapter Nine). Insecticide treatments sometimes reduce diversity and indirectly cause a pest outbreak. Before the days of DDT, red-banded leafrollers (Fig. 10–2C) and European red mites in apple orchards were controlled by a variety of parasitic and predaceous arthropods. Use of DDT* and, later, other synthetic organic insecticides, killed these predators; populations of leafrollers and mites then increased to damaging levels (Harman, 1948).

A final way in which insects become pests is by downward adjustment of the economic injury level due to changes in people's activities and expectations. The spruce budworm (Fig. 10–2D) is becoming more important as a pest because of increased demand for pulpwood from coniferous forests of Canada, Maine, and Minnesota (Morris, 1963). Many North Americans now demand food that is nearly insect free and will not settle for less. It was not always so; prior to the introduction of synthetic organic insecticides (about 1947), an 80 per cent reduction in codling moth infestation was the best apple growers could do, and the apple-eating public was satisfied if only one apple of five was wormy. Then DDT and, later, other chemicals enabled growers to produce apples up to 99 per cent free of codling moth larvae. Concomitantly, consumer expectations increased, effectively lowering the economic injury level to its present 1 per cent for apples sold as fresh fruit.

KINDS OF DAMAGE

Insect pests attack practically every commodity of plant or animal origin used by human beings, and some attack people directly as well. Insects also affect mankind in a variety of indirect ways. To adequately catalogue the variety among insect pests requires a separate book; good compilations are those of Davidson and Peairs (1966), Metcalf et al. (1962), Pfadt (1971), Westcott (1973) and Metcalf and Luckmann (1975), which contain descriptions, life histories, and illustrations of major North American insect pests.

Insects may cause direct damage by feeding on something in which people are interested. A host of mandibulate insects, particularly Orthoptera and larval Lepidoptera and Coleoptera, eat crop plants in the field. Others (especially some Coleoptera and Lepidoptera) attack food in storage and transit. Caterpillars, bark beetles, and borers attack standing trees, while termites, carpenter ants, and powder-post beetles sometimes reduce wooden structures to sawdust.

Insects may also cause indirect damage. Tomato hornworms, apple mites, and Colorado potato beetles eat the leaves of their respective host plants, indirectly reducing yields of tomatoes, apples, and potatoes. More unusual is the damage done by some Orthoptera and Homoptera whose females oviposit in twigs (Fig. 10–3). Severe infestations of such insects (e.g., the periodical cicada) may weaken fruit-laden twigs in orchards, with resulting breakage, lowered yield,

---

*Mention in this book of this or any other insecticide for a specific use *does not in any way* constitute endorsement or recommendation of the insecticide.

Figure 10–3.   Scarring of apple twig from oviposition by tree cricket.

and possible entry of disease into broken twig ends. Many insects, particularly ectoparasites with piercing-sucking mouthparts, are severe problems not because of the fluid they remove but because of the diseases they transmit to plants, livestock, and humans. Disease, in a broad sense, includes both specific reactions of hosts to attack and the introduction of a pathogenic microorganism (discussed in detail in Chapter Eleven). Insects themselves are a form of indirect damage when they or their fragments occur as contamination in foods.

Finally, there are "psychological pests"—insects that do no real damage on their own but whose mere presence is disturbing. A huge beetle that blunders into an outdoor cocktail party is in this category. Many people consider all insects merely as "bugs" to be destroyed as quickly as possible. Extreme fear of insects, **entomophobia,** may lead to delusions of attack by nonexistent insects (Pomerantz, 1959).

CONTROL TECHNIQUES

An array of chemical, biological, cultural, and physical control techniques exists to reduce pest numbers below economic injury levels. For the last few decades, synthetic chemicals have been the backbone of most insect control programs. Though this will continue, researchers are devoting increased attention to integrating a variety of control measures into each pest situation (Metcalf and Luckmann, 1975).

CHEMICAL CONTROL

Synthetic organic insecticides have been widely used in North America and other parts of the world to control infestations of insect pests. Insecticides are particularly suited to Type B (see Fig. 10–1C) pest situations in which a very large proportion of the pest population is killed. Synthetic insecticides have several advantages over other control methods: they kill rather quickly, they may be reapplied as needed, their purchase price and cost of application are moderate, and they usually reduce pest numbers to exceedingly low densities. Unfortunately, they also have a number of potentially very serious disadvantages.

Kenaga and End (1974) list 254 commercial and experimental insecticides in use today in the United States. New ones are added annually, and sometimes, after great debate, some are removed from the market. Early schemes of insecticide classification recognized **stomach** and **contact** poisons as discrete groupings. Stomach poisons must be ingested before they can take effect, while contact poisons are absorbed through the external cuticle and epidermis. More recently, insecticides have been categorized by chemical structure, and this approach will be followed here. O'Brien (1967) and Kenaga and End (1974) cover insecticide characteristics in detail.

Inorganic insecticides formed the basis of most chemical control until World War II. Most compounds containing arsenic, fluoride, mercury, sulfur, thallium, and copper have been replaced by newer, less persistent organic compounds. Some inorganic insecticides, for example, lead arsenate, are extremely persistent in soils of ecosystems to which they have been applied. Residues of lead arsenate in a few Ohio apple orchards have prevented normal growth of new stock. **Organic insecticides** are the mainstay of most chemical control programs and are sufficiently diverse to warrant separate consideration here of botanicals, organochlorines, organophosphates, and carbamates.

Botanical insecticides are compounds that have evolved in plants, apparently to ward off insect attack. The compounds are extracted from commercially grown plants: nicotine from tobacco, pyrethrum from a chrysanthemum species, and rotenone from derris root. Of these, pyrethrins (chemical components of pyrethrum) are the most widely used, particularly in household aerosol sprays. Piperonyl butoxide is often added to enhance the effect of pyrethrins. This enhancement of one chemical by another is **synergism**; piperonyl butoxide is a synergist. Pyrethrum kills by interrupting nerve impulse transmission along axons (O'Brien, 1967), often with great speed. This is an additional selling point for household insecticides when a person wants an insect dead fast. When taken orally, pyrethrum is not very toxic to mammals, and it breaks down quickly on exposure to air and sunlight, making it a useful but expensive household insecticide. The other botanicals are not so widely used. Recently, several manufacturers have developed synthetic pyrethrins, which are currently being tested for eventual commercial use.

Organochlorine, or **chlorinated hydrocarbon,** insecticides include a variety of chlorine-containing compounds, the most famous (or notorious) of which is DDT. Other commonly used chlorinated hydrocarbons are aldrin, chlordane, dieldrin, heptachlor, lindane, and methoxychlor. All are contact and stomach poisons that, when absorbed through the integument, interfere with the nervous system. Most organochlorines are very stable, long-lasting compounds; traces of them may be detectable in soils more than 10 years after use (Menzie, 1972). They are soluble in fats and are stored in bodies of animals to be passed along food chains, occasionally with serious physiological effects on carnivores. Recent concern over unknown side effects of chlorinated hydrocarbon residues has led to restrictions in domestic use of several insecticides especially DDT, aldrin, chlordane, and heptachlor. Methoxychlor is less toxic than the others (see Table 10–1) and does not leave such lasting residues. Long-residual insecticides are very useful, however, in controlling structural pests, such as termites and powder-post beetles.

Organophosphorus compounds are nerve poisons that inhibit activity of cholinesterase at nerve synapses (Chapter Five) in mammals, at least. The mode of poisoning is probably similar in insects. Organophosphates include parathion, diazinon, malathion, and a host of less often used insecticides.

Some compounds (e. g., parathion and TEPP) are exceedingly toxic to mammals (Table 10–1), and spilling a few drops of concentrate on your skin may result in a trip to the hospital — or the morgue. Other compounds (e.g., malathion) are only slightly toxic and are rather safe to use. None has the long-term residual effect of organochlorines, nor are organophosphates stored in fats or concentrated in food chains in appreciable amounts. However, some (e.g., demeton and phorate) are systemic poisons, which are absorbed into living plants or livestock, thereby rendering the sap or blood poisonous to those insects who would feed on it. Finally, some organophosphates disperse as fumigants in air. Dichlorvos is one that is impregnated in a wax strip to be hung in a closed area; the insecticide is released slowly as a vapor.

Carbamate insecticides are also nerve poisons; the most widely used is carbaryl. Although carbaryl is rather harmless to humans, it is very toxic to a huge array of insects, including, unfortunately, honey bees and parasitic Hymenoptera. Like pyrethrum, carbaryl breaks down to harmless residues very quickly, so it is useful for food crops that must be treated close to harvest time. There are other, less broadly applied carbamates, including a few, like aldicarb, that are extremely hazardous to people and must be applied with great care.

Oils clog insects' spiracles and thereby cut off oxygen; several types are used as insecticides. Oils are particularly helpful in controlling aphids, mites, and scale insects on fruit trees or woody ornamentals in early spring just as buds are breaking. Later on, oils cannot be applied because of potential damage to the plants (phytotoxicity). No cases of insect resistance to oils have as yet been discovered.

Fumigants are useful insecticides in enclosed spaces, particularly grain elevators, mills, and greenhouses. They are gases that enter the insect through the spiracles and tracheae. Hydrogen cyanide and methyl bromide are commonly applied commercially; both are extremely hazardous to people and are best handled by professional exterminators. Paradichlorobenzene and naphthalene exist as crystals that slowly release gases that repel and are mildly toxic to clothes moths and carpet beetles. Chances are that you store your winter clothes with moth flakes or mothballs concocted from one of these compounds.

Finally, the arsenal includes **biological insecticides,** bacterial spores or virus particles formulated for application as sprays or dusts. These are, of course, not organic chemicals, but they are subject to the same testing procedures and legal restrictions as chemical poisons. *Bacillus thuringiensis* causes a bacterial disease of larval Lepidoptera (and a few flies and earthworms). It is particularly useful when parasitoids or predators are to be conserved or when vegetables are nearing harvest and an appropriate chemical might leave illegal residues. Also available is *Bacillus popillae,* which causes a disease specific to Japanese beetle larvae and other Scarabaeidae. Recently, a nuclear polyhedrosis virus (NPV) of *Heliothis* larvae has been registered for application to cotton bollworm (*Heliothis zea*) infestations. Much effort is currently being directed to development of specific microbial insecticides.

Insecticides are seldom used in pure concentrated form, though recent technical advances have made low-volume, high-concentration application equipment more readily available, especially to tree fruit producers and those involved in aerial application. Most insecticides are sold mixed with an inert substance and are formulated for dry application as dusts and granules or for wet application as emulsifiable concentrates, wettable powders, or aerosols. The concentrate as formulated is usually further diluted with an inert (nontoxic) carrier: fine clay particles for dusts, coarser vermiculite or ground peanut shells for granules, and (usually) water for liquid formulations. Which to use depends on the pest situation and available application equipment. Fronk (1971) discusses application equipment in more detail, and Figure 10–4 illustrates a range of commonly used devices.

Figure 10–4. Insecticide application equipment. *A,* Speed sprayer for applying liquid insecticide to fruit trees. (Photo courtesy of F. E. Myers & Bros. Co.) *B,* Power duster for applying dusts to tree crops. (Photo courtesy of John Bean Division, FMC Corp.) *C,* Granule applicator for applying granular insecticide to row crops at planting time; it attaches to tractor. (Photo courtesy of Noble Division, Royal Industries.) *D,* Hand applicator for small amounts of insecticide, suitable for home use.

Insecticide Development and Use

Insecticide manufacturers are subject to the provisions of the Federal Insecticide, Fungicide, and Rodenticide Act (revised 1972), which stipulates that rather exhaustive testing must be done before the product may be registered, or labelled, for public sale and use. The Subcommittee on Insect Pests (1969) gives a detailed discussion of registration procedures; generally, these include formulation and toxicity studies, field tests, and long-term tests.

Formulation studies include synthesizing a "candidate" insecticide, screening it for activity (does it kill insects?), and testing its chemical characteristics, particularly stability (does it break down too quickly?), wettability (will it gum up the sprayer?) and ease and convenience of handling. The candidate insecticide is then subjected to **toxicity** studies on a variety of laboratory animals. Small populations of houseflies, cockroaches, fish, rats, and rabbits are each exposed to a different concentration of the chemical either in feed (oral) or as a surface application (dermal). Low doses have little or no effect, whereas high doses kill most or all of the test animals. Between these extremes lies a point at which about 50 per cent of a test population is killed; this is the "lethal dose for 50 per cent mortality," or $L.D._{50}$. Rarely will precisely 50 per cent of test animals be killed, but $L.D._{50}$ is calculated by appropriate statistical methods. $L.D._{50}$ is an indication of the toxicity of a chemical to vertebrates and insects; the lower the $L.D._{50}$, the more toxic the insecticide. An "ideal" insecticide thus has a high mammalian $L.D._{50}$. Table 10–1 lists oral and dermal toxicities of some common insecticides.

The next step in insecticide development is field testing by both the manufacturer and governmental agencies, especially the United States Department of Agriculture (USDA) and state agricultural experiment stations. Here, the compound is applied to naturally occurring pest populations in field plots. Its efficacy (proportion of pests killed) is evaluated in relation to untreated control plots and (when possible) to currently recommended chemicals in as many geographic locations, soil types, and crop varieties as practicable. Several concentrations are applied, and experimenters carefully note any evidence of phytotoxicity or animal injury (if the compound is being considered for livestock insect pest control). Small samples of crop, soil, and water runoff are also periodically collected from the test plots for detection of residual amounts of insecticide. This indicates the disappearance rate of a compound under field conditions. If a chemical is applied to a livestock feed such as alfalfa, residue samples are also taken from meat, milk, or eggs of animals that have eaten treated feed.

Finally, ongoing feeding trials commence in which sublethal amounts of insecticide are fed to laboratory mammals (rats and dogs, usually) over at least three generations. Any unusual effects are noted, particularly any increase in incidence of cancers (carcinogenicity) or birth defects (teratogenicity) in treated populations.

Detailed data from all these studies are submitted to the federal Environmental Protection Agency (EPA) as part of an application for registration in accordance with the 1972 law. EPA may (or may not) approve the insecticide; only after being approved can it be labelled for sale to and use by the public. The label as approved by EPA stipulates the precise uses for the chemical, and it can be applied legally only for those uses. If it is labelled only for cutworms on cabbages, one should not spray it on bean-infesting aphids, or even on cabbage

Table 10-1. CLASSIFICATION AND TOXICITY OF SELECTED INSECTICIDES*

| Category | Chemical | L.D.$_{50}$† (mg./kg. in lab rats) | |
		ORAL	DERMAL
Inorganic	lead arsenate	1050	>2400
Botanical	nicotine sulfate	83	285
	pyrethrum	820	2060
	rotenone	50–75	>940
Chlorinated hydrocarbon	aldrin	60	98
	chlordane	430	690
	dieldrin	46	60
	DDT	118	2150
	heptachlor	162	250
	lindane	91	900
	methoxychlor	5000	>6000
Organophosphorus	diazinon	76	455
	malathion	1000	4444
	parathion (ethyl)	3.6	6.8
	systox	6	14
	TEPP	1.05	2.4
Carbamate	aldicarb	1	5
	carbaryl	500	>4000
	carbofuran	5	885
Social drugs	aspirin	1000–2000	—
	caffeine	100–500	—
	ethanol	5000–13000	—
	nicotine (sulfate)	83	285

*From Subcommittee on Insect Pests. 1969. Insect-pest management and control. Principles of plant and animal pest management. Vol. 3. Nat. Acad. Sci., Washington, D.C.
†L.D.$_{50}$ is the lethal dose for 50 per cent mortality; i.e., the dose at which 50 per cent of the laboratory animals are killed.

aphids. After a careful study of toxicity and residue data, the EPA sets **tolerance** limits (the maximum legal amount of residue allowable on or in a commodity) and waiting periods (the length of time necessary between application of insecticide and harvest to ensure that tolerance limits are not exceeded). The EPA also stipulates that appropriate warnings must be on the label, particularly for the more highly toxic insecticides.

The latest information on what insecticides are labelled for particular uses is best obtained through state agricultural extension offices. Extension entomology specialists usually publish booklets containing recommendations for insect problems in their state. Their recommendations are based on knowledge of available, labelled insecticides plus local entomological research that may indicate which of several labelled insecticides may be best for local use. If you have an insect pest problem, that is the place to go.

Problems of Insecticide Use

Chemical insecticides are by far the most widely used insect control method, and this widespread use is a major factor in growing high-quality, pest-free produce. Insecticides are not without several disadvantages, however, some of which are potentially very serious and are stimulating further research on alternative control methods. These disadvantages are: hazard to nontarget organisms, resistance, and development of secondary pest outbreaks. In these days of oil shortage, cost of application may also become a disadvantage to insecticide use.

Acute hazard exists, especially for the insecticide applicator and his immediate associates but also for anyone who is in contact with the concentrated chemical. In the United States, perhaps fewer than 100 people are killed annually by insecticides (Subcommittee on Insect Pests, 1969); many are children under five years old who drink the poison, often from an unlabelled temporary container. Almost all insecticide accidents are avoidable if one reads the label and follows the directions. Wildlife, fish, and livestock may be inadvertently affected by insecticide drift, a particular problem on windy days.

Chronic hazard is more insidious because a real danger is often very difficult to prove experimentally. The effects of tiny residual amounts of long-lasting insecticides like DDT in the environment and in human tissues are therefore not well understood. It is now well documented that **biological magnification** of chlorinated hydrocarbon insecticides occurs in natural food chains (Table 10–2), owing to concentration of these chemicals in fatty tissues. These high amounts of insecticides alter eggshell synthesis and embryonic development in eagles, peregrine falcons, pelicans, and perhaps other carnivorous birds (Cope, 1971). Recent precipitous declines in populations of these birds are at least partially due to chronic insecticide poisoning.

Evidence of direct chronic danger to humans is lacking so far. Some chlorinated hydrocarbons cause cancer when fed in large concentrations to laboratory mice, but there is no proof yet that existing low levels of DDT and other insecticides in human tissues are detrimental (Quinby et al., 1965; W.H.O., 1971). Apparently a balance occurs between absorption and excretion, and excess amounts are eliminated. The public alarm raised over insecticide residues (Carson, 1962; Graham, 1970) is partially justified, however, and we should guard against indiscriminate use of long-lasting chemicals until we are more certain of the chronic effects from exposure to low levels.

Of graver concern, particularly to growers and entomologists, is insecticide resistance, the evolution of insect strains that resist insecticides (Chapter Two). Insecticide resistance may be physiological (when an insect possesses detoxifying enzymes) or behavioral. Widespread use of DDT has resulted in the evolution of hyperirritable *Anopheles* mosquitoes that avoid DDT-treated walls (Hoskins,

Table 10–2. CONCENTRATIONS OF DDT AND RELATED RESIDUES
IN FOOD CHAIN ASSOCIATED WITH LAKE MICHIGAN*

Location	Average Residue (p.p.m.)
Bottom mud	0.014
Shrimp	0.44
Small fish	4.5
Herring gulls	98.8

*From Woodwell, G. M., W. M. Malcolm, R. H. Whittaker. 1969. A-bombs, bugbombs, and us. *In* Shepherd, P., and D. McKinley (eds.). The Subversive Science—Essays Toward an Ecology of Man. Houghton Mifflin Company, Boston, pp. 230–241. Copyright © 1969 by Houghton Mifflin Company. Reprinted by permission of the publisher. Original data from Brookhaven National Laboratory Report No. 9842, 1966.

1963). Insects that resist one insecticide may at the same time develop resistance to other insecticides of the same chemical group **(class-resistance)** or to chemicals from a different chemical class **(cross-resistance).** Probably close to 300 insect pest species have some degree of resistance (Brown, 1968).

Development of secondary pests is another complication of insecticide use. When lead arsenate (a stomach poison) was the main control for codling moth on apples, both the red-banded leafroller and the European red mite were controlled by a complex of natural enemies. Introduction of DDT (a contact poison) and, later, other synthetic organic chemicals, reduced populations of predators and parasitoids of leafrollers and red mites to the point that densities of both exceeded economic injury levels, and commercial fruit growers now must contend with both these secondary pests in addition to the codling moth. Secondary pest problems have occurred on a variety of other crops following introduction of synthetic organic insecticides.

BIOLOGICAL CONTROL

Biological control, or **biocontrol,** in its narrow sense is the importation, augmentation, and manipulation of natural enemies to control insect pest populations (Clausen, 1956). More recently (DeBach, 1964; Huffaker, 1971) this definition has been enlarged to include sterilization, behavioral control, plant resistance, and other control methods that have a "biological" basis and density-dependent effect; however, I here consider biological control in its earlier, narrow sense. Importation and enhancement of natural enemies, once established, has advantages over chemical control—to wit, safety, permanence, and economy. The effects of biological control agents, predators, parasites, or pathogens, are density-dependent, however, (Chapter Eight) and therefore are best suited to Type A pest situations (see Fig. 10–1*C*) in which a small pest population may be tolerated.

Biological control most often involves release of natural enemies to control a pest that has accidentally been introduced to an area where it does not normally occur. The premise is that many insect populations are regulated by predators, parasites, and pathogens in their homeland but escape this control and establish much higher densities in their new home. Importation of appropriate natural enemies should then restore the original balance. In practice, a minority (about 20 per cent) of such attempts at biological control have been successful, and none has succeeded on an annual cultivated crop. From another standpoint, however, most insect species are not pests, and DeBach (1974) attributes this to natural biological control exerted by effective, naturally occurring predation and parasitism.

Release of exotic natural enemies has occasionally been spectacularly successful. In the early 1880's, the infant California citrus industry was threatened with premature demise through the depredations of the cottony-cushion scale, *Icerya purchasi* (Fig. 10–5), which sucks sap in great quantity and thereby reduces yield and mars appearance of oranges, grapefruit, and lemons. It was determined that the scale hailed originally from Australia, and a researcher was sent there to search for its natural enemies. He returned with an assortment of entomophagous insects, including the vedalia beetle, a small ladybird. These beetles were established on an enclosed orange tree from which they gobbled

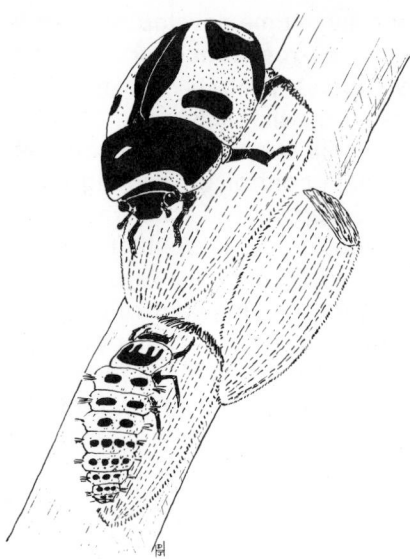

Figure 10–5. Adult and larva vedalia beetles eating cottony-cushion scales.

very nearly all the cottony-cushion scales within a few weeks. When the cage was
removed, the beetles wandered throughout the orchard, voraciously decimating
scale populations. Vedalia beetles exported to other orchards did the same, and
within a very few years, the density of cottony-cushion scales was brought below
the economic injury level.

Much biological control research has centered in California, partly spurred
on by the vedalia success and partly because of the preponderance of orchard
crops there. Beginning largely with empirical work, California researchers (e.g.,
DeBach, 1964) developed lists of favorable characteristics to be sought in
biocontrol agents. The most important indicators of success are: (1) high reproductive capacity and dispersal ability (preferably greater than those of the pest);
(2) ability to locate prey (or host) at low density; (3) synchrony with host life
cycle; (4) tolerance of range of climatic extremes in which prey survives; (5)
monophagy, or at least oligophagy, showing preference for the pest before alternate foods. Alternate food may be very important, particularly when agent and
pest numbers are not well synchronized. Force (1972) pointed out that the first
and second indicators are characteristic of r-strategists (see Tables 8–8, and
8–9), which may be the more uncommon parasitoids and predators in the native
land of a pest, where (presumably) reasonably stable relationships have coevolved. Ehler and van den Bosch (1974) showed that r-strategist parasitoids
exerted most of the biological control over populations of cabbage loopers on
cotton. More quantitative characteristics of useful biological control agents
should be sought to aid in determining which natural enemies to release.

An ongoing controversy in biological control research is whether it is best
to release a single "best" biological control agent or whether several species,
each of which attacks the pest, will effect greater control. Turnbull and Chant
(1961) and others have argued that several natural enemy species may compete for
a host, with potentially negative results in control. In Chapter Nine I cited some

examples of competition among introduced parasitoids. In most cases, however, it seems that introduction of a complex of natural enemies increases overall host mortality even though the biocontrol agents compete (Huffaker et al., 1971; DeBach, 1974). To increase the diversity of pests' natural enemies, the USDA and the (British) Commonwealth Institute of Biological Control maintain overseas laboratories whose personnel scour the neighboring countryside for promising agents of biological control. These are reared in the laboratory and, if successful, shipped to the United States, where they are reared in quarantine to make certain that no unwanted species (particularly hyperparasitoids) are included. After several generations in the laboratory, parasitoids or predators are released in insecticide-free field plots from which, if all goes well, they disperse and effect some control on their hosts.

If, as often happens, a biological control agent fails to exert significant control on a pest population, it may be possible to augment the agents' activities not only by additional release of it and other parasitoid or predator species but also by habitat alteration. Leaving weedy areas around fields or staggering cutting times for field crops (when possible) leaves cover and alternate food sources for natural enemies. Hagen and Tassan (1970) concocted a nutritious, sugary bait, "Wheast," that encouraged lacewings to remain in fields when aphids were at low densities. When aphid numbers increased, lacewings were numerous enough to prevent a severe pest outbreak. Augmenting the effects of natural enemies by such cultural practices is integrated control, to which we shall return shortly.

Vertebrate predators, particularly bats, birds, frogs, and fish, consume vast quantities of insects and are sometimes very effective natural control agents. The role of gulls in rescuing the crops of Utah pioneers from hordes of Mormon crickets is legendary. However, few vertebrates have been specifically imported as biological control agents. Notable examples have been the giant toad, *Bufo marinus,* the mosquito-fish *Gambusia,* and several other fish that have been dispersed throughout much of the tropics to control mosquitoes (James and Harwood, 1969). Biological control of insects was a partial basis for the scandalously misled introduction of starlings and house sparrows into North America (Elton, 1958).

Exotic insects have been used successfully in biological control of weeds; such beneficial insects are discussed in Chapter Twelve.

Sterilization

One of the newer "biological" control methods that shows great promise in insect control is sterilization, either by release of sterile insects into naturally occurring pest populations or by chemically sterilizing insects in natural populations through the use of baits. Insects for release are sterilized by exposing pupae to x-rays or gamma radiation. Some chemicals induce sterility in female insects and may one day prove useful in control. Both radiation and chemosterilants disrupt chromosome replication and thereby prevent the cell divisions of normal gametogenesis.

Baumhover et al. (1955) and Knipling (1955, 1960) pioneered in sterilization against the screwworm fly, *Cochliomyia hominivorax.* Screwworm fly females oviposit within open sores of livestock and the larvae feed therein, enlarging the sore and attracting more flies until fatal infestation results. The fly was thus a

Table 10–3. REPORTED CASES OF SCREWWORM INFESTATION IN LIVESTOCK OF SOUTHWESTERN UNITED STATES, 1962–1974*

Year	Cases
Before 1962	>1,000,000/year
1962	50,000
	(eradication begun in 1962)
1963	6,259
1964	237
1965	1,060
	(entire U.S.-Mexican border included)
1966	1,883
1967	872
1968	9,877
1969	219
1970	153
1971	473
1972	95,668
1973	14,976
1974	7,267

*From Cooperative Economic Insect Report. 1963–1975. USDA Animal and Plant Health Inspection Service, Washington, D.C.

major livestock pest in the southern United States, as it still is throughout much of Latin America. After years of research, USDA personnel developed procedures for mass-rearing male screwworm flies, sterilizing them with gamma radiation, and releasing them within infested areas. The sterile males are normal in all other respects, pursuing mates with libido nearly equal to that of wild flies. Female screwworms mate but once; the first male deposits within her an accessory gland secretion inhibiting further mating behavior. If he is sterile, her eggs will never hatch. Screwworm population density is rather low in nature, and thus it was (and is) possible to release from laboratory cultures a superabundance of sterile flies to quickly overwhelm the existing population. Within a few years after initial releases, screwworms were eradicated from a large portion of their former range (Table 10–3). Despite some temporary setbacks, releases of sterile male screwworm flies (1.8×10^8 weekly) continue along the United States-Mexico border, with additional releases soon to occur within Mexico.

This highly effective and specific control method has shown promise when experimentally applied on local populations of other insects, such as mosquitoes (Patterson et al., 1970), stable flies (LaBrecque et al., 1972) and melon flies (Steiner et al., 1965). Sterilization is most effective on localized populations of low density, though it could be used in conjunction with other methods that temporarily reduce high densities to levels at which sterile-male release would be practicable. Techniques for handling large numbers of sterile insects, together with new methods for sterilization, remain to be perfected for many insects potentially amenable to sterilization. For instance, radiation doses necessary to sterilize male tsetse flies (*Glossina* spp.) also render many of these same flies incapable of flight (Dame and Schmidt, 1970). Sterilization, when it works, can be an almost ideal insect control method, being very specific to a particular pest species. Sterilization is potentially capable of eradication (complete elimination of a pest), something that classical chemical and biological controls have failed to do.

BEHAVIORAL CONTROLS

A number of insect pests have been controlled by methods that affect their behavior, particularly orientation. Attractants are used to lure insects to an "untimely doom," or perhaps merely to prevent normal orientation to food and mates. Repellents are used to prevent insect attack and to keep insects away from commodities, livestock, or persons.

Among attractants, it has been known for millennia that moths and other nocturnal insects are attracted to light sources, and more recently it has been noted that ultraviolet light is most efficient in attracting many insects. Ultraviolet light is used in a variety of commercially available insect traps that kill the attracted insects by electrocution, drowning, or shredding in a fan. Such traps are useful around lighted outdoor buildings, such as ice cream stands, where night-flying insects are a problem (among other things, they fall into the ice cream). Ultraviolet light traps have recently significantly reduced numbers of hickory shuckworm (Tedders et al., 1972) and cucumber beetles (Barrett et al., 1971) in experimental plots and may therefore be of broader commercial use in the future.

Chemical attractants, particularly sex pheromones, are now receiving much attention for their potential not only in controlling insects but also in eradicating pests from local areas. Disparlure, a synthetic pheromone of the gypsy moth, is used as an attractant in sticky traps throughout the northeastern United States (Fig. 10–6); it attracts male moths at extremely low densities and thus effectively detects incipient infestations outside the quarantine area (Fig. 10–7). Disparlure also has shown promise in local control of low-density gypsy moth populations, at least in limited experiments (Beroza and Knipling, 1972). Both sex pheromones and host-plant attractants have reduced infestations of bark beetles

Figure 10–6. Gypsy moth trap. The inside is covered with sticky glue and has pheromone source.

GYPSY MOTH QUARANTINES

U. S. DEPARTMENT OF AGRICULTURE
ANIMAL AND PLANT HEALTH INSPECTION SERVICE
PLANT PROTECTION AND QUARANTINE PROGRAMS
AND CANADA DEPARTMENT OF AGRICULTURE
COOPERATING WITH AFFECTED STATES

Figure 10–7. Area of gypsy moth quarantine, 1972. (From USDA map.)

among logs in experimental plots (Rudinsky et al., 1972), and synthetic fruit oils combined with a chemical sterilant have eliminated *Dacus* fruit flies from Rota Island in the South Pacific. Pheromones can be combined with insecticide-impregnated traps or can be used as a "confusion" technique (Beroza and Knipling, 1972), being applied as a broadcast spray and thus rendering natural pheromone sources ("sexy" female moths) indistinguishable from the rest of the environment. Attractants are also useful in conjunction with other control methods in integrated control programs. Attractants have the same advantage as the sterile male technique in that they are highly specific to the pest insects in question.

Repellents currently are in wider commercial use than attractants. Of particular note are topical repellents that humans apply to themselves to drive away biting flies, ticks, and chiggers. Repellents are not insecticides; they merely inhibit an insect from alighting and feeding, and some cause the insect to turn away and go elsewhere. Repellents are useful when insecticide applications are impracticable or undesirable. In the "canoe country" of Minnesota and northwestern Ontario and in the mountains of New England and New York, hordes of bloodthirsty black flies rampage after hikers and fisherpeople in late spring. Black fly larvae are aquatic and live in running water, and to treat these streams with enough insecticide to kill black fly larvae would do serious harm to the very fish populations that the outdoorspeople pursue and on which depend the livelihoods of local motel and bait-shop owners. Dimethylphthalate ("Deet") is perhaps the most widely used repellent, though all marketed repellents give some degree of protection. I find that cigar smoke keeps many biting flies at bay. Sulfur dust around sock tops repels chiggers and ticks.

Repellents are also of limited use in livestock and crop protection. Pyrethrum is both an insecticide and a repellent for biting flies of cattle, and wood impregnated with creosote repels termites and carpenter ants. Aluminum foil laid down between rows of flower crops repels aphids that normally rest on the undersides of leaves; they orient to the surface opposite the sun's rays, which are incident to *both* surfaces if foil is present. This involves quite an investment in foil and is obviously limited to high-value crops.

INSECT HORMONES AND ENZYMES

Still at the experimental and developmental stage but showing promise for insect control is the use of insect hormones and hormone analogs (synthetic chemicals that cause the same physiological effects as natural hormones but are chemically different). Juvenile hormones or their analogs (juvenoids) have effectively prevented metamorphosis of dung-infesting fly larvae and grain beetles. Ecdysones cause molting abnormalities in test pests. **Chitinase,** which normally breaks down old cuticle as the new is formed before molting, also has control possibilities. When combined with *Bacillus thuringiensis,* chitinase hastened the penetration of the bacteria into spruce budworm larvae, speeding the onset of disease and hence the decline of budworm populations in forest plots (Smirnoff et al., 1973).

CULTURAL AND PHYSICAL CONTROL

Included here are a variety of control measures that vary from planting insect-resistant crop varieties to the ubiquitous window screen and fly swatter. Hundreds of cultural and physical methods exist, of which I shall give but a few examples. The range of cultural and physical controls is limited only by humanity's ingenuity. These controls work best when directed at the most vulnerable stage of the insect; the difference between them is that a physical control is directed specifically at insects, while in cultural control, insects are destroyed as a result of normal or slightly modified agricultural or silvicultural practices.

Plant (and animal) **resistance** is a form of cultural control that uses crop varieties that resist insect attack, either naturally or after selective breeding. Painter (1951), a pioneer in plant resistance, recognized three types: tolerance, nonpreference, and antibiosis. **Tolerance** is the ability of a plant (or animal) to outgrow and repair insect damage. Most corn varieties produce new prop roots when the old are attacked by rootworms. Tolerance is closely related to plant vigor; dense, well-watered, and well-fertilized corn (or lawns) tolerate chinch bug populations that decimate sparser, water-stressed plants. **Nonpreference** is the apparent unwillingness of pest insects to feed or oviposit on a plant because of chemical or physical characteristics that interfere with normal feeding behavior. Hairy-stemmed clover varieties evidently irritate probing aphids, whose populations there do not reach the densities found on smooth-stemmed clovers. Similarly, bristly oat leaves inhibit oviposition by cereal leaf beetle. In **antibiosis,** a plant may contain chemicals that inhibit insect growth, development, or survival, or it may lack a required nutrient. Toxins in the "Pawnee" wheat variety inhibit the growth of Hessian fly larvae on stems; fewer adults are produced, and these lay fewer eggs (Painter, 1951), so that infestations decrease (Fig. 10–8). Where it exists, or once it has been developed, plant (or animal) resistance is cumulative, persistent, and low in cost. However, development is lengthy and expensive; it took 20 years to breed high-yielding wheat resistant to Hessian fly. In addition, plant resistance and other cultural-physical controls are most applicable to Type A pest situations since small pest populations inevitably do survive.

Animal resistance has not been as well utilized as plant resistance, partly because of longer generation times, greater investment per organism, and the need to breed for yields. Some cattle are more resistant than others to biting flies, ticks and lice, and some sheep varieties resist wool maggots (Subcommittee on Insect Pests, 1969). Native antelopes of East Africa resist **nagana,** a disease transmitted by bites of the tsetse fly (Chapter Eleven), and it may be possible to raise some of the larger antelope species for meat and milk in areas now unavailable for cattle grazing because of tsetse infestations.

Plowing, tilling, and crop rotation are useful cultural controls, especially for soil-inhabiting insects. In the northern United States, fall plowing exposes overwintering pupae of cutworms, armyworms, hornworms, grape berry moths, and a host of other insects to lethal low temperatures and predation by birds and mammals. Permitting swine to forage in corn stubble has a similar effect. Ventilating grain elevators and mills during subzero (Fahrenheit) temperatures controls pests of stored grains, and if you have a freezer, you can do the same to beetle-infested flour. Lethal high temperatures are sometimes effective; cutting alfalfa hay in June often leaves large numbers of alfalfa weevil larvae to starve and desiccate in the sun (Casagrande and Stehr, 1973). Alfalfa weevils (and other insects) have also been controlled by flame cultivation in which gas flames are directed at the soil surface to overheat litter and the first few centimeters of soil. This destroys overwintering insects, though its use is limited to periods when plants are dormant.

Sanitation, to remove insects' food supplies and breeding places, is a useful control method. Many flies breed in manure or vegetable compost, and fly numbers can be greatly curtailed by eliminating these substances or at least removing them from near barns, feedlots, and residences. Draining of stagnant

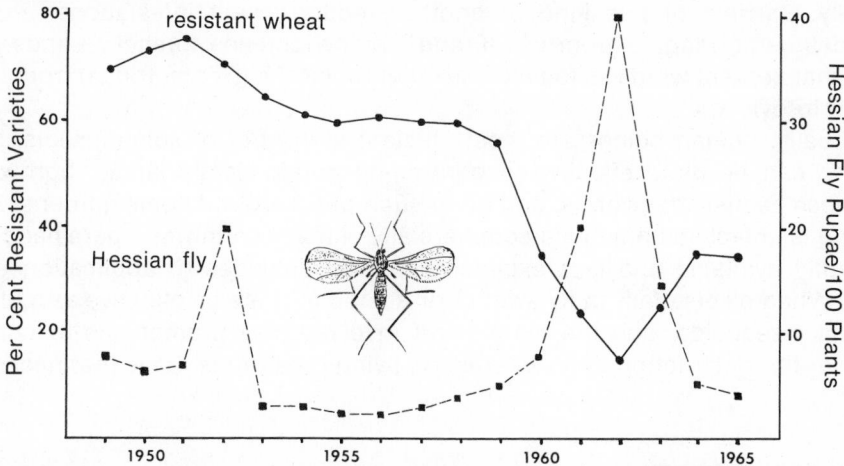

Figure 10–8. Relationship between plantings of resistant wheat and Hessian fly infestations in north central Kansas, 1949 to 1965. (From Subcommittee on Insect Pests, 1969. Insect-Pest Management and Control. Principles of Plant and Animal Pest Management, Vol. 3. Nat. Acad. Sci. Washington, D.C.)

water from swamps, old tires, rain gutters, and other collecting places eliminates mosquito larvae, though draining of wetlands and straightening and deepening of streams have other profound ecological effects that should be considered before valuable habitats are altered in the name of mosquito control. Crop plants can sometimes be removed from insect attack. Hessian fly adults have a very short, predictable fall flight period, and by planting winter wheat after the "fly-free date" for a given locality (Fig. 10–9), a producer can avoid this insect almost

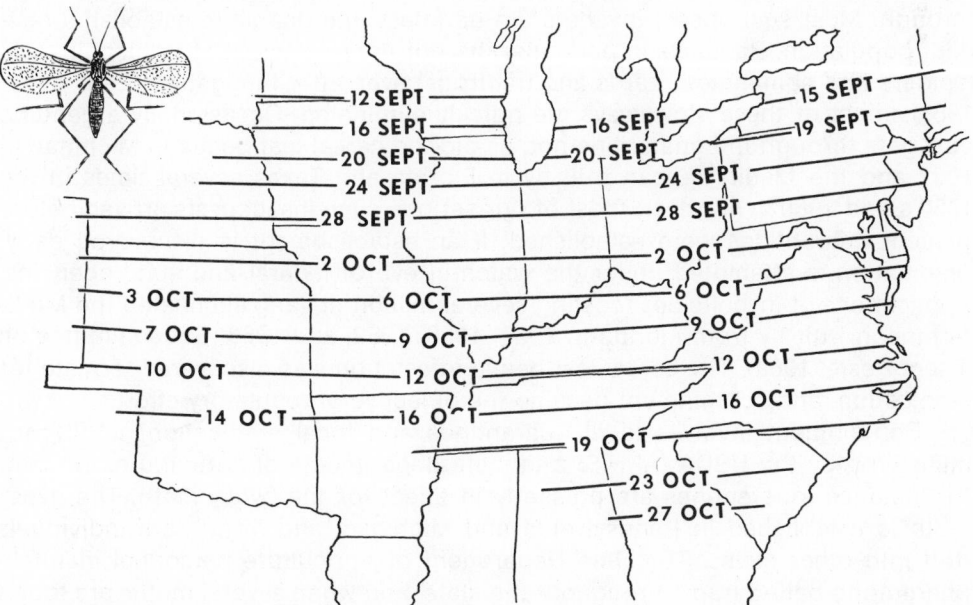

Figure 10–9. Fly-free dates: earliest planting dates to avoid Hessian fly infestations in winter wheat in the United States. (From USDA map.)

entirely. Barriers of one kind or another reduce insect infestations, and this includes items ranging from well-fitting window screens to sticky bands about trees that prevent wingless female cankerworm moths (Geometridae) from climbing up to oviposit.

Finally, human beings are most efficient at control of some insects. Handpicking can be quite effective in controlling potato beetle larvae, hornworms, Japanese beetles, bagworms, and other such pests around home gardens. Handpicking is in fact still practiced commercially in many countries where hand labor is readily available and less expensive than insecticides or application equipment. When all else fails, a fly swatter or a shod foot are as effective as a blast of aerosol insecticide, and the extra effort involved may prompt one to consider whether the destruction of an interesting living creature is really that necessary.

REGULATORY CONTROL

Many, and perhaps most, insect pest problems originate when an insect population becomes newly established in an area where there is abundant food and few specific predators, parasites, or competitors. Because of this, the United States and many other countries have established **quarantines** to exclude potential pests. With widespread high-speed travel, people are transporting more items more quickly than ever before, and effective quarantines consequently are of increasing importance in slowing the spread of unwanted pests. Stationed at all ports of entry into the United States are personnel of the Animal and Plant Health Inspection Service (APHIS), who inspect all incoming persons and goods, particularly plant material, that might harbor insects or plant pathogens. APHIS inspectors intercepted over 15,000 infested items in 1974 (Cooperative Economic Insect Report, 1975), including several potentially very serious crop pests.

Inspection cannot uncover everything, and inevitably insect-infested items get through. Most such insect invaders are harmless and unable to establish a resident population. Bananas, in particular, harbor an assortment of tropical insects (spiders and sometimes lizards and treefrogs) even after fumigation (Eads et al., 1966); most of these stowaways are quickly eliminated. Occasionally a genuine pest gets through the quarantine net, as did the cereal leaf beetle in Michigan in 1962 and the Mediterranean fruit fly in Florida and Texas several times in the 1950's and 1960's; however, most of our serious alien insect pests arrived before present quarantines were established. If an establishment is discovered early, eradication is attempted under the watchful eye of federal and state agencies. Applications of insecticides (costing several million dollars) eliminated the Mediterranean fruit fly from Florida in 1929, 1956, 1962, and 1963 (Subcommittee on Insect Pests, 1969). The cereal leaf beetle infestation was discovered too late for eradication, and containment became the objective of regulatory efforts.

Containment involves local quarantines and local eradication, jointly administered by the USDA (APHIS) and state departments of agriculture. In Ohio, for instance, quarantines are presently in effect for the gypsy moth. The gypsy moth is established in Pennsylvania and Michigan, and from there individuals drift into other states. The Ohio Department of Agriculture personnel maintain pheromone-baited traps throughout the state, and when several moths are found in one location, the local area is treated with insecticide. Gypsy moths were thus eradicated locally within Ohio in 1972 and 1975. Undoubtedly, the gypsy moth, along with most other established pests, will eventually spread into all suitable habitats. Containment merely retards this spread, permitting growers a few more crops without a particular pest while researchers buy a little time in their search for more effective controls. Containment works best against insects that disperse slowly like the Japanese beetle and gypsy moth. The cereal leaf beetle spread throughout the eastern United States within ten years, despite quarantine efforts.

INTEGRATED CONTROL AND MANAGEMENT

The shortcomings of chemical control, together with limitations of biological, cultural, and physical controls used alone, have led to **integrated control,** the simultaneous use of several different control methods (Stern et al., 1959). Integrated controls have been developed for a variety of crop systems (agroecosystems). Their development and use depend on ever greater knowledge of pest life histories and population dynamics.

As an example, consider integrated control of apple pests in several northeastern and midwestern states. Apples are attacked by as great a variety of insects as any other crop (Fig. 10–10). Codling moths, leafrollers, plum curculios, and apple maggots are major pests of the fruit, while other insects feed on sap or leaves and reduce yields. Several caterpillar species eat apple leaves, and cerambycid and scolytid beetle larvae bore in branches and trunk. Apple producers must also contend with mice, deer, and several serious plant diseases. At least one major pest is present in an orchard at any time throughout the growing season, so

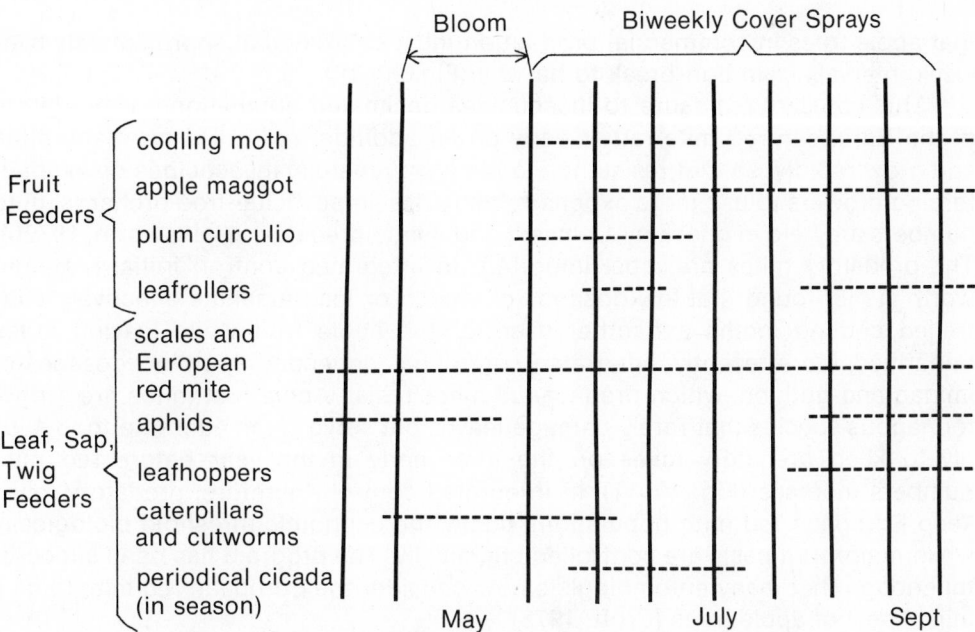

Figure 10–10. Apple pest system. Dashed horizontal lines indicate major activity period for insect adults and mites in orchard. Solid vertical lines indicate times for insecticide applications to trees in commercial production.

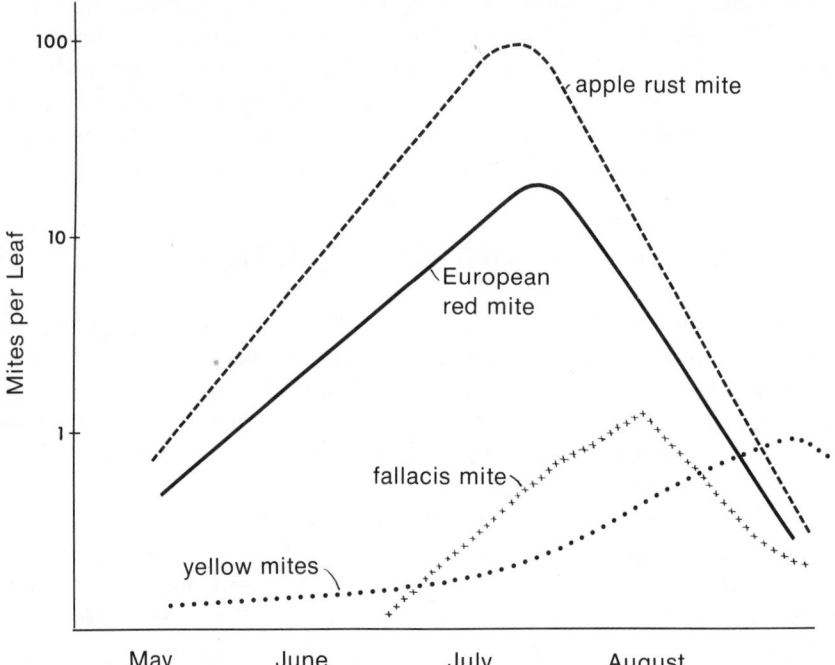

Figure 10–11. Seasonal changes in densities of mite species in southeast Ohio apple orchards. Phytophagous mites: apple rust mite, dashed line; European red mite, solid line. Predaceous mites: yellow mite. (Stigmaeidae), dotted line; fallacis mite (Phytoseiidae), crosses. (Data from Holdsworth, R. P., Jr. 1972. European red mite predators and their management. Proc. Ohio State Hort. Soc. 125th Ann. Mtg., pp. 86–88.)

that apple trees in commercial production must be treated at approximately two-week intervals from bud-break to harvest (Fig. 10–10).

This constant exposure to insecticides decimated populations of predators of the European red mite rather early on. In addition, red mites lay many eggs and grow rapidly, so that resistance to many commercial insecticides developed, forcing growers to use more expensive miticides. In pesticide-free orchards, mite numbers are held in check by 11 insect and 3 mite predators (Holdsworth, 1972b). The predatory mites are most important in integrated control; initially, Holdsworth (1968) found that low dosages of imidan or lead arsenate effectively controlled codling moths and other pests of the apple fruit while leaving mites unharmed. More recently, integrated control has depended upon low dosages of imidan and guthion, which predaceous mites resist. Apple rust mites are a phytophagous species that rarely damage leaves but serve as an alternate food supply to keep predatory mites on the trees early in the year before red mite numbers increase (Fig. 10–11). In integrated control, therefore, predatory mites keep European red mite populations below the economic threshold biologically while major fruit pests are controlled chemically. The program has been successful enough that many entomologists now consider the European red mite to be a minor pest of apple trees (Croft, 1975).

Implicit in integrated control is the fact that pest populations must be carefully monitored. This in turn depends on: (1) adequate estimation of the economic threshold; (2) accurate (and inexpensive) methods of estimating pest population density; and (3) acceptance of small (subeconomic) numbers of insects by growers and consumers. Such integrated-control pest management projects involving corn, alfalfa, cotton, tobacco, and other crops have resulted in significant savings in insecticide costs with reduction of the pesticide "load" in the environment. In tobacco and cotton crops, scouts sampled fields weekly and counted insects in a standard sample. Scouts' reports were processed by computer, and if the economic threshold was exceeded, the grower was advised to treat with insecticide. In some cotton fields, insecticide applications were reduced from 18 to 2 per season (Ganyard, 1973). In Illinois and Indiana, a computer model predicts alfalfa weevil populations several weeks in advance, based on temperature and plant development (Giese et al., 1975). A grower thus knows in advance whether or not he or she will have to use insecticide. Integrated pest management is well suited to many insect pest situations but not to all. The lower the economic threshold, the greater the dependence on chemical control with its attendant problems. Existing economic injury levels for some crop and garden pests could probably be increased but not those for insects that transmit disease. Here, a single insect may be too many, as is pointed out in the next chapter.

SUMMARY

This chapter discusses negative aspects of our relationship with insects. Insect pests are defined as those whose population density exceeds an arbitrarily defined *economic injury level.* Events that may lead to an insect's becoming a pest are discussed.

Insects whose numbers exceed the economic injury level may be controlled and managed by successful application of one or more control techniques. This chapter reviews the development and use of insecticides, parasites and predators, sterilization, hormones, pheromones, and cultural/physical controls. Some very successful programs of insect pest management utilize several methods concurrently to achieve *integrated control.*

Chapter Eleven

Insects and Disease

INTRODUCTION

A fundamental relationship between humanity and insects involves those insects that cause, or transmit, diseases of humans, livestock, pets, poultry, and plants. In the study of insect-borne disease, several disciplines, notably plant pathology, microbiology, epidemiology, immunology, and medicine, interrelate with entomology. The same general principles of transmission of disease by insects apply whether one is considering aster yellows of lettuce or bubonic plague in humans. Characteristically, insect vectors of disease pathogens have a very low economic injury level; even one mosquito bite is too many if you thereby contract malaria. Insect-borne diseases have had major impact on human history. Plague, which is transmitted from rats to people by fleas, killed an estimated 25 per cent of the population of Western Europe between 1348 and 1350 (Langer, 1964). Epidemic typhus, transmitted between people by lice, has produced catastrophic epidemics, particularly in wartime; Zinsser (1938) documented several major military campaigns whose outcomes were altered by typhus outbreaks. Until World War I, disease-related deaths outnumbered battle deaths for all wars for which we have such statistics. Only in the past century have industrialized countries adequately controlled insect-borne diseases, and many are still rampant, especially in the tropics. Much of east central Africa would be suitable for cattle grazing and human habitation were it not for tsetse flies, which are vectors of African sleeping sickness and nagana. Even in North America, plague exists in some rodent populations (Kartman et al., 1958), and isolated human cases appear annually. Epidemics are yet possible, particularly when societal disruptions occur. In South Vietnam, reported plague cases rose from 353 in 1966 to 4725 in 1967 as refugees became more crowded in unsanitary conditions (James and Harwood, 1969). The potential threat is compounded when one realizes that most of the almost 300 cases of insecticide resistance documented by Brown (1968) involve insects of public health importance.

DIRECT EFFECTS OF INSECT DAMAGE

In its broadest sense, disease includes any abnormal condition that interferes with normal growth, development, and maintenance functions. Any insect

376

Table 11-1. INSECTS AND ARACHNIDS THAT CAUSE DISEASE
BY DIRECT ATTACKS ON MAN AND ANIMALS

Disease Symptom	Agent
Bites, blood loss	chiggers (Acarina: Trombiculidae); bed bugs (Cimicidae); horse flies* and deer flies* (Tabanidae); stable flies (Muscidae); dog, cat, human fleas (Pulicidae); vectors of mammalian diseases listed in Table 11-3
Eye irritation Stinging, envenomization	eye gnats (Chloropidae); face flies (Muscidae); eye moths (several families); ants;* bees;* wasps* (Hymenoptera); scorpions (Scorpionida); black widow* and brown recluse spiders* (Arachnida); rarely, large centipedes
Allergic reaction	In particular, blister beetles (Meloidae); some larval Lepidoptera (especially Eucleidae); house dust mites (Acarina); however, stings or bites of any arthropod may elicit allergic reaction
Subsurface body infestation	myiasis—bot flies (Oestridae and Hypodermatidae), screwworm (Calliphoridae) scabies mites

*Only females bite or sting.

attack upon a plant or animal for food or defense may produce abnormal symptoms and thus could be termed a disease (e.g., wilting of plants following wounding by sucking insects). In practice, however, direct effects due to insect attack are considered disease only if the symptoms are systemic—that is, if insect attack causes general abnormal symptoms or at least a reaction somewhere other than the point of initial attack. Table 11-1 lists insects that cause direct symptoms through direct attacks, and some of these are discussed in the following sections.

INSECT AND ARACHNID BITES

Insects with sucking mouthparts usually inject saliva when they feed (Chapter Four). This saliva may cause a general systemic or tissue reaction in the host plant or animal. Plant galls (see Fig. 9–23) thus are sometimes considered a disease (Carter, 1973). Saliva of the potato leafhopper blocks conducting vessels in alfalfa and potato leaves, resulting in V-shaped yellow areas called "hopperburn" (Fig. 11–1). Swelling and itching accompany bites of mosquitoes, horse flies, black flies, bed bugs and other biting insects. Apparently proteins and other chemical constituents of the injected saliva trigger a defensive reaction by the victim's antibodies.

Bites of most insects are not serious, though the temporary itching caused by chiggers is maddening, and black fly bites sometimes swell disproportionately to the tiny insect that caused the bite. Insects that feed on blood are in most cases well adapted to taking only a small drink without eliciting a serious allergic reaction in the host. This ensures that the host will live to provide a blood meal another day.

Exceptions to this rule of relative harmlessness are the bites of some arachnids. Besides transmitting microorganisms (see Table 11–2), ticks sometimes inject enough saliva in the several days during which they feed on a host to cause a

Figure 11–1. "Hopperburn," yellowing of leaf tip caused by feeding by leafhopper, which apparently blocks circulation in midrib.

systemic reaction, **tick paralysis**, in both humans and domestic animals (particularly cattle). Tick paralysis can be fatal if untreated, but symptoms usually disappear rapidly following removal of the offending tick(s) (James and Harwood, 1969). Two spider genera (in the United States; more in tropical areas) have unusually potent bites. Black widows (Fig. 11–2A) (*Latrodectus* spp.) are common in protected places such as hollow logs and outbuildings and bite defensively if they or their webs are disturbed. Their poison is a potent nerve toxin, and an untreated bite may prove fatal, particularly to very young or very old people. James and Harwood (1969) report that most bites occur in outdoor privies, the spider generally

Table 11–2. MAJOR GROUPS OF ARTHROPOD VECTORS OF
PLANT AND ANIMAL PATHOGENS

Order	Family	Disease	Reference
Homoptera	Aphididae (aphids*)	Plant viruses (mosaics and yellows)	Watson and Plumb, 1972
	Cicadellidae (leafhoppers*)	Plant yellows viruses A few plant viruses	Ishihara, 1969
Coleoptera	Chrysomelidae (leaf beetles), corn flea beetle, cucumber beetles	Bacterial wilt of corn and cucumbers	Carter, 1973
	Scolytidae (bark beetles)	Dutch elm disease	Carter, 1973
Anoplura	Pediculidae (human louse)	Typhus†‡	Zinsser, 1938
Siphonaptera	Pulicidae (Oriental rat flea)	Plague, typhus†‡	James and Harwood, 1969
Diptera	Culicidae (female mosquitoes*)	Malaria,† yellow fever,† dengue,† encephalitis, filariasis†	James and Harwood, 1969
	Psychodidae (female sand flies*)	Leishmaniasis†	James and Harwood, 1969
	Simuliidae (female black flies*)	Onchocerciasis†	James and Harwood, 1969

	Muscidae
	    tsetse fly†
	    house fly
		Trypanosomiasis
		Suspected: dysentery, typhoid,‡ cholera, salmonella, polio-myelitis, anthrax, leprosy, hepatitis, and others
			James and Harwood, 1969

Hemiptera	Reduviidae *Triatoma* spp.	Trypanosomiasis (Chagas' disease)	James and Harwood, 1969
Acarina	Ixodidae (ticks)	Rocky Mountain spotted fever Tularemia, Colorado tick fever	James and Harwood, 1969
	Eriophyidae (mites)*	Plant viruses	Carter, 1973

*Not all species transmit, and pathogen-vector relationship is often species-specific.
†Not established in United States or Canada.
‡**Typhus** is a rickettsial disease transmitted by lice and fleas. **Typhoid** is a bacterial disease spread by contact with feces, by flies, by contaminated water, etc.

B

Figure 11–2. Dangerous spiders. *A,* Black widow. (USDA photo.) *B,* Brown recluse.

sinking her chelicerae into that portion of the human anatomy closest to the seat. Recluse spiders (*Loxosceles* spp.) (Fig. 11–2*B*) are denizens of outdoor debris in the southern United States and of attics, basements, and outbuildings farther north. The bite is rarely fatal, though a painful, necrotic wound forms that is slow to heal (Atkins et al., 1958). Both black widow and recluse spiders are secretive and easily avoided; they do not seek out humans to bite but do so only in self-defense. Tarantulas, much feared for their "deadly" bite, are usually quite harmless and, indeed, must be induced to bite (Baerg, 1958). The venom of North American species produces a reaction no more severe than a bee sting.

Rarely will loss of blood from insect bites cause disability or death. Heavy tick infestations on livestock may weaken animals through blood loss; Hunter and Hooker (1907) reported that ticks removed up to 200 lb. of blood yearly from cattle in heavily tick-infested pasture. Up to 10,000 horn flies (Muscidae) may infest a single cow, and though they are small (3–4 mm.), each consumes blood twice a day. A heavy infestation can thereby weaken an animal, making it more susceptible to other ailments and reducing milk yields.

Plant feeders may be more serious. Hemiptera and Homoptera of several species commonly cause significant sap loss from plants, resulting in wilting, flower- and fruit-drop, and sometimes death. Aphids, scale insects, and plant bugs (Miridae) are the major sap-sucking plant pests.

IRRITATION

A few insects, particularly eye gnats (Chloropidae, genus *Hippelates*) and face flies (Fig. 11–3), feed on liquid bodily secretions of humans and domestic animals. The eye gnats are most troublesome, for large numbers will irritate and annoy the host while feeding or flying about looking for a place to land. Occasionally, one may become entrapped in eye fluids, causing inflammation and the risk of injury or infection. It is suspected that these flies transmit bacteria causing *conjunctivitis,* or pinkeye, a disease of both cattle and people. Other insects of several orders may accidentally cause eye irritation. Bombardier beetles (see Fig. 9–11) and some Tenebrionidae squirt tremendously irritating defensive chemicals. Hemolymph of blister beetles (Meloidae) contains a potent defensive irritant, cantharidin, that can cause a blistering skin rash or serious eye damage.

Caterpillars of several families bear stinging or urticating hairs (setae), combined with one-celled poison glands. Whoever rashly handles these caterpillars (Fig. 11–4) will surely develop a severe rash, and such hairs in the eyes can cause blindness. Cattle develop mouth blisters when grazing on range infested with the range caterpillar *Hemileuca oliviae* (James and Harwood, 1969).

STINGING INSECTS

In aculeate Hymenoptera (ants, bees, and wasps), the ovipositor has become modified into a sting for injecting poisons produced by enlarged secondary glands. Most such poisons are apparently complex chemical mixtures that disrupt transmission of nerve impulses and break down cells in the recipient.

Figure 11-3. Face flies on cow. (Photo by G. Berkey, courtesy of P. R. Heller and Ohio Agricultural Research and Development Center.)

Most severe stinging incidents result from accidental or intended disturbance of honey bee or bumble bee colonies or those of hornets, yellow jackets (*Vespula* spp.), or fire or harvester ants (in the United States). The nest inhabitants swarm out and sting en masse; a few hundred stings may well provoke a serious and perhaps fatal reaction in a human (James and Harwood, 1969). Solitary Hymenoptera and more docile social species like *Polistes*, paper wasps, also sting when disturbed. A small number of persons (about 2 per cent) are exceedingly sensitive to stings of Hymenoptera and react to the small amount of protein in the venom. For these persons, a single bee sting may be fatal, but fortunately an-

Figure 11-4. Io moth caterpillar (Saturniidae), showing poisonous spines.

tigens are available for annual desensitizing injections preceding bee season. Many beekeepers have become more resistant to honey bee stings after repeated exposure; however, others have experienced progressively greater susceptibility (James and Harwood, 1969). Allergies can develop to other insects as well, and quite a few researchers have realized with frustration that they have developed an allergy to their experimental cockroaches, house flies, or alfalfa weevils.

MYIASIS

Myiasis is a condition caused by infestation of humans or other animals by larval Diptera. (Plant pathologists do not consider maggot infestation of plants to be a disease.) Flies of several species oviposit on wild and domestic animals and, occasionally, on people. The resulting maggots may feed within the digestive tract (horse bots) or the nasal passages (sheep, goat, and deer bots) or under the skin where they produce a warble (see Fig. 4–21E) (warble fly and human bot fly). In most cases, a light infestation causes little permanent damage; an exception is the screwworm fly (Chapter Ten) that develops in open, festering, and progressively larger wounds. If left untreated, screwworm-infested livestock usually die.

Myiasis of humans is rather rare in temperate or dry climates. Most cases occur among persons who are intimately associated with the more normal livestock host of the fly. Sheep bot females sometimes larviposit in the eyes or nose of sheepherders. The larvae cause great irritation initially but die within a few days without feeding or developing further. The human bot fly of tropical America does not select hosts directly but instead oviposits on a mosquito (or other small arthropod). When the mosquito lands on a host, the bot fly eggs hatch and larvae make their way through the skin to feed. Dunn (1930), a truly dedicated scientist, allowed two of these to develop to maturity in his arm and described in detail the "sharp itching" followed by the "excruciating pain" he experienced over the next 50 days and 15.5 hours. Screwworm flies oviposit readily in human wounds, and at least one fatality has resulted (James and Harwood, 1969). Other fly larvae are sometimes passed in excrement or vomited. Many such incidents seem to have resulted from eating maggot-infested food rather than from direct infestation.

TRANSMISSION OF PATHOGENS

Transmission of pathogenic microorganisms is by far the most important interrelationship between people, arthropods, and disease. Insects and arachnids that transmit disease-causing microorganisms are called **vectors,** and Table 11–2 lists major groups of arthropod vectors and the major disease pathogens spread by each. More information on the biology, appearance, habits, and relationships of these arthropod groups can be found in Chapter Three. As one might expect, most have sucking mouthparts with which pathogens may be injected directly into hosts.

Disease-causing microorganisms transmitted by arthropods were probably originally (evolutionarily) associated with these vectors exclusively and only later

Table 11–3. MAJOR GROUPS OF PATHOGENS*

Group	Disease
Viruses	plant mosaics, yellows yellow fever dengue encephalitis poliomyelitis
Mycoplasma	plant yellows
Rickettsiae	typhus Rocky Mountain spotted fever
Bacteria	bacterial wilt (corn) fireblight (apples) anthrax plague
Fungi	Dutch elm disease
Protozoa	malaria leishmaniasis trypanosomiasis (including nagana and Chagas' disease)
Nematodes	onchocerciasis filariasis elephantiasis

*This list is restricted to pathogens discussed in the text.

developed in host plants, livestock, or humans. Kramer (1963) arrived at this hypothesis because most insect-borne pathogens are less virulent or damaging in their arthropod hosts than in a diseased plant or animal. Coevolution between many pathogens and their vectors has led to commensalism (Chapter Nine), while the relationship between pathogen and vertebrate host is still parasitism. Table 11–3 lists major groups of pathogens in animals and plants and the diseases they cause. Volk and Wheeler (1973) is a useful reference for further information about characteristics of pathogens.

To implicate a vector in disease transmission one must demonstrate actual movement of the pathogen from a diseased to an uninfected host under controlled conditions. Plant viruses characteristically cause wilting, dwarfing (Fig. 11–5), and color changes, especially yellow mottling. Feeding by phytophagous mites causes the same problems, and many mite species cause viruslike symptoms in plants, while about a dozen plant viruses actually are transmitted by mites (Slykhuis, 1969). There are quite a few cases in which disease transmission by mites or insects is suspected but unproven. Cockroaches conceivably could crawl directly to your food pantry from sewerage contaminated with pathogens of typhoid, cholera, hepatitis, or polio. This possibility has been demonstrated in laboratory studies, but there is only circumstantial evidence that cockroaches spread such diseases under natural conditions (James and Harwood, 1969). The human body louse is a proven vector of typhus, whereas its little relative, the crab louse, has never been implicated in disease transmission under natural conditions despite the family resemblance.

Figure 11-5. Maize plant stunted by maize chlorotic dwarf virus, transmitted by leafhoppers. (Photo by G. Berkey, courtesy of L. R. Nault and Ohio Agricultural Research and Development Center.)

MECHANICAL TRANSMISSION

Many disease-causing microorganisms potentially can be spread from diseased to healthy insects or people by mechanical means, merely by contamination of the insect vector as it moves around on, or in, a diseased organism or its excrement. Like almost everything else, all insects are covered with bacterial and fungal spores and living microbes, and we should be thankful that rather few regularly transmit disease this way. Almost any spore may cling to an insect, and therefore, even when mechanical transmission is demonstrable in laboratory studies, it may still be questionable whether there is significant transmission of the same pathogens in nature, even by such filth-inhabiting insects as cockroaches and flies. Most mechanically transmitted pathogens can be maintained and transmitted mechanically without insects. House flies feed and breed on human (and other) excrement and are also given to walking about on food for human consumption. Cockroaches also are partial to both sewers and pantries. Microorganisms causing dysentery, salmonella, typhoid, cholera, leprosy, tuberculosis, and hepatitis, together with eggs of intestinal tapeworms and nematodes, all may occur in human excrement. Flies and cockroaches are therefore vectors by implication if not by experimental demonstration (James and Harwood, 1969).

Several fungi are spread by mechanical means, and one of the more important ones causes Dutch elm disease. Bark beetles reared in diseased trees carry the fungus to nearby (usually within ¼ mile) healthy trees, and females establish the fungus there when they tunnel beneath the bark to oviposit. The fungus rapidly reproduces, blocking water conduction in the plant; characteristically a few upper branches die first, and over several years, progressively more and more branches die. Elm species and varieties differ in susceptibility; the American elm is very susceptible, and this has had serious aesthetic consequences in areas where these were the dominant shade tree (Fig. 11–6).

An important mechanism for mechanical transmission by insects is introduction of a pathogen during feeding. The pathogen remains essentially unchanged during its transportation to the next victim and can be spread almost immediate-

Figure 11–6. Dutch elm disease. *A,* Elm tree before introduction of disease. *B,* Same tree after epidemic of Dutch elm disease. (Photos by C. C. Powell, Jr.)

ly; there is no "latent period." Many mechanically transmitted pathogens are not specific to a particular host. Most are transmissible by introduction into any wound, whether caused by insect mouthparts or not.

Many plant viruses and mycoplasmas are mechanically transmitted by aphids and are consequently called **stylet-borne** or "nonpersistent" viruses (Kennedy et al., 1962). Characteristically, they are picked up as aphids make feeding probes in infected hosts and then must be rather quickly inoculated into an uninfected host for they lose infectivity after several hours. The quantity, duration, and location of aphid feeding probes (Fig. 11–7) are important in the spread of stylet-borne viruses. McClean and Kinsey (1964) pioneered microelectronic recordings of aphid probes in which they wired aphids and plants so that a feeding probe completed an electric circuit. They thereby demonstrated that very short, exploratory probes did not usually penetrate plant cells or vessels and likely would not result in viral infection. Polyphagous aphid species are the most important vectors of nonpersistent viruses because they probe within a variety of host plants during a short period of time. The green peach aphid, *Myzus persicae,* has been shown to transmit more than 50 different plant viruses (van Emden et al., 1969).

BIOLOGICAL TRANSMISSION

A number of pathogens develop within the arthropod vector before being transmitted to a vertebrate or plant host. Such biological transmission occurs in one of three ways: **Propagative** (or persistent) pathogens merely multiply within

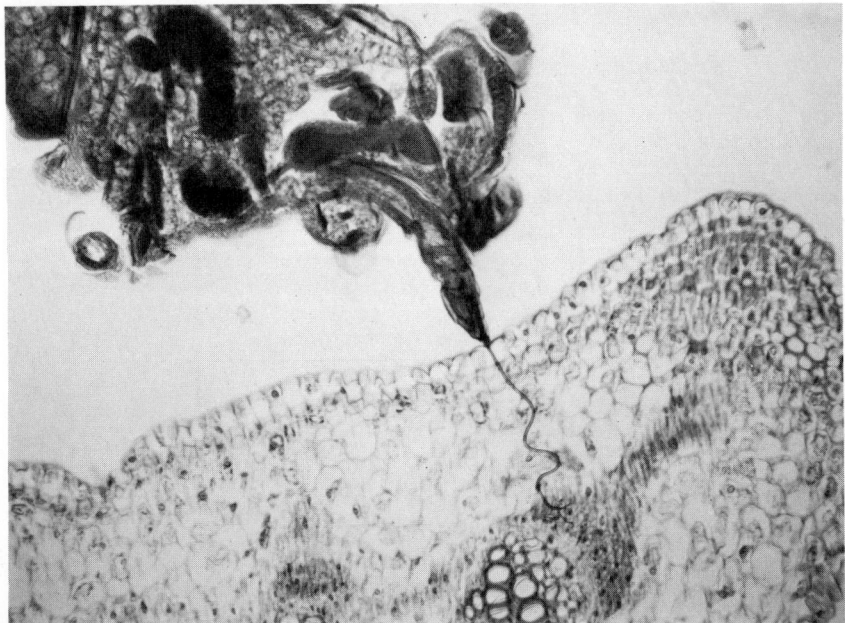

Figure 11–7. Cross section of aphid and plant stem, showing probe by aphid mouthparts into phloem vessels. (Photo courtesy of L. R. Nault and Ohio Agricultural Research and Development Center.)

their arthropod vector. **Cyclopropagative** pathogens not only multiply but also transform within the arthropod. Finally, **cyclodevelopmental** pathogens transform, without multiplication, within the arthropod.

Epidemic typhus is an example of a propagative rickettsial disease of humans; the vector is the human body louse, *Pediculus humanus.* Rickettsiae multiply within the louse, eventually killing it. While alive, the louse transmits typhus rickettsiae in biting its host. The pathogen can also be introduced when a person crushes an infected louse or its feces in a cut or scratch. The disease is always debilitating and sometimes fatal in people; survivors may become **reservoirs** of the disease. A similar but milder form of typhus (murine typhus) is transmitted from rodents to people by fleas (Zinsser, 1938).

An equally serious disease is plague, a propagative bacterial disease spread from rodents to humans by bites of fleas. In past epidemics, the principal source of disease was probably the black rat *(Rattus rattus)* and the major vector, the Oriental rat flea *(Xenopsylla cheopis).* Plague is mainly a disease of rodents and is continuously present in many wild rodent populations, particularly those of the western United States (Kartman et al., 1958). Plague bacilli ingested by a flea multiply in its digestive tract, blocking it so that the flea becomes hungrier, bites more frequently, and regurgitates gut contents when feeding. Spread of plague requires association between people and rats, and this usually occurs in crowded, unsanitary conditions.

In the southeastern and western United States, Rocky Mountain spotted fever is a propagative rickettsial disease transmitted by ticks, chiefly *Dermacentor* species. Several rather common woodland species transmit the pathogen, though the incidence of disease in ticks is normally low — less than one per cent. There is a 9- to 12-day latent period before an infected tick can transmit spotted fever (Parker, 1928), but once established, the rickettsiae remain infective throughout the tick's life and may be transmitted to subsequent generations via tick eggs (transovarially). Outdoorspeople run the greatest risk of contracting Rocky Mountain spotted fever.

Several bacterial pathogens of plants are propagative. Bacterial wilts of corn and cucurbits (melons, squash, etc.) are spread by flea beetles and cucumber beetles respectively. The adult beetles chew holes in the leaves and then may contaminate these wounds with their feces. If the feces contain *Xanthomonas stewartii* (from corn flea beetles) or *Erwinia tracheiphila* (from cucumber beetles), these multiply, and they and their toxic by-products spread through the plant's vascular system. The results are wilting, yellowing, reduced yield, and sometimes death. *Erwinia* reproduces within the beetle's gut, where it apparently does little harm but does overwinter (Carter, 1973); the beetle is thus a disease reservoir as well as a vector. Fire blight is a bacterial disease of apples (and other orchard fruit) that causes oozing from cankers (growths) on branches and trunk. During apple blossom time, ants visit both cankers and blossoms, transporting bacteria to the latter. The pathogens may be transferred by other means: once the disease is established in blossoms, it is very quickly spread through an orchard by bees (Keitt and Ivanov, 1941). The blossom clusters blacken and fall off, the whole orchard looks as though it had been singed, and the grower can forget about selling fruit that year.

Aster yellows is a propagative virus disease spread from asters to lettuce by the six-spotted leafhopper. The virus is taken in when the insect feeds, and virus particles move through the midgut lining into the hemolymph. There follows a latent period when they multiply in the salivary glands and very likely in other tissues, such as the fat body (Sylvester, 1969). The latent period ends when infective viruses are injected along with saliva into the phloem of healthy plants. Once they become infective, persistent plant viruses remain in the vector for the rest of its life, and some are incorporated into the insect's eggs, to reproduce in the next leafhopper generation (Watson and Plumb, 1972).

Perhaps the most important of cyclopropagative diseases is malaria, a cyclic protozoan disease that has played a major role in the history of human colonization and land use. Though popularly considered to be a tropical disease, malaria was a major scourge of western Europe and North America until the advent of widespread mosquito control programs. Even so, more than 2000 cases were reported in the United States in 1967 (James and Harwood, 1969), mostly among military personnel returning from Vietnam.

Human malaria is caused by four *Plasmodium* species and transmitted by *Anopheles* mosquitoes (many species). *Homo sapiens* is the principal reservoir, but two *Plasmodium* species also infest chimpanzees (Rodhain, 1948). The life cycle of a representative plasmodium is outlined by James and Harwood (1969) as follows: An *Anopheles* female ingests male and female plasmodia from a malarial victim (Fig. 11–8). These cells fuse and migrate to the gut wall, where they multiply in a cyst. This bursts and the resulting sporozoites migrate to the salivary glands, from whence they are injected into another person. This "sexual cycle" takes at least a week, during which the mosquito does not yet transmit the disease. After injection, the plasmodia move to the liver, then into the general circulation where they periodically invade and multiply in red blood cells. Their cyclic reproduction in blood cells causes typical chills, high fever, fatigue, and weakness in the victim, sometimes with fatal results.

African sleeping sickness, a form of trypanosomiasis, is as severe as malaria but is localized to tropical Africa, where it is spread by several species of tsetse flies (*Glossina* spp.) (Fig. 11–9). Several protozoans of the genus *Trypanosoma* are responsible for the disease in humans and for a related disease, nagana, in livestock. Large areas of east and central Africa have been unsuited to economic

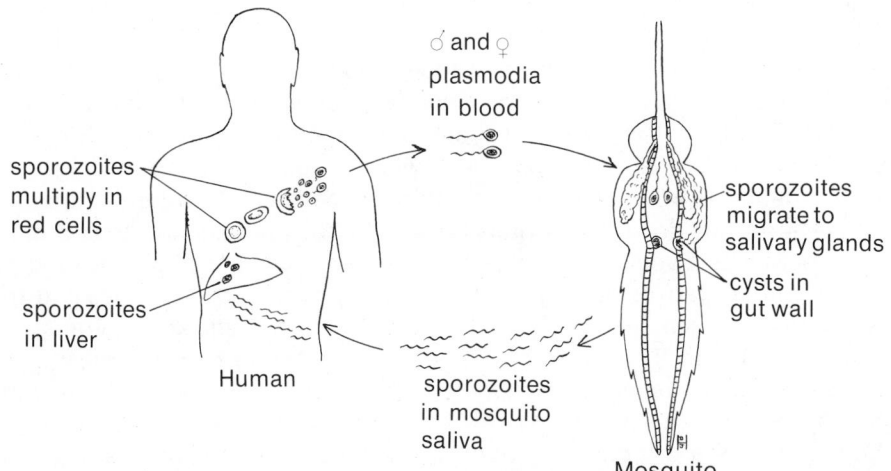

Figure 11–8. Cyclic development of malaria; sexual phase in mosquito and asexual phase in human. (Modified from James, M. T., and R. F. Harwood. 1969. Herms' Medical Entomology. 6th ed. Macmillan Publishing Co., Inc., New York. © The Macmillan Co. 1969.)

Figure 11–9. Tsetse fly, *Glossina* spp., vector of trypanosomiasis (African sleeping sickness and nagana). (Photo by and courtesy of W. A. Foster.)

development, even livestock grazing, because of the ravages of trypanosomiasis; Buxton (1955) cited an epidemic near Lake Victoria that killed 67 per cent of the local human population around 1900. Natives of west Africa associated the disease with bites of tsetse flies many years before Europeans experimentally verified the mode of transmission. Transmission is similar to that in malaria; i.e., there is an 18-day latent period while the protozoans multiply and move to the tsetse's salivary glands (James and Harwood, 1969). Thereafter the insect can transmit the pathogen. Rarely, mechanical transmission occurs by regurgitation in the first day or two. In humans, dogs, horses, and camels, the trypanosomes move to the cerebrospinal fluid and cause progressive lethargy and often death. Cattle become extremely weak but usually survive; swine are generally unaffected. Many of the large wild mammals of Africa are tolerant of *Trypanosoma* and serve as reservoirs, which greatly complicates management of sleeping sickness and nagana (Willett, 1963).

Cyclodevelopmental pathogens, which transform without multiplication, are mostly worms. Several insect species transmit roundworms that are parasites of people or domestic animals. Particularly in the tropics, biting Diptera transmit microscopic blood-infesting larval roundworms, **filariae**. Black flies transmit filariae that cause onchocerciasis, or "river blindness," so called because the worm larvae invade the eyes and optic nerves. Black flies evidently ingest worm larvae from the host's skin, and these worms move through the stomach wall to develop further in the thoracic muscles. When the fly bites, the worms emerge from the fly and enter through the host's skin (DeLeon and Duke, 1966). Filariae that are transmitted via mosquitoes often reproduce in sufficient quantity to form nodules that block lymphatic circulation, causing arms, legs, or scrotum to swell to grotesque proportions (elephantiasis). Heartworm of dogs and cats is an increasingly important veterinary health problem in the United States. In this disease, filarial roundworms, transmitted by mosquitoes, concentrate in the heart and major arteries and may block circulation to the lungs.

EPIDEMIOLOGY

Epidemiology is the study of how diseases are maintained and spread, with emphasis on the conditions necessary for infecting many individuals over a wide area more or less simultaneously. Thorough understanding of the epidemiology of insect-borne diseases is a prerequisite to their control. The epidemiology of any arthropod-borne disease has three foci: pathogen, vector, and host (Fig. 11–10). These are equally important, and changes in any one may be sufficient to commence or end an epidemic. For instance, in plague the pathogen is a bacterium, *Yersinia pestis.* Its usual hosts are rodents, both wild rodents (e.g., ground squirrels, voles, wood rats) and semidomestic rats. The principal vector is the Oriental rat flea, which transmits *Yersinia pestis* from rodent to rodent. People become infected when bitten by an infected rat flea.

Many biological (and cultural) attributes of pathogen, vector, and host are important in determining whether or not an arthropod-borne disease becomes epidemic. Density and physical condition of the host are important. Cases of plague are most frequent when humans and rodents, especially rats, are in close proximity. Furthermore, persons who are unhealthy and undernourished generally have less resistance to the disease. By overwhelming the defenses of its human host, plague may progress from bubonic form (transmitted by fleas) to pneumonic plague, transmitted by droplet infection through coughs and sneezes. Obviously, once established in human populations, plague can spread much more rapidly by droplets than by fleas.

The biology of vectors is also important in epidemiology. James and Harwood (1969) suggested that the more vital biological parameters are: (1) population density, (2) proportion harboring pathogens, (3) longevity, (4) dispersal, (5)

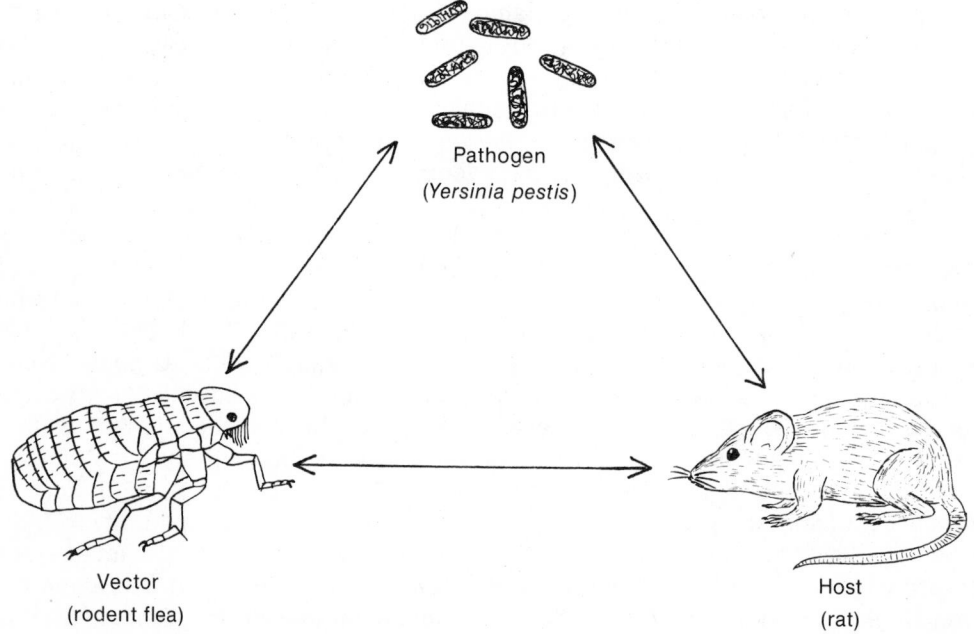

Pathogen
(*Yersinia pestis*)

Vector
(rodent flea)

Host
(rat)

Figure 11–10. Interrelationship of pathogen, vector, and host in epidemiology of plague.

frequency of biting, and (6) host range. For instance, the frequency of fleas' biting increases greatly when the insects are infested with plague bacilli. Many bloodsucking arthropods bite for energy and water as well as blood, so that high humidity may lower the frequency of biting. Rat fleas bite a number of mammalian hosts, whereas lice are very host-specific and are less likely to be interspecific disease vectors. Epidemiology may depend on whether people are a primary (preferred) or secondary host; we are secondary for the Oriental rat flea and primary for the human body louse. In summary, epidemiology requires a thorough understanding of the life system of a disease.

CONTROL

Once epidemiology of a disease is at least partially understood, potential weak links in the pathogen-vector-host interrelationship may be recognized, suggesting practical possibilities for controlling the disease. Control of an arthropod-borne disease is usually a community-wide effort coordinated and applied by public agencies, especially with diseases of livestock and humans. This is necessary because of the wide range of some arthropod vectors, such as mosquitoes and black flies, and the societal consequences of major disease epidemics. The classic notion of economic injury level (Chapter Ten) hardly applies to a disease such as plague in which a single case left untreated may shortly spread to many persons. Even the one case is too many if one has reasonably high regard for human life.

Control of insect-born diseases is often a prerequisite to further economic development. In 1883, the French commenced construction of a canal across Panama, but they suffered heavy losses from yellow fever and malaria and the project was abandoned. It remained for an American, Walter Reed, to establish the epidemiological connection between yellow fever and *Aedes* mosquitoes. The Panama Canal was then completed after a thorough mosquito control campaign. Worldwide control of yellow fever, malaria, and other arthropod-borne diseases has had a notable effect in reducing human death rates. Lack of corresponding reduction in birth rates is a major factor in worldwide population growth and its attendant societal problems.

Generally, management of insect-borne disease seeks to break the epidemiological interrelationship (Fig. 11–10) by measures directed at the pathogen, vector, or host, or sometimes at all three. The ultimate, locally attainable goal of disease management is eradication, total elimination of the pathogen from its host. Principles of disease management are discussed in terms of control of plague, malaria, trypanosomiasis, Rocky Mountain spotted fever, and Dutch elm disease.

PLAGUE

Plague management primarily depends on breaking the vector-host relationship between the vector fleas and human beings. Plague is maintained as an endemic disease in wild rodents and house rats, and a major step in its elimination is a vigorous program of rodent (especially rat) control around human habitations. (There are several other good reasons for controlling rats.) Where economic and social factors preclude effective rodent control, insecticide sprays in joint rat and human dwellings have been effective, and vaccines are available for persons who are occupationally exposed to the disease (McCrumb, 1975). Most of the very few recent cases of plague in the United States have involved hunters or small children who handle dead rodents. As with all communicable diseases, it is best that human cases be identified, isolated, and treated as quickly as possible before the disease begins to spread.

MALARIA

Malaria is an example of a disease that has been controlled by measures directed at both pathogen and vector. For many years, quinine, a naturally occurring plant alkaloid from the South American cinchona tree, was useful in controlling *Plasmodium* reproduction in humans. More recently, synthetic drugs have been used successfully to control malaria in victims and to provide partial protection to exposed persons (Rollo, 1965). Such antimalarial drugs greatly reduced the number of cases among American military personnel in Asia during World War II and subsequent wars.

Direct and indirect control of mosquitoes is perhaps the most important factor in malaria management, particularly in its initial phases. Surface applications of DDT (and, more recently, other chemicals) to interior walls of dwellings have greatly reduced domestic *Anopheles* mosquito populations in malarial areas. Sanitation, from installing tightly fitting screening to draining of breeding ponds near human habitations, also reduces *Anopheles* numbers and breaks the cycle. When feasible, such measures are useful in controlling mosquito vectors of other diseases, though total elimination of breeding sites is impossible and, in irrigated areas, undesirable. If mosquito and *Plasmodium* numbers are reduced for three or four years, malaria can be eliminated entirely, as it has from the United States and most of western Europe, Japan, and Russia. Eradication of malaria in the tropics is vastly complicated by the existence of isolated pockets of the disease and lack of equipment and technical personnel. Even "eradicated" malaria is kept at bay only by prompt reporting, isolating, and treating of individual cases.

ROCKY MOUNTAIN SPOTTED FEVER

This disease is endemic in the United States where ticks serve as both vector and primary reservoir. Eradication is virtually impossible because of the difficulty, and undesirability, of covering millions of square kilometers of woodlands with enough pesticide to control ticks. Consequently, practical control of the disease involves reducing chances for exposure. Effective repellents prevent ticks' attachment, and prompt inspection for and removal of ticks after exposure is effective, particularly because a tick must remain attached for at least several hours in order to transmit Rocky Mountain spotted fever. Obviously, the disease is avoidable if one simply stays out of tick-infested woodlands and pastures during spring and early summer.

TRYPANOSOMIASIS AND NAGANA

Several species of tsetse-fly–borne trypanosomes have effectively prevented colonization and economic development of millions of square kilometers in Africa. Both humans and livestock are affected (by different *Trypanosoma* species). Control of the diseases is based on control of vectors, *Glossina* species, by insecticidal applications to brushy areas in which the flies rest, and experimentally, removal of brush has greatly reduced local tsetse numbers (Willett, 1963). Isolation and treatment of individual cases is important because people are the major reservoir for human trypanosomiasis. Nagana and trypanosomiasis were not widespread in Africa until major population shifts into east and central Africa occurred, following colonization by Europeans in the nineteenth century. Wild game animals have evolved resistance to trypanosomes but harbor the parasite causing nagana. This raises potential conflicts in management: Shall game animals be eliminated from most of east Africa to permit cattle grazing? Even when confined to national parks, wild game are a source of nagana infection for cattle grazing near (or within) park boundaries. Immunization of livestock has helped in management of other insect-borne diseases (e.g., equine encephalitis), though as yet no effective immunization exists for trypanosomes. Alternatively, some of the larger game animals, particularly larger antelopes, might be grazed and raised for milk, meat, and blood in nagana-infested areas. Preliminary results from antelope ranching have been encouraging (Myers, 1971).

DUTCH ELM DISEASE

Management of Dutch elm disease focuses on all three points in epidemiology: vector, pathogen, and host. Elm bark beetles are susceptible to insecticidal sprays, though problems in timing and coverage exist: The adult beetles are active for but a short time (usually June and September) on the bark surface, and to get uniform coverage over all the cracks and crannies in the bark of a large elm tree is nearly impossible. A single female beetle that gets through may be sufficient to introduce the disease. Systemic insecticides, especially bidrin, are sometimes effective but are expensive and difficult or hazardous to apply. Elm bark beetles do orient to pheromones and host plant attractants (Peacock et al., 1973), but these chemicals have not yet provided effective control.

Recently a systemic fungicide, benomyl, has been used successfully as both an injection and a foliar spray against the causative fungus of Dutch elm disease. Benomyl is useful in protecting healthy trees but is of limited effectiveness in diseased trees because the fungus blocks plant circulation and thereby prevents movement of the systemic fungicide.

The most effective, and least popular, management tool for Dutch elm disease is sanitation. Immediate removal of dead trees, stumps, and elm logs prior to emergence of the next adult beetle brood is most effective. Ideally, elms should be cut down and destroyed as soon as disease symptoms are noticed and confirmed. People are understandably reluctant to do this, even though the disease is invariably fatal and the elm will die within a few years. Fortunately for elm lovers, hybrid elms and hardy species resist Dutch elm disease and may be planted in infested areas.

SUMMARY

Insects are of major importance because of their relationship to diseases of humans, domestic animals, and cultivated plants. Insects and related arthropods can cause disease directly by side effects of bites or stings, especially those species that habitually parasitize domestic animals or people. Of even greater health significance are those arthropod vectors that transmit pathogens: viruses, mycoplasma, bacteria, fungi, protozoa, and roundworms. Transmission may occur indirectly by contagion or directly through feeding. Some pathogens are very specific to both a particular host and vector and must pass part of their life cycle in each. Knowledge of the interrelationship—epidemiology—among pathogen, vector, and host is a prerequisite to effective management of arthropod-borne diseases. This is illustrated by brief discussions of plague, malaria, Rocky Mountain spotted fever, trypanosomiasis, and Dutch elm disease.

Chapter Twelve

Beneficial Aspects

INTRODUCTION

Beneficial relationships between insects and people generally are not accorded the same importance as harmful relationships. Perhaps our preoccupation with noxious arthropods results from the immediacy and obviousness of such damage as chewed leaves, wormy apples, and bee stings. Nonetheless, many more insect species are beneficial to humanity's interests, because they are important links in terrestrial and aquatic ecosystems (Chapter Nine), and a number of insects also provide more obvious economic benefits. We derive from insects both goods (honey, silk, lac, food) and services (biological control, pollination, research).

HONEY AND BEESWAX

The most ubiquitous insect-produced product is probably honey, a viscous, sugary concentrate formed from nectar within the stomach of the honey bee, *Apis mellifera* (Apidae). Throughout most of human history honey was the only available sweetener; use of refined sugar has become widespread only in this century. Honey is storable for long periods without refrigeration, for microorganisms cannot thrive in such a concentrated solution. Honey is used in many products and is also fermented to produce mead, a staple alcoholic beverage of northern Europe in the days of the Vikings and the Merrie Men of Sherwood Forest.

Beeswax is secreted by abdominal glands (see Fig. 6–11) and assembled into comb; this is harvested along with honey. Even in these days of synthetic waxes and paraffins, beeswax finds use; beeswax candles, being nearly smokeless and dripless, are prized as church candles. Beeswax is also (in my opinion) the best material available for waxing bowstrings to prevent unraveling.

The honey bee is one of the few domesticated insects, in the sense that colonies are managed for maximum production of honey and wax. (Honey bees are, however, perfectly capable of survival in the wild.) Beekeepers cage bees in the sort of box pictured in Figure 12–1. Essentially, the social life of the bee in such a hive is similar to that outlined in Chapter Six, except that beekeepers generally buy newly mated queens and "requeen" hives annually. Also, lest bees mix honey with "brood" (larvae and pupae), a wire grid, or "queen excluder" is

395

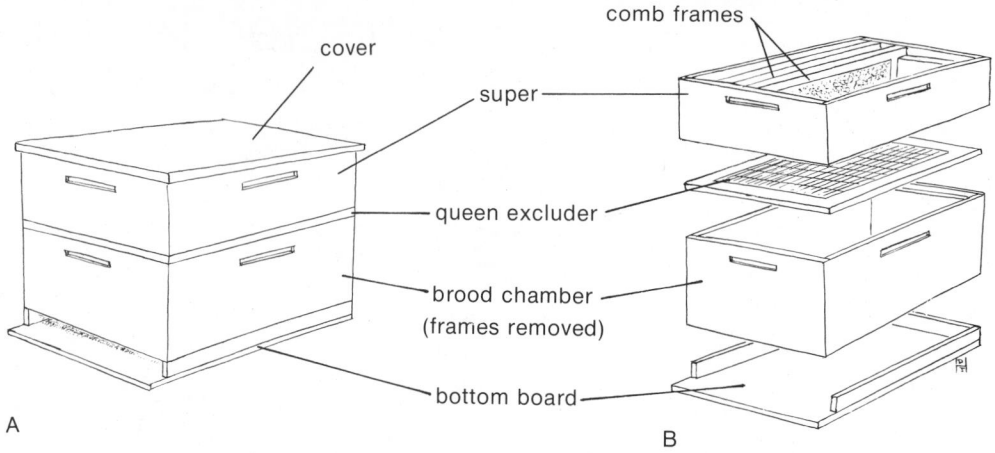

Figure 12–1.   Commercial beehive. *A*, Intact. *B*, Separated to show parts.

placed between upper and lower boxes of a hive. The queen cannot get through the screen because she is larger than the workers, so no eggs are laid in the upper combs. The beekeeper furthermore may assist the bees by providing a foundation (of beeswax, metal, or nylon) on which bees can build new comb. He or she usually feeds the bees sugar water and soybean-based cakes during winter or inclement weather to assure a strong colony during the "honey flow," when flowers are blooming profusely.

SILK, LAC, AND OTHER PRODUCTS

Since about 2500 B.C., the Chinese have grown the commercial silkworm, *Bombyx mori* (Fig. 12–2). Though insects of many orders produce it, the silk of only a few, mostly Lepidoptera, has found commercial use. *Bombyx mori* is especially valuable, for boiling the cocoon loosens the silk and one long strand can then be unreeled. Alas for the silkworm, this must be done before the adult emerges, because it will break through the strand on emergence. Sericulture, the growing of silkworms and harvesting of silk, was for many centuries a closely guarded secret in the Orient; it was not until eggs were smuggled to Constantinople in 550 A.D. that sericulture began in the West. Sericulture is labor-intensive because larvae must be tended and cocoons unreeled by hand; thus silk has become expensive and recently has lost much ground to similar but less expensive synthetic fibers. Most silkworm silk goes into the manufacture of clothing, although some is used for surgical thread. The breeding and pampering of *Bombyx mori* for 4500 years has resulted in evolution of larvae with degenerate prolegs that no longer permit them to climb their food plant, mulberry. They must be fed and therefore are thoroughly domesticated. None has been found in the wild.

Silk from other insects or spiders has found occasional utility. A unique use of the silk from black widow spiders is for crosshairs on optical equipment, including gun- and bombsights. Black widow silk is of uniform thickness and resists shock and vibration. Many of the B-17's used in American air raids over

Europe in World War II were equipped with bombsights having crosshairs of spider silk.

Lac is a sticky, honeydew-like substance secreted by a scale insect, *Laccifer lacca,* of India, Pakistan, and southeast Asia. Lac deposits often coat branches of shrubs to a depth of several millimeters. The twigs are harvested and some (brood lac) are tied to uninfested trees to spread the infestation. The rest are ground up, then heated to melt the lac, which is then separated from the sticks and other debris, dried, and flaked. These lac flakes are the main ingredient in

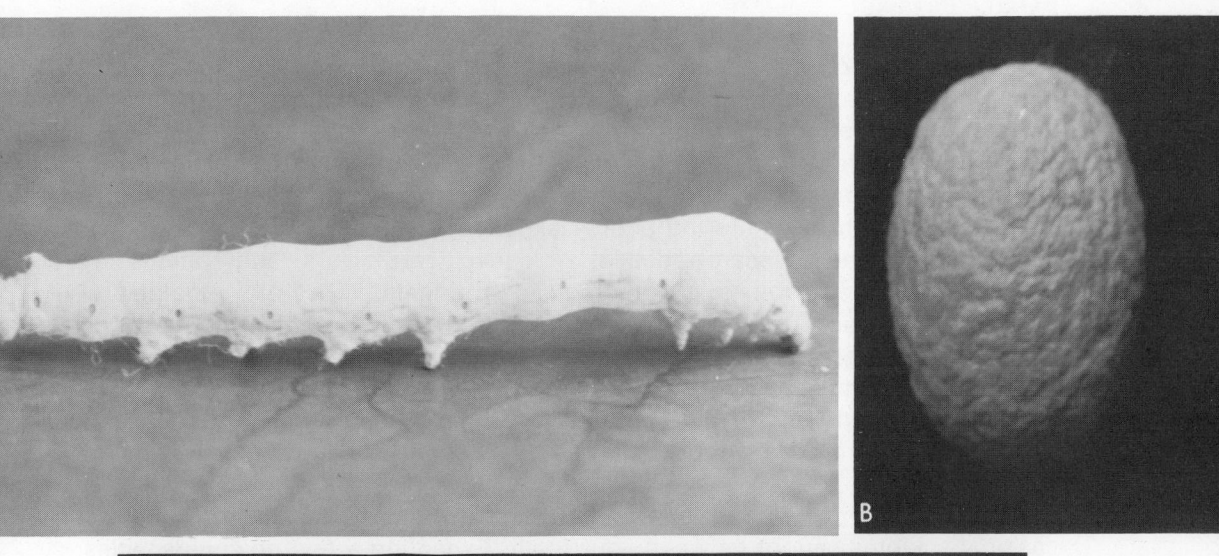

Figure 12–2. The silkworm, *Bombyx mori. A,* Larva. *B,* Cocoon. *C,* Adult.

shellac. In recent years, shellac has faced stiff competition from synthetic wax- or vinyl-based varnishes, which are less expensive to produce.

Several insect products are, or were, used as dyes for cloth. Cochineal was one of the most important; it is a red pigment extracted from scale insects of prickly pear cactus in Mexico. Insect galls are a source of a wide variety of dyes. Recently, most insect-based dyes have been unable to compete with less expensive and more colorfast synthetic dyes.

FOOD

Insects are rich in protein and micronutrients, and were it not for our corporate squeamishness, insects would be valuable additions to American diets. Certainly, they are more nutritious than potato chips or soda pop. Insects are a staple dietary item for many of the world's people who live off the land out of choice or desperation. The insects that are most often eaten are large and/or numerous enough to justify the energy expended in gathering them. Termites, grubworms (larvae of scarab beetles), cicadas, caterpillars, and locusts are perhaps most often eaten by entomological "gourmets." They are a major protein source for many "primitive" people today, and formerly some American Indians subsisted largely on grubs and locusts. In the United States, insects are available for eating mostly as novelty items: canned grasshoppers or caterpillars, chocolate-covered bees or ants, and so forth. Mexican producers of mescal, a liquor distilled from agave plants, traditionally bottle a larva along with the beverage.

There is nothing wrong with eating most insects if you do not mind occasional sclerites caught between your teeth. Excepting a few noxious species, almost all insects can be eaten, and it seems somewhat incongruous that we do not better utilize this outstanding nutrient source that constantly walks, flies, and crawls among us. Taylor (1975) has more information about what insects to eat, with appropriate recipes.

POLLINATION

A most important service rendered us by insects is pollination of flowers. Flowers will not produce seeds or fruit unless pollen is transferred from the male anthers to the female pistil. Some pollination is accomplished by wind, particularly among grasses (including corn and wheat) and some trees (conifers, willows, some nuts), and other flowers are self-pollinating. However, the majority, by far, of fruit and vegetable crops are pollinated by insects. Apples, pears, cherries, grapes, tomatoes, melons, beans, and cotton are just a few examples. Even leaf or root crops, such as cabbage, lettuce, carrots, and turnips, are ultimately dependent on pollinators, without which their seed could not be produced. The importance of insect pollinators was well illustrated following English colonization of New Zealand and the subsequent introduction of red clover. Clover grew well on the islands but did not produce seed well; native insects evidently could not pollinate the plant. After European bumble bees were introduced, clover in New Zealand began to yield seed in quantity (Cumber, 1954).

A wide variety of insects are capable of pollinating. Most insects that visit flowers may in their search for nectar pick up pollen and by accident transfer it to another blossom. Hymenoptera probably pollinate more flowers than all other orders combined, though Diptera, Lepidoptera, and Coleoptera are important too. Floral adaptations sometimes have coevolved with specific insects who alone can pollinate them; examples are yucca moths and yucca, *Ophrys* orchids and bees, and bumble bees and red clover. Other flowers can be pollinated by any insect that happens to tread thereon. In the United States and throughout the world, the most important single insect pollinator is the honey bee. This is true partly because the honey bee visits a variety of flowers but restricts each foraging trip to a single plant species (von Frisch, 1950) and is therefore a very efficient pollinator. Also, this insect is often the most readily available pollinator; it is the only species that a fruit grower can rent in quantity for pollination.

BIOLOGICAL CONTROL

In addition to the obvious importance of parasitic and predaceous insects in preserving ecological systems, many species have been used specifically as agents of biological control. I discussed biological control of pest insects in Chapter Ten. Specific agents of biological control of insects are mainly parasitic wasps or flies (Tachinidae) and predatory beetles (Coccinellidae and Carabidae), lacewings (Chrysopidae), and mites.

Phytophagous insects have been successfully used in several instances to control weeds biologically. Andres and Goeden (1971) documented over 50 cases of successful biological control of weeds. A classic case is control of prickly pear cactus in Australia (Dodd, 1959). This plant, native to North and South America, was introduced to Australia, where it was planted as an ornamental. Unfortunately, prickly pear survived so well in the Australian climate that it became a pest, rendering millions of rangeland acres unsuitable for sheep and cattle grazing (Fig. 12–3A). Search for natural enemies of prickly pear revealed, among others, the South American cactus moth, *Cactoblastis cactorum,* whose larvae ate prickly pear specifically and voraciously. Within a few years following their release into Australia, larvae of *C. cactorum* had decimated the extensive stands of prickly pear (Fig. 12–3B). Moth and plant are both now uncommon, and isolated stands of prickly pear survive only until *Cactoblastis* finds them.

In the United States, outstanding success has been attained in controlling Klamath weed on western rangelands (Huffaker and Kennett, 1959) and alligator-weed in southeastern waterways, both by Chrysomelidae (Andres and Goeden, 1971). Obviously, in investigations of potential agents of weed control, diet is a most important consideration, and plant-feeding insects are very closely screened as to food-plant preferences. It certainly would not do, for instance, to introduce a thistle-eating insect to control these weeds in eastern pastures, only to have it spread to California and decimate the artichoke crop. Most biological agents for weed control have been selected for very narrow food preferences.

An unusual use of beneficial insects in biological control occurred in the case of bovine dung in Australia. When Europeans introduced cattle and sheep to Australia, they simultaneously introduced dung that native dung beetles (Scarabaeidae) literally could not handle. The native beetles were eminently specialized for breaking up and burying kangaroo droppings, but cow dung was

A

B

Figure 12–3. Control of prickly pear in Australia by *Cactoblastis cactorum* (Pyralidae). *A*, Prickly pear plot before importation of moth. *B*, Same scene 3 years later, after establishment of moth. (From Dodd, A. P. 1959. The biological control of prickly pear in Australia. *In* Keast, A., R. L. Cocker, and C. L. Christian (eds.). Biogeography and Ecology in Australia. Monographs in Biology, Vol. VIII. Dr. W. Junk, The Hague.)

simply too much for them. As the dung piled higher, it covered up to 10 per cent of some pastures and provided plenty of food for larvae of biting flies. In desperation, the Australian government dispatched entomologists to tropical east Africa, which supports an incredible diversity of dung beetles. A selection of the most industrious rollers of bovine dung was introduced, and in a short time, dung ceased to be a major problem for stockmen in the Australian outback.

INSECTS IN BIOLOGY AND MEDICINE

Insects, with their short life cycle, high reproductive rate, and (sometimes) easily obtainable diets, are ideally suited to mass-rearing for biological studies. Many insect species have thus assisted scientists in their efforts to unravel the secrets of living systems. Among the insects that have contributed tremendously to our knowledge of biology are:

1. Pomace flies (*Drosophila* species, principally *D. melanogaster*), much used by geneticists. *Drosophila* feed readily on fruit or artificial media and have large, easily observed chromosomes in cells of the salivary glands. The flies crossbreed freely and, since many different genetic variations occur, are very useful in analyzing patterns of inheritance.

2. The bloodsucking bug *Rhodnius* (Reduviidae). Wigglesworth (1936, 1959, 1963, 1964, 1972) and associates in Britain have thoroughly investigated the relationship among feeding, hormonal secretion, and metamorphosis in the bug. Conveniently, it needs a blood meal to molt or produce eggs and survives various operations and manipulations in the course of study.

3. The saturniid moth, *Hyalophora cecropia*. It has an obligate pupal diapause determined by photoperiod. It is large, eminently rearable, and dissectable and has thereby provided important information on metamorphosis and the nature of diapause.

4. Cockroaches of several species, particularly the domestic pests. They feed contentedly on many readily available foods (e.g., dog biscuits). They are important components of studies on behavior and development and are one group used in standard determination of the L.D.$_{50}$'s (see p. 360) of experimental insecticides.

5. Flies, particularly the house fly, *Musca domestica,* and blow flies (Calliphoridae). In the laboratory the former eats artificial diet and the latter, meat. Both lay many eggs, grow well in containers, and have short enough lifespans that many generations can pass in a year. One may observe significant numerical and genetic changes during that time, and flies have thereby added much to our knowledge of population ecology.

6. Grain-eating beetles, especially *Tribolium* species. These have short lives, lay many eggs, and are among the easiest insects to rear. They too have provided much useful knowledge about genetics, population processes, and tolerance ranges of insects to specific physical factors.

7. Social insects, especially the honey bee, *Apis mellifera.* The colonial insects are very suitable subjects for study of insect behavior and its relation to genetics. They display a wide variety of behavioral patterns, as insects go.

Many insects have been reared in quantity (Smith, 1966) as subjects for study; the seven just discussed are outstanding examples, but others have been almost as important. Still other species are incapable (so far) of survival under laboratory conditions but nonetheless have been of major importance to scientists. Obviously, all named insects have been studied, at least to the point of description.

Before our present age of synthetic drugs and sophisticated surgical equipment, insects found many medical uses. Maggots were once utilized in treatment of infected wounds and bones, for it was noted that soldiers with maggot-infested wounds were less likely to develop gangrene. Maggots secrete a bacterial inhibitor, allantoin, that promotes healing, and this has subsequently been synthesized and used in wound treatment. At one time, the maggots themselves were reared in aseptic conditions, then placed in wounds to clean them out.

Cantharidin is a drug made from the powdered bodies of a blister beetle, the "Spanish fly." It is an irritant, and while it is useful in treating some urogenital conditions, its legendary aphrodisiac effect is questionable, and its unauthorized use can be dangerous.

Surgeons have used ants to suture lacerations (LeClercq, 1969). Ants clamp their mandibles together and close a cut when applied to it; their bodies may then be cut away, leaving the head with the jaws permanently locked shut. When the ant heads dry, they crumble away, and by then the wound is usually healed. Ant heads may not seem as neat and tidy as surgical thread or tape, but they will do in a pinch.

ENJOYMENT

At the outset, I stated that this book is mostly about scientific study of insects. On another level, insects may be seen as objects of enjoyment for humanity. Certainly, brightly colored adult Lepidoptera are favorites, whether their wings decorate trays and lampshades or whether a living butterfly suddenly appears on a sunny day late in March to remind us that the gloom of winter is soon to end. Fireflies, too, are things of great beauty and give an added dimension to summer evenings. A chorus of crickets and katydids likewise may provide great enjoyment in the coolness of the day. Those of us who study insects scientifically may tend to lose our wonder and awe of insects as we discover how they function, but this need not necessarily be so. Insect-watching, like bird-watching, can and should be done for pure enjoyment, even by entomologists. Such moments of relaxation, far from being a waste of time, are absolutely necessary if humanity is to retain any corporate sanity in a progressively more insulated, mechanized, and regimented environment.

References

Aldrich, J. M., and L. A. Turley. 1899. A balloon-making fly. Amer. Nat. *33*:809–12.

Alexander, R. D., and W. L. Brown, Jr. 1963. Mating behavior and the origin of insect wings. Univ. Michigan Occas. Pap. Mus. Zool. No. 628.

Alexander, R. D., and T. M. Moore. 1962. The evolutionary relationships of 17- and 13-year cicadas, and three new species (Homoptera, Cicadidae, *Magicicada*). Univ. Michigan Misc. Publ. Mus. Zool. No. 121.

Alloway, T. M. 1972. Learning and memory in insects. Ann. Rev. Entomol. *17*:43–56.

Andres, L. A., and R. D. Goeden. 1971. The biological control of weeds by introduced natural enemies. *In* Huffaker, C. B. (ed.). Biological Control. Plenum Publishing Corp., New York, pp. 143–164.

Andrewartha, H. G. 1961. Introduction to the Study of Animal Populations. University of Chicago Press, Chicago, 281 pp.

Andrewartha, H. G., and L. C. Birch. 1954. The Distribution and Abundance of Animals. University of Chicago Press, Chicago, 782 pp.

Armbrust, E. J., and G. G. Gyrisco. 1968. The influence of some physical and biological factors on the phototactic response of the alfalfa weevil, *Hypera postica*. Ann. Entomol. Soc. Amer. *61*:1561–66.

Arnett, R. H., Jr. 1968. The Beetles of the United States, a Manual for Identification. The Catholic University of America Press, Washington, D. C., 1112 pp.

Arnold, J. W., and S. S. Sohi. 1974. Hemocytes of *Malacosoma disstria* Hübner. Morphology of the cells in fresh blood and after cultivation in vitro. Canad. J. Zool. *52*:481–84.

Arthur, A. P. 1966. Associative learning in *Itoplectis conquisitor* (Say) (Hymenoptera:Ichneumonidae). Canad. Entomol. *98*:213–23.

Askew, R. R. 1971. Parasitic Insects. American Elsevier Publishing Co., Inc., New York, 316 pp.

Atkins, J. A. C., W. Wingo, W. A. Sodeman, and J. E. Flynn. 1958. Necrotic arachnidism. Amer. J. Trop. Med. Hyg. *7*:165–184.

Baerends, G. P. 1941. Fortpflanzungsverhalten und Orientierung der Grabwespe *Ammophila campestris*. Jur. Tidjschr. Entomol. *84*:68–275.

Baerg, W. J. 1929. Some poisonous arthropods of North and Central America. Trans. 4th Int. Cong. Entomol. *2*:418–38.

Baerg, W. J. 1958. The tarantula. University of Kansas Press, Lawrence, 88 pp.

Baker, H. G., and I. Baker. 1973. Amino-acids in nectar and their evolutionary significance. Nature *241*:543–45.

Bakker, K. 1969. Selection for rate of growth and its influence on competitive ability of larvae of *Drosophila melanogaster*. Neth. J. Zool. *19*:541–95.

Baltensweiler, W. 1968. The cyclic population dynamics of the grey larch tortrix, *Zeiraphera griseana* Hübner (= *Semasia diniana* Guenée) (Lepidoptera:Tortricidae). *In* Southwood, T. R. E. (ed.): Insect abundance. Royal Entomol. Soc. London *4*:88–97.

Barber, H. S. 1951. North American fireflies of the genus *Photuris*. Smiths. Inst. Misc. Coll. *117*:1–58.

Barnes, R. D. 1974. Invertebrate Zoology. 3rd ed. W. B. Saunders Co., Philadelphia, 870 pp.

Baron, S. R. 1972. The Desert Locust. Methuen & Co. Ltd., London, 228 pp.

Barrett, J. R., Jr., H. O. Deay, and J. G. Hartsock. 1971. Reduction in insect damage to cucumbers, tomatoes, and sweet corn through use of electric light traps. J. Econ. Entomol. *64*:1241–49.

Baumhover, A. H., A. J. Graham, B. A. Bitter, D. E. Hopkins, W. D. New, F. H. Dudley, and R. C. Bushland. 1955. Screw-worm control through release of sterilized flies. J. Econ. Entomol. *48*:462–66.

Beck, S. D. 1963. Physiology and ecology of photoperiodism. Bull. Entomol. Soc. Amer. 9:8–16.

Beck, S. D. 1973. Photoperiodism and biological clocks. In Tipton, V. J. (ed.). Syllabus/Introductory Entomology. Brigham Young University Press, Provo, Utah, pp. 299–306.

Beirne, B. P. 1956. Leafhoppers (Homoptera:Cicadellidae) of Canada and Alaska. Canad. Entomol. Suppl. 2:1–180.

Beirne, B. P. 1970. Effects of precipitation on crop insects. Canad. Entomol. 102:1360–73.

Benett, L. 1973. Effectiveness and flight of small insects. Ann. Entomol. Soc. Amer. 66:1187–90.

Benfield, E. F. 1974. Autohemorrhage in two stoneflies (Plecoptera) and its effectiveness as a defense mechanism. Ann. Entomol. Soc. Amer. 67:739–42.

Bergerard, J. 1972. Environmental and physiological control of sex determination and differentiation. Ann. Rev. Entomol. 17:57–74.

Beroza, M., and E. F. Knipling. 1972. Gypsy moth control with the sex attractant pheromone. Science 177:19–27.

Berridge, M. J., and J. L. Oschman. 1972. Transporting Epithelia. Academic Press, Inc., New York.

Bess, H. A., R. van den Bosch, and F. H. Haramoto. 1961. Fruit fly parasites and their activities in Hawaii. Proc. Hawaiian Entomol. Soc. 17:367–78.

Bey-Bienko, G. Y. 1962. On the general classification of insects. Entomol. Rev. 41:3–10.

Bignell, D. E. 1973. Digestion. In Tipton, V. J. (ed.). Syllabus/Introductory Entomology. Brigham Young University Press, Provo, Utah, pp. 279–95.

Birch, L. C. 1953. Experimental background to the study of the distribution and abundance of insects. III. The relations between innate capacity for increase and survival of different species of beetles living together on the same food. Evolution 7:136–44.

Bishop, O. N. 1966. Statistics for Biology: A Practical Guide for the Experimental Biologist. Houghton-Mifflin Co., Boston, 182 pp.

Blackwelder, R. E. 1967. Taxonomy: A Text and Reference Book. John Wiley & Sons, Inc., New York, 698 pp.

Blaine, W. D., and S. E. Dixon. 1973. The effect of juvenile hormone on the function of the accessory gland of the adult male cockroach, Periplaneta americana (Orthoptera:Blattidae). Canad. Entomol. 105:1275–80.

Blatchley, W. S. 1920. Orthoptera of Northeastern America, with Especial Reference to the Faunas of Indiana and Florida. Nature Publishing Co., Indianapolis, 784 pp.

Blatchley, W. S. 1926. Heteroptera or True Bugs of Eastern North America, with Especial Reference to the Faunas of Indiana and Florida. Nature Publishing Co., Indianapolis, 1386 pp.

Blest, A. D. 1957. The function of eyespot patterns in the Lepidoptera. Behaviour 11:209–56.

Bohart, R. M. 1941. A revision of the Strepsiptera with special reference to the species of North America. Univ. Calif. Publ. Entomol. 7:91–159.

Bonhag, P. F. 1959. Histological and histochemical studies on the ovary of the American cockroach, Periplaneta americana (L.). Univ. Calif. Publ. Entomol. 16:81–124.

Borror, D. J., and D. M. DeLong. 1971. An Introduction to the Study of Insects. 3rd ed. Holt, Rinehart and Winston, Inc., New York, 812 pp.

Borror, D. J., D. M. DeLong, and C. A. Triplehorn. 1976. An Introduction to the Study of Insects. 4th ed. Holt, Rinehart and Winston, Inc., New York.

Borror, D. J., and R. E. White. 1970. A Field Guide to the Insects of America North of Mexico. Houghton-Mifflin Co., Boston, 404 pp.

Bowers, W. S., and C. C. Blickenstaff. 1966. Hormonal termination of diapause in the alfalfa weevil. Science 154:1673–74.

Bowers, W. S., L. R. Nault, R. E. Webb, and S. R. Dutky. 1972. Aphid alarm pheromone: isolation, identification, synthesis. Science 177:1121–22.

Brammer, J. D., and R. H. White. 1969. Vitamin A deficiency: effect on mosquito eye ultrastructure. Science 163:821–23.

Brian, M. V., and M. S. Blum. 1969. The influence of Myrmica queen head extracts on larval growth. J. Ins. Physiol. 15:2213–23.

Britton, W. E. 1923. The Hemiptera or sucking insects of Connecticut. Conn. State Geol. Nat. Hist. Bull. 34, 807 pp.

Broadhead, E. 1958. The psocid fauna of larch trees in northern England—an ecological study of mixed populations exploiting a common resource. J. Anim. Ecol. 27:217–63.

Brower, J. V. Z. 1958a. Experimental studies of mimicry in some North American butterflies. I. The monarch, Danaus plexippus and the viceroy, Limenitis archippus archippus. Evolution 12:32–47.

Brower, J. V. Z. 1958b. Experimental studies of mimicry in some North American butterflies. II. Battus philenor and Papilio troilus, P. polyxenes and P. glaucus. Evolution 12:123–36.

Brower, J. V. Z. 1960. Experimental studies of mimicry. IV. The reactions of starlings to different proportions of models and mimics. Amer. Nat. 94:271–82.

Brower, L. P. 1969. Ecological chemistry. Sci. Amer. 220(2):22–29.

Brown, A. W. A. 1968. Insecticide resistance comes of age. Bull. Entomol. Soc. Amer. 14:3–9.

Brown, L. R. 1973. Postembryonic development. In Tipton, V. J. (ed.). Syllabus/Introductory Entomology. Brigham Young University Press, Provo, Utah, pp. 125–56.

Brown, W. L., Jr., and E. O. Wilson. 1958. Character displacement. Syst. Zool. 5:49–64.

Brues, C. T., A. L. Melander, and F. M. Carpenter. 1954. Classification of insects. Bull. Mus. Comp. Zool. 73:1–917.

Buck, J. B. 1953. Physical properties and chemical composition of insect blood. In Roeder, K. D. (ed.). Insect Physiology. John Wiley & Sons, Inc., New York, pp. 147–90.

Burges, H. D., and N. W. Hussey (eds.). 1971.

Microbial Control of Insects and Mites. Academic Press, Inc., New York, 861 pp.

Bursell, E. 1970. An Introduction to Insect Physiology. Academic Press, Inc., New York, 276 pp.

Bush, G. L. 1969. Sympatric host race formation and speciation in frugivorous flies of the genus *Rhagoletis* (Diptera:Tephritidae). Evolution *23*:237–51.

Buxton, P. A. 1955. The Natural History of Tsetse Flies. H. K. Lewis, London.

Caldwell, R. L., and M. A. Rankin. 1972. Effects of a juvenile hormone mimic on flight in the milkweed bug *Oncopeltus fasciatus*. Gen. Comp. Endocrinol. *19*:601–5.

Carayon, J. 1964. Un cas d'offrande nuptiale chez les Hétéroptères. C. R. Acad. Sci. (Paris) *259*:4815–18.

Cardé, R. T. 1971. Aspects of reproductive isolation in the *Holomelina aurantiaca* complex (Lepidoptera:Arctiidae). Ph.D. thesis, Cornell University, Ithaca, N. Y.

Cardé, R. T., and W. L. Roelofs. 1973. Temperature modification of male sex pheromone response and factors affecting female calling in *Holomelina immaculata* (Lepidoptera:Arctiidae). Canad. Entomol. *105*:1505–12.

Carpenter, F. M. 1953. The geological history and evolution of insects. Amer. Sci. *41*:256–70.

Carpenter, F. M. 1973. Geological history and evolution of insects. *In* Tipton, V. J. (ed.). Syllabus/Introductory Entomology. Brigham Young University Press, Provo, Utah, pp. 77–88.

Carrell, J. E., and T. Eisner. 1974. Cantharidin: potent feeding deterrent to insects. Science *183*:755–57.

Carson, H. L., D. E. Hardy, H. T. Spieth, and W. S. Stone. 1970. The evolutionary biology of the Hawaiian Drosophilidae. *In* Hecht, M. K., and W. C. Steere (eds.). Essays in Evolution and Genetics in Honor of Theodosius Dobzhansky. Appleton-Century-Crofts, New York, pp. 473–543.

Carson, R. L. 1962. Silent Spring. Houghton-Mifflin Co., Boston, 368 pp.

Carter, W. 1973. Insects in Relation to Plant Disease. 2nd ed. John Wiley & Sons, Inc., New York, 759 pp.

Carthy, J. D. 1958. An Introduction to the Behaviour of Invertebrates. George Allen & Unwin Ltd., London.

Casagrande, R. A., and F. W. Stehr. 1973. Evaluating the effects of harvesting alfalfa on alfalfa weevil (Coleoptera:Curculionidae) and parasite populations in Michigan. Canad. Entomol. *105*:1119–28.

Chambers, D. L., R. T. Cunningham, R. W. Lichty, and R. B. Thrailkill. 1974. Pest control by attractants: a case study demonstrating economy, specificity, and environmental acceptability. BioScience *24*:150–52.

Chandler, H. P. 1956. Megaloptera. *In* Usinger, R. L. (ed.). Aquatic Insects of California. University of California Press, Berkeley, pp. 229–33.

Chapman, R. F. 1969. The Insects: Structure and Function. American Elsevier Publishing Co., Inc., New York, 819 pp.

Chapman, R. F. 1971. The Insects: Structure and Function. 2nd ed. American Elsevier Publishing Co., Inc., New York.

Chapman, R. N. 1928. The quantitative analysis of environmental factors. Ecology *9*:111–22.

Chauvin, R. 1967. The World of an Insect. McGraw-Hill Book Co., New York, 256 pp.

Christiansen, K. 1964. Bionomics of Collembola. Ann. Rev. Entomol. *9*:147–78.

Christophers, S. R. 1960. *Aedes aegypti* (L.), the Yellow Fever Mosquito: Its Life History, Bionomics, and Structure. Cambridge University Press, New York, 738 pp.

Church, N. S. 1960. Heat loss and the body temperature of flying insects. II. Heat conduction within the body and its loss by radiation and convection. J. Exp. Biol. *37*:186–212.

Cisne, J. L. 1974. Trilobites and the origin of arthropods. Science *186*:13–18.

Clark, L. R., P. W. Geier, R. D. Hughes, and R. F. Morris. 1967. The Ecology of Insect Populations in Theory and Practice. Methuen & Co. Ltd., London, 232 pp.

Clausen, C. P. 1956. Biological control of insect pests in the continental United States. USDA Tech. Bull. *1139*:1–151.

Cloudsley-Thompson, J. L. 1958. Spiders, Scorpions, Centipedes, and Mites: the Ecology and Natural History of Woodlice, Myriapods, and Arachnids. Pergamon Press, Inc., New York, 228 pp.

Coad, B. R. 1931. Insects captured by airplane are found at surprising heights. USDA Yearbook, pp. 320–23.

Cole, F. R. 1971. The Flies of Western North America. University of California Press, Berkeley, 693 pp.

Colwell, R. K. 1973. Competition and coexistence in a simple tropical community. Amer. Nat. *107*:737–60.

Comstock, J. H., and J. G. Needham. 1899. The wings of insects. Comstock, Ithaca, N. Y., 124 pp.

Cooperative Economic Insect Report. 1963–1975. USDA Animal and Plant Health Inspection Service, Washington, D. C.

Cope, O. B. 1971. Interactions between pesticides and wildlife. Ann. Rev. Entomol. *16*:325–64.

Corbet, P. S. 1963. A Biology of Dragonflies. Quadrangle Books Inc., Chicago, 247 pp.

Cothran, W. R., and C. G. Summers. 1974. Visual economic thresholds and potential pesticide abuse: alfalfa weevils, an example. Environ. Entomol. *3*:891–94.

Cotter, W. B. 1974. Social facilitation and development in *Ephestia kühniella*. Z. Science *183*: 747–48.

Creighton, W. S. 1950. The ants of North America. Bull. Mus. Comp. Zool. *104*:1–585.

Croft, B. A. 1975. Tree fruit pest management. *In* Metcalf, R. L., and W. H. Luckmann (eds.). Introduction to Insect Pest Management. John Wiley & Sons, Inc., New York. pp. 471–507.

Crombie, A. C. 1945. On competition between different species of graminivorous insects. Proc. Roy. Entomol. Soc. (Ser. B.) *132*:362–95.

Crowson, R. A. 1955. The Natural Classification of the Families of Coleoptera. Nathaniel & Lloyd, London, 187 pp.

Cumber, R. A. 1954. The life-cycle of bumble-bees in New Zealand. N. Z. J. Sci. Tech. Bull. *36*:95–107.

Cummins, K. W. 1964. Factors limiting the micro-distribution of larvae of the caddisflies *Pycnopsyche lepida* (Hagen) and *Pycnopsyche guttifer* (Walker) in a Michigan stream (Trichoptera: Limnephilidae). Ecol. Monog. *34*:271–95.

Curran, C. H. 1934. The Families and Genera of North American Diptera. Published by the author, New York, 512 pp.

DaCosta, C. P., and C. M. Jones. 1971. Cucumber beetle resistance and mite susceptibility controlled by the bitter gene in *Cucumis sativus*. *Science 172*:1145–46.

Dadd, R. H. 1963. Feeding behavior and nutrition in grasshoppers and locusts. Adv. Ins. Physiol. *1*:47–109.

Dadd, R. H. 1973. Insect nutrition: current developments and metabolic implications. Ann. Rev. Entomol. *18*:381–420.

Dalton, S. 1975. Borne on the Wind. Reader's Digest Press, New York, 160 pp.

Dame, D. A., and C. H. Schmidt. 1970. The sterile-male technique against tsetse flies, *Glossina* spp. Bull. Entomol. Soc. Amer. *16*:24–30.

Davey, K. G. 1965. Reproduction in the insects. W. H. Freeman and Co., Publishers, San Francisco, 96 pp.

Davidson, R. H., and L. M. Peairs. 1966. Insect Pests of Farm, Garden and Orchard. 6th ed. John Wiley & Sons, Inc. New York, 675 pp.

Day, W. C. 1956. Ephemeroptera. *In* Usinger, R. L. (ed.). Aquatic Insects of California. University of California Press, Berkeley, pp. 79–105.

DeBach, P. (ed.). 1964. Biological Control of Insect Pests and Weeds. Reinhold Publishing Corp. New York, 844 pp.

DeBach, P. 1974. Biological Control by Natural Enemies. Cambridge University Press, Cambridge, England, 323 pp.

DeBach, P., and R. A. Sundby. 1963. Competitive displacement between ecological homologues. Hilgardia *34*:105–66.

DeFoliart, G. R. 1975. Insects as a source of protein. Bull. Entomol. Soc. Amer. *21*:161–63.

DeLeon, J. R., and B. O. L. Duke. 1966. Experimental studies on the transmission of Guatemalan and West African strains of *Onchocerca volvulus* by *Simulium ochraceum, S. metallicum*, and *S. callidum*. Trans. Roy. Soc. Trop. Med. Hyg. *60*:735–52.

DeLong, D. M. 1948. The leafhoppers, or Cicadellidae, of Illinois (Eurymelinae–Balcluthinae). Ill. Nat. Hist. Surv. Bull. *24*:97–376.

Denning, D. G. 1956. Trichoptera. *In* Usinger, R. L. (ed.). Aquatic Insects of California. University of California Press, Berkeley, pp. 237–70.

Dethier, V. G. 1962. To Know a Fly. Holden-Day, Inc., San Francisco, 119 pp.

Dethier, V. G. 1963. The physiology of Insect Senses. John Wiley & Sons, Inc., New York, 266 pp.

Dingle, H. 1972. Migration strategies of insects. Science *175*:1327–35.

Dixon, A. F. G. 1973. Biology of Aphids. Studies in Biology No. 44. Edward Arnold, London, 58 pp.

Dobzhansky, T. 1950. Evolution in the tropics. Amer. Sci. *38*:209–21.

Dodd, A. P. 1959. The biological control of prickly-pear in Australia. *In* Keast, A., R. L. Crocker, and C. L. Christian (eds.). Biogeography and Ecology in Australia. Monographs in Biology, Vol. VIII. Dr. W. Junk, The Hague, pp. 565–77.

Dominick, R. D., and C. R. Edwards. 1970. The Moths of America North of Mexico. P. W. Classey, London (several vols.).

Dowell, R. V. 1976. Ovary structure and biology of alfalfa weevil parasites. Ann. Entomol. Soc. Amer. (submitted for publication).

Dowell, R. V., and D. J. Horn. 1976. Adaptive strategies of larval parasitoids of alfalfa weevil. Canad. Entomol. (in press).

Dunn, L. H. 1930. Rearing the larvae of *Dermatobia hominis* Linn. in man. Psyche 37:327–42.

Eads, R. B., E. G. Campos, and H. A. Trevino. 1966. Quarantine problems associated with the importation of bananas from Mexico. J. Econ. Entomol. *59*:896–99.

Eaton, J. L. 1971. Insect photoreceptor: an internal ocellus is present in sphinx moths. Science *173*:822–3.

Eberhard, M. J. W. 1969. The social biology of polistine wasps. Univ. Michigan Misc. Publ. Mus. Zool. No. 140.

Edmunds, G. F. 1962. The principles applied in determining the hierarchic level of the higher categories of Ephemeroptera. Syst. Zool. *11*:22–31.

Edney, E. B. 1967. Water balance in desert arthropods. Science *156*:1059–66.

Edney, E. B. 1973. Water regulation. *In* Tipton, V. J. (ed.). Syllabus/Introductory Entomology. Brigham Young University Press, Provo, Utah, pp. 267–78.

Edwards, G. A. 1960. Insect micromorphology. Ann. Rev. Entomol. *5*:17–34.

Ehler, L. E., and R. van den Bosch. 1974. An analysis of the natural biological control of *Trichoplusia ni* (Lepidoptera: Noctuidae) on cotton in California. Canad. Entomol. *106*:1067–73.

Ehrlich, P. R., and A. E. Ehrlich. 1961. How to Know the Butterflies. William C. Brown Co., Publishers, Dubuque, Iowa. 262 pp.

Ehrlich, P. R., and P. H. Raven. 1964. Butterflies and plants: a study in coevolution. Evolution *18*:586–608.

Ehrlich, P. R., and P. H. Raven. 1967. Butterflies and plants. Sci. Amer. *216*(6):104–13.

Eisenstein, E. M., and M. J. Cohen. 1965. Learning in an isolated prothoracic insect ganglion. Anim. Behav. *13*:104–8.

Eisner, T. 1970. Chemical defense against predation in arthropods. *In* Sondheimer, E., and J. B. Simeone (eds.). Chemical Ecology. Academic Press, Inc., New York, pp. 157–217.

Eisner, T., J. S. Johnessee, J. Carrel, L. B. Hendry, and J. Meinwald. 1974. Defensive use by an insect of a plant resin. Science *184*:996–99.

Eisner, T., and J. Meinwald. 1966. Defensive secretions of arthropods. Science *153*:1341–50.

Elton, C. S. 1958. The ecology of invasions by animals and plants. Methuen & Co. Ltd., London, 181 pp.

Embree, D. G. 1965. The population dynamics of the winter moth in Nova Scotia. Mem. Entomol. Soc. Can. *46*:1–57.

Emden, H. F. van, V. F. Eastop, R. D. Hughes, and M. J. Way. 1969. The ecology of *Myzus persicae*. Ann. Rev. Entomol. *14*:197–270.

Emden, H. F., van, V. F. Eastop, R. D. Hughes, and M. J. Way. 1969. The ecology of *Myzus persicae*. Ann. Rev. Entomo. *14*:197–270.

Emden, H. F. van, and G. C. Williams. 1974. Insect stability and diversity in agro-ecosystems. Ann. Rev. Entomol. *19*:455–76.

Engelmann, F. 1970. The Physiology of Insect Reproduction. Pergamon Press Ltd., Oxford, 307 pp.

Entomological Society of America. 1970. Common Names of Insects Approved by the Entomological Society of America. Entomol. Soc. Amer., College Park, Maryland, 36 pp.

Errington, P. L. 1963. Muskrat Populations. Iowa State University Press, Ames, 665 pp.

Esten, W. N., and C. J. Mason. 1908. Sources of bacteria in milk. Bull. Conn. Agr. Expt. Sta. *51*:94–98.

Evans, F. C., and W. W. Murdoch. 1968. Taxonomic composition, trophic structure, and seasonal occurrence in a grassland insect community. J. Anim. Ecol. *37*:259–73.

Evans, H. E. 1966. Life on a Little-known Planet. Dell Publishing Co., Inc., New York, 318 pp.

Evans, H. E., and R. W. Matthews. 1973. Systematics and nesting behavior of Australian *Bembix* sand wasps (Hymenoptera, Sphecidae). Mem. Amer. Entomol. Inst. No. 20., 386 pp.

Fager, E. W. 1968. The community of invertebrates in decaying oak wood. J. Anim. Ecol. *37*:121–42.

Feeny, P. 1970. Seasonal changes in oak leaf tannins and nutrients as a cause of spring feeding by winter moth caterpillars. Ecology *51*:565–81.

Ferris, G. F. 1937–1955. Atlas of the Scale Insects of North America. Stanford University Press, Palo Alto (7 vols.).

Fischer, A. G. 1960. Latitudinal variations in organic diversity. Evolution *14*:64–81.

Flanders, S. E. 1956. The mechanism of sex-ratio regulation in the parasitic Hymenoptera. Ins. Soc. *3*:325–34.

Forbes, S. A. 1906. The corn root-aphis and its attendant ant. Bull. U.S. Div. Entomol. *60*:29–39.

Force, D. C. 1970. Competition among four hymenopterous parasites of an endemic insect host. Ann. Entomol. Soc. Amer. *63*:1675–88.

Force, D. C. 1972. r- and K-strategists in endemic host-parasitoid communities. Bull. Entomol. Soc. Amer. *18*:135–37.

Foster, W. A. 1967. Hormone-mediated nutritional control of sexual behavior in male dung flies. Science *158*:1596–97.

Fox, I. 1940. Fleas of Eastern United States. Iowa State College Press, Ames, 191 pp.

Fox, L. R. 1975. Cannibalism in natural populations. Ann. Rev. Ecol. Syst. *6*:87–106.

Fox, R. M., and J. W. Fox. 1964. Introduction to Comparative Entomology. Reinhold Publishing Corp., New York, 450 pp.

Fraenkel, G. 1932. Die Flugreflexe der Insekten und ihre Koordination. Z. vergl. Physiol. *16*:371–93.

Fraenkel, G., and D. L. Gunn. 1961. The Orientation of Animals. Dover Publications, Inc., New York, 376 pp.

Free, J. B., and C. G. Butler. 1959. Bumblebees. Macmillan Publishing Co., Inc., New York, 208 pp.

Frisch, K. von. 1950. Bees: Their Vision, Chemical Senses, and Language. Cornell University Press, Ithaca, 119 pp.

Frisch, K. von. 1967. The Dance Language and Orientation of Bees. Harvard University Press, Cambridge, 566 pp.

Frisch, K. von. 1974. Decoding the language of the bee. Science *185*:663–68.

Froeschner, R. C. 1947. Notes and keys to the Neuroptera of Missouri. Ann. Entomol. Soc. Amer. *40*:123–36.

Fronk, W. D. 1971. Insecticide application equipment. *In* Pfadt, R. E. (ed.). Fundamentals of Applied Entomology. 2nd ed. Macmillan Publishing Co., Inc., New York, pp. 219–41.

Furniss, M. M., L. N. Kline, R. F. Schmitz, and J. A. Rudinsky. 1972. Tests of three pheromones to induce or disrupt aggregation of douglas-fir beetles (Coleoptera:Scolytidae) on live trees. Ann. Entomol. Soc. Amer. *65*:1227–32.

Ganyard, M. C., and H. C. Ellis. 1973 (unpubl.). North Carolina tobacco pest management. 3rd annual report. USDA, Washington, D. C.

Gause, G. F. 1934. The Struggle for Existence. The Williams & Wilkins Co., Baltimore, 163 pp.

Geiger, R. 1965. The Climate Near the Ground. Harvard University Press, Cambridge, 611 pp.

Ghiradella, H., D. Aneshansley, T. Eisner, R. E. Silberglied, and H. E. Hinton. 1972. Ultraviolet reflection of a male butterfly: interference color caused by thin-layer elaboration of wing scales. Science *178*:1214–17.

Gibo, D. L., R. M. Yarascavitch, and H. E. Dew.

1974. Thermoregulation in colonies of *Vespula arenaria* and *V. maculata* (Hymenoptera: Vespidae) under normal conditions and under cold stress. Canad. Entomol. *106*:503–07.

Gibson, W. P., and R. C. Berberet. 1974. Histological studies on encapsulation of *Bathyplectes curculionis* eggs by larvae of the alfalfa weevil. Ann. Entomol. Soc. Amer. 67:588–90.

Giese, R. L., R. M. Peart, and R. T. Huber. 1975. Pest management. Science *187*:1045–52.

Gilbert, L. E. 1971. Butterfly-plant coevolution: has *Passiflora adenopoda* won the selectional race with heliconiine butterflies? Science *172*:585–86.

Gilbert, L. E. 1972. Pollen feeding and reproductive biology of *Heliconius* butterflies. Proc. Nat. Acad. Sci. *69*:1403–07.

Gilbert, L. I., and D. S. King. 1973. Physiology of growth and development: endocrine aspects. *In* Rockstein, M. (ed.). The Physiology of Insecta, Vol. 1. 2nd ed. Academic Press, Inc., New York, pp. 249–370.

Gilmour, D. 1961. The Biochemistry of Insects. Academic Press, Inc., New York, 343 pp.

Gilmour, D. 1965. The Metabolism of Insects. W. H. Freeman and Co., Publishers, San Francisco, 195 pp.

Gleason, H. A., and A. Cronquist. 1964. The Natural Geography of Plants. Columbia University Press, New York, 420 pp.

Glick, P. A. 1939. The distribution of insects, spiders, and mites in the air. USDA Tech. Bull. No. 673, 150 pp.

Goetsch, W. 1967. Ants. University of Michigan Press, Ann Arbor.

Goldsmith, T. H., and L. T. Warner. 1964. Vitamin A in the vision of insects. J. Gen. Physiol. 47:433–41.

Goodchild, A. J. P. 1966. Evolution of the alimentary canal in the Hemiptera. Biol. Rev. *41*:97–140.

Gould, J. L. 1975. Honey bee recruitment: the dance-language controversy. Science *189*:685–93.

Graham, F., Jr. 1970. Since Silent Spring. Houghton-Mifflin Co., Boston.

Grégoire, C. 1964. Hemolymph coagulation. *In* Rockstein, M. (ed.). The Physiology of Insecta, Vol. 3. Academic Press, Inc., New York, pp. 153–88.

Gupta, A. P. 1969. Studies of the blood of Meloidae (Coleoptera). I. The haemocytes of *Epicauta cinerea* (Forster), and a synonymy of haemocyte terminologies. Cytologia *34*:300–44.

Gurney, A. B. 1938. A synopsis of the order Zoraptera, with notes on the biology of *Zorotypus hubbardi* Caudell. Proc. Entomol. Soc. Wash. *40*:57–87.

Hagan, H. R. 1951. Embryology of the Viviparous Insects. The Ronald Press Co., New York, 472 pp.

Hagedorn, H. H. 1974. The control of vitellogenesis in the mosquito, *Aedes aegypti*. Amer. Zool. *14*:1207–17.

Hagen, K. S., and R. L. Tassan. 1970. The influence of food Wheast® and related *Saccharomyces fragilis* yeast products on the fecundity of *Chrysopa carnea* (Neuroptera:Chrysopidae). Canad. Entomol. *102*:806–11.

Hagstrum, D. W., and W. R. Hagstrum. 1970. A simple device for producing fluctuating temperatures, with an evaluation of the ecological significance of fluctuating temperatures. Ann. Entomol. Soc. Amer. *63*:1385–89.

Hamilton, W. D. 1964. The genetical evolution of social behaviour. I and II. J. Theoret. Biol. 7:1–52.

Hamilton, W. J., III. 1971. Competition and thermoregulatory behavior of the Namib Desert tenebrionid beetle genus *Cardiosis*. Ecology *52*:810–22.

Happ, G. M., and T. Eisner. 1961. Hemorrhage in a coccinellid beetle and its repellent effect on ants. Science *134*:329–31.

Harcourt, D. G. 1969. The development and use of life tables in the study of natural insect populations. Ann. Rev. Entomol. *14*:175–96.

Harcourt, D. G. 1970. Crop life tables as a pest management tool. Canad. Entomol. *102*:950–55.

Harker, J. E. 1961. Diurnal rhythms. Ann. Rev. Entomol. *6*:131–46.

Harman, S. W. 1948. The red banded leafroller as an apple pest in New York. N. Y. State Agr. Expt. Sta. Bull. No. 733.

Hatch, M. H. 1953–1975. The beetles of the Pacific Northwest. University of Washington Publications in Biology, Seattle, Washington (5 vols.).

Haydak, M. H. 1957. Changes with age in the appearance of some internal organs of the honeybee. Bee World *38*:197–207.

Headley, J. C. 1972. Economics of agricultural pest control. Ann. Rev. Entomol. *17*:273–86.

Heath, J. E., and P. A. Adams. 1965. Temperature regulation in the sphinx moth during flight. Nature *205*:309–10.

Heatwole, H., and D. M. Davis. 1965. Ecology of three sympatric species of parasitic insects of the genus *Megarhyssa* (Hymenoptera: Ichneumonidae). Ecology *46*:140–50.

Heed, W. B., and H. W. Kircher. 1965. Unique sterol in the ecology and nutrition of *Drosophila pachea*. Science *149*:758–61.

Heinrich, B. 1972. Energetics of temperature regulation and foraging in a bumblebee, *Bombus terricola* Kirby. J. Comp. Physiol. 77:49–64.

Heinrich, B., and P. H. Raven. 1972. Energetics and pollination ecology. Science *176*:597–602.

Helfer, J. R. 1963. How to Know the Grasshoppers, Cockroaches and their Allies. William C. Brown Co., Publishers, Dubuque, Iowa, 353 pp.

Heller, P. R. 1976. Biology of *Aleochara tristis* in relation to biological control of the face fly. Ph.D. thesis, Ohio State University, Columbus.

Hess, R., W. C. Allee, and K. P. Schmidt. 1937. Ecological animal geography. John Wiley & Sons, Inc., New York, 597 pp.

Hink, W. F., and J. D. Briggs. 1968. Bactericidal factors in haemolymph from normal and immune wax moth larvae, *Galleria mellonella*. J. Ins. Physiol. *14*:1025–34.

Hinton, H. E. 1955. Protective devices of endopterygote pupae. Trans. Brit. Entomol. Soc. *12*:49–92.

Hinton, H. E. 1960a. Insect eggshells. Sci. Amer. *223*(2):84–91.

Hinton, H. E. 1960b. Cryptobiosis in the larva of *Polypedilum vanderplanki* Hint. (Chrionomidae). J. Ins. Physiol. *5*:286–300.

Hinton, H. E. 1964. Sperm transfer in insects and the evolution of haemocoelic insemination. *In* Highnam, K. C. (ed.). Royal Entomol. Soc. London, Symposium No. 3. Insect Reproduction, pp. 95–107.

Holdsworth, R. P., Jr. 1968. Integrated control: effect on European red mite and its more important predators. J. Econ. Entomol. *61*:1602–07.

Holdsworth, R. P., Jr. 1972a. Major predators of the European red mite on apple in Ohio. Ohio Agr. Res. Dev. Cen. Res. Circ. No. 192.

Holdsworth, R. P., Jr. 1972b. European red mite predators and their management. Proc. Ohio State Hort. Soc. 125th Ann. Mtg., pp. 86–88.

Holland, W. J. 1913. The Moth Book. Doubleday, Page and Co., New York, 479 pp.

Holling, C. S. 1959. Some characteristics of simple types of predation and parasitism. Canad. Entomol. *91*:385–98.

Holling, C. S. 1965. The functional response of predators to prey density and its role in mimicry and population regulation. Mem. Entomol. Soc. Can. *45*:1–60.

Hori, K. 1974. Plant growth-promoting factor in the salivary gland of the bug, *Lygus disponsi*. J. Ins. Physiol. *20*:1623–27.

Horn, D. J. 1971. The relationship between a parasite, *Tetrastichus incertus* (Hymenoptera:Eulophidae), and its host, the alfalfa weevil, *Hypera postica* (Coleoptera: Curculionidae), in New York. Canad. Entomol. *103*:83–94.

Horn, D. J. 1974. Observations on primary and secondary parasitoids of California oakworm, *Phryganidia californica*, pupae. Pan-Pac. Entomol. *50*:53–59.

Horn, D. J. 1975. Life tables for the alfalfa weevil in Ohio. Proc. North Centr. Branch Entomol. Soc. Amer. *30*:98.

Horn, H. S. 1968. Regulation of animal numbers: a model counter-example. Ecology *49*:776–78.

Horridge, G. A. 1965. Arthropoda: details of groups. *In* Bullock, T. H., and G. A. Horridge (eds.). Structure and Function in the Nervous System of Invertebrates, Vol. II. W. H. Freeman and Co., Publishers, San Francisco, pp. 1165–1270.

Hoskins, W. M. 1963. Resistance to insecticides. Internat. Rev. Trop. Med. *2*:119–74.

Hottes, F. C., and T. H. Frison. 1931. The plant lice, or Aphididae, of Illinois. Ill. Nat. Hist. Surv. Bull. *19*:21–477.

Hoy, R. R., and R. C. Paul. 1973. Genetic control of song specificity in crickets. Science *180*:82–83.

Hoyle, G. 1973. Muscle and its neural control. *In* Tipton, V. J. (ed.). Syllabus/Introductory Entomology. Brigham Young University Press, Provo, Utah.

Hsieh, F., S. J. Roberts, and E. J. Armbrust. 1974. Developmental rate and population dynamics of alfalfa weevil larvae. Envir. Entomol. *3*:593–97.

Hubbard, C. A. 1947. Fleas of Western North America. Iowa State College Press, Ames, 533 pp.

Huffaker, C. B. 1958. Experimental studies on predation: dispersion factors and predator-prey oscillations. Hilgardia *27*:343–83.

Huffaker, C. B. (ed.). 1971. Biological Control. Plenum Publishing Corp. New York, 511 pp.

Huffaker, C. B., and W. K. Kennett. 1959. A ten-year study of vegetational changes associated with biological control of Klamath weed. J. Range Man. *12*:69–82.

Huffaker, C. B., P. S. Messenger, and P. DeBach. 1971. The natural enemy component in natural control and the theory of biological control. *In* Huffaker, C. B. (ed.). Biological Control. Plenum Publishing Corp., New York, pp. 16–67.

Hughes, G. M. 1965. Neuronal pathways in the insect central nervous system. *In* Treherne, J. E., and J. W. L. Beament (eds.). The Physiology of the Insect Central Nervous System. Academic Press, Inc., New York, pp. 79–112.

Hunter, W. D., and W. A. Hooker. 1907. Information concerning the North American fever tick. USDA Bur. Entomol. Bull. No. 72.

Hurlbert, S. H. 1971. The nonconcept of species diversity: a critique and alternative parameters. Ecology *52*:577–86.

Hutchins, R. E. 1966. Insects. Prentice-Hall, Inc., Englewood Cliffs, N. J., 324 pp.

Hylton, A. R. 1966. Histopathological changes with age in the flight muscles of the African mosquito, *Eretmapodites chrysogaster*. J. Invert. Pathol. *8*:75–8.

Imms, A. D. 1957. A General Textbook of Entomology. 9th ed. Methuen & Co. Ltd., London.

Ishihara, T. 1969. Families and genera of leafhopper vectors. *In* Maramorosch, K. (ed.). Viruses, Vectors, and Vegetation. John Wiley & Sons, Inc., New York.

Istock, C. A. 1973. Population characteristics of a species ensemble of waterboatmen (Corixidae). Ecology *54*:535–44.

Ives, W. G. H. 1964. Problems encountered in the development of life tables for insects. Proc. Entomol. Soc. Manitoba *20*:34–44.

Ives, W. G. H. 1973. Heat units and outbreaks of the forest tent caterpillar, *Malacosoma disstria* (Lepidoptera: Lasiocampidae). Canad. Entomol. *105*:529–43.

James, M. T., and R. F. Harwood. 1969. Herm's Medical Entomology. 6th ed. Macmillan Publishing Co., Inc., New York, 484 pp.

Janzen, D. H. 1966. Coevolution of mutualism between ants and acacias in Central America. Evolution 20:249–75.

Janzen, D. H. 1967. Interaction of the bull's horn acacia (*Acacia cornigera* L.) with an ant cohabitant (*Pseudomyrmex ferruginea* Smith) in eastern Mexico. Univ. Kans. Sci. Bull. 47:315–558.

Janzen, D. H. 1971. Escape of *Cassia grandis* L. beans from predators in time and space. Ecology 52:964–79.

Jaques, H. E. 1951. How To Know the Beetles. William C. Brown Co., Publishers, Dubuque, Iowa. 372 pp.

Johannsen, O. A., and F. H. Butt. 1941. Embryology of Insects and Myriapods. McGraw-Hill Book Co., New York, 462 pp.

Johnson, C. G. 1969. Migration and dispersal of insects by flight. Methuen & Co. Ltd., London, 763 pp.

Jones, J. C. 1964. The circulatory system of insects. *In* Rockstein, M. (ed.). The Physiology of Insecta, Vol. 3. Academic Press, Inc., New York, pp. 1–107.

Kaiser, H. 1974. Die Regelung der Individuendichte bei Libellenmännchen (*Aeschna cyanea*, Odonata). Eine Analyse mit systemtheoretischem Ansatz. Oecologia 14:53–74.

Kanwisher, J. W. 1966. Tracheal gas dynamics in pupae of the cecropia silkworm. Biol. Bull. Marine Biol. Lab Woods Hole 130:96–105.

Kartman, L., V. I. Miles, and F. M. Prince. 1958. Ecological studies of wild rodent plague in the San Francisco Bay region of California. I. Introduction. Amer. J. Trop. Med. Hyg. 7:112–24.

Kaston, B. J., and E. Kaston. 1953. How To Know the Spiders. William C. Brown Co., Publishers, Dubuque, Iowa, 220 pp.

Keeton, W. T. 1972. Biological Science. 2nd ed. W. W. Norton & Co., Inc., New York, 888 pp.

Keitt, G. W., and S. S. Ivanov. 1941. Transmission of fire blight by bees and its relation to nectar concentrations of apple and pear blossoms. J. Ag. Res. 62:745–53.

Kenaga, E. E., and C. S. End. 1974. Commercial and experimental organic insecticides. Entomol. Soc. Amer. Spec. Publ. No. 74-1. 77 pp.

Kennedy, J. S., M. F. Day, and V. F. Eastop. 1962. A conspectus of aphids as vectors of plant viruses. Comm. Inst. Entomol. Publ., London.

Kennedy, J. S., and D. Marsh. 1974. Pheromone-regulated anemotaxis in flying moths. Science 184:999–1001.

Kerr, G. E. 1974. Visual and acoustical communicative behavior in *Dissosteira carolina* (Orthoptera:Acrididae). Canad. Entomol. 106:263–72.

Kettlewell, H. B. D. 1973. The Evolution of Melanism. The Study of a Recurring Necessity; with Special Reference to Industrial Melanism in the Lepidoptera. Clarendon Press, Oxford, 423 pp.

Key, K. H. L. 1945. The general ecological characteristics of the outbreak areas and outbreak years of the Australian plague locust (*Chortoicetes terminifera* Walk.). Bull. C.S.I.R.O. 186:1–127.

King, P. E. 1975. Pycnogonids. Hutchinson Publishing Group Ltd., London. 144 pp.

Kleinjan, J. E., and T. E. Mittler. 1975. A chemical influence of ants on wing development in aphids. Entomol. Exp. Appl. 18:384–88.

Klomp, H. 1966. The dynamics of a field population of the pine looper, *Bupalus piniarius* L. (Lepidoptera: Geometridae). Adv. Ecol. Res. 3:207–305.

Klomp, H. 1968. A seventeen-year study of the abundance of the pine looper, *Bupalus piniarius* L. (Lepidoptera: Geometridae). *In* Southwood, T. R. E. (ed.). Insect Abundance. Roy. Entomol. Soc. Symp. No. 4. Royal Entomological Society, London.

Klots, A. B. 1951. A Field Guide to the Butterflies of North America, East of the Great Plains. Houghton-Mifflin Co., Boston, 349 pp.

Knabke, J. J., and A. A. Grigarick. 1971. Biology of the African earwig *Euborellia cincticollis* (Gerstaecker) in California and comparative notes on *Euboriella annulipes* (Lucas). Hilgardia 41:157–94.

Knipling, E. F. 1955. Possibilities of insect control or eradication through the use of sexually sterile males. J. Econ. Entomol. 48:459–62.

Knipling, E. F. 1960. The eradication of the screw-worm fly. Sci. Amer. 203(4):54–61.

Kramer, J. P. 1963. Pathogens of vertebrates and plants as pathogens of their acarine and insect vectors. *In* Steinhaus, E. A. (ed.). Insect pathology, an advanced treatise. 1:251–72.

Krebs, C. J. 1972. Ecology: the Experimental Analysis of Distribution and Abundance. Harper & Row, Publishers, New York, 694 pp.

Krieger, R. I., P. P. Feeny, and C. F. Wilkinson. 1971. Detoxication enzymes in the guts of caterpillars: an evolutionary answer to plant defenses? Science 172:579–81.

Krogh, A., and E. Zeuthen. 1941. The mechanism of flight preparation in some insects. J. Exp. Biol. 18:1–10.

Kulman, H. M. 1971. Effects of insect defoliation on growth and mortality of trees. Ann. Rev. Entomol. 16:289–324.

LaBrecque, G. C., D. W. Meifert, and J. Rye, Jr. 1972. Experimental control of stable flies, *Stomoxys calcitrans* (Diptera: Muscidae), by releases of chemosterilized adults. Canad. Entomol. 104:885–87.

Lack, D. 1966. Population Studies of Birds. Oxford University Press, New York, 341 pp.

Langer, W. L. 1964. The black death. Sci. Amer. 211(2):114–21.

Larsen, J. R., Jr. 1973. Sensory receptors. *In* Tipton, V. J. (ed.). Syllabus/Introductory Entomology. Brigham Young University Press, Provo, Utah, pp. 197–219.

Leclercq, M. 1969. Entomological Parasitology. Pergamon Press, Inc., Elmsford, N.Y., 158 pp.

Leech, H. B., and H. P. Chandler. 1956. Coleoptera. *In* Usinger, R. L. (ed.). Aquatic Insects of California. University of California Press, Berkeley, pp. 293–371.

Leius, K. 1967. Food sources and preferences of adults of a parasite, *Scambus buolianae* (Hym.:

Ichn.), and their consequences. Canad. Entomol. *99*:865–71.

Leonard, D. E. 1974. Recent developments in ecology and control of the gypsy moth. Ann. Rev. Entomol. *19*:197–230.

Leopold, R. A., and M. E. Degrullier. 1973. Sperm penetration of housefly eggs: evidence for involvement of a female accessory secretion. Science *181*:555–57.

Levins, R., and R. H. MacArthur. 1969. An hypothesis to explain the incidence of monophagy. Ecology *50*:910–11.

Lewis, D. R. 1973. A study of factors influencing the sex ratio of *Microctonus aethiops.* M.S. Thesis, Ohio State University, Columbus, 64 pp.

Lewis, T. 1973. Thrips: Their Biology, Ecology, and Economic Importance. Academic Press, New York, 349 pp.

Lindauer, M. 1965. Social behavior and mutual communication. *In* Rockstein, M. (ed.). The Physiology of Insecta, Vol. 2. Academic Press, New York, pp. 123–86.

Lindauer, M., and H. Martin. 1972. Magnetic effect on dancing bees. *In* NASA Symposium SP-262, Animal Orientation and Navigation. U.S. Government Printing Office, pp. 559–67.

Lindroth, C. H. 1957. Faunal Relationships Between North America and Europe. John Wiley & Sons, Inc., New York.

Linsley, E. G., T. Eisner, and A. B. Klots. 1961. Mimetic assemblages of sibling species of lycid beetles. Evolution *15*:15–29.

Linsley, E. G., J. W. MacSwain, and P. H. Raven. 1963. Comparative behavior of bees and Onagraceae. Univ. Calif. Publ. Entomol. *33*:1–92.

Lloyd, J. E. 1965. Aggressive mimicry in *Photuris:* firefly femmes fatales. Science *149*:653–54.

Lloyd, J. E. 1971. Bioluminescent communication in insects. Ann. Rev. Entomol. *16*:97–122.

Lloyd, J. E. 1973. Fireflies of Melanesia: bioluminescence, mating behavior, and synchronous flashing (Coleoptera: Lampyridae). Env. Entomol. 2:991–1008.

Lloyd, J. E. 1975. Aggressive mimicry in *Photuris* fireflies: signal repertoires by femmes fatales. Science *187*:452–53.

Lloyd, M. 1965. Laboratory studies with confined cannibalistic populations of flour beetles *(Tribolium castaneum)* in a cold-dry environment. I. Data for 24 unmanipulated populations. Tribolium Info. Bull. *8*:88–123.

Lloyd, M., and H. S. Dybas. 1966. The periodical cicada problem. I. Population ecology. Evolution *20*:133–49.

Loucks, O. L. 1970. Evolution of diversity, efficiency, and community stability. Amer. Zool. *10*:17–25.

Luck, R. F. 1971. An appraisal of two methods of analyzing insect life tables. Canad. Entomol. *103*:1261–71.

Lüscher, M. 1969. Die Bedeutung des Juvenilhormons für die Differenzierung der Soldaten bei Termite *Kalotermes flavicollis.* Proc. 6th Cong. Int. Union for Study of Social Insects, Bern, Switzerland, pp. 165–70.

Lutz, F. E. 1936. Fieldbook of Insects. 4th ed. G. P. Putnam's Sons, New York, 510 pp.

MacArthur, R. H., and E. O. Wilson. 1967. The Theory of Island Biogeography. Princeton University Press, Princeton, 203 pp.

Maddrell, S. H. P. 1971. The mechanisms of insect excretory systems. Adv. Ins. Physiol. *8*:199–331.

Mansingh, A. 1971. Physiological classification of dormancies in insects. Canad. Entomol. *103*:983–1009.

Manton, S. M. 1949. Studies on Onychophora. VII. The early embryonic stages of *Peripatopsis,* and some general considerations concerning the morphology and phylogeny of the arthropods. Phil. Trans. Roy. Soc. Ser. B. *233*:483–580.

Manton, S. M. 1964. Mandibular mechanisms and the evolution of arthropods. Phil. Trans. Roy. Soc. Ser. B. *247*:1–183.

Manton, S. M. 1972. The evolution of arthropod locomotory mechanisms. 10. Locomotory habits, morphology, and evolution of the hexapod classes. Zool. J. Linn. Soc. London *51*:203–400.

Maramorosch, K. (ed.). 1969. Viruses, Vectors, and Vegetation. John Wiley & Sons, Inc., New York, 666 pp.

Martynov, A. S. 1925. Über zwei Grundtypen der Flügel bei den Insecten und Ihre Evolution. Z. Morph. Oekol. Tiere *4*:465–501.

Matthewman, W. G., and D. P. Pielou. 1971. Arthropods inhabiting the sporophores of *Fomes fomentarius* (Polyporaceae) in Gatineau Park, Quebec. Canad. Entomol. *103*:775–847.

Mattson, W. J., and N. D. Addy. 1975. Phytophagous insects as regulators of forest primary production. Science *190*:515–22.

May, R. M. 1974. Stability and Complexity in Model Ecosystems. 2nd ed. Princeton University Press, Princeton, 265 pp.

Mayr, E. 1974. Behavior programs and evolutionary strategies. Amer. Sci. *62*:650–59.

McAlpine, J. F., and J. E. H. Martin. 1969. Canadian amber—a paleontological treasure-chest. Canad. Entomol. *101*:819–38.

McClean, D. L., and M. G. Kinsey. 1964. A technique for electronically recording aphid feeding and salivation. Nature *202*:1358–59.

McClure, M. S., and P. W. Price. 1975. Competition among sympatric *Erythroneura* leafhoppers (Homoptera:Cicadellidae) on American sycamore. Ecology *56*:1388–97.

McCrumb, F. R., Jr. 1975. Plague. *In* Beeson, P. B., and W. McDermott (eds.). Cecil-Loeb Textbook of Medicine. 14th ed. W. B. Saunders Co., Philadelphia.

McKenzie, H. L. 1967. Mealybugs of California. University of California Press, Berkeley, 525 pp.

McKittrick, F. A. 1964. Evolutionary studies of cockroaches. Cornell Univ. Agr. Expt. Sta. Mem. 389, 199 pp.

Melius, M. E., Jr., and W. H. Telfer. 1969. An autoradiographic analysis of yolk deposition in the cortex of the cecropia moth oocyte. J. Morphol. *129*:1–15.

Menzie, C. M. 1972. Fate of pesticides in the environment. Ann. Rev. Entomol. *17*:199–222.

Metcalf, C. L., C. P. Flint, and R. L. Metcalf. 1962. Destructive and Useful Insects. 4th ed. McGraw-Hill Book Co., New York, 1087 pp.

Metcalf, R. L., and W. H. Luckmann (eds.). 1975. Introduction to Insect Pest Management. John Wiley & Sons, Inc., New York, 587 pp.

Michener, C. D. 1944. Comparative external morphology, phylogeny, and a classification of the bees (Hymenoptera). Bull. Amer. Mus. Nat. Hist. *82*:151–326.

Michener, C. D. 1969. Comparative social behavior of bees. Ann. Rev. Entomol. *14*:299–342.

Miller, L. A. 1975. The behaviour of flying green lacewings, *Chrysopa carnea,* in the presence of ultrasound. J. Ins. Physiol. *21*:209–19.

Miller, T. A. 1973. Circulation. *In* Tipton, V. J. (ed.). Syllabus/Introductory Entomology. Brigham Young University Press, Provo, Utah, pp. 233–38.

Milne, A. 1952. Features of the ecology and control of the sheep tick, *Ixodes ricinus* L., in Britain. Ann. Appl. Biol. *39*:144–46.

Mitchell, R. 1974. The evolution of thermophily in hot springs. Quart. Rev. Biol. *49*:229–42.

Mitsuhashi, J., and K. Koyama. 1974. Folic acid as a dietary factor affecting the wing morph of the planthopper, *Laodelphax striatellus* (Hemiptera, Delphacidae). Entomol. Exptl. Appl. *17*:77–82.

Mittler, T. E., 1958. Studies on the feeding and nutrition of *Tuberolachnus salignus* (Gmelin) (Homoptera, Aphididae) III. The nitrogen economy. J. Exptl. Biol. *35*:626–38.

Mockford, E. L. 1951. The Psocoptera of Indiana. Proc. Ind. Acad. Sci. *60*:192–204.

Mockford, E. L., and A. B. Gurney. 1956. A review of the psocids, or book-lice and bark-lice, of Texas (Psocoptera). J. Washn. Acad. Sci. *46*:353–68.

Mohr, C. O. 1943. Cattle droppings as ecological units. Ecol. Monog. *13*:275–98.

Mook, L. J. 1963. Birds and the spruce budworm. *In* Morris, R. F. (ed.). The dynamics of epidemic spruce budworm populations. Mem. Entomol. Soc. Can. *31*:268–71.

Moore, T. E. 1973. Acoustical communication in insects. *In* Tipton, V. J. (ed.). Syllabus/Introductory Entomology. Brigham Young University Press, Provo, Utah, pp. 307–23.

Morris, R. F. 1959. Single-factor analysis in population dynamics. Ecology *40*:580–88.

Morris, R. F. 1960. Sampling insect populations. Ann. Rev. Entomol. *5*:243–64.

Morris, R. F. (ed.). 1963. The dynamics of epidemic spruce budworm populations. Mem. Entomol. Soc. Can. *31*:1–332.

Muller, J. 1826. Zur vergleichenden Physiologie des Gesichtsinnes des Menschen und der Tierre. Leipzig.

Murdoch, W. W., F. C. Evans, and C. H. Peterson. 1972. Diversity and pattern in plants and insects. Ecology *53*:819–29.

Myers, N. 1971. Wildlife and development in Uganda. BioScience *21*:1071–75.

Neal. J. W., Jr., and W. E. Bickley. 1971. A study of *Microctonus aethiops* (Nees), a braconid parasite of the alfalfa weevil, *Hypera postica* (Gyllenhal). Univ. Md. Agr. Exp. Sta. Sci. Article No. 1668.

Needham, J. G., and P. W. Claassen. 1925. A monograph of the Plecoptera or stone-flies of America north of Mexico. Thomas Say Foundation Publ. No. 2., 397 pp.

Needham, J. G., J. R. Traver, and Y-c. Hsu. 1957. The Biology of Mayflies, with a Systematic Account of North American Species. 2nd ed. Comstock Publishing Associates, Ithaca, N.Y., 759 pp.

Needham, J. G., and M. J. Westfall, Jr. 1955. A Manual of the Dragonflies of North America (Anisoptera). University of California Press, Los Angeles, 615 pp.

Nicholson, A. J. 1933. The balance of animal populations. J. Anim. Ecol. *2*:132–78.

Nicholson, A. J. 1954. An outline of the dynamics of animal populations. Austr. J. Zool. *2*:9–65.

Nickerson, B. 1956. Pigmentation of hoppers of the desert locust in relation to phase colouration. Anti-Locust Bull. 24, 34 pp.

Nicol, D. 1966. Cope's rule and precambrian and cambrian invertebrates. J. Paleontol. *40*:1397–99.

Novák, V. J. A. 1975. Insect Hormones. 4th ed. John Wiley & Sons, Inc., New York, 600 pp.

O'Brien, R. D. 1967. Insecticides, Action and Metabolism. Academic Press, Inc., New York, 332 pp.

Odum, E. P. 1971. Fundamentals of Ecology. 3rd ed. W. B. Saunders Co., Philadelphia, 574 pp.

Oldroyd, H. 1964. The Natural History of Flies. George Weidenfeld & Nicolson Ltd., London, 324 pp.

Opler, P. A. 1973. Fossil lepidopterous leaf mines demonstrate the age of some insect-plant relationships. Science *179*:1321–23.

Opler, P. A. 1974. Biology, ecology, and host specificity of Microlepidoptera associated with *Quercus agrifolia* (Fagaceae). Univ. Calif. Publ. Entomol. *75*:1–83.

Paine, R. T. 1966. Food web complexity and species diversity. Amer. Nat. *100*:65–75.

Painter, R. H. 1951. Insect Resistance in Crop Plants. Macmillan Publishing Co., Inc., New York, 520 pp.

Park, T. 1954. Experimental studies of interspecies competition. II. Temperature, humidity and competition in two species of *Tribolium.* Physiol. Zool. *27*:177–238.

Parker, R. R. 1928. Rocky Mountain spotted fever. Montana State Board Entomol. Bien. Rep. 7:39–62.

Patten, B. P. (ed.). 1971. Systems Analysis in

Ecology, Vol. 1. Academic Press, Inc., New York.

Patterson, R. S., D. E. Weidhaas, H. R. Ford, and C. S. Lofgren. 1970. Suppression and elimination of an island population of *Culex pipiens quinquefasciatus* with sterile males. Science *168*:1368–70.

Patton, R. L. 1963. Introductory Insect Physiology. W. B. Saunders Co., Philadelphia, 245 pp.

Patton, R. L., and R. A. Flint. 1959. Variation in blood cell count with a molt. Ann. Entomol. Soc. Amer. *52*:240–42.

Peacock, J. W., R. M. Silverstein, A. C. Lincoln, and J. B. Simeone. 1973. Laboratory investigations of the frass of *Scolytus multistriatus* (Coleoptera:Scolytidae) as a source of pheromone. Env. Entomol. *2*:355–59.

Pfadt, R. E. 1971. Fundamentals of Applied Entomology. 2nd ed. Macmillan Publishing Co., Inc., New York, 693 pp.

Pianka, E. R. 1970. On r- and K-selection. Amer. Nat. *104*:592–97.

Pianka, E. R. 1973. Evolutionary Ecology. Harper & Row Publishers, New York.

Piepho, H., and H. Meyer. 1951. Reaktionen der Schmetterlingshaut auf Häutunghormone. Biol. Zentralblatt *70*:252–60.

Pimentel, D. 1961. Species diversity and insect population outbreaks. Ann. Entomol. Soc. Amer. *54*:76–86.

Pimentel, D., W. P. Nagel, and J. L. Madden. 1963. Space-time structure of the environment and the survival of parasite-host systems. Amer. Nat. *97*:141–67.

Pomerantz, C. 1959. Arthropods and psychic disturbances. Bull. Entomol. Soc. Amer. *5*:65–67.

Potts, W. H., and C. H. N. Jackson. 1953. The Shinyanga game destruction experiment. Bull. Entomol. Res. *43*:365–74.

Powell, J. A., and R. A. Mackie. 1966. Biological interrelationships of moths and *Yucca whipplei* (Lepidoptera:Gelechiidae, Blastobasidae, Prodoxidae). Univ. Calif. Publ. Entomol. *42*:1–59.

Powell, J. M. 1971. The arthropod fauna collected from the comandra blister rust, *Cronartium comandrae,* on lodgepole pine in Alberta. Canad. Entomol. *103*:908–18.

Pratt, H. D., and R. F. Darsie, Jr. 1975. Highlights in medical entomology in 1974. Bull. Entomol. Soc. Amer. *21*:173–76.

Price, P. W. 1970a. Trail odors: recognition by insects parasitic on cocoons. Science *170*:546–7.

Price, P. W. 1970b. Characteristics permitting coexistence among parasitoids of a sawfly in Quebec. Ecology *51*:445–54.

Price, P. W. 1975. Insect Ecology. John Wiley & Sons, Inc., New York, 514 pp.

Pringle, J. W. S. 1954. A physiological analysis of cicada song. J. Exp. Biol. *31*:525–60.

Pringle, J. W. S. 1957. Insect Flight. Cambridge University Press, Cambridge, 132 pp.

Putnam, W. L. 1970. Some effects of wind on the European red mite, *Panonychus ulmi* (Acarina:Tetranychidae). Canad. Entomol. *102*: 659–67.

Puttler, B. 1967. Interrelationship of *Hypera postica* and *Bathyplectes curculionis* in the eastern United States with particular reference to encapsulation of parasite eggs by alfalfa weevil larvae. Ann. Entomol. Soc. Amer. *60*:1031–38.

Quinby, G. E., W. J. Hayes, Jr., J. F. Armstrong, and W. F. Durham. 1965. DDT storage in the United States population. J.A.M.A. *191*:175–79.

Rabb, R. L., and F. E. Guthrie (eds.). 1970. Concepts of Pest Management. North Carolina State University Press, Raleigh, 242 pp.

Rainey, R. C. 1963. Meteorology and the migration of desert locusts. Anti-Locust Mem. *7*:1–115.

Ramsay, J. A. 1964. The rectal complex of the mealworm *Tenebrio molitor* L. (Coleoptera:Tenebrionidae). Phil. Trans. Roy. Soc. Ser. B. *248*:279–314.

Rathcke, B. J., and R. W. Poole. 1975. Coevolutionary race continues: butterfly larval adaptation to plant trichomes. Science *189*:175–76.

Regnier, F. E., and E. O. Wilson. 1968. The alarm-defence system of the ant *Lasius alienus.* J. Ins. Physiol. *15*:893–98.

Rentz, D. C. 1972. The lock and key as an isolating mechanism in katydids. Amer. Sci. *60*:750–55.

Rettenmeyer, C. W. 1963. Behavioral studies of army ants. Kans. Univ. Sci. Bull. *44*:281–465.

Rettenmeyer, C. W. 1970. Insect mimicry. Ann. Rev. Entomol. *15*:43–74.

Ribbands, C. R. 1953. The Behaviour and Social Life of Honeybees. Bee Research Association Ltd., London, 352 pp.

Richards, O. W. 1953. The Social Insects. Harper & Row Publishers, New York, 219 pp.

Richter, J. H., D. R. Jensen, V. R. Noonkester, J. B. Kreasky, M. W. Stimmann, and W. W. Wolf. 1973. Remote radar sensing: atmospheric structure and insects. Science *180*:1176–78.

Riddiford, L. M. 1967. Trans-2-hexenal: mating stimulant for polyphemus moths. Science *158*:139–41.

Riley, R. G., R. M. Silverstein, and J. C. Moser. 1974. Biological responses of *Atta texana* to its alarm pheromone and the enantiomer of the pheromone. Science *183*:760–62.

Robbins, W. E., J. N. Kaplanis, J. A. Svoboda, and M. J. Thompson. 1971. Steroid metabolism in insects. Ann. Rev. Entomol. *16*:53–72.

Rockstein, M., and J. Miquel. 1973. Aging in insects. *In* Rockstein, M. (ed.). The Physiology of Insecta, Vol. 1. 2nd ed. Academic Press, Inc. New York, pp. 371–478.

Rodhain, J. 1948. Susceptibility of the chimpanzee to *Plasmodium malariae* of human origin. Amer. J. Trop. Med. Hyg. *28*:629–31.

Roeder, K. D. 1967. Nerve Cells and Insect Behavior. Harvard University Press, Cambridge, 238 pp.

Roeder, K. D., and A. E. Treat. 1961. The detection and evasion of bats by moths. Amer. Sci. 49:135–48.

Rollo, I. M. 1965. Drugs used in the chemotherapy of malaria. In Goodman, L. S., and A. Gilman (eds.). The Pharmacological Basis of Therapeutics. Macmillian Publishing Co., Inc., pp. 1087–1117.

Romoser, W. S. 1973. The Science of Entomology. Macmillan Publishing Co., Inc., New York, 449 pp.

Root, R. B. 1973. Organization of a plant-arthropod association in simple and diverse habitats: the fauna of collards (Brassica oleracea). Ecol. Monogr. 43:95–124.

Ross, E. S. 1944. A revision of the Embioptera, or webspinners, of the New World. Proc. U. S. Nat. Mus. 94:401–504.

Ross, H. H. 1944. The caddisflies, or Trichoptera, of Illinois. Ill. Nat. Hist. Surv. Bull. 23:1–326.

Ross, H. H. 1957. Principles of natural coexistence indicated by leafhopper populations. Evolution 11:113–29.

Ross, H. H. 1965. A Textbook of Entomology. 3rd ed. John Wiley & Sons, Inc., New York, 539 pp.

Rothschild, M. 1965. Fleas. Sci. Amer. 213(6):44–53.

Rudinsky, J. A., M. M. Furniss, L. N. Kline, and R. F. Schmitz. 1972. Attraction and repression of Dendroctonus pseudotsugae (Coleoptera:Scolytidae) by three synthetic pheromones in traps in Oregon and Idaho. Canad. Entomol. 104:815–22.

Russell, P. F. 1958. Malaria in the world today. Amer. J. Publ. Health 47:414–20.

Sahota, T. S. 1969. Hormonal control of ovarian development and metamorphosis in Malacosoma pluviale. Canad. J. Zool. 47:917–20.

Salt, G. 1961. Competition among insect parasitoids. In Mechanisms in biological competition. Symp. Soc. Exptl. Biol. 15:96–119.

Salt, G. 1965. Experimental studies in insect parasitism. XIII. The haemocytic reaction of a caterpillar to eggs of its habitual parasite. Proc. Roy. Entomol. Soc. Ser. B. 162:303–18.

Salt, R. W. 1961. Principles of insect cold-hardiness. Ann. Rev. Entomol. 6:55–74.

Sanders, H. L. 1968. Marine benthic diversity: a comparative study. Amer. Nat. 102:243–82.

Saunders, D. S. 1962. Age determination for female tsetse flies and the age composition of samples of Glossina pallidipes Aust., G. palpalis fuscipes Newst and G. brevipalpis Newst. Bull. Entomol. Res. 53:579–95.

Savory, T. 1964. Arachnida. Academic Press, Inc., New York, 291 pp.

Schaller, F. 1971. Indirect sperm transfer by soil arthropods. Ann. Rev. Entomol. 16:407–46.

Schedl, K. E. 1956 (1958). Breeding habits of arboricole insects in central Africa. Proc. 10th Int. Cong. Entomol. 1:183–97.

Schildknecht, H., and K. Holoubek. 1961. Die Bombardierkafer und ihre Explosionschemie

V. Mitteilung uber insekten Abwehrstoffe. Angew. Chem. 73:1–6.

Schmidt, P. 1913. Biol. Zentralblatt. 33:193–207.

Schmidt-Nielsen, B. M. 1973. Excretion. In Tipton, V. J. (ed.). Syllabus/Introductory Entomology. Brigham Young University Press, Provo, Utah, pp. 249–65.

Schmidt-Nielsen, K. 1972. Locomotion: energy cost of swimming, flying, and running. Science 177:222–28.

Schuchert, C., and C. O. Dunbar. 1933. A Textbook of Geology. Part II. Historical Geology. 3rd ed. John Wiley & Sons, Inc., New York.

Scott, H. G. 1961. Collembola: pictorial keys to the nearctic genera. Ann. Entomol. Soc. Amer. 54:104–13.

Scudder, G. G. E. 1973. Recent advances in the higher systematics and phylogenetic concepts in entomology. Canad. Entomol. 105:1251–63.

Seevers, C. H. 1965. The systematics, evolution, and zoogeography of staphylinid beetles associated with army ants (Coleoptera: Staphylinidae). Fieldiana-Zoology 47:137–351.

Seidel, F. 1929. Untersuchungen über das Bildungsprinzip der Keimanlage im Ei der Libelle Platycnemis pennipes. Roux' Arch. Entwicklungmech. Organismen 119:322–440.

Seidel, F. 1963. Analyse des Differenzierungsverlaufs im Insektenei (Gryllus) mittels UV- und Röntgenbestrahlungen. Zool. Anz. Suppl. 27:121–43.

Shapiro, A. M. 1974. Beak-mark frequency as an index of seasonal predation intensity on common butterflies. Amer. Nat. 108:229–32.

Sharov, A. G. 1966. Basic Arthropodan Stock, with Special Reference to Insects. Pergamon Press, Inc., Elmsford, N.Y., 271 pp.

Shepherd, J. G. 1975. A polypeptide sperm activator from male saturniid moths. J. Ins. Physiol. 21:9–22.

Silberglied, R. E. 1973 (unpubl.). Ultraviolet reflections and communication in butterflies. Paper presented at the National Meeting of the Entomological Society of America, Dallas, Tex.

Simberloff, D. S., and E. O. Wilson. 1969. Experimental zoogeography of islands: the colonization of empty islands. Ecology 50:278–96.

Skaife, S. H. 1961. Dwellers in Darkness. Doubleday & Co., Inc., Garden City, N.Y. 180 pp.

Sláma, K., and C. M. Williams. 1966. The juvenile hormone. V. The sensitivity of the bug, Pyrrhocoris apterus, to a hormonally active factor in American paper-pulp. Biol. Bull. 130:235–46.

Slykhuis, J. T. 1969. Mites as vectors of plant viruses. In Maramorosch, K. (ed.). Viruses, Vectors, and Vegetation. John Wiley & Sons, Inc., New York.

Smart, J., and N. F. Hughes. 1973. The insect and the plant: progressive palaeoecological integration. In Emden, H. F. van, (ed.). Insect-plant relationships. Roy. Entomol. Soc. London, Symposium No. 6, pp. 145–55.

Smirnoff, W. A., J. J. Fettes, and R. Desaulniers. 1973. Aerial spraying of a Bacillus thuringiensis-chitinase formulation for control of the spruce budworm (Lepidoptera:Tortricidae). Canad. Entomol. *105*:1535–44.

Smith, C. N. (ed.). 1966. Insect Colonization and Mass Production. Academic Press, Inc., New York, 618 pp.

Smith, D. S. 1963. The organization and innervation of the luminescent organ in a firefly, *Photuris pennsylvanica* (Coleoptera). J. Cell Biol. *16*:323–59.

Smith, D. S. 1965. Synapses in the insect nervous system. *In* Treherne, J. E., and J W. L. Beament. The Physiology of the Insect Central Nervous System. Academic Press, Inc., New York, pp. 39–57.

Smith, J. N. 1955. Detoxication mechanisms in insects. Biol. Rev. *30*:455–75.

Smith, L. M. 1960. The family Projapygidae and Anajapygidae (Diplura) in North America. Ann. Entomol. Soc. Amer. *53*:575–83.

Smith, R. F., T. E. Mittler, and C. N. Smith, (eds.). 1973. History of Entomology. Annual Reviews Inc., Palo Alto, 517 pp.

Sneath, P. H. A., and R. H. Sokal. 1973. Numerical Taxonomy. 2nd ed. W. H. Freeman and Co. Publishers, San Francisco, 573 pp.

Snodgrass, R. E. 1925. Anatomy and Physiology of the Honeybee. McGraw-Hill Book Co., New York.

Snodgrass, R. E. 1935. Principles of Insect Morphology. McGraw-Hill Book Co., New York, 667 pp.

Snodgrass, R. E. 1944. The feeding apparatus of biting and sucking insects affecting men and animals. Smiths. Inst. Misc. Coll. *104*:1–113.

Snow, K. R. 1970. The Arachnids: An Introduction. Columbia University Press, New York, 84 pp.

Solomon, M. E. 1949. The natural control of animal populations. J. Anim. Ecol. *18*:1–35.

Southwood, T. R. E. 1961. The number of insect species associated with various trees. J. Anim. Ecol. *31*:1–8.

Southwood, T. R. E. 1966. Ecological Methods, with Particular Reference to the Study of Insect Populations. Methuen & Co. Ltd., London, 391 pp.

Southwood, T. R. E., and M. J. Way, 1970. Ecological background to pest management. *In* Rabb, R. L., and F. E. Guthrie (eds.). Concepts of Pest Management. North Carolina State University Press, Raleigh, pp. 6–28.

Spradbery, J. P. 1973. Wasps: An Account of the Biology and Natural History of Solitary and Social Wasps. University of Washington Press, Seattle, 408 pp.

Springett, B. P. 1968. Aspects of the relationship between burying beetles, *Necrophorus* spp., and the mite, *Poecilochirus necrophori* Vitz. J. Anim. Ecol. *37*:417–24.

Srivastava, P. N., and J. L. Auclair. 1974. Effect of amino acid concentration on diet uptake and performance by the pea aphid, *Acyrthosiphon pisum* (Homoptera:Aphididae). Canad. Entomol. *106*:149–56.

Stairs, G. R. 1972. Pathogenic microorganisms in the regulation of forest insect populations. Ann. Rev. Entomol. *17*:355–72.

Stannard, L. J., Jr., 1968. The thrips, or Thysanoptera, of Illinois. Ill. Nat. Hist. Surv. Bull. *29*:215–552.

Steiner, L. F., E. J. Harris, W. C. Mitchell, M. S. Fujimoto, and L. D. Christenson. 1965. Melon fly eradication by overflooding with sterile flies. J. Econ. Entomol. *58*:519–22.

Steinhaus, E. A. (ed.). 1963. Invertebrate Pathology: an advanced treatise. Academic Press, Inc., New York.

Stern, V. M., R. F. Smith, R. van den Bosch, and K. S. Hagen. 1959. The integration of chemical and biological control of the spotted alfalfa aphid. The integrated control concept. Hilgardia *29*:81–101.

Subcommittee on Insect Pests. 1969. Insect-pest management and control. Principles of plant and animal pest management, Vol. 3. National Academy of Science, Washington, D. C., 508 pp.

Suomalainen, E. 1962. Significance of parthenogenesis in the evolution of insects. Ann. Rev. Entomol. *7*:349–66.

Swihart, S. L., W. C. Gordon, and R. J. Machwart. 1974. Reflections on the eyes of butterflies. J. Ins. Physiol. *20*:359–81.

Sylvester, E. S. 1969. *In* Maramorosch, K. (ed.). Viruses, Vectors, and Vegetation. John Wiley & Sons, Inc., New York.

Tanada, Y. 1965. Factors affecting the susceptibility of insects to viruses. Entomophaga *10*:139–50.

Tauber, O. E., and J. F. Yeager. 1936. On the total hemolymph cell counts in insects. Ann. Entomol. Soc. Amer. *28*:229–40.

Taylor, R. L. 1975. Butterflies in My Stomach: Insects in Human Nutrition. Woodbridge Press, Santa Barbara, 224 pp.

Tedders, W. L., Jr., J. G. Hartsock, and M. Osburn. 1972. Suppression of hickory shuckworm in a pecan orchard with black-light traps. J. Econ. Entomol. *65*:148–55.

Thorsteinson, A. J. 1960. Host selection in phytophagous insects. Ann. Rev. Entomol. *5*:193–218.

Tinbergen, N., and W. Kruyt. 1938. Über die Orientierung des Bienenwolfes *(Philanthus triangulum* Fabr.). III. Die Bevorzugung bestimmer Wegmarken. Z. vergl. Physiol. *25*:292–334.

Townes, H. K., and M. Townes. 1959–1962. Ichneumon-flies of America north of Mexico. Amer. Entomol. Inst. Ann Arbor, Mich. (Several vols.)

Trager, W. 1953. Nutrition. *In* Roeder, K. D. (ed.). Insect Physiology. John Wiley & Sons, Inc., New York, pp. 350–86.

Truman, J. W. 1973. How moths "turn on": a study of the action of hormones on the nervous system. Amer. Sci. *61*:700–06.

Turnbull, A. L., and D. A. Chant. 1961. The practice and theory of biological control of insects in Canada. Canad. J. Zool. *39*:697–753.

Tuxen, S. L. 1964. The protura: a revision of the species of the world, with keys for determination. Hermann, Paris, 360 pp.

Ullyet, G. C. 1947. Mortality factors in populations of *Plutella maculipennis* Curtis (Tineidae:Lepidoptera), and their relation to the problem of control. Entomol. Mem. Dept. Agr. Union of South Africa 2:77–202.

Urquhart, F. A. 1960. The Monarch Butterfly. University of Toronto Press, Toronto, 361 pp.

Usinger, R. L. (ed.). 1956. Aquatic Insects of California. University of California Press, Berkeley, 508 pp.

Utida, S. 1957. Cyclic fluctuations of population density intrinsic to the host-parasite system. Ecology 38:442–49.

Varley, G. C., and G. R. Gradwell. 1968. Population models for the winter moth. *In* Southwood, T. R. E. (ed.). Insect Abundance. Roy. Entomol. Soc. London Symp. No. 4, pp. 132–42.

Varley, G. C., and G. R. Gradwell. 1970. Recent advances in insect population dynamics. Ann. Rev. Entomol. 15:1–24.

Varley, G. C., G. R. Gradwell, and M. P. Hassell. 1973. Insect Population Ecology: An Analytical Approach. University of California Press, Berkeley, 212 pp.

Viereck, H. L. 1916. The Hymenoptera, or wasp-like insects, of Connecticut. Bull. Geol. Nat. Hist. Surv. State of Conn. 22:1–844.

Volk, W. A., and M. F. Wheeler. 1973. Basic Microbiology. J. B. Lippincott Co., Philadelphia, 592 pp.

Waldbauer, G. P. 1962. The mouth parts of female *Psorophora ciliata* (Diptera, Culicidae), with a new interpretation of the functions of the labral muscles. J. Morphol. 111:201–15.

Walker, E. M. 1953. The Odonata of Canada and Alaska. Vol. 1, General, the Zygoptera—damselflies. University of Toronto Press, Toronto.

Walker, E. M. 1958. The Odonata of Canada and Alaska. Vol. 2, The Anisoptera—4 Families. University of Toronto Press, Toronto.

Walker, E. M., and P. S. Corbet. 1975. The Odonata of Canada and Alaska, Vol. 3. University of Toronto Press, Toronto.

Walker, T. J., and D. Dew. 1972. Wing movements of calling katydids: fiddling finesse. Science 178:174–6.

Wasmann, E. 1925. Die Amiesenmimikry. Abhandl. zur theoret. Biol. 19:1–164.

Watson, M. A., and R. T. Plumb. 1972. Transmission of plant-pathogenic viruses by aphids. Ann. Rev. Entomol. 17:425–52.

Watt, W. B. 1968. Adaptive significance of pigment polymorphisms in *Colias* butterflies. I. Variation of melanin pigment in relation to thermoregulation. Evolution 22:437–58.

Weber, N. A. 1966. Fungus-growing ants. Science 153:587–604.

Weis-Fogh, T. 1964. Functional design of the tracheal system of flying insects as compared with the avian lung. J. Exp. Biol. 41:207–27.

Weiss, B. A., and T. C. Schneirla. 1967. Inter-situational transfer in the ant *Formica schaufussi* as tested in a two-phase single choice-point maze. Behaviour 28:269–79.

Welch, H. E. 1965. Entomophilic nematodes. Ann. Rev. Entomol. 10:275–302.

Wellington, W. G. 1957. Individual differences as a factor in population dynamics: the development of a problem. Canad. J. Zool. 35:293–323.

Wellington, W. G. 1960. Qualitative changes in natural populations during changes in abundance. Canad. J. Zool. 38:289–314.

Wellington, W. G. 1964. Qualitative changes in unstable environments. Canad. Entomol. 96:436–51.

Wellington, W. G. 1974. Bumblebee ocelli and navigation at dusk. Science 183:550–51.

Went, D. F. 1971. *In vitro* culture of eggs and embryos of the viviparous paedogenetic gall-midge *Heteropeza pygmaea*. J. Exp. Zool. 177:301–12.

Westcott, C. 1973. The Gardener's Bug Book. 4th ed. Doubleday & Co., Inc., New York, 689 pp.

Whedon, A. D. 1938. The aortic diverticula of the Odonata. J. Morphol. 63:229–61.

Wheeler, A. G., Jr. 1971. A study of the arthropod fauna of alfalfa. Ph.D. thesis, Cornell University, Ithaca, N.Y., 332 pp.

Wheeler, A. G., Jr. 1974. Studies on the arthropod fauna of alfalfa. VI. Plant bugs (Miridae). Canad. Entomol. 106:1267–75.

White, M. J. D. 1964. Cytogenetic mechanisms in insect reproduction. *In* Highnam, K. C. (ed.). Insect Reproduction. Royal Entomol. Soc. London Symp. No. 3., pp. 1–12.

White, T. C. R. 1974. A hypothesis to explain outbreaks of looper caterpillars, with special reference to populations of *Selidosema suavis* in a plantation of *Pinus radiata* in New Zealand. Oecologia 16:279–301.

Whitehead, A. T. 1973. Respiration. *In* Tipton, V. J. (ed.). Syllabus/Introductory Entomology. Brigham Young University Press, Provo, Utah, pp. 239–48.

Whittaker, R. H. 1962. Classification of natural communities. Bot. Rev. 28:1–239.

Whittaker, R. H., and P. P. Feeny. 1971. Allelochemics: chemical interactions between species. Science 171:757–770.

Whitten, J. M. 1964. Connective tissue membranes and their apparent role in transporting neurosecretory and other secretory products in insects. Gen. Comp. Endocrinol. 4:176–92.

Whitten, J. M. 1972. Comparative anatomy of the tracheal system. Ann. Rev. Entomol. 17:373–402.

Wickler, W. 1968. Mimicry in plants and animals. McGraw-Hill Book Co., New York, 253 pp.

Wigglesworth, V. B. 1936. The function of the corpus allatum in the growth and reproduction of *Rhodnius prolixus* (Hemiptera). Quart. J. Microsc. Sci. 79:91–121.

Wigglesworth, V. B. 1959. The Control of Growth and Form: A Study of the Epidermal Cell in an Insect. Cornell University Press, Ithaca, N.Y. 140 pp.

Wigglesworth, V. B. 1963. Origin of wings in insects. Nature *197*:97–8.

Wigglesworth, V. B. 1964. The Life of Insects. World Publishing Co., New York, 359 pp.

Wigglesworth, V. B. 1972. The principles of Insect Physiology. 7th ed. Chapman & Hall Ltd., London, 827 pp.

Wilbur, D. J. 1971. Stored grain insects. *In* Pfadt, R. E. (ed.). Fundamentals of Applied Entomology. 2nd ed. Macmillan Publishing Co., Inc., New York, pp. 495–522.

Wilde, J. de, and J. A. de Boer. 1969. Humoral and nervous pathways in photoperiodic induction of diapause in *Leptinotarsa decemlineata.* J. Ins. Physiol. *15*:661–75.

Wilde, J. de, and A. De Loof. 1973a. Reproduction. *In* Rockstein, M. (ed.). The Physiology of Insecta, Vol. 1. 2nd ed. Academic Press, Inc., New York, pp. 12–95.

Wilde, J. de, and A. de Loof. 1973b. Reproduction: endocrine control. *In* Rockstein, M. (ed.). The Physiology of Insecta, Vol. 1. 2nd ed. Academic Press, Inc., New York. pp. 97–157.

Willett, K. C. 1963. Trypanosomiasis and the tsetse fly problem in Africa. Ann. Rev. Entomol. *8*:197–214.

Williams, F. X. 1956. Life history studies of *Pepsis* and *Hemipepsis* wasps in California (Hymenoptera:Pompilidae). Ann. Entomol. Soc. Amer. *49*:447–66.

Willis, J. H. 1974. Morphogenetic action of insect hormones. Ann. Rev. Entomol. *19*:97–115.

Wilson, E. O. 1971. The Insect Societies. Harvard University Press, Cambridge, 548 pp.

Wilson, E. O., and T. Eisner. 1957. Quantitative studies of liquid food transmission in ants. Ins. Soc. *4*:157–66.

Wilson, E. O., T. Eisner, W. R. Briggs, R. E. Dickerson, R. L. Metzenberg, R. D. O'Brien, M. Susman, and W. E. Boggs. 1973. Life on Earth. Sinauer Associates, Stanford, Conn., 1059 pp.

Wood, T. K. 1974. Aggregating behavior of *Umbonia crassicornis* (Homoptera:Membracidae). Canad. Entomol. *106*:169–73.

Wood, T. K., and G. K. Morris. 1974. Studies on the function of the Membracid pronotum (Homoptera) I. Occurrence and distribution of articulated hairs. Canad. Entomol. *106*:143–48.

Woodwell, G. M., W. M. Malcolm, and R. H. Whittaker. 1969. A-bombs, bugbombs, and us. *In* Shepard, P., and D. McKinley (eds.). The Subversive Science—Essays Toward an Ecology of Man. Houghton Mifflin Co., Boston, pp. 230–41.

World Health Organization. 1971. The place of DDT in operations against malaria and other vector-borne diseases. Appendix 14, Official Records of the World Health Organization, No. 190. World Health Organization, Geneva, pp. 176–82.

Wynne-Edwards, V. C. 1962. Animal Dispersion in Relation to Social Behavior. Oliver and Boyd Ltd., Edinburgh and London, 653 pp.

Yajima, H. 1960. Studies on embryonic determination of the harlequin-fly, *Chironomus dorsalis.* I. Effect of centrifugation and of its combination with constriction and puncturing. J. Embryol. Exp. Morphol. *8*:198–215.

Yamamoto, R. T. 1974. Induction of host-plant specificity in the tobacco hornworm, *Manduca sexta.* J. Ins. Physiol. *20*:641–50.

Youssef, N. N. 1973. Embryology. *In* Tipton, V. J. (ed.). Syllabus/Introductory Entomology. Brigham Young University Press, Provo, Utah, pp. 109–124.

Zinsser, H. 1938. Rats, Lice, and History. Little, Brown and Co., Boston, 301 pp.

Index

Note: Page numbers in *italics* indicate illustrations; *t* indicates tables.